# The Police in America

*Seventh Edition*

# The Police in America

*An Introduction*

**Samuel Walker**

*University of Nebraska at Omaha*

**Charles M. Katz**

*Arizona State University*

THE POLICE IN AMERICA: AN INTRODUCTION, SEVENTH EDITION

Published by McGraw-Hill, a business unit of The McGraw-Hill Companies, Inc., 1221 Avenue of the Americas, New York, NY 10020. Copyright © 2011 by The McGraw-Hill Companies, Inc. All rights reserved. Previous editions © 2008, 2005 and 2002. No part of this publication may be reproduced or distributed in any form or by any means, or stored in a database or retrieval system, without the prior written consent of The McGraw-Hill Companies, Inc., including, but not limited to, in any network or other electronic storage or transmission, or broadcast for distance learning.

Some ancillaries, including electronic and print components, may not be available to customers outside the United States.

 This book is printed on acid-free paper.

1 2 3 4 5 6 7 8 9 0 WFR/WFR 1 0 9 8 7 6 5 4 3 2 1 0

ISBN 978-0-07-811149-5
MHID 0-07-811149-8

Vice President & Editor-in-Chief: *Mike Ryan*
VP EDP / Central Publishing Services: *Kimberly Meriwether David*
Publisher: *Mike Ryan*
Sponsoring Editor: *Katie Stevens*
Managing Editor: *Meghan Campbell*
Marketing Manager: *Pamela S. Cooper*
Sr. Project Manager: *Lisa A. Bruflodt*
Design Coordinator: *Margarite Reynolds*
Photo Research: *Nora Agbayani*
USE Cover Image Credit: *Untitled Organisation*
Production Supervisor: *Sue Culbertson*
Media Project Manager: *Jami Woy*
Compositor: *Aptara®, Inc.*
Typeface: *10/12 Times New Roman*
Printer: *Worldcolor*

All credits appearing on page or at the end of the book are considered to be an extension of the copyright page.

**Library of Congress Cataloging-in-Publication Data**

Walker, Samuel, 1942-
    The police in America : an introduction / Samuel Walker, Charles M. Katz.—7th ed.
       p. cm.
    ISBN-13: 978-0-07-811149-5
    ISBN-10: 0-07-811149-8
    1. Police—United States. 2. Police administration—United States. I. Title.
    HV8139.W35 2010
    363.20973—dc22
                                                                2009045528

www.mhhe.com

# About the Authors

***Dr. Samuel Walker***   Dr. Samuel Walker is Professor Emeritus at the University of Nebraska at Omaha, where he taught for 31 years before retiring in 2005. He is the author of 13 books on policing, criminal justice policy, and civil liberties. He continues to write and consult in the area of police accountability, with a special interest in police early intervention systems and federal litigation against police misconduct.

***Dr. Charles Katz***   Dr. Charles Katz is the Watts Family Director of the Center for Violence Prevention and Community safety and is an Associate Professor in the School of Criminology and Criminal Justice at Arizona State University. Dr. Katz earned his Ph.D. in Criminal Justice from the University of Nebraska at Omaha in 1997. He is coauthor *of Policing Gangs in America* (2006) and numerous articles on policing and gangs. He is currently working with several large metropolitan police agencies evaluating programs and practices.

# Contents in Brief

# Contents

# Preface

*The Police in America: An Introduction* provides a comprehensive introduction to the foundations of policing in the United States today. Descriptive and analytical, the text is designed to offer undergraduate students a balanced and up-to-date overview of who the police are and what they do, the problems they face, and the many reforms and innovations that have taken place in policing. The book is designed primarily for undergraduate students enrolled in their first police or law enforcement course—such as introduction to policing, police and society, or law enforcement systems.

## Changes in the Seventh Edition

The seventh edition of *The Police in America* has undergone extensive revision. In response to reviewer feedback, we have not only updated all the statistical information but also provided new examples of several important issues throughout the book. We have also included coverage of the latest research and practices in policing. Some of the most important changes we have made for the seventh edition are as follows:

- Chapter 1, "Police and Society," has been enhanced to include an in-depth discussion of the role of the local police in homeland security, and presents recent trends in award-winning problem-oriented policing practices.
- Chapter 3, "The Contemporary Law Enforcement Industry," has been revised and updated to include a discussion on interagency cooperation on matters related to homeland security, and presents new information on trends related to coroners and medical examiners.
- Chapter 4, "Police Organizations," has been shortened to increase student attention on contemporary issues affecting police organization and management, and material focusing on new managerial practices has been included. Additionally, our coverage of police organizational theory has been expanded to include a section on a life-course perspective of police organizations.
- Chapter 8, "Peacekeeping and Order Maintenance," has been expanded to include greater discussion of the police response to domestic violence and provides increased attention to recent trends in mandatory arrest laws and the impact of dual arrest on domestic violence. The chapter also includes new material on the police response to the mentally ill and recent strategies to reduce the demand for prostitution.
- Chapter 9, "The Police and Crime," was shortened to increase student attention on contemporary crime issues. Material focusing on the manipulation

of official clearance rates was added, along with expanded discussion of the use of DNA by the police to solve homicides and problems associated with eyewitness identification.

- Chapter 10, "Innovations in Police Strategy" includes new material on research examining the relationship between disorder and crime. It also includes updated information on the impact of community policing in poor and minority communities, the role of problem-oriented policing in San Diego, and innovative police strategies to address problems associated with home foreclosures.

## Overview of the Contents

Part I, "Foundations," provides students with an introduction to policing in America. It explains the role of the police in the United States, along with the realities of police work and the many factors that shape policing. It also traces the history of the police from the creation of the first modern police department through the many new developments that can be found in policing today. The section concludes with a discussion of the characteristics of the contemporary law enforcement industry, including a section on the Department of Homeland Security.

Part II "Officers and Organizations," begins with an explanation of the characteristics of police organization, the role and influence of police unions, and a discussion of the theoretical rationales for why police organizations behave the way that they do. It also includes an explanation of police recruitment, selection, and training practices, as well as a discussion of the characteristics of American police officers. The section covers the reality shock that officers encounter when beginning their job, the concept of police culture, and the relationship between the attitudes of the police and the behavior of the police.

Part III, "Police Work," includes explanations of what the police do and how they do it. Among the subjects covered are the functions of patrol, the delivery of services, and the effectiveness of traditional policing strategies. This section also discusses the various problems that the police face while on the job and the strategies they use to respond to these problems. The section closes with a discussion of innovations in police strategy, such as community-oriented policing, problem-oriented policing, and zero-tolerance policing.

Part IV, "Issues in Policing," covers the various problems that police officers and police organizations encounter. The chapter on police discretion explains the nature of police discretion, sources of discretion, and how police organizations have attempted to control discretion. The section also includes a chapter on police-community relations. Attention is placed on citizen perception of the police, police perceptions of citizens, and sources of police–community relations problems. Special emphasis is placed on race and ethnicity and its implications for policing in the United States. This section includes chapters on police corruption and police accountability, which discuss different types of police misbehavior and the different strategies that are used to hold the police accountable.

Part V, "Challengers for a New Century," concludes the book with a chapter on the future of policing in America.

# Pedagogy

A number of learning devices are included to make the text easier to teach and, for students, easier to learn, enlivening the material with practical, concrete examples and applications:

- A new box called *Police in Focus* provides a discussion of a series of important issues in policing. This features is designed to highlight particularly important points and can serve as the basis for class discussion. In each case, references are provided for students who want to pursue the issue further.
- Sidebars in every chapter expound upon important concept and feature contemporary issues related to the chapter discussion.
- For easy reference to the boxed features (Police in Focus and Sidebars), a separate listing has been added after the contents in the front of the book.
- Cross-reference icons direct students to material elsewhere in the text that can further illuminated chapter topics.
- Chapter-opening outlines guide students through the chapter.
- Key terms are highlighted in the margins, boldfaced in the text, listed at the end of the chapter, and defined in a comprehensive glossary at the end of the book.
- Internet exercises at the end of each chapter can be used by students for further Web-based study.
- An end-of-the-chapter case study—a real-world example that highlights a major concept or idea from the chapter—enables students to begin applying what they have read, and discussion questions following the case study stimulate classroom discussion.

# Supplements

Visit our Online Learning Center Web site at www.mhhe.com/walker7.

## For the Student

On the student side of this free Web site are multiple-choice and true-false self-quizzes for each chapter, chapter outlines, Internet exercises, and summaries.

## For the Instructor

The instructor side of the Web site comprises all student content and a password-protected *Instructor's Manual and Test Bank*. A PowerPoint presentation, chapter by chapter, features text and exhibits to encourage student discussion.

# Acknowledgments

Samuel Walker would like to thank his colleagues and the University of Nebraska at Omaha for creating a supporting academic environment. He also wishes to thank several of his graduate students who have not only helped tack down particular bits of information from time to time but also provided a sounding board for how particular issues should be covered in this book. Sam would especially like to thank former student and coauthor Chuck Katz for agreeing to share the work on producing this edition as well as the fifth and sixth editions. For Sam, it has been as much of a pleasure to work with Chuck as a colleague as it was to work with him as a student just a few years ago.

Charles Katz would like to thank the many people who have contributed to the completion of this edition and to acknowledge his colleagues at Arizona State University who have always been supportive and who have been willing to lend a helpful hand when asked. Special thanks, too, to four people in particular: to Charles's parents and his wife Keri, who have always been loving and supportive (this book, and his other work, is just as much a result of their dedication and efforts as his own) and to his coauthor Sam Walker. Sam has always been supportive, whether it be professionally or personally, and his insights continue to influence Charles today.

**Samuel Walker**
**Charles M. Katz**

# Foundations

# Police and Society

## Chapter Outline

More than 30 years ago, Jerome Skolnick posed the fundamental question, "For what social purpose do police exist?"[1] Why do we have police? What purpose do they serve? What do we want them to do? What do they do that other government agencies do not do? How do we want them to do these things? These are basic questions related to the police role in society.

Too often the answers to these questions are vague and simplistic. People say the police should "protect and serve" or "enforce the law." Such answers, however, avoid all the important issues. Policing is extremely complex, involving difficult questions about the police role, the fair treatment of citizens, police organizations, and the recruitment, training, and supervision of police officers.

## The Goals of This Book

Several innovations in policing such as community-oriented policing, problem-oriented policing, and zero-tolerance policing have raised new questions about the police role. These new strategies represent a different role for the police compared with the "professional" style of policing that prevailed as a result of the professionalization movement (1900–1980).[2] These innovations reopen all of the basic questions about how we should organize and deliver police services, whom we should recruit, and how we should evaluate them.

The purpose of this book is not to argue for or against any one of these innovations in policing. It is to provide the necessary background information about policing to help you, the reader, discuss these innovations intelligently. This book seeks to describe what police do (see Chapter 7); the many problems that arise, such as the exercise of discretion (Chapter 11), police-community relations (Chapter 12), how police officers are selected and who police officers are (Chapters 5 and 6); and how police organizations operate (Chapter 4). It seeks to describe what policing has been in the past (Chapter 2), what it is today, and what it could be in the future (Chapters 10 and 15).

However, before we begin, in this chapter we provide you with a foundation for understanding the police in America. Specifically, this chapter defines the police and police agencies, the myths and realities of police work, the factors that shape the police role, and the various forms of policing that are possible.

# A Definition of Terms

## What Is a Law Enforcement Agency?

What do we mean when we talk about a police or law enforcement agency? The question is not as simple as it might seem. Many different kinds of government agencies have some responsibility for enforcing the law and/or providing protection: state parks departments, federal agencies such as the U.S. Supreme Court Police, some college campus police.

This book focuses only on **general service law enforcement agencies:** those that are regularly engaged in (1) preventing crime, (2) investigating crimes and apprehending criminals, (3) maintaining order, and (4) providing other miscellaneous services.

*general service law enforcement agencies*

This definition excludes many government regulatory agencies whose personnel often have law enforcement powers. It excludes investigatory and prosecutorial agencies, such as state bureaus of criminal investigation, coroner's offices, and constables. It also excludes corrections agencies, even though in many states their officers are legally peace officers with arrest power.

# Who Is a Police Officer?

**police officer**

**peace officer**

The term **police officer** is often used interchangeably with **peace officer.** There is an important distinction, however. All police officers are peace officers, but all peace officers are not police officers. The legal status of peace officers is defined by statute. Iowa law, for example, designates eight categories of peace officer, the last coming under the catchall phrase: "all other persons so designated." California law gives peace officer status to more than thirty different occupations.

Peace officer status grants certain powers and provides certain legal protections that ordinary citizens do not have. Under the English common-law standard, all citizens have the power to make a "citizen's arrest." Private citizens can also shoot to kill under certain limited circumstances. Sworn peace officers, however, have broader power in taking these actions and have somewhat greater protection from liability when they are acting "in good faith" in carrying out an official duty.

# Myths, Realities, and Possibilities

At the outset it is necessary to sort out the myths, realities, and possibilities of policing. The myths include the many erroneous ideas about what the police do and what they should do. The realities include what the police in fact do on a day-to-day basis and what role they play in society. The possibilities include the ways in which policing could be different from what it is today.

For a full discussion of patrol time allocated to law enforcement, see Chapter 7.

# Myths about Policing

Policing is surrounded by many myths and stereotypes.[3] One of the enduring myths is that police are primarily crime fighters. According to this view, police devote most of their efforts to enforcing the criminal law: patrolling to deter crime, investigating crimes, and arresting criminals. Some people believe that this is what the police *should* do. A lot of the rhetoric about the police reflects the **crime-fighter image:** the idea of the police as a "thin blue line," fighting a war on crime.[4]

**crime-fighter image**

For a brief explanation of peacekeeping and order maintenance, see Chapter 8.

The crime-fighter image, however, is not an accurate description of what the police do. Only about one-third of a patrol officer's activities are devoted to criminal law enforcement. The typical police officer rarely makes a felony arrest and almost never fires a weapon in his or her entire career. Most police work is best described as peacekeeping, order maintenance, or problem solving.

## Sources of the Crime-Fighter Image

The myth of the crime fighter endures for many reasons. The entertainment media play a major role in popularizing it. Movies and television police shows feature crime-related stories because they offer drama, fast-paced action, and violence. Think for a moment about the latest Hollywood cop movie: How many car chases

# Police in Focus

## *The CSI Effect*

Over the past several years, television shows focusing on criminal investigations have become the most watched in the country—so much so that some of these programs have resulted in a number of spin-offs. Today, we have *CSI: Crime Science Investigators; CSI: New York; CSI: Miami; Law & Order; Law & Order: Criminal Intent;* and *Law & Order: Special Victims Unit.* Television shows focused on forensic science, such as *Bones, Numbers, Crossing Jordan,* and *Forensic Files,* are almost as popular. Due to their popularity these programs have had such a substantial effect on the criminal justice system that many police officials, prosecutors, and judges have begun to call it the "*CSI* effect."

*CSI*-type shows depict crime scene investigators and scientists as the persons primarily responsible for solving complex crimes, with police officers merely being their assistants. These television programs have projected an image that the police have high-tech labs at their beck and call and that crime labs are well staffed with medical doctors, forensic anthropologists, and well-educated crime scene investigators. They depict crime scientists running endless numbers of scientific tests and laboratory experiments that are provided back to the police within hours, and they portray their scientific evidence as nearly infallible, with the capacity to detect and solve almost any crime.

The fact is that most arrests are made by patrol officers through traditional policing strategies, such as responding to 911 calls for service and observing crime on the streets. Most local law enforcement agencies do not employ a forensic anthropologist or criminal profiler to investigate crime; rather patrol officers and detectives are responsible for investigating crimes. Crime scene investigators are not permitted to investigate crimes but are responsible for collecting evidence. For example, they measure tire tread marks to determine the speed at which a car was driving before an accident occurred; they collect shell casings where shootings occur and collect fingerprints from crime scenes. Additionally, crime scene investigators do not conduct lab experiments with the evidence they collect, but it is many times sent to often poorly staffed and equipped regional or state crime labs that take weeks and even months to process it.

Regardless, *CSI*-type television programs have had a profound impact on the work of both police and prosecutors. These shows have heightened a jury's expectations about the scope and nature of evidence that should be presented at trial. In some jurisdictions when prosecutors do not introduce some forms of evidence into the record, such as fingerprints and DNA, they work with police investigators on the stand to explain why this evidence has not been presented to the court. This is largely because prosecutors have found that when they do not educate juries about why some forms of evidence have not been presented in court, juries take the "lack of expected evidence" as cause for reasonable doubt. For example, in one Illinois case jurors "acquitted a man accused of stabbing his estranged girlfriend because police didn't test her bloody bed sheets for DNA. The man went back to prison on a parole violation and stabbed his ex again when he got out—this time fatally." In another case the Los Angeles district attorney was so frustrated with jurors who acquitted actor Robert Blake of the murder of his wife that he publicly called the jurors "incredibly stupid" and blamed Blake's acquittal on the *CSI* effect.*

*Kit R. Roane, "The CSI Effect," *U.S. News & World Report,* April 25, 2005. Accessed at http://www.usnews.com/usnews/culture/articles/050425/25csi.htm on February 28, 2006.

were there? How many shoot-outs? The typical domestic disturbance, which in real life is a common police situation, does not offer the same kind of dramatic possibilities.

The news media are equally guilty of overemphasizing police crime fighting. A recent study of crime and the news media concluded that "crime stories are frequently presented and prominently displayed," and the number of these stories is "large in comparison with other topics."[5] A serious crime is a newsworthy event. There is a victim who engages our sympathies, a story, and then an arrest that offers dramatic visuals of the suspect in custody. A typical night's work for a patrol officer, by way of contrast, does not offer much in the way of dramatic news.

The police perpetuate the crime-fighter image themselves. Official press releases and annual reports emphasize crime and arrests. Crime fighting is a way for the police to tell the public they are doing something and doing something important. Peter Manning argues that the police deliberately adopted the crime-fighter role image as a way of staking claim to a domain of professional expertise that they, and they alone, could control.[6]

## Consequences of the Crime-Fighter Image

For a full discussion of peacekeeping and order maintenance, see Chapter 8.

Because it does not present an accurate picture of what the police do, the crime-fighter image creates a number of serious problems.[7] Most important, it ignores the order maintenance and peacekeeping activities that consume most police time and effort (for further reading see Chapters 7 and 8). This prevents us from intelligently evaluating police performance. The emphasis on crime fighting also creates unrealistic public expectations about the ability of the police to prevent crime and catch criminals. Movies and TV shows strengthen the impression that the police are highly successful in solving crimes, when in fact only 20 percent of all reported index crimes are solved.

For a full discussion of how successful the police are in solving crimes, see Chapter 9.

The police themselves suffer from this distorted image. Police chiefs cannot effectively manage their departments when so much attention is given to only one small part of their activities. The crime-fighter image also creates role conflict for individual police officers. By placing a premium on detective work and devaluing patrol work, it creates a contradiction between what patrol officers value and what they actually do.[8]

## The Realities of Policing

police role

The reality of policing is that the police play an extremely complex role in today's society. This role involves many different tasks. Herman Goldstein warns that "anyone attempting to construct a workable definition of the **police role** will typically come away with old images shattered and a new-found appreciation for the intricacies of police work."[9]

Many studies of police work document the complexity of the police role. For example, the Police Services Study (PSS), which was the last study conducted of its kind, examined 26,418 calls for service to the police in three metropolitan areas.[10] As the data in Exhibit 1–1 indicate, only 19 percent of the calls involve crime, and only 2 percent of the total involve violent crime.

The data in Exhibit 1–1 also illustrate how ambiguous police work is. The situations in the category of interpersonal conflict, for example, may involve a potential crime (e.g., assault), or pose a serious risk to the officer or another person (e.g., a mentally disturbed person with a gun), or merely be an argument and some noise.

One of the most important aspects of policing is that officers exercise enormous discretion in handling these situations. Take, for example, the case of Mr. and Mrs. Jones. One night the neighbors overhear the couple arguing and call the police. After the police arrive and are faced with the dispute, should they warn Mr. and Mrs. Jones, ask one of them to leave the premises, arrest one of them, or try to mediate the dispute? These are difficult choices, requiring good judgment and human relations skills. It is not a simple matter of making an arrest, as the crime-fighter image suggests.

For a full discussion on police discretion, see Chapter 11.

The American Bar Association's *Standards Relating to the Urban Police Function* illustrates the complexity of the police role by identifying eleven different police responsibilities (Exhibit 1–2).[11]

The ABA list illustrates three ways in which the police role is extremely complex. First, it involves a wide variety of tasks. Only a few deal with criminal law enforcement.

Second, many of the tasks are extremely vague. Resolving conflict, for example, raises a number of difficult questions. What kinds of situations represent conflicts that require police intervention? What is the best response to a conflict situation? Should officers always make arrests in domestic disputes, for example? If not, what should they do?

Third, different responsibilities often conflict with each other. Police are responsible for both maintaining order and protecting constitutional liberties, for example. In the case of a large political demonstration, the police have to balance the First Amendment rights of the protesters and the need to maintain order and protect the rights of other people to use the streets and sidewalks.

As Goldstein points out, "The police, by the very nature of their function, are an anomaly in a free society."[12] On the one hand, we expect them to exercise coercive force: to restrain people when they are out of control, to arrest them when they break the law, and in some extreme cases to use deadly force. At the same time, however, we expect the police to protect the individual freedoms that are the essential part of a democratic society. The tension between freedom and constraint is one of the central problems in American policing.[13]

## Factors That Shape the Police Role

Several factors contribute to the complexity of the police role. Most important is the fact that police services are available 24 hours a day. The telephone makes it possible to call the police at any hour and for any problem. The police, moreover, have encouraged people to call and have promised to respond to those calls. Goldstein argues that the police end up handling many problems "because no other means has been found to solve them. They are the residual problems of society."[14] Policing

EXHIBIT 1–1

## Citizen Calls for Police Services, by General Problem Types and Subcategories

| Type of Problem | Number of Calls | Percent of Total | Percent of Category |
|---|---|---|---|
| **Violent Crimes** | **642** | **2** | |
| 1. Homicide | 9 | | 1 |
| 2. Sexual attack | 26 | | 4 |
| 3. Robbery | 118 | | 18 |
| 4. Aggravated assault | 74 | | 12 |
| 5. Simple assault | 351 | | 55 |
| 6. Child abuse | 38 | | 6 |
| 7. Kidnapping | 26 | | 4 |
| **Nonviolent Crimes** | **4,489** | **17** | |
| 1. Burglary and break-ins | 1,544 | | 34 |
| 2. Theft | 1,389 | | 31 |
| 3. Motor vehicle theft | 284 | | 6 |
| 4. Vandalism, arson | 866 | | 19 |
| 5. Problems with money/credit/documents | 209 | | 5 |
| 6. Crimes against the family | 29 | | 1 |
| 7. Leaving the scene | 168 | | 4 |
| **Interpersonal Conflict** | **1,763** | **7** | |
| 1. Domestic conflict | 694 | | 39 |
| 2. Nondomestic arguments | 335 | | 19 |
| 3. Nondomestic threats | 277 | | 16 |
| 4. Nondomestic fights | 457 | | 26 |
| **Medical Assistance** | **810** | **3** | |
| 1. Medical assistance | 274 | | 34 |
| 2. Death | 38 | | 5 |
| 3. Suicide | 34 | | 4 |
| 4. Emergency transport | 203 | | 25 |
| 5. Personal injury, traffic accident | 261 | | 32 |
| **Traffic Problems** | **2,467** | **9** | |
| 1. Property damage, traffic accident | 1,141 | | 46 |
| 2. Vehicle violation | 543 | | 22 |
| 3. Traffic-flow problem | 322 | | 13 |
| 4. Moving violation | 292 | | 12 |
| 5. Abandoned vehicle | 169 | | 7 |
| **Dependent Persons** | **774** | **3** | |
| 1. Drunk | 146 | | 19 |
| 2. Missing persons | 318 | | 41 |
| 3. Juvenile runaway | 121 | | 16 |
| 4. Subject of police concern | 134 | | 17 |
| 5. Mentally disordered | 55 | | 7 |
| **Public Nuisances** | **3,002** | **11** | |
| 1. Annoyance, harassment | 980 | | 33 |
| 2. Noise disturbance | 984 | | 33 |
| 3. Trespassing, unwanted entry | 302 | | 10 |

EXHIBIT 1 – 1    (continued)

| Type of Problem | Number of Calls | Percent of Total | Percent of Category |
|---|---|---|---|
| 4. Alcohol, drug violations | 130 | | 4 |
| 5. Public morals | 124 | | 4 |
| 6. Juvenile problem | 439 | | 15 |
| 7. Ordinance violations | 43 | | 1 |
| **Suspicious Circumstances** | **1,248** | | **5** |
| 1. Suspicious person | 674 | | 54 |
| 2. Suspicious property condition | 475 | | 38 |
| 3. Dangerous person or situation | 99 | | 8 |
| **Assistance** | **3,039** | **12** | |
| 1. Animal problem | 755 | | 25 |
| 2. Property check | 616 | | 20 |
| 3. Escorts and transports | 86 | | 3 |
| 4. Utility problem | 438 | | 14 |
| 5. Property discovery | 240 | | 8 |
| 6. Assistance to motorist | 154 | | 5 |
| 7. Fires, alarms | 112 | | 4 |
| 8. Crank calls | 114 | | 4 |
| 9. Unspecified requests | 425 | | 14 |
| 10. Other requests | 99 | | 3 |
| **Citizen Wants Information** | **5,558** | **21** | |
| 1. Information, unspecified | 248 | | 4 |
| 2. Information, police-related | 1,262 | | 23 |
| 3. Information about specific case | 1,865 | | 34 |
| 4. Information, nonpolice-related | 577 | | 10 |
| 5. Road directions | 189 | | 3 |
| 6. Directions, nontraffic | 55 | | 1 |
| 7. Requests for specific unit | 1,362 | | 25 |
| **Citizen Wants to Give Information** | **1,993** | **8** | |
| 1. General information | 1,090 | | 55 |
| 2. Return of property | 156 | | 8 |
| 3. False alarm | 176 | | 9 |
| 4. Complaint against specific officer | 105 | | 5 |
| 5. Complaint against police in general | 350 | | 18 |
| 6. Compliments for police | 20 | | 1 |
| 7. Hospital report to police | 96 | | 5 |
| **Internal Operations** | **633** | **2** | |
| 1. Internal legal procedures | 63 | | 10 |
| 2. Internal assistance request | 134 | | 21 |
| 3. Officer wants to give information | 298 | | 47 |
| 4. Officer wants information | 132 | | 21 |
| 5. Other internal procedures | 6 | | 1 |
| Total calls | 26,418 | 100 | |

Source: Eric J. Scott, *Calls for Service: Citizen Demand and Initial Police Response* (Washington DC: Government Printing Office, 1981), pp. 28–30.

## EXHIBIT 1–2

### Police Roles and Responsibilities

1. Identify criminal offenders and criminal activity and, when appropriate, apprehend offenders and participate in subsequent court proceedings.
2. Reduce the opportunities for the commission of some crimes through preventive patrol and other measures.
3. Aid individuals who are in danger of physical harm.
4. Protect constitutional guarantees.
5. Facilitate the movement of people and vehicles.
6. Assist those who cannot care for themselves.
7. Resolve conflict.
8. Identify problems that are potentially serious law enforcement or government problems.
9. Create and maintain a feeling of security in the community.
10. Promote and preserve civil order.
11. Provide other services on an emergency basis.

*Source:* American Bar Association, *Standards Relating to the Urban Police Function,* 2nd ed. (Boston: Little, Brown, 1980), pp. 1–31 to 1–32, Standard 1–2.2, "Major Current Responsibilities of Police."

involves society's "dirty work": the tasks that no one else wants to do.[15] People call the police when everything else has failed.

The public wants a general-purpose emergency service, available to handle problems that arise. This job falls to the police. It would be extremely expensive to maintain a number of additional specialized agencies—one that deals only with domestic disturbances, for example, or one that responds only to mental illness situations. The 24-hour availability of the police gives them an extremely heavy workload. Many calls do not necessarily require a sworn police officer with arrest power. Also, some of these calls require someone with professional expertise (some mental health incidents, for example). As a result, the police are generalists, expected to handle a wide range of situations, but with only limited training and expertise in family problems, mental illness, or alcohol and drug abuse.

The complexity of the police role was not really planned. For the most part, it just happened. The police acquired many responsibilities simply because they were the only agency available. The telephone made it convenient for people to call the police, and so they did (for further reading see Chapter 2). The debate over the police role today raises basic questions about whether we really want the police to do all these things.

## The Authority to Use Force

The authority to use force is one of the most important factors shaping the police role. In this crucial respect, the police are different from other professionals such as teachers, social workers, or doctors. In one of the most important essays on policing, Egon Bittner argues that the capacity to use **coercive force** is the defining feature of the police.[16] Force includes the power to take someone's life (deadly

coercive force

force), the use of physical force, and the power to deprive people of their liberty through arrest.

Bittner quickly adds that the authority to use force is not unlimited. First, it is limited by law. The police cannot lawfully shoot to kill anyone. The power to arrest is also limited by the law. Second, officers may use force only in the performance of their job. They may not use force, for example, to settle a private dispute. Third, officers may not use force maliciously or frivolously. They may not arrest, harass, or abuse citizens for personal spite or amusement.

The authority to use force has implications that go far beyond its actual use. Bittner argues that it is latent and ever present, defining relations between officers and citizens. He observes: "There can be no doubt that this feature of police work is uppermost in the minds of people who solicit police aid."[17] People call the police because they want an officer to settle a problem: to arrest someone, to get someone to calm down, or to have someone removed from the home. People generally defer to police authority. In the vast majority of situations, citizens comply with police officer requests, suggestions, or threats.[18]

## Social Control

The police are part of the broader system of social control. Stanley Cohen defines **social control** as "the organized ways in which society responds to behavior and people it regards as deviant, problematic, worrying, threatening, troublesome or undesirable in some way or another."[19] There are three different types of social control: private, parochial, and public. The most basic form of social control is at the private level. This is also referred to as a primary form of social control. At the private level social control is carried out by family, friends, and other informal social groups that have the capacity to exercise social control through criticism, praise, ostracism, and even violence. The second form of social control is at the parochial level and is also known as *secondary social control*. At the parochial level social control is exercised by community organizations such as schools, churches, neighborhood groups, and businesses that often have a stake in individual behavior, but do not have the same sentimental attachment as those at the private level. Social control levied by those at the parochial level, for example, can take the form of a verbal reprimand by a neighbor or sanctions meted out by a school principal or church official. The third form of social control is exercised at the public level. At the public level social control is exercised by governmental organizations such as the police and regulatory agencies. This form of social control is often called to action when other strategies exercised by the private and parochial levels have failed.[20]

social control

## The Police and Social Control

To be clear, social control exercised by the police is not the same as repression or enforced conformity. The distinguishing feature of a democratic society is the existence of mechanisms for peaceful political change (see Sidebar 1–1). Constitutional guarantees of freedom of speech, press, and assembly facilitate peaceful change by allowing new and controversial ideas to be heard. As the ABA list of

For a full discussion on the impact of the telephone on policing, see Chapter 2.

## The Principles of Democratic Policing

As a result of the conflict in Bosnia and Herzegovina, the warring factions and several other interested parties came together in Youngstown, Ohio, to discuss the principles to guide the development of a new police force in the country. As part of what was later called the "Youngstown Accord," seven principles were established to guide policing in both established and emerging democracies across the world. These seven principles were:

1. The police must operate in accordance with democratic principles.

2. The police as recipients of public trust should be considered as professionals whose conduct must be governed by a professional code.

3. The police must have as their highest priority the protection of life.

4. The police must serve the community and consider themselves accountable to the community.

5. The police must recognize that protection of life and property is the primary function of police operations.

6. The police must conduct their activities with respect for human dignity and basic human rights.

7. The police are expected to discharge their duties in a nondiscriminatory manner.

### Suggested Exercise

1. In groups of four or five, discuss whether you think American policing is characterized by democratic principles.

2. Discuss which principles you believe are more closely adhered to in American policing.

3. Should these principles be adopted by all law enforcement agencies in the United States?

*Source:* Adapted from Jeremy Travis, 2000, "Policing in Transition," *Police Practice & Research: An International Journal,* 1(1): pp. 31–40.

---

police tasks indicates (Exhibit 1–2 ), preserving constitutional rights is part of the police role.

The police contribute to social control through both their law enforcement and order maintenance responsibilities. Their task is to preserve the norms of society by deterring crime and arresting people who violate the criminal law, which embodies those norms. The police presence in society is also intended to preserve order by serving as a deterrent to misconduct and by providing a quick-response mechanism for potential or low-level problems.

The capacity of the police to exercise complete social control is extremely limited, however. As we will learn in Chapter 7, routine patrol has only a limited effect on crime, and as we will see in Chapter 9, the ability of the police to identify and arrest criminal suspects is extremely limited.

Experts now recognize that the police are heavily dependent on citizens in carrying out their responsibilities. Police depend on people to report crimes, to provide information about suspects, to cooperate in investigations, and so on. For this reason, many experts refer to citizens as "coproducers" of police services.[21]

In the colonial era (1600–1840s), before we had the modern police, citizens were the primary agents of social control. Behavior was regulated by comments, warnings, or rebukes by family, friends, and neighbors.[22] The creation of the modern police, as a large professional bureaucracy, transferred that responsibility away from citizens (for further reading see Chapter 2). The community-policing movement is an attempt to restore and develop the role of citizens as coproducers of police services. In important respects, the police are the last resort in the system of social control. We call the police when everything else has failed. The primary social control mechanism is the family. Peer groups, community groups, religious institutions, and the schools are also important. When these mechanisms fail and a person breaks the law, we call the police.

## The Police and Social Control Systems

The police are part of several different systems of social control. First, and most important, they are the "gatekeepers" of the criminal justice system. The decision by a police officer to make an arrest initiates most criminal cases. The decision not to arrest keeps the incident out of the system.[23] Thus, the police determine the workload for the criminal justice system. At the same time, police efforts are deeply affected by the actions of other criminal justice agencies.

For a full discussion of the creation of the modern police, see Chapter 2.

Second, the police are an important part of the social welfare system. They are often the first contact that official agencies have with social problems such as delinquency, family problems, drug abuse, and alcoholism. The police often refer individuals to social service agencies. The police are also an important part of the mental health system. Patrol units are routinely called to situations where someone is believed to be mentally ill. The officer has the responsibility of determining whether the person is in fact mentally ill and requires hospitalization. Goldstein argues that we need to recognize the fact that this is what police actually do, and we should develop alternatives to the criminal justice system for dealing with these situations.[24]

For a full discussion of the organization and responsibilities of the Sheriff, see Chapter 3.

Third, the police are an important part of the political system. In a democratic society, the political system ensures public control and accountability of the police. The people, acting through their elected representatives, determine police policy, such as community policing, or not, and aggressive enforcement of traffic laws, or not. In the case of the sheriff, the people directly elect the top law enforcement official.

For a full discussion of the history of police corruption, see Chapter 2.

Political control of law enforcement agencies represents one of the central dilemmas of policing a democratic society. On the one hand, the people have a fundamental right to control their government agencies. At the same time, however, politics have historically been the source of much corruption and abuse of law enforcement powers. Striking the balance between popular control and professional standards is another one of the basic tensions in American policing.

In important respects, the police are symbols of the political system. They are the most visible manifestation of power and authority in society. The badge, the gun,

For a full discussion of the history of the police, see Chapter 2.

and the billy club are potent visual reminders of the ultimate power of the police in maintaining the existing social and political system. As a result, attitudes toward the police are influenced by people's attitudes toward the political system generally. Arthur Niederhoffer describes the police officer as "a 'Rorschach' in uniform." People project upon the officer their attitudes about a wide range of issues.[25]

# Possibilities

The form of policing we currently have is not the only one that is possible. The idea that the police do not and cannot change is a myth. The history of the police indicates that they have changed dramatically over the years (for further reading see Chapter 2).[26] In *Police for the Future,* David H. Bayley argues that we have a choice—a political choice about different possibilities for policing.[27] The real question is, What kind of policing do we want to create?

Bayley argues that we should take the crime prevention role of the police seriously. He believes the police, as traditionally organized, cannot effectively prevent crime. But he does see the possibility of more effective crime prevention if we choose to decentralize police departments and give more responsibility to neighborhood police officers (NPOs). This approach takes police departments and stands them on their heads, giving more decision-making responsibility to the officers at the bottom of the organization. Executives at the top of the organization would coordinate rather than command, as they do in the traditional quasi-military-style organization.[28]

Is Bayley's proposal sound? Would it achieve its goals without doing more harm to society? The purpose of this book is not to provide prescriptive yes or no answers to these questions. Instead, our purpose is to provide a factual, up-to-date description of policing today so that we can make informed decisions about the choices that are available—choices that are based on evidence, not subjective beliefs.

Let's consider some of the alternative possibilities for the police.

## Problem-Oriented Policing

Herman Goldstein

problem-oriented policing

**Herman Goldstein**'s concept of **problem-oriented policing** (POP) represents a different approach to the complexity of the police role. He argues that the police should disaggregate their workload, identify recurring problems, and develop strategies to reduce or eliminate those problems. Instead of thinking in terms of general categories of crime and disorder, the police should identify particular kinds of crime (drug dealing, drunk driving) and disorder (rowdy juveniles, chronic alcoholics in the neighborhood) and develop appropriate responses. POP represents a proactive approach, very different from the reactive approach of simply responding to 911 calls. It involves research and planning, as well as a shift from individual calls for service to a concern with underlying problems. The category of disorder, for example, would be disaggregated into separate problems: domestic disturbances, juvenile rowdiness, and chronic alcoholism on the street. A different strategy would be developed for each one.[29]

One of the first experiments in problem-oriented policing occurred in **Newport News,** Virginia, in the mid-1980s. The program focused on burglaries in the New Briarfield apartments, one of the worst low-income housing units in the city. The project began by analyzing crime patterns in the area and conducting an opinion survey of apartment complex residents. The survey discovered that deteriorated buildings contributed to many burglaries. Windows and doors were easily broken into, vacant apartments created havens for criminals, and deteriorated conditions created an atmosphere of despair and powerlessness among the residents.[30]

Newport News

Police officers assigned to New Briarfield responded by attempting to improve the physical condition of the buildings. One officer negotiated the settlement of a dispute with the private trash hauler that resulted in the removal of accumulated garbage. Abandoned refrigerators and other dangers to children were also removed. The police department organized a meeting of government agencies that had some responsibility for the housing project: the fire department, the Department of Public Works, the Redevelopment and Housing Authority, and so on. The purpose of the meeting was to develop a coordinated strategy to improve conditions in the complex. One officer organized a tenants' group to pressure city officials into making short-term improvements in the apartments.

POP in Newport News represented a new role for the police. Officers functioned as community organizers and brokers of government services, mediating between citizens and other agencies.

Today, police departments around the world practice problem-oriented policing. To facilitate its practice the San Diego police department and the Police Executive Research Forum (PERF) have cohosted the International Problem-Oriented Policing (POP) Conference every year since 1990. At the conference are hundreds of representatives from police agencies and academic institutions who come together to discuss the direction of problem-oriented policing and to share information about problem-oriented policing strategies.[31] Each year the **Herman Goldstein Award** is presented at the conference to recognize the most innovative and successful problem-oriented policing project implemented by a police agency. Recent award winners have been the Mid-City Graffiti Project, San Diego Police Department, San Diego, CA US (2000); Operation Cobra: Tackling Vehicle Crime in the City of Portsmouth Hampshire Constabulary, Hampshire, UK (2004); and Operation Pasture, Lancashire Constabulary, Lancashire, UK (2008). The award was created to honor Herman Goldstein, who developed the concept of problem-oriented policing.[32]

Herman Goldstein Award

## Community Policing

One of the more popular approaches to policing today is **community policing.** Community policing alters the basic philosophy of policing. It holds that the police should work closely with community residents, instead of being an inward-looking bureaucracy; that they should emphasize crime prevention, as opposed to law enforcement; and that they should decentralize the decision-making authority to rank-and-file officers, as opposed to the top-down military-style organization.[33]

community policing

Community-policing programs take many different forms.[34] Some emphasize disorder and quality-of-life issues, while others focus on serious crime.

In Chicago, the police department has instituted the **Chicago Alternative Policing Strategy** (CAPS). At the root of the CAPS plan is the idea that the whole police department, not just a specialized unit, should become intimately involved with a partner within the community. As part of this strategy, officers are permanently assigned to neighborhoods to enhance their knowledge about the community in which they work and to allow the officers and the neighborhood residents to get to know one another on a personal level. Under CAPS the police department requires officers to meet with neighborhood residents regularly to discuss problems in the community and to develop strategies to solve them. Once neighborhood residents identify problems, officers mobilize the necessary resources to address them. While there are a number of obstacles to implementing CAPS, independent research is beginning to show that the strategy has been successful in reducing social disorder and fear of crime in black communities and is successful in building a stronger relationship between the police and the community.[35]

## Zero-Tolerance Policing

**zero-tolerance policing**

New York City adopted a policy of **zero-tolerance policing** in the 1990s. This approach concentrates on relatively minor quality-of-life issues, such as urinating in public and "fare-beating" (jumping over the subway turnstiles to avoid paying the fare). George Kelling and Catherine Coles argue that tough enforcement on minor crimes directly contributes to a significant reduction in serious crime. Some fare-beaters, for example, were found to be carrying weapons in violation of the law. The weapons were then seized and the persons were arrested on more serious gun charges. The crime rate in New York City began to fall dramatically in 1992, and by 1997 it was at the lowest level in 30 years.[36] These results led police agencies across the world to adopt zero-tolerance policing.

Critics of the zero-tolerance policy, however, argue that it encourages police abuse of citizens. And, in fact, complaints against New York City police officers increased in the 1990s. From 1994 through 1996 the police department paid out over $70 million for police misconduct.[37] These allegations raise the question of whether it is possible to have tough law enforcement while at the same time respecting the rights of citizens.

## The Implications of Change

It is easy to talk about dramatic changes in policing. For example, advocates of community policing believe that it represents a new era in American policing. Translating ideas into practice is extremely difficult, however. Consider, for example, the case of **team policing.** It was a radical innovation in the early 1970s, involving restructuring police operations along neighborhood lines and decentralizing decision-making authority. At one point a large number of police departments said they were doing team policing.[38] And then, suddenly, the team-policing movement collapsed and it vanished.[39] Obviously, something went wrong. Most analysts conclude that team-policing experiments were poorly planned, with little attention given to important operational details.[40]

**team policing**

## Police in Focus

### *The Role of Local Police in Homeland Security*

Since September 11, 2001, some local police agencies have become involved in matters related to homeland security. Maguire and King note that since 9/11 the police are "developing new areas of investigative experience, cooperating much more with federal law enforcement and intelligence agencies, working more closely with the military, increasing their levels of surveillance over their communities, and paying more attention to the safety of critical infrastructure."[a] The first municipal police agency to expend a significant amount of resources toward homeland security was the New York City Police Department (NYPD). In 2002, Police Commissioner Raymond W. Kelly established a Counterterrorism Bureau. As a result, New York City police officers are stationed in such cities as London, Tel Aviv, and Hamburg, working on a variety of issues involving counterterrorism.

Some critics believe that this kind of attention to homeland security diverts attention and resources away from more traditional policing responsibilities. Regardless, the day-to-day activities of most general service law enforcement agencies, and most police officers, do not involve addressing issues related to homeland security. This is because police agencies typically focus on issues of local concern, and center their officers' attention on small subsections of communities called *beats* and *precincts*. Unless a suspected terrorist is believed to be in the agency's jurisdiction, most local police departments do not expend a substantial amount of resources toward searches for terrorists. On the other hand, some local police agencies have become more involved with protecting particular places from potential terrorist activity. This effort has largely involved developing emergency response plans and providing preventative patrols in locations where the risks of terrorism are higher, such as stadiums, parks, and other locations that host large public gatherings.[b] Therefore, while some local police agencies participate in homeland security efforts, homeland security plays a small role in most police organizations.

[a]Maguire, Edward & William King (2004). Trends in the policing industry, *Annals of the American Academy of Political and Social Sciences*, 593, 15–41.
[b]Thacher, David (2005). The local role in homeland security, *Law & Society Review*, 39, 3: 635–676.

No matter what a police department decides to do—community policing, problem-oriented policing, zero-tolerance policing, or traditional-style policing—a number of basic issues must be faced.

- **Mission.** What is the primary mission of the department—law enforcement, order maintenance, service, crime prevention, or some combination of all four? How is that mission expressed? How do citizens know what it is? How do officers know what it is? Does the department have a written mission statement? If so, what does it say?
- **Patrol Operations.** What is the place of basic preventive patrol operations in the mission of the department? Is it the central aspect of departmental activities? Or is it only one part of a multitask mission? If it is central, how efficiently is it currently being operated? What improvements need to be made? These issues are covered in Chapter 7.
- **Calls for Service.** Does the department respond to each and every call for service? Does the department attempt to manage the call-for-service workload through differential response? These issues are also covered in Chapter 7.

- **Discretion.** What policies does the department maintain to control police officer discretion? What is the current policy on use of deadly force? Is there a written policy on handling domestic violence incidents? Is there a written policy on dealing with mentally ill citizens? These issues are covered in Chapter 11.
- **Police–Community Relations.** How are the department's relations with racial and ethnic minority communities? Is there a high level of tension and conflict? What kinds of programs does the department maintain to improve police–community relations? These issues are covered in Chapter 12.
- **Corruption.** Does the department have a reputation for corruption? If it does, what evidence is there to support this reputation? Does the department have a specific anticorruption program? These issues are covered in Chapter 13.
- **Accountability.** What accountability mechanisms exist in local law enforcement agencies? Is there a citizen review board? Does the police chief have civil service protection, or can he or she be fired at will? What kind of data are published in the annual report? Does this report provide information that allows you to make a meaningful judgment about the performance of the department? See Chapter 14 for a discussion of these issues.
- **Personnel.** What are the minimum recruitment standards for a law enforcement agency? What is the educational level for the department as a whole? How long is the preservice training program? Does the curriculum contain a section on ethics? Is there a field training component? Is the training program consistent with the stated mission of the department? What is the racial, ethnic, and gender composition of the different departments? Does the composition of particular departments match the composition of the local population? Personnel issues are covered in Chapters 5 and 6.
- **Organization.** What is the organizational structure of the department? Is it consistent with recommended standards? If there is a community-policing program, is it departmentwide or carried out by a special unit? Does a recognized police union represent the rank-and-file officers? How powerful is the union? What influence does it have over department policy? These issues are covered in Chapter 4.

 **Case Study**

## *Reality-Based Police Television: Does "Reality Television" Distort Reality?*

Beginning in 1989 with the television debut of *Cops,* reality-based police shows have been in the forefront of "reality" television, paving the way for other live action, uncensored documentary programs. These in-depth programs look into law enforcement—with their use of real-time video footage featuring real cops and criminal suspects—and appeal to many viewers, as indicated by their consistently high ratings. Some proponents of these programs contend that they help the public to understand police work and the criminal justice system. However, some critics believe that reality-based police shows are more interested in high ratings than pursuing a journalistic truth and that they present violent, one-dimensional depictions of law enforcement.

The National Television Violence Study found that for four straight television seasons (1994–1998) every reality-based police show contained visual violence. Today, these programs continue to show live footage or dramatic reenactments of violent events, which leave many researchers concerned about the effects this content has on viewers. In addition, the number of reality specials that combine unusually violent video clips under sensationalistic program topics has risen, and they often feature fatal police car chases and police shoot-outs that highlight the dangerous, and often tragic, elements of police work. Murder, aggravated assault, and robbery are also depicted on police programs at a much higher rate than they actually occur in real life.

Reality-based police programs have been criticized for distorting the truth by offering a one-sided view of events to television audiences, usually from the police officer's standpoint. Although police programs feature real stories and use live footage, critics argue that the editing process produces overly positive portrayals of law enforcement officers and their work. For example, studies show that reality police programs overrepresent the percentage of crimes that are cleared or solved by law enforcement personnel. More than 60 percent of crime stories featured on shows are solved, but success rates for police departments are typically much lower. Police work is also portrayed as continually exciting; rarely does television depict the job's day-to-day tedium, such as paperwork and other office duties. Audiences are only afforded a look into dramatic moments captured during active duty while in the squad car, receiving radio calls, or at a suspect's home ready to execute a search/arrest warrant.

Some people are skeptical about the portrayals of officers featured on reality police programs, claiming that they are acutely aware of being filmed and may conduct themselves accordingly. Their meticulously professional and solicitous behavior can be perceived as an act, rather than a true representation. Furthermore, reality-based police shows depend on police departments' voluntary participation, so the programs have an interest in maintaining favorable relationships with the police. Casting officers in a negative light would jeopardize that rapport.

Others criticize police shows for how they portray certain ethnic groups. Studies have found that programs tend to underrepresent African Americans and overrepresent whites as police officers. Minority groups are also portrayed as committing a greater share of crime on television than they do in real life, while white people are rarely portrayed as criminal suspects. Such ethnic representations may contribute to and perpetuate racial stereotyping.

*Source:* Adapted from *Reality-Based Police Programs*. 2000. Issue Briefs. Studio City, CA: Mediascope Press; or it can be viewed at **http://www.mediascope.org/pubs/ibriefs/rbpp.htm.**

---

# Summary

Why do we have police? Jerome Skolnick's question, with which we opened this chapter, cannot be avoided. As this chapter has indicated, we cannot be satisfied with simplistic answers like "to protect and serve." The police role is extremely complex. First, we must decide which tasks we want the police to emphasize: law enforcement? crime prevention? order maintenance? Second, we need to decide how we want the police to carry out those tasks. Third, we need to decide what kind of officers we want for these tasks, including what selection criteria we want to use, what kind of training officers will receive, and how they will be supervised. We need to decide how we are going to hold the police accountable for the tasks we ask them to carry out.

All of these questions are extremely complex. This book is designed to provide a basic introduction to the police in America so that we can discuss policing in an informed manner.

## Key Terms

general service law enforcement
   agencies, 3
police officer, 4
peace officer, 4
crime-fighter image, 4
police role, 6

coercive force, 10
social control, 11
Herman Goldstein, 14
problem-oriented policing, 14
Newport News, 15
Herman Goldstein Award, 15

community policing, 15
Chicago Alternative Policing
   Strategy, 16
zero-tolerance policing, 16
team policing, 16

## For Discussion

1. Divide into groups and discuss the various functions/roles that the police play in communities. Which functions should the police continue to perform and which functions should be eliminated? How much time should the police devote to each function?

2. Discuss the question raised by Jerome Skolnick: "Why do we have police?"
3. Discuss how the police are part of the system of social control.
4. Discuss how the myths of policing impact the public's expectations of police work.
5. What factors influence the police role?

## Internet Exercises

**Exercise 1** Many police departments have placed their mission statements on the Web. Locate the Web sites for several departments. Which ones have mission statements? How do they compare?

**Exercise 2** Check out the Web site **www.officer. com.** It offers a number of resources to the public and police officers on issues relating to policing, including information on your local police department, police associations, and employment opportunities. Examine the site closely; it will provide you with a number of Web links that you will need to use over the course of the semester.

## Notes

1. Jerome H. Skolnick, *Justice without Trial: Law Enforcement in a Democratic Society,* 3rd ed. (New York: Macmillan, 1994), p. 1.
2. George L. Kelling and Mark H. Moore, *The Evolving Strategy of Policing,* "Perspectives on Policing," No. 4 (Washington DC: Government Printing Office, 1988); Samuel Walker, *A Critical*

*History of Police Reform* (Lexington, MA: Lexington Books, 1977).
3. David H. Bayley, *Police for the Future* (New York: Oxford University Press, 1994), Ch. 1.
4. Egon Bittner, *The Functions of the Police in Modern Society* (Cambridge, MA: Olgeschlager, Gunn, and Hain, 1980).

# Flashback: Moments in American Police History

## The First American Police Officer

The day the first American police officer went out on patrol, he had received no training, patrolled on foot, had no two-way radio, could not be dispatched through a 911 system, and carried no weapon. Moreover, he had little education, received no formal preservice training, and had no manual of policies or procedures. Policing in 1838, in short, was completely different from what it is today.

## Flash Forward: 1950

The 1950 police officer worked in a very different situation. He probably had a high school education (and he was definitely a male, because there were no women on patrol for another sixteen years), may have had some brief academy training but no in-service training, and had a policy and procedure manual, which, however, contained no policies on when to use deadly force, how to handle domestic violence incidents, or when to do a high-speed pursuit. He did not have to worry about any Supreme Court rulings on police procedure, and did not worry too much about being disciplined if he beat up someone with his billy club. Policing had changed a lot since 1838, but was still a long way from where it would be in 2010.

    The police today are the product of their history. This chapter examines the history of the American police, from its roots in England and colonial America down to present-day issues related to community policing, racial profiling, and other matters.

# Why Study Police History?

Why study police history? The history of the American police can help us understand policing today. Many people believe the police do not change. That is a myth. In fact, American policing has changed tremendously, even in the last several years. David Bayley argues that "the last decade of the twentieth century may be the most creative period in policing since the modern police officer was put onto the streets of London in 1829."[1]

Studying this history can help us understand how and why important changes occur. Racial profiling, for example, is nothing new. The police–community relations problem has a long history. It is useful to understand why it continues despite many reforms intended to eliminate discrimination. The patrol car revolutionized police work, and it is important to understand both its positive contributions and its negative effects.

# The English Heritage

**English heritage**

American policing is a product of its **English heritage.** The English colonists brought a criminal justice system as part of their cultural baggage. This heritage included the English common law, the high value placed on individual rights, the court systems and forms of punishment, and different law enforcement agencies.[2]

The English heritage contributed three enduring features to American policing. The first is a tradition of limited police authority. The Anglo American legal tradition places a high value on individual liberty and on governmental authority.[3] In the United States, these limits are embodied in the Bill of Rights. Continental European countries, by contrast, give their law enforcement agencies much broader powers. German citizens, for example, are required to carry identity cards and report changes of address to police authorities.

The second feature is a tradition of local control of law enforcement agencies. Almost every other country in the world has a centralized, national police force.

The third feature, which is a consequence of local control, is a highly decentralized and fragmented system of law enforcement. The United States is unique in

---

**SIDEBAR        2 – 1**

## *The Relevance of History*

The study of police history can:

1. Highlight the fact of change.
2. Put current problems into perspective.
3. Help us understand which reforms have worked.
4. Alert us to the unintended consequences of reforms.

having about 15,000 separate law enforcement agencies, subject only to minimal coordination and very little national control or regulation.[4]

Formal law enforcement agencies emerged in England in the thirteenth century, and over the years evolved in an unsystematic fashion. Responsibility for law enforcement and keeping the peace was shared by the constable, the sheriff, and the justice of the peace. Private citizens, however, retained much of the responsibility for law enforcement, pursuing offenders on their own and initiating criminal cases. This approach was brought to America and persisted into the nineteenth century.[5]

## Creation of the Modern Police: London, 1829

**Robert Peel** is the "father" of modern policing. An important political leader in England, he fought for over 30 years to improve law enforcement in that country. By the early 1900s, the old system of law enforcement collapsed under the impact of urbanization and industrialization. London suffered from poverty, disorder, ethnic conflict, and crime. The 1780 Gordon riots, a clash between Irish immigrants and English citizens, triggered a 50-year debate over how to provide better public safety. Peel finally persuaded Parliament to create the **London Metropolitan Police** in 1829. It is recognized as the first modern police force, and officers are still known as "Bobbies" in honor of Peel.[6]

**Robert Peel**

**London Metropolitan Police**

What exactly is "modern" about the type of policing created by Peel? The three core elements involve the mission, strategy, and organizational structure of the police.

The mission of Peel's new police was **crime prevention.** This reflected the utilitarian idea that it is better to prevent crime than to respond after the fact. Before the London Police, all law enforcement was reactive, responding to crimes that had been committed.

**crime prevention**

The strategy for implementing the mission of crime prevention was preventive patrol. Peel introduced the idea of officers patrolling fixed "beats" to maintain a visible police presence throughout the community. This presence was designed to deter crime.

The organizational structure for organizing police operations was borrowed from the military. This included a hierarchical organization, uniforms, rank designations, and an authoritarian system of command and discipline. This "quasi-military" style still exists in American police administration today.

The modern police represented a new concept in social control. Allan Silver argues that a continuous presence of police reflected a growing "demand for order" in urban industrial society.[7] David Bayley, meanwhile, argues that to accomplish this the modern police are "public, specialized, and professional."[8] Public, or government, agencies have the primary responsibility for public safety. They have a specialized mission of law enforcement and crime prevention. Finally, they are professional in the sense that they are full-time, paid employees. Bayley cautions that these characteristics did not appear all at once. Although 1829 is traditionally cited as the birth of the London police, in reality all the new features did not appear for many decades. The American police, in particular, were slow to become fully "modern."

### *Contributions of the English Heritage to American Policing*

1. Tradition of limited police authority.
2. Tradition of local control.
3. Decentralized and fragmented police system.

# Law Enforcement in Colonial America

When the first English colonists in America created their own law enforcement agencies, they borrowed from their English heritage (Sidebar 2–2). The three important institutions were the sheriff, the constable, and the watch. In the new environment of America, however, these institutions acquired distinctive American features.[9]

The sheriff was the most important law enforcement official in America. Appointed by the colonial governor, the sheriff had a very broad role that included law enforcement, collecting taxes, supervising elections, maintaining bridges and roads, and other miscellaneous duties.[10]

The constable also had responsibility for enforcing the law and carrying out certain legal duties. Initially an elective position, the constable gradually evolved into a semiprofessional appointed office. In Boston and several other cities, the office of constable became a desirable and often lucrative position.[11]

**the watch**

**The watch** most resembled the modern-day police. Watchmen patrolled the city to guard against fires, crime, and disorder. At first there was only a night watch. As towns grew larger, they added a day watch. Boston created its first watch in 1634. Following the English tradition, all adult males were expected to serve as watchmen. Many men tried to avoid this duty, either by outright evasion or by paying others to serve in their place. Eventually, the watch evolved into a paid professional position.[12]

The slave patrol was a distinctly American form of law enforcement. In southern states where slavery existed, it was intended to guard against slave revolts and capture runaway slaves. In some respects, the slave patrols were actually the first modern police forces in this country. The Charleston, South Carolina, slave patrol had about 100 officers in 1837 and was far larger than any northern city police force at that time.[13]

## EXHIBIT 2–1

### Law Enforcement Institutions in Colonial America

Sheriff
Constable
Watch
   Night watch
   Day watch
Slave Patrol

## The Quality of Colonial Law Enforcement

Colonial law enforcement was inefficient, corrupt, and affected by political interference. Contrary to popular myth, there was never a "golden age" of efficiency, effectiveness, and integrity in American policing.

With respect to crime, the sheriff, the constable, and the watch had little capacity to prevent crime or apprehend offenders. They were reactive, responding to complaints brought to them. Although watchmen patrolled, they were too few in number to really prevent crime. They did not have enough personnel to investigate many crimes. Crime victims could not easily report crimes. Finally, the sheriff and the watchmen were paid by fees for particular services. As a result, they had greater incentive to work on their civil responsibilities, which offered more certain payment, than on criminal law enforcement.[14]

Colonial agencies were also ill-equipped to maintain order. With very few watchmen on duty, there was little they could do in response to public drunkenness, disputes, or **riots.** Cities were in fact very disorderly in those years. Nor could citizens easily report disturbances. Finally, providing both routine and emergency service to the public, as today's police do, was not a regular part of the sheriff's or the constable's job.

In practice, ordinary citizens played a major role in maintaining social control through informal means: a comment, a warning, or a rebuke from friends or neighbors, or a "trial" by the church congregation for misbehavior. This system worked because communities were small and homogeneous. There was much face-to-face contact, and people shared the same basic values. Eventually, however, the system broke down as communities grew into larger, diverse towns and cities.[15]

If policing was ineffective in cities and towns, it was almost nonexistent on the frontier. Organized government did not appear in many areas for decades. As a result, settlers relied on their own resources and often took the law into their own hands. The result was a terrible tradition of vigilantism that lasted into the twentieth century, and represented some of the worst aspects of American criminal justice. Frequently, mobs drove out of town or even killed people whom they did not like. The lynching of African Americans was used to maintain the system of racial segregation in the South.[16]

Corruption appeared very early. The criminal law was even more moralistic than today, with many restrictions on drinking, gambling, and sexual practices. As a result, people bribed law enforcement officials to overlook violation of the law.

**riots**

## The First Modern American Police

Modern police forces were established in the United States in the 1830s and 1840s. As in England, the old system of law enforcement broke down under the impact of urbanization, industrialization, and immigration. In the 1830s, a wave of riots struck American cities. Boston had major riots in 1834, 1835, and 1837. Philadelphia, New York, Cincinnati, Detroit, and other cities all had major disturbances. In 1838, Abraham Lincoln, then a member of the Illinois state legislature, warned of the "increasing disregard for law which pervades the country."[17]

Compare these early riots with the urban racial violence of the 1960s.

Many riots were clashes between different ethnic groups: Irish or German immigrants versus native-born English Protestants. Other riots were economic in nature: angry depositors vandalized failed banks, for example. Moral issues also produced violence. People objecting to medical research on cadavers attacked hospitals; residents of Detroit staged several "whorehouse riots," attempting to close down houses of prostitution. Finally, pro-slavery whites attacked abolitionists and free black citizens in northern cities.[18]

Despite the breakdown in law and order, Americans moved very slowly in creating new police forces. New York City did not create a new police force until 1845, 11 years after the first serious riots. Philadelphia could not make up its mind, creating and abolishing several different law enforcement agencies between 1834 and 1854, before finally creating a consolidated, citywide police force on the London model.[19]

Americans were very uncertain about the new police. The idea of a continual police presence on the streets brought back memories of the hated British colonial army. Many people were afraid their political opponents would control the police and use them to their advantage. Finally, taxpayers simply did not want to pay for a public police force.

Many of the first American police departments were basically expanded versions of the existing watch system. The Boston police department had only nine officers in 1838. The first American police officers did not wear uniforms, or carry weapons, and were identified only by a distinctive hat and badge. Weapons did not become standard police equipment until the late nineteenth century, in response to rising levels of crime and violence.

Americans borrowed most of the features of modern policing from London: the mission of crime prevention, the strategy of visible patrol over fixed beats, and the quasi-military organizational structure. The structure of political control of the police, however, was very different. The United States was a far more democratic country than Britain. American voters—although only white males with property until the latter part of the nineteenth century—exercised direct control over all government agencies. London residents, by contrast, had no direct control over their police. As a result, American police departments were immediately immersed in local politics, a situation that led to many serious problems. The commissioners of the London police, freed from political influence, were able to maintain high personnel standards.[20]

## The "Political Era" in American Policing, 1830s–1900

Politics influenced every aspect of American policing in the nineteenth century, and the period from the 1830s to 1900 is often called the "political era" (see Exhibit 2–2). Inefficiency, corruption, and lack of professionalism were the chief results.[21]

### A Lack of Personnel Standards

Police departments in the political era had no personnel standards as we understand them today. Officers were selected entirely on the basis of their political connections.

**Three Eras of American Policing**
I    The political era: 1830s–1900
II   The professional era: 1900–1960s
III  The era of conflicting pressures: 1960s–present

Men with no formal education, those in bad health, and those with criminal records were hired. There were a few female matrons for the jail, but no female sworn officers until the early twentieth century. In New York City, a $300 payment to the Tammany Hall political machine was the only requirement for a job on the police force.[22]

In most departments, recruits received no formal preservice training. They were handed a badge, a baton, and a copy of the department rules (if one existed), and then sent out on patrol duty. Cincinnati created one of the first police academies in 1888, but it lasted only a few years. New York City established a School of Pistol Practice in 1895, but offered no training in any other aspect of policing until 1909. Even then, a 1913 investigation found it gave no tests and all recruits were automatically passed.[23]

Police officers had no job security and could be fired at will. In some cases, almost all the officers were fired after an election. Nonetheless, it was an attractive job because salaries were generally higher than those for most blue collar jobs. In 1880 officers in most big cities earned $900 a year, compared with $450 for factory workers.

Jobs on the police force were a major form of **patronage,** which local politicians used to reward their friends. Consequently, the composition of departments reflected the ethnic and religious makeup of the cities. When Irish Americans began to win political power, they appointed their friends as police officers. When Barney McGinniskin became the first Irish American police officer in Boston in 1851, it provoked major protests from the English and Protestant establishment in the city. Many German Americans served as police officers in Cleveland, Cincinnati, Milwaukee, and St. Louis, where German immigration was heavy. After the Civil War, some African Americans were appointed police officers in northern cities where the Republicans, the party of Abraham Lincoln, were in power.

**patronage**

## Patrol Work in the Political Era

Routine police patrol in the political era was hopelessly inefficient. Officers patrolled on foot and were spread very thin. In Chicago, beats were three and four miles long. In many cities entire areas were not patrolled at all. The telephone did not exist, and so it was impossible for citizens to call about crime and disorder. And with no patrol cars, officers could not have responded anyway.

Supervision was weak or nonexistent. Sergeants also patrolled on foot and could not keep track of the officers under their command. Many reports from those years indicate that officers easily evaded duty and spent much of their time in saloons and barbershops. Bad weather—rain, snow, and extremely hot weather—encouraged officers to spend their time in bars or barbershops.

For a full discussion of contemporary police patrol work, see Chapter 7.

The first primitive communications systems involved a network of call boxes that allowed patrol officers to call precinct stations. Officers soon learned to sabotage them, however: leaving receivers off the hook (which took the early systems out of operation), or lying about where they actually were.[24] The lack of an effective communications system made it difficult if not impossible for citizens to contact the police. In the event of a crime or disturbance, a citizen had to go out into the street and find an officer.

## The Police and the Public

There was never a "golden age" of policing where the police were friendly, knowledgeable about their neighborhoods, and enjoyed good relations with the public. There were so few police officers they could not possibly have known many people on their beats. There was a high turnover rate among officers, and the population was even more mobile than today. Many reports, moreover, indicate that many police officers drank on duty and frequently used excessive physical force. As a result, citizens were very disrespectful. Juvenile gangs, for example, made a sport of throwing rocks at the police or taunting them. People who were arrested often fought back, causing officers to use excessive force.[25]

Historian Christopher Thale, analyzing the records of officer assignments in New York City in the nineteenth century, convincingly argues that it was "not mathematically plausible" for officers to know many people on their beats First, the composition of neighborhoods constantly changed under the pressure of massive immigration. Second, officer assignments were not stable. When the New York City Police Department was first established, officers were required to live in their precinct. This policy was often ignored, however, and then abolished in 1857. The pressure of providing police services forced the department to assign officers where they were needed, particularly in new and growing neighborhoods. Thale concludes that citizens "experienced not 'the' cop on the beat, but 'the cops.'"[26]

In addition to the instability of assignments, police–citizen relations were characterized by ethnic and religious tensions. The New York City Police Department was largely Irish Catholic, and officers were often hostile to or even brutal toward the new Italian and Jewish immigrants. In short, long before the introduction of the police car in the twentieth century, American urban policing was highly impersonal and marked by police–citizen conflict. The idea of the friendly "neighborhood cop" is pure myth.

What went wrong with American policing? In a provocative comparative study, Wilbur Miller argues that the London police became highly professional, while the American police were completely unprofessional. The difference was that the Commissioners of the London Metropolitan Police were free from political interference and able to maintain high personnel standards. As a result, London Bobbies eventually won public respect. By contrast, the lack of adequate supervision in America tolerated police misconduct, and the result was public disrespect. From the very start, in short, police in the two countries went in different directions.[27]

American police officers eventually began to carry firearms in response to increasing citizen violence. As late as 1880 the police in Brooklyn (then an independent city of 500,000 people) were unarmed. In some cities weapons were optional or carried at the discretion of a sergeant. As crime and violence increased in the late 1800s, however, officers began to carry firearms as standard equipment.

The role of the police was very different in the political era from what it is today. The police were a major social welfare institution. Precinct stations provided lodging to the homeless. The Philadelphia police gave shelter to over 100,000 people a year during the 1880s. This began to change around 1900. The police professionalized, concentrating on crime, and care for the poor became the responsibility of professional social work agencies.[28]

## Corruption and Politics

George W. Plunkitt represented everything that was wrong with American policing in the nineteenth century. Plunkitt was a district leader for Tammany Hall, the social club that controlled New York City politics for several generations. He is a famous historical figure because he explained in writing exactly how corruption worked.

Corruption, Plunkitt explained, was the essence of democracy. His Tammany Hall organization "always stood for rewardin' the men that won the victory." Jobs on the police department were one of the major rewards he and other political leaders had to offer. Running a political organization was expensive, and Tammany Hall funded itself through kickbacks from people it rewarded or payoffs from gamblers and prostitutes. Why did police corruption last so long? Plunkitt explained that the people "knew just what they were doin'." They liked the rewards they received and were not offended by the illegal activity.[29]

Police corruption was epidemic in the nineteenth century. Historian Mark Haller argues that corruption was one of the main functions of local government, and the police were only one part of the problem.[30] The police took payoffs for not enforcing laws on drinking, gambling, and prostitution. The money was then divided among officers at all ranks. Corruption extended to personnel decisions. Officers often had to pay bribes for promotion. The cost of obtaining a promotion was compensated for by the greater opportunities for graft. The New York City police

For a full discussion of police corruption, see Chapter 13.

---

SIDEBAR        2 – 3

### *The Diary of a Police Officer: Boston, 1895*

We know very little about what police officers actually did in the early years. Most of the evidence comes from reformers or journalists seeking to expose corruption and inefficiency. Their reports are inherently biased. An 1895 diary of Boston police officer Stillman S. Wakeman provides a rare glimpse into actual police work 100 years ago.

Officer Wakeman was "an officer of the neighborhood." He spent most of his time on patrol responding to little problems that neighborhood residents brought to him: disputes, minor property crimes, and so on. He spent relatively little time on major offenses: murder, rape, robbery. He resolved most of the problems informally, acting as a neighborhood magistrate. His role was remarkably similar to that of contemporary patrol officers. He was reactive and a problem solver. The major difference was the absence of modern police technology: the patrol car and the 911 telephone system.

*Source:* Alexander von Hoffman, "An Officer of the Neighborhood: A Boston Patrolman on the Beat in 1895," *Journal of Social History 26* (Winter 1992): pp. 309–30.

commissioner, forced to resign in 1894, admitted that he had amassed a personal fortune of over $350,000 (equivalent to millions in today's dollars).[31]

Corruption served important social and political ends. Alcohol was an important symbolic issue in American politics. Protestant Americans saw sobriety as a badge of respectability and self-discipline. They sought to impose their morality on working class immigrant groups, especially the Irish and Germans, by limiting or outlawing drinking. For blue collar immigrants, the neighborhood saloon was not only a place to relax (remember: people in those days did not have large homes with recreation rooms), but an important social institution and often the base of operations for political machines. Thus, the attack on drinking was also an attack on working-class social life and political power. Working-class immigrants fought back by gaining political control of the police, and simply not enforcing the laws on drinking.[32]

## Immigration, Discrimination, and Police Corruption

On December 3, 1882, the New York City Police arrested 137 people for violating the "Sunday Closing Law." The crackdown was a dramatic reversal of traditional practice. Laws requiring businesses to close on Sunday had been on the books since the colonial period but were usually ignored. The new enforcement effort, and the controversy that lasted for many years afterward, illustrates the connection between immigration, ethnic and religious discrimination, and police corruption.[33]

Almost all of those arrested that Sunday in 1882 were Jewish small businessmen: butchers, barbers, bakers, and so forth. They worked on Sunday because their religious beliefs required them to close on Saturday to observe the Jewish Sabbath. Complying with the state law meant they would be closed two days a week, while their non-Jewish competitors only had to close for one day.

As the battle over enforcement of the Sunday closing law continued for many years, several patterns emerged, according to cultural historian Batya Miller. "Reform" mayors, who were generally Protestant, were the most vigorous in enforcing the laws. Future U.S. President Theodore Roosevelt, who served as New York police commissioner from 1895 to 1897, advocated strict enforcement, for example. The Tammany Hall political machine, dominated by Irish Catholics, on the other hand, tended to ignore the law when it was in power. This did not mean that Jewish businessmen were free of discrimination, however. Tammany Hall politicians were notorious for corruption, and they extorted a $5 fee from street peddlers to avoid being arrested. In fact, police officers marked the carts of those who did not pay with chalk, indicating to other officers that they were fair game for arrest. At the same time, police brutality against Jews by Irish Catholic officers was "not uncommon" according to Miller.

In short, cultural conflict over religious holidays was at the heart of arbitrary enforcement of the laws, corruption, police brutality, and deeper ethnic and religious conflict in city politics. This was no "golden age" of good law enforcement.

## The Failure of Police Reform

Political reformers made police corruption a major issue during the nineteenth century. Their efforts were generally unsuccessful. The reformers concentrated on changing the formal structure of control of police departments, usually by creating a board of police commissioners appointed by the governor or the legislature. This struggle for control reflected divisions along the lines of political parties, ethnic groups, and urban and rural perspectives. New York created the first state-controlled police commission in 1857. In many cities, the battle for control of the police was endless. Cincinnati underwent ten major changes in the form of police control between 1859 and 1910. (This system of state control continues today with St. Louis and Kansas City, Missouri.)[34]

Even when the reformers won, however, they did not succeed in improving the quality of policing. Their reform agenda emphasized replacing "bad" people (their political opponents) with "good" people (their own supporters). They did not have any substantive ideas about police administration, and did not improve recruitment standards, training, or supervision. Also, looking at it from today's perspective, we can see that they did not give any attention to use of excessive force or race discrimination—two issues that are of paramount concern today.

For a full discussion of current police accountability measures and their impact, see Chapter 14.

**Theodore Roosevelt**

**Theodore Roosevelt,** who was later president of the United States (1901 to 1909), is one of the most famous people in American history. Yet few people are aware that he earlier served as a police commissioner of New York City between 1895 and 1897. As commissioner he fought against the corrupt Tammany Hall political machine and tried to eliminate corruption and inefficiency in the NYPD.

His leadership style was vigorous and flamboyant, as he went out on the streets at night, catching officers in saloons or sleeping on the job. He tried to raise personnel standards and ensure enforcement of the liquor laws, but with little success. He made a lot of headlines (which, of course, advanced his political career) but did not achieve any lasting changes in the NYPD. Like other reformers of his day, he did not have a good theory of police administration. Corruption and inefficiency continued long after he resigned in 1897.[35]

## The Impact of the Police on Society

Did the early American police departments reduce crime and disorder? Did a young man in the slums of Cincinnati or Baltimore refrain from committing a burglary or robbery because he was afraid of being caught? Did the presence of patrol officers on the street help to maintain order? Probably not.

Historians debate the impact of the police on society. Cities did become more orderly as the nineteenth century progressed, and some historians argue that the police contributed to this. Other historians, however, argue that the police were so few in number that they could not possibly have deterred crime. The growth of order, they argue, was more a result of a natural adaptation to urban life. The daily routine of urban life—reporting to work every day at the same hour—cultivated habits of self-discipline and order. The police, according to this view, played a supporting role at best.[36]

The role of the police in labor relations during the nineteenth century is also a matter of debate among historians. Marxist historians argue that the police served the interests of business and were used to harass labor unions and break strikes. American labor relations during these years were extremely violent. Management fought unions, and many strikes led to violence. In some communities, particularly those with coal and steel industries, strikes were virtual civil war. In many cities, however, the police were friendly to organized labor, mainly because they came from the same blue-collar communities, and refused to serve the interests of businessmen.[37]

In the end, while the modern police were created to deal with the problems of crime and disorder, they mainly succeeded in becoming a social and political problem themselves. The rampant corruption and inefficiency set in motion generations of reform efforts that continue today.

# The Professional Era, 1900–1960

American policing underwent a dramatic change in the twentieth century. The two principal forces for change were an organized movement for police professionalism, and the introduction of modern technology, particularly the telephone and the patrol car.

## The Professionalization Movement

**August Vollmer**

If Robert Peel was the father of the modern police, **August Vollmer** was the father of American police professionalism. Vollmer served as chief of police in Berkeley, California, from 1905 to 1932 and, more than any other person, defined the reform agenda that continues to influence policing today. He is most famous for advocating higher education for police officers, hiring college graduates in Berkeley and organizing the first college-level police science courses at the University of California in 1916. In that respect, he is also the father of modern criminal justice education. Vollmer also served as a consultant to many local police departments and national commissions. In 1923 he took a year's leave from Berkeley to serve as chief of the Los Angeles police department. He also wrote the 1931 Wickersham Commission *Report on Police,* which summarized the reform agenda of modern management for police departments and higher recruitment standards for officers. A number of his students went on to become reform police chiefs in California and other states.[38]

Vollmer was part of a new generation of leaders at the turn of the century who launched an organized effort to professionalize the police. Police reform was part of a much broader political movement known as progressivism between 1900 and 1917. Progressive reformers sought to regulate big business, eliminate child labor, improve social welfare services, and reform local government, as well as professionalize the police.[39]

## The Reform Agenda

**professionalization movement**

The **professionalization movement** developed a specific agenda of reform (see Exhibit 2–3). First, the reformers defined policing as a profession. This meant that the police should be public servants with a professional obligation to serve the entire community on a nonpartisan basis. Second, reformers sought to eliminate the influence of politics on policing. Third, they argued for hiring qualified chief executives to head police departments, people who had proven ability to manage a large organization. Arthur Woods, a prominent lawyer, served as police commissioner in New York City from 1914 to 1917, while Philadelphia hired Marine Corps General Smedley Butler to head its police department from 1911 to 1915.[40]

## EXHIBIT 2-3

### The Reform Agenda of the Professionalization Movement

1. Define policing as a profession.
2. Eliminate political influence from policing.
3. Appoint qualified chief executives.
4. Raise personnel standards.
5. Introduce principles of modern management.
6. Create specialized units.

Fourth, the reformers tried to raise personnel standards for rank-and-file officers. This included establishing minimum recruitment requirements of intelligence, health, and moral character. New York City created the first permanent police training academy in 1895. In most cities the process of reform was painfully slow. Some cities did not offer any meaningful training until the 1950s.

Fifth, professionalism meant applying modern management principles to police departments. This involved centralizing command and control and making efficient use of personnel. Until then, police chiefs had exercised little real control; captains in neighborhood precincts and their political friends had the real power. Reformers closed precinct stations and used the new communications technology to control both middle management personnel and officers on the street.

Sixth, reformers created the first specialized units devoted to traffic, juveniles, and vice. Previously, police departments had only patrol and detective units. Specialization, however, increased the size and complexity of the police bureaucracy, increasing the challenge of managing departments.

Juvenile units led to a historic innovation: the first female sworn officers. Until then, policing had been an all-male occupation. The Portland (Oregon) police hired the first policewoman, Lola Baldwin, as a juvenile specialist in 1905.

**Alice Stebbins Wells** became the real leader of the policewomen's movement. She joined the Los Angeles Police Department in 1910, and was soon active at the national level. She organized the International Association of Policewomen in 1915, and gave many talks around the country about the role of policewomen. By 1919 over sixty police departments employed female officers. Wells shared the dominant values of her time regarding women, however, which limited their role in policing.

The first policewomen did not perform regular patrol duty, usually did not wear uniforms, did not carry weapons, and had only limited arrest powers. Policewomen advocates argued that women were specially qualified to work with children and that they should not handle regular police duties.[41]

**Alice Stebbins Wells**

For a full discussion of women in policing, see Chapter 6.

## The Impact of Professionalization

Professionalization progressed very slowly. By 1920 Milwaukee, Cincinnati, and Berkeley had emerged as leaders in the field. Most other departments, however, remained mired in corruption and inefficiency. August Vollmer spent 1923 and 1924 trying to reform the Los Angeles police, but gave up in despair and returned to

Berkeley. Chicago seemed to resist all efforts at reform. In some cities, the police made notable steps forward, only to slide backward a few years later. Philadelphia implemented many reforms between 1911 and 1915, only to have all progress wiped out when the city's old political machine regained control.[42]

Despite these failures, the professionalization movement reformers achieved some important successes. The idea of professionalism was established as the goal for modern policing. Reformed departments also became models for other cities.

## The New Police Subculture

Professionalization also introduced some new problems in policing. Reform increased the military ethos of police departments, adding parades, close-order drills, and military-style commendations. The command system became far more authoritarian than it had been in the old days.

The rank-and-file police officer became the forgotten person, not respected by reformers who placed their hopes on strong administrators. As a result, the rank and file retreated into an isolated and alienated police subculture that opposed most reforms.[43]

The most dramatic expression of the new police subculture was the emergence of police unions. As policing became a profession and officers thought in terms of the job as a career, they demanded better salaries and a voice in decisions affecting their jobs. The problem reached crisis proportions during World War I, when increases in the cost of living eroded the value of police salaries. This set the stage for the 1919 **Boston police strike,** one of the most famous events in police history. Salaries for Boston police officers had not been raised in nearly 20 years. When their demand for a 20 percent raise was rejected, they voted to form a union. Police Commissioner Edwin U. Curtis then suspended the union leaders, and 1,117 officers went out on strike, leaving only 427 on duty. Violence and disorder erupted throughout the city. Massachusetts Governor Calvin Coolidge called out the state militia and won national fame for his comment, "There is no right to strike against the public safety by anybody, anywhere, at any time." The strike quickly collapsed and all the strikers were fired.[44]

**Boston police strike**

The violence in Boston produced a national backlash against police unions, and police unions in other cities disappeared. Police unionism was dead until the 1960s, but the problem of an alienated rank and file remained.

Professionalism also created new problems in police administration. As departments grew in size and created new specialized units, they became increasingly complex bureaucracies, which required increasingly sophisticated management. Managing police organizations continued to be a major challenge into the twenty-first century.

## Police and Racial Minorities

Conflict between the police and the African American community also appeared during the World War I years. Major race riots erupted in East St. Louis, Illinois (1917), and in Chicago and other cities in 1919. Investigations of these riots found race discrimination by the police prior to and during the riots. In some cases, officers joined in the rioting themselves. The Chicago Riot Commission recommended several steps to improve police–community relations, but virtually nothing was done to either hire more African American officers or eliminate race discrimination in police work.[45]

Even when some departments outside the south hired a few African American officers, they usually assigned them to the black community. Most southern police departments hired no African American officers at all, while some put them in a second-class category, assigning them only to the black community and not allowing them to arrest whites. Conflict between the police and the African American community remained a serious problem in all parts of the country, but it did not receive any serious attention until the riots of the 1960s.[46]

For a full discussion of police–community relations, see Chapter 12.

## New Law Enforcement Agencies

Two important new law enforcement agencies appeared in the years before World War I: the state police and the Bureau of Investigation.

Several states created state-level law enforcement agencies in the nineteenth century, but they remained relatively unimportant. The Texas Rangers were established in 1835. The Pennsylvania State Constabulary, created in 1905, was the first modern state police force, but was not typical of most others. It was a highly centralized, militaristic agency that concentrated on controlling strikes. Business leaders felt that local police and the militia were unreliable during strikes. Organized labor bitterly attacked the Constabulary, denouncing its officers as "cossacks."[47]

Other states soon created their own agencies. About half were highway patrols, limited to traffic enforcement, while the other half were general law enforcement agencies. While business interests wanted Pennsylvania-style agencies, organized labor in several states was able to limit their powers or block their creation altogether.[48]

The Bureau of Investigation was established in 1908 by executive order of President Theodore Roosevelt. (It was renamed the Federal Bureau of Investigation in 1935.) Until then, the federal government had no full-time criminal investigation agency. Private detective agencies were sometimes used under contract on an as-needed basis. The new Bureau of Investigation was immediately involved in scandal. Some agents were caught opening the mail of one senator who had opposed creating the Bureau. In 1919 and 1920, in the Palmer Raids, the Bureau conducted a massive roundup of alleged political radicals, accompanied by gross violations of due process. More scandals followed in the 1920s, as the Bureau continued to engage in political spying.[49]

## Technology Revolutionizes Policing

Some of the most important changes in policing were the result of modern technology, especially **communications technology.** The patrol car, the two-way radio, and the telephone revolutionized patrol work, the nature of police–citizen contacts, and police management (see Exhibit 2–4).[50]

**communications technology**

The patrol car first appeared just before World War I and by the 1920s was in widespread use. The police adopted it in part because they had to keep up with citizens and criminals who were now driving cars. Even more important, police chiefs believed the patrol car would make possible efficient and effective patrol coverage. Patrolling by car would allow officers to cover their beats more intensively, and

---

### EXHIBIT 2–4

## The Technological Revolution in Policing

| New Technology | Impact |
|---|---|
| Telephone | Citizens can easily call the police |
| Two-way radio | Quick dispatch of police to calls |
| | Constant supervision of patrol officers |
| Patrol car | Quick response to citizen calls |
| | Efficient patrol coverage |
| | Isolation of patrol officers |

---

chiefs believed this would deter crime more effectively than foot patrol. Also, patrol officers could respond quickly to crimes and calls for service. American police departments steadily converted from foot to motor patrol, and by the 1960s only a few major cities still relied heavily on foot patrol.

The patrol car had important unintended consequences, however, that created new problems. It removed the officer from the street and reduced informal contact with law-abiding citizens. The police became isolated from the public, and racial minorities in particular saw the police as an occupying army. This problem remained hidden until the police–community relations crisis of the 1960s.

The two-way radio became widespread in the late 1930s and had two important consequences. First, it allowed departments to dispatch officers in response to citizen calls for service. Second, it revolutionized police supervision by allowing the department to maintain continuous contact with patrol officers.

The telephone was invented in 1877, but it did not have a great impact on policing until it was linked with the patrol car and the two-way radio in the mid-twentieth century. Together, the three pieces of technology completed a new communications link between citizens and the police. Citizens could now easily call the police; the two-way radio enabled the department to dispatch a patrol car immediately; and the patrol car allowed the officer to reach the scene quickly.

Police departments encouraged people to call, promising an immediate response. Gradually, citizens became socialized into the habit of "calling the cops" to handle even the smallest problems. Over time, Americans developed higher expectations about the quality of life because they could now call someone to deal with all sorts of problems. As a result, the call workload steadily increased. When the rising number of calls overloaded the police, they responded by adding more officers, more patrol cars, and more sophisticated communications systems. More resources, however, only encouraged more calls, and the process repeated itself. This process continued until the idea of community policing questioned the importance of responding to each and every call for service.[51]

Telephone-generated calls for service altered the nature of police–citizen contacts. Previously, police officers rarely entered private dwellings. Patrolling on foot, they had no way of learning about problems in private areas. Nor did citizens have any way of summoning the police. The new technology made it possible for citizens to invite the police into their homes. The result was a complex and contradictory change in police–citizen contacts. While the patrol car isolated the police from people on the streets, the telephone brought police officers into people's living rooms, kitchens, and bedrooms. There, officers became involved in the most intimate domestic problems: domestic disputes, alcohol abuse, parent–child conflicts, and other social problems.[52]

# New Directions in Police Administration, 1930–1960

## The Wickersham Commission Report

In 1929 President Herbert Hoover created the **Wickersham Commission,** officially the National Commission on Law Observance and Enforcement, to conduct the first national study of the American criminal justice system. The commission published fourteen reports in 1931, but the most important was the *Report on Lawlessness in Law Enforcement.* The report shocked the nation with its expose of "the third degree— the inflicting of pain, physical or mental, to extract confessions or statements." Police abuse, it concluded, "is extensively practiced." The report found that police routinely beat suspects, threatened them with worse punishment, and held them illegally for protracted questioning. It cited examples of a suspect who was held by the ankles from a third-story window, and another who was forced to stand in the morgue with his hand on the body of a murder victim. The chief of police in Buffalo, New York, openly declared that he would violate the Constitution if he felt he had to.[53]

**Wickersham Commission**

The Wickersham report inspired a new generation of police administrators who made new efforts to professionalize the police.

## Professionalization Continues

Influenced by August Vollmer, California police departments took the lead in professionalization from the 1920s through the 1960s. Vollmer's protégés became police chiefs throughout the state, spreading the reform agenda. The first undergraduate law enforcement program was established at San Jose State College in 1931. California also developed a system of regional training for police officers in the late 1930s.[54]

**O. W. Wilson** was Vollmer's most famous protégé, and he was the most prominent leader of the professionalization movement from the late 1930s through the end of the 1960s. He served as chief of police in Wichita, Kansas, from 1928 to 1935, Dean of the University of California School of Criminology from 1950 to 1960, and Superintendent of the Chicago police from 1960 to 1967.

**O. W. Wilson**

Wilson made his greatest impact through his two textbooks on police management: the International City Management Association's *Municipal Police Administration* and his own *Police Administration* (1950). The latter book became the informal "bible" of police administration, influencing a generation of police chiefs.[55]

Wilson's major contribution to police management involved the efficient management of personnel, particularly patrol officers. In 1941 he developed a formula for assigning patrol officers on the basis of a workload formula that reflected reported crime and calls for service. This formula, refined and updated through modern management information systems, is still used by police departments today.

## Simmering Racial and Ethnic Relations

Despite the progress in professionalization, the reformers did almost nothing to improve relations with racial and ethnic minority communities. They completely ignored the recommendations of the report on the 1919 Chicago race riot. In 1943 another wave of racial violence swept the country, with serious disturbances in Detroit, New York City, and Los Angeles. The Detroit riot was very serious, disrupting production of tanks and other vehicles needed in World War II.

The 1943 Los Angeles riot brought attention to growing conflict between the police and the Latino community. Often referred to as the "Zoot Suit" riot, the violence was the product of many factors. The population of Los Angeles was changing, with an increase in immigrants from Mexico. In addition to discrimination in employment and housing, the Latino community experienced brutality and discrimination at the hands of the police. World War II added another volatile element, as many U.S. Navy personnel were usually on leave in the city. The news media encouraged the idea that young Mexican Americans were responsible for an increase in crime and juvenile delinquency. And because many Latino youth wore the so-called zoot suit, it became both a stereotype and a symbol of the violence that erupted in 1943. The riots broke out on June 3, 1943, and lasted for a week. Although recommendations were made to improve police-community relations, little was done in the years that followed.[56]

The riots of the 1940s gave birth to the modern police-community relations movements. A number of departments created special police-community relations units and offered the first training programs on race relations. The most significant progress occurred in California. These reforms, however, were very limited and did not prevent the even more serious race relations crisis of the 1960s.

## J. Edgar Hoover and the War on Crime

**J. Edgar Hoover**

The most important new figure in American law enforcement in the 1930s was the director of the Bureau of Investigation, **J. Edgar Hoover.** He was appointed director of the Bureau in 1924 after a series of scandals. Capitalizing on public fears about a national crime wave in the 1930s, he increased the size and scope of the Bureau's activities. In 1930 he won control of the new Uniform Crime Reports (UCR) system. In 1934 a set of new federal laws gave the FBI increased jurisdiction, including authority to arrest criminals who crossed state lines in order to avoid prosecution. The following year the FBI opened its National Police Academy, which trained Bureau agents and, by invitation, some local police officers.[57]

Hoover was a master at public relations, skillfully manipulating the media to project an image of the FBI agent as the paragon of professionalism: dedicated, honest, trained, and relentlessly efficient. Some of Hoover's reputation was deserved. FBI agents were far better educated and trained than local police officers. There was an ugly underside to Hoover's long career (1924–1972) as leader of the Bureau, however. He exaggerated the FBI's role in several famous cases—John Dillinger, Pretty Boy Floyd—and manipulated crime data to create an exaggerated impression of the Bureau's effectiveness. He concentrated on small-time bank robbers, while ignoring organized crime, white-collar crime, and violations of federal civil rights laws. Even worse, Hoover spied on citizens in violation of their constitutional rights, compiling secret files on political groups. The most notorious case involved his secret attempt to destroy Dr. Martin Luther King, Jr. as a civil rights leader. Hoover's misuse of power did not become known until after his death in 1972.[58]

Hoover's FBI had a powerful impact on local police. The emphasis on education and training established a new model for personnel standards. The introduction of the UCR, the development of the Ten Most Wanted list, and the creation of the FBI crime lab all served to emphasize crime fighting at the expense of other aspects of policing.

# The Police Crisis of the 1960s

## The Police and the Supreme Court

**police and the Supreme Court**

Ernesto Miranda was just an ordinary career criminal. Between the ages of 14 and 18 he had been arrested six times and imprisoned four times. On the evening of March 2, 1963, he raped a young woman in Phoenix, Arizona. His arrest 11 days later set the stage for one of the most famous Supreme Court decisions in American history. In *Miranda v. Arizona* (1966), the Court overturned his conviction and ruled that police officers had to advise suspects of their right to remain silent and their right to an attorney before being interrogated.[59]

In a postscript to the famous decision, Ernesto Miranda himself was retried, convicted, and sentenced to prison for the original 1963 rape. After he was paroled, he returned to Phoenix and worked as a deliveryman. On the night of January 31, 1976, at age 34, he got into a fight while playing poker in a bar and was stabbed to death. When one of his two assailants was arrested, the police officers followed the law and read him his *Miranda* rights.

The *Miranda* decision was only one of several famous cases where the Supreme Court established constitutional standards for the police and for other parts of the criminal justice system. In *Mapp v. Ohio,* the Court held that evidence gathered in an illegal search and seizure could not be used against the defendant. These

---

**EXHIBIT 2–5**

### Conflicting Pressures of the Police, 1960 to Present

Intervention of the Supreme Court

High crime rates; fear of crime; political reaction

Riots; PCR crisis; PCR programs

Research and experimentation

Traditional professionalization (recruitment standards, patrol management)

Affirmative action (race and gender)

Administrative control of discretion (deadly force, domestic violence, pursuits)

Community policing

Problem-oriented policing

Citizen oversight

decisions provoked an enormous political controversy. The police and their supporters claimed that the Court had "handcuffed" them in the fight against crime. Conservative politicians accused the Court of favoring the rights of criminals over the
rights of victims and law-abiding citizens.[60]

## The Police and Civil Rights

The civil rights movement entered a new militant phase in the 1960s, challenging
race discrimination in all areas of American life. On February 1, 1960, African
American college students launched sit-ins to protest segregated lunch counters in
the South. This inspired civil rights groups to challenge employment and housing
discrimination in all parts of the country. Activists also attacked race discrimination
and physical brutality by the police.[61]

As civil rights protests rose, the white police officer in the black ghetto became
a symbol of white power and authority. Studies of deadly force found that police officers shot and killed African American citizens about eight times as often as white
citizens. Because of employment discrimination, meanwhile, African Americans
were seriously underrepresented as police officers.

Tensions between the police and the African American community finally exploded in a nationwide wave of riots between 1964 and 1968. Many riots were sparked
by an incident involving the police. The 1964 New York City riot began after a white
off-duty officer shot and killed a black teenager. The 1965 riot in the Watts district of
**Kerner Commission**    Los Angeles was sparked by a simple traffic stop. The **Kerner Commission,** appointed to study the riots, counted over 200 violent disorders in 1967 alone.[62]

In response to the crisis, police departments established special police–community
relations (PCR) units. PCR programs included speaking to community groups and
schools, "ride-along" programs that allowed citizens to view police work from the
perspective of the police officer, and neighborhood storefront offices to facilitate
communication with citizens. A Justice Department report, however, found that these
programs had little impact on day-to-day police work and did little to improve police–
community relations.[63]

Civil rights leaders demanded the hiring of more African American officers
and the creation of citizen review boards to investigate citizen complaints of excessive force. Although the 1964 Civil Rights Act outlawed race discrimination in employment, minority employment made little progress until the 1980s. The demand
for civilian review was also unsuccessful at first. The Philadelphia Police Advisory
Board (PAB), created in 1958, was abolished in 1967 under pressure from the police
union. The police union in New York City succeeded in abolishing a citizen-dominated
Civilian Complaint Review Board (CCRB) in 1966. By the end of the 1960s, even
though the riots had stopped, relations between the police and minority communities
remained tense.[64]

## The Police in the National Spotlight

**police–community**    Rising public concern about crime, riots, and the **police–community relations crisis**
**relations crisis**    stimulated a series of national reports on the police that greatly enhanced knowledge
about policing and made a set of recommendations for improving the American police.

The American Bar Foundation (ABF) conducted the first field observations of police work (1955–1957) and found that police officers exercised broad discretion and that most police work involved noncriminal activity.[65]

The President's Commission on Law Enforcement and Administration of Justice (known as the **President's Crime Commission**) (1965–1967) conducted a comprehensive study of the entire criminal justice system, including the police, and sponsored some important police research. The Commission's *Task Force Report: The Police* included a thoughtful analysis of the complexity of the police role and the fact that only a relatively small part of police work was devoted to criminal law enforcement. The commission sponsored Albert Reiss and Donald Black's observational study of patrol officers, which produced important findings on police discretion. The Commission's report, *The Challenge of Crime in a Free Society* (1967), endorsed the traditional agenda of professionalization: higher recruitment standards, more training, and better management and supervision, but also called for controls over police discretion.[66]

**President's Crime Commission**

The National Advisory Commission on Civil Disorders, popularly known as the Kerner Commission, was created after the riots of 1967 to study the national crisis in race relations (see Sidebar 2–4). Its report found "deep hostility between police and ghetto communities as a primary cause of the disorders." It recommended that routine police operations be changed "to ensure proper individual conduct and to eliminate abrasive practices," that more African American police officers be hired, and that police departments improve their procedures for handling citizen complaints.[67]

The Kerner Commission questioned some of the traditional assumptions about police professionalization. It noted that "many of the serious disturbances took place in cities whose police are among the best led, best organized, best trained, and most professional in the country." It pointed out that the patrol car removed the officer from the street and isolated the police from ordinary citizens.[68]

Chief William Parker of the Los Angeles Police Department (LAPD) illustrated the commission's point about how aggressive crime fighting aggravated

---

**S I D E B A R        2 – 4**

## *Riot Commission Reports in Historical Perspective*

| | |
|---|---|
| 1919 Chicago | Chicago Commission on Race Relations, Race Riot, *The Negro in Chicago: A Study of Race Relations and a Race Riot.* (Chicago: University of Chicago Press, 1922). |
| 1960s | National Advisory Commission on Civil Disorders, *Report* (New York: Bantam Books, 1968). |

**Exercise:** Compare the report on the 1919 Chicago race riot and the Kerner Commission report on the racial disturbances of the 1960s.

1. Are there any significant differences in the causes of the riots?
2. Are there any differences in the recommendations related to improved police-community relations in the two reports?

police–community relations. Parker was nationally recognized for turning the LAPD into what was then widely regarded as the most professional department in the country. Parker took command of a notoriously corrupt LAPD in 1950 and quickly asserted strict control over it. He instituted high personnel standards, modern management principles, and an aggressive anticrime approach to policing. Like J. Edgar Hoover, Parker was a master of public relations. Working closely with Jack Webb, he helped the television program "Dragnet" become one of the top-rated programs, and it projected an image of the LAPD as flawlessly professional and efficient.[69]

Parker's style of policing came at a price, however. The aggressive law enforcement tactics aggravated conflict with minority communities, and the LAPD's famous disciplinary system overlooked officer use of excessive force. Historian Martin Schiesl argues that officers "under the direction of strong-willed chiefs, confused professional obligations with the unrestrained use of power and undermined the civil liberties of racial minorities and politically active groups.[70] Civil rights groups protested, but Parker tolerated no criticism and accused the NAACP and the ACLU of supporting the criminal element. Parker's legacy lived on in the LAPD long after he retired. The LAPD generated national controversy as a result of the 1991 beating of Rodney King and again in 1999 with the Rampart scandal. In both cases the LAPD was accused of tolerating excessive use of force, particularly against racial and ethnic minorities, and of failing to discipline its officers.[71]

In 1973 the American Bar Association (ABA) published its *Standards Relating to the Urban Police Function*. Most important, the *Standards* recommended policy guidelines to control the exercise of police discretion. This proved to be very influential, and in the years ahead police departments developed written policies over use of deadly force, high speed pursuits, and the handling of domestic violence incidents.[72]

Finally, to help raise the standards of police departments, a process for accrediting police departments was established. Accreditation had long existed as a means of professional self-regulation in other occupations claiming status as a profession: law, medicine, and education, for example. The Commission on Accreditation for Law Enforcement Agencies (CALEA) published its first set of *Standards for Law Enforcement Agencies* in 1983.[73]

## The Research Revolution

An explosion in police research began in the 1960s, producing a substantial body of knowledge about patrol work, criminal investigation, police officer attitudes, and other important aspects of policing.

Much of this research was funded by the federal government, first through the Law Enforcement Assistance Administration (LEAA) (1968–1976), and later the National Institute of Justice (NIJ). In 1970 the Ford Foundation established the Police Foundation with a grant of $30 million. The foundation sponsored some of the most important police research, including the Kansas City Preventive Patrol Experiment. Later, the Police Executive Research Forum (PERF), a professional association of big-city police managers, emerged as the leader of innovation in policing.

**Kansas City Preventive Patrol Experiment**

Some of the most important research undermined traditional assumptions about policing. The **Kansas City Preventive Patrol Experiment** (1972–1973)

---

**S I D E B A R      2 – 5**

### The Research Revolution: An Assessment

In 2004 the National Academy of Sciences published a comprehensive assessment of research on the police. The report, *Fairness and Effectiveness in Policing: The Evidence,* evaluated all of the available research on the police. It found that while the research revolution has produced much useful knowledge about certain subjects, such as routine police patrol and police–citizen interactions, there are many aspects of policing about which we know very little.

*Source:* National Academy of Science, *Fairness and Effectiveness in Policing: The Evidence* (Washington DC: National Academy Press, 2004).

---

tested the effect of different levels of patrol on crime, and found that increased patrol did not reduce crime, while reduced patrol did not lead to an increase in crime or public fear of crime. These findings had a profound effect on thinking about the police, and laid the foundation for the development of community policing a few years later.[74]

Other studies, meanwhile, questioned the value of rapid police response. Faster response time did not result in more arrests. Few calls involved crimes in progress, and most crime victims did not call the police immediately.[75] The Rand Corporation study of criminal investigation, meanwhile, shattered traditional myths about detective work. Most crimes are solved through information obtained by the first officer on the scene, using information from victims or witnesses. Follow-up detective work, of the kind portrayed in the movies and on television, is actually relatively unproductive, and involves routine paperwork.[76]

With respect to police officers' attitudes and behavior, William Westley identified a distinct police subculture, characterized by hostility toward the public, group solidarity, and secrecy. Jerome Skolnick followed up on this insight and found that policing has a distinct working environment, dominated by danger and exercise of authority. The pressure to achieve results in the form of arrests and convictions, moreover, encourages officers to violate legal procedures. Other studies also found that police officers' attitudes are shaped by the nature of police work, including the culture of the organization, and not by their personal background characteristics such as education or race.[77]

The mounting body of research had a significant effect on police reform. The studies that questioned the deterrent effect of patrol and identified the important role of citizens in solving crimes laid the foundation for the community policing movement. James J. Fyfe's pioneering study of deadly force, meanwhile, indicated that written policies could effectively control police discretion in the use of firearms.[78]

---

# New Developments in Policing, 1970–2010

The American police changed significantly from the 1970s to the present. The characteristics of officers changed dramatically; officers worked in a very different organizational environment; and new ideas about the police role emerged.[79]

## The Changing Police Officer

The profile of the American police officer changed significantly beginning in the 1970s. The employment of racial and ethnic minority officers increased significantly. Underrepresentation of African American officers on big-city police departments was one of the major complaints raised by civil rights groups. The Kerner Commission found that in 1967 African Americans represented 34 percent of the population of Cleveland but only 7 percent of the police officers; in Oakland, they were 31 percent of the population but only 4 percent of the officers. As a result of aggressive minority hiring efforts, the number of African American officers increased significantly. Similar progress was made in the employment of Latino officers in many departments. By the 1990s African American officers were a majority in Detroit, Washington, and Atlanta. In 2006, the San Antonio, Texas, police department consisted of 48 percent white officers, 46 percent Hispanic officers, and 6 percent African American officers. African Americans served as police chief in New York City, Los Angeles, Atlanta, Chicago, Houston, and many other cities.[80]

For a full discussion of affirmative action in police employment, see Chapter 5.

Felicia Shpritzer made history in breaking down the barriers against women in policing. She joined the New York City police department in 1942 and, following the model established by Alice Stebbins Wells and the other pioneer policewomen, served almost 20 years in the juvenile unit. In 1961, she and five other female officers applied for promotion to sergeant. Their applications were rejected, and in fact they were not even allowed to take the promotional exam. They sued, and in 1963 the courts declared the NYPD policy illegal and ordered the department to allow them to take the exam. The following year, 126 policewomen took the exam; Shpritzer and one other woman passed. The other woman, Gertrude Schimmel, became the first female captain in the NYPD in 1971. Shpritzer died in December 2000 at age 87.[81]

Traditional barriers to women in policing collapsed under the impact of the 1964 Civil Rights Act, which barred discrimination on the basis of sex, and the women's movement. By the mid-1990s, the percentage of female officers in most big-city departments was about 13 percent. Additionally, departments eliminated requirements (such as minimum height or special strength tests) that had discriminated against female applicants. In an important breakthrough, female officers were assigned to routine patrol duty for the first time in 1968. Evaluations of female officers on patrol in Washington DC, and New York City found their performance to be as effective as that of comparable groups of male officers.[82]

Penny Harrington broke another barrier in 1985 when she was appointed chief of the Portland, Oregon, police department. She was the first woman to head a large police department. (There had been several female chiefs since 1919, but all involved small agencies, according to historian Dorothy Schulz.) Harrington was followed by Elizabeth Watson, appointed chief of the Houston, Texas, police department in 1990. Since then a number of women have served as chiefs of large city and state law enforcement agencies.[83]

Police departments also began to recruit college students. In the early 1960s, the typical officer had only a high school education. The federal government, meanwhile, encouraged the development of college criminal justice programs. While only 20 percent of all sworn officers had any college education in 1960, the figure had risen to 65 percent by 1988.[84]

Preservice training improved dramatically. The length of training increased from an average of about 300 hours in the 1960s to over 1,000 hours in many departments by the 1990s. The more professional departments added a field training component to the traditional academy program. Police academy curricula added units on race relations, domestic violence, and ethics. New York and California had introduced mandatory training for all police officers in 1959, and eventually every state had a training and certification requirement. Previously, many small police and sheriff's departments offered no preservice training whatsoever.[85]

## The Control of Police Discretion

In response to recommendations by the ABA and the President's Crime Commission, police departments instituted procedures to control police discretion (see Chapter 11). These involved written policies covering search and seizure, interrogations, and other aspects of police work. Particularly important were the policies on the use of deadly force, handling domestic violence, and high-speed pursuits. Policies were collected in the standard operating procedure (SOP) manual, which became the basic tool of police management. They were part of a general movement to control the exercise of discretion in all criminal justice agencies.[86]

The control of deadly force was one of the most important reforms. Research indicated that police shot eight African Americans for every white citizen. The racial disparity was especially great with respect to unarmed citizens. Many of the 1960s riots were sparked by a shooting incident. Most police departments at that time either had no policy on deadly force or relied on state statutes that permitted the shooting of unarmed suspects under the fleeing-felon rule. In the early 1970s, they began to adopt a more restrictive "defense-of-life" rule. Pioneering research by James J. Fyfe found that the New York City police department's new policy in 1972 reduced firearms discharges by 30 percent. Within just a few years, other departments adopted similar policies. As a result, the number of citizens shot and killed by the police nationwide dropped substantially between 1970 and 1984. Even more important, the ratio of blacks to whites shot and killed fell by 50 percent.[87]

Rising public concern about domestic violence led to a revolution in police policy in that area as well. Women's groups sued the police in New York, Oakland, and other cities for failing to arrest men who had committed domestic assault. These suits produced departmental policies prescribing mandatory arrest. Soon, other departments across the country adopted similar policies. This trend received a strong boost when a Police Foundation study found that arrest deterred future violence more effectively than either mediation or separation. Although subsequent studies failed to confirm this effect, mandatory arrest policies remained popular.[88]

## The Emergence of Police Unions

**Police unions** spread rapidly in the 1960s and by the 1970s were a powerful force in American policing. Officers were angry and alienated over Supreme Court rulings, criticisms by civil rights groups, poor salaries and benefits, and arbitrary disciplinary practices by police chiefs.[89]

**police unions**

Unions had a dramatic impact on police administration. They won significant improvements in salaries and benefits for officers, along with grievance procedures that protected the rights of officers in disciplinary hearings. The result was a revolution in police management. Police chiefs were no longer all-powerful, and now had to negotiate with unions over many management issues. Many reformers were alarmed about the growth of police unions. Unions tended to resist innovations and were particularly hostile to attempts to improve police–community relations.[90]

## The Spread of Citizen Oversight of Police

Citizen complaint review procedures are discussed in Chapter 14, on Police Accountability.

Citizen oversight of the police also spread beginning in the 1980s. The creation of civilian review boards to handle citizen complaints was one of the major demands of civil rights groups since the 1960s. They argued that because of the police subculture, police departments were not capable of conducting independent and fair investigations of complaints. In the 1990s a new form of citizen oversight appeared: the police auditor. Police auditors in San Jose and Portland, Oregon, examined police department policies and procedures, and recommended changes that would help to reduce citizen complaints. By the late 1990s, almost every major city had some form of citizen oversight of the police, either a review board or an auditor.[91]

The Special Counsel to the Los Angeles Sheriff's Department has the longest record of oversight. Between 1993 and mid-2009 it had issued 26 reports on the department, covering a wide range of subjects. They included use of force, the cost of litigation against the police, foot pursuits of suspects, recruitment procedures, and the status of women in the department. In each case, the Special Counsel made recommendations for improvement. Sheriff Lee Baca in 2002 created the Office of Independent Review as an additional form of oversight. The OIR investigated critical incidents and made recommendations for changes in policies where they were needed.[92]

## A New Paradigm: Community Policing and Problem-Oriented Policing

**community policing**

The most important new development in policing in the 1980s and 1990s was the advent of **community policing** (COP) and problem-oriented policing (POP). Both represented a new paradigm for policing.

Community policing holds that police departments should develop partnerships with neighborhood residents, develop programs addressing specific problems, and give rank-and-file officers more decision-making freedom with regard to how to deal with particular problems on their beats. In the seminal article "Broken Windows," James Q. Wilson and George L. Kelling summed up the recent research on policing: that patrol had only limited deterrent effect on crime, that faster response times did not increase arrests, and that the capacity of detectives to solve crimes was limited. This research suggested two important points: that the police could not fight crime by themselves, but were very dependent upon citizens, and that the police could reduce fear by concentrating on less serious quality-of-life problems (e.g., "broken windows").[93]

Departments all across the country adopted COP. The most ambitious program was in Chicago, where Chicago Alternative Policing Strategy (CAPS) was a citywide effort. The core element of CAPS was a series of regular neighborhood meetings between police and residents for the purpose of identifying neighborhood problems and developing solutions. An evaluation of CAPS found that it did result in greater citizen involvement with the police, improved cooperation between the police and other government agencies (e.g., sanitation), a decline in neighborhood problems, and improved public perceptions of the police department.[94]

The concept of problem-oriented policing was developed by Herman Goldstein. It holds that instead of thinking in terms of global concepts such as "crime" and "disorder," the police should address particular problems and develop creative responses to each one. Instead of crime fighters, officers should be problem solvers, planners, and community organizers.[95]

In the first POP experiment, officers in Newport News, Virginia, attacked crime in a deteriorated housing project by helping the residents organize to improve conditions in the project itself. This included pressuring both government agencies and private companies to fulfill their responsibilities regarding building conditions and sanitation. The Center on Problem-Oriented Policing in Madison, Wisconsin, provides resource materials on POP and organizes an annual POP Conference. Police departments compete for the Herman Goldstein Award for the outstanding POP project each year.[96]

Advocates of community policing hailed it as a new era in policing. As early as 1988 Kelling argued that "a quiet revolution is reshaping American policing."[97] The U.S. Justice Department encouraged the growth of community policing through the Office of Community Oriented Policing Services (known as the COPS office), which distributed the money for hiring 100,000 new officers. Many police departments received federal funds for additional officers and established community policing programs. Several studies attempted to measure the impact of the additional officers on crime, but they reached conflicting findings. Some departments, like Chicago, made serious COP efforts. Others, however, adopted the label COP or POP, but did not really change police operations.

Whatever the impact of community policing, by the late 1990s the American police were in the midst of an extraordinary period of innovation. Police chiefs across the country were open to experimentation and evaluation. David Bayley argues that "the last decade of the twentieth century may be the most creative period in policing since the modern police officer was put onto the streets of London in 1829."[98]

## Racial Profiling and Discrimination

Despite the many positive gains made by the police in the previous 30 years, tensions between the police and racial and ethnic minority groups reemerged as a serious problem in the late 1990s. A report by Human Rights Watch in 1998 concluded that "race continues to play a central role in police brutality in the United States."[99] Several incidents gained focused national attention on the issue of police and race. The 1991 beating of Rodney King by Los Angeles police officers was videotaped by a bystander and provided dramatic visual evidence of police use of excessive force. Massive riots broke out in Los Angeles and other cities in 1992 when four officers involved in the beating were acquitted of criminal charges (three were subsequently convicted on federal criminal charges).[100] A vicious assault on Abner Louima by New York City officers in 1997 and the fatal shooting of the unarmed Amadou Diallo inflamed the police–community relations problem. Many observers blamed the race relations crisis in New York City on its zero-tolerance policing policy that involved aggressive enforcement of laws against minor crimes such as public urination and graffiti.[101]

On the morning of May 8, 1992, Robert Wilkins was driving on Interstate 95 in Maryland with three members of his family. They were returning to Washington DC, from the funeral of a family member in Chicago. They were stopped by an officer of the Maryland State Police who told them to get out of the car and then asked for permission to search the car. Wilkins, an attorney and a graduate of Harvard Law School, informed the officer that without an arrest of the driver a search would be illegal. The officer ignored this advice and made the four family members stand in the rain while they waited for the agency's drug dog to arrive. The dog eventually found no trace of drugs, and Wilkins was finally given a $105 speeding ticket. Wilkins believed not only that the traffic stop was illegal but that he was stopped only because he is African American. This traffic stop eventually led to a major lawsuit (*Wilkins v. Maryland*) that sparked national controversy over the practice of **racial profiling,** or what some people called "driving while black."[102]

**racial profiling**

Civil rights leaders charged that the police stopped African American drivers solely on the basis of their race and not on the basis of any suspected criminal activity. Data presented as part of an ACLU lawsuit against the Maryland State Police indicated that while African Americans represented only 17 percent of all drivers on Interstate 95 and 18 percent of all observed traffic law violators, they represented 72.9 percent of all drivers stopped by the state police. Additionally, among those drivers stopped, 81.3 percent of those searched after being stopped were African American. Many observers argued that racial profiling, particularly on interstate highways, was a result of the national "war on drugs," and that police officers stereotyped both African Americans and Hispanics as drug dealers.[103]

Several strategies developed to combat racial profiling. Civil rights groups advocated the collection of data on traffic stops for the purpose of documenting police practices. Some states passed laws requiring all law enforcement agencies to collect data. The San Diego Police Department began collecting data voluntarily, and issuing reports on the data. Other departments did the same. The Police Executive Research Forum published a report with a recommended policy on when race can and cannot be used in law enforcement. A number of departments adopted new policies to prohibit racial profiling (see Ch. 12).

## Police Reform Through Federal Litigation

For a full discussion of federal "pattern or practice" litigation, see Chapter 14.

A race riot erupted in Cincinnati in April 2001 after the fifteenth fatal shooting of an African American male in five years. In response, the U.S. Justice Department brought a "pattern or practice" suit against the Cincinnati Police Department. Meanwhile, the ACLU and other groups had already filed racial profiling suits against the department. The suits resulted in two settlement agreements. The Justice Department suit ended with a Memorandum of Agreement in 2002 that required the department to institute a number of management reforms designed to control the use of force and to improve the supervision of officers and the citizen complaint process. The settlement of the ACLU suit required the Cincinnati Police Department to adopt problem-oriented policing as a way of ending police practices that encouraged use of force incidents.[104]

Federal litigation against police departments was authorized by the 1994 Violent Crime Control Act. Section 14141 of the law allowed the Civil Rights Division of the Justice Department to sue law enforcement agencies if a "pattern or practice" of violations of citizens rights existed. The Justice Department sued the Pittsburgh Police Department, the New Jersey State Police, the Los Angeles Police Department, Cincinnati, and other agencies under the law. Settlements of these suits resulted in consent decrees or memoranda of agreement that required the departments to improve their use of force policies and citizen complaint procedures, and to implement an early intervention system (EIS) that would track officer performance. Each settlement also included a court-appointed monitor to oversee implementation of the required reforms.[105]

By 2009, the court-appointed monitors had found substantial improvements in the Pittsburgh, Cincinnati, and Washington DC police departments and the New Jersey State Police. The monitor for the Cincinnati Police Department, for example, concluded in late 2008 that "The City of Cincinnati is now in a very different situation than it was in 2002." The Cincinnati Police Department "has improved its training, its policies and procedures, its investigations of uses of force and citizen complaints, its risk management and its accountability."[106] The Monitor for the Washington DC police department, meanwhile, concluded in 2008 that as a result of the court-ordered reforms, "the department has substantially transformed itself for the better since the late 1990s."[107] Monitors in Pittsburgh and for the New Jersey State Police reported similar positive results.

# Into the Twenty-First Century

In the first decade of the twenty-first century, the American police faced a number of challenges. Community policing and problem-oriented policing were important innovations that in some cases had brought about genuine change. Sustaining those reforms remained a challenge, however. Some progress had been made in reducing excessive use of force and ending racial discrimination, but racial and ethnic tensions continued to plague many departments.

The war on terrorism following the attack on September 11, 2001, presented the police with new challenges. Homeland security efforts diverted attention and resources away from traditional police priorities. The war in Iraq, meanwhile, resulted in the temporary loss of many officers who served in the military Reserves or National Guard. Finally, the economic crisis that struck the nation in 2008 strained police department budgets, causing them to delay the hiring of new officers or in some cases even to lay off existing officers.

Much had changed since the first American police departments were created in the 1830s. Policing was completely different from what it had been as recently as the 1960s. In most respects, policing was far more professional than ever before. Major challenges still remained, however.

 **Case Study**

*Police Patrol Practices*

Although police administrators may take steps to attempt to eliminate misconduct by individual police officers, many departments have adopted patrol practices that, in the words of one commenter, have "replaced harassment by individual patrolmen with harassment by entire departments."

These practices, sometimes known as *"aggressive preventative patrol,"* take a number of forms, but invariably they involve a large number of police–citizen contacts initiated by police rather than in response to a call for help or service. *One such practice utilizes a roving task force,* which moves into high crime districts without prior notice and conducts intensive, often indiscriminate, street stops and searches. A number of persons who might legitimately be described as suspicious are stopped. But so also are persons who the beat patrolman would know are respected members of the community. Such tasks forces are often deliberately moved from place to place, making it impossible for its members to know the people with whom they come in contact.

*In some cities aggressive patrol is not limited to special task forces.* The beat patrolman himself is expected to participate and to file a minimum number of stop-and-frisk or field interrogation reports for each tour of duty. This pressure to produce, or a lack of familiarity with the neighborhood and its people, may lead to widespread use of these techniques without adequate differentiation between genuinely suspicious behavior and behavior that is suspicious to a particular officer merely because it is unfamiliar. *Police administrators, pressed by public concern about crime, have instituted such patrol practices often without weighing their tension-creating effects* and the resulting relationship to civil disorder.

*Motorization of police* is another aspect of patrol that has affected law enforcement in the ghetto. The patrolman comes to see the city through a windshield and hear about it over a police radio. To him, the area increasingly comes to consist only of lawbreakers. To the ghetto resident, the policeman comes increasingly to be only an enforcer.

*Loss of contact between the police officer and the community he serves adversely affects law enforcement.* If an officer has never met, does not know, and cannot understand the language and habits of the people in the area he patrols, he cannot do an effective police job. His ability to detect truly suspicious behavior is impaired. He deprives himself of important sources of information. *He fails to know those persons with an "equity" in the community*—homeowners, small businessmen, professional men, persons who are anxious to support proper law enforcement—and thus sacrifices the contributions they can make to maintaining community order.

*Source:* Excerpt from the Kerner Commission Report, 1968, pp. 304–305. Emphasis added.

## Summary: The Lessons of the Past

American policing has changed dramatically throughout its history. Viewed from the perspective of three hundred years, the major change was the creation of the modern police: a large, specialized bureaucratic agency devoted to crime control and order maintenance. From the perspective of 100 years, American police departments have changed from inefficient and corrupt political organizations to enterprises with a nonpartisan professional mission.

From the perspective of the last 30 years, we can see vast improvements in personnel standards and systems of accountability, including the values of due process and equal protection. The research revolution has produced an impressive body of knowledge about policing. There is a new candor about police discretion and about the limits of the police's ability to control crime. And, as David Bayley argues, the police are remarkably open to innovation and experimentation.[108]

The legacy of the past continues to weigh heavily on the police. Problems of abuse of authority—excessive force, corruption—continue to plague many departments. Conflict between the police and racial and ethnic minority communities remains a problem in nearly every city. And despite the many community policing experiments, routine police work in most cities has not changed that much in 30 years: Officers patrol in cars and answer their 911 calls. In a comprehensive review of recent developments in policing, Stephen Mastrofski concludes that "the patrol officers of today can be expected to do their job by and large as they did a decade ago and as they will do a decade hence."[109]

History offers many lessons about the American police. It dramatizes the fact that policing is always changing. Some of these changes are the result of planned innovation, while others are the result of external social changes. At the same time, history illustrates the extent to which many aspects of policing, including some serious problems, endure.

## Key Terms

English heritage, 24
Robert Peel, 25
London Metropolitan Police, 25
crime prevention, 25
the watch, 26
riots, 27
patronage, 29
Theodore Roosevelt, 33
August Vollmer, 34

professionalization movement, 34
Alice Stebbins Wells, 35
Boston police strike, 36
communications technology, 37
Wickersham Commission, 39
O. W. Wilson, 39
J. Edgar Hoover, 40
police and the Supreme Court, 41
Kerner Commission, 42

police–community relations
    crisis, 42
President's Crime
    Commission, 43
Kansas City Preventive Patrol
    Experiment, 44
police unions, 47
community policing, 48
racial profiling, 50

## For Discussion

*The 1968 Kerner Commission Report on urban riots identified a number of police practices that created problems with racial and ethnic minority communities. Has anything changed in the years since? Specifically:*

1. Do some police departments still engage in "aggressive preventative patrol"? Can you

identify any departments that do? Is the New York City zero-tolerance anticrime program the same thing with just a different name? Find some articles on zero tolerance and examine the similarities.

2. Do some departments use roving anticrime task forces? What about the Street Crime Unit in the New York City police department? Did the

policies of the SCU lead to the controversial shooting of Amadou Diallo in 1999? Find some articles on the Diallo case and discuss whether there are any similarities.

3. The Kerner Commission concluded that automobile patrol alienated officers from the community. Have any departments taken steps to overcome this problem? How? Do some departments use more foot patrol than they did in the 1960s? Is it effective in improving police–

community relations? Find an evaluation of a foot patrol program. Did it make a difference in terms of citizen attitudes toward the police?

4. Are community-policing programs effective in improving police–community relations? Can you find specific examples? Find some material on community policing in San Diego. What, exactly, does it consist of? Is there persuasive evidence that it is effective in both controlling crime and maintaining good police–community relations?

## Internet Exercises

Many police departments include material on the history of the department in their annual report and/or on their Web site.

**Exercise 1** Go to www.officer.com and click on "Agencies." Select several police departments and check their Web sites for historical material.

**Exercise 2** Find several department history pages on local police department web pages. What subjects do they cover? What do they not cover? In your opinion, do they cover the really important changes in policing discussed in this chapter?

## Notes

1. David Bayley, *Police for the Future* (New York: Oxford University Press, 1994), p. 126.
2. Samuel Walker, *Popular Justice: A History of American Criminal Justice,* 2nd ed. (New York: Oxford University Press, 1998), Ch. 1.
3. T. A. Critchley, *A History of Police in England and Wales,* 2nd ed. (Montclair, NJ: Patterson Smith, 1972).
4. Bureau of Justice Statistics, *Local Police Departments, 2003* (Washington DC: Department of Justice, 2006).
5. Allen Steinberg, *The Transformation of Criminal Justice, Philadelphia, 1800–1880* (Chapel Hill: University of North Carolina Press, 1989).
6. Critchley, *A History of Police in England and Wales,* Ch. 2.
7. Allan Silver, "The Demand for Order in Civil Society: A Review of Some Themes in the History of Urban Crime, Police, and Riot," in David J. Bordua, ed., *The Police: Six Sociological Essays* (New York: John Wiley, 1967), pp. 12–13.
8. David Bayley, *Patterns of Policing: A Comparative International Analysis* (New Brunswick, NJ: Rutgers University Press, 1985), p. 23.
9. Walker, *Popular Justice,* Ch. 1
10. Julian P. Boyd, "The Sheriff in Colonial North Carolina," *North Carolina Historical Review* 5 (1928): pp. 151–81.
11. Roger Lane, *Policing the City* (New York: Atheneum, 1971), Ch. 1.
12. Ibid.
13. Sally E. Hadden, *Slave Patrols: Law and Violence in Virginia and the Carolinas* (Cambridge: Harvard University Press, 2001).
14. Douglas Greenberg, *Crime and Law Enforcement in the Colony of New York, 1691–1776* (Ithaca, NY: Cornell University Press, 1976).
15. Walker, *Popular Justice,* Ch.1.
16. Richard Maxwell Brown, *Strain of Violence: Historical Studies of American Violence and Vigilantism* (New York: Oxford University Press, 1975).
17. Richard Hofstadter and Michael V. Wallace, eds. *American Violence: A Documentary History* (New York: Vintage Books, 1971).
18. Ibid.
19. Steinberg, *The Transformation of Criminal Justice,* pp. 119–49.

20. Wilbur R. Miller, *Cops and Bobbies: Police Authority in New York and London, 1830–1870* (Chicago: University of Chicago Press, 1977).

21. Samuel Walker, *A Critical History of Police Reform* (Lexington: Lexington Books, 1977). Robert Fogelson, *Big City Police* (Cambridge, MA: Harvard University Press, 1977).

22. Jay Stuart Berman, *Police Administration and Progressive Reform: Theodore Roosevelt as Police Commissioner of New York* (New York: Greenwood Press, 1987), p. 71.

23. Walker, *A Critical History of Police Reform,* pp. 71–72.

24. Jonathan Rubenstein, *City Police* (New York: Ballantine Books, 1974), pp. 15–22.

25. Walker, *A Critical History of Police Reform,* pp. 14–19. Miller, *Cops and Bobbies.*

26. Christopher Thale, "Assigned to Patrol: Neighborhoods, Police, and Changing Deployment Practices in New York City Before 1930," *Journal of Social History* 37 (No. 4, 2004): pp. 1037–64.

27. Miller, *Cops and Bobbies.*

28. Eric H. Monkkonen, *Police in Urban America, 1860–1920* (Cambridge, England: Cambridge University Press, 1981).

29. William L. Riordan, ed., *Plunkitt of Tammany Hall* (New York: Dutton, 1963).

30. Mark Haller, "Historical Roots of Police Behavior: Chicago, 1890–1925," *Law and Society Review* 10 (Winter 1976): pp. 303–24.

31. Berman, *Police Administration and Progressive Reform,* p. 51.

32. Ibid.

33. Batya Miller, "Enforcement of the Sunday Closing Law on the Lower East Side, 1882–1903," *American Jewish History* 91 (June 2003): pp. 269–86.

34. James F. Richardson, *The New York Police: Colonial Times to 1901.* (New York: Oxford University Press, 1970). Walker, *A Critical History of Police Reform.*

35. Berman, *Police Administration and Progressive Reform.*

36. Roger Lane, *Violent Death in the City* (Cambridge, MA: Harvard University Press: 1979). Walker, *Popular Justice,* pp. 66–69.

37. Sidney L. Harring, *Policing a Class Society: The Experience of American Cities, 1865–1915* (New Brunswick, NJ: Rutgers University Press, 1983). Walker, *A Critical History of Police Reform.*

38. Gene E. Carte and Elaine H. Carte, *Police Reform in the United States: The Era of August Vollmer* (Berkeley: University of California Press, 1975).

39. Walker, *A Critical History of Police Reform.*

40. Ibid.

41. Dorothy Moses Schulz, *From Social Worker to Crimefighter: Women in United States Municipal Policing* (Westport, CT: Praeger, 1995).

42. Walker, *A Critical History of Police Reform.*

43. Ibid.

44. Francis Russell, *A City in Terror: 1919—The Boston Police Strike* (New York: Viking Press, 1975).

45. Chicago Commission on Race Relations, *The Negro in Chicago* (Chicago: University of Chicago Press, 1922).

46. W. Marvin Dulaney, *Black Police in America* (Bloomington: Indiana University Press, 1996).

47. Walker, *Popular Justice,* p. 140.

48. H. Kenneth Bechtel, *State Police in the United States: A Socio-Historical Analysis* (Westport, CT: Greenwood, 1995).

49. Curt Gentry, *J. Edgar Hoover: The Man and the Secrets* (New York: W. W. Norton, 1991).

50. Samuel Walker, "'Broken Windows' and Fractured History: The Use and Misuse of History in Recent Police Patrol Analysis," *Justice Quarterly* I (March 1984): pp. 77–90.

51. Malcolm K. Sparrow, Mark H. Moore, and David M. Kennedy, *Beyond 911: A New Era for Policing* (New York: Basic Books, 1990).

52. Walker, "'Broken Windows' and Fractured History."

53. National Commission on Law Observance and Enforcement, *Report on Lawlessness in Law Enforcement* (Washington DC: Government Printing Office, 1931).

54. Carte and Carte, *Police Reform in the United States.*

55. William J. Bopp, *O. W.: O. W. Wilson and the Search for a Police Profession* (Port Washington, NY: Kennikat Press, 1977). O. W. Wilson, *Police Administration* (New York: McGraw-Hill, 1950).

56. Edward J. Escobar, *Race, Police, and the Making of a Political Identity: Mexican Americans and the Los Angeles Police Department, 1900–1945* (Berkeley: University of California Press, 1999).

57. Gentry, *J. Edgar Hoover: The Man and the Secrets.*

58. Richard Gid Powers, *G-Men: Hoover's FBI in American Popular Culture* (Carbondale: Southern Illinois University Press, 1983). Athan G. Theoharis and John Stuart Cox, *The Boss: J. Edgar Hoover and the Great American Inquisition* (Philadelphia: Temple University Press, 1988).

59. Liva Baker, *Miranda* (New York: Atheneum, 1983).

60. Richard A. Leo, *Police Interrogation and American Justice* (Cambridge: Harvard University Press, 2008).

61. Walker, *Popular Justice*, pp. 180–85. Chevigny, *Police Power* (New York: Vintage Books, 1969).

62. National Advisory Commission on Civil Disorders, *Report* (New York: Bantam Books, 1968), pp. 315–16, 321–22.

63. Department of Justice, *Improving Police/Community Relations* (Washington DC: Government Printing Office, 1973).

64. Samuel Walker, *Police Accountability: The Role of Citizen Oversight* (Belmont, CA: Wadsworth, 2001), Ch. 2.

65. Samuel Walker, "Origins of the Contemporary Criminal Justice Paradigm: The American Bar Foundation Survey, 1953–1969," *Justice Quarterly* 9 (March 1992): pp. 47–76.

66. President's Commission on Law Enforcement and Administration of Justice, *The Challenge of Crime in a Free Society* (Washington DC: Government Printing Office, 1967). President's Commission on Law Enforcement and Administration of Justice, *Task Force Report: The Police* (Washington DC: Governmental Printing Office, 1967).

67. National Advisory Commission on Civil Disorders, *Report*.

68. Ibid., p. 301

69. Lou Cannon, *Official Negligence: How Rodney King and the Riots Changed Los Angeles and the LAPD* (New York: Times Books, 1997), Ch. 3.

70. Martin Schiesl, "Behind the Shield: Social Discontent and the Los Angeles Police Since 1950," in Martin Schiesl and Mark Morrall Dodge, eds., *City of Promise: Race and Historical Change in Los Angeles* (Claremont: Regina Books, 2006), p. 166.

71. Christopher Commission, *Report of the Independent Commission on the Los Angeles Police Department* (Los Angeles: The Christopher Commission, 1991).

72. American Bar Association, *Standards Relating to the Urban Police Function*, 2nd ed. (Boston, Little, Brown, 1980).

73. Commission on Accreditation for Law Enforcement Agencies, *Standards for Law Enforcement Agencies*, 4th ed. (Fairfax, VA: CALEA, 1999).

74. George L. Kelling et al., *The Kansas City Preventive Patrol Experiment* (Washington DC: The Police Foundation, 1974).

75. Department of Justice, *Response Time Analysis* (Washington, DC: Government Printing Office, 1978).

76. Peter Greenwood, *The Criminal Investigation Process* (Santa Monica, CA: Rand, 1975).

77. William A. Westley, *Violence and the Police* (Cambridge, MA: MIT Press, 1970). Jerome Skolnick, *Justice without Trial: Law Enforcement in a Democratic Society*, 3rd ed. (New York: Macmillan, 1994).

78. James J. Fyfe, "Administrative Interventions on Police Shooting Discretion: An Empirical Analysis," *Journal of Criminal Justice* 7 (Winter 1979): pp. 309–23.

79. Samuel Walker, "Between Two Worlds: The President's Crime Commission and the Police, 1967–1992," in John A. Conley, ed., *The 1967 President's Crime Commission Report: Its Impact 25 Years Later* (Cincinnati, OH: Anderson Publishing, 1994), pp. 21–35.

80. National Advisory Commission on Civil Disorder, *Report*, pp. 321–22. Bureau of Justice Statistics, *Law Enforcement Management and Administrative Statistics, 2000* (Washington DC: Government Printing Office, 2004). San Antonio Police Department Web site: www.sanantonio.gov\sapd.

81. "Felicia Shpritzer Dies at 87; Broke Police Gender Barrier," *The New York Times,* December 31, 2000.

82. Susan E. Martin, *Women on the Move: The Status of Women in Policing* (Washington DC: The Police Foundation, 1990). Peter B. Bloch and Deborah Anderson, *Policewomen on Patrol: Final Report* (Washington DC: The Police Foundation, 1974).

83. Dorothy Moses Schulz, "Women Police Chiefs: A Statistical Profile," *Police Quarterly* 6 (September 2003): pp. 330–45.

84. David L. Carter et al., *The State of Police Education* (Washington DC: Police Executive Research Forum, 1989).

85. International Association of Directors of Law Enforcement Standards and Training, *Sourcebook of Standards and Training Information* (Charlotte: University of North Carolina at Charlotte, 1993). Bureau of Justice Statistics, *Law Enforcement Management and Administrative Statistics, 1999.* (Washington DC: Department of Justice, 2001).

86. Samuel Walker, "Historical Roots of the Legal Control of Police Behavior," in David Weisburd and Craig Uchida, eds., *Police Innovation and the Rule of Law* (New York: Springer, 1991), pp. 32–55. Samuel Walker, *Taming the System: The Control of Discretion in Criminal Justice, 1950–1990* (New York: Oxford University Press, 1993). pp. 21–53.

87. Fyfe, "Administrative Interventions on Police Shooting Discretion: An Empirical Analysis." William A. Geller and Michael Scott, *Deadly Force:*

*What We Know* (Washington DC: Police Executive Research Forum, 1992).

88. Lawrence W. Sherman, *Policing Domestic Violence* (New York: The Free Press, 1992).

89. Hervey A. Juris and Peter Feuille, *Police Unionism* (Lexington, MA: Lexington Books, 1973).

90. Samuel Walker, "The Neglect of Police Unions: Exploring One of the Most Important Areas of American Policing," *Police Practice and Research,* 9 (May 2008): 95–112.

91. Samuel Walker, *Police Accountability: The Role of Citizen Oversight* (Belmont: Wadsworth, 2001).

92. Merrick Bobb, *25th Semiannual Report of the Special Counsel* (Los Angeles: PARC, July 2008). All the Special Counsel reports are available at www.parc.info.

93. James Q. Wilson and George L. Kelling, "Broken Windows: The Police and Neighborhood Safety," *Atlantic Monthly* 249 (March 1982): pp. 29–38.

94. Wesley G. Skogan and Susan M. Hartnett, *Community Policing, Chicago Style* (New York: Oxford University Press, 1997).

95. Michael S. Scott, *Problem-Oriented Policing: Reflections on the First Twenty Years* (Washington DC: Department of Justice, 2000).

96. John E. Eck and William Spelman, *Problem-Solving: Problem Oriented Policing in Newport News* (Washington DC: PERF, 1987).

97. George L. Kelling, "Police and Communities: The Quiet Revolution," *Perspectives on Policing* (Washington DC: Government Printing Office, 1988).

98. Bayley, *Police for the Future*, p. 101.

99. Human Rights Watch, *Shielded from Justice: Police Brutality and Accountability in the United States* (New York: Human Rights Watch, 1998), p. 39.

100. Cannon, *Official Negligence*. Jerome H. Skolnick and James J. Fyfe, *Above the Law* (New York: Free Press, 1993).

101. George L. Kelling and Catherine M. Coles, *Fixing Broken Windows* (New York: Free Press, 1996).

102. Details of the case are in David Harris, "'Driving While Black' and All Other Traffic Offenses: The Supreme Court and Pretextual Traffic Stops," *Journal of Criminal Law and Criminology* 87, no. 2 (1997): pp. 563–64. David A. Harris, *Profiles in Injustice: Why Racial Profiling Cannot Work* (New York: The New Press, 2002).

103. ACLU, *Driving While Black* (New York: ACLU, 1999).

104. Samuel Walker, *The New World of Police Accountability* (Thousand Oaks, CA: Sage, 2005). Information about federal "pattern or practice" litigation is available at www.usdoj.gov/crt/split.

105. Samuel Walker and Morgan Macdonald, "An Alternative Remedy for Police Misconduct: A Model State 'Pattern or Practice' Statute," *George Mason Civil Rights Law Journal,* 19 (2009): pp. 479–552.

106. City of Cincinnati, *Independent Monitor's Final Report* (December 2008), p. 36.

107. Michael Bromwich, *Twenty-Third Report of the Independent Monitor* (January 31, 2008), p. 3.

108. Bayley, *Police for the Future,* p. 126.

109. Stephen D. Mastrofski, "The Prospects of Change in Police Patrol: A Decade in Review," *American Journal of Police* IX, no. 3 (1990): p. 62.

# The Contemporary Law Enforcement Industry

## Chapter Outline

# Basic Features of American Law Enforcement

Law enforcement in the United States is a large and extremely complex enterprise. There are almost 18,000 federal, state, and local agencies, along with a private security industry that employs over a million additional people.

Several basic features characterize the law enforcement industry. Most important is the tradition of **local political control.** The primary responsibility for police protection rests with local governments: cities and counties. This tradition was inherited from England during the colonial period.

**local political control**

As a result, American policing is highly fragmented.[1] There is no formal, centralized system for coordinating or regulating all the different agencies. There are some mechanisms for federal and state regulation of local police. They are discussed later in this chapter.

For further reading see Chapter 2.

Fragmentation produces tremendous variety. Police services are provided by four different levels of government: city, county, state, and federal. Agencies at each level have very different roles and responsibilities. Within each category, moreover, there is tremendous variety. The six largest police departments—New York City, Chicago, Los Angeles, Philadelphia, Houston, and Detroit—are very different from the 9,555 police departments with fewer than 25 officers.[2]

As a result of this variety, it is very difficult to generalize about American policing. All police departments have some characteristics in common, but most generalizations about the "typical" police department are extremely risky. Writing about the county sheriff, David N. Falcone and L. Edward Wells reject the common assumption that "policing is policing" and argue that the sheriff "represents a historically different mode of policing that needs to be distinguished more clearly from municipal policing."[3]

## An "Industry" Perspective

Because of its fragmentation and variety, it is useful to take an industry perspective on American law enforcement. This approach provides a comprehensive picture of all the different producers of police services in a particular area.[4]

The industry approach also provides a consumer's perspective on policing. On a typical day, the average citizen receives police services from several different agencies. Consider the case of Mr. and Mrs. Smith. The small local police department patrols their suburban neighborhood. Mrs. Smith works downtown, where she is

## *Basic Sources on Law Enforcement Agencies*

The most comprehensive source of data on American law enforcement agencies is the report from the Bureau of Justice Statistics (BJS), *Law Enforcement Management and Administrative Statistics*. The most recent report is for 2004. You should look for a new report in 2010.

Additional data can be found in the FBI's Uniform Crime Reports (UCR), published annually.

Many law enforcement agencies now maintain their own Web site, which provides information about organizational structure and current programs.

served by the big-city police department. Mr. Smith is a sales representative and drives through small towns and areas patrolled by the county sheriff. The office building where Mrs. Smith works hires private security guards. On her way home, Mrs. Smith drives on the Interstate highway, which is patrolled by the state patrol. Meanwhile, the Federal Bureau of Investigation (FBI), the Drug Enforcement Agency (DEA), and other federal agencies are at work investigating various violations of federal law.

Exhibit 3–1 indicates the various components of the law enforcement industry.

**EXHIBIT 3–1**

### Components of the American Law Enforcement Industry

**Government Agencies**

*Local*
   Municipal police
   County police
   County sheriffs

*State*
   State police
   Bureaus of criminal investigation

*Federal*
   Federal law enforcement agencies
   Military law enforcement

*Special district police*
   Public schools
   Transit police
   College and university police

*Native American tribal police*

**Private Security**
   Private security firms
   Security personnel

# An International Perspective

A quick look at law enforcement in other countries provides a useful perspective on the decentralization and **fragmentation** of American law enforcement.

**fragmentation**

England, with a population one-fourth that of the United States, has forty-three police departments: forty-one provincial departments and two police forces in London. This is half the number of law enforcement agencies in the state of Nebraska (total of ninety-three). All forty-three agencies are administered by the home secretary, who is one of the top officials in the national government (and in some respects the equivalent of the attorney general in the United States). Each provincial department also answers to a local police commission. The home secretary has the power to issue administrative regulations on personnel and police operations. Additionally, each of the forty-three police departments receives 51 percent of its annual budget from the home secretary's office, giving it the power to enforce regulations.[5]

The Japanese police system also balances central coordination with local control. The National Police Agency is responsible for coordinating the operations of the forty-seven prefectural police. Each prefecture is officially independent, but the National Police Agency can recommend operational standards and, as in England, provides a significant part of each local agency's budget.[6]

# Size and Scope of the Law Enforcement Industry

## The Number of Law Enforcement Agencies

There are just under 18,000 law enforcement agencies in the United States. This includes 12,766 local police departments, 3,067 sheriff's departments, 49 state police agencies, 1,481 special police agencies, and 65 federal agencies (Exhibit 3–2).[7]

---

**EXHIBIT 3–2**

**Employment by State and Local Law Enforcement Agencies in the United States, 2004**

| Type of Agency | Number of agencies | Number of Employees | | | | | |
|---|---|---|---|---|---|---|---|
| | | Full-Time | | | Part-Time | | |
| | | Total | Sworn | Civilian | Total | Sworn | Civilian |
| Total | 17,876 | 1,076,897 | 731,903 | 344,994 | 105,252 | 45,982 | 59,270 |
| Local police | 12,766 | 573,152 | 446,974 | 126,178 | 62,693 | 28,712 | 33,981 |
| Sheriff | 3,067 | 326,531 | 175,018 | 151,513 | 27,004 | 11,784 | 15,220 |
| State police | 49 | 89,265 | 58,190 | 31,075 | 708 | 31 | 677 |
| Special jurisdiction | 1,481 | 85,126 | 49,398 | 35,728 | 14,342 | 5,063 | 9,279 |
| Constable/marshal | 513 | 2,823 | 2,323 | 500 | 505 | 392 | 113 |

*Source:* Bureau of Justice Statistics, Census of State and Local Law Enforcement Agencies, 2004 (Washington DC: Government Printing Office, 2007).

## EXHIBIT 3–3

### State and Local Law Enforcement Agencies, by Number of Sworn Personnel, 2004

| Number of Sworn Personnel* | Agencies | | Full-Time Sworn Personnel | |
|---|---|---|---|---|
| | Number | Percentage | Number | Percentage |
| All sizes | 17,876 | 100 | 731,903 | 100 |
| 1,000 or more | 79 | 0.4 | 222,201 | 30.4 |
| 500–999 | 89 | 0.5 | 60,943 | 8.3 |
| 250–499 | 217 | 1.2 | 75,157 | 10.3 |
| 100–249 | 714 | 4.0 | 106,964 | 14.6 |
| 50–99 | 1,259 | 7.0 | 86,558 | 11.8 |
| 25–49 | 2,304 | 12.9 | 79,374 | 10.8 |
| 10–24 | 4,213 | 23.6 | 65,563 | 9.0 |
| 5–9 | 3,513 | 19.7 | 23,524 | 3.2 |
| 2–4 | 3,286 | 18.4 | 9,699 | 1.3 |
| 0–1 | 2,202 | 12.3 | 1,920 | 0.3 |

*Detail may not add to total because of rounding.

Source: Bureau of Justice Statistics, *Census of State and Local Law Enforcement Agencies, 2004.* (Washington DC: Government Printing Office, 2007).

### *The Myth of 40,000 Agencies*

For many years there was great controversy over exactly how many law enforcement agencies exist in the United States. In 1967 the President's Crime Commission incorrectly reported that there were 40,000 agencies, repeating an unconfirmed figure that had been used for years.[8] The correct figure is about 18,000 state and local agencies.

The typical police department is very small. As Exhibit 3–3 indicates, about half (50.4 percent) have nine or fewer sworn officers. The 168 largest departments, which represent less than 1 percent of the departments, employ about 40 percent of all full-time sworn officers.[9]

## The Number of Law Enforcement Personnel

In 2004 there were 731,903 full-time sworn law enforcement officers employed by local and state law enforcement agencies (Exhibit 3–2). In addition there were 105,000 federal law enforcement officers authorized to carry firearms and make arrests in 2004 (this figure, however, does not include military law enforcement personnel).[10] The number of state and local law enforcement personnel has grown significantly since 1992. By 2004 there were about 27 percent more full-time employees than in 1992.[11]

## Understanding Law Enforcement Personnel Data

There is often much confusion about law enforcement personnel data. The important question is, How much police protection does a community receive? The *total number of employees* includes clerical staff and civilian specialists in computers, criminal-istics, and so on. The *number of sworn officers* refers to those employees who are legally recognized as police officers, with full arrest power and the like.

It is also important to distinguish between an agency's **authorized strength** and the number of sworn officers *currently employed*. Because of retirements, resig-nations, and terminations, most departments are below their authorized strength. The annual average attrition rate is about 5 percent.[12] Hiring is often delayed as a way of allowing the city or county to cope with a budget shortfall.[13]

Thus, if you want to know the level of police protection in Cleveland, for example, you need to determine the number of full-time sworn officers currently employed.

**authorized strength**

## Civilianization

Civilianization is the process of replacing sworn officers with nonsworn personnel for certain positions. Today about 33 percent of all local police department employ-ees are civilians. This represents an increase from 11.1 percent in 1960 and 18.4 per-cent in 1980. Nonsworn personnel have been increasingly used as dispatchers, research and planning specialists, crime-data analysts, and computer technicians.[14]

There are several reasons for utilizing **civilians** in police work. First, they free up sworn officers for critical police work that requires a trained and experienced officer. Second, they possess needed expertise in such areas as computers or data analysis. Third, in many cases they are less expensive than sworn officers, thereby representing a cost saving.[15] For these reasons, a number of experts use the propor-tion of civilian employees within a police agency as an indicator of departmental professionalism.[16]

**civilians**

## The Police–Population Ratio

The standard measure for the level of police protection in a community is the **police–population ratio.** This is usually expressed as the number of sworn offi-cers per thousand residents. The national average for local agencies is 2.5 sworn officers per thousand. The ratio for large cities with populations of 250,000 or more is 2.5. Small cities (population 50,000 to 99,999) have the lowest ratio (1.8 per thousand).[17]

There is tremendous variation in the police–population ratios among big cities. Washington DC has a ratio of 6.3 per thousand residents, compared with 4.4 in Detroit and 1.6 in San Diego.[18] There is no clear relationship between the police–population ratio and the crime rate. In many respects, instead of higher levels of po-lice protection producing lower crime rates, higher crime rates lead to the employment of more police.[19] The relationship of the police–population ratio to the crime rate is discussed in detail in Chapter 7.

**police–population ratio**

## The Cost of Police Protection

Law enforcement is an extremely expensive enterprise. Each year local government agencies spend a total of $57.5 billion on police services. This represents about

30 percent of all criminal justice system expenditures. These figures do not, however, include the cost of private security. The cost of police protection increased about 545 percent between 1977 and 2003. Expenditures for corrections increased more than twice as fast (1,173 percent) in the same period, mainly as a result of the soaring prison populations.[20]

Law enforcement is a labor-intensive industry. Personnel costs, including salaries and fringe benefits, consume about 85 to 90 percent of an agency's budget. For this reason, the efficiency of a police department depends heavily on how well it manages its personnel and what percentage of officers it places in patrol and investigative units (see Chapter 7).

# The Fragmentation Issue

In 1967 the President's Crime Commission concluded that "a fundamental problem confronting law enforcement today is that of fragmented crime repression efforts resulting from the large number of uncoordinated local governments and law enforcement agencies."[21]

The commission published a map of the Detroit metropolitan area indicating the eighty-five agencies in the area. As Exhibit 3–4 indicates, almost half of these agencies had twenty or fewer officers.

The major problem, according to the critics, is a lack of coordination between agencies in the same geographic area. Criminals do not respect political boundaries. In a large metropolitan area, a burglar may commit crimes in several different communities, each with its own police force. Auto-theft rings are often multistate operations. Detectives in one police department may have information that would help solve a series of crimes in a neighboring jurisdiction. In many instances, however, agencies compete rather than cooperate with one another.

Second, fragmentation of responsibility can also lead to crime displacement, especially with respect to vice crimes. One community may adopt a policy of strict enforcement of laws against gambling or prostitution. This often has the effect of driving vice activities to a neighboring jurisdiction, where different community standards exist.

Third, many experts believe there is a serious problem of duplication of services, with the resulting increase in costs. A city police department and the local

---

**SIDEBAR    3 – 2**

### *Exercise: Studying the Fragmentation Problem in Your Area*

1. Prepare a map and accompanying table indicating the number of law enforcement agencies in your metropolitan area, the names of these agencies, and the number of sworn officers in each.

2. Research the nature of any contract or collaborative arrangements between these agencies (e.g., shared communications systems, jail services).

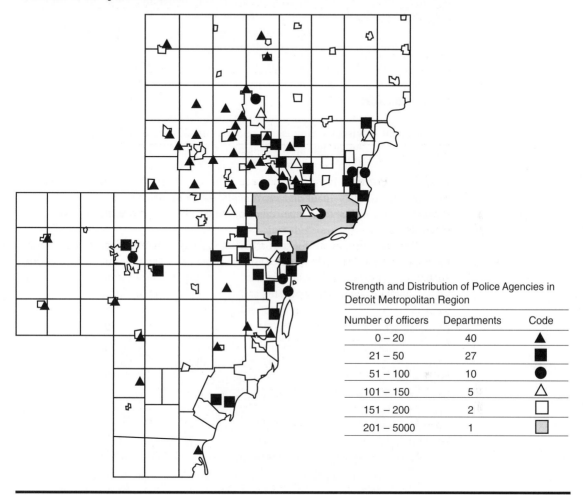

## EXHIBIT 3–4

**Detroit Metropolitan Area**

Strength and Distribution of Police Agencies in Detroit Metropolitan Region

| Number of officers | Departments | Code |
|---|---|---|
| 0 – 20 | 40 | ▲ |
| 21 – 50 | 27 | ■ |
| 51 – 100 | 10 | ● |
| 101 – 150 | 5 | △ |
| 151 – 200 | 2 | □ |
| 201 – 5000 | 1 | ▨ |

sheriff's department may both operate their own 911 telephone systems and their own training academies. Several agencies in the same area may operate their own crime laboratories.

Fourth, fragmentation leads to inconsistent standards. Law enforcement agencies in the same area may have very different recruitment standards, training programs, and salary scales. In countries with a single national police force, uniform standards are established at the national level. In England, which has a tradition of local control of the police, minimum national standards are achieved through a process of inspection and financial incentives. The Home Office inspects each of the forty-three local police constabularies annually.

# Alternatives to Fragmentation

The fragmentation problem is not easily solved. The independence of local governments is deeply rooted in American history. The principle of local control, not just of police but of schools and other government services, is deeply rooted in American political culture. There has always been a very strong fear of a national police force and suspicion of federal control of schools and police.

The major remedies for fragmentation include the following:

## *Consolidation*

Some experts argue that small agencies should be consolidated into larger ones.[22] The National Advisory Commission on Criminal Justice Standards and Goals recommended the consolidation of all agencies with ten or fewer sworn officers (or more than half of the current total).[23] In a few urban areas, the city police and the sheriff's department have been merged. The Charlotte, North Carolina, and the Mecklenburg County Sheriff's Departments, for example, were merged in the early 1990s. Some cities, meanwhile, have combined police and fire departments into a single agency.[24]

Consolidation of police and sheriff's departments has made little progress, however. Both are large bureaucracies that do not want to give up their autonomy. Also, there are practical problems related to merging different entrance requirements, salary schedules, and pension systems.

## *Contracting*

A second alternative to fragmentation is for small agencies to contract with larger agencies for specific services. About half of all cities and counties contract with other governmental units for various services. These contracts cover everything from sewage disposal to tax assessment and water supply. The most common criminal justice services include jails and detention facilities and police–fire communications systems.[25] In many cases, the county sheriff maintains the 911 service for small towns in the area. In other cases, small towns contract with the sheriff for all police services. The Los Angeles County Sheriff's Department, for example, contracts with forty-one separate towns. These contracts account for over $400 million in revenue each year.[26]

# The Fragmentation Problem Reconsidered

Some experts believe the fragmentation problem may not be as serious as others have argued. The Police Services Study (PSS) undertook the first systematic research on the issue in the 1970s, examining the activities of 1,827 law enforcement agencies in 80 medium-sized metropolitan areas. Contrary to the traditional image of fragmentation, the study found that "informal interagency assistance is common," and "strict duplication of services is almost nonexistent in the production of direct police services."[27]

With respect to patrol, for example, informal arrangements involving coordination, sharing, or alternating responsibility were common. No areas were left completely unpatrolled; nor were areas being patrolled by two or more agencies. With respect to auxiliary services, small police departments routinely had access to crime laboratories, training academies, communications systems, and other services provided by larger agencies.

Even more important, the PSS concluded that small police departments were not necessarily less efficient than large departments. Small departments put a higher percentage of their officers on the street, performing direct police services. Larger departments did not necessarily achieve any advantages of scale.[28] Larger agencies had more complex bureaucratic structures, with the result that a smaller percentage of officers were available for direct police services. Gary Cordner found that among Maryland agencies, the complexity of the community social structure, not the size of the agency, was most important in determining the effectiveness of criminal investigation: The less complex the community, the more effective the police.[29]

Finally, the emphasis on decentralized policing under community policing suggests that small local law enforcement agencies might be preferable to large consolidated agencies.[30]

# Municipal Police

Municipal or city police are the most important component of American law enforcement. In 2004 they represented 71 percent of all law enforcement agencies and employed 61 percent of all sworn officers.[31]

---

**SIDEBAR   3 – 3**

## U.S. Police Protection Level Compared to Those of Other Countries

Researchers have just begun to compare the level of police protection in the United States to those of other countries. Below is a table of countries and the number of police officers per thousand residents. As a group, identify three reasons why the level of police in the United States is higher than in some countries but lower than in others.

### Sworn Police Officers per Thousand Residents

| Nation | Number | Nation | Number |
|---|---|---|---|
| Russia | 8.65 | Colombia | 2.48 |
| Kuwait | 6.30 | England and Wales | 2.42 |
| Hong Kong | 5.42 | Turkey | 2.26 |
| Israel | 4.47 | Syria | 1.98 |
| Panama | 4.20 | Japan | 1.81 |
| Lebanon | 4.18 | Canada | 1.79 |
| Austria | 3.57 | Finland | 1.53 |
| Peru | 3.16 | Norway | 1.37 |
| Czech Republic | 2.87 | Nigeria | 1.09 |
| United States | 2.50 | | |

*Source:* Adapted from Edward Maguire and Rebecca Schulte-Murray, Issues and Patterns in the Comparative International Study of Police Strength, *International Journal of Comparative Sociology* 42, 1–2 (2001): pp. 75–99.

municipal police

Even more important, **municipal police** play a more complex role than any other type of law enforcement agency. The external environment heavily influences all agencies.[32] Cities, and big cities in particular, represent the most complex environments, particularly in terms of the diversity of the population. City police departments have the heaviest responsibility for dealing with serious crime, which is disproportionately concentrated in cities. They are also responsible for difficult order maintenance problems and are asked to provide a wide range of emergency services.[33]

Among all municipal police departments, a few very large departments play a disproportionately important role. A Police Foundation report on the big six police departments—New York, Los Angeles, Chicago, Houston, Philadelphia, Detroit—found that they are responsible for 7.5 percent of the U.S. population but face 23 percent of all violent crime, including 34 percent of all robberies.[34] Although these six represent a tiny fraction of all departments, they employ almost 13 percent of all sworn officers. The New York City police department towers over all others, with 35,973 sworn officers. Chicago is second with about 13,000 officers.[35]

The big departments dominate public thinking about the police. Events in New York or Los Angeles—the Rodney King case, for example—are reported by the national news media. Moreover, a disproportionate amount of the research on policing has been conducted in New York, Chicago, Los Angeles, Philadelphia, Boston, and Washington. Much less is known about medium-sized police departments, and almost no research has been done on small departments, even though they are more representative of policing in America.

The typical municipal police department is in a small town. Slightly more than half (50.4 percent) employ fewer than ten sworn officers.[36] Small town and rural police operate in a very different context than big-city police. There is less serious crime than in urban areas. The majority of calls for police service involve noncriminal events and minor disturbances.[37] In one study, traffic problems accounted for 25 percent of all calls, public disturbances accounted for 19 percent, family disturbances represented 18 percent, and stray dogs another 11 percent. (The remaining 27 percent were miscellaneous calls.)[38]

## County Police

county police

A few areas are served by **county police** departments. They are essentially municipal police that operate on a countywide basis, but do not have any of the non-law-enforcement roles of the county sheriff (see Exhibit 3–5). Less than 1 percent of all local departments are county police. The largest are Suffolk County police (2,692 sworn officers) and New York State's Nassau County police (2,574 sworn officers).[39]

# The County Sheriff

There are 3,067 sheriff's departments in the United States.[40] The county sheriff's office is unique among American law enforcement agencies, in terms of both its legal status and its role.[41]

## EXHIBIT 3–5

### Responsibilities of Sherrif's Departments

| Function | Percentage of Agencies |
|---|---|
| Routine patrol | 98% |
| Crime investigation | 92 |
| Enforcement of traffic laws | 90 |
| Process serving | 99 |
| Court security | 94 |
| Jail operations | 76 |
| Search and rescue | 56 |

Source: Adapted from Bureau of Justice Statistics, *Sheriff's Departments, 2003* (Washington DC: Government Printing Office, 2006).

The legal status of the **sheriff** is unique because in thirty-seven states it is a **sheriff** constitutional office, whose responsibilities are defined in the state constitution. Also, sheriffs are elected in all but two states. (In Rhode Island they are appointed by the governor; in Hawaii they are appointed by the chief justice of the state supreme court.) As elected officials, sheriffs are directly involved in partisan politics in ways that municipal police chiefs are not. Historically, in rural areas the sheriff was the most powerful politician in the county.[42]

## The Role of the Sheriff

Sheriffs have a unique role in that they serve all three components of the criminal justice system: law enforcement, courts, and corrections. As Exhibit 3–5 indicates, almost all sheriff's departments perform the basic law enforcement functions of patrolling and investigating crimes. Almost all serve the courts by process serving (subpoenas, etc.) and providing security for the courts. In many urban areas, sheriffs spend more time on civil court duties than on criminal law enforcement. Furthermore, 76 percent of all sheriff's departments maintain the county jail. In most big cities the jail is operated by a separate department of corrections.[43]

Lee Brown identified four different models of sheriff's departments, according to their responsibilities: (1) full-service model sheriff's departments carry out law enforcement, judicial, and correctional duties; (2) law enforcement model agencies carry out only law enforcement duties, with other responsibilities assumed by separate agencies; (3) civil-judicial model agencies handle only court-related duties (e.g., counties in Connecticut and Rhode Island); and (4) correctional-judicial model agencies (e.g., San Francisco County) handle all responsibilities except law enforcement.[44]

The distribution of sheriff's departments resembles that of the municipal police. There are a few very large departments and many small ones. The largest is the Los Angeles County sheriff's department, which had 8,622 sworn officers in 2004. About 24 percent of all sheriff's departments, however, have fewer than 10 sworn officers.[45]

# Other Local Agencies

The American law enforcement picture is complicated by the existence of other local agencies that have some law enforcement responsibilities.

## The Constable

constable

Like the sheriff, the **constable** is an office whose roots can be traced back to colonial America. Urbanization and the consequent growth of city departments have stripped the constable's office of most of its functions. The Advisory Commission on Intergovernmental Relations found it to be "of minor importance" and recommended its abolition.[46]

For a full discussion on policing in colonial America, see Chapter 2.

There are few constables left in the United States today. Depending on the state, constables can be elected or appointed, and their role and function is defined by state constitution. Modern constables typically work within the county court system. They are responsible for serving warrants and subpoenas, transporting prisoners, and providing security for district judges. They also work with county commissioners to post delinquent tax notices and assist attorneys in serving divorce papers.[47]

## The Coroner/Medical Examiner

coroner

The office of the **coroner,** or medical examiner, is often considered a law enforcement agency because it has the responsibility to investigate crimes. Medical examiners and coroners' offices are responsible for a wide range of activities including investigating death scenes, conducting autopsies, and determining the cause of violent or unexpected deaths. A Bureau of Justice Statistics special report found a total of 1,998 coroners or medical examiners in the United States.[48]

Coroners and medical examiners are usually employed by a state, county, or city agency. The type of "death investigator" used by a jurisdiction is typically mandated by law. The Bureau of Justice Statistics reported that "16 states had a centralized statewide medical examiner system, 14 states had a county coroner system, 7 had a county medical examiner system, and 13 had a mixed county medical examiner and coroner system."[49]

There are a number of important distinctions between coroners and medical examiners. First, coroners are typically not trained as physicians and have received little, if any, medical training; whereas medical examiners are physicians and often have received special training in death investigation. Second, coroners are typically elected to their position; medical examiners are usually appointed by an elected official. Third, while both are responsible for the investigation of deaths, medical examiners are expected to rely heavily on their medical expertise to understand the cause of death.[50]

The Centers for Disease Control (CDC) reports that about 20 percent of deaths in the United States are investigated by a coroner or medical examiner. While guidelines vary on which deaths are required to be investigated, most jurisdictions require that the following types of deaths be investigated:

- Deaths due to homicide, suicide, or accidental causes such as car crashes, falls, burns, or the ingestion of drugs.
- Sudden or suspicious deaths, deaths from sudden infant death syndrome (SIDS), and unattended deaths.

- Deaths caused by an agent or disease constituting a threat to public health.
- Deaths that occur at a workplace.
- Deaths of people who were in custody, confinement, or who were institutionalized.
- Deaths of people to be cremated.[51]

## Special District Police

**Special district police** agencies serve particular government agencies. The Los Angeles School District, for example, has its own police force. Some urban transit systems maintain separate law enforcement agencies. The Metropolitan Transit Police Force in the Washington DC subway system overlaps three different political jurisdictions: the District of Columbia, Virginia, and Maryland.[52]

    College and university campus police are an important example of special district police.[53] About three-fourths of the campus security forces at colleges and universities with 2,500 or more students are state certified law enforcement agencies. Their officers have general arrest powers, often carry firearms, are certified by the state, and participate in the FBI's Uniform Crime Reports (UCR) system. Today, the nation's 750 law enforcement agencies that serve universities employ about 13,000 sworn officers. The other colleges and universities use private security or their own nonsworn security officers.[54]

**special district police**

## Tribal Police

A unique aspect of American criminal justice is that many Native American tribes maintain their own separate criminal justice systems, including **tribal police** departments, on their reservations. Native American tribes are separate nations, which

**tribal police**

---

### SIDEBAR 3 – 4

### *Getting to Know Your Campus Police*

1. Is your campus police agency a certified law enforcement agency?

2. If so, what state-mandated training do they receive? How many hours of training? What is the content of the curriculum? Who provides the training?

3. If it is not, what are the recruitment standards? What kind of training do officers receive? Who provides the training?

4. If your campus police agency is a certified law enforcement agency, does it file the required UCR report?

5. If not, does it file an annual crime report anyway?

6. Are your campus police officers armed? What kind of training in firearms use do they receive? What kind of retraining or recertification are the officers required to receive?

7. Does your campus police agency have a written deadly force policy? What does that policy say? (See Chapter 14 on deadly force policies.)

## EXHIBIT 3-6

### Types of Indian Police Departments and Their Characteristics

| Type of Law Enforcement Program | Public Law 93-638 | BIA | Self-Governance | Tribal Funded |
|---|---|---|---|---|
| **Administered by** | Tribe | Federal government | Tribe | Tribe |
| **Officers are employees of** | Tribe | Federal government | Tribe | Tribe |
| **Funding** | Federal (often with tribal contribution) | Federal government | Tribe | Tribe |

signed treaties with the United States government and retain a significant degree of legal autonomy. In a number of important respects, tribes and reservations are not subject to federal or state law (see Exhibit 3–6 ).[55]

While there are roughly 330 Indian reservations in the United States, there are about 200 police agencies whose primary responsibility is to provide police services in Indian Country. This is largely because the Bureau of Indian Affairs (BIA) provides police services to more than one reservation and many tribes are not entitled to their own police department. Historically, policing Indian Country has been the responsibility of the BIA. The BIA is located in the U.S. Department of the Interior. Today, however, there are a number of different administrative arrangements that are used to police Indian nations.[56]

The most common administrative arrangement is for the tribe's police agency to be created under the Indian Self-Determination and Education Assistance Act of 1975. This act, also known as Public Law 93-638, gives Indian nations the right to establish their own organizational framework and to establish their own performance standards for their police department. While officers and civilians in these agencies are considered tribal employees, they are typically funded with federal monies. The majority of Indian police departments are configured in this way.[57]

The second most common administrative arrangement in Indian Country is for the Bureau of Indian Affairs (BIA) to assume policing responsibilities. About 64 Indian nations still rely on the BIA for policing. Under this model all staff are federal employees and work under the authority of the BIA. Many Indian nations that are policed by the BIA are assigned a local BIA superintendent who assumes many of the responsibilities granted to chiefs of police in municipal police departments. BIA superintendents of small tribes are often administratively responsible for more than one tribe.[58] There are about 37 police agencies operated by the BIA.[59]

A less popular administrative arrangement is self-governance. Under this model, Indian nations contract with the BIA for policing services. Because the BIA is paid through block grants, the Indian nation is afforded a higher degree of organizational freedom. The least used administrative arrangement is the Tribally Funded

Indian Police Department. While this model affords Indian nation's complete control over their police services, most Indian nations do not have the financial resources for such an agency.[60]

Most tribally operated police agencies are small. Only seven tribal police agencies have fifty or more full-time sworn officers, and about one-third have fewer than five officers. These agencies are also typically responsible for policing relatively small populations that are dispersed over large land areas, making officers' jobs difficult to manage.[61]

## State Law Enforcement Agencies

State law enforcement agencies fall into three categories: state police, highway patrols, and state investigative agencies. This book will focus on the first two, since they are regarded as general service law enforcement agencies.[62]

**State police** are defined as agencies "having statewide police powers for both traffic regulation and criminal investigations." **Highway patrol** are defined as agencies having "statewide authority to enforce traffic regulations and arrest non-traffic violators under their jurisdiction."[63]

**state police**
**highway patrol**

There are forty-nine general service state law enforcement agencies in the United States; Hawaii is the only state without one. These agencies are divided about equally between state police and highway patrol. Several states have more than one law enforcement agency. California, for example, maintains both the California Highway Patrol and the California Division of Law Enforcement; in Ohio there is both the Ohio Highway Patrol and the Ohio Bureau of Criminal Identification and Investigation. The roles and missions of state law enforcement agencies are defined by state law, and hence vary widely from state to state.

There is considerable variation in the administrative structure of state law enforcement agencies. One report found that "almost every possibility" exists. Several states have an umbrella agency containing a number of different departments responsible for various services. The New Jersey Department of Public Safety includes eight divisions: Division of Law, State Police, Division of Motor Vehicles, Division of Alcoholic Beverage Control, Division of Criminal Justice, Division of Consumer Affairs, Police Training Commission, and State Athletic Commissioner.

### *Roles and Responsibilities*

State police and highway patrol provide a variety of law enforcement services. In terms of patrol, state police have concurrent or shared responsibility with local police agencies. In about half of the states, the state police or highway patrol agency has the primary responsibility for enforcing traffic laws on the main highways.[64]

State laws vary regarding responsibility for criminal investigation. In some states, the state police have general responsibility; in others, the investigative powers are limited. About half of all state agencies provide crime lab services (ballistics, drug testing) for local police departments. Finally, 77.6 percent of state police agencies operate a training academy. In some states, they are responsible for training recruits from local police departments.[65]

# Federal Law Enforcement Agencies

The federal component of the law enforcement industry is relatively small but more complex than generally recognized. It is estimated that there are 105,000 full-time federal law enforcement employees. This figure includes all personnel "authorized to carry firearms and make arrests." It does not include military police, however.[66]

There is no agreement about the exact size of federal law enforcement activities. The confusion is due to the fact that many federal agencies have enforcement or regulatory powers. Most are not general service agencies, as defined above. They do not provide the basic services of protection and criminal investigation.

Seventeen federal law enforcement agencies employ 500 or more sworn officers. The U.S. Customs and Border Protection is the largest with 27,705 full-time officers, followed by the Federal Bureau of Prisons with 15,214 officers, and the Federal Bureau of Investigation with 12,242 officers. The Drug Enforcement Agency (DEA) employs 4,400 officers. The complexity and variety of federal law enforcement are indicated by the fact that the largest agencies include the U.S. Fish and Wildlife Service (708 officers) and the U.S. Forest Service (600 officers).[67]

The role of each federal agency is specified by federal statute. In important respects, federal agencies have a far less complex role than that of municipal agencies. Federal agents do not have the ambiguous and difficult order maintenance responsibilities, do not maintain 911 emergency telephone services, and are not asked to handle vague "disturbance" calls.

We discuss the role of the largest federal law enforcement agencies in the United States in the next section.

# Federal Law Enforcement after September 11, 2001

After September 11, 2001, there was a substantial movement led by President George W. Bush to alter the organizational structure of federal law enforcement in the United States.

He restructured federal law enforcement roles and responsibilities into two departments: the Department of Homeland Security and the Department of Justice (see Exhibit 3–7).

---

### EXHIBIT 3–7

### Largest Federal Law Enforcement Employers and Their Departments

| Department of Homeland Security | Department of Justice |
|---|---|
| Bureau of Customs and Border Protection | Drug Enforcement Administration |
| Bureau of Immigration and Customs Enforcement | Federal Bureau of Investigation |
| Federal Emergency Management Agency | Bureau of Alcohol, Tobacco, |
| Transportation Security Administration | Firearms, and Explosives |
| U.S. Coast Guard | U.S. Marshals Service |
| U.S. Secret Service | |

## The Department of Homeland Security

On November 25, 2002, the Homeland Security Act was passed, creating the Department of Homeland Security (DHS), a new cabinet-level department that is responsible for activities pertaining to homeland security. This act launched the largest government reorganization since 1947.[68] Twenty-two agencies, and about 170,000 employees, all with functions related to homeland security, were organizationally moved to the Department of Homeland Security (DHS). The six largest federal law enforcement employers with DHS are:

- Customs and Border Protection (CBP)
- Immigration and Customs Enforcement (ICE)
- Federal Emergency Management Agency (FEMA)
- Transportation Security Administration (TSA)
- U.S. Coast Guard
- U.S. Secret Service

***Customs and Border Protection (CBP).***    Many of the functions formerly carried out by the Customs Service, the INS Inspection Service, the Border Patrol, and the Agricultural Quarantine Inspection program were combined into the Bureau of Customs and Border Protection (CBP). The CBP is currently responsible for ensuring that persons and cargo enter the United States legally and safely through official ports of entry. It works to prevent illegal immigration and the smuggling of controlled substances, weapons of mass destruction (WMD), and illegal and diseased plants and animals into the country.[69]

***Immigration and Customs Enforcement (ICE).***    Immigration and Customs Enforcement (ICE) is the Department of Homeland Security's largest investigative bureau. It conducts many of the functions formerly carried out by the U.S. Customs Service, the Immigration and Naturalization Service, and the Federal Protective Service. ICE is responsible for the enforcement of immigration and customs laws, the protection of many federal buildings, and air and marine enforcement. ICE is comprised of four divisions: (1) the Office of Investigations is responsible for investigating such issues as human smuggling, drugs, weapons, and other contraband; (2) the Office of Detention and Removal is responsible for deporting illegal immigrants; (3) the Office of Protective Services is responsible for policing over 8,800 federal buildings and facilities; and (4) the Office of Intelligence is responsible for collecting, maintaining, and disseminating strategic and tactical intelligence for the other three ICE divisions and for DHS.[70]

***Federal Emergency Management Agency (FEMA).***    The Federal Emergency Management Agency (FEMA) was first established in 1979 and became part of DHS on March 1, 2003. It currently employs 2,600 full-time employees and has almost 4,000 standby personnel who are available for deployment after disasters if required. FEMA is responsible for preparing for, preventing, and responding to natural and man-made disasters. FEMA typically does not work alone, but coordinates and partners with government, private, and nonprofit organizations to manage emergency preparedness and response efforts.[71]

***Transportation Security Administration (TSA).***    The Transportation Security Administration (TSA) was created on September 11, 2001, in direct response to the terrorist attacks on September 11, 2001. TSA is responsible for protecting the nation's transportation system. While many people are aware of its responsibility for maintaining security at airports, it is also responsible for other transportation systems including roads, railways, seaports, bridges, and pipelines.[72] The TSA is the largest employer within the Department of Homeland Security, employing more than 69,000 persons.[73]

***U.S. Coast Guard.***    The U.S. Coast Guard was originally established by Alexander Hamilton in 1790 as the Revenue Cutter Service, under the Department of Transportation. While the U.S. Coast Guard has been administratively housed in many government agencies over the years, it was transferred to the Department of Transportation in 1967, and moved to the Department of Homeland Security on March 1, 2003. The U.S. Coast Guard is a multifunctional, multimission service that has missions that are both security and nonsecurity related.[74] For example, it is responsible for security missions such as port, waterway, and coastal security; drug interdiction; migrant interdiction; and defense readiness. It is also responsible for conducting nonsecurity missions such as maritime safety, search and rescue, protecting the environment and living marine resources, and ice operations. As such, the U.S. Coast Guard is unique in that it has been granted authority and responsibilities that are similar to both the military and the police.

***U.S. Secret Service.***    The U.S. Secret Service was originally established in 1865 for the purpose of investigating the counterfeiting of U.S. currency. Today, it has a wide array of investigative responsibilities and is responsible for the protection of current and former U.S. presidents, vice presidents, and their immediate family members. Many of their investigative responsibilities were changed with the advent of more sophisticated forms of communication.[75] The U.S. Secret Service is currently responsible for investigating "crimes that involve financial institution fraud, computer and telecommunication fraud, false identification documents, access device fraud, advance fee fraud, electronic funds transfer, and money laundering."[76]

## *The Department of Justice*

In 1870, Congress established the Department of Justice with the attorney general as its administrative head. Congress made the Department of Justice responsible for enforcing and prosecuting all federal laws.[77] While the structure of the Department of Justice has changed, its fundamental mission has remained the same. The five largest Department of Justice agencies are:

- Drug Enforcement Administration
- Federal Bureau of Investigation
- Bureau of Alcohol, Tobacco, Firearms, and Explosives
- U.S. Marshals Service
- Federal Bureau of Prisons

***Drug Enforcement Administration (DEA).***    The mission of the Drug Enforcement Administration (DEA) is to enforce federal laws and regulations pertaining to controlled substances. The primary focus of its law enforcement efforts is on those individuals and organizations who grow, manufacture, and distribute illegal drugs. Therefore, its mission is primarily dedicated to reducing the supply of illegal drugs to residents in the United States. For example, DEA agents investigate individuals involved in high-level drug trafficking within the United States and investigate individuals who traffic major amounts of illegal drugs into the United States. They also work with local police agencies to reduce the availability of illegal drugs at the street level and work with foreign governments to eradicate crops associated with illegal drugs.[78] The DEA is staffed with about 5,300 special agents who are supported by 5,600 staff.[79]

***Federal Bureau of Investigation (FBI).***   The role of the FBI has historically been shaped by administrative and political factors. Under J. Edgar Hoover (1924–1972), the FBI concentrated its efforts on investigating alleged "subversives" and apprehending bank robbers and stolen cars. Critics charged that the FBI ignored white-collar crime, organized crime, and violations of the civil rights of minorities. After Hoover's death it was discovered that, under his direction, the FBI had committed many violations of citizens' rights: it was guilty of spying on individuals and groups because of their political beliefs, conducting illegal wiretaps, and even burglarizing the offices of groups it was spying on.[80] However, since Hoover's death, subsequent FBI directors reoriented the Bureau's mission, placing more emphasis on white-collar crime, organized crime, and political corruption.

In 2002, after the terrorist attacks on the World Trade Center and the Pentagon, the FBI announced that it was going to make a fundamental change in its mission, which would focus first on preventing future terrorist attacks. In particular, the FBI crafted a new mandate that focused on ten priorities.

1. Protect the United States from terrorist attack.
2. Protect the United States against foreign intelligence operations and espionage.
3. Protect the United States against cyber-based attacks and high technology crimes.
4. Combat public corruption at all levels.
5. Protect civil rights.
6. Combat transnational and national criminal organizations and enterprises.
7. Combat major white-collar crime.
8. Combat significant violent crime.
9. Support federal, state, local, and international partners.
10. Upgrade technology to successfully perform the FBI's mission.[81]

***Bureau of Alcohol, Tobacco, Firearms, and Explosives (ATF).***   In 2003, under the Homeland Security Act, the law enforcement functions of the U.S. Bureau of Alcohol, Tobacco, Firearms, and Explosives (ATF) were transferred from the U.S. Treasury Department to the Department of Justice. First, ATF is responsible for enforcing federal firearms laws. It investigates firearms trafficking and identifies and arrests armed career criminals. Second, it is responsible for regulating the explosives-related

## Police in Focus

### *Looking for a Job with the FBI?*

A lot of students are curious about the qualifications needed for a job with the FBI. Below are many of the frequently asked questions about employment with the FBI and the answers to them.

#### What are the qualifications for the special agent position?

To qualify for training as a special agent, an individual must be a U.S. citizen and have reached his or her twenty-third but not thirty-seventh birthday. All candidates must possess a valid driver's license and must pass a polygraph examination, a drug test, and a color vision test. Other requirements include uncorrected vision not worse than 20/200 and corrected 20/20 in one eye and not worse than 20/40 in the other eye. Applicants must possess a four-year degree from a college or university accredited by one of the regional or national institutional associations recognized by the U.S. secretary of education.

#### What about a background investigation?

Applicants are thoroughly investigated for FBI employment. The background investigation takes from one to four months and encompasses contacting former and current employers, references, social acquaintances, and neighbors, as well as reviewing school, credit, arrest, medical, and military records.

The complete background investigation is assessed before a final decision on employment is rendered.

#### Do certain degrees provide a more desirable educational background for the special agent position?

The FBI does not recommend particular courses or schools. Any degrees that develop research and analytical skills are desirable educational backgrounds. For example, a law degree is a desirable asset because special agents are charged with the duty of investigating violations of federal laws of the United States. An accounting degree is also desirable because special agents trace financial transactions and review complex accounting records in criminal investigations. Special agent accountants often testify in such cases as expert witnesses.

#### How can I obtain an application for FBI employment?

You can apply for jobs at the FBI, including special agent, online at fbijobs.com. If you don't have access to the Internet, please contact the applicant coordinator or special agent recruiter of the FBI field office nearest your residence.

*Source:* The above information was adapted and obtained from https://www.fbijobs.gov/Faq.asp.

---

industry to prevent terrorists and criminals from coming into possession of explosives and to ensure that those in possession of explosives are properly licensed. It also provides training to federal, state, and local officials for the detection, handling, and destruction of explosives. Last, ATF is responsible for enforcing federal laws as they pertain to the collection of federal taxes on alcohol and tobacco products.[82]

***U.S. Marshals Service.*** The U.S. Marshals Service, established in 1789, is the nation's oldest federal law enforcement agency. The U.S. Marshals Service is responsible for providing security to the federal courts, housing federal detainees, and conducting fugitive investigations. Each year U.S. marshals arrest more than 35,000 persons wanted by federal law enforcement agencies, such as the FBI, DEA, and ATF, and house over 54,000 detainees through cooperative agreements with local, state, and private jails. The U.S. Marshals Service is also responsible for administering the nation's witness protection program. Since 1971 it has provided new identities and relocated 7,800 witnesses and about 10,000 of their family members.[83]

---

# The Private Security Industry

Private security is an important part of American law enforcement. Its exact size is difficult to determine because it involves many small, private agencies, part-time employees, and security personnel that are employed by private businesses. It is estimated that there are as many as 90,000 private security organizations that employ over 2 million people.[84] Elizabeth Joh reports that this amounts to roughly three private security officers for every one public police officer in America. She further points to the fact that it is estimated the United States spends twice as much money on private policing as it does on public policing.[85] The above estimates include the following categories of jobs: private detectives and investigators, patrol services, security guards, loss prevention specialists, gaming officers and investigators, and armored car services. Brian Forst points out that Sears, Roebuck employs about 6,000 security guards, which is significantly more personnel than almost any metropolitan police department.[86]

Today private security firms are responsible for patrolling and providing protection at public and private housing complexes, gated communities, business parks, malls, office complexes, power plants, and airports.[87] They have also begun to play a major role in traffic regulation through the operation of cameras that detect red-light running and automated radar stations for administering speeding tickets. One news story providing an example of the extent of private security in American life made the following statement: "There are certain areas in Florida—home of Wackenhut HQ—where your housing estate is policed by Wackenhut, you get on the train to go to work and that's policed by Wackenhut, and you get to work and the corporate office is policed by Wackenhut. And if you do something wrong, you end up in a Wackenhut prison."[88]

Private police organizations display four characteristics that differentiate themselves from the public police. First, private police organizations focus on more than crime. They also concern themselves with broader issues such as property, personal assets, and general consumer satisfaction. Second, private police organizations have many more alternatives at their disposal for addressing problems. For example, they can have employees fired, ban persons from establishments, fine those who do not follow policies and guidelines, as well as pursue prosecution in the criminal courts. As such, private police have much more discretion in how they resolve problems. Third, private police organizations place significantly more emphasis on the prevention of problems. Public police organizations have traditionally emphasized reacting to problems after they occur, whereas private police invest more of their resources in the prevention of problems before they occur. Fourth, private police primarily concern themselves with matters occurring on, or with, private property. For instance, private police are typically associated with large privately held spaces such as malls, housing developments, and business complexes.[89]

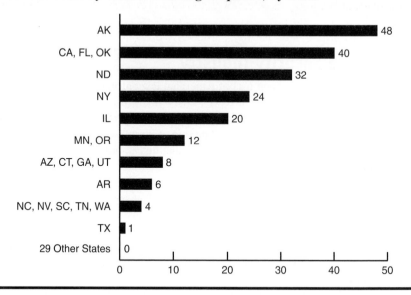

## EXHIBIT 3–8

### Hours of Security Guard Training Required, by State

*Source:* Service Employees International Union (SEIU), "Report Card on Security Standards," October 12, 2004, http://www.seiu.org/building/security/statesecuritygrades.cfm.

The size of the private security industry raises a number of important issues. The first is the quality of private security personnel. Requirements for employment are minimal, and in many cases, training is nonexistent. States each have their own laws regarding minimum training qualifications for being a private security officer (see Exhibit 3–8). In 2004 thirteen states required security personnel to undergo eight or more hours of training; however, twenty-nine states did not require any training at all. By 2006 the latter number had risen to thirty-one. Similarly, in 2006 twenty-one states did not require private security officers to be licensed, and sixteen states did not require a criminal background check.[90] The result is that in many states private security is often the last resort for people unable to find other jobs.

Second, there are few federal, state, or local laws that guide private police conduct. The courts have repeatedly articulated that the laws that guide the behavior of public police officers are not applicable to private security. For example, the Supreme Court has ruled that decisions such as *Miranda* and *Mapp* only apply to public police, and private security officers are not bound by these decisions. Likewise, few states have sought to enact legislation to guide private security conduct and instead have chosen to hold private security officers accountable in the same way as they do private citizens.

Third, there are problems related to cooperation between public and private police. In large part this appears to be a consequence of the attitudes and beliefs held by each group about the other. Research indicates that private police officers believe that public police officers do not respect them, are more concerned with making arrests and less concerned about crime prevention, and are generally unwilling to share information with them. Similar studies examining public police reveal that they perceive private police to be unprofessional, too client-oriented, and often unwilling to prosecute.[91]

This last problem has become particularly pronounced since the terrorist attacks on September 11, 2001. The 9/11 commission noted that 85 percent of the nation's critical infrastructures are protected by private security organizations[92] and roughly 5 percent of all private police are responsible for guarding and protecting a critical infrastructure or asset.[93] For example, private police are responsible for protecting nuclear power plants, major financial institutions, chemical facilities, and water plants. Advisers to Congress have begun to publicly question the wisdom of placing the nation's most valuable assets in the hands of those who are so poorly trained and who earn less than half the average salary of the police.[94]

# Minimum Standards: American Style

Unlike most other countries, the United States does not have a national police system. There is no federal agency responsible for supervising local agencies or ensuring minimum standards. In England each local department receives half of its budget from the national government and undergoes a regular inspection as part of the process.[95] Nonetheless, there are some minimum standards for law enforcement agencies in the United States that are required by federal and state governments. The process for developing and enforcing these standards, however, is not systematic.

## The Role of the Federal Government

The most important set of national standards are the decisions of the U.S. Supreme Court related to police procedures. Decisions such as *Mapp v. Ohio, Miranda v. Arizona,* and *Tennessee v. Garner* set minimum national standards based on provisions of the U.S. Constitution. Beginning in the 1960s, these and other Supreme Court decisions were a major instrument of reform, forcing departments to significantly improve personnel standards and management and supervision.[96]

For a full discussion on these court decisions, see Chapters 2, 11, and 14.

Relying on the Supreme Court to define minimum standards for police has serious limitations, however. First, most aspects of policing do not raise issues of constitutional law—for example, the length of police academy training or the content of that training. Second, enforcing Supreme Court decisions is extremely difficult. A police department may systematically violate the *Miranda* requirement; it is enforced only when someone is convicted and then appeals that conviction on the basis of the *Miranda* decision.[97]

Congress has passed a number of laws that directly apply to state and local law enforcement agencies. Most important is the 1964 Civil Rights Act, which prohibits discrimination on the basis of race, color, national origin, religion, or sex. Local and state agencies are forbidden to discriminate in recruitment, promotion, or assignment of officers.[98] The law, however, does not cover many police personnel issues. It does not, for example, establish minimum standards for recruitment or training. No federal law specifies a minimum level of education for police recruits.

Nor does any law require a minimum police–population ratio or set standards for patrol operations.

Office of Community-
Oriented Police Services
(COPS)

The U.S. Department of Justice also uses grants to encourage changes in policing. For example, the 1994 Violent Crime Control Act provided funds for 100,000 officers. The program was administered through the **Office of Community-Oriented Police Services (COPS),** and money was granted only if the local agency developed a plan for implementing community policing.[99]

## The Role of State Governments

State governments also set minimum standards for police in a number of areas. State supreme courts rule on issues under their state constitutions. State codes of criminal procedure also define what police must do and what they may not do.

The most important role of state governments has been to require the licensing or certification of all sworn officers. In particular, this includes mandatory preservice training. New York and California were pioneers in this area in 1959, and by the 1970s every state had some kind of certification requirement. Prior to this time, it was not uncommon in small departments for officers to have no preservice training whatsoever.[100]

In a further development of this approach, some states have adopted procedures for delicensing or decertifying police officers. In Florida, for example, when an officer's license is revoked by the state, that person is not eligible to be employed by any other law enforcement agency in the state.[101] In most states, however, it is possible for an officer to be fired by one police department and then hired by another.

## Accreditation

accreditation

A final approach to establishing minimum national standards in policing is through **accreditation.**[102] Accreditation is a process of professional self-regulation, similar to those processes that exist in medicine, law, education, and other occupations. The Commission on Accreditation of Law Enforcement Agencies (CALEA) was established in 1979. The fourth edition of its *Standards for Law Enforcement* includes separate standards. Some standards are mandatory, while others are only recommended.[103]

The major weakness with accreditation is that it is a voluntary process. There is no penalty for a police department not being accredited. By comparison, a nonaccredited educational institution is not eligible for certain federal funds, and graduates from nonaccredited institutions find that their credits are not accepted by other schools.[104]

The process of becoming accredited is expensive, in terms of both the formal CALEA fees and the staff time required to meet the various standards.[105] However, by 2008 CALEA had accredited 746 agencies.[106]

Critics question the impact of accreditation on police work. Mastrofski suggests that accreditation standards "add[s] to the proliferation of rules in already rule-suffused bureaucracies, without appreciably affecting patterns of police behavior."[107] Others, however, have found that accreditation has a positive impact on police organizations. For example, McCabe and Fajardo reported that accredited agencies, when compared to nonaccredited agencies, are more likely to require more training, have higher minimum educational requirements for new officers, and are twice as likely to require drug testing for sworn officers. Agencies that are accredited were also found to be more likely to have specialized units to respond to child abuse and to enforce drug laws.[108]

In short, American law enforcement agencies must meet *some* minimum standards. These standards cover only a limited range of issues, and there is no system for developing and implementing a comprehensive set of standards.

---

 # Case Study

## *Interagency Coordination: A Case Study of the 2005 London Train Bombings*

On July 7, 2005, at approximately 8:50 a.m., a series of bombs exploded on three London Underground trains. One hour later, a fourth bomb exploded on the upper deck of a bus in Tavistock Square. The attacks—the work of four suicide bombers—marked the deadliest bombings in London since World War II and the first suicide attacks in modern Western Europe.

The response of London's emergency services and transportation system to the bombings is considered the city's most comprehensive and complex response ever to a terrorist attack. [1] Responding agencies faced challenges during and immediately after the attacks, but major problems in emergency coordination were minimized because London officials had established relationships with one another and had practiced agreed-upon procedures. Consequently, everyone knew their roles and responsibilities; a command and control system was up and running quickly; and mutual aid agreements—planned out in advance—were successfully initiated and applied.

This case study is based on research regarding the multiagency response to the London attacks, including barriers and ways to overcome them. As part of that National Institute of Justice-funded study, Stro and Eyerman interviewed officials from law enforcement, fire and medical services, and public health agencies who were directly involved in the July 2005 London response. [2] The authors asked about their role during the response, the strategies for coordination that facilitated it, the barriers they encountered, and possible strategies for improving coordination among agencies responding to emergencies.

### Why Do Emergency Coordination Efforts Fail?

Like the U.K., the United States faces a range of potential threats that would require a quick and coordinated response by many agencies. Our nation's capacity to prepare for and respond to terrorist attacks, natural disasters and other large-scale emergencies—especially ones involving simultaneous attacks at different locations—hinges on the ability of agencies to communicate with one another, share resources, and coordinate and execute a joint effort.

Researchers who study coordinated emergency response have identified both barriers and promising practices to help law enforcement and public health agencies improve interagency support during such situations. First and foremost, we know that multiagency coordination is a challenge at all levels. Even small problems can be exacerbated when crises occur in several places simultaneously or when reports by the media heighten public panic. Overlapping jurisdictions and responsibilities in emergency response can compound budget concerns, interagency friction, and miscommunication.

In their research, they found four general barriers to interagency coordination:

- **Communication.** Agencies tend to develop their own jargon based on their areas of focus and internal workings. The subsequent lack of a common language often impedes cross-agency communication.
- **Leadership.** Coordinated planning and response require an ongoing commitment from agency leaders. Response can fail when a leader of a critical partner agency is unwilling to commit qualified staff and resources because he or she is unconvinced of the benefits to the agency.
- **Cultural differences.** Although public safety and health officials share the common goal of saving lives, each agency develops its own cultural standards of behavior that reflect the educational and social backgrounds of its staff, organizational hierarchy, leadership style, and core mission.
- **Legal and structural differences.** Each agency has a unique internal hierarchy, different processes for working through the chain of command, legal limitations, and varying geographical and topical jurisdictions. These differences can discourage, delay, or prohibit joint planning initiatives.

To identify promising practices that can be used to resolve coordination barriers in the United States and elsewhere, the authors examined London's response in relation to a general coordination model. Applying this model—just one coordination model among many—to the 2005 bombings response provides an interesting look at some of the following interagency coordination promising practices.

## The London Bombings: Declaring a 'Major' Incident

London's public safety agencies have been collaborating for a long time. In 1973, city leaders formed the London Emergency Services Liaison Panel (LESLP), with representatives from the London Metropolitan Police Service, City of London Police, British Transport Police, London Fire Brigade, London Ambulance Service, and local London authorities. LESLP developed a manual, *Major Incident Procedure Manual,* [3] which is the core memorandum among the members and includes a comprehensive outline upon which London's coordination model of emergency response is founded.

The manual defines "major incident" broadly so that any emergency response agency can declare a major incident and thus increase the likelihood that multiple agencies will respond immediately. A key facet of the London bombing response was, in fact, rapid recognition and declaration of a major incident.

## London's Standardized Command Structure

LESLP's manual also describes the responsibilities of each agency during any major incident and defines the general roles that relevant personnel perform on the scene. The roles are defined by three levels of leadership: Gold, Silver, and Bronze. [4] The three levels of command are used across the U.K. for all large-scale emergencies. Consequently, relevant agencies are familiar with the roles and responsibilities of each level.

In addition, all agencies have agreed that the U.K.'s law enforcement serves as the coordination lead. Thus, there is no confusion about which agency is in charge during a major incident. Because these procedures were already in place at the time of the 2005 bombings, there was limited confusion about the roles and responsibilities of responding agencies.

## Joint Training and Planning

The anti-terrorism branch of the London Metropolitan Police Service hosts quarterly joint exercises, known as the Hanover Series, to practice what to do in the event of a major incident. Partner agencies and other stakeholders meet in the outskirts of London for weekend tabletop exercises that increase everyone's knowledge of roles and responsibilities. According to emergency service personnel, the practice sessions also increase familiarity with other key personnel, provide the opportunity to test procedures and rehearse the standardized LESLP command and control system, and help agencies learn how to respond and react collectively.

The exercises use the Silver and Gold components of LESLP's command and control structure and therefore help reinforce and improve multiagency coordination. Perhaps most importantly, the scenarios introduced during the Hanover Series are grounded in practical, wide-ranging incidents that require in-depth planning and response duties. These exercises usually reflect local, national and international events and address a series of issues to improve multiagency cooperation.

## One Voice, One Message

Having a single media spokesperson can help ensure that consistent information is released to the public in a timely manner. It can also help avoid conflicting and confusing statements from different agencies. Shortly after the 2005 bombings, the Metropolitan Police Service assumed the lead position of a joint media "cell" and convened a group of public information officials from partnering agencies and the central government. The group met quickly after the bombings to agree upon roles and responsibilities and to develop a joint message. It provided the public—via the media—with a constant stream of information that helped to restore calm and ultimately to identify the bombers.

## Developing a National Coordination Model

Since 2001, there has been an increased emphasis on multiagency planning and response, and efforts have been taken in the United States and elsewhere to develop coordinated approaches. In public safety and homeland security, informal agreements between agencies can serve as a first step toward minimizing barriers to coordination. Informal agreements can allow agency leaders to achieve their goals through cooperation rather than direct competition and can help clarify each agency's expectations. After working relationships have been established, agencies may then decide to develop more formal agreements that describe the planning, collaboration and training elements discussed above.

The July 2005 bombings in London are just one example of a complex event that required extensive response planning and training. Other examples include public health outbreaks, serial violence like the D.C.-area sniper attacks and natural disasters like Hurricane Katrina. Identifying and developing a national coordination model—and learning from earlier cases—should greatly improve our nation's abilities to respond to terrorist attack or other major homeland security events.

## Notes

[1] London Regional Resilience Forum, *Looking Back, Moving Forward. The Multi-Agency Debrief: Lessons Identified and Progress Since the Terrorist Events of 7 July 2005* (pdf, 61 pages) Exit Notice , London: Government Office for London, 2006.

[2] The authors thank the London planning and response community for their candid and thoughtful participation in this study; this project would not have been possible without their support.

[3] London Emergency Services Liaison Panel (LESLP), *Major Incident Procedure Manual, Sixth Edition,* London: Metropolitan Police Service, 2004.

[4] These levels of command are often called "strategic," "tactical" and "operational." In London's emergency command structure, these roles are not related to rank within or across agencies.

*Source:* Adapted from Kevin J. Strom and Joe Eyerman's "Interagency Coordination: A Case Study of the 2005 London Train Bombings," *National Institute of Justice Journal* 260 (2008), http://www.ojp.usdoj.gov/nij/journals/260/interagency-coordination.htm (accessed February 16, 2009).

## Summary

Law enforcement is an extremely complex activity in the United States. The delivery of police services is fragmented among thousands of city, county, state, special district, federal, and private security agencies. There are tremendous differences in the size, role, and activities of these different agencies. Consequently, it is extremely difficult to generalize about the police in America.

## Key Terms

local political control, 59
fragmentation, 60
authorized strength, 63
civilians, 63
police–population ratio, 63
municipal police, 68

county police, 68
sheriff, 69
constable, 70
coroner, 70
special district police, 71
tribal police, 71

state police, 73
highway patrol, 73
Office of Community-Oriented
    Police Services (COPS), 82
accreditation, 82

## For Discussion

1. Go to your campus law enforcement agency's headquarters and request a copy of last year's campus crime statistics. Ask the desk attendant how many full-time employees work for the agency. Ask how many are sworn officers and how many are nonsworn officers. As a class,

discuss whether you think there are too many or too few personnel working for your campus law enforcement agency in light of the campus's reported crime problem.

2. What are some of the advantages and disadvantages of civilianization?

3. What are the strengths and weaknesses of leaving the primary responsibility for police protection to local governments versus the federal or state government?

4. The military has rarely been used for local crime control. When, if ever, would the use of the military be acceptable to address local crime problems?

## Internet Exercises

**Exercise 1** Go to a Web site of an agency in your region and find out (a) the total number of employees who are authorized to work for the agency, (b) the total number of sworn officers authorized to work for the agency, and (c) the total number of employees who are currently employed by the agency.

**Exercise 2** Go to the Web site www.calea.org. Examine the process that a police department must go through to become accredited by CALEA.

**Exercise 3** Go to the Web sites of your police and sheriff's departments and find out what services are duplicated by the two agencies.

**Exercise 4** Go to the Web site www.OJP.USDOJ. gov/bjs. Look for law enforcement and administrative statistics online. Compare your local agency to others in your state.

## Notes

1. Elinor Ostrom, Roger Parks, and Gordon P. Whitaker, *Patterns of Metropolitan Policing* (Cambridge, MA: Ballinger, 1978).

2. Bureau of Justice Statistics, *Local Police Departments, 2003* (Washington DC: Government Printing Office, 2006).

3. David N. Falcone and L. Edward Wells, "The County Sheriff as a Distinctive Policing Modality," *American Journal of Police* XIV, no. 3/4 (1995): pp. 123–24.

4. Ostrom, Parks, and Whitaker, *Patterns of Metropolitan Policing.*

5. Richard J. Terrill, *World Criminal Justice Systems: A Survey,* 3rd ed. (Cincinnati, OH: Anderson, 1997), pp. 12–13.

6. Ibid., pp. 246–48.

7. Bureau of Justice Statistics, *Local Police Departments, 2003* (Washington DC: Government Printing Office, 2006); Bureau of Justice Statistics, *Federal Law Enforcement Officers, 2004* (Washington DC: Government Printing Office, 2006).

8. President's Commission on Law Enforcement and Administration of Justice, *The Challenge of Crime in a Free Society* (Washington DC: Government Printing Office, 1967).

9. Bureau of Justice Statistics, *Local Police Departments, 2003.*

10. Bureau of Justice Statistics, *Local Police Departments, 2003,* Bureau of Justice Statistics, *Federal Law Enforcement Officers, 2004.*

11. Bureau of Justice Statistics, *Census of State and Local Law Enforcement Agencies, 2004.* (Washington DC: Government Printing Office, 2007.

12. Christopher Koper, Edward Maguire, and Gretchen Moore, *Hiring and Retention Issues in Police Agencies* (Washington DC: Urban Institute, 2001).

13. James J. Fyfe, "Police Personnel Practices, 1986," *Municipal Yearbook 1987* (Washington DC: ICMA, 1987), Table 3/2, p. 17.

14. Bruce L. Heininger and Janine Urbanek, "Civilianization of the American Police: 1970–1980," *Journal of Police Science and Administration* 11 (1983): pp. 200–205; William King and Edward Maguire, "Police Civilianization, 1950–2000: Change or Continuity?" presented at the American Society of Criminology (November 2000); Bureau of Justice Statistics, *Local Police Departments, 2000.*

15. David Bayley, *Police for the Future* (New York: Oxford University Press, 1994).

16. Edward Maguire, *Organizational Structure in American Police Agencies* (Albany, NY: SUNY Press, 2003).

17. Bureau of Justice Statistics, *Local Police Departments, 2003.*

18. Bureau of Justice Statistics, *Police Departments in Large Cities, 1990–2000* (Washington DC: Government Printing Office, 2002).

19. Thomas B. Marvell and Carlisle E. Moody, "Specification Problems, Police Levels, and Crime Rates," *Criminology* 34 (November 1996): 609–46.

20. Bureau of Justice Statistics, *Justice Expenditure and Employment in the United States, 2003* (Washington DC: Government Printing Office, 2006).

21. President's Commission on Law Enforcement and Administration of Justice, *Task Force Report: The Police* (Washington DC: Government Printing Office, 1967), p. 68.

22. Terry W. Koepsell and Charles M. Girard, *Small Police Agency Consolidation: Suggested Approaches* (Washington DC: Government Printing Office, 1979).

23. National Advisory Commission on Criminal Justice Standards and Goals, *Police* (Washington DC: Government Printing Office, 1973), pp. 73–76.

24. International City Management Association, *Public Safety Departments: Combining the Police and Fire Functions* (Washington DC: ICMA, July 1976).

25. International City Management Association, "Intergovernmental Service Arrangements and the Transfer of Functions," *Baseline Data Report* 16 (June 1984).

26. http://www.lasd.org/divisions/hqtrs/contract_law. html; Information retrieved on December 4, 2003.

27. Ostrom, Parks, and Whitaker, *Patterns of Metropolitan Policing.*

28. Ibid., pp. xxi, 101.

29. Gary W. Cordner, "Police Agency Size and Investigative Effectiveness," *Journal of Criminal Justice* 17, no. 1 (1989): p. 153.

30. Weisheit, Falcone, and Wells, *Crime and Policing in Rural and Small-Town America,* pp. 69–73.

31. Bureau of Justice Statistics, *Census of State and Local Law Enforcement Agencies, 2004.*

32. John P. Crank and Robert Langworthy, "An Institutional Perspective on Policing," *Journal of Criminal Law and Criminology* 83, no. 2 (1992): pp. 341–46.

33. Herman Goldstein, *Policing a Free Society* (Cambridge, MA: Ballinger, 1977).

34. Anthony Pate and Edwin E. Hamilton, *The Big Six: Policing America's Largest Cities* (Washington DC: The Police Foundation, 1991).

35. Bureau of Justice Statistics, *Local Police Departments, 2003.*

36. Ibid.

37. Ralph A. Weisheit, David N. Falcone, and L. Edward Wells, *Crime and Policing in Rural and Small-Town America: An Overview of the Issues* (Washington DC: Government Printing Office, 1995).

38. John F. Galliher et al., "Small-Town Police: Troubles, Tasks, and Publics," *Journal of Police Science and Administration* 3 (March 1975): pp. 19–28.

39. Bureau of Justice Statistics. *Census of State and Local Law Enforcement Agencies, 2004.* (Washington DC: Government Printing Office, 2007.

40. Bureau of Justice Statistics. *Census of State and Local Law Enforcement Agencies, 2004.* (Washington DC: Government Printing Office, 2007.

41. Falcone and Wells, "The County Sheriff as a Distinctive Policing Modality."

42. National Sheriff's Association, *County Law Enforcement: Assessment of Capabilities and Needs* (Washington DC: National Sheriff's Association, 1976).

43. Bureau of Justice Statistics, *Law Enforcement Management and Administrative Statistics, 1999.*

44. Lee P. Brown, "The Role of the Sheriff," in Alvin W. Cohn, ed., *The Future of Policing* (Beverly Hills, CA: Sage, 1978), pp. 227–28.

45. Bureau of Justice Statistics, *Sheriffs Departments, 2004.*

46. U.S. Advisory Commission on Intergovernmental Relations, *State and Local Relations in the Criminal Justice System* (Washington DC: Government Printing Office, 1971), p. 28.

47. National Constable Association, Who Is and What Is a Constable? Available at http://www.angelfire.com/ la/nationalconstable/. Accessed December 2, 2003.

48. Bureau of Justice Statistics, Medical Examiners' and Coroners' Offices, 2004 (Washington DC: Government Printing Office, 2007).

49. Ibid, pg. 1.

50. Ibid.; The National Association of Medical Examiners, "So You Want to Be a Medical Detective," http://www.thename.org/medical_ detective.htm (December 2, 2003).

51. CDC Division of Public Health Surveillance and Informatics, "About MECISP," http://www.cdc.gov/epo/dphsi/mecisp/about.htm (December 2, 2003).

52. Martin Hannon, "The Metro Transit Police Force: America's First Tri-State, Multi-Jurisdictional Police Force," *FBI Law Enforcement Bulletin* 47 (November 1978): pp. 16–22.

53. John J. Sloan, "The Modern Campus Police: An Analysis of Their Evolution, Structure, and Function," *American Journal of Police* XI, no. 2 (1992): pp. 85–104.

54. Bureau of Justice Statistics, Campus Law Enforcement Agencies, 2004–2005 (Washington DC: Government Printing Office, 2008).

55. Ken Peak, "Criminal Justice, Law, and Policy in Indian Country: A Historical Perspective," *Journal of Criminal Justice* 17, no. 5 (1989): pp. 393–407.

56. Stewart Wakeling, Miriam Jorgensen, Susan Michaelson, and Manley Begay, *Policing on American Indian Reservations.* National Institute of Justice: (Washington DC: National Institute of Justice, 2001).

57. Ibid.

58. Ibid.

59. Bureau of Justice Statistics, *Tribal Law Enforcement* (Washington DC: Government Printing Office).

60. Wakeling, Jorgensen, Michaelson, and Begay, *Policing on American Indian Reservations.*

61. Bureau of Justice Statistics, *Tribal Law Enforcement* (Washington DC: Government Printing Office).

62. Donald A. Torres, *Handbook of State Police, Highway Patrols, and Investigative Agencies* (New York: Greenwood Press, 1987).

63. Ibid., p. 12.

64. Department of Justice, *Profile of State and Local Law Enforcement Agencies 1987* (Washington DC: Government Printing Office, 1989).

65. Ibid.

66. Bureau of Justice Statistics, *Federal Law Enforcement Officers, 2004.*

67. Ibid.

68. Bureau of Justice Statistics, *Federal Law Enforcement Officers, 2002* (Washington DC: Government Printing Office, 2003).

69. U.S. Customs and Border Protection: Budget in Brief, February 7, 2006. Accessed at http://www.cbp.gov/xp/cgov/newsroom/fact_sheets/budget/ on April 13, 2006.

70. U.S. Immigration and Customs Enforcement Organization. Accessed at http://www.ice.gov/graphics/about/organization on April 13, 2006.

71. FEMA: About FEMA. Accessed at http://fema.gov/about/index.shtm on April 13, 2006.

72. TSA Strategic Plan Executive Summary Letter from the Assistant Secretary. Accessed at http://www.tsa.gov/interweb/assetlibrary/788TSA.final(Sept.6).pdf on April 13, 2006.

73. TRACREPORTS, Department of Homeland Security Employment Levels by Organizational Component, March 2003. Accessed at http://trac.syr.edu/tracreports/tracdhs/030825/dhs_org.html on April 13, 2006.

74. Coast Guard Overview, Mission and History. Accessed at http://uscg.mil/hq/g-cp/comrel/factfile/factcards/overview.html on April 13, 2006.

75. US Secret Service: Protection. Accessed at http://www.secretservice.gov/protection.shtml on April 13, 2006.

76. US Secret Service: Investigations. Accessed at http://www.secretservice.gov/investigations.shtml on April 13, 2006.

77. About DOJ. Accessed at http://www.usdoj.gov/02organizations/ on April 14, 2006.

78. DEA Mission Statement. Accessed at http://www.dea.gov/agency/mission.htm on April 14, 2006.

79. DEA Staffing & Budget. Accessed at http://www.dea.gov/agency/staffing.htm on April 14, 2006.

80. Curt Gentry, *J. Edgar Hoover: The Man and the Secrets* (New York: Norton, 1991).

81. Department of Justice, *FBI Reorganization Fact Sheet* (Washington DC: Government Printing Office, 2002).

82. ATF 2003 Performance and Accountability Report. Accessed at http://www.atf.gov/pub/gen_pub/2003annrpt/discussionandanalysis.pdf on April 14, 2006.

83. U.S. Department of Justice, *United States Marshals Service Fact Sheet* (Washington DC: Government Printing Office, 2006).

84. U.S. Department of Justice, *National Policy Summit: Building Private Security/Public Policing Partnerships to Prevent and Respond to Terrorism and Public Disorder* (Washington DC: International Association of Chiefs of Police, 2005).

85. Elizabeth Joh, "The Paradox of Private Policing," *The Journal of Criminal Law & Criminology* 95, no. 1 (2004): pp. 49–131.

86. Brian Forst, "The Privatization and Civilianization of Policing," in Charles Friel, ed., *Criminal Justice,* 2 (2000): pp. 19–79.

87. Bud Hazelkorn, "Making Crime Pay," *San Francisco Chronicle,* August 17, 2003, p. 1.

88. Ibid.

89. Elizabeth Joh, "The Paradox of Private Policing," *The Journal of Criminal Law & Criminology* 95, no. 1 (2004): pp. 49–131; Clifford Shearing, "Private Security: Implications for Social Control," in K.R.E McCormick & L.A. Visano, eds. *Understanding Policing* (Toronto: Canadian Scholars Press, 1992): p. 521.

90. About the Industry. Accessed at http://www.seiu.org/property/security/aboutindustry/ on April 15, 2006.

91. Don Hummer and Mahesh Nalla, "Modeling Future Relations between the Private and Public Sectors of Law Enforcement." *Criminal Justice Studies* 16, no. 2 (2003): pp. 87–96.

92. The 9/11 Commission Report, Executive Summary, www.9-11commission.gov.

93. Paul Parfomak, "Guarding America: Security Guards and U.S. Critical Infrastructure Protection" (Washington DC: Congressional Research Service, 2004).

94. Ibid.

95. Terrill, *World Criminal Justice Systems,* pp. 9–25.

96. Samuel Walker, "Historical Roots of the Legal Control of Police Behavior," in David Weisburd and Craig Uchida, eds., *Police Innovation and Control of the Police* (New York: Springer, 1993), pp. 32–55.

97. Anthony Amsterdam, "Perspectives on the Fourth Amendment," *Minnesota Law Review* 58 (1974): p. 428.

98. Susan E. Martin, *On the Move: The Status of Women in Policing* (Washington DC: The Police Foundation, 1990), pp. 11–24.

99. Department of Justice, *COPS Office Report* (Washington DC: Government Printing Office, 1997).

100. International Association of Directors of Law Enforcement Standards and Training, *Sourcebook of Standards and Training Information* (Charlotte: University of North Carolina at Charlotte, 1993).

101. Roger Goldman and Stephen Puro, "Decertification of Police: An Alternative to Traditional Remedies for Police Misconduct," *Hastings Constitutional Law Quarterly* 15 (Fall 1987): pp. 45–80.

102. Jack Pearson, "National Accreditation: A Valuable Management Tool," in James J. Fyfe, ed., *Police Management Today: Issues and Case Studies* (Washington DC: ICMA, 1985), pp. 45–48.

103. See www.calea.org. Commission on Accreditation for Law Enforcement Agencies, *Standards for Law Enforcement Agencies,* 4th ed. (Fairfax, VA: CALEA, 1999).

104. Stephen D. Mastrofski, "Police Agency Accreditation: The Prospects of Reform," *American Journal of Police* VI, no. 2 (1986): pp. 45–81.

105. W. E. Eastman, "National Accreditation: A Costly, Unneeded Make-Work Scheme," in Fyfe, ed., *Police Management Today,* pp. 49–54.

106. http://www.calea.org/Online/Clients/ CALEAAWARDS.pdf, Accessed February 16, 2009.

107. Stephen D. Mastrofski, "The Prospects of Change in Police Patrol: A Decade in Review," *American Journal of Police* IX, no. 2 (1990): p. 25.

108. Kimberly McCabe and Robin Fajardo, "Law Enforcement Accreditation: A National Comparison of Accredited vs. Nonaccredited Agencies," *Journal of Criminal Justice* 29 (2001): pp. 127–31.

# Officers and Organizations

# Police Organizations

Police services are delivered to the public through organizations. The quality of policing depends on how well a department is organized and managed. Some critics argue that the nature of police organizations is a major problem in policing: that the departments are isolated from the public, resist change, and do not make good use of their personnel.

This chapter examines the dominant features of American law enforcement organizations. Some of those features are unique to police organizations, while others are common to all large bureaucracies. The chapter identifies the major strengths and weaknesses of the prevailing style of organization and discusses alternative ways of organizing police work. It also discusses the impact of both civil service and police unions on police organizations. The chapter concludes with a discussion of organizational theory and its application to understanding police organizations.

## The Quasi-Military Style of Police Organizations

American law enforcement agencies are organized along quasi-military lines.[1] That is, they resemble the military in some but not all respects. This style of organization originated with Robert Peel's plan for the London Metropolitan Police in 1829 and was adopted by American police departments.

For a full discussion of the Robert Peel and the London Metropolitan Police, see Chapter 2.

The police resemble the military in the following respects. First, police officers wear uniforms. Second, police departments use military-style rank designations, such as sergeant, lieutenant, and captain. Third, the command structure is hierarchical, with commands flowing from the top. Fourth, the organizational style is authoritarian, with penalties for failing to obey orders. Fifth, police officers carry weapons and have the legal authority to use deadly force, physical force, and to deprive people of their liberty through arrest.

At the same time, however, the police are different from the military in several important respects. First, the police serve a citizen population rather than fight a foreign enemy. Second, they provide services designed to help people, and these services are often requested by individual citizens. Third, they are constrained by laws protecting the rights of citizens. Fourth, they routinely exercise individual discretion, whereas military personnel are trained and expected to operate as members of military units.[2]

For a full discussion on police discretion, see Chapter 11.

### Criticisms of the Quasi-Military Style

Many experts believe that the **quasi-military style** is inappropriate for the police. They argue that, first, the military ethos cultivates an "us versus them" attitude that is used to justify mistreatment of citizens. Second, it encourages the idea of a "war on crime" that is inappropriate for serving a citizen population.[3] Third, the authoritarian command style is contrary to democratic principles of participation. Fourth, the authoritarian style produces low morale, and the rigid rank structure fails to provide sufficient job satisfaction for police officers.

**quasi-military style**

```
S I D E B A R        4 – 1
```

## The Myth of the Military Model

For years the police organizational structure has been said to be modeled after the military. A recent essay by Thomas Cowper, a former Marine and 17-year veteran of the New York State Police, argues that this perception is the result of several "wrong" assumptions. In particular, he states that the military and policing professions differ in terms of organizational characteristics and operational activities. With respect to organizational characteristics, he argues that the military is founded on the idea of teamwork and leadership, while the police profession emphasizes individuality, monitoring (from a variety of distances), and supervision. Cowper believes that military leaders are schooled in the art of war to more effectively perform their job and innately have the ability to promote esprit and heighten morale; whereas police leaders, he argues, are not highly trained on matters of concern to their profession and only monitor the activities of their subordinates to ensure that they follow policies. Similarly, he adds that while police officers act as a "lone ranger" on patrol, rarely working with others in their department, soldiers work closely as a team, producing a more effective result. With regard to operational strategy, Cowper points out that the military has one mission—to wage war—whereas the police have several missions: crime fighting, order maintenance, and service. Additionally, he argues that the military engages in proactive operations, while police work is primarily reactive in nature.

1. Discuss whether or not you think that Cowper is correct in his characterization of the military and police professions.

2. As a class, discuss other differences between the military and the police.

3. As a class, discuss similarities between the military and the police.

*Source:* Adapted from Thomas Cowper, "The Myth of the Military Model of Leadership in Law Enforcement," *Police Quarterly* 3, no. 3 (2000): pp. 228–46.

In the 1960s and early 1970s, some critics argued that the police should deemphasize their military image, primarily in order to improve police–community relations. Specifically, they suggested using civilian-style blazers rather than military-style uniforms. A few small police departments experimented with using blazers. For example, the Menlo Park (California) police department found that they created no serious problems. The Lakewood (Colorado) police department adopted blazers and did not use the traditional rank designations when the department was first organized in the 1970s. After a few years, however, it returned to the traditional style. Problems arose because the public image of the police was so closely associated with military-style uniforms that it was difficult for the department to depart from the norm.[4]

In recent years some scholars have noted a shift back toward the militarization of the police. Peter Kraska, the foremost expert on the matter, points out that since the end of the cold war a militaristic culture has begun to sweep back through police organizations. He contends that this phenomenon is most clearly seen in the rise in the number of police paramilitary units created throughout the United States in recent years. Police paramilitary units, which are often regarded as the most elite in a police agency, employ a very strict military command structure, train similarly to elite military units, and handle high-risk situations (their sole purpose) that are in progress and that call for use-of-force specialists. Kraska further notes that officers in these units typically wear battle dress uniforms (BDUs), combat boots, Kevlar helmets, and carry specialized weapons such as machine guns, sniper rifles, CS gas, and surveillance equipment.[5]

# Police Departments as Organizations

The quasi-military aspect is only one feature of American police departments. To understand how police departments operate, and how they deliver services to the public, it is necessary to understand them as *organizations*. Many of the problems in policing are related to organizational features. It is important to also understand why these features exist and what positive contributions they make.

## The Dominant Style of American Police Organizations

American police departments are remarkably similar in terms of organizational structure and administrative style. The typical police department is a complex **bureaucracy,** with a hierarchical structure and an authoritarian management style.    **bureaucracy** The only exceptions to this rule are the very small departments, which have simple organizational structures and more informal management styles. At the same time, all but the very smallest agencies are governed by some form of civil service rules that regulate personnel policies. Finally, most of the large police departments are legally bound by collective bargaining contracts with unions representing rank-and-file officers.

## Police Organizations as Bureaucracies

The modern police department is a bureaucratic organization, as are other large organizations in modern society: private corporations, universities, religious organizations, government agencies, and so on. Police departments share similar characteristics of bureaucracy with these other organizations.[6]

     The bureaucratic form of organization exists because it is the most efficient means that has been developed for organizing and directing many different activities in the pursuit of a common goal. This does not mean that the bureaucratic form is completely efficient, but only that no other organizational form has been found that is better able to carry out multiple tasks simultaneously in the pursuit of a common goal.

     The modern bureaucracy has the following characteristics:[7]

1. It is a complex organization performing many different tasks in pursuit of a common goal.
2. The different tasks are grouped into separate divisions, or "bureaus" (hence the term bureaucracy).
3. The organizational structure is hierarchical or pyramidal, with a clear division of labor between workers, first-line supervisors, and chief executives.
4. Responsibility for specific tasks is delegated to lower-ranking employees.

5. There is a clear chain of command, which indicates who is responsible for each task and who is responsible for supervising each employee.

6. There is a clear unity of command, so that each employee answers to one and only one supervisor.

7. Written rules and regulations are designed to ensure uniformity and consistency.

8. Information flows up and down through the organization according to the chain of command.

9. There are clear career paths by which personnel move upward through the organization in an orderly fashion.

The modern police bureaucracy began to emerge in the early 20th century, as a part of the professionalization movement.[8] With the creation of new specialized units (traffic, juvenile, vice, training, etc.), departments became more complex organizations. The new field of police management developed in order to help cope with this new complexity. Experts borrowed modern management principles from business administration and applied them to police administration. The leaders of this movement were **August Vollmer, Bruce Smith,** and **O. W. Wilson.** Wilson's textbook, *Police Administration,* became the unofficial bible on the subject by the 1950s.[9]

For example, see Exhibit 4–1, which is the organizational chart of the Phoenix Police Department. It is representative of other big-city police departments and illustrates the main features of the modern police bureaucracy.

First, as is evident in the chart, the Phoenix Police Department's organizational structure is pyramidal, reflecting a hierarchical management style. Second, the organization is structured to be able to perform many different tasks simultaneously: patrol, traffic, criminal investigation, records, training, planning and research, and so on. Third, the Phoenix Police Department has grouped together related tasks in a logical fashion: patrol and related functions are organizationally located in a patrol division, criminal investigation is in another division, professional standards in another, and so on.

Fourth, the lines of authority in the Phoenix Police Department are clear, with responsibility for supervision flowing from the chief of police down through the organization. It is possible to identify who is responsible for particular tasks. This approach reflects the principle of unity of supervision: each person reports to one supervisor. Under the principle of span of control, each supervisor is responsible for a limited number of people. In the patrol units, the ideal span of control involves a sergeant supervising between eight and twelve patrol officers.

The degree of specialization in a police department depends on the size of the community, the nature of its problems, and the size of the department itself.[10] The police department in a medium-sized city with relatively little serious crime does not need a separate homicide unit. The police department in a big city with many murders does need, and can afford to create, a homicide unit. Small and medium-sized departments cannot afford to maintain their own training academies. These tasks can be performed more efficiently for them by a state agency that serves many departments.

What is not evident from the organizational chart is the set of rules governing employee behavior. Police departments rely on written rules and collect them in a standard operating procedure (SOP) manual or policy manual. Also, the career paths for officers will be indicated in its civil service procedures.

**August Vollmer**

**Bruce Smith**

**O. W. Wilson**

For a full discussion on the use of written policies and administrative rulemaking, see Chapter 11, and Chapter 14.

EXHIBIT 4–1

# Phoenix Police Department Organizational Chart, July 2008

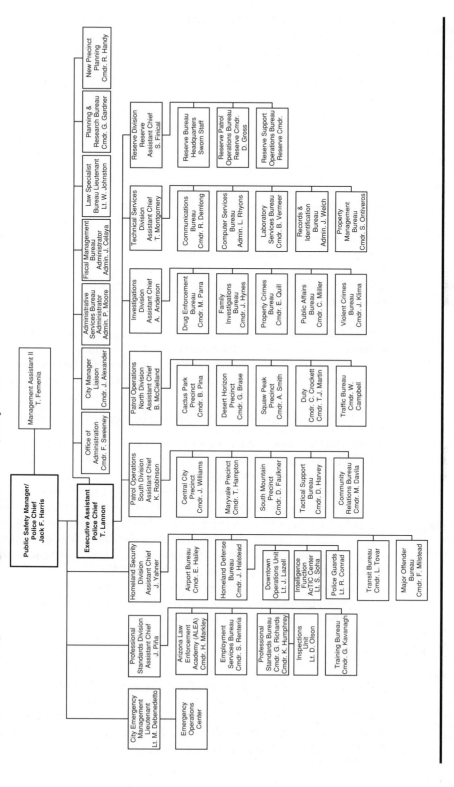

For a full discussion on the relationship between the police and ethnic communities, see Chapter 12.

For a full discussion on citizen review of the police, see Chapter 14.

For a full discussion on the control of police discretion and police misconduct through bureaucratization, see Chapter 11 and Chapter 13.

For a full discussion on the impact of written rules on police discretion, see Chapter 11.

For a full discussion of rules on the use of deadly force and response to domestic violence, see Chapter 8, and Chapter 11.

## The Problems with Bureaucracy

There are several major criticisms of the bureaucratic form of organization, all of which apply to police organizations.[11] First, bureaucracies are often rigid, inflexible, and unable to adapt to external changes. Thus, for example, many business administration experts argue that American corporations have failed to adapt to changing markets and the new global economy. Police departments have often failed to respond to changes in patterns of crime and in the composition of the communities they serve.[12]

Second, communication within the organization often breaks down. Important information does not reach the people who need it. As a result, bad decisions are made, or the organization pursues conflicting goals.

Third, bureaucracies tend to become inward looking, self-serving, and isolated from the people they serve. Organizational self-protection and survival take precedence over the basic goals of the organization. Thus, businesses are accused of not catering to customer demands, universities are accused of not serving the needs of students, and police departments are accused of being isolated from the public. The problem of isolation is particularly acute with respect to police–community relations, as police departments have been accused of not listening to the concerns of racial- and ethnic-minority communities.

Fourth, bureaucracies are accused of not using the talents of their employees and even stifling creativity.[13] Many observers have found serious morale problems among rank-and-file police officers and argue that departments need to provide officers with greater opportunities at work and more flexibility to perform their duties.

## The Positive Contributions of Bureaucracy in Policing

Because the problems associated with bureaucracies are often the topic of conversation, their positive contributions are often overlooked. These contributions are best appreciated from a historical perspective.

A comparison of the typical police department in 1900 with the typical big-city department today illustrates the contributions of the modern bureaucracy. The police department of 1900 was very unspecialized, with only two units, patrol and detective. The development of many specialties—juvenile, traffic, community relations, training, and criminalistics—has required the growth of complex organizations that have the capacity to coordinate all of these activities.[14]

The control of police discretion and the reduction of misconduct have also been achieved through bureaucratic principles. Written rules on the use of deadly force or the response to domestic violence represent the technique of administrative rulemaking. The paperwork involved in this approach is characteristic of bureaucracies.[15]

## Informal Aspects of Police Organizations

The formal aspects of police organizations represent only one part of their actual operations. Every organization has important informal aspects, which are often referred to as office politics.[16] Dorothy Guyot argues that "within police departments, as in any formal organization, there are subdivisions, hierarchies, status groupings, and other formal arrangements. There are also informal relationships, cliques, friend-ship patterns, and temporary collaborations."

For example, information does not always flow up and down the organization in the manner prescribed by the organizational chart. Sensitive and potentially em-barrassing information is often withheld. Rank-and-file officers cover up each other's mistakes. Sergeants cover up mistakes by officers under their command because it would reflect poorly on their own performance. In some important re-spects, chief executives do not want to know about certain things. This allows them to publicly deny that such things exist when questioned by the news media or members of the public.

At the same time, however, information does flow to friends in the organiza-tion, outside of the prescribed channels. Such information is often referred to as gossip. Gossip falls into two general categories: true and false information. Gossip that is false is created and circulated to discredit someone. Gossip that is true is of-ten useful. It may be important to know, for example, that someone is planning to retire or leave the organization, or that a person is in serious trouble because of mistakes on the job.

John Crank argues that within almost all police departments there are "cliques," or informal networks of officers. These cliques, Crank explains, are formed to pro-tect officers from "administrative bullshit." There are two types of protective cliques: vertical and horizontal. **Vertical cliques** are formed between lower and higher rank-ing officers. These cliques oftentimes have a shared understanding of situations and problems and work together to address them in an agreeable manner. **Horizontal cliques** are formed between similarly ranked officers. Most horizontal cliques are created to protect line officers from supervisory oversight and accountability.[17]

**vertical cliques**

**horizontal cliques**

Cliques in a police department are often based on work groups. Officers who work together day in and day out, on patrol or as detectives, tend to develop close personal ties. They see things from the perspective of their unit and, when a conflict arises, defend their colleagues, even if they know their colleagues are wrong.

One dysfunctional result of this process is rivalry among different units. Patrol officers often resent the higher status that detectives enjoy. There are also rivalries between patrol officers assigned to different shifts. To a certain extent, the seniority system aggravates these tensions, as the evening shift gets the younger officers while the day shift has the older officers.

At the same time, there are cliques throughout the organization based on per-sonal friendships. Often these cliques originated in shared experiences as members of the same recruit class or members of the same patrol crew. The folklore of polic-ing includes the belief that some police officers develop closer relationships with their partners than with their spouses. A partner is someone who can understand the unpleasant aspects of policing that an officer would not want to discuss at home.

Friendship patterns become important in the management of a police depart-ment. Westley found that a police chief needs both information about what is going on in the organization and people to perform sensitive tasks. As a result the chief re-lies on "a group of favorites within the department whom he can depend on to handle delicate assignments."[18] A chief maintains this network of friends by handing out rewards in the form of favorable assignments and by punishing real or imagined en-emies by giving them low-status assignments.

# Bureaucracy and Police Professionalism

The bureaucratic aspects of policing conflict in many ways with the professionalism as understood in other occupations. In law, medicine, and education, a professional is someone with special expertise, resulting from extensive training and experience, who exercises independent judgment about critical events. The doctor, for example, makes critical decisions about diagnosis and treatment of patients. The professional is not expected to follow a rigid set of rules.[19]

For a full discussion on formal, written rules, see Chapter 14.

**police professionalism**

The bureaucratic aspects of policing represent a different approach to the control of behavior. First, the quasi-military nature of police organizations has emphasized hierarchical command and control rather than collegial decision making. Second, police organizations attempt to control police officer behavior through formal, written rules.

Because of the history of the American police, **police professionalism** acquired a special meaning. Professionalism meant the same thing as bureaucratization. Thus, the professional departments were the ones that adopted O. W. Wilson's principles of police administration: specialization, hierarchy, clear lines of authority, written rules and policies, and so on. Professional departments were the ones in which officers did their job "by the book," meaning that they followed written departmental rules.[20]

To a certain extent, however, the professional autonomy of the traditional professions is disappearing. Doctors increasingly work in large hospitals or medical facilities. Like other bureaucracies, these organizations impose formal controls over doctors' behavior. Lawyers increasingly work in large law firms or corporations, which also seek to control the lawyers' behavior by monitoring the number of hours billed.

# Changing Police Organizations

For a full discussion on police discretion, see Chapter 11.

There is much dissatisfaction with the current state of police organizations. There are two schools of thought on how to improve them. The dominant school of thought accepts the basic principles of bureaucratic organization and seeks to apply them more effectively. Advocates of this approach, for example, support greater control of discretion through written rules.[21] The other school of thought seeks to use alternative decision-making procedures that operate within the existing formal structure.

## Community Policing

**decentralize**

**deformalize**

Community policing represents an alternative to the traditional form of police organizations. Traditional police organizations are extremely bureaucratic structures, which are said to necessarily limit the effectiveness and efficiency of the police because of the many impersonal rules, the lack of discretion officers are permitted to use, and the hierarchical nature of the organizational structure. Accordingly, community policing attempts to modify the police organization through debureaucratization. Specifically, it attempts to **decentralize** decision making both territorially and administratively. This requires the police to place greater responsibility on rank-and-file officers at the neighborhood level and to become more responsive to neighborhood residents. It also requires the police to **deformalize,** eliminating many of the rules and policies that often stifle creativity and do not encourage problem solving. Under community policing, organizations are also encouraged to **despecialize** functions. This means replacing specialized units with neighborhood officers, who are more knowledgeable about the problems that face their neighborhood. Finally, community policing attempts to **delayerize,** decreasing the amount of social and administrative distance between the beat officer and the chief of police. This, reformers argue, will increase the speed at which decisions are made and will empower beat officers. In this respect, community policing responds to the standard criticisms of bureaucracies (see above).[22]

**despecialize**

**delayerize**

Whether or not organizations have been able to accomplish these goals is still a matter of debate. The most definitive study to date was conducted by Edward Maguire, who analyzed survey data collected between 1990 and 1998 from 353 large municipal police departments across the United States. Maguire found some support for the view that the community policing movement was having an impact on the organizational structure of police agencies. In particular, he found that in the 1990s large police departments across the country were becoming less centralized and less bureaucratic, and were increasingly relying on civilians to perform police work. On the other hand, over the same period police departments did not decrease the amount of social or administrative distance between line officers and the chief of police and did not reduce their reliance on specialized units.[23]

---

**SIDEBAR      4 – 2**

## *Toward a Life-Course Perspective of Police Organizations*

William King recently proposed a new and innovative strategy for understanding police organizations and police organizational change. He argues that all police organizations, like people, go through stages of development that have significant impact on their structure and behavior. King stipulates that police organizations go through several stages or events. Two of these events are inevitable: organizational birth and death; and the other four stages—all of which may or may not be experienced by a police organization—include early founding effects, growth, decline, and crisis.

**Organizational Birth.** All police organizations had to have been created at some point. King points out that, depending on the time and place, history has shown that several factors have led to the creation of police organizations, such as increases in crime, riots, public drunkenness, and class conflict. He further points out that a number of local police agencies have been created in the U.S. over the past 20 years, but that scholars do not have a strong understanding of why they were created.

**Early Founding Effects.** Soon after creation the police organization develops routines, structures, and behaviors that are "imprinted" into the organization. King calls these early founding effects. He maintains that the founders of the organization, and other like police organizations, set the template for how the police organization will be structured and managed and how it will behave. As a consequence, King posits that early decisions made by the police organization have a substantial impact on its trajectory for a very long period of time.

**Growth.** King states that some police organizations go through periods of substantial growth. If an organization goes through a period of growth, this growth is accompanied not

---

continued

**SIDEBAR     4 – 2 (continued)**

only by increased hiring and training, but also provides substantial amounts of opportunity for existing employees. For example, as a police organization grows there is increased potential for promotion, increased opportunity for the creation of specialized units, and increased potential for rewards. Organizations that are growing are also typically viewed as successful, which often results in increases in resources that are available to the organization.

**Decline.** On the other hand, King maintains that some organizations experience periods of decline. This occurs when there is a reduction in the number of employees in the police organization. This is often viewed as a sign that the organization is failing. Promotions are more difficult to obtain; employees are asked to serve in multiple roles; and they are expected to do more with a reduction in resources.

**Crisis.** Many police organizations endure crises. King explains that crises can occur inside or outside of the police organization. An externally generated crisis might include increased crime rate or reduction in budget. Internally generated crises might include police corruption, excessive use of force, or a labor dispute. How a police organization adapts to crises has the potential to have a significant impact on whether it experiences a period of growth or decline.

**The Disbanding of Police Organizations.** King notes that most people are familiar with a business failing or going bankrupt, but few are familiar with the disbanding of a police organization. However, he points out that it is more common than many believe. For example, over the last three decades 117 local police agencies in Ohio were disbanded. Most of these agencies were relatively small, and served small communities. He also points out that some of the largest police organizations in the country have been disbanded. These include the New York City school, and transit, and housing police agencies, and the Compton, California, and Lauderdale, Florida, Police Departments. King argues that the life-course perspective calls on policymakers and scholars to better understand why a police organization might disband and what existing police organizations might learn from those that do.

1. Discuss whether you think that King is correct is his characterization of police organizations having a life course.

2. As a class, discuss the characteristics of a declining police organization and the impact that it could have on police productivity.

*Source:* Adapted from William R. King, "Toward a Life-Course Perspective of Police Organizations." *Journal of Research in Crime and Delinquency* 2009, 46: 213–44.

## Task Forces

An alternative to changing the structure of police organizations is to develop decision-making procedures that operate within the existing formal structure. One example is the use of **task forces** consisting of officers from different ranks within the same agency. A task force on drug enforcement, for example, might include a captain, a lieutenant, two sergeants, and three police officers. An interagency task force allows the police chief to select particular officers from different ranks, based on their talents rather than just their rank.

The interagency task force approach addresses several problems related to the traditional police organizational structure. It recognizes the fact that many officers at the lowest rank are competent to make intelligent decisions about police policy. Involving them offers them greater job satisfaction, prepares them for supervisory

**task forces**

responsibilities later in their careers, and increases the likelihood that innovations will be accepted within the organization.

The success of interagency task forces has led a number of law enforcement organizations to adopt multiagency task forces. Multiagency task forces operate as special law enforcement organizations, usually with multijurisdictional authority, created through formal agreements between several governmental agencies for the purpose of more effectively and efficiently combating specific crime problems.[24] It is estimated that there are between 900 and 1,100 multiagency task forces funded by the federal government alone.[25]

Multiagency task forces typically consist of two or more sworn officers from several participating agencies, with each agency donating personnel and equipment. Often one of the participating agencies is selected as the lead agency to coordinate law enforcement efforts. Arizona's Anti-Gang Task Force, for example, consists of sworn officers from many of the state's larger cities as well as agents from a number of federal law enforcement agencies. The Anti-Gang Task Force is organizationally led and coordinated by the state's Department of Public Safety. This task force, while responsible for gang enforcement, is also responsible for managing gang intelligence for all law enforcement agencies in the state—a specialized function that is too expensive and time intensive for many of the police agencies in the state.

Phillips notes that there are five major advantages to using multiagency task forces: (1) they eliminate the duplication of services in surrounding communities; (2) they afford smaller agencies services that they otherwise might not be able to afford; (3) they result in the benefit of shared resource management; (4) they allow officers to work in jurisdictions where they might not otherwise have authority; and (5) they increase the amount of information that officers have at their disposal.[26]

# COMPSTAT

Over the past two decades police organizations have been increasing the amount of technology they employ to more effectively and efficiently make use of their resources. However, it was not until 1994, when the New York City Police Department, led by Commissioner William Bratton, implemented **COMPSTAT** (short for compare stats), that technology was used as an organizational tool to achieve crime control through accountability. In the New York City Police Department the COMPSTAT model attempts to blend timely intelligence, effective tactics, rapid deployment of personnel, and relentless follow-up and assessment.[27] Under COMPSTAT the police department continuously collects arrest, calls for service, and complaint data from each precinct or beat within the agency, and analyzes them for reporting purposes at that level. This organizational model of management in New York City places the responsibility for crime control on precinct commanders. At weekly meetings crime trends are examined, and precinct commanders are "grilled" about the strategies that they have used to control crime in their precinct. Commanders who are not successful in reducing crime are reassigned to less prestigious and demanding positions.[28]

Weisburd and his associates performed an exhaustive study examining the adoption of COMPSTAT across the county and the primary goals associated with

**COMPSTAT**

## EXHIBIT 4-2

### Has Your Department Implemented a COMPSTAT-Like Program?

| Department Size | Percent Yes | Percent No, but Planning | Percent No |
|---|---|---|---|
| Small department (50–99 sworn) | 11.0 | 29.3 | 59.8 |
| Large department (100+ sworn) | 32.6 | 25.6 | 41.8 |

Due to rounding, rows may not add to 100.

*Source:* David Weisburd, Stephen Mastrofski, Rosann Greenspan, and James Willis, "The Growth of Compstat in American Policing," *Police Foundation Reports* (Washington DC: Police Foundation: April 2004).

the strategy. They found that there were six key elements or features associated with COMPSTAT.[29]

1. COMPSTAT clarifies the department's mission, goals, and values.
2. COMPSTAT holds managers within the organization accountable.
3. Organizational power and authority are transferred to commanders who are responsible for geographic areas.
4. Resources are transferred to commanders who are responsible for geographic areas.
5. Data are used to identify problems and to evaluate success and failure.
6. Middle managers are expected to use innovative problem-solving tactics.

Since its implementation in New York City, COMPSTAT has been hailed as one of the most important organizational innovations in American policing. This is in large part because a number of policy makers and police officials claimed that COMPSTAT was responsible for the dramatic drop in crime in New York City. Following the implementation of COMPSTAT, index crimes in New York City decreased by 55 percent, compared with 24 percent in other large cities. Similarly, during the same period, homicides in New York City decreased by 66 percent, compared with a decrease of 24 percent in other cities. As a result, the model has been implemented in a number of police departments across the country.[30] A survey of 615 police agencies across the country showed that about 33 percent of large police departments and 11 percent of small departments use a COMPSTAT-like program. Furthermore, over 25 percent of large and small departments are planning to implement COMPSTAT soon.[31]

A number of critics, however, have pointed out that the decrease in crime came at the expense of due process and morale. Citizen complaints escalated dramatically as commanders were required to use more aggressive policing strategies. For example, complaints against the police for conducting illegal searches increased 135 percent in the first two years. Likewise, many police managers in the New York City Police Department complained that COMPSTAT was no more than a numbers game that was used to foster fear among management. Those managers who did not increase arrests and decrease crime in the areas they commanded were subject to public embarrassment by police executives who scolded them in COMPSTAT meetings.[32]

# Civil Service

**Civil service** procedures are a major feature of American police organizations. Civil service represents a set of formal and legally binding procedures governing personnel decisions. Civil service is nearly universal. With the exception of some of the very smallest departments, police departments in the United States operate under some form of civil service. The purpose of civil service is to ensure that personnel decisions are based on objective criteria, and not on favoritism, bias, and political influence.

State law or local ordinance establishes civil service systems. In most cities, ultimate authority over personnel procedures rests with a board or commission consisting of three to five persons. The mayor or a city manager government unit typically appoints board members for a specified term. The board sets basic policy and hires a personnel director to administer policy on a day-to-day basis.[33]

The civil service agency and the police department share responsibility for personnel policies. Civil service agencies are responsible for developing job descriptions and pay scales, developing recruitment procedures, developing and administering recruitment tests, certifying qualified applicants, developing promotional criteria, developing and administering promotional tests, developing disciplinary procedures, and hearing appeals of disciplinary actions. Police departments provide input on job descriptions, participate in recruiting, conduct some of the recruitment tests, and select recruits from certified lists.

Civil service systems reinforce the hierarchical structure of police departments. William King points out that there are four formal hierarchies (typically outlined under civil service systems) that stratify organizational members.[34] First, there is a **rewards hierarchy.** This hierarchy typically corresponds with an officer's rank and seniority within the department. It does not, however, typically correspond with individual skill or performance.

Second, officers are differentiated on the basis of a **seniority hierarchy.** Officers with more years of service are typically paid more and are given advantage over which shifts and jobs they are assigned.

Third, officers are differentiated on the basis of a **status hierarchy**—their assigned status within the police department. Officers who are assigned to a specialized unit, such as detective, or who occupy a particular job in the department, such as special assistant to the chief, typically have greater authority and responsibility in particular situations. In these cases an officer who occupies an assigned status can have command and control over those who outrank him or her. However, an officer carries the title and authority only while assigned or appointed to a particular job; if reassigned, the person loses both the title and the authority.

Fourth, officers are differentiated on the basis of a **rank hierarchy.** An officer carries his or her rank permanently, until promoted (demotions are extremely rare under civil service). For example, an officer holding the rank of sergeant is restricted to those jobs designated for sergeants by civil service job descriptions.

Civil service creates a number of problems for police organizations. First, it limits the power of police chiefs in making personnel decisions. A chief cannot hire, fire, or promote those people at will. Nor can a chief change existing personnel standards at will (e.g., impose a college education requirement for all new recruits).

**civil service**

**rewards hierarchy**

**seniority hierarchy**

**status hierarchy**

**rank hierarchy**

Second, it limits the opportunities and incentives for individual officers. Officers cannot earn financial bonuses or receive rapid promotions for exceptional performance.

Third, many critics argue that the provisions for discipline make it extremely difficult for chiefs to terminate bad officers or even to discipline officers for poor performance.

# Police Unions

**police union**

Police unions are another structural feature of police organizations. A **police union** is an organization legally authorized to represent police officers in collective bargaining with the employer. Under American labor law, employers are required to recognize and negotiate with democratically chosen unions. Police unions are extremely powerful, and union contracts are an important feature of police organizations.

## Aspects of Police Unions

The majority of sworn police officers in the United States today are members of police unions. According to the Law Enforcement Management and Administrative Statistics (LEMAS) survey, officers are represented by unions in 73 percent of all municipal police departments and 43 percent of all sheriffs' departments.[35] Almost all of the big and medium-sized cities have police unions, while small city and county departments (10 sworn officers or fewer) do not. Although union membership has been declining in the private sector of the economy, it has been growing in the public sector. The police are not the most heavily unionized group of public employees. A higher percentage of firefighters and public school teachers are members of unions.[36]

Unlike other parts of the economy, there is no single national union that represents all police officers. The United Automobile Workers, for example, represents all employees in the automobile industry; the Teamsters union represents all truck drivers, and so on. Police unions are fragmented among several different national federations. Today, there are three major police unions:

1. **Fraternal Order of Police.** The Fraternal Order of Police (FOP) is the oldest and largest police organization. It represents about 50 percent of law enforcement officers in the nation. Today it is reported that the FOP has 325,000 members.[37]

2. **International Union of Police Associations.** The International Union of Police Associations (IUPA) is one of 89 chartered unions affiliated with the AFL-CIO. However, in recent years the AFL-CIO has not provided the IUPA with much assistance. It is estimated that the IUPA has 35,000 members.[38]

3. **Teamsters Law Enforcement League.** The Teamsters Law Enforcement League, which is a division of the International Brotherhood of Teamsters, is perhaps the most controversial police union given its historical involvement with organized crime. Like the IUPA, the Teamsters Law

Enforcement League is affiliated with the AFL-CIO. The Teamsters mostly represents officers in suburban and rural law enforcement agencies. Today it is estimated that the Teamsters represents about 15,000 officers in 225 police organizations.[39]

## Collective Bargaining

**Collective bargaining** is defined as "the method of determining conditions of employment through bilateral negotiations." The basic principles of collective bargaining are that (1) employees have a legal right to form unions of their own choosing, (2) employers must recognize employee unions, (3) employees have a right to participate in negotiations over working conditions, and (4) employers are required to negotiate with the union's designated representatives. The process is designed to provide a structured framework for settling differences between employers and employees.[40]

**collective bargaining**

In some departments, the union represents all of the officers except the chief. In others, it represents all of the officers from the rank of captain on down; deputy chiefs are excluded on the grounds that they are part of management. In some large departments there are separate unions for different ranks: one for police officers, one for sergeants, and so on. In these cases, the chief must negotiate with two and, in some cases, three unions. There may also be a separate union for the civilian employees.

The 1935 National Labor Relations Act defined the scope of collective bargaining as "wages, hours, and other conditions of employment." The scope of conditions of employment is ambiguous and subject to negotiations. It generally excludes management rights issues, such as the right to recruit, assign, transfer, or promote employees. In some cities, however, the union has won the right to control such issues as patrol staffing.[41]

## Grievance Procedures

One of the most important conditions of work involves disciplinary procedures. Almost all police unions have formal grievance procedures designed to protect officers against unfair discipline. Grievance procedures provide due process for employees.

The typical grievance procedure (see Exhibit 4–3) requires that an officer be notified (usually in writing) about a disciplinary action, that the officer has the right to a hearing, the right to an attorney, and the right to appeal any disciplinary action. In some instances, these procedures are referred to as the police officers' bill of rights (see Exhibit 4–4).

## Unions and Shared Governance

Collective bargaining represents a form of shared management. Unions give officers a voice in some, but not all, decisions about the operation of the department. The major impact of police unions, therefore, has been to greatly reduce the power of police chiefs. Prior to the late 1960s, chiefs had an almost completely free hand in managing their departments.

**EXHIBIT 4–3**

## Article 8: Grievance Procedure

**Step 1**   An employee or Union who has a grievance shall present the same, in writing, to the Police Chief, or his designated representative, within ten (10) working days from the date on which the employee or Union became aware of the grievance. The written grievance must set forth the sections and articles of this Agreement upon which the matter of interpretation or application is involved. The Chief, or his designated representative, will respond to the grievant in writing within ten (10) working days from the date on which the written grievance was received.

**Step 2**   If satisfactory settlement is not reached under Step 1 hereof, then the aggrieved employee or Union may, within ten (10) working days of receipt of the Chief's response to Step 1 hereof appeal the Chief's decision to the Department Head, or his designated representative, who shall have ten (10) working days in which to respond, in writing, to the employee.

**Step 3**   In the event the employee or Union is still dissatisfied with the response of the Department Head, or his designated representative, then the employee or Union may, within ten (10) working days from the date of the response given by the Department Head or his designated representative, appeal said decision, in writing to the Labor Relations Director, or his designated representative. The Labor Relations Director or his designated representative shall respond to the grievant, in writing, within ten (10) working days from the date on which the grievance appeal was received. An extension on the time period may be granted when mutually agreed to by the Labor Relations Director and the Union.

**Step 4**   If satisfactory settlement is not reached under Step 3 hereof, either the aggrieved employee, the Union, or the City of Omaha by and through the Labor Relations Director, or his representative shall, within twenty (20) working days from the expiration of the limits as set forth in Step 3 or any extension thereof as set forth in Section 3, by written notice to the other party, request arbitration. The City shall furnish the Union with a copy of any such notice sent or received requesting arbitration.

The arbitration proceeding shall be conducted by an arbitrator to be mutually selected by the parties within thirty (30) calendar days after the submission of written demand for arbitration. The UNION shall at its discretion become a party for the purpose of selecting an arbitrator. The UNION and the grievant shall together be considered one party. If the parties are unable to mutually agree as to the selection of an arbitrator within such time limit and either party continues to demand arbitration, the parties shall jointly request the Federal Mediation and Conciliation Service to provide a list of five (5) arbitrators. Each party shall have the right to strike two (2) names from the list of arbitrators as submitted. The party requesting arbitration shall have the right to strike the first name and the other party shall then strike one name with the same process being repeated so that the person remaining on the list shall be the arbitrator.

*Source:* Omaha Police Department, "Union Contract," *Standard Operating Procedure Manual,* pp. 12–13.

# EXHIBIT 4-4

## Florida Police Officers' Bill of Rights

### 112.532 Law Enforcement Officers' and Correctional Officers' Rights

All law enforcement officers and correctional officers employed by or appointed to a law enforcement agency or a correctional agency shall have the following rights and privileges:

1. **Rights of Law Enforcement Officers and Correctional Officers While under Investigation.** Whenever a law enforcement officer or correctional officer is under investigation and subject to interrogation by members of his or her agency for any reason that could lead to disciplinary action, suspension, demotion, or dismissal, the interrogation must be conducted under the following conditions:

   a    The interrogation shall be conducted at a reasonable hour, preferably at a time when the law enforcement officer or correctional officer is on duty, unless the seriousness of the investigation is of such a degree that immediate action is required.

   b    The interrogation shall take place either at the office of the command of the investigating officer or at the office of the local precinct, police unit, or correctional unit in which the incident allegedly occurred, as designated by the investigating officer or agency.

   c    The law enforcement officer or correctional officer under investigation shall be informed of the rank, name, and command of the officer in charge of the investigation, the interrogating officer, and all persons present during the interrogation. All questions directed to the officer under interrogation shall be asked by or through one interrogator during any one investigative interrogation, unless specifically waived by the officer under investigation.

   d    The law enforcement officer or correctional officer under investigation must be informed of the nature of the investigation before any interrogation begins and he or she must be informed of the names of all complainants. All identifiable witnesses shall be interviewed, whenever possible, prior to the beginning of the investigative interview of the accused officer. The complaint, all witness statements, including all other existing subject officer statements, and all other existing evidence, including, but not limited to, incident reports, GPS locator information, and audio or video recordings relating to the incident under investigation, must be provided to each officer who is the subject of the complaint before the beginning of any investigative interview of that officer. An officer, after being informed of the right to review witness statements, may voluntarily waive the provisions of this paragraph and provide a voluntary statement at any time.

   e    Interrogating sessions shall be for reasonable periods and shall be timed to allow for such personal necessities and rest periods as are reasonably necessary.

   f    The law enforcement officer or correctional officer under interrogation may not be subjected to offensive language or be threatened with transfer, dismissal, or disciplinary action. A promise or reward may not be made as an inducement to answer any questions.

   g    The formal interrogation of a law enforcement officer or correctional officer, including all recess periods, must be recorded on audio tape, or otherwise

continued

**E X H I B I T   4 – 4   (continued)**

preserved in such a manner as to allow a transcript to be prepared, and there shall be no unrecorded questions or statements. Upon the request of the interrogated officer, a copy of any recording of the interrogation session must be made available to the interrogated officer no later than 72 hours, excluding holidays and weekends, following said interrogation.

h   If the law enforcement officer or correctional officer under interrogation is under arrest, or is likely to be placed under arrest as a result of the interrogation, he or she shall be completely informed of all his or her rights before commencing the interrogation.

i   At the request of any law enforcement officer or correctional officer under investigation, he or she has the right to be represented by counsel or any other representative of his or her choice, who shall be present at all times during the interrogation whenever the interrogation relates to the officer's continued fitness for law enforcement or correctional service.

j   Notwithstanding the rights and privileges provided by this part, this part does not limit the right of an agency to discipline or to pursue criminal changes against an officer.

*Source:* Florida Statutes, Sec. 112.532.

The chief, for example, might announce a plan to add a fourth patrol shift. The union might argue that this represents a change in working conditions, because the officers involved will have to work different hours. The chief will reply that his power to create a fourth shift is a management right. The two sides will try to settle this disagreement informally. If they cannot, the union may file a grievance under the contract. Contracts normally contain a formal grievance procedure to settle these conflicts.

## Impasse Settlement and Strikes

When the union and the city or county cannot agree on a contract, an impasse exists. In the private sector, the union often goes out on strike, or the employer conducts a lockout of the employees. Police strikes are illegal in many states, and other impasse settlement procedures exist, such as mandatory mediation, fact finding, or arbitration.

Strikes are the most controversial aspect of police unionism. Many people argue that the police have absolutely no right to strike: that it is unprofessional and that it creates a serious danger to the public. Police unions reply that they should have the same right to strike as other unions. Withholding one's labor is the ultimate weapon that working people have to force the employer to reach an agreement. Most union leaders, however, are opposed to strikes either because they are illegal in that state or because of the negative public reaction.[42]

Instead of actual strikes, police officers occasionally engage in job actions, defined as a deliberate disruption of normally assigned duties. One example is the "blue flu," where many officers do not go to work, claiming they are sick.[43] In some cases, such as in San Francisco in 1975, police officers tried to exert pressure on the city by refusing to write any traffic tickets or writing massive numbers of tickets.[44] A police strike is a major crisis for the community. Police strikes in Baltimore (1974), San Francisco (1975), and New Orleans (1979) resulted in violence and disorder. In many strikes, some officers remain on duty, feeling a sense of obligation to the community.

Police strikes are actually very rare, and there have been very few since the 1970s. Public school teachers strike far more often than police officers do. Even in the private sector, the number of strikes has declined substantially since the 1970s.[45]

## The Impact of Police Unions

Police unions have had a powerful impact on American policing. Most important, they have produced significant improvements in police officer salaries and benefits. In the mid-1960s many police departments were having great difficulty recruiting and holding qualified officers. By the late 1980s the picture had changed dramatically. Police departments generally had many applicants for each opening and were able to recruit people with at least some college education. In other words, jobs with the police department were competitive with other jobs that a person with some college education might consider.

For a full discussion on beginning police work, see Chapter 6, and Chapter 15.

Jihong Zhao and Nicholas Lovrich performed one of the few studies examining the impact of collective bargaining on police compensation. They reported that about 70 percent of today's large police agencies engage in collective bargaining. Agencies that do not engage in collective bargaining were found to be less likely to receive hazardous duty pay, shift differential pay, and education incentive pay. The researcher's findings led them to conclude that collective bargaining is a successful strategy for "the advocacy of policies promoting the well-being of police personnel."[46]

Police officers have also experienced other benefits as a consequence of police unions. For example, police unions have radically altered the process of police management, reducing the power of chiefs and introducing a process of shared governance. Similarly, unions have introduced due process into union discipline procedures, limiting the power of police chiefs to arbitrarily or unfairly discipline officers.

On the other hand, several scholars and police executives claim that police unions are a serious obstacle to change in police organizations. Over the last several decades unions have been found to hinder the development of police professionalism. For example, in many cities they have fought the implementation of civilian review boards, lateral entry, changes in department policies, disciplinary procedures, and promotion procedures. They have also been associated with restricting management's ability to efficiently run a police department by opposing different policies associated with manpower allocation, one-officer cars, the implementation of a fourth shift, and changes in overtime procedures.[47]

## Police Organizations and Their Environment

There are three primary theories that have been used by researchers to understand police organizational structures and operational strategies: contingency theory, institutional theory, and resource dependency theory. Each of these models emphasizes the importance of understanding the environment in which the police operate and how that environment impacts police organizations.

## Contingency Theory

**contingency theory**

**Contingency theory** has emerged as the dominant theoretical framework for understanding the structures and practices of police organizations. The underlying premise of contingency theory is the belief that organizations are created and structured to achieve specific goals, such as crime control. According to contingency theory, organizations are rational entities, adopting organizational structures and operational activities that are most effective and efficient in achieving specific goals. It is argued that organizations that fail to make the appropriate adjustments to the environmental contingencies they face will not prosper and, in some cases, will not survive.[48]

Solomon Zhao, a leading police organizational theorist, contends that contingency theory, therefore, makes two primary assumptions about police organizations. The first is that police organizations "must adapt themselves to the external environment when their existing goals are affected by changes in their operating conditions." The second is that police organizations must be dynamic so that they maintain "fit" between themselves and their environment over time. A good fit between a police organization and its environment results in higher performance. Zhao points out that these two underlying assumptions make contingency theory well suited for helping students of police organizations understand why law enforcement agencies change their organizational arrangements and operational strategies.[49]

Contingency theory has often been used by researchers and policymakers to understand police innovation. For example, Inglewood, California, faced a growing gang problem in the early 1970s. In response to the proliferation of gangs and gang-related problems, the police department established a police gang unit to enhance the success of departmental crime control efforts. Similarly, many researchers and policymakers have argued that community-oriented policing has been adopted because past attempts by the police to control crime have failed.[50]

## Institutional Theory

**institutional theory**

**Institutional theory** holds that police organizations are social institutions that operate in relation to their external social and political environment. The central premise of institutional theory, as applied to the police, is a belief that the organization and activities of the police must be understood in the context of their institutional environment. Institutional environment, here, refers to powerful actors, called sovereigns, who have the capacity to influence the policies and decisions of police organizations.[51] Sovereigns in a given community might include, but are not necessarily limited to, the mayor, city council, special-interest groups, citizens, and other criminal justice agencies.

Within the institutional perspective it is argued that the organization and activities performed by the police do not necessarily reflect rationality. That is, police departments do not create organizational structures or engage in operational activities simply because they are more efficient and/or more effective. Instead, police departments create organizational structures and engage in operational activities because they reflect the ideas and values that are shared by their institutional environment.[52] Therefore, institutional theory holds that for police departments to establish legitimacy, their organizational structures and operational activities must be performed in accordance with the ideas and beliefs that are held by various powerful actors within their environment.[53] Those police organizations that conform to the ideas and beliefs that are prescribed to them by their external environment are more likely to obtain "cultural support" and, henceforth, improve their chances for organizational survival.[54] Conversely, those organizations that do not conform to the ideas and beliefs that are held by their institutional environment are at risk of being perceived as useless or unimportant, and may lose any legitimacy that was previously granted by their institutional environment.[55]

Charles Katz examined the utility of institutional theory in his ethnographic study of the establishment of one police gang unit. Katz found that the institutional pressures placed on the police department had a significant impact on the creation of the gang unit. Observations and internal documents showed that the city had only a minor gang problem that did not substantiate the need for a specialized gang unit. However, the gang unit was created because of external pressures exerted on the chief of police by powerful local political, business, and community stakeholders and that, once created, the unit's strategic response was largely driven by its need to incorporate the ideas and beliefs of sovereigns in its environment. As such, he reported that attempting to measure and account for key elements of the environment in which police organizations operate can be important for understanding existing organizational arrangement and operational activities.[56]

## Resource Dependency Theory

**Resource dependency theory** suggests that organizations must obtain resources to survive, and that to obtain these resources they must engage in exchanges with other organizations in their environment. This, resource dependency theorists argue, requires organizations to alter their organizational structure and/or operational strategy so that it accommodates others in their environment who have the capacity to provide much-needed resources. As a consequence, resource dependency theorists argue that those in an organization's environment that have the capacity to provide resources necessarily have indirect or direct power through resource exchanges. At the same time, proponents of resource dependency theory hold that organizations are not simply passive organisms at the mercy of others in their environment, but also have the capacity to influence their environment to ensure the flow of resources.[57] Organizations actively scan their environment for opportunities that may provide access to valuable resources.[58] Adherents of resource dependency theory maintain that while environmental factors influence the structure and activities of organizations, organizations also have the ability to influence the environment in which they operate to ensure the flow of resources.[59] Thus, at the core of resource dependency theory is the belief that organizational structures and practices are adopted to meet resource needs, rather than to increase the efficiency or effectiveness of the police organization.[60]

**resource dependency theory**

Only a few studies to date have used resource dependency theory to understand police organizations. Katz, Maguire, and Roncek, who examined 285 police agencies across the country, found that even when controlling for the amount of gang-related crime, departments that received external funding for gang-control functions were about 4.8 times more likely to have established a specialized gang unit than agencies that had not received funding. They argued that gang units might have been created because of the plentiful resources that were available for crime-control efforts aimed at gangs rather than because there was a real and growing gang problem.[61] Similarly, Maguire, Zhao, and Lovrich argue that one of the reasons so many police agencies have implemented community-oriented policing is to obtain their share of the $8.8 billion to be distributed by the Department of Justice to facilitate community policing.[62]

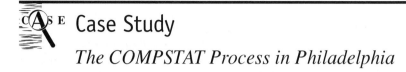

# C A S E  Case Study
## *The COMPSTAT Process in Philadelphia*

On the basis of COMPSTAT principles, the Philadelphia Police Department has developed a process that ensures that the whole of the department is actively involved in the fight against crime.

The process begins with the collection, analysis, and mapping of accurate and timely crime information. This is the job of the department's Crime Analysis and Mapping Unit, established in September 1997 with the help of federal funds provided through the Local Law Enforcement Block Grant. This unit, staffed by civilians who are experts in the use of geographical information systems, produces as many as 2,000 maps a week. Crime in each police district is broken down by type and then further analyzed to identify the place of occurrence as well as the time of day, day of week, and week of the year of occurrence. Homicides, rapes, robberies, and aggravated assaults are broken down into those committed with and without guns. Aggravated assaults are further classified as domestic or nondomestic. Burglaries are listed as residential or commercial. Thefts are classified as retail theft, theft from person, theft from an auto, and auto theft. Data are also captured involving shooting victims, shooting incidents, gun arrests, and gun seizures.

Each map displays this information not only about current crime but also about the previous month's. This enables commanders to assess the impact and effectiveness of anti-crime strategies. Drug patterns are shown overlaying the crime data. Because narcotics are often the driving force behind violent crime, district maps display narcotic arrests of both buyers and sellers along with reported crime.

Crime is not the only data analyzed and mapped. The number of arrests and the number of cases still requiring investigation are also shown. Still other maps highlight police activity such as vehicle and pedestrian investigations and moving and parking violations. The 911 calls in each district are also tallied, including the percentage of these that were unfounded. This data is captured both electronically and through manual means. After the data is aggregated, it is incorporated in the form of a COMPSTAT Process Data Form. This completed form is then transmitted to the department's officials and all police district commanders.

This statistical information is the basis for weekly meetings where the police commissioner and his entire top management team plan and coordinate the department's fight against crime. These meetings, known as COMPSTAT meetings, normally take place on Thursday mornings, begin at 7:30 a.m., and last for about three hours.

The maps prepared by the Mapping Unit are projected onto a large screen in the front of the room, and the district commanders responsible for the mapped districts are questioned on what the maps reveal. "Hot spots" of serious crimes and other problems such as quality of life offenses are discussed in detail and commanders are expected to describe their tactical plans for dealing with them. Commanders are also asked to report on the efficacy of actions they have taken to tackle issues identified during their previous COMPSTAT appearance, normally about a month ago.

Two of the department's six Patrol Bureau Divisions and their corresponding Detective Bureau Divisions are featured at a COMPSTAT meeting each week for a period of three weeks. Every fourth week, the meeting focuses on the department's specialized units, including SWAT, Canine, Mounted, Aviation, Bomb Disposal, Environmental Response, Marine, and Accident Investigation. At these meetings, performance measures, such as the number of cases involving barricaded persons handled by the SWAT Unit, the number of vehicle pursuits in which Aviation Unit officers were engaged, and the number of code enforcement violations issued by the Environmental Response Unit, are identified and discussed.

The data examined at COMPSTAT meetings is normally seven days old, as this is the time it takes to prepare the maps for discussion. Commanders use this time span to prepare for COMPSTAT meetings. They research and analyze the results of deployment strategies, disposition of offenders, multiple clearances, crime patterns, and other relevant data to prepare themselves for the inquiries that will be made at their next COMPSTAT meeting.

To augment the data analysis process further, the department is presently extending intranet access to each district to permit daily district-level crime mapping. Using this resource, commanders have the ability to review crime in a real-time environment. These visual aids will enable patrol and special unit officers to deploy their personnel much more flexibly and rapidly. For example, district commanders who are online are able to create, view and print crime maps using data layers to look at their own crime patterns on a daily basis. Charts may also be created to analyze crime patterns based on day of week, tour, time, etc. Stolen and recovered vehicles can also be tracked showing both locations. Individual incident (INCT) checks can be made for specific locations.

Analysis based on demographics is being incorporated into the intranet to allow district commanders to understand the characteristics of the neighborhoods within their district, based on census information. Firearm tracking will also be added so that guns can be linked to crimes committed throughout the city.

An essential feature of the COMPSTAT process, and one that is generally believed to account for its dramatic success in reducing crime in Philadelphia, is the freedom that the police commissioner gives to his district commanders to deploy their resources as they judge to be most effective. But with this freedom goes accountability and responsibility: it is at the COMPSTAT meeting that the commanders are required to justify their decisions and are held accountable for them.

Present at each COMPSTAT meeting are the police commissioner himself, his five deputy commissioners, and the chiefs of the Patrol, Training, Special Operations, and Quality Assurance Bureaus. Also in attendance are the commanders of the department's specialized and support units such as Highway Patrol, Major Crimes, Special Victims, Homicide, and Internal Affairs, as well as representatives of the suburban, transit, and local university police departments. Parole and probation officers and representatives from the district attorney's office and other city agencies also regularly attend. The sessions are open to the media and they are usually well attended by them. These partnerships are essential ingredients in the department's efforts to reduce crime in Philadelphia. In this way, the COMPSTAT process ensures that everyone in the city who has a contribution to make in fighting crime is involved in the process of planning this fight and monitoring its progress.

The department's Incident Reporting System (INCT) computer program, which was implemented in mid-1997, is the source of the crime statistics. After a police officer prepares an incident report, it is classified in accordance with the federally mandated Uniform Crime Reporting (UCR) standards. An investigative control number is assigned. The data is then entered into an online application and is available for the district and investigative commanders to review. District commanders have a five-day window in which to revise incorrectly coded incident reports. The revisions must be documented prior to the INCT system being changed. In the case of Part I crimes (murder, rape, robbery, etc.), the investigator must submit a follow-up report in order to comply with UCR reporting procedures. The COMPSTAT maps are prepared on the basis of this information. The maps are delivered to commanders prior to the COMPSTAT meeting so that they can prepare their comments and plans.

To ensure that the information used to prepare the COMPSTAT maps is both timely and accurate, the police commissioner has established a Quality Assurance Bureau that reports directly to him. Headed by a chief inspector, the bureau carries out regular audits of the reports prepared by police officers. The bureau is advised by an independent expert from the University of Pennsylvania.

*Source:* Adapted from "Philadelphia Police Department: CompStat Meetings." The URL of the page is: http://www.ppdonline.org/hq_compstat2.php. Downloaded on April 30, 2009.

## Summary

Police organizations are a critical element in policing. They are the instruments through which police services are organized and delivered to the public. Many police problems are associated with the problems of bureaucracy. Past attempts to restructure police departments, such as team policing, have not been successful. More recent attempts, such as community policing and COMPSTAT, represent efforts to revitalize police organizations by making them more open and responsive to the communities they serve and to changing social conditions.

## Key Terms

quasi-military style, 93
bureaucracy, 95
August Vollmer, 96
Bruce Smith, 96
O. W. Wilson, 96
vertical cliques, 99
horizontal cliques, 99
police professionalism, 100

decentralize, 100
deformalize, 100
despecialize, 101
delayerize, 101
task forces, 102
COMPSTAT, 103
civil service, 105
rewards hierarchy, 105

seniority hierarchy, 105
status hierarchy, 105
rank hierarchy, 105
police union, 106
collective bargaining, 107
contingency theory, 112
institutional theory, 112
resource dependency theory, 113

## For Discussion

1. If you were a police chief, how would you organize your department? For example, would it have many specialized units? Would it have many or few rules?

2. How has police professionalism been enhanced in the last 20 years?

3. Explain the difference between a centralized and decentralized organization. What are the advantages and disadvantages of each?

4. Explain how police unions affect police departments today.

5. What are some of the advantages and disadvantages of specialization?

## Internet Exercises

**Exercise 1** Many police departments have their organizational charts on their Web sites. Find the organizational charts for several of each size department: very large (3,000 sworn officers), large (700-plus sworn officers), medium-sized (200 to 700 sworn officers), and small (under 100 sworn officers). What are the obvious differences? How do they compare in terms of degree of specialization?

**Exercise 2** Go to http://www.iupa.org/ to learn about the International Union of Police Associations. After reading the article, discuss the benefits and limitations of police unions.

## Notes

1. Egon Bittner, *Aspects of Police Work* (Boston: Northeastern University Press, 1990), pp. 136–147.
2. Ibid.
3. Ibid., pp. 132–136.
4. James H. Tenzel, Lowell Storms, and Harvey Sweatwood, "Symbols and Behavior: An Experiment in Altering the Police Role," *Journal of Police Science and Administration* 4, no. 1 (1976): pp. 21–28.
5. Peter Kraska and Louis Cubellis, "Militarizing Mayberry and Beyond: Making Sense of American Paramilitary Policing," *Justice Quarterly* 14, no. 4 (1997): pp. 607–30.

6. William R. King, "Bending Granite Revisited: The Command Rank Structure of American Police Organizations," *Policing* 26, no. 2 (2003): pp. 208–30.
7. Charles Perrow, *Complex Organizations: A Critical Essay* (New York: Random House, 1986).
8. Samuel Walker, *A Critical History of Police Reform* (Lexington, MA: Lexington Books, 1977).
9. James Fyfe, Jack Greene, William Walsh, O.W. Wilson, and Roy C. McLaren, *Police Administration,* 5th ed. (New York; McGraw-Hill, 1997).
10. Charles M. Katz, Edward Maguire, and Dennis Roncek, "The Creation of Specialized Police Gang

Units: A Macro-Level Analysis of Contingency, Social Threat, and Resource Dependency Explanations," *Policing* 25, no. 3 (2002): pp. 472–506.

11. James Q. Wilson, *Bureaucracy* (New York: Basic Books, 1989).

12. Henry I DeGeneste and John P. Sullivan, *Policing a Multicultural Community* (Washington DC: PERF, 1997).

13. Perrow, *Complex Organizations.*

14. Walker, *A Critical History of Police Reform.*

15. Samuel Walker, "Legal Control of Police Behavior," in D. Weisburd and C. Uchida, eds., *Police Innovation and Control of the Police* (New York: Springer-Verlag, 1993), pp. 32–55.

16. John Crank, *Understanding Police Culture,* 2nd ed. (Cincinnati: Anderson Publishing, 2004).

17. John P. Crank, "The Influence of Environmental and Organizational Factors on Police Style in Urban and Rural Environments," *Journal of Research in Crime & Delinquency* 27 (May 1990): pp. 166–90

18. Westley, *Violence and the Police,* p. 23.

19. Steven Brint, *In an Age of Experts: The Changing Role of Professionals in Politics and Public Life* (Princeton: Princeton University Press, 1994).

20. Jihong Zhao, *Why Police Organizations Change* (Washington DC: Police Executive Research Forum, 1996).

21. Samuel Walker, *Taming the System* (New York: Oxford University Press, 1994).

22. Edward Maguire, "Structural Change in Large Municipal Police Organizations during the Community Policing Era," *Justice Quarterly* 14, no. 3 (1997): pp. 547–676; Stephen Mastrofski and Richard Ritti, "Making Sense of Community Policing: A Theory-Based Analysis," presented at the annual meeting of the American Society of Criminology, Boston (1995).

23. Edward Maguire and Yeunhee Shin, "Structural Change in Large Police Agencies during the 1990s," *Policing* 26, no. 2 (2003): pp. 251–75.

24. Jihong (Solomon) Zhao, *Evaluation on the Implementation of Total Quality Management in the Omaha Police Department: An Interim Report* (Omaha: 1998).

25. Peter W. Phillips, "De Facto Police Consolidation: The Multi-Jurisdictional Task Force," *Police Forum* 9, no. 3 (1999): pp. 1–5; G. Orvis, "The Evolution of the Crime Task Force and Its Use in the Twenty-First Century," presented at the annual meeting of the Academy of Criminal Justice Sciences, Orlando (1999).

26. Terry Dunworth, P. Hayes, and A. Saiger, *National Assessment of the Byrne Formula Grant Program* (Washington DC: National Institute of Justice, 1997).

27. Phillips, "De Facto Police Consolidation: The Multi-Jurisdictional Task Force."

28. David H. Bayley, *Police for the Future* (New York: Oxford University Press, 1994), p. 101.

29. U.S. Department of Justice, *Mapping Out Crime* (Washington DC: National Partnership for Reinventing Government, 1999).

30. John Eck and Edward Maguire, "Have Changes in Policing Reduced Violent Crime? An Assessment of the Evidence," in Alfred Blumstein and Joel Wallman, eds., *The Crime Drop in America* (Cambridge, England: Cambridge University Press, 2000), pp. 207–65.

31. David Weisburd, Stephen Mastrofski, Ann McNally, Rosann Greenspan, and James Willis, "Reforming to Preserve: COMPSTAT and Strategic Problem Solving in American Policing," *Criminology and Public Policy* 2, no. 3 (2003): pp. 421–56.

32. Robert Davis and Mateu-Gelabert, *Respectful and Effective Policing: Two Examples in the South Bronx* (New York: Vera Institute of Justice, March 1999).

33. George W. Griesinger, Jeffrey S. Slovak, and Joseph J. Molkup, *Civil Service Systems: Their Impact on Police Administration* (Washington DC: Government Printing Office, 1979).

34. William R. King, "The Hierarchical Nature of Police Organizations: Conception and Measurement," Unpublished paper (Bowling Green, OH: Bowling Green University, 2003).

35. Bureau of Justice Statistics, *Law Enforcement Management and Administrative Statistics, 1997* (Washington DC: Government Printing Office, 1999), p. xiv.

36. Bureau of the Census, *Statistical Abstract of the United States, 1997* (Washington DC: Government Printing Office, 1997), pp. 438–42.

37. John Burpo, Ron DeLord, and Michael Shannon, *Police Association Power, Politics, and Confrontation* (Springfield: Charles C. Thomas Publisher, 1997); Accessed at http://www.grandlodgefop.org/ on May 1, 2009.

38. John Burpo, Ron DeLord, and Michael Shannon, *Police Association Power, Politics, and Confrontation* (Springfield: Charles C. Thomas Publisher, 1997);

39. Ibid.

40. International Association of Chiefs of Police, *Guidelines and Papers from the National*

*Symposium on Police Labor Relations* (Washington DC: IACP, 1974).

41. Michael T. Leibig and Robert B. Kliesmet, *Police Unions and the Law: A Handbook for Police Organizers* (Washington DC: Institute for Police Research, 1988).

42. Jack Steiber, *Public Employee Unionism: Structure and Growth* (Washington DC: The Brookings Institution, 1973), pp. 159–92.

43. Margaret Levi, *Bureaucratic Insurgency* (Lexington, MA: Lexington Books, 1977), pp. 91–130.

44. William J. Bopp, "The San Francisco Police Strike of 1975: A Case Study," *Journal of Police Science and Administration* 5, no. 1 (1977): 32–42.

45. Bureau of the Census, *Statistical Abstract of the United States,* 1997, p. 439.

46. Jihong Zhao and Nicolas Lovrish, "Collective Bargaining and the Police," *Policing* 20, 3 (1997): pp. 508–18.

47. Colleen Kadleck, Police Employee Organizations, *Policing* 26, 2 (2003): pp. 341–50.

48. Lex Donaldson, *American Anti-Management Theories of Organization* (Cambridge, UK: Cambridge University Press, 1995); Charles M. Katz, Edward R. Maguire, and Dennis W. Roncek, "The Creation of Specialized Police Gang Units."; Stephen Mastrofski, "Community Policing and Police Organizational Structure," pp. 161–89, in Jean-Paul Brodeur, ed., *How to Recognize Good Policing* (Thousand Oaks, CA: Sage, 1998).

49. Jihong "Solomon" Zhao, Ni He, and Nicholas Lovrich, "Community Policing: Did It Change the Basic Functions of Policing in the 1990?" *Justice Quarterly* 20, no. 4 (2003): pp. 697–724.

50. Charles M. Katz, Edward R. Maguire, and Dennis W. Roncek, "The Creation of Specialized Police Gang Units."

51. John Crank and Robert Langworthy, "An Institutional Perspective of Policing," *The Journal of Criminal Law and Criminology* 83 (1992): pp. 338–63; Paul Di Maggio and Walter Powell, "The Iron Cage Revisited: Institutional Isomorphism and Collective Rationality in Organizational Fields," in Walter Powell and Paul Di Maggio, eds., *The New Institutionalism in Organizational Analysis* (Chicago:

University of Chicago Press, 1991); John Meyer and Brian Rowan, "Institutionalized Organizations: Formal Structure as Myth and Ceremony," *American Journal of Sociology* 83 (1977): pp. 340–48.

52. John Meyer and Brian Rowan, "Institutionalized Organizations: Formal Structure as Myth and Ceremony." *American Journal of Sociology* 83 (1977): pp. 340–48.

53. John Meyer and Brian Rowan, "Institutionalized Organizations"; John Crank and Robert Langworthy, "An Institutional Perspective of Policing"; John Crank, "Watchman and Community: Myth and Institutionalization in Policing," *Law and Society Review* 29 (1994): pp. 135–351.

54. John Meyer and Brian Rowan, "Institutionalized Organizations."

55. John Crank and Robert Langworthy, "An Institutional Perspective of Policing."

56. John Crank and Robert Langworthy, "An Institutional Perspective of Policing," *The Journal of Criminal Law and Criminology* 83 (1992): pp. 338–63

57. Charles Katz, "The Establishment of a Police Gang Unit: An Examination of Organizational and Environmental Factors." *Criminology,* 39 (2001): 37–75.

58. Donaldson, *American Anti-Management Theories of Organization;* Katz, Maguire, and Roncek, "The Creation of Specialized Police Gang Units."

59. William Scott, "Introduction," in J. M. Meyer and W. R. Scott, eds., *Organizational Environments* (London: Sage Publications, 1992).

60. Lex Donaldson, *American Anti-management Theories of Organization* (Cambridge: Cambridge University Press, 1995). R. H. Hall, *Organizations; Structures, Processes, and Outcome* (Upper Saddle River: Prentice Hall, 1999). P. S. Tolbert and L. G. Zucker, "The Institutionalization of Institutional Theory," in S. R. Clegg, C. Hardy, and W. R. Nord, eds., *The Handbook of Organizational Studies* (Thousand Oaks, CA: Sage, 1997).

61. Katz, Maguire, and Roncek, "The Creation of Specialized Gang Units."

62. Ed Maguire, Jihong Zhao, and Nicholas Lovrich, "Dimensions of Community Policing," unpublished manuscript (Omaha, Nebraska).

# Police Officers I: Entering Police Work

# The Changing American Police Officer

*The Police Tapes,* produced in the mid-1970s, is an award-winning documentary of New York City police officers engaged in routine police work. Watching it today, you immediately notice that police work hasn't changed, but there is only one officer who is not white and there are no female officers at all.

Forty years ago officers were almost all male, almost all white, and typically had only a high school education. Today, there are substantial numbers of female, African American and Hispanic officers (Exhibit 5–1). In some departments, African American or Hispanic officers are in a minority. Most police officers today have some college education, many have undergraduate college degrees, and a number have masters' degrees. There are openly gay or lesbian officers in many departments. All of these changes have had a significant impact on police organizations and the police subculture.

The Los Angeles Police Department dramatizes the extent of the change. In January 2009 the LAPD was 41 percent Latino, 38 percent non-Latino white, 12 percent African American, and 7 percent Asian. In 1986, Latinos were only 16.5 percent of the department, while African Americans were 12.4 percent.[1]

This chapter approaches policing from the perspective of occupational sociology. It examines policing in terms of the kinds of people who are recruited into

## EXHIBIT 5–1

### Racial and Ethnic Minority and Female Officers, 1990–2000

**Percentage of All Sworn Officers in Cities with Population of 500,000–999,999**

|      | African American | Hispanic | Female |
|------|------------------|----------|--------|
| 1990 | 25.2             | 11.4     | 12.3   |
| 2000 | 27.0             | 17.5     | 16.8   |

*Source:* Bureau of Justice Statistics, *Police Departments in Large Cities, 1990–2000* (Washington DC: U.S. Justice Department, 2002). Available at www.ncjrs.org. NCJ 175703.

police work, how different factors influence that selection process, and what happens to officers once they are hired. It attempts to explain how these different factors influence the attitudes and behavior of police officers on the job.

# Aspects of the Personnel Process

## A Career Perspective

Working for a law enforcement agency is more than a job; it's a *career*. It begins with recruitment and continues through to retirement. For some officers, it continues after retirement. Many retired officers have second careers, as officers in other departments or in jobs where they use their police experience as consultants or in education.

**career perspective**

A **career perspective** helps to understand how police officers interact with law enforcement organizations. Far too much attention is given to the recruitment stage—the entry requirements, the testing and hiring, and so on. Maintaining high-quality police services is a complicated process, however. It requires departments to hire *and retain* the best officers. This means paying close attention to all the stages of officer careers. Many departments have personnel problems because they:

- Hire good recruits, but do not train them properly.
- Train their officers well, but do not supervise them adequately.
- Do not have good personnel evaluation systems that recognize good performance.
- Fail to discipline officers whose performance is unprofessional.
- Fail to provide career opportunities that promote good morale and help retain good officers.
- Do not promote the best officers.

## Beyond Stereotypes of Cops

How many times have you heard someone make a statement such as "All cops are _____"? How many jokes have you heard about police officers spending all their time at donut shops? How often have you heard someone say that people become cops because they like to use force? Statements and jokes of this sort reflect negative stereotypes about police officers. At the same time, how many times have you heard someone say that police officers do no wrong or, more likely, that they have such dangerous and stressful jobs that we should never criticize them for maybe using a little too much force in some situations? This point of view reflects a positive stereotype about police officers.

**stereotypes about cops**

**Stereotypes about cops** heavily influence the public image of who police are, what they believe, and how they act. These stereotypes fall into two categories. On one side, a negative stereotype views officers as uneducated, untrained, prejudiced, brutal, and corrupt. On the other side, a positive stereotype views them as heroic saints, risking their lives in the face of hostility from the public, the media, and the courts. Arthur Niederhoffer characterizes the police officer as "a 'Rorschach' in uniform. . . . To people in trouble the police officer is a savior," but to others he is "a fierce ogre."[2]

Neither stereotype is accurate. As Bayley and Mendelsohn conclude in their study of police–community relations in Denver, the average police officer is rather average.[3] Police officers do not differ significantly from the general population in terms of their values and political beliefs. The special nature of police work does, however, encourage certain attitudes and behaviors, and there is a distinct police subculture among officers. (The relationship of police officer attitudes to behavior is examined in Chapter 6.)

Inaccurate stereotypes about policing affect the recruitment of new officers. The National Center for Women and Policing argues that stereotypes emphasizing officer use of force and the need for physical size and strength discourage women from considering careers in policing.[4] In reality, most police work is uneventful, and police–citizen encounters primarily require communication skills (see Chapter 4).

## The Personnel Process: A Shared Responsibility

Personnel decisions in policing are a shared responsibility. Police departments control some of the decisions, but other government agencies, such as the **civil service system** and/or the city personnel department, control the others. A police chief, for example, cannot unilaterally change recruitment standards (e.g., raise the minimum educational requirement) or fire an officer and be sure the decision will stand (the officer has the right to appeal, under the union contract and/or the civil service system).

**civil service system**

The lack of complete control over personnel decisions is often an emotional issue among police chiefs. At a national chiefs' meeting a few years ago, a police chief from Texas described how he fired an officer for using excessive force only to have the officer reinstated on appeal. The chief received a burst of applause from his fellow chiefs when he declared that this particular officer never belonged in law enforcement in the first place, but there was nothing he could do about it.

Typically, the civil service agency has the responsibility for (1) developing job descriptions; (2) establishing the minimum standards required for each position; (3) developing tests for each position; (4) announcing job openings; (5) conducting some, but not all, of the tests; and (6) certifying a list of persons to be hired or promoted. Police departments, meanwhile, generally (1) advise the civil service agency on job descriptions, requirements, and tests; (2) conduct some of the recruiting; and (3) administer some of the tests.[5] Civil service systems are discussed in more detail in Chapter 4.

---

# Recruitment

To hire good officers, a department must first attract a pool of good applicants. The recruitment process includes three separate elements: (1) the minimum qualifications, (2) the recruitment effort, and (3) the applicant's decision to apply for a position.

## What Kind of Job? What Kind of Person?

Before establishing the formal entry requirements for any job, it is important first to define the nature of the job. What does it involve? What kind of tasks are performed? What skills and qualities are best suited for that job? This process involves a job task analysis.

---

**EXHIBIT 5-2**

### San Diego Police Department: Job Dimensions for Police Officers

| | |
|---|---|
| Integrity | Observational Skills |
| Interest in People | Learning Ability |
| Interpersonal Sensitivity | Appearance |
| Communication Skills | Dependability |
| Problem Solving Ability | Physical Ability |
| Judgment Under Pressure | Desire for Self-Improvement |
| Willingness to Confront Problems | Operation of a Motor Vehicle |
| Credibility as a Witness | |

---

*Source:* San Diego Police Department web site: www.sandiego.gov/police/recruiting/about/dimensions.shtml

On its Web site, the San Diego Police Department lists the Job Dimensions for Police Officers (Exhibit 5–2). The top categories are Integrity, Interest in People, Interpersonal Sensitivity, Communication Skills, and Problem Solving Ability. Notice that the qualities associated with the old stereotypes about police are either ranked very low (physical ability) or not listed at all (strength, height).

## Minimum Qualifications

### Age

Is a person who is 21 years old mature enough to be a police officer? Does a 21-year-old have sufficient work experience and emotional maturity to be able to handle the stress and complex demands of police work? Some experts believe that police departments should raise the **minimum age level** for recruits. Most law enforcement agencies require all applicants to be at least 21 years old. In several states (e.g., Georgia, Pennsylvania), the state certification standards only require that an applicant be 18 years old.[6]

**minimum age level**

In the past, most police departments had maximum age limits for recruits. Typically you could not be older than 35 to be eligible for employment. This limit was primarily designed to reduce financial strains on pension systems by officers who would retire after fewer years on the job than younger officers. Federal law banning age discrimination has forced most departments to eliminate these limits, however.[7]

### Height and Weight

Can you be too short to be a police officer? Thirty years ago, nearly all police departments (85 percent) required officers to be at least 5 feet 8 inches tall.[8] This requirement reflected the old stereotype that police work frequently involves physical confrontations with suspects and that officers need to be physically imposing in order to gain the respect of citizens. As will be discussed in Chapter 7, however, police work rarely involves physical confrontations. Citizens generally comply with officers' requests, and communication skills and good judgment are considered more important for police work than physical strength.

# EXHIBIT 5-3

## Minimum Education Requirements for Recruits, 2003

| Percentage of<br>Departments Requiring | All Departments | Departments in cities with population<br>between 500,000–999,999 |
|---|---|---|
| Four-year college degree | 1% | 5% |
| Two-year college degree | 9 | 9 |
| Some college | 8 | 13 |
| High school diploma | 81 | 72 |

*Source:* Bureau of Justice Statistics, *Local Police Departments, 2003* (Washington DC: U.S. Justice Department, 2006). Table 16. Available at www.ncjrs.org. NCJ 210118.

The old height requirements were challenged in lawsuits arguing that they discriminated against women, Hispanic Americans, and Asian Americans. Only a handful of big-city departments still had minimum height requirements by 1994.[9]

Departments today require that *weight be proportional to height*. But as everyone can see, many police officers are overweight. In some cases they are seriously overweight relative to their height. Why are they still on the force? Traditionally, law enforcement agencies have not enforced fitness standards throughout officers' careers. This practice has begun to change. The Ohio State Highway Patrol began a fitness program in 1992, with penalties for veteran officers who did not meet the standards.[10]

## Education

The vast majority (81 percent) of police departments in 2003 required only a high school education or the equivalent (Exhibit 5–3). Requirements are much higher in big city departments, however. In 2003, 5 percent of the departments in cities with populations between 500,000 and 999,999 required a college degree, compared with only 1 percent of all departments. Another 9 percent in this group required two years of college.[11]

Minimum entry requirements, however, do not reflect actual hiring practices. Departments often hire applicants with *more* than the required minimum level of education. The average recruit in the San Diego police department in the late 1980s had two years of college, despite the fact that there was no formal college education requirement. By 1988, 65.2 percent of all sworn officers in the United States had some college education, and 22.6 percent had undergraduate or graduate degrees.[12] The Chicago Police Department in 2009 required applicants to have at least 60 semester (or 90 quarter) hours of credit from an accredited college or university.[13]

## Require a College Degree?

Some people argue that all police officers should have a college degree. They believe this would improve policing in three ways. First, higher education will *shape the values* of students and make them better understand the complex role of the police in a democratic society. Second, it will *improve on-the-street performance* by giving them the capacity to make better judgments. Third, people who have pursued a college education have exhibited a desire for self-improvement, and this trait is likely to make them more professional police officers.[14]

In addition, police officers need to deal with the complex and constantly changing law of criminal procedure and need to raise their requirements to keep pace with rising levels of education in society. Between 1960 and 2004 the percentage of adults completing high school doubled, from 41 to 84.2 percent, and the percentage graduating from college tripled, from 7.7 to 25.2 percent. Finally, community policing and problem-oriented policing ask police officers to be planners and problem solvers, and a college education is good preparation for these tasks.[15]

Some people argue that requiring a college degree limits the pool of applicants and has a disparate impact on racial minorities who have been the victims of inferior schooling. In 2004, 26 percent of all white Americans had completed four years of college or more, compared with 16 percent of African Americans, and 10.3 percent of Hispanic Americans.

In 1985, however, federal courts upheld a requirement by the Dallas police department that recruits have at least 45 hours of college education with a minimum average of C. A 1991 Police Executive Research Forum (PERF) discussion paper concluded that "there appears to be an adequate pool of both minority and majority college-educated men and women interested in police employment" to justify a college requirement.[16]

There is no conclusive evidence that officers with college degrees perform more effectively than those without degrees. The National Academy of Sciences reviewed the subject and found serious methodological problems in both assessing the content of college education courses and in the measures used to evaluate police performance. Michael D. White's study illustrated the problem of simply counting the number of college credit hours. He found that the number of college credit hours recruits had did not predict how well they would perform in the academy. Interestingly, however, reading level was the most powerful predictor of their performance.[17]

Some evidence, however, suggests that officers with relatively more education are more likely to become dissatisfied with their jobs than officers with less education. Dantzker found relatively lower levels of job stress among officers with only a high school education compared to those with college degrees. He suggested that college-educated officers may become "more easily frustrated with how the police system actually works, and with how their police agencies failed to accept and utilize their knowledge and skills."[18]

### *Criminal Record*

**criminal record**

Should someone with a **criminal record** be eligible to work as a police officer? Some experts argue that a criminal record of any sort should automatically disqualify an applicant on the grounds that it indicates a lack of ethical standards. Others argue in favor of a variable standard, depending on the nature of the offense (felony or misdemeanor, adult or juvenile), the number of offenses, and how recently the last offense was committed.

A Justice Department survey found that 95 percent of all departments refuse to hire anyone with an adult felony conviction, while 75 percent reject those with a juvenile felony conviction. Only 30 percent, however, automatically reject applicants with either an adult or a juvenile misdemeanor conviction. While 20 percent reject those with an adult felony arrest but no conviction, 25 percent reject those with a juvenile arrest but no conviction.[19]

Drug offenses pose the most difficult questions. On one hand, officers with any kind of drug involvement history are far more likely to become corrupt. On the other hand, drug use is extremely prevalent in today's society. According to the National Survey on Drug Use and Health, 54 percent of persons 18 to 25 (the age of potential police recruits) report having used marijuana.[20] Rejecting all of them would severely limit the applicant pool. Some experts suggest that applicants should be considered as long as the drug involvement was limited to "experimentation" rather than heavy use, to "soft" drugs (marijuana) rather than "hard" drugs (heroin), and as long as there had been no use for several years.

### Residency Requirements

Should police officers be required to live in the city they police? Does this make better officers than officers who live outside the city? The American Civil Liberties Union believes it does make a difference. In a 1994 report it found that 83 percent of all Los Angeles police officers lived outside the city of Los Angeles. It argued that police officers must be "a true part of the community they patrol" and not appear to be "an outside hired force."[21]

**Residency requirements** are a major controversy across the country. About one-quarter of all city police departments require their officers to live within the city or county. Residency requirements are intended to heighten officers' familiarity with the community and heighten their commitment to its well-being. Opponents of residency requirements argue that it infringes on the freedom of officers to choose where they live. Others argue that residency does not predict a person's behavior as a police officer. There is no thorough study of this issue. We really don't know the impact of residence on police performance. In one small indicator, New York City officers who live outside the city receive fewer citizen complaints than officers who live inside the city.[22]

**residency requirements**

For coverage of alternative strategies for getting officers to be more involved in the communities they police, see Chapter 10.

## Recruitment Effort

The size and quality of the applicant pool depend in part on a department's recruitment effort. An active effort will produce a larger pool, more of whom are likely to be highly qualified. If a department wants to increase the representation of college-educated, African American, Hispanic, or female officers, it needs to direct recruitment efforts toward those groups. To recruit more Hispanic applicants, for example, it needs to meet with Hispanic community groups and leaders.

Historically, police departments did not actively recruit. This practice gave people with political or family ties to the police department an advantage, since they were most likely to hear about hiring opportunities. Open recruitment efforts, including public advertising of opportunities, are required by law today. The 1994 Academy of Criminal Justice Sciences (ACJS) survey of recruitment, selection, and training standards found that 90 percent of all departments had a special recruitment strategy for minorities, slightly more than half (52.5 percent) had a special strategy for recruiting women, 37.3 percent actively sought veterans and college graduates, while 20 percent had a special program for recruiting people with prior police experience.[23]

## Choosing Law Enforcement as a Career

### Applicants' Motivations

Why do people want to become police officers? One stereotype holds that some people choose law enforcement for reasons that make them unsuited for police work: a desire to use force, for example. Research has refuted this stereotype, however.

Surveys of recruits and new police officers consistently indicate that they choose law enforcement for two main reasons: the nature of police work and the material benefits of the job. A survey of male and female officers in two Midwestern police departments found that they listed the top five reasons for choosing policing as a career in the following rank order: (1) "help people," (2) "job security," (3) "fight crime," (4) "excitement of the job," and (5) "prestige of the job." There were no significant differences between the male and female officers. Contrary to the negative stereotypes about police, recruits appear to be relatively idealistic, perhaps even slightly more than the average person. Significantly, both male and female officers ranked "authority/power" ninth out of a total of eleven items. In short, applicants are not primarily motivated by a desire to enforce the law or to use force against other people.[24]

The appeal of jobs with a police department often depends on the state of the economy and how the pay and benefits of a police job compare with those of other jobs available to the applicant. In 1999 and 2000 police departments in New York City, Los Angeles, and many other cities had difficulty attracting recruits because of the strong economy and the availability of other good jobs. In the recession of 2008–2009, however, police officer jobs were very attractive.

**job security**

Police officers enjoy a high degree of **job security** because of civil service rules and police union contract provisions that make it very difficult to fire officers.[25] After the probationary period, officers can be fired only for a specific cause, and any officer who is terminated has the right to appeal. Job security is a particularly appealing factor for individuals whose family experience included periodic unemployment.

Research has consistently found that racial-minority applicants are motivated by the same factors as white recruits: the nature of the work and the material benefits of the job. In a study of African American officers in New York City, Nicholas Alex concludes that "the motives of the white policeman for choosing police work seem little different from those of the black policeman."[26] Some studies, however, have found that economic factors are a little more important for African Americans than for whites.

Family connection is another factor that has some impact on choosing law enforcement as a career. Some applicants are motivated by the fact that they have a parent, a brother or sister, or some other relative who is a police officer. In the 1960s over half of all sergeants in the Chicago police department had a relative on the force. Because of past discrimination, African Americans, Hispanics, and women are less likely to have a family member to provide a role model or encouragement for choosing law enforcement as a career.[27]

Some applicants do not have clearly defined goals when they apply. They "drift" into police work, often after trying several other jobs.[28] Among those with clear goals, meanwhile, career expectations are often not fulfilled. Persons expecting an exciting job discover that patrol work is often very boring. Others, expecting good opportunities for advancement, are disappointed by the limited opportunities in police organizations.

## Barriers to Recruitment

Some potential applicants face informal barriers to applying for police jobs. The negative image of the police in their community causes some African Americans not to apply. In a survey of high school seniors, Kaminski found that African Americans were significantly less likely to accept a job with the Albany police department if it were offered to them.[29]

Many women do not apply because they see policing as a traditionally male occupation. The culture of policing still has a heavily masculine tone, emphasizing aggressiveness, psychological toughness, and physical strength.[30] The need for great physical strength, however, is a myth. It is very low on the list of the San Diego Police Department Job Dimensions (Exhibit 5–2). And see the discussion of "myths" about women and policing by the Charlotte-Mecklenburg, North Carolina, Police Department in the Police in Focus on p. 135.

# Selecting Officers from the Recruit Pool

## Selection Tests

Once there is a pool of applicants, a series of tests are used to select a group of new recruits. These tests include written and medical exams, a background check, and interviews of finalists. About 25 percent use a polygraph or lie detector (see Exhibit 5–4).[31]

### EXHIBIT 5–4

### Screening Methods Used by Local Police Departments, 2003

**Percentage of Departments Using Method**

| Method | All Departments | Departments in cities with populations 500,000–999,999 |
|---|---|---|
| Personal interview | 98% | 100% |
| Criminal record check | 99 | 100 |
| Background investigation | 98 | 100 |
| Driving record check | 96 | 100 |
| Medical exam | 85 | 100 |
| Psychological evaluation | 67 | 100 |
| Drug test | 73 | 95 |
| Written aptitude test | 43 | 84 |
| Physical agility test | 50 | 86 |
| Polygraph exam | 25 | 64 |

*Source:* Bureau of Justice Statistics, *Local Police Departments, 2003* (Washington DC: Government Printing Office, 2006), p. 8.

One problem with the recruitment and selection process in some jurisdictions is that it sometimes takes many months. Long delays cause some applicants to drop out; they either find other jobs or lose interest. Cohen found that delay accounted for a significant degree of attrition among minority applicants in New York City. Nearly 60 percent of black applicants who passed the initial written and physical examinations dropped out before the background investigation phase. This compared with an overall dropout rate of 18 percent.[32]

Of all the largest police departments (populations 100,000 or more), 90 percent test job applicants for drug use, and 80 percent of them also require drug tests of all officers. Some administer mandatory drug tests to both sworn and civilian employees, some use random tests, and others test employees when drug use is suspected.[33]

**oral interviews**

**Oral interviews** of applicant finalists are used by almost all big-city police departments. Interviews typically last about 45 minutes and involve two or three interviewers. Interviews can detect attitudes that might be incompatible with good police work (e.g., arrogance, inability to listen, extreme passivity, racial bias). The ACJS survey found that interviews explore such areas as common sense, verbal communication skills, motivation, appearance, quick thinking, racism, compassion, sexism, and patience. Interviews are time-consuming and expensive, however, and open the door to possible bias on the part of the interviewers. To ensure consistency and eliminate potential bias, most departments use a standardized interview format, have a structured marking sheet, and train their interviewers.[34]

Can a 45-minute interview really determine who will be a good police officer? Can an interview determine how a person will perform as a police officer? William G. Doerner correlated oral interview scores in the Florida state law enforcement training academy with subsequent performance records. He found a "persistent inability of this selection technique to isolate suitable candidates" for law enforcement.[35]

## Background Investigations

Background investigation of applicants is perhaps the most important part of the selection process. A thorough investigation can identify factors related to job performance as a police officer: a good work record in previous jobs, the ability to get along with people, the absence of disciplinary problems in school or jobs. It can also identify a criminal record, prior involvement with drugs, or behavior problems in school or on jobs.

**background investigations**

Virtually all big-city departments conduct **background investigations.** These investigations cover previous employment, possible criminal records, interviews with neighbors, a check of educational attainment, a review of the applicant's financial status, and a home visit.[36]

Poorly conducted background investigations open the door to subjective judgments and bias. In 1972, Anthony Bouza, deputy chief inspector of the New York City police department, argued that character investigations traditionally reflected the "biases of the investigating sergeant." This was especially true of African American and Hispanic applicants being interviewed and assessed by white sergeants. The NYPD adopted standardized procedures in an effort to eliminate bias.[37]

## Police in Focus

### *What Qualities Make a Good Police Officer?*

What qualities make someone a good police officer? The state of California Peace Officers Standards and Training (POST) Commission conducts psychological screening that examines eleven dimensions of applicants' attitudes. These dimensions include:

1. *Social competence:* The ability to "read" people and be aware of the impact of their own words and behavior on others.
2. *Adaptability/flexibility:* The ability to change gears and easily adjust to sudden changes in demands.
3. *Impulse control/attention to safety:* The ability to think before acting.

4. *Integrity/ethics:* High standards of personal conduct.
5. *Emotional regulation and stress tolerance:* The ability to maintain composure and stay in control.
6. *Decision making and judgment:* Common sense, "street smarts," and the ability to size up situations quickly.

*Source:* Ellen Scrivner, *Innovations in Police Recruitment and Hiring: Hiring in the Spirit of Service* (Washington DC: Department of Justice, 2005).

The Washington DC police department had a very bad experience in the early 1990s when it failed to conduct good background investigations. Congress had directed the department to quickly hire an additional 2,000 officers. The department then abandoned its standard background investigations. A large number of applicants submitted false references and work histories that were never checked. Some applicants even had serious criminal histories. As a result, a number of those hired became corrupt officers involved in drug activity. The department paid a terrible price in terms of negative publicity, loss of public respect, damage to department morale, and dollar costs related to firing those officers and hiring new ones.[38]

# Predicting Police Officer Performance

Can we predict who will become a good police officer? Are there any specific factors that help to predict which applicants are likely to be the best possible officers and which ones should not be hired at all?

Some studies have attempted to correlate background characteristics with subsequent performance records. Cohen and Chaiken studied 1,608 New York City police officers hired in 1957. Thirty-three background characteristics were examined, including race, age, IQ, father's occupation, previous occupational history (last job, number of jobs, and so on), military record, marital status, education, and criminal record. The only factor that correlated with good on-the-job performance (as indicated by their official records), however, was the recruit training score. The study concluded that it is not possible to predict which individuals will become good officers on the basis of background characteristics.[39]

In a review of selection procedures commonly used by police departments, J. Douglas Grant and Joan Grant conclude that "efforts to improve the quality of police officer performance by screening out those recruits who will not make good police officers have generally been unsuccessful." They argue that existing preemployment psychological tests, such as the widely used MMPI, do not successfully predict future behavior as a police officer.[40]

Similar problems affect widely used selection criteria. Many applicants, for example, have two years of college education. Some of them are likely to be excellent police officers, but others are not. At best, written tests screen out the illiterate and very poorly educated. The applicant who has superior academic skills and who might, for example, make an excellent researcher might not be able to work with people under conditions of stress. Psychological tests do not necessarily identify people who have good judgment.

A study of Tallahassee, Florida, police recruits found that neither preemployment psychological test scores (the MMPI and CPI tests were used) nor a clinical assessment by a psychologist correlated with recruits' performance ratings during field training.[41] The 1991 Christopher Commission, reviewing psychological evaluations given to LAPD applicants, concluded that "this initial screening can identify obvious social misfits in the grossest sense, but cannot test for more subtle abnormalities which may make an individual ill-suited to be a police officer, such as poor impulse control and the proclivity toward violence."[42]

# Equal Employment Opportunity

## The Law of Equal Employment Opportunity

**Title VII of the 1964 Civil Rights Act**

Employment discrimination on the basis of race, ethnicity, or sex is illegal in the United States. The underemployment of minorities and women in policing continues to be a major controversy. Under **Title VII of the 1964 Civil Rights Act,** it is unlawful for an employer "to fail or refuse to hire or to discharge any individual, or otherwise to discriminate against any individual . . . because of such individual's race, color, religion, sex, or national origin." The 1972 Equal Employment Opportunity Act extended the coverage of the 1964 law to state and local governments, which include police and sheriffs' departments.

State and local civil rights laws also prohibit employment discrimination. Virtually all cover discrimination on the basis of race, religion, age, and national origin. Some state laws cover other categories not covered by federal law. Several states and over sixty cities, for example, prohibit discrimination on the basis of sexual orientation, meaning that employers may not discriminate against homosexuals.

## Job-Related Qualifications

Is a handicapped person qualified for a job as a police officer? It is easy to answer this question about a paraplegic person who cannot walk a patrol beat, chase a suspect, or subdue a person who is physically resisting arrest. But what about a person who only suffers from some limited use of one hand? What about the person with a moderate speech impediment?

**bona fide occupational qualifications (BFOQ)**

Equal employment opportunity laws do not guarantee anyone a job. Employers may establish **bona fide occupational qualifications (BFOQ)** and refuse to hire

---

**S I D E B A R          5 – 1**

## Title VII, 1964 Civil Rights Act

SEC. 703. (a) It shall be an unlawful employment practice for an employer—

1. to fail or refuse to hire or to discharge any individual, or otherwise to discriminate against any individual with respect to his compensation, terms, conditions, or privileges of employment, because of such individual's race, color, religion, sex, or national origin; or

2. to limit, segregate, or classify his employees in any way which would deprive or tend to deprive any individual of employment opportunities or otherwise adversely affect his status as an employee, because of such individual's race, color, religion, sex, or national origin.

---

people who do not possess those qualifications. A BFOQ is any requirement that is "reasonably necessary to the normal operation of that particular business."[43]

A few examples illustrate how BFOQs apply to policing. Since driving a patrol car is one of the basic tasks of a police officer, a department can legitimately refuse to hire someone who cannot drive a car because of a certain handicap. On the other hand, the old height requirements are not job-related because it has not been demonstrated that people shorter than 5 feet 8 inches cannot effectively perform police work. In *Davis v. City of Dallas,* the Fifth Circuit Court of Appeals ruled that a requirement of 45 hours of college credits was reasonably related to the job of a police officer, on the grounds that officers are expected to exercise judgment in complex and difficult situations.[44]

The 1990 Americans with Disabilities Act (ADA) has added a new element to police employment practices. There are a number of issues that have not been resolved by the courts as to what conditions represent a disability and which disabilities legitimately disqualify a person from employment as a police officer.[45]

## "Not Your Father's Police Department": Diversity in Policing

It's "Not Your Father's Police Department," argues law professor David Sklansky. The changing face of the American police officer has resulted in many changes in policing. The traditional police subculture (see Chapter 6) is a thing of the past. In its place is a far more complex set of attitudes, and in some cases, different behavior.[46]

The employment of racial- and ethnic-minority police officers has increased significantly over the last forty years. In the mid-1960s, African Americans represented only 3.6 percent of all sworn police officers. The figure rose to 6 percent in 1973, 7.6 percent in 1982, and 11.7 percent by 2000. Hispanics represented 8.3 percent of all officers in 2000 (up from 6.2 percent in 1993, and 4.8 percent in 1988).[47]

It is important to note, however, that these trend data are not strictly comparable because national surveys over the years used different samples: some used all police departments, while others used only large departments. Obtaining long-term data on Hispanic employment is difficult, if not impossible, because early surveys did not ask for data on Hispanic officers.

The aggregate data on racial- and ethnic-minority employment are somewhat misleading, however, because racial and ethnic minorities are not evenly distributed throughout the United States. African Americans are concentrated in the South and the big cities across the country. Hispanic Americans are concentrated in particular cities in the Southwest, East, and South.

The most useful measure of employment practices is the extent to which a police department *reflects the composition of the community it serves*. Federal courts have used the percentage of minorities in the local adult workforce as the standard in settling employment discrimination suits. The CALEA *Standards for Law Enforcement Agencies* recommend that departments have "a ratio of minority group employees in approximate proportion to the makeup of the agency's law enforcement service community."[48]

**equal employment opportunity (EEO) index**

Lewis and Walker independently developed an **equal employment opportunity (EEO) index** to measure the extent to which a police department reflects the community it serves. The EEO index is computed by dividing the percentage of a particular minority group on the police force by the percentage in the population of the local community. Thus, if a community is 30 percent Hispanic and the police department is 15 percent Hispanic, the EEO index is 0.50.[49]

The EEO index is useful for measuring the employment performance of individual cities, for measuring change over time, and for taking into account the changing racial and ethnic composition of cities. A police department, for example, might hire more Hispanic officers, but if the Hispanic population of the city also increases, it may still be unrepresentative of the community.

Racial- and ethnic-minority employment has increased significantly in many departments in recent years, although some still lag behind. And in some departments people of color now represent a majority of all sworn officers. The Law Enforcement Management and Administrative Statistics (LEMAS) data indicate that in 1997 the Miami, Florida, police department was 53 percent Hispanic, 26 percent African American, and 20 percent white. The Atlanta, Georgia, police department was 58 percent African American, 40 percent white, and 1 percent Hispanic. The San Antonio, Texas, police department is today 46 percent Hispanic, 48 percent white, and 6 percent African American.

## African American Officers

In the 1960s, the underrepresentation of African Americans as police officers was a major contributor to the urban riots and the police–community relations crisis. The problem was particularly acute in cities with large minority populations. In 1966 African Americans represented 23 percent of the population of Oakland, California, but only 2.3 percent of the police officers (resulting in an index of 0.10). African Americans were 30 percent of the population of Detroit in 1966, but only 3.9 percent of the police officers (for an index of 0.13). Similar disparities were found in Chicago, Cleveland, and other cities.

One of the major avenues for increasing the number of African American officers has been employment discrimination litigation under Title VII of the 1964 Civil Rights Act. The concept of affirmative action and the issue of hiring quotas are discussed later in this chapter.

# Hispanic and Latino Officers

Special considerations relate to the employment of **Hispanic and Latino officers.** The 2000 Census found that the American population is changing rapidly, and the Hispanic population is growing even faster than most experts had expected. As a result, police departments increasingly serve communities where large numbers of people speak Spanish. Since the ability to communicate with people is the most important aspect of police work, it is important that police departments take active steps to ensure that they are able to communicate with Spanish-speaking people.[50]

**Hispanic and Latino officers**

The ability to speak a second language can be considered a legitimate BFOQ. Some departments subscribe to translation services that allow them to handle 911 calls in languages other than English. Having an adequate number of Spanish-speaking officers on the force is also extremely important.

Police departments can take several steps to increase the number of Hispanic officers. They can first contact community groups and leaders in the Hispanic community and arrange for personal meetings with potential applicants. A second approach might be to offer incentive pay for officers who are bilingual. Higher pay for bilingual officers is justified on the grounds that officers should receive additional compensation if they have special skills that help the department fulfill its mission. The National Latino Peace Officers Association (LPOA) helped to initiate a bilingual pay program with the California Highway Patrol in the 1970s.[51]

A former barrier to the employment of Hispanics in policing was the minimum height requirement. In 1976, the LPOA testified before the California State Personnel Board, along with a group representing Japanese Americans, and succeeded in ending the height requirement for the California Highway Patrol. Since then, minimum height requirements have been eliminated across the country.

## Police in Focus

### *Women in the Charlotte-Mecklenburg (North Carolina) Police Department*

The Charlotte-Mecklenburg, North Carolina, Police Department Web site has a special section devoted to recruiting women. In one section, current female officers describe their careers in the department. Another section debunks some myths about women and policing. Two of those myths are:

*Myth: Police work requires people who are physically imposing.*
*Fact: Police work is not all about size and muscles. You do have to pass a job-related physical ability test, but good general physical conditioning is more important than size or strength.*

*Myth: Women police are faced with a lot more situations where they must use a gun.*
*Fact: Police officers must sometimes make life and death decisions. There may be an incident which causes any officer to use deadly force. Officers receive over 120 hours of training specifically in firearms, shoot-don't-shoot scenarios, use of force, and legal training which helps prepare them for this type of situation. Statistically, though, the majority of men and women police officers retire from law enforcement without ever having to use deadly force.*

*Source:* Charlotte-Mecklenburg Police Department, at www.charmeck.org.

# Women in Policing

Lucy Duvall, one of the first female officers in Cleveland, Ohio, had a difficult and often humiliating experience as a rookie officer. The department's precinct stations did not have separate locker rooms or restrooms for women. Some of the male officers who resented womens' presence on the force deliberately changed clothes in front of them, as a form of subtle harassment.[52]

As more women entered policing, many department policies had to be changed. Old rules on hair falling below the collar were not consistent with common women's hairstyles. Police departments had to develop policies for pregnant officers. The federal Pregnancy Discrimination Act prohibits employment discrimination on the basis of pregnancy, childbirth, or any pregnancy-related medical condition.[53]

Prior to the late 1960s, police departments hired only a few women, restricted to a separate job category of "policewoman," excluded them from many assignments, including patrol, and in some departments barred them from promotion above a certain rank. Everything began to change in the late 1960s when the 1964 Civil Rights Act outlawed employment discrimination and female officers were assigned to patrol duty on an equal basis with men. Nonetheless, many forms of covert discrimination continue to exist. As a result, women are still underrepresented in police departments relative to their presence in the work force. The percentage of all sworn officers who are women increased from 2 percent in 1972 to 4.2 percent in 1978 and 10.6 percent in 2000. The National Center for Women in Policing found that women represented 13.8 percent of all sworn officers in 1998 in large departments, up from 10.6 percent in 1990. The percentage of **female officers** is generally higher in large police departments, but reaches 20 percent in only a handful of departments. Yet, in 2003, women made up over 46 percent of the adult labor force.

**female officers**

Female officers are concentrated in the lower ranks. They represent only 7.5 percent of top command positions and 9.6 percent of supervisory positions. Of the ten city departments with the largest percentage of female officers, eight were, or at some point had been, under a consent decree to hire more women. Among big-city police departments, Pittsburgh had the highest percentage of female officers, with 24.8 percent. Washington DC was a close second with 24.6 percent.[54]

# Barriers to Women in Policing

The 1998 report by the National Center for Women and Policing found a number of barriers to the employment of women. Entrance examinations that emphasize upper body physical strength favor men. There is no evidence, however, that great physical strength (as opposed to good health) affects an officer's ability to perform well. On-the-job discrimination, particularly sexual harassment and discriminatory assignments, either discourages women from applying or encourages them to resign their jobs. Many police departments, meanwhile, recruit heavily from the military, which is a male-dominated occupation. Finally, some police departments embrace an old-fashioned model of policing, emphasizing aggressiveness and authoritarianism that is unappealing to many potential women applicants.

Several police departments today make special efforts to overcome barriers to women, and have special features on their Web sites (see Charlotte-Mecklenberg at www.charmek.org).

# Gay and Lesbian Officers

Sergeant Charles Cochrane, Jr., of the New York City police department took a bold step in 1982, announcing that he was gay and planned to form an organization of gay officers in the NYPD. As a staff psychologist with the NYPD later explained, the words *gay* and *police* "did not fit together comfortably in American society [at that time] let alone in the NYPD." Four years earlier, the mayor of New York City had banned employment discrimination against homosexuals in all city agencies. The head of the police union angrily denounced the policy, arguing that it would "do more harm than good." In his view, police officers form very close working relationships with their colleagues and the employment of homosexual officers would undermine cohesion among the rank and file.[55]

Gay and lesbian people have become increasingly open as working police officers in recent years. Some departments actively recruit gay and lesbian officers. In some jurisdictions, state and local law prohibits discrimination on the basis of sexual orientation, and in jurisdictions with large gay and lesbian populations, serving the community requires serving that segment of the population. Having officers who are gay and lesbian who can serve as liaisons helps to advance a police department's mission.

How well do lesbian and gay officers fit into a police department? A study of the San Diego police department found no major conflict. Interviews with officers determined that lesbian and gay officers have experienced some subtle forms of discrimination and do not always feel respected by other officers, but in general there were no serious problems.[56]

# Achieving Diversity in Police Employment

Almost all experts in policing argue that police departments should maintain a diverse workforce that reflects the communities they serve. The U.S. Supreme Court has held that diversity is a "compelling state interest." Diversity in employment has three basic goals:

- To ensure that the employer is not discriminating and is in compliance with equal employment opportunity laws;
- To improve police service, because some experts believe that racial and ethnic minority officers will be better able to serve minority communities;
- To improve the image of a police department and lead to better police–community relations with a workforce that reflects the community.

## Employment Discrimination Suits

Employment discrimination suits under Title VII of the 1964 Civil Rights Act have been a major factor in increasing the number of minorities and women in policing. Successful suits produce a number of different results. First, they can result in direct benefit to the plaintiffs, including financial damages. Second, they often result in a court order eliminating tests or procedures that were discriminatory (e.g., height requirements that discriminated against women and Hispanics). Third, there may be a court-ordered affirmative action plan with specific goals and timetables for future recruiting.

For a full discussion of the importance of race and ethnicity in policing, see Chapter 12.

In 1980 the Los Angeles police department signed a consent decree with the U.S. Justice Department awarding $2 million in back pay and agreeing that 45 percent of all new recruits would be African American or Hispanic, and 20 percent of all new recruits would be women. By 1990, the department had met its target of having 10.9 percent African American officers out of the total force, but was still short of its goal on Hispanic officers (20 versus 24.6 percent target) and women (12 versus 20 percent target).

## The Controversy over Affirmative Action

affirmative action

The most controversial issue in police employment is **affirmative action.** The concept of affirmative action means that an employer must take positive steps (hence, "affirmative action") to remedy past discrimination. Affirmative action originated in 1965, with presidential Executive Order 11246 requiring all federal contractors to develop written affirmative action programs. Today, all private employers and government agencies receiving federal funds are required to have affirmative action plans. The basic premise of affirmative action is that simply ending discrimination (as required by the 1964 Civil Rights Act) does not automatically correct for the legacy of past discrimination.

An affirmative action plan consists of several elements. The employer must (1) conduct a census of current employees, (2) identify underutilization or concentration

---

**SIDEBAR     5 – 2**

### *Hiring Quotas: Fair or Unfair?*

A number of employment discrimination lawsuits have been settled through consent decrees that include a hiring quota for women, African Americans, or Latinos. A typical example would be the requirement that 40 percent of all new recruits be female until a specified target is reached.

Are quotas fair or unfair? Consider the following example.

Assume that a department is operating under a 40 percent quota for women. It plans to hire fifty new officers, and therefore, twenty must be women and thirty will be men. When all the test scores are compiled, the twentieth-highest-scoring female applicant has a combined score of 82 out of 100. She is hired. A male applicant who has a combined score of 83 ranked thirty-first on the men's list. He is not hired. Is this system fair? Consider the following questions. Is it fair to the male applicant who had a higher score but was not hired? Is it fair to women as a group, who have historically been denied employment with the police?

How significant is the difference between a score of 83 and a score of 82? Do those numbers really predict who will be the better police officer? How reliable are the tests that went into that composite score? If they used a general intelligence test, does it really identify who will be an effective police officer? Does a difference of a few points on a standard psychological test indicate that the person with the slightly higher score will be the better police officer? (Point of fact: The department set a combined score of 70 as the minimum for employment. Anyone with a score of 69 or lower could not be hired.)

The courts have upheld quota systems as a remedy for past discrimination. If you feel this system is unfair, what strategy would you recommend for remedying past discrimination?

of minorities and women, and (3) develop a recruiting plan to correct any under-utilization. The U.S. Equal Employment Opportunity Commission defines underutilization as "having fewer minorities or women in a particular job category than would reasonably be expected by their presence in the relevant labor market."[57] The EEO index (see p. 134) is a useful tool for identifying underutilization. Concentration is defined as the overrepresentation of minorities or women in the lowest-level job categories.

## The Question of Quotas

Affirmative action does not necessarily involve the use of quotas in hiring. Opponents of affirmative action argue that quotas involve an illegal form of **reverse discrimination.** White officers, for example, challenged the Detroit one-for-one promotion plan. In 1996, California voters approved Proposition 209, which outlawed affirmative action in state agencies.

**reverse discrimination**

Opponents of affirmative action also argue that it lowers personnel standards by forcing the employer to hire people with lower qualifications. But a PERF study found a steady rise in the levels of education among police officers from the 1960s through the late 1980s, a period that included affirmative action programs. The educational levels of white, African American, and Hispanic officers in 1988, moreover, were nearly comparable. It found that 62.2 percent of whites had some college credits, compared with 67.5 percent of Hispanics and 63.2 percent of African Americans.[58]

The question of whether affirmative action results in lower personnel standards depends on how a police department implements its affirmative action plan. If, for example, an agency hires people who do not meet the normal minimum standards, then it is lowering its standards. The intent of affirmative action is to prod employers to recruit more aggressively in order to find qualified employees. If an agency cannot meet a quota, the proper course of action is to suspend the hiring process and conduct a more vigorous recruitment effort in order to increase the size of the applicant pool.

Some critics of affirmative action cite the example of the Washington DC police department, which conducted a major hiring campaign in the early 1990s and in the process failed to conduct the standard background investigations of applicants. As a result, many unqualified officers were hired, some of whom had criminal records and eventually became corrupt officers.[59]

Two aspects of the Washington DC experience deserve comment. First, expedited hiring was directed by Congress not to increase the number of minority officers but to put more officers on the street. Second, whatever the goals of the expedited hiring, the department was irresponsible in failing to conduct standard background checks.

Do affirmative action programs achieve their goals? There is conflicting evidence on this question. Susan Martin's research on women in policing found that departments with affirmative action plans did, in fact, have a higher percentage of women in their applicant pools. And partly as a result, they hired more women as police recruits.[60] With respect to the employment of African American officers, however, a national survey of 281 police departments found that the presence of an affirmative action plan had only modest impact. The most important explanation of the employment of African American officers was the size of the African American population in the local community.[61]

## Diversity as a "Compelling State Interest"

The constitutionality of affirmative action programs is uncertain at this point. In 2003 the U.S. Supreme Court issued two decisions involving the University of Michigan. It declared unconstitutional the undergraduate admission program that automatically awarded extra points to minority applicants, because this approach was not "narrowly tailored" to achieve the goal of racial diversity. But it upheld the use of race in the law school's admission program where race is only one of many factors considered, including grades, the quality of an applicant's undergraduate college, a personal statement, letters of recommendation, and so on. In 2007, however, in two school integration cases, the Court disallowed the use of race in assigning students. These decisions suggest that the Court might declare affirmative action[62] programs in employment unconstitutional."[63]

# Police Training

## The Police Academy

**preservice training**

Significant improvements have been made in **preservice training** in police academies. The typical training period is much longer than before, covers more subjects, and is required by state law. About three-quarters of all big-city police departments operate their own police academy (officers in small departments are typically trained in state training academies).[64]

The average length of preservice training programs tripled between the 1950s and 2000, increasing from about 300 to over 1,400 hours, including both classroom and field training. In 2003, big city departments provided an average of about 1,400 hours of training, divided between over 920 hours of classroom training and 561 hours of field training. Departments in small cities typically provide much less training.[65]

The police academy experience serves several functions. First, it provides formal training. Second, it is a process for weeding out recruits who prove to be

## EXHIBIT 5–5

### Preservice Training Requirements, 2003

| Average Number of Hours Required | Classroom Academy Training | Field Training |
| --- | --- | --- |
| All Departments | 628 | 326 |
| Departments in Cities with Populations of 500,000–999,999 | 920 | 561 |

*Source:* Bureau of Justice Statistics, Local Police Departments, 2003 (Washington DC: U.S. Justice Department, 2006), Table 17.

## Police in Focus

### *What Is Taught in Training Academies?*

What do they teach in law enforcement training academies? And how much time do they devote to different subjects? The Bureau of Justice Statistics surveyed state and local training academies and found the median number of hours devoted to each of the following subjects:

*Source:* Bureau of Justice Statistics, *State and Local Law Enforcement Training Academies, 2002* (Washington DC: Department of Justice, 2005). Available at www.ncjrs.org, NCJ 204030.

| | |
|---|---|
| Firearms skills | 60 hours |
| Investigations | 45 |
| Self-defense | 44 |
| Criminal law | 40 |
| Constitutional law | 11 |
| Cultural diversity | 8 |
| Ethics and integrity | 8 |
| Community policing | 8 |

unqualified. An average of about 10 percent of all recruits fail the police academy training program, according to the ACJS survey.[66] Third, it is a rite of passage that socializes recruits into the police subculture. This subculture includes a strong ethos of identification with the profession, the department, and fellow officers.[67]

The content of police academy curricula has changed significantly, with less emphasis on the purely technical aspects of policing (e.g., effecting an arrest, booking a suspect, firing a weapon) and more on the legal and behavioral aspects. One survey found that in the 1950s, 93 percent of all firearms-related training time involved skill development in shooting; almost no time was devoted to the legal aspects of when an officer could fire a weapon or to the general issue of discretion in shooting.[68] Gradually, new subjects have been added to training curricula, including human relations, domestic violence, and ethics.

Police academy instructors vary according to background, expertise, and orientation toward education. In an observational study of three police academies, Berg developed a typology of five different categories of instructors. "Police academics" were sworn police officers who had obtained college credentials and used college-style teaching techniques. "Police careerists" were sworn officers who relied primarily on "war stories" of the lessons of their experience. "Maladaptive generalists" were officers who were not prepared to teach, who offered personal advice, and who sometimes contradicted departmental policy. "Legalists" were instructors who confined their teaching to legal issues. Finally, "civilians" were people who were not sworn officers but were specialists in some particular area.[69]

## Field Training

To supplement classroom academy training, most departments also operate field training programs. These involve practical experience in police work under the supervision of an experienced **field training officer (FTO).** A 1986 UPDATE survey found that nearly two-thirds (64 percent) of the departments had a field training

**field training officer (FTO)**

### EXHIBIT 5–6

**Tampa, Florida, Police Department Field Training and Evaluation Program (FTEP)**

**10 Reasons for a Field Training & Evaluation Program**

- A Court approved procedure, within EEOC Guidelines, for dealing with Affirmative Action Issues is provided.
- Increased support for management and administrative policies.
- The possibility of negligent hiring, retention, training, and supervision issues are reduced.
- The cost of training is controlled in that non-qualified persons are not retained by the agency.
- Standardization of training and evaluation procedure is established.
- Individual competency is identified for promotional purposes; supervisory skills are practiced by line personnel prior to promotion.
- Another career path is available to the line Officer.
- Line Officers become more involved in decision making and work in a participative environment.
- The Probationary Officer assimilates job skills more rapidly with Field Training Officer guidance.
- Field Training Officers become more capable, knowledgeable and safer as a result of their role model responsibilities.

*Source:* Tampa, Florida, Police Department Web site, www.tampagov.net.

program. More than half (57 percent) indicated that their program was directly modeled after the innovative San Jose program created in 1972.

The original San Jose FTO program consisted of sixteen weeks of classroom training, followed by fourteen weeks of field training. During field training, the recruit is assigned to three different FTOs for four-week periods each, followed by a final two weeks with the original FTO. Each FTO makes daily reports on the recruit's performance, and supervisors complete weekly evaluation reports.[70]

FTO programs also vary in quality. A sex discrimination suit by female officers in one department exposed serious problems with the existing informal postacademy field training program. The officers alleged that the field training officers were biased against them. The suit found that the FTO program had no curriculum, no performance evaluation system based on actual tasks, and no training for the field training officers. The suit resulted in a new and improved FTO program.[71] This particular case illustrates the way in which employment discrimination suits often result in general reforms of police department policies and practices.

## State Training and Certification

One of the most important changes in police training in the past thirty years has been the development of state laws requiring preservice training for all officers.

California and New York were the first states to adopt this requirement in 1959. In 1965, 85 percent of all officers received no preservice training. By the early 1980s, every state had some form of mandated training. State-mandated training has had a tremendous impact over the years.[72]

In most states, small departments send their new officers to a state training academy or program certified by the state. Some programs are operated through community colleges. The separate police academies run by the large police departments are similarly certified by the state. The minimum state training requirements are usually lower, in terms of the number of hours of training, than the programs operated by big-city police academies. Officers who complete state training are then certified or licensed as peace officers in the state.

If a police officer has been fired by one department, should he or she be hired by another law enforcement agency? Many people worry about the problem of the "gypsy cops" who move from one department to another despite bad performance histories. There has never been any national registry of officers and their career patterns. An applicant may simply lie and not tell a police department that he or she was fired by another department. Many small agencies may not have the resources to do a thorough background investigation. Some, in fact, may not care. One partial solution to this problem is state certification of officers with procedures for **decertification.**[73]

**decertification**

A majority of states (thirty-nine) now have procedures for decertifying officers by revoking their license to work as police officers in the state. Decertification addresses the problem of officers who are fired from one department for misconduct but are then hired by another. If they are decertified, this is not possible. The process does not, however, prevent the fired officer from being hired in another state (assuming the individual meets the requirements and the hiring department does not check the person's work history).[74]

Florida was one of the first states to adopt a comprehensive decertification process. Between 1976 and 1983 the Florida Criminal Justice Standards and Training Commission took action against 148 officers. It decertified 132, suspended 14, and placed 2 on probation. Most cases involved private or departmental misconduct; only 22 of the 148 involved official misconduct.[75]

## Shortcomings of Current Police Training

Do police training programs cover the really important aspects of police work? This book later explains that officers routinely exercise tremendous discretion (Chapter 11). They also deal with a lot of difficult social problems such as domestic disputes and mental health problems (Chapter 8). Only some of these incidents involve an arrest. Use of deadly force, moreover, is a very rare event. Do police training programs adequately cover the kinds of situations that occur most frequently, or are they too heavily weighted toward criminal law enforcement and infrequent critical incidents?

Despite the recent improvements, police training programs suffer from a number of limitations. Many programs still do not cover important subjects, such as discretion, the use of informants, and ethics. Also, preservice training by itself may not adequately prepare officers for the tasks they face. A one-hour police academy lecture on spouse abuse, for example, may have no effect on how officers handle a domestic violence incident months or years later. A short session on mental illness may not prepare officers to recognize serious mental illness or provide adequate guidance on how to handle mentally ill people.

The Detroit police department conducted an experimental training program for recruits on dealing with crime victims. An evaluation found that crime victims did not rate officers who had received the training any better than officers who had not been through the program. (Both groups of officers, in fact, received very high ratings.) Even more serious, all recruits experienced a significant change in attitudes after being out on the street, developing significantly less positive attitudes toward the public.[76]

McNamara found a similar shift in attitudes after one year on the street in a study of New York City recruits.[77] These findings lend support to the argument advanced by Skolnick that the working environment of policing—rather than background characteristics or training—is the principal factor in shaping police officer attitudes and behavior.[78] The police subculture is discussed in more detail in Chapter 6.

Because of persistent police–community relations problems (Chapter 12), most departments have introduced race relations, human relations, or cultural diversity training into the curriculum. A review of cultural diversity training programs, however, found that the content has not changed much since the 1960s, that they tend to perpetuate negative stereotypes about racial and ethnic minorities, and that they focus on the attitudes of individual officers and ignore the policies of the department as a whole.[79]

Alpert, Smith, and Watters argue that "mere classroom training" on issues such as race relations "is insufficient." In particular, they recommend experimenting with training officers in communication skills with racial and ethnic groups "other than their own."[80]

## The Probationary Period

Upon completing preservice training, a recruit is sworn in and assigned to regular duty. The officer is on probationary status for a period that may range from six months to two years, depending upon the department (some departments count the time in training as part of this period). In 1994 the average length was about one year.[81]

probationary period

During the **probationary period** an officer can be dismissed without cause. After the probationary period is completed, dismissal must be based on cause under rules established by the local civil service regulations and/or police union contract.

An average of about 7 percent of all recruits were rejected during their probationary period in 2003.[82] Susan Martin found significant differences in how departments used the probationary period, however. In Phoenix, 47 percent of all officers who left the department were on probation at the time. This included 26 percent of all female recruits and 14 percent of all males. In Washington DC, however, only 15 percent of those leaving the department were in the probationary phase (representing 5 percent of both males and females).[83]

Many experts argue that a longer probationary period permits more time for observing performance and an opportunity to dismiss those whose performance is unsatisfactory. In Philadelphia the six-month probationary period includes nineteen weeks of academy training, leaving only a seven-week period of on-the-street experience. A report found this "insufficient to allow supervisors to determine whether a particular candidate is qualified to be a police officer" and recommended at least a six-month probationary period following completion of academy training.[84]

# Case Study

*Excerpt from the President's Commission on Law Enforcement and Administration of Justice,* The Challenge of Crime in a Free Society

*The Commission recommends:*

**Police departments should take immediate steps to establish a minimum requirement of a baccalaureate degree for all supervisory and executive positions.**

The long-range objective for high-ranking officers should be advanced degrees in the law, sociology, criminology, police or public administration, business management, or some other appropriate specialty. Of equal importance with his education is a police candidate's aptitude for the job: his intelligence, his moral character, his emotional stability, his social attitudes. The consequences of putting on the street officers who, however highly educated, are prejudiced, or slow witted, or hot tempered, or timid, or dishonest are too obvious to require detailed discussion. Thorough personal screening of police candidates is a clear necessity. The amount of thoroughness with which local departments screen candidates varies enormously. Some departments screen quite sketchily; others, including those in many of the biggest cities, make in-depth background investigations, administer intelligence tests and interview candidates exhaustively. However, it is fair to say that even the most thorough departments do not evaluate reliably the personal traits and characteristics that contribute to good police work, not because they lack the desire to do so but because a technique for doing so does not exist. Clearly this is a field in which intensive research is needed.

*Source:* President's Commission on Law Enforcement and Administration of Justice, *The Challenge of Crime in a Free Society* (Washington DC: Government Printing Office, 1967), p. 110.

# Summary

The profile of the American police officer has changed significantly over the past twenty-five years. There are now more racial-minority, female, and college-educated officers than ever before. Many old personnel practices have been eliminated because they discriminated against particular groups.

Meanwhile, the training of officers has improved substantially during the same period. In short, the police recruit of today is a very different kind of person from the recruit of twenty-five years ago.

## Key Terms

career perspective, 122
stereotypes about cops, 122
civil service system, 123
minimum age level, 124
criminal record, 126
residency requirements, 127
job security, 128
oral interviews, 130

background investigations, 130
Title VII of the 1964 Civil
  Rights Act, 132
bona fide occupational
  qualifications (BFOQ), 132
equal employment opportunity
  (EEO) index, 134
Hispanic and Latino officers, 135

female officers, 136
affirmative action, 138
reverse discrimination, 139
preservice training, 140
field training officer (FTO), 141
decertification, 143
probationary period, 144

## For Discussion

Over thirty years ago, the President's Crime Commission recommended that all police officers have an undergraduate baccalaureate degree. When the commission made this recommendation, there was very little research on policing (either on police work or on police officers). We have learned much more about policing since then.

In light of this research, discuss the commission's recommendation.

1. Is it a good strategy for improving policing?
2. What are the underlying assumptions of this approach?
3. What evidence do we have that it improves policing?

## Internet Exercises

**Exercise 1** How do the recruitment standards for the law enforcement agencies in your area compare with those in other parts of the country? First, select a list of agencies in your area. Choose either the agencies in your immediate metropolitan area (which would include the major city police department and suburban departments) or the state, or, for example, a multistate region if applicable (say, for example, the Kansas City area, which would include two states and a combination of city and suburban departments). Second, use the Web to identify the minimum qualifications for each agency. Most (but not all) agencies post employment criteria on their Web site. Third, compile the data in a table that is easily readable. Are there any significant differences in employment standards by size of agency or other factor? Does any particular agency appear to have relatively low standards?

**Exercise 2** Some police departments have special hiring provisions for applicants who are bilingual. This represents an effort to increase the number of officers who can speak Spanish, or Vietnamese, or some other language. Often, the special provision involves granting extra points in the application process. First, identify cities with large Hispanic/Latino and/or Asian populations. Data from the 2000 Census are available on the Web. One place to start looking would be **www.refdesk.com.** Then, search the Web sites of the police departments in those cities (**www.officer.com**). Identify any cities that are making special efforts to hire bilingual officers. How prevalent are such efforts? What special provisions do these efforts involve?

# Notes

1. "Change Has Come to the LAPD Too," *Los Angeles Times,* January 21, 2009. 1986 data from Christopher Commission, *Report of the Independent Commission on the Los Angeles Police Department* (Los Angeles: The Commission, 1991), p. 23. Available at www.parc.info.

2. Arthur Niederhoffer, *Behind the Shield: The Police in Urban Society* (Garden City, NY: Anchor Books, 1967), p. 1.

3. David H. Bayley and Harold Mendelsohn, *Minorities and the Police: Confrontation in America* (New York: The Free Press, 1969).

4. National Center for Women and Policing, *Recruiting and Retaining Women: A Self-Assessment Guide for Law Enforcement* (Los Angeles: National Center for Women and Policing, 2001), p. 43. www.womenandpolicing.org.

5. George W. Griesinger, Jeffrey S. Slovak, and Joseph J. Molkup, *Civil Service Systems: Their Impact on Police Administration* (Washington DC: Government Printing Office, 1979).

6. Pennsylvania, Municipal Police Officers Standards and Training Council Regulations. www.mpostc.state.pa.us/.

7. Robert Langworthy, Thomas Hughes, and Beth Sanders, *Law Enforcement Recruitment, Selection and Training: A Survey of Major Police Departments in the U.S.* (Highland Heights, KY: ACJS, 1995), p. 24.

8. President's Commission on Law Enforcement and Administration of Justice, *Task Force Report: The Police* (Washington DC: Government Printing Office, 1967), p. 130.

9. Langworthy, Hughes, and Sanders, *Law Enforcement Recruitment, Selection and Training,* p. 24.

10. "Weighty Matters: Court Rules Against Ohio Troopers in Fitness-Standards Suit," *Law Enforcement News* (February 2, 1997), p. 1.

11. Bureau of Justice Statistics, *Local Police Departments, 2003* (Washington DC: Government Printing Office, 2006). Available at www.ncjrs.gov.

12. David L. Carter, Allen D. Sapp, and Darrell W. Stephens, *The State of Police Education* (Washington DC: Police Executive Research Forum, 1989), p. 84.

13. Chicago Police Department, "Career Information." https://chicagopolice.org.

14. Michael Heidingsfield, "Six Reasons to Require College Education for Police Officers," *Subject to Debate* 9 (December 1995): pp. 5–7; President's Commission on Law Enforcement and Administration of Justice, *The Challenge of Crime in a Free Society* (Washington DC: Government Printing Office, 1967), p. 109.

15. Wesley G. Skogan and Susan M. Hartnett, *Community Policing, Chicago Style* (New York: Oxford University Press, 1997), pp. 70–109.

16. David L. Carter, Allen D. Sapp, and Darrel W. Stephens, "Higher Education as a Bona Fide Occupational Qualification (BFOQ) for Police: A Blueprint," *American Journal of Police* 7 (Fall 1988): pp. 1–27; *Davis v. City of Dallas,* 777 F.2d 205 (5th Cir. 1985); David L. Carter and Allen D. Sapp, *Police Education and Minority Recruitment: The Impact of a College Requirement* (Washington DC: PERF, 1991); p. 27.

17. Michael D. White, "Identifying Good Cops Early: Predicting Recruit Performance in the Academy," *Police Quarterly,* (2008): pp. 27–49.

18. M. L. Dantzker, "Do College Education Requirements for Police Create an Overeducation Problem?" *Subject to Debate* 9 (December 1995): p. 4.

19. Griesinger et al., *Civil Service Systems,* p. 102.

20. Department of Health and Human Services, *2002 National Survey on Drug Use and Public Health* (Washington DC: Department of Health and Human Services, 2003), Table 1.1b. Available at www.samhsa.gov.

21. American Civil Liberties Union of Southern California, *From the Outside In: Residency Patterns within the Los Angeles Police Department* (Los Angeles: ACLU-Southern California, 1994): p. i.

22. Bureau of Justice Statistics, *Law Enforcement Management and Administrative Statistics, 2000* (Washington DC: Department of Justice, 2004). www.ncjrs.org. NCJ 2033350; Langworthy, Hughes, and Sanders, *Law Enforcement Recruitment, Selection and Training,* p. 24; New York City Civilian Complaint Review Board, *Annual Report 1993* (New York: CCRB, 1993): p. 28. www.nyc.gov/html/ccrb/home/html.

23. Langworthy, Hughes, and Sanders, *Law Enforcement Recruitment, Selection and Training,* p. 23.

24. M. Steven Meagher and Nancy Yentes, "Choosing a Career in Policing: A Comparison of Male and Female Perceptions," *Journal of Police Science and Administration* 14, no. 4 (1986): pp. 320–27; Virginia B. Ermer, "Recruitment of Female Police

Officers in New York City," *Journal of Criminal Justice* 6, no. 3 (Fall 1978): pp. 233–46.

25. Griesinger et al., *Civil Service Systems.*

26. Nicholas Alex, *New York Cops Talk Back* (New York: John Wiley, 1976): p. 9.

27. Ermer, "Recruitment of Female Police Officers"; James Q. Wilson, "Generational and Ethnic Differences among Career Police Officers," *American Journal of Sociology* 69 (March 1964): p. 526.

28. Bayley and Mendelsohn, *Minorities and the Police,* p. 30.

29. Robert J. Kaminski, "Police Minority Recruitment: Predicting Who Will Say Yes to an Offer for a Job as a Cop," *Journal of Criminal Justice* 21 (1993): pp. 395–409.

30. Susan E. Martin, *On the Move*: *The Status of Women in Policing* (Washington DC: The Police Foundation, 1990).

31. Langworthy, Hughes, and Sanders, *Law Enforcement Recruitment, Training and Selection,* p. 26.

32. Bernard Cohen, "Minority Retention in the New York City Police Department: A Policy Study," *Criminology* 11 (November 1973): pp. 287–306.

33. Bureau of Justice Statistics, *Local Police Departments, 2003,* p. 8.

34. Langworthy, Hughes, and Sanders, *Law Enforcement Recruitment, Selection and Training,* p. 27.

35. William G. Doerner, "The Utility of the Oral Interview Board in Selecting Police Academy Admissions," *Policing* 20, no. 4 (1997): p. 784.

36. Langworthy, Hughes, and Sanders, *Law Enforcement Recruitment, Selection and Training,* p. 29.

37. Anthony V. Bouza, "The Policeman's Character Investigation: Lowered Standards or Changing Times?" *Journal of Criminal Law, Criminology, and Police Science* 63 (March 1972): pp. 120–24.

38. "D.C. Police Force Still Paying for Two-Year Hiring Spree," *Washington Post* (August 28, 1994).

39. Bernard Cohen and Jan M. Chaiken, *Police Background Characteristics and Performance* (Lexington, MA: Lexington Books, 1973): pp. 87, 90–91.

40. J. Douglas Grant and Joan Grant, "Officer Selection and the Prevention of Abuse of Force," in W.A. Geller and H. Toch, eds., *And Justice for All* (Washington DC: PERF, 1995): pp. 161–62.

41. Benjamin S. Wright, William G. Doerner, and John C. Speir, "Pre-employment Psychological Testing as a Predictor of Police Performance during an FTO Program," *American Journal of Police,* IX, no. 4 (1990): pp. 65–84.

42. Christopher Commission, *Report of the Independent Commission on the Los Angeles Police Department,* p. 110.

43. Paula Rubin, *Civil Rights and Criminal Justice: Employment Discrimination Overview* (Washington DC: Government Printing Office, 1995): p. 102.

44. *Davis v. City of Dallas,* 777 F.2d 205.

45. Paula N. Rubin, *The Americans With Disabilities Act and Criminal Justice: An Overview* (Washington DC: Government Printing Office, 1993). www.ncjrs.org, NCJ 155061.

46. David Alan Sklansky, "Not Your Father's Police Department: Making Sense of the New Demographics of Law Enforcement," *Journal of Criminal Law and Criminology,* 96 (Spring 2006): 1209–1213.

47. The data appear in various reports which do not always present them in the same form. Bureau of Justice Statistics, *Police Departments in Large Cities, 1990–2000* (Washington DC: Department of Justice, 2002). www.ncjrs.org, NCJ 175703.

48. CALEA, Standards for Law Enforcement Agencies, 4th ed. (Fairfax, VA: CALEA, 1998). www.calea.org.

49. Samuel Walker, *Employment of Black and Hispanic Police Officers* (Omaha: University of Nebraska at Omaha, 1983); William G. Lewis, "Toward a Representative Bureaucracy," *Public Administration Review,* 49 (May–June, 1989): pp. 257–67.

50. Leigh Herbst and Samuel Walker, "Language Barriers in the Delivery of Police Services," *Journal of Criminal Justice* 29 (July 2001): pp. 1–12.

51. National Latino Peace Officers Association, "History" (www.nlpoa.com/history), p. 4.

52. Tamar Husansky and Pat Sparling,—*Working Vice: The True Story of Lt. Lucy Duvall—America's First Woman Vice Squad Chief* (New York: Harper Paperbacks, 1993).

53. National Center for Women and Policing, *Equality Denied: The Status of Women in Policing* (Los Angeles: National Center for Women and Policing, 1998). www.womenandpolicing.org.

54. National Center for Women and Policing, *Equality Denied,* pp. 2, 10.

55. Patrick Suraci, Ph.D., "The Beginning of GOAL" (www.goalny.org).

56. Aaron Belkin and Jason McNichol, "Pink and Blue: Outcomes Associated With the Integration of Open Gay and Lesbian Personnel in the San Diego Police Department," *Police Quarterly* 5 (March 2002): pp. 63–95.

57. U.S. Equal Employment Opportunity Commission, *Affirmative Action and Equal Employment,* Vol. 1

(Washington DC: Government Printing Office, 1974), p. 23.

58. David L. Carter, Allen D. Sapp, and Darrel W. Stephens, *The State of Police Education* (Washington DC: Police Executive Research Forum, 1988).

59. "D.C. Police Force Paying for Two-Year Hiring Spree," *Washington Post,* August 28, 1994.

60. Martin, *On the Move,* p. 39

61. Jihong Zhao and Nicholas Lovrich, "Determinants of Minority Employment in American Municipal Police Agencies: The Representation of African American Officers," *Journal of Criminal Justice* 26, no. 4 (1998): pp. 267–78.

62. Ibid.

63. *Gratz v. Bollinger,* 539 US 244 (2003); *Grutter v. Bollinger,* 539 US 306 (2003); *Parents Involved in Community Schools v. Seattle,* 551 U.S. 701 (2007); *Meredith v. Jefferson County,* 551 U.S. 782 (2007).

64. Langworthy, Hughes, and Sanders, *Law Enforcement Recruitment, Selection and Training,* p. 32.

65. Thomas M. Frost and Magnus J. Seng, "The Administration of Police Training, A Thirty Year Perspective," *Journal of Police Science and Administration* 12 (March 1984): pp. 66–73; Bureau of Justice Statistics, *Local Police Departments, 2003.*

66. Langworthy, Hughes, and Sanders, *Law Enforcement Recruitment, Selection and Training,* p. 32.

67. William A. Westley, *Violence and the Police* (Cambridge, MA: MIT Press, 1970): pp. 153–59; Richard N. Harris, *Police Academy: An Inside View* (New York: John Wiley, 1973).

68. Frost and Seng, "Police Entry-Level Curriculum: A Thirty Year Perspective," *Journal of Police Science and Administration,* 12 (September 1984): p. 254.

69. Bruce L. Berg, "Who Should Teach Police: A Typology and Assessment of Police Academy Instructors," *American Journal of Police* IX, no. 2 (1990): pp. 79–100.

70. Michael S. Campbell, *Field Training for Police Officers: State of the Art* (Washington DC: Government Printing Office, 1986).

71. William G. Doerner and E. Britt Patterson, "The Influence of Race and Gender Upon Rookie Evaluations of their Field Training Officers," *American Journal of Police* XI, no. 2 (1992): pp. 23–36.

72. Richard C. Lumb, ed., *Sourcebook of Standards and Training Information in the United States* (Charlotte University of North Carolina at Charlotte, 1993); President's Commission on Law Enforcement and Administration of Justice, *Task Force Report: The Police,* p. 138.

73. J. Middleton-Hope, "Misconduct Among Previously Experienced Officers: Issues in the Recruitment and Hiring of 'Gypsy cops'," *St. Louis University Public Law Review* 22 (No. 1, 2003): pp. 173–184.

74. Steven Puro, Roger Goldman, and William C. Smith, "Police Decertification: Changing Patterns among the States, 1985–1995," *Policing 20,* no. 3 (1997): pp. 481–96.

75. Roger Goldman and Steven Puro, "Decertification of Police: An Alternative to Traditional Remedies for Police Misconduct," *Hastings Constitutional Law Quarterly* 15 (Fall 1987): pp. 45–80.

76. Arthur J. Lurigio and Dennis P. Rosenbaum, "The Travails of the Detroit Police–Victims Experiment: Assumptions and Important Lessons," *American Journal of Police* XI, no. 3 (1992): pp. 1–34.

77. McNamara, "Uncertainties in Police Work."

78. Jerome H. Skolnick, *Justice without Trial,* 3rd ed. (New York: Macmillan, 1994).

79. Jerome L. Blakemore, David Barlow, and Deborah L. Padgett, "From the Classroom to the Community: Introducing Process in Police Diversity Training," *Police Studies* XVIII, no. 1 (1995): pp. 71–83.

80. Geoffrey P. Alpert, William C. Smith, and Daniel Watters, "Implications of the Rodney King Beating," *Criminal Law Bulletin* 28 (September–October 1992): p. 477.

81. Langworthy, Hughes, and Sanders, *Law Enforcement Recruitment, Selection, and Training,* p. 39.

82. Bureau of Justice Statistics, *Local Police Departments, 2003,* Table 8.

83. Martin, *On the Move,* pp. 131–32.

84. Philadelphia Police Study Task Force, *Philadelphia and Its Police: Toward a New Partnership* (Philadelphia: City of Philadelphia, 1986): p. 94.

# Police Officers II: On the Job

A fter completing the probationary period, a police officer becomes a full-fledged sworn officer, and begins a career. Many factors influence the course of a career. Some officers are promoted, while others remain at the rank of police officer for their entire careers. Some quit, while some are fired. Officers' attitudes about the job, the profession, the department, and citizens often change over time. This chapter examines the experience of being on the job as a police officer.

# Reality Shock: Beginning Police Work

The first weeks and months on the job for a new police officer are often a rude awakening. In his classic study of the police subculture, Westley calls the experience **"reality shock."**[1] The new officer quickly encounters the unpleasant aspects of dealing with the public, the criminal justice system, and the department.

**reality shock**

## Encountering Citizens

Police officer attitudes toward the public change significantly during the first weeks and months on the job. McNamara found that the percentage of officers agreeing with the statement "Patrolmen almost never receive the cooperation from the public that is needed to handle police work properly" rose from 35 percent at the beginning of academy training to 50 percent after two years on the job.[2] A similar change in attitudes occurred among new Detroit police officers After four months on the job, officers gave substantially lower ranking to the importance of "listening attentively when the victim expresses feelings or emotions."[3]

Changes in officers' attitudes are partly the result of encountering **hostility from citizens.** As explained in Chapter 5, most officers enter law enforcement

**hostility from citizens**

because they want to work with people and help the community. Even though citizen hostility is statistically infrequent (about 10 percent of all encounters), officers tend to remember such experiences. Recalling unpleasant or traumatic experiences is a phenomenon common to all people.[4]

Officers particularly resent official complaints filed by citizens, which are then investigated by the department's internal affairs unit or an external citizen oversight agency. A study by the Denver Office of the Independent Monitor, however, found that much of the resentment involves the process of investigating complaints. As a result of reforms instituted by the OIM, officer satisfaction with the process rose from 12 percent to 34 percent. Even more dramatically, the percentage of officers reporting that the information they provided to investigators was taken seriously rose from 24 percent before the reforms to 78 percent afterwards.[5]

Officers also react to being stereotyped, as citizens respond to their uniform, badge, and gun, rather than to them as individuals. As is the case with racial stereotyping, people find it unpleasant to be treated as a category rather than as an individual. Additionally, many citizens feel uncomfortable around a person with arrest powers. To avoid these reactions, police officers tend to socialize primarily with other officers, thereby increasing their isolation from the public.[6]

Police officer attitudes also change because they perform society's "dirty work," handling unpleasant tasks that no one else wants to perform or is able to handle. The police see humanity at its worst. They are the first people to find the murder victim, or the victim of rape, domestic violence, or child abuse. In one study, for example, officers ranked dealing with an abused child as the most stressful kind of situation they encounter.[7] These experiences accumulate over time, and eventually give officers a very negative view of humanity.

Additionally, when police officers refer to "the public," they include the news media and elected officials. They are generally very unhappy with the news media, seeing it emphasizing the negative aspects of policing (an officer-involved shooting, allegations of excessive force) and ignoring the positive aspects. Police officers also believe that elected officials ("politicians") try to interfere with police operations (e.g., demanding more patrol coverage in their neighborhood) and do not understand the basic elements of policing.

## Encountering the Criminal Justice System

**insiders**

A second shock involves learning about the criminal justice system. Police officers are **"insiders,"** who get to see firsthand how the system works. They see arrests dismissed, or serious crimes plea-bargained to lesser offenses. They observe incompetent prosecutors, defense attorneys, and judges. As a result, many become cynical about the ability of the system to be fair and effective. Generally, police officers believe that the courts are too lenient.[8] Only 27 percent of police officers in Washington DC expressed trust in the courts, compared with 63 percent who expressed trust in their department commanders.[9]

Officers also often feel they are not respected by lawyers and judges. When they testify in court, defense attorneys challenge the quality of their work, and judges sometimes exclude evidence or confessions they have obtained.[10]

# Encountering the Department

When researchers asked New York City police officers what they disliked about being a cop, most cited aspects of their own department, not hostility from citizens. The most frequently mentioned problem was that the leadership of their department "doesn't care" about them, followed by "precinct-level supervisors." "Lack of respect from the public" was third in this survey.[11]

The survey of NYPD officers documents the disillusionment of new officers with their own department. They discover that **"department politics"** affects decisions about assignments and promotion. They discover that some of their supervisors are incompetent and that hard work is not rewarded.[12]

**department politics**

As in other large organizations, conflict exists between the rank and file and the top command. A study of Washington DC police officers found that while 82 percent were satisfied with their jobs and 87 percent expressed trust in their fellow officers, 63 percent trusted their commanders and only 51 percent expressed trust in the chief of police.[13] Conflict between the rank and file and top management is now channeled through police unions (see Chapter 4) and is often handled through an established grievance procedure. Finally, as discussed below, many police departments are characterized by internal conflicts along racial, ethnic, and gender lines.

# Initial Assignment

## Impact of the Seniority System

New officers are typically assigned to patrol duty, usually in high-crime areas and on the evening shift. Assignments in most police departments are governed by civil service procedures or union contracts that embody the principle of **seniority.** Officers with more experience have first priority in requesting assignments. This leaves the least desirable assignments to the new officers.[14]

**seniority**

The seniority principle has both good and bad points. On the positive side, it eliminates favoritism and discrimination. In the 1960s, for example, the President's Crime Commission found that some departments assigned their worst officers to black neighborhoods.[15] On the negative side, it means that the least experienced officers get the most difficult assignments: patrolling the highest-crime neighborhoods on the busiest shift with the most crime and calls for service. A related consequence is that in departments that have significantly improved their personnel standards, the younger officers are likely to be better qualified and better trained for such work than the older officers. At the same time, in departments that have recently hired significant numbers of racial and ethnic minority or female officers, they will be disproportionately represented in the least desirable assignments, such as assignment to high-crime precincts.[16]

# The Idea of a Unique Police Subculture

Is there a unique police subculture? Are there a set of attitudes and behaviors among police officers that are fundamentally different from those in other occupations? This section reviews the original concept of a police subculture and then examines the recent criticisms of that concept.

> ### SIDEBAR     6 – 1
>
> ### *Issue for Discussion: The Impact of the Seniority System*
>
> The seniority system means that rookie officers will generally be assigned to patrol in the highest-crime neighborhoods during the busiest shift (usually 4:00 P.M. to midnight) when most of the serious crime occurs.
>
> Is this a good system for assigning officers? Does it result in the best police service in those times and places that demand the most skill?
>
> Discuss the major drawbacks to this system. What are the advantages? Can you devise an alternative system?

## The Original Concept

**police subculture**

William Westley tells a poignant and revealing story about his pioneering research on the **police subculture.** When his interviews in the Gary, Indiana, police department began to touch on a particularly sensitive subject, the officers stopped talking to him. Eventually, he explained to a sergeant that his career would be ruined if he could not complete his research. The sergeant then "gave the officers hell" for not helping him, and immediately afterward they were extremely cooperative. Westley's experience illuminates two aspects of the police subculture: on the one hand, an attitude of secrecy toward outsiders studying the department, and on the other hand, a genuine eagerness to help someone having difficulty with his assignment. The basic point is that the so-called police subculture is an extremely complex phenomenon.[17]

Westley's study approached the police from the perspective of occupational sociology, seeking "to isolate and identify the major social norms governing police conduct, and to describe the way in which they influence police action in specific situations."[18] He concluded that a distinct subculture exists among police officers, emphasizing secrecy, solidarity, and violence. In his view, police officers view the public as the "enemy" and believe that they are justified in lying to protect other officers from criticism by citizens, and also in using force against citizens.

Selective contact with the public, Westley argues, is one of the main sources of the police subculture. Officers rarely meet the average person but, instead, meet people with problems who often resent police presence. Officers also resent the fact that the other professionals they routinely deal with—lawyers, news reporters, social workers, and so on—have negative attitudes about the police.[19] In the face of perceived public hostility, Westley continues, officers believe they can rely only on their fellow officers in times of crisis. Among the officers he interviewed, 73 percent thought citizens were hostile to the police.[20]

**group solidarity**

Hostility to the public encourages a strong sense of **group solidarity.** An officer in Washington DC explains that "I've been working with my partner now for two and one-half years. I think I know more about him than his wife does . . . He knows everything about me: I think you get a certain relationship when you work together with a partner.[21] The very nature of police work—working closely together, often spending long hours together in a patrol car, facing the same uncertainties and danger—fosters a very strong sense of group solidarity.

**Secrecy** is a consequence of both public hostility and group solidarity. Secrecy serves "as a shield against the attacks of the outside world." Secrecy, in turn, justifies lying. Westley asked officers if they would report a fellow officer who took money from a citizen (a person arrested for drunkenness). A total of 73 percent said they would not. Westley concluded that most officers believed that "illegal action is preferable to breaking the secrecy of the group."[22] A national study by the Police Foundation found that over half (52.4 percent) of all officers agree with the statement that "it is not unusual for a police officer to turn a blind eye to improper conduct by other officers."[23]

**secrecy**

An important aspect of secrecy is the **"code of silence,"** which involves not testifying against other officers accused of misconduct, for example, in a citizen complaint. The Christopher Commission reported a Los Angeles police officer saying, "It is basically a non-written rule that you do not roll over, tell on your partner, your companion."[24] In the Police Foundation study, almost 17 percent believed that the "code of silence is an essential part" of good policing.[25] The code of silence is perhaps the most serious obstacle to police accountability and the reduction of both corruption and police use of excessive force (see Chapter 14)

**code of silence**

For a discussion of the impact of the "code of silence" on investigations of police corruption, see Chapter 13.

Westley also found that public hostility and group solidarity justify violence against citizens. Officers feel a need to use force to maintain respect in encounters with citizens. More than a third of the officers (39 percent) surveyed by Westley thought that they were justified in using force when faced with citizen disrespect. Two-thirds of the

---

**SIDEBAR    6 – 2**

## *The Code of Silence in Operation*

The pervasiveness of the code of silence is itself alarming. But what we found particularly troubling is that it often appears to be strongest where corruption is most frequent. This is because the loyalty ethic is particularly powerful in crime-ridden precincts where officers most depend upon each other for their safety each day—and where fear and alienation from the community are most rampant. Thus, the code of silence influences honest officers in the very precincts where their assistance is needed most.

The pervasiveness of the code of silence is bolstered by the grave consequences for violating it: Officers who report misconduct are ostracized and harassed; become targets of complaints and even physical threats; and are made to fear that they will be left alone on the streets in a time of crisis. This draconian enforcement of the code of silence fuels corruption because it makes corrupt cops feel protected and invulnerable. As former police officer Bernard Cawley testified at the public hearings:

Question: Were you ever afraid that one of your fellow officers might turn you in?

Answer: Never.

Question: Why not?

Answer: Because it was the Blue Wall of Silence. Cops don't tell on cops. And if they did tell on them, just say if a cop decided to tell on me, his career's ruined. He's going to be labeled as a rat. So if he's got fifteen more years to go on the job, he's going to be miserable because it follows you wherever you go.

*Source:* Mollen Commission, *Report of the Commission to Investigate Allegations of Police Corruption and the Anti-Corruption Procedures of the Police Department* (New York: Mollen Commission, 1994). Available at www.parc.info.

officers (66 percent) gave some rationalization for the illegal use of force.[26] In a more recent study, the Police Foundation survey found that about one-quarter (24.5 percent) of all officers agree that "it is sometimes acceptable to use more force than is legally allowable to control someone who physically assaults an officer."[27]

Jerome Skolnick expanded on Westley's concept of a police subculture in his classic study, *Justice Without Trial*. He found that police officers develop a "working personality" shaped by two aspects of the police role: danger and authority. Because the potential for danger is an ever-present feature of police work, officers become routinely suspicious of all people. Officers develop a "perceptual shorthand" of visual cues associated with people they believe are criminals or potentially dangerous. These visual cues include gender, age, apparent income level, styles of clothing and behavior, and in many cases race or ethnicity. The cues become a form of stereotyping involving young low-income racial and ethnic minority men, and is the basis of racial profiling.[28] This aspect of the police subculture is a major contributor to police–community relations problems (Chapter 12).

## The Capacity to Use Force

Egon Bittner, in another classic essay, expanded on Skolnick's argument about police authority. He argues that the capacity to use force is the defining feature of the police, distinguishing them from other occupations.[29] Bittner points out that no other occupation has the power to deprive people of their liberty (arrest), use physical force, and take human life. These powers are inherent in the police role and apply to every sworn officer. The uniform, the badge, and an officer's weapon are the convenient symbols of these unique powers. Citizens are very aware of these symbols and the power they represent. An officer rarely has to explicitly remind someone that he or she could be arrested.

## Danger: Potential versus Actual

Police work is dangerous. Officers are killed and injured in the line of duty every year. But danger plays out in complex ways in the minds of police officers. Skolnick argues that the *potential* for danger, especially attacks by citizens, also shapes the police subculture. The potential for danger is omnipresent, even if actual danger occurs only rarely. Occupational safety data show that police work is not the most dangerous occupation. Mining and construction consistently have higher rates of on-the-job deaths.[30] Danger in policing is also very different from danger in other occupations. In policing, threats involve criminal violence, while in other occupations danger involves accidents. In fact, measured in terms of felonious killings of police officers, police work has actually become much safer in the last 20 years. The felonious death rate per 100,000 officers fell by almost two-thirds between 1976 and 1998 (see Exhibit 6–1).[31]

## Conflicting Demands: Law versus Order

Skolnick also argued that policing involves a conflict between the demands of law and the demands of order. To maintain order, officers are under pressure to "produce," meaning getting results through arrests and convictions. The law, however, limits

## EXHIBIT 6-1

### Felonious Death Rate per 100,000 Police Officers

Police Officers Murdered by Felons,
Rate per 100,000 Officers

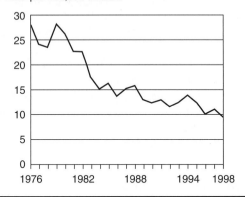

police powers in order to protect the rights of individual citizens. The result of this conflict is that officers feel pressured to evade or bend the rules to obtain physical evidence or confessions.[32] The Police Foundation found that almost half (42.9 percent) of all officers agree that "always following the rules is not compatible with getting the job done." In his classic study, Herbert Packer defines the tension between the demand for results and the rule of law as a conflict between "crime control" values and "due process" values.[33]

# New Perspectives on the Police Subculture

David Sklansky argues persuasively that because of the dramatic changes in the demographic composition of law enforcement agencies over the past 35 years, it is "Not Your Father's Police Department" anymore. One result is that the traditional view of the police subculture is no longer relevant. "Police officers are far less unified today and far less likely to have an us-them view of civilians."[34]

The original concept of a police subculture developed by Westley and Skolnick has been criticized as methodologically flawed. Reviewing the literature, Joel Lefkowitz concludes that "a significant portion of the relevant literature is primarily mere opinion." Moreover, "almost all of the research studies reviewed are methodologically inadequate to the task of supporting reasonable inferences" about the existence or origins of a police personality. Much of the early research was impressionistic (e.g., Skolnick), based on small samples (e.g., Westley), or imprecise in the specification of key concepts.[35]

Lefkowitz concludes that the personalities of police officers "do differ in systematic ways from the rest of the population, but differ in an evaluatively neutral sense." In short, police officers are somewhat different, but their personality traits are not pathological. In their study of Denver police officers, Bayley and Mendelsohn found that "on all personality scales the data show that policemen are absolutely average people." Research on police officers' reasons for choosing law enforcement as a career has consistently found that most seek to help people and to serve the community (see Chapter 5). Recruits, in short, are rather idealistic when they enter policing. The officers surveyed by Bayley and Mendelsohn were somewhat more conservative politically than the population at large, but were not authoritarian in any pathological sense.[36]

## Herbert's Dimensions of the Police Subculture

The most comprehensive critique of the traditional view of the police subculture concept is offered by Steve Herbert. Based on his ethnographic study of the Los Angeles Police Department, he identified six different factors that shape and help to explain police officer behavior.[37]

1. *The law.* Even though officers exercise broad discretion (see Chapter 11), the law defines the boundaries of permissible actions.
2. *Bureaucratic control.* Officers do not act completely alone. They are subject to control by other members of the department and the criminal justice system bureaucracy: supervisors, defense attorneys, prosecutors, and judges.
3. *A culture of "adventure/machismo."* Herbert found that, in Los Angeles, officers put a high premium on active and aggressive police work. They respect other officers with this style of work and do not respect more passive officers.
4. *Safety.* A concern for personal safety shapes how officers behave in different situations. This point is close to Skolnick's argument about how danger shapes the police subculture.
5. *Competence.* Officers take pride in their own competence and respect other officers they believe are competent. Having to call in officers from other units to help with calls (referred to as "dropping calls") is a sign of lack of competence. This point is true of all professions, and not unique to the police.
6. *Morality.* Officers make moral judgments about people, and regard some people as "good" and others as "bad." "Good" people deserve more respect and better treatment than "bad" people.

Herbert's main point is that the traditional concept of the police subculture is too limited, and fails to take into account the influence of other factors. Equally important, the dominant elements of the traditional concept painted a very negative image of policing (secrecy, lying, violence). The factors identified by Herbert are morally neutral, and in some respects present a favorable view of the police (e.g., competence, morality).

After considering both the traditional concept and the new perspectives on the police subculture, the safest conclusion is that the attitudes and behavior of police officers are extremely complex, subject to many different factors, and should not be reduced to oversimplified stereotypes. As the next section explains, moreover, they have changed over time with the arrival of officers with different backgrounds.

# The Changing Rank and File

The original concept of a police subculture is ahistorical because it fails to take into account the changes in the composition of the rank and file over the past 40 years.[38] The initial research was conducted in the 1950s and 1960s when American police officers were overwhelmingly male, white, and typically with no college education. Today there are significant numbers of African American, Hispanic, female, and college-educated officers. Robin Haarr argues that "the initial concept of a single, unified occupational culture is now being replaced by an alternative conceptualization of diversity, variation, and contrast within the police organization and occupation."[39]

## The Impact of Women Police Officers

Susan Martin found that the introduction of women into policing broke up the traditional solidarity of the work group. Women officers, for example, do not share the same outside interests as male officers: hunting, fishing, and cars. She also argues that policewomen "alter the rules of the game" of how to act as a police officer. Traditional masculine characteristics of not expressing emotion publicly and of settling disputes physically are no longer appropriate. Expressions of friendship, which were acceptable between two male officers, are problematic between officers of different sexes.[40]

Martin also found significant differences among the male officers, especially in terms of their attitudes toward women officers. The **traditionals** were committed to the image of policing as dangerous work involving aggressive action and requiring physical strength. The **moderns,** on the other hand, accept policewomen relatively easily, recognizing that police work rarely calls for physical strength and accepting the idea that job opportunities should be open to everyone on the basis of individual merit. The **moderates** were somewhere in between, with many accepting the idea of policewomen in principle but unhappy about women on patrol duty.[41]

**traditionals**

**moderns**

**moderates**

Martin's research exposed the fact that the original research on the police subculture failed to take into account important differences in attitudes among male officers.

Women today have become more integrated into policing. A number of women have served as chiefs of big city police departments, and many serve in top command positions. Martin and Jurik report that "the resistance faced by the first women on patrol was blatant, malicious, widespread, organized, and sometimes life-threatening." With the passage of time, the hostility has become less blatant and more subtle.[42] The Police Foundation study of officer attitudes toward abuse of authority found no significant differences between male and female officers. This could be the result of either female officers adapting the existing police subculture or a process of self-selection by which only women who are likely to adapt to the police subculture seek law enforcement jobs.[43]

Although the percentage of women in policing has increased, there appears to be an invisible "glass ceiling" at both the entry level and in terms of promotion. The overall percentage of women among sworn officers remains at around 13 to 14 percent, and has not increased significantly in recent years. Also, in 1998 there were only 12 departments

# Police in Focus

## *The Brass Ceiling: Penny Harrington's Road to Police Chief*

Penny Harrington made history in January 1985 when she was appointed chief of the Portland, Oregon, Police Department. There had been women chiefs of small-town departments before, but she was the first female chief of a big-city department. Portland had 940 sworn officers in 1985.

Harrington's career illuminated some important milestones in the history of women and policing. When she joined the Portland Police Bureau in 1964, she was assigned to the women's protective division, the only assignment open to female officers. Female recruits were required to have a college degree (Harrington graduated from Michigan State University), while males only needed a high school diploma. They were paid less than male officers, and not issued regular uniforms. Protective division officers investigated only sex offenses and juvenile cases. In 1971 Portland finally eliminated the categories of "policewoman" and "policeman," creating a gender-neutral "police officer" category. Harrington was promoted to sergeant in 1972, and in 1975 became the first female sergeant to supervise male patrol officers.

*Source:* Dorothy Moses Schulz, *Breaking the Brass Ceiling: Women Police Chiefs and Their Paths to the Top* (New York: Praeger, 2004).

where women were more than 20 percent of all officers. Also, the number of women officers in supervisory and command positions remains small (Exhibit 6–2).

Sexism continues to exist in many police departments. Archbold and Schulz found that most (79 percent) of the female officers in one department felt they had to work harder than male officers. Most felt they had been treated differently and at some point had been treated like tokens. Nonetheless, the same percentage indicated they did not feel isolated on their jobs, and most (64 percent) would recommend law

## EXHIBIT 6–2

### Percentage of Sworn Law Enforcement Officers by Rank and Gender, 2001

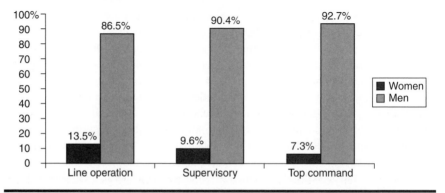

*Source:* National Center for Women and Policing, Equality Denied: The Status of Women in Policing: 2001 (Los Angeles: National Center for Women and Policing, 2002). Available at www.feminist.org. Reprinted by permission of Ms. Magazine, © 2001.

enforcement as a career to other women. The remaining 36 percent said it would depend on the women involved. Importantly, none of the female officers would not recommend law enforcement as a career.[44] Comparisons of the performance of male and female officers have found only slight differences in their handling of routine police work.

## Women Officers on Patrol

The major change in policing in the 1970s was the assignment of women officers to patrol duty. Previously, women had been confined to juvenile and vice units (see Chapter 2). Did the assignment of women to patrol make a difference in policing? Do female officers behave differently than male officers?

The Police Foundation conducted the first systematic study of female officers on routine patrol duty. It compared comparable groups of 86 male and 86 female new officers. It found that male and female officers performed in a generally similar manner. There were some slight differences in performance, involving arrests for example, but they were not significant. Female officers were less likely to engage in conduct unbecoming an officer. Most important, there were no observed incidents that cast doubt on the capacity of female officers to handle patrol duty.[45]

A study of patrol officers in New York City compared 41 male and 41 female officers in 1975 and 1976. The female officers' style of police work was "almost indistinguishable" from that of male officers. Both used different verbal and nonverbal techniques to control situations at virtually identical rates. Particularly important, female officers used force at exactly the same rate as male officers. Although the female officers were "slightly less active" than the male officers, "civilians rated the female officers more competent, pleasant, and respectful."[46] A more recent study in a large suburban police department also found no statistically significant differences in the use of force by male and female officers.[47]

The National Center for Women in Policing (NCWP) makes a bold claim: Police departments should hire more women officers because "female officers are less likely to use excessive force."[48] Is this true? Does the evidence support this claim?

The NCWP argument was based on data from the Los Angeles police department indicating that male officers were much more likely to be "problem" officers. They cost the city $63.4 million in damage awards between 1990 and 1999, compared with only $2.8 million for female officers. Females represented 18 percent of the LAPD officers, but were responsible for only 4.4 percent of the total damage awards. Kathy Spillar, head of the Feminist Majority, co-sponsor of the study, argues that "the single most fundamental reform that the LAPD could make would be to gender balance its police force.[49]

Data on citizen complaints also indicate a difference between male and female officers in this area. In both New York City and San Jose, female officers receive fewer complaints than male officers.[50] Additionally, a national evaluation of police early intervention systems (Chapter 14) finds that women officers are less likely than male officers to be identified as potential "problem" officers as a result of citizen complaints and use of force incidents.[51]

In the end, the data indicate that in terms of routine policing—day-to-day patrol, crime-fighting, and order maintenance—there are no significant differences between male and female officers. In this respect, female officers have not changed the police subculture in terms of behavior. At the same time, however, in terms of problematic behavior—excessive force, citizen complaints—female officers are somewhat different than male officers.

## Sexual Harassment on the Job

**sexual harassment**

Sexual harassment of female officers is a problem in policing, as it is in most organizations. **Sexual harassment** is defined as unwanted sexual advances, offensive sexually-related behavior (e.g., dirty jokes), or discrimination in assignments or promotion.

How do female officers respond to sexual harassment incidents? In interviews with 117 female officers, Chaiyavej and Morash found that only 19 percent reported the incidents to an authority. The most common responses were "hinting dissatisfaction" (61 percent), deflecting the offensive behavior (57 percent), or directly protesting to the offending person (52 percent).[52]

One reason victims of sexual harassment typically do not file complaints is that departments do not take them seriously and fail to investigate complaints and discipline guilty officers. In response to a series of sexual harassment lawsuits, the Los Angeles Sheriff's Department revised its policies and practices. A subsequent investigation found that as a result the department was responding more

---

**SIDEBAR    6 – 3**

### *Officer Race and Use of Force*

In several cities, African American officers have spoken out publicly on the issue of police use of force, criticizing their own departments and in some cases the police union, which is dominated by white officers.[1]

African American officers are also more likely to support innovation and change. They are more supportive of citizen oversight of the police than white officers.[2] And in their study of community policing in Chicago, Skogan and Hartnett found that African American officers were far more receptive to change and supportive of community policing.[3]

A Police Foundation study found that African American officers are far more likely to believe that the police use excessive force against both racial and ethnic minorities and poor people. Nearly half of all African American officers (47.7 percent) agreed with the statement that police officers are more likely to use force against blacks, compared with only 4.5 percent of white officers. By nearly the same margin, African American officers agreed that police officers are more likely to use force against poor people. Interestingly, the survey did not find differences between male and female officers on the same issues, suggesting that race is a far more powerful factor in shaping officer attitudes than is gender.[4]

[1]"Black Officers Take on the LAPD and Protective League: An Interview with Sgt. Leonard Ross," *Policing by Consent* (October 1995): pp. 8–9.
[2]Weisburd et al., *Police Officer Attitudes toward Abuse of Authority.*
[3]Wesley G. Skogan and Susan M. Hartnett, *Community Policing, Chicago Style* (New York: Oxford University Press, 1997).
[4]Weisburd et al., *Police Attitudes toward Abuse of Authority.*

quickly to allegations, conducting speedier and more thorough investigations, and had ended its practice of imposing only lenient discipline on officers found guilty of harassment.[53]

## African American Officers

In a remarkable break with the traditional police subculture, the National Black Police Officers Association published a pamphlet on police brutality urging officers to report misconduct by other officers. An officer who witnesses brutality should "report the incident to your supervisor, whether or not he/she is supportive." No other police officer organization had ever urged its officers to report misconduct. This position reflects some of the differences between African American and white rank-and-file officers.[54]

Are there significant differences in the behavior of **African American officers** and white officers? Civil rights leaders have always urged police departments to hire more African American and Hispanic officers as a way to improve police–community relations. They argue that these officers will have more rapport with the African American community and will not discriminate in arrests or other police actions.[55] Does the evidence support this argument? Do racial and ethnic minority officers police differently than white officers?

**African American officers**

To answer the question, it is important to recognize that there are significant differences among African American officers. In a study done in the 1960s, Alex found a generational difference between the older and younger African American officers. The younger officers were more likely to be assertive and willing to express their criticisms of the department than older officers.[56] Today, African American officers in departments where they are represented in significant numbers are less likely to feel isolated than were their older colleagues who were few in number and often isolated. A different dynamic exists in departments today (e.g., Detroit, Washington DC) where African American officers are the majority. (Irlbeck found important variations among Latino police officers. See below.)

In terms of conduct on the street, there appears to be no significant difference between African American and other police officers. Reiss found no significant differences in the use of force by white and African American officers.[57] Similarly, official data on citizen complaints in New York City and San Jose indicate that white, African American, and Hispanic officers receive complaints in proportion to their presence in a police department.[58] On the critical issue of deadly force, Fyfe found that, after controlling for place of assignment, white and African American officers fired their weapons at the same rate. The most powerful predictor of use of deadly force was the nature of the precinct where officers were assigned. Not surprisingly, officers assigned to high-crime precincts in New York City used deadly force more frequently than those assigned to low-crime precincts. Within each type of precinct, white and black officers used deadly force at essentially the same rate.[59]

Some important differences have been found in the attitudes of African American and white officers. In a survey of 522 police officers assigned to minority-group neighborhoods in 13 large cities, Peter Rossi found that African American officers had more positive attitudes toward their assigned districts. They are less likely than white officers to rate the assignment as more difficult than other assignments, three times more likely to live in the precinct where they work, and more likely to have friends there. The African American officers are also more likely to believe that the residents of the area where they are assigned are "honest" and "industrious."[60]

## Hispanic/Latino Officers

The employment of Hispanic/Latino Americans in policing has been increasing significantly in recent years. There are significant differences among Hispanic or Latino officers, just as there are among African American officers. Dawn Irlbeck interviewed 100 percent of the Hispanic officers in one Midwestern police department and found complex patterns of identity. A few identified themselves entirely as police officers, while many had dual identities as both police officers and members of the Hispanic community. None, however, identified completely with the Hispanic community. Those who had dual identities used their identification with and knowledge about the Hispanic community as a guide and resource in their police work. This did not involve leniency toward Hispanic offenders, however.[61]

**Hispanic officers**

In a number of departments today, Hispanic officers are the majority, as is the case with African American officers (see above). In an earlier study where they were a minority, Carter found that **Hispanic officers** believed that the department discriminated against them in promotions and also against Hispanic citizens.[62]

Unfortunately, there are no studies that systematically compare the behavior of Hispanic police officers with white and African American officers, with respect to arrest patterns and use of force. As already noted, in New York City and San Jose, Hispanic officers receive citizen complaints in direct proportion to their representation in the department.

## Gay and Lesbian Officers

A number of police officers are lesbian or gay. In some departments they are open about their sexual orientation, and have formed their own organizations. The Gay Officer Action League (GOAL) in New York City began publishing a newsletter in 1982. By 1992 at least ten police departments openly recruited **lesbian and gay officers.** Some of these departments are in states where antidiscrimination laws cover sexual orientation. Others are in cities with large lesbian and gay communities, and they have officers designated as liaisons to them.[63]

**lesbian and gay officers**

Lesbian and gay officers represent a clear challenge to the traditional stereotype of policing as a tough, macho, male occupation. In New York City the police union, along with a coalition of twenty-five religious and social organizations, attempted to block the police department's program for recruiting lesbian and gay officers.

A survey of gay and lesbian officers found that they chose law enforcement as a career for the same reasons people have traditionally chosen it: 41 percent cited job security, career opportunity, and civic duty as the three top reasons they chose policing (see Chapter 5 on this issue). Many, however, experienced discrimination on the job. Two-thirds (67 percent) reported homophobic talk on the job and 51 percent reported being treated like an outsider. Nearly a quarter (22 percent) cited barriers to promotion, and 17 percent saw barriers in assignment because of their sexual orientation.[64]

There are, however, no studies of the performance of gay and lesbian officers.

# The Intersection of Gender, Race, Ethnicity, and Sexual Identity

A comment by an African American female supervisor interviewed by Susan Martin illustrates the complex relationships resulting from increased diversity within police departments. This supervisor had problems with a white male officer under her command. After he transferred, however, he had similar problems with his new male supervisor. She concluded that "it wasn't a female thing . . . but at the time I couldn't be sure . . . I felt he was rebelling against me because I was a female lieutenant and a black lieutenant."[65] In short, relationships among officers of different genders, races, and ethnicities are extremely complex, and it is often difficult to determine which is the primary factor in any given situation.

In many departments some tension and conflict exist among racial, ethnic, and gender groups. Haarr found that white officers believed they were being discriminated against because promotions and preferred assignments were being given to African American officers who were less qualified.[66]

As is the case in much of American society, a pattern of self-segregation exists in police departments. In a midwestern police department, Robin Haarr found limited day-to-day interaction between officers of different race or gender. She measured interaction in terms of daily "meets" between officers, including handling calls together, backing each other up, eating meals together, and gossiping or joking. White male officers largely interacted with other white male officers. Most (75 percent) of the African American male officers indicated they mainly interacted with other male officers (either African American or white). The three African American female officers interacted primarily with other African American officers, either male or female. White female officers interacted mainly with other female officers, rather than with partners or former partners. Finally, at roll call, officers "separated themselves spatially by race and gender as to where they sat and whom they interacted with."[67]

Divisions along racial, ethnic, and gender lines are reflected in the fact that groups form separate social and fraternal associations representing African American, Hispanic, and female officers. There are also national associations of African American, Hispanic, and female officers. In many departments, the recognized police union (e.g., the official collective bargaining organization) reflects the views of the white officers.

After reviewing all the available research, the National Academy of Sciences concluded that "there is no credible evidence that officers of different racial or ethnic backgrounds perform differently during interactions with citizens *simply because of race or ethnicity*" (emphasis added).[68] Consequently, merely increasing the number of African American or Hispanic officers will not *by itself* change the quality of policing in a department.

This does not mean that increasing the racial or ethnic diversity of a department is not important. First, employment discrimination is illegal. Second, the composition of a department affects how it is perceived in the community. A department that does not employ a sufficient number of racial or ethnic minority officers is likely to have police–community relations problems. Third, as discussed above, officers of different racial or ethnic background often have different views about the community and about policing. Thus, they bring different perspectives to the department.

## Levels of Education

The profile of the American police officer has been changing because of rising educational levels. In the 1960s, 80 percent of all sworn officers had only a high school education. By 1988 the figure had fallen to 34.8 percent. The percentage of officers with a four-year college degree rose from 2.7 to 22.6 percent in the same period.[69] In many departments there is an **education generation gap** between the younger, better-educated officers and the veteran officers with less education.

**education generation gap**

Does education make a difference in police performance? Is a police officer with a college education more effective than an officer with only a high school diploma? There is no strong evidence that officers with college education behave differently on the street than officers with less education.[70] One study, however, did find that college-educated officers tended to receive fewer complaints than officers with less education.[71]

The research on the relationship between education and performance has been very weak. The National Academy of Sciences identified the following problems with the research on this subject.[72]

First, studies have not used good measures of police officer behavior and performance. This highlights the much larger problem of how to measure officer performance. The number of arrests is not a good measure because some officers have more opportunity to make arrests, while the total number does not reflect the quality of the arrests (measured by convictions). A low number of citizen complaints or use of force incidents, meanwhile, may only indicate that an officer has not initiated much activity.

Second, studies have not taken into account the content of educational programs. The number of college credit hours does not reflect either what courses were taken or the quality of the instruction.

Third, studies have not controlled for the effects of other factors that influence officer behavior and performance. Individuals with a strong commitment to self-improvement are also likely to have continued their education. The factors that cause them to seek more education also shape their performance as officers.

## Cohort Effects on Performance

Throughout society there are generation gaps: conflicts between young people and old people, between children and their parents. These conflicts involve clothes, hairstyles, music, lifestyle, and issues of morality. In the 1960s there were deep conflicts between generations over the Vietnam War. Then and now there are conflicts over sexual morality. Similar conflicts exist within police departments. Social scientists refer to these as **cohort effects.** That is, the officers hired in one decade will have different ideas and lifestyles than officers hired in later decades.

**cohort effects**

As new groups of officers enter policing, the dominant attitudes of rank-and-file officers also change over time. While officers at any one point in time might react negatively to a dramatic change in policing (e.g., a Supreme Court decision, the introduction of community policing), new cohorts of officers arrive to find these circumstances an established fact of life.

Skolnick's study in the 1960s found that officers were hostile to Supreme Court decisions placing limits on searches and seizures and interrogations. From their perspective, the rulings were something new that changed the rules of policing.[73] Forty years later, a new generation of officers takes the exclusionary rule and the Miranda warning as established parts of policing. A study of narcotics officers in Chicago in the 1980s, meanwhile, found a high degree of support for the exclusionary rule. On the whole, officers did not regard it as a barrier to effective police work, and many officers felt that it played an important role in deterring police misconduct.[74]

Along the same lines, Reuss-Ianni found two cultures among police officers in the department she studied. One group identified with the old **street cop culture** that values street experience and a tough, personalized way of dealing with people on the street. The other group identified with the new bureaucratic style of written rules and formal procedures for dealing with both police work on the street and departmental governance. This latter group is more accepting of, for example, Supreme Court rules on police practices, along with other formal procedures designed to control discretion (Chapter 11) and ensure police accountability (Chapter 14).[75]

**street cop culture**

## Organizational Effects on Attitudes and Performance

Police departments vary, and these differences affect the attitudes and behavior of officers in them. Milner, for example, found a higher degree of support for the *Miranda* decision in the more professionalized departments than in the less professionalized ones.[76] In short, the informal culture of a police organization affects officer attitudes toward certain important subjects.

## Attitudes toward Community Policing

"Can we affect crime?" asked a Chicago police officer. "Not really," he said, answering his own question. "We can't control the social fabric. It can't be done." These comments reflect the negative attitude toward community policing held by many tradition-bound officers. Other Chicago officers, however, are more favorable toward community policing, agreeing with the idea that "police officers should work with citizens to try and solve problems in their beat."[77]

For this reason, the community-policing program in Chicago (Chicago Alternative Policing Strategy, or CAPS) made a special effort in "winning the hearts and minds" of the rank and file. Skogan's evaluation of CAPS found significant differences of opinion among Chicago officers regarding community policing. Older officers and African American officers were consistently more supportive of community policing. African American officers were "ready for change," while white officers were satisfied with the status quo and most pessimistic about the likely success of CAPS.[78]

In a review of evaluations of community policing in twelve different cities, Lurigio and Rosenbaum found that involvement in community policing had a somewhat positive effect on officer attitudes (and on citizen perceptions of the police). Officers were generally more likely to have increased job satisfaction and motivation, as well as improved relationships with both citizens and coworkers. Lurigio and Rosenbaum cautioned against being overly optimistic about the impact of community policing on officer attitudes, but there is some evidence that changes in the police organization can affect officer attitudes.[79]

# The Relationship between Attitudes and Behavior

The graduate students observing police work in Boston, Chicago, and Washington DC in Albert Reiss's pioneering study for the President's Crime Commission observed more than 75 percent of the officers making racially prejudiced statements. They did not, however, observe a pattern of systematic mistreatment of African Americans, either in terms of disrespect or discriminatory arrests.[80] The contradictions in this study illustrate the complex relationship between the attitudes and behavior of police officers.

**attitudes and behaviors**

Common sense suggests a direct relationship between **attitudes and behavior:** that people who express prejudicial *attitudes* about race, ethnicity, or gender will automatically *behave* in a discriminatory manner. In practice, this is not necessarily true. The National Academy of Sciences reviewed the literature and found only "weak relationships between specific officer attitudes and behavior."[81] Terrill and Mastrofski, for example, found no relationship between officers' attitudes and their use of coercive force.[82]

Several factors mediate the effect of attitudes on officer behavior. First, police officers are constrained by the police bureaucracy and the criminal justice system. An arrest comes to the attention of other officials: the officer's sergeant, the prosecutor and defense attorney, and a judge. All review the officer's performance and have the power to correct any gross abuse of power. The prosecutor can reject the charges, and a judge can exclude evidence or confessions that were obtained improperly. These factors illustrate Herbert's point about the impact of the criminal justice bureaucracy on the police subculture. The result is that an officer is not free to act solely on the basis of his or her personal prejudices.[83]

A second constraint is the possibility of a citizen complaint or a lawsuit. Either one could affect an officer's career. Third, in a professional department with high standards of conduct, supervisors will advise officers that both prejudicial statements and discriminatory actions are contrary to the values of the department and could result in disciplinary action.

# Styles of Police Work

Conducting a series of ride-alongs with patrol sergeants in the Wilshire Division of the Los Angeles Police Department in 1993 and 1994, Herbert observed that officers used different labels to describe the work styles of their fellow officers. Some were called "hardchargers": active, often aggressive officers who would volunteer to handle potentially dangerous situations, and enjoyed the excitement of high-speed pursuits. Some others, meanwhile, were labeled "station queens" because they were seen as avoiding danger.[84]

**active officers**

Individual officers have different work styles; some work very hard, some do as little as possible. The same is true in every organization. **Active officers** (1) initiate more contacts with citizens (field interrogations, traffic stops, building checks); (2) back up officers on other calls, even when not dispatched to that call; (3) assert control of situations with citizens; and (4) make more arrests. **Passive officers**

**passive officers**

(1) initiate few contacts with citizens; (2) respond only to calls to which they are

dispatched; and (3) make few traffic stops, field interrogations, and arrests. Data on arrests, traffic stops, and field interrogations consistently indicate that a few officers are very productive, while some other officers engage in little activity.[85]

Bayley and Garofalo observed officers responding to specific situations, and found that active officers were more likely to take charge of the situation by asking probing questions, requesting citizens to explain themselves, and giving direction or advice to the people involved. Passive officers, by contrast, were more likely to just observe a situation, take notes, and leave without taking any specific action.[86]

# Moving Through Police Careers

## Salaries and Benefits

The salaries and **fringe benefits** offered police officers in most departments are generally one of the most attractive aspects of jobs in law enforcement.[87] They are one of the main reasons why people choose law enforcement as a career (see Chapter 5). Salaries are rigidly structured by civil service procedures and/or union contracts, however. Pay is tied to an officer's rank. Typically, there are several pay steps at the rank of police officer, which an officer gains through seniority or special assignment.

**fringe benefits**

**Job security** has always been very important in policing. Because of civil service rules and police union contracts, it is extremely difficult to fire an officer, except for criminal conduct. It is extremely difficult to fire an officer simply for doing little work.

**job security**

The only way to achieve a significant pay increase is through promotion. Unlike employees in the private sector, a police chief cannot reward an outstanding officer through a bonus or discretionary pay increase. Thus, there are no immediate financial rewards for outstanding performance.

Most departments offer additional pay for certain assignments or qualifications. The 2000 LEMAS data indicate that 68 percent of all municipal departments offer incentive pay for college education, 26 percent offer hazardous duty pay for certain assignments, and 47 percent provide shift differential pay. Another 32 percent offer various forms of merit pay increases.[88]

The major source of additional pay is overtime. Certain assignments, particularly those that involve frequent court appearances such as criminal investigation and traffic, offer the greatest opportunities for overtime pay.

## In-Service Training

Ensuring high levels of professionalism requires a comprehensive training program that includes (1) preservice academy training, (2) a field training program (both covered in Chapter 5), and (3) regular in-service training.

Experts argue that regular in-service training is important because officers may forget their academy training or slip into unacceptable habits under the pressure of the job. They also need to be trained over new laws, court decisions, or department policies. California requires all officers to receive 24 hours of in-service training every year over what it labels "perishable skills." These include use of force, traffic stops, and communication skills. The term "perishable skills" is a recognition that an officer can easily lose them.

## California P.O.S.T. Requirements for Continuing Professional Training (CPT)

**2-2. Perishable Skills:** All regular and specialized peace officers below middle management position (i.e., officers and first level supervisors) assigned to patrol, traffic, or investigation, who routinely effect the physical arrest of criminal suspects, are required to complete a minimum of 14 hours of POST-certified training (Perishable Skills and Communications) as part of the CPT requirement. A minimum of 12 hours of this requirement in each two-year period shall contain perishable skills training including a minimum of 4 hours of each of the three following courses which have been specifically designated by POST as satisfying this requirement:

1. Arrest and Control
2. Driver Training/Awareness or Driving Simulator
3. Tactical Firearms* or Force Options Simulator

*Tactical Firearms training courses involve tactical situations, judgment and application. Basic marksmanship and routine qualification do not satisfy the requirements.

Level I and Level II Reserve Officers are not required to complete Perishable Skills Training.

**2-3. Communications:** All regular and specialized peace officers below middle management position (i.e., officers and first level supervisors) assigned to patrol, traffic, or investigation, and who routinely effect the physical arrest of criminal suspects are required to complete a minimum of 2 hours of this requirement in each two year period in tactical or interpersonal communications training. Level I and Level II Reserve Officers are not required to complete Perishable Skills Communications Training.

*Questions for Discussion:* What is meant by "perishable skills"? Why are these particular skills considered "perishable"? Why does the State of California consider them so important?

In-service training can take several forms. States generally require all sworn officers to be recertified annually in the use of their firearms. Equally important is training over procedures for dealing with citizens. The most important is annual in-service training, in a classroom setting away from the job. In addition, many departments conduct training at roll call at the start of regular shifts. Finally, supervisors can train officers under their command on an informal, as-needed basis. In what is often called "coaching," a sergeant who observes an officer making a small mistake can take that officer aside and instruct him or her on proper procedure.

In-service training requirements and practices vary widely around the country. Several states mandate annual in-service training. The state of Utah, for example, requires 40 hours a year of in-service training. North Carolina requires 24 hours, divided among 4 hours of firearms qualification, 12 hours on required topics, and 8 hours on topics chosen by the department. In 2008 the required 12 hours included 4 hours on legal updates, 2 hours on career survival, 2 hours on juvenile minority sensitivity, and 4 hours on response to critical incidents.[89] Some states have no required annual in-service training.

Although common sense suggests that training is important, there is unfortunately little research investigating the impact of training programs. Studying the impact of in-service training encounters the same problems affecting research on the impact of college education (see the discussion on p. 166). There are no valid measures of officer performance, no measures of the content of the training or the quality of instruction, and there is a failure to isolate the effects of training from other factors that influence performance.[90]

The organizational culture of a department has an impact on training. Training over the use of force, for example, will be undermined if a department does not have good policies on force or does not supervise well and enforce its policies. Training on race relations and human relations will be undermined if a department does not have a good citizen complaint process and does not discipline officers who receive valid complaints for rudeness or for using racial or ethnic slurs.

# Career Development

The lack of opportunities for career development is recognized as a problem in American police departments. **Career development** involves opportunities to use one's talents and develop expertise in a particular area. In a two-wave survey of Detroit police officers, over half in both 1978 (53 percent) and 1988 (54 percent) indicated low satisfaction with the opportunity for career advancement. Few (10 percent in 1978 and 16 percent in 1988) expressed high satisfaction with the advancement opportunities. Traditionally, the two main career opportunities are promotion to higher rank and assignment to a preferred unit such as criminal investigation or traffic.

**career development**

To promote career development, many departments have educational incentive programs where officers receive additional pay based on their level of education. The Cincinnati Police department went even further in 2008, creating a Chief's Scholar Program. The department assigned three officers to attend the University of Cincinnati to obtain a Masters Degree in Criminal Justice as part of their regular duty assignment. As part of its Strategic Plan, meanwhile, the department also developed a Succession Planning program to prepare officers for vacancies created by anticipated retirements. The Lincoln, Nebraska, Police Department developed a similar program to mentor younger officers to prepare them for future command responsibilities.[91]

## Promotion

Opportunities for **promotion** are typically very limited in policing. First, civil service regulations usually require an officer to serve a certain number of years in rank before being eligible to apply for promotion. Time-in-rank requirements typically range from two to five years.[92]

**promotion**

Second, there are only a few openings at higher rank. Additionally, promotions are often affected by the city or county's financial condition. In a time of financial

---

## *Studying Your Own Community*

What are the requirements for in-service training among the law enforcement agencies in your community? Is there a state requirement? If so, how many hours and in what subjects? Do local agencies have their own requirements? Do they go beyond what is required by state law? What subjects are required to be covered every year beyond firearms recertification?

---

crisis, postponing hiring and promotions is an easy way to save money. The national financial crisis of 2008–2009 forced many law enforcement agencies to either cancel or postpone recruit classes and/or postpone or cancel promotions.

Third, promotions are based on a formal testing process, typically involving a written examination and an oral interview. Supervisory positions require different skills than on-the-street police work: directing other people, writing performance evaluations, dealing with performance problems, etc. It is not clear that the testing procedures select people who have the proper skills. Interviews are generally conducted by the chief of police, a committee of high-ranking officers, and often members of the local civil service agency group.[93] Some departments use the assessment center technique, which attempts to evaluate the ability of the applicant to handle the job being sought.

Several studies have found that a "glass ceiling" exists with regard to female officers, and women are underrepresented in higher ranks. Interestingly, Archbold and Schulz found that even though over half the female officers felt that promotional opportunities were "very good" or "good" in their department, many were reluctant to test for sergeant because of a perception they would be promoted only because they were female. Almost half (43 percent) could mention a potential male "sponsor" to help them with promotion, but this also appeared to have a negative effect.[94]

## Assignment to Special Units

**special unit**    An important career opportunity involves assignment to a **special unit:** criminal investigation, training, juvenile, and so on. These assignments are typically at the discretion of the chief. Traditionally, giving these assignments to friends or allies was one of the ways a chief maintained control over a department.

Assignments must be within the officer's rank. A sergeant, for example, cannot be assigned as commander of a unit if that position is designated a lieutenant's position. The rigidity of these personnel classification systems limits both the career opportunities for individual officers and the management flexibility of the chief executive.[95]

Special assignments play an important role in promotional opportunities. Serving in a number of special units gives an officer broad experience, an opportunity to become known to other officers, and to establish a reputation for ability.

In all law enforcement agencies certain assignments are regarded as highly desirable by rank-and-file officers. These are sometimes referred to as **"coveted"**
**"coveted" assignments**    **assignments.** Officers prefer these assignments for two reasons. First, they are

usually challenging assignments that are more interesting than basic patrol. Second, experience in these assignments often helps gain promotion to higher rank.

A study of the Los Angeles Sheriff's Department identified the following "coveted" assignments: Special Enforcement Bureau, Narcotics Bureau, and Station Detectives. All three involve specialized crime-fighting activities. In most departments, detective and crime-related assignments are the most desired. At the same time, the study identified "high-profile" assignments that tend to bring the officer "to the attention of persons in a position to notice and promote him or her." In the LASD, the three most significant "high-profile" assignments for deputies are Operations Deputy, Recruitment Training Bureau, and Field Training Officer.[96]

Exclusion of certain groups from coveted positions has been an important form of employment discrimination. The LASD study, for example, found that female officers were less than 2 percent of all Special Enforcement Bureau deputies and less than 3 percent of all Field Training Officers. Exclusion from such assignments creates barriers to promotion.

## Lateral Entry

The opportunity to move to other police departments was traditionally very limited in American departments. Someone transferring from another department lost all seniority and had to start as a rookie officer. This was a serious impediment to career development. In other professions, someone can move to a different organization without losing seniority and often to a higher position with better pay.

Some experts regard lateral entry as a potential means of enhancing police professionalism. They argue that it would create greater career opportunities for talented and ambitious officers and would allow departments to bring in fresh blood and new ideas. **Lateral entry** is opposed because officers jealously guard the few   **lateral entry**
promotional opportunities that do arise in a department and resent the idea of outsiders getting these jobs.[97]

Personnel policies have been changing, and many departments now offer lateral entry programs. The Los Angeles Police Department has had a lateral entry program that admits people with state POST certification and prior experience with another agency. They are required to take an abbreviated four-week training course, and on the salary schedule are given one year of credit for every two years of previous experience (up to a maximum of six years). They can also advance one step for 60 hours of college credits (2.0 GPA required) and two steps for an undergraduate degree.[98]

## Outside Employment

A significant number of police officers supplement their incomes with **outside em-**   **outside employment**
**ployment.** In addition, officers who are frustrated by the lack of career opportunities look for challenges and rewards outside the department. Many of those jobs are in private security, where the officer wears his or her police uniform. A 1988 Justice Department study found that half of all officers in some departments work off duty and in uniform.[99]

Outside employment creates a number of potential problems. First, it may diminish an officer's commitment to his or her job with the police department. A study of arrest productivity among New York City police officers found that those officers who held outside jobs made significantly fewer arrests than officers who did not. Apparently, officers were deterred from making arrests out of fear that the resulting court appearances would interfere with their outside work.[100]

Second, off-duty work in uniform creates potential conflicts of interest. An off-duty officer working in a bar, for example, may be caught between the duty to enforce the law and the interests of the bar owner. Finally, outside work in uniform may lower the dignity of the department.[101]

The San Jose independent police auditor exposed another conflict of interest by pointing out that some officers working off duty were hiring their supervisors as employees on those jobs. This practice potentially undermines discipline in the department, as a supervisor might be afraid to discipline an officer under his or her command out of fear of being fired from the off-duty job.[102]

# Performance Evaluations

In any professionally-managed organization, employee performance evaluations are extremely important. Regular evaluations serve to identify good performance that can be rewarded and poor performance that needs to be corrected. The following sections review the challenges associated with performance evaluations in policing.

## Traditional Performance Evaluations

**performance evaluations**

New York City police officer Michael Dowd received outstanding **performance evaluations.** His 1987 evaluation concluded that he had "excellent street knowledge" and could "easily become a role model for others to emulate."[103] Unfortunately, the Mollen Commission investigating corruption in the NYPD found that he was one of the most brutal and corrupt officers in the police department.

Effective performance evaluations are a critical part of a police department's personnel system. An effective system should identify and reward good performance, establish a basis for which officers deserve promotion, identify inadequate performance, and provide a basis for correcting those performance problems. The CALEA accreditation standards state that "a written directive requires that a performance evaluation of each employee be conducted and documented at least annually."[104]

Performance evaluations do not always reflect an officer's actual performance. The Christopher Commission, for example, found that some of the Los Angeles officers with the highest number of citizen complaints had received excellent performance evaluations.[105] One of the most damning indictments of police personnel evaluation procedures was made by the Los Angeles Police Department (LAPD) about its own system. In the wake of the Rampart Area corruption scandal in 2000, the department undertook a full-scale Board of Inquiry investigation that resulted in a 350-page report. The report concluded that "our personnel evaluations have little or no credibility at any level in the organization . . ." It recommended major changes "so that it can be relied upon as a true measure of performance."[106]

Some departments, however, do not conduct regular performance evaluations. The Pittsburgh Police Bureau, for example, did not conduct regular performance evaluations prior to a 1997 consent decree with the U.S. Justice Department to settle a suit over officer use of excessive force.[107]

## Problems with Performance Evaluations

Traditional police performance evaluation systems have been heavily criticized. A 1977 Police Foundation report concluded that "the current status of performance appraisal systems is discouragingly low."[108] Changes over the next 20 years resulted in only marginal improvements. A 1997 report by the Community Policing Consortium concluded that "most performance evaluations currently used by police agencies do not reflect the work officers do."[109]

The problems with traditional performance evaluations include the following issues. First, the definitions are often not clear. They do not explain, for example, how effective police work is to be measured. Second, because of the "halo effect," officers rated high on one factor are likely to be rated high on all others. Third, because of the "central tendency" phenomenon, the ratings of all officers tend to cluster around one numerical level. Finally, through "grade inflation," there is a tendency to rate everyone highly.[110]

---

**S I D E B A R          6 – 6**

### *Identifying "Top Performing" Officers*

One of the most difficult issues in police performance evaluations has been how to identify the best officers. Traditionally, evaluations have been based on reputations, which are often based on particular incidents (i.e., a major arrest). The challenge is to document good performance in routine situations over the course of a year. Early intervention systems (EIS) offer a method of identifying "top performing" officers. EIS (see Chapter 14) were originally developed to identify "problem" officers, for example, officers who use force more often than other officers. The data in an EIS computerized database can also be used to identify good officers.

The method of analysis involves the ratio between officers' activity levels on desired activities (e.g., arrests) with problematic incidents (e.g., citizen complaints). Thus, what is the ratio between complaints and arrests? Let's say Officer A makes 100 arrests and receives 1 citizen complaint. Officer B, working the same patrol assignment, makes 20 arrests and receives 3 citizen complaints. The resulting ratios are:

**Complaints/Arrests**
**Officer A:**    1/100
**Officer B:**    3/20

Clearly, Officer A is a top performer. He or she is engaging in important police work—making arrests—without generating many citizen complaints. Officer B does a lot less work and is apparently doing something that offends citizens. The department can use these data to reward Officer A and initiate counseling or retraining for Officer B.

*Source:* Samuel Walker, *Early Intervention Systems for Law Enforcement Agencies: A Planning and Management Guide* (Washington DC: Department of Justice, 2003).

An officer may be very skilled at defusing conflicts among people (e.g., in a domestic situation or a bar fight). Doing that successfully provides a very important service to the public. It prevents possible harm to people, keeps the neighborhood quiet, and avoids arrest and the potential use of force. Yet, traditional personnel evaluation systems are not good at identifying and rewarding this skill.

Performance evaluations may also reflect patterns of racial, ethnic, or gender bias within a department. There is some indication that African American and Hispanic officers are more likely to be cited for departmental violations. Martin and Jurik argue that traditional performance criteria such as aggressiveness are male-oriented and inevitably biased against female officers.[111]

Traditionally, an officer might gain a "halo effect" because of an arrest in a highly publicized crime. Arrests, however, are not necessarily a good measure of overall performance. First, the number of arrests does not necessarily reflect the quality of the arrests. A high-quality arrest is defined as a conviction on a felony charge. Second, arrests are only one small part of an officer's job. Most patrol work involves order maintenance and peacekeeping (see Chapter 8.)[112]

Police personnel systems have also traditionally focused on punishing misconduct rather than rewarding good behavior. Critics have called police organizations "punishment-centered bureaucracies."[113] There are elaborate rules that can be used, often selectively, to catch and punish officers, but few methods for positively rewarding officers. An independent report sponsored by the police union in Los Angeles following the Rampart scandal concluded that supervisors often harassed officers by citing them for minor violations of department policy while ignoring major forms of misconduct such as use of excessive force.

A more positive view of police personnel evaluation emerged from Bayley and Garofalo's study of New York City police officers. Officers in three precincts were asked in confidence to identify three other officers they thought were "particularly skilled at handling conflict situations." The officers receiving the highest scores were then matched with comparison groups in the same precincts. An analysis of 467 police–citizen encounters involving potential violence found that officers rated highly by their peers handled situations differently than the members of the comparison groups. They were more likely to take charge of situations, less likely to simply stand by and observe, more likely to probe with questions and ask citizens to explain themselves, and more likely to verbally defuse situations. They were less likely to threaten the use of physical force, more likely to request people to disperse, and less likely to order people to do so.[114]

Bayley and Garofalo found that peer evaluations corresponded with observed differences in officer behavior. More important, the officers who were rated more highly by their peers and who performed better on the job also received higher ratings in official departmental evaluations. They received higher ratings in such categories as appearance, community relations skills, impartiality, decision making, ethics, and street knowledge.[115]

The Charlotte-Macklenburg, North Carolina, Police Department has added a new dimension to performance evaluations by incorporating problem solving. Officers are evaluated on the number or quality of the POP projects they have initiated. This helps to institutionalize problem-oriented policing throughout the department.

# Job Satisfaction and Job Stress

## The Sources of Job Satisfaction

What do police officers like about their jobs? What factors cause them stress on the job? Several studies have found that contrary to what many people think, officers are more stressed out by what their own department does than by what citizens on the street do. A survey of community policing officers in New York City found that in response to the question "What do you dislike about being a cop?" the most frequently cited factor was "department/headquarters doesn't care" (mentioned by 58.2 percent of the officers). Another 22.4 percent mentioned "precinct level supervisors." Meanwhile, "lack of respect from the public" ranked third and was mentioned by only 16.4 percent of the officers.[116]

The factors associated with **job satisfaction** in policing fall into five general categories:[117]

**job satisfaction**

1. *The nature of police work,* including working with people, serving the community, the excitement of the work
2. *Organizational factors,* including recognition for good performance, opportunities for advancement, support from the organization leaders
3. *Relations with the community,* including cooperation from citizens in encounters, presence or absence of overt conflict with citizens, positive feedback for good performance
4. *Relations with the media and political leaders,* including positive or negative coverage in the news media, positive support from political leaders, the presence or absence of direct political interference from political leaders
5. *Personal or family factors,* including family environment that understands police work, presence or absence of conflict between job and family responsibilities, presence or absence of family problems (e.g., divorce, problems with children, and so on)

A majority of police officers are generally satisfied with their jobs. In Washington DC, 82 percent indicated that they were satisfied or very satisfied. A study of Detroit police officers found that, in 1988, 61 percent expressed medium satisfaction and 8 percent expressed high satisfaction. This represented lower levels of satisfaction than 10 years earlier, when 53 percent expressed medium and 28 percent expressed high satisfaction with their jobs. About three-quarters (78 percent) said they would choose law enforcement again as a career, but 64 percent also said that the work is stressful. Few of the Detroit officers indicated that they felt low satisfaction in terms of job fulfillment (3 percent in 1978 and 8 percent in 1988), defined in terms of freedom to make decisions and overall feelings of accomplishment.[118]

## The Sources of Job Stress

There is some disagreement over whether policing is more stressful than other demanding occupations. Some studies have reported higher rates of suicide, alcoholism, heart attack, and divorce among police officers compared with the general population. A study of suicides in New York City between 1964 and 1973 found a rate of 17.2 per 100,000 among police officers, compared with 8.3 per 100,000 for the city as a whole and 11 per 100,000 for males in the city. Some studies claimed to find divorce rates as high as 30 percent in some police departments, but it was not clear that the rate for police officers was significantly higher than for the general population in the areas studied.[119]

The threat of danger is a basic element of police work that creates stress. Threatening incidents, such as physical assaults in the form of being attacked with a weapon, are statistically infrequent. The number of police officers feloniously killed in the line of duty, in fact, fell by 50 percent between the 1970s and 1990s, and averages less than 70 a year nationwide at present.[120] In fact, measured in terms of on-the-job deaths, mining, construction, and farming are considerably more dangerous. The fatality rate in coal mining was 30 per 100,000 employees in 2000, compared with 21 in agriculture and 13 in construction. The rate for law enforcement is about 20 per 100,000, including both accidental and felonious deaths.[121]

Citizen disrespect and challenges to police authority are another source of on-the-job stress. Even though such incidents are statistically infrequent, they loom large in an officer's consciousness. Equally important is the problem of boredom. Routine patrol work often involves long periods of inactivity. Shifting suddenly from inactivity to a high state of readiness is also a source of stress. Another major cause of stress in policing involves dealing with extreme human suffering. Officers regularly handle people who have been killed or seriously injured, or who are in a state of extreme psychological disorder.

The police department itself is a major source of stress. For many officers it is more serious than problems arising from dealing with the public. Officers often feel that command officers do not support them adequately, that incompetent officers are given preferred assignments because of personal friendships, and that the department changes policies in reaction to criticism from the media or politicians.[122]

Female police officers experience special gender-related forms of stress, such as sexual harassment or lack of acceptance by male police officers.[123] Additionally, female officers often have greater child care responsibilities than male officers and take more sick leave in order to handle them. African American and Hispanic officers also experience discrimination within their department, often in terms of exclusion from preferred assignments.

## Community Policing and Job Satisfaction

For a full discussion of community policing, see Chapter 10.

Many advocates of community policing (COP) argue that it leads to greater job satisfaction for officers than traditional policing does. According to this view, under COP officers will be less isolated from the communities they serve, will have greater autonomy in their work, will not be subject to as many rigid rules, will have the opportunity for greater personal development, and will be able to see the results of their work.

In an innovative approach to the study of police officer job satisfaction, Brody, DeMarco, and Lovrich surveyed both police officers and non-police employees in twelve governments in Washington State. Also, they compared police officers in terms of the level of COP implementation by the police department (as measured by the amount of COP funding and a survey of police chief executives regarding COP strategies and philosophies). Departments were classified as high, medium, or low COP implementation. Finally, the study used eleven measures of job satisfaction.[124]

The study found that the adoption of COP raised the level of job satisfaction among police officers and reduced the gap in levels of satisfaction between police and non-police employees. The positive effects were confined, however, to departments with a high commitment to COP. In departments with only a medium COP commitment, levels of job satisfaction in some arenas were actually lower than in departments with a low COP commitment. The authors of the study speculate that an incomplete commitment to COP may cause confusion and frustration among officers. This finding has important implications for reform and organizational change. It suggests that a half-hearted and incomplete change effort may be worse than not attempting any organizational change at all.

## Coping with Job Stress

Until recently, few police departments tried to help officers in **coping with job stress**. They either ignored the problem or assigned an officer with obvious problems to an easier job. For their part, troubled officers either relied on the support of their fellow officers or internalized their problems—a response that often led to alcohol abuse, mental illness, or even suicide.[125]

**coping with job stress**

Today, many police departments maintain programs to help officers cope with the pressures of the job and/or other personal problems. These programs take several different forms. Some use mental health professionals, while others rely on peer support. Mental health professionals are employed either on a contract/referral basis or as full-time staff members of an employee assistance program (EAP). Many EAPs serve all city or county employees. Many experts regard peer counseling as particularly valuable, since the officer can relate well to the counselor as a fellow police officer. Also, some peer counselors can provide a role model of having dealt, for example, with an alcohol abuse problem.[126]

One of the key issues in employee assistance programs is confidentiality. Officers seek out assistance when they are assured that the information will not be used

---

**SIDEBAR    6 – 7**

### *Peer Officer Support Programs*

To help officers cope with stress and problems that affect their performance, some departments have created peer officer support programs. In the Los Angeles Sheriff's Department (LASD) a few officers in each unit are selected to serve in the peer support program. They are not paid for this assignment but receive 40 hours of training. Their role is to be available to talk with officers who are having problems, such as family issues, substance abuse, or on-the-job performance problems. As fellow officers they are people an officer with problems can relate to. Their conversations are strictly confidential.

*Source:* Samuel Walker, Stacy Osnick Milligan, and Anna Berke, *Supervision and Intervention within Early Intervention Systems: A Guide for Law Enforcement Chief Executives* (Washington DC: Police Executive Research Forum, 2005), pp. 24–25.

against them in a disciplinary action. Some EAPs have been damaged by unauthorized leaks of information or by the belief that such leaks occur.[127] Many officers refuse to seek professional help when they are having problems because of the traditional macho image of police officers as tough individuals who can handle any problem.

# The Rights of Police Officers

Police officers enjoy the same civil and constitutional rights as other citizens, subject only to certain limitations related to the special circumstances of law enforcement. These include the constitutional rights of freedom of speech and association, due process of law, and privacy. The U.S. Supreme Court ruled in the 1966 *Garrity* case that "policemen[sic], like teachers and lawyers, are not relegated to a watered-down version of constitutional rights."[128]

In 1981 the American Civil Liberties Union published a short handbook entitled *The Rights of Police Officers,* which summarizes these rights.[129] Under the First Amendment, police officers may not be barred from employment or be disciplined for private political or religious activities. Thus, a police officer has a constitutional right to belong to unpopular political or religious organizations. Political or religious activity on the job is not permitted, however. The right of freedom of speech includes, to a limited extent, the right of an officer to criticize his or her own department publicly. Generally, a department may not discipline an officer if the public criticism involves matters of policy.

Polygraph examinations are a special case with respect to the right to privacy. The federal Polygraph Protection Act prohibits employers from using lie detectors in recruitment. Law enforcement agencies, however, are exempted and may administer polygraph tests to job applicants.

## The Police Officer's Bill of Rights

Officers also enjoy procedural due process protections on the job. They may not be fired or disciplined without adequate cause. Due process in personnel decisions is guaranteed in part by existing civil service regulations, by union contract in some departments, and by a police officer's "bill of rights" in Maryland, Florida, and other states.

About fourteen states have enacted laws creating a Police Officer's Bill of Rights. These laws create special due process protections for officers who are under investigation for alleged misconduct. Similar protections are found in the collective bargaining agreements between rank and file officers and the department. These laws and union contracts typically require that an officer under investigation has a right to be informed of the nature of the allegations, to have an attorney or representative present during interrogations, and to be able to appeal any adverse disciplinary decision.

Many civil rights activists argue that the protections in Police Officer Bills of Rights improperly protect officers who are guilty of misconduct by making it difficult for the department to investigate the allegations against them. A content analysis of the fourteen state laws found a mixed picture. Provisions such as the right to notice of the charges and the right to an attorney are basic due process rights that all employees should enjoy. Keenan and Walker found that some state laws and collective bargaining agreements, however, contain provisions that do impede investigations and are an impediment to accountability. The Maryland state law holds that an officer cannot be interrogated by anyone other than a sworn police officer. This provision makes it impossible to create an independent civilian oversight agency to handle citizen complaints. Some other laws and contracts provide "waiting periods" of up to forty-eight hours before an officer suspected of misconduct can be interviewed. It is believed that this allows a guilty officer time to create a cover story about the incident. A similar waiting period would not be tolerated in criminal investigations. In short, police officers are entitled to the basic due process rights that all citizens are entitled to, but the provisions of some laws do impede the investigation of alleged misconduct.[130]

## Turnover: Leaving Police Work

Every year, about 5 percent of all police officers leave their jobs. This **turnover,** or attrition, rate appears to have been steady since the 1960s. Officers leave police work because of retirement, death, dismissal, voluntary resignation, or layoffs resulting from financial constraints.[131]

turnover

Martin found that women leave policing at a slightly higher rate than men (6.3 percent annually, compared with 4.6 percent), but for reasons other than retirement. Women are more likely to resign voluntarily (4.3 versus 3.0 percent) and to be terminated involuntarily (1.2 versus 0.6 percent). Women officers experience a more hostile work environment. Women, especially single parents, have greater difficulty combining work with family responsibilities. Inadequate pregnancy leave policies make it difficult or impossible for women to have children and continue to work.[132]

Doerner found significantly higher attrition rates for female officers, both African American and white, compared with male officers in the Tallahassee police department. He suggests that this pattern raises an issue of concern for affirmative action programs, which focus almost exclusively on recruitment and ignore long-term employment patterns.[133]

Relatively little research has been done on the reasons for voluntary resignation. A Memphis study of police officers who resigned found that dissatisfaction with opportunities for promotion and with department policies was more important than inadequate pay and benefits or the feeling that their efforts were not being appreciated. Not all officers who are unhappy choose to resign, however. The Memphis study concludes that "dissatisfaction is a necessary but not a sufficient condition to cause resignation." As is the case with employees in all occupations, the decision is made in the context of many different personal, familial, and economic factors, including perceived career alternatives. The Memphis study identifies several key "turning points" leading to the decision to resign. These include, in order of importance, (1) the feeling that one's career had stagnated (e.g., "I just can't see any future in being a police officer."); (2) a particularly intense experience that brought accumulated frustrations to a head; (3) lack of a sense of fulfillment on the job; (4) family considerations; (5) the conduct of coworkers; (6) a particular department policy or policies; and (7) new employment opportunities.[134]

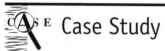

# Case Study

*National Center for Women and Policing (Excerpt)*

## Underrepresentation of Women Hurts Law Enforcement

National and international research shows conclusively that increasing the numbers of women in police departments measurably reduces police violence and improves police effectiveness and service to communities. The studies also show that women officers respond more effectively than their male counterparts to violence against women, which accounts for up to 50 percent of all calls to police. Yet this record stands in stark contrast to women's dramatic underrepresentation in police departments, where they make up 13.8 percent of sworn officers nationwide.

## Escalating Cost of Police Brutality

Study after study shows that women officers are not as likely as their male counterparts to be involved in the use of excessive force. As a result, the underrepresentation of women in policing is contributing to and exacerbating law enforcement's excessive force problems. The actual and potential liability for cities and states is staggering, with lawsuits due to excessive force by male law enforcement personnel costing millions of dollars of taxpayer money every year.

## Ineffective Response to Domestic Violence

Domestic violence is the single major cause of injury to women, and yet the majority of these violent crimes against women go unreported and uninvestigated by law enforcement agencies. At the same time, law enforcement officers who commit domestic abuse are routinely ignored or exonerated, often leading to tragic results. With studies showing that as many as 40 percent of male law enforcement officers commit domestic abuse, more women law enforcement officers can serve as a strong force to promote a more effective response by agencies to domestic violence cases that occur both within police departments and communitywide.

## Damaged Police–Community Relations

Women favor a community-oriented approach to policing that is rooted in strong interpersonal and communication skills and that emphasizes conflict resolution over force. Women tend to rely on their verbal skills over employing the use of force. With greater numbers of women, this highly effective model of policing will increasingly improve the public image of law enforcement agencies as well as have a positive impact on police–community relations nationwide.

## Costly Sexual Harassment and Sexual Discrimination Lawsuits

Law enforcement agencies have tolerated workplace environments that are openly hostile and discriminatory towards female employees, forcing women to bring

successful lawsuits against their agencies. The ongoing serious underrepresentation of women in policing leads to greater numbers of incidents of sexual harassment and discrimination. Increasing the number of women, treating women
equally on the job, and holding women to fair hiring and promotion practices will
reduce the enormous costs resulting from widespread lawsuits.

*Source:* National Center for Women and Policing, *Equality Denied* (1998), p. 5.

## Summary

Careers in law enforcement are subject to many different influences. Most popular stereotypes about police officer attitudes and behavior are not supported by the evidence. There is no evidence that a particular type of person is attracted to law enforcement or that this explains police behavior. The evidence does suggest, however, that certain aspects of police work do have a powerful influence on both attitudes and behavior. At the same time, it is evident that recent changes in police employment patterns have brought a new diversity to the rank and file. Racial and ethnic minorities and women bring different expectations to policing. Law enforcement careers are heavily influenced by factors associated with police departments, particularly the opportunities for career advancement. The nature of police organizations is explored in more detail in Chapter 4.

## Key Terms

reality shock, 151
hostility from citizens, 151
insiders, 152
department politics, 153
seniority, 153
police subculture, 154
group solidarity, 154
secrecy, 155
code of silence, 155
traditionals, 159
moderns, 159
moderates, 159

sexual harassment, 162
African American
    officers, 163
Hispanic officers, 164
lesbian and gay officers, 164
education generation
    gap, 166
cohort effects, 166
street cop culture, 167
attitudes and behavior, 168
active officers, 168
passive officers, 168

fringe benefits, 169
job security, 169
career development, 171
promotion, 171
special unit, 172
"coveted" assignments, 172
lateral entry, 173
outside employment, 173
performance evaluations, 174
job satisfaction, 177
coping with job stress, 179
turnover, 181

## For Discussion

The National Center for Women and Policing argues that adding more women officers to a police department will produce a number of benefits.

1. Is this argument sound?
2. What evidence does the center cite?

3. Is the evidence persuasive?
4. Is there any contrary evidence that is ignored?
5. What does the center's argument say about the culture of policing?

# Internet Exercise

**The Diverse Police Subculture on the Web**

Many organizations representing different groups of police officers maintain their own Web sites. Check out the Web sites for such groups as the National Hispanic Police Association, the International Association of Women Police, the Emerald Society of Boston, the Federation of Lesbian and Gay Police Organizations, and others. Whom do these organizations represent? Do they provide their membership figures? What do they do? What activities do they sponsor? Do they offer any reports or other literature?

# Notes

1. William A. Westley, *Violence and the Police* (Cambridge, MA: MIT Press, 1970), pp. 159–60.
2. John H. McNamara, "Uncertainties in Police Work: The Relevance of Police Recruits' Backgrounds and Training," in David J. Bordua, ed., *The Police, Six Sociological Essays* (New York: Wiley, 1967), pp. 163–252.
3. Arthur J. Luirgio and Dennis P. Rosenbaum, "The Travails of the Detroit Police-Victims Experiment: Assumptions and Important Lessons," *American Journal of Police* XI, no. 3 (1992): p. 24.
4. Albert Reiss, *The Police and the Public* (New Haven, CT: Yale University Press, 1971): p. 51; John A. Groger, *Memory and Remembering: Everyday Memory in Context* (New York: Longman, 1997); pp. 189–97.
5. Joseph De Angelis, *Assessing the Impact of the Office of the Independent Monitor on Complainant and Officer Satisfaction* (Denver: Office of the Independent Monitor, 2008). Available at www.denvergov.org/OIM/.
6. John P. Clark, "Isolation of the Police: A Comparison of the British and American Situations," *Journal of Criminal Law, Criminology, and Police Science* 56 (September 1965): pp. 307–19.
7. Westley, *Violence and the Police*, pp. 18–19; Stephen B. Perrott and Donald M. Taylor, "Crime Fighting, Law Enforcement and Service Provider Role Orientations in Community-Based Police Officers," *American Journal of Police* XIV, no. 3/4 (1995): p. 182.
8. Westley, *Violence and the Police*.
9. Richard Seltzer, Sucre Aone, and Gwendolyn Howard, "Police Satisfaction with Their Jobs: Arresting Officers in the District of Columbia," *Police Studies* 19, no. 4 (1996): p. 33.
10. Westley, *Violence and the Police*, pp. 76–82.
11. Jerome E. McElroy, Colleen A. Consgrove, and Susan Sadd, *Community Policing: The CPOP in New York* (Newbury Park, CA: Sage, 1993), p. 27.
12. John Van Maanen, "Police Socialization: A Longitudinal Examination of Job Attitudes in an Urban Police Department," *Administrative Science Quarterly* 20 (June 1975): p. 222.
13. Seltzer, Aone, and Howard, "Police Satisfaction with Their Jobs: Arresting Officers in the District of Columbia," p. 33.
14. George W. Griesinger, Jeffrey S. Slovak, and Joseph J. Molkup, *Civil Service Systems: Their Impact on Police Administration* (Washington DC: Government Printing Office, 1979); James L. O'Neill and Michael A. Cushing, *The Impact of Shift Work on Police Officers* (Washington DC: PERF, 1991).
15. President's Commission on Law Enforcement and Administration of Justice, *Task Force Report: The Police* (Washington DC: Government Printing Office, 1967), p. 165.
16. James J. Fyfe, "Who Shoots? A Look at Officer Race and Police Shooting," *Journal of Police Science and Administration* 9 (December 1981): p. 373.
17. Westley, *Violence and the Police,* p. viii.
18. Ibid., p. 11.
19. Ibid., pp. 76–82.
20. Ibid.
21. Susan Martin, *Breaking and Entering: Police Women on Patrol* (Berkeley: University of California Press, 1980), p. 97.
22. Ibid., p. 113.
23. David Weisburd and Rosann Greenspan, with Edwin E. Hamilton, Hubert Williams, and Kellie Bryant, *Police Attitudes toward Abuse of Authority: Findings from a National Study* (Washington DC: Department of Justice, 2000). www.ncjrs.org. NCJ 181312.
24. Christopher Commission, *Report of the Independent Commission to Investigate the Los Angeles Police*

*Department* (Los Angeles: City of Los Angles, 1991): pp. 168–71. www.parc.info.

25. Weisburd et al., *Police Attitudes toward Abuse of Authority.*

26. Westley, *Violence and the Police,* pp. 121–22.

27. Weisburd et al., *Police Attitudes toward Abuse of Authority.*

28. Jerome H. Skolnick, *Justice Without Trial: Law Enforcement in Democratic Society,* 3rd ed. (New York: Macmillan, 1994), pp. 44–47.

29. Egon Bittner, "The Functions of the Police in Modern Society," in Bittner, *Aspects of Police Work* (Boston: Northeastern University Press, 1990), pp. 120–32.

30. Bureau of the Census, *Statistical Abstract of the United States, 2002* (Washington DC: Government Printing Office, 2002), Table 626.

31. Bureau of Justice Statistics, *Policing and Homicide, 1976–98: Justifiable Homicide by Police, Police Officers Murdered by Felons* (Washington DC: Government Printing Office, 2000). www.ncjrs.org. NCJ 180987.

32. Skolnick, *Justice Without Trial,* pp. 1–21, 199–223.

33. Herbert Packer, *The Limits of the Criminal Sanction* (Stanford: Stanford University Press, 1968), Ch. 8.

34. David Sklansky, "Not Your Father's Police Department: Making Sense of the New Demographics of Law Enforcement," *Journal of Criminal Law and Criminology* 96 (Spring 2006): pp. 1209–1248.

35. Joel Lefkowitz, "Psychological Attributes of Policemen: A Review of Research and Opinion," *Journal of Social Issues* 31, no. 1 (1975): pp. 3–26.

36. David H. Bayley and Harold Mendelsohn, *Minorities and the Police* (New York: The Free Press, 1969), pp. 15–18.

37. Steve Herbert, "Police Subculture Reconsidered," *Criminology* 36, no. 2 (1998): pp. 343–68.

38. Samuel Walker, "Racial-Minority and Female Employment in Policing: The Implications of 'Glacial Change,'" *Crime and Delinquency* 31 (October 1985): pp. 555–72.

39. Robin N. Haarr, "Patterns of Interaction in a Police Patrol Bureau: Race and Gender Barriers to Integration," *Justice Quarterly* 14 (March 1997): p. 53.

40. Martin, *Breaking and Entering,* pp. 79–108.

41. Ibid., pp. 102–7.

42. Susan Ehrlich Martin and Nancy Jurik, *Doing Justice, Doing Gender: Women in Law and Criminal Justice Occupations* (Thousand Oaks, CA: Sage, 1996), p. 68; Susan E. Martin, *On the Move:*

*The Status of Women in Policing* (Washington DC: The Police Foundation, 1990).

43. Weisburd et. al., *Police Attitudes toward Abuse of Authority.*

44. Carol A. Archbold and Dorothy Moses Schulz, "Making Rank: The Lingering Effects of Tokenism on Female Police Officers' Promotion Aspirations," *Police Quarterly* 11 (March 2008): pp. 50–73.

45. Peter B. Bloch and Deborah Anderson, *Policewomen on Patrol: Final Report* (Washington DC: The Police Foundation, 1974). The various studies are summarized in Martin and Jurik, *Doing Justice, Doing Gender: Women in Law and Criminal Justice Occupations,* Chs. 3, 4. For a critique of these studies, however, see Merry Morash and Jack R. Greene, "Evaluating Women on Patrol: A Critique of Contemporary Wisdom," *Evaluation Review* 10 (April 1986): pp. 230–55.

46. Joyce L. Sichel, Lucy N. Friedman, Janice C. Quint, and Michael E. Smith, *Women on Patrol: A Pilot Study of Police Performance in New York City* (Washington DC: Government Printing Office, 1978).

47. Peter B. Hoffman and Edward R. Hickey, "Use of Force by Female Police Officers," *Journal of Criminal Justice* 33 (March–April 2005): pp. 145–51.

48. National Center for Women and Policing, *Men, Women, and Police Excessive Force: A Tale of Two Genders* (Los Angeles: National Center for Women and Policing, 2002); Kimberly A. Lonsway, *Hiring and Retaining More Women: The Advantages to Law Enforcement Agencies* (Los Angeles: National Center for Women and Policing, 2000). www. womenandpolicing.org

49. National Center for Women and Policing, *Men, Women, and Police Excessive Force.*

50. San Jose, Independent Police Auditor, *Annual Report 2006* (San Jose, CA: City of San Jose, 2007), p. 51. www.cityofsanjoseca.gov/ipa/. New York City, Civilian Complaint Review Board, *Status Report, January–December 2007* (New York: CCRB, 2008), Table 11. www.nyc.gov/html/ccrb/home/html.

51. Samuel Walker, *Early Intervention Systems for Law Enforcement Agencies: A Planning and Management Guide* (Washington DC: Department of Justice, 2003). www.cops.usdoj.gov.

52. Somvadee Chaiyavej and Merry Morash, "Reasons for Policewomen's Assertive and Passive Reactions to Sexual Harassment," *Police Quarterly* 12 (2009): pp. 63–85.

53. Merrick Bobb, *13th Semiannual Report of the Special Counsel to the Los Angeles Sheriff's Department* (Los Angeles: PARC, December 2000), pp. 57–74. www.parc.info.

54. National Black Police Officers Association, *Police Brutality: How to Stop the Violence* (Washington DC: NBPOA, nd.).

55. President's Commission on Law Enforcement and Administration of Justice, *The Challenge of Crime in a Free Society* (Washington DC: Government Printing Office, 1967), pp. 101–2.

56. Nicholas Alex, *Black in Blue* (Englewood Cliffs, NJ: Prentice-Hall, 1969).

57. Albert Reiss, "Police Brutality—Answers to Key Questions," *Transaction* 5 (July–August, 1968): pp. 10–19.

58. New York City, Civilian Complaint Review Board, *Status Report, January–December 2007,* Table 9. www.nyc.gov/html/ccrb/home/html. San Jose, Independent Police Auditor, *Annual Report, 2007,* p. 50. www.cityofsanjose.gov/ipa/.

59. Fyfe, "Who Shoots? A Look at Officer Race and Police Shooting," pp. 367–82.

60. Peter H. Rossi et al., *The Roots of Urban Discontent: Public Policy, Municipal Institutions, and the Ghetto* (New York: John Wiley, 1974).

61. Dawn Irlbeck, "Latino Police Officers: Patterns of Ethnic Self-Identity and Latino Community Attachment," *Police Quarterly* 11 (December 2008): pp. 468–95.

62. David L. Carter, "Hispanic Police Officers' Perceptions of Discrimination," *Police Studies* 9 (Winter 1986): pp. 204–10.

63. Stephen Leinen, *Gay Cops* (New Brunswick, NJ: Rutgers University Press, 1993).

64. Roddrick Colvin, "Shared Perceptions Among Lesbian and Gay Police Officers: Barriers and Opportunities in the Law Enforcement Work Environment," *Police Quarterly* 12 (2009): pp. 86–101.

65. Susan E. Martin, "Outsider Within the Station House: The Impact of Race and Gender on Black Women Police," *Social Problems* 41 (August 1994): p. 393.

66. Haarr, "Patterns of Interaction in a Police Patrol Bureau," p. 65.

67. Ibid.

68. National Academy of Sciences, *Fairness and Effectiveness in Policing: The Evidence* (Washington DC: National Academy Press, 2004), p. 148.

69. David L. Carter, Allen D. Sapp, and Darrel W. Stephens, *The State of Police Education* (Washington DC: Police Executive Research Forum, 1989), p. 38.

70. Lawrence W. Sherman, *The Quality of Police Education* (San Francisco: Jossey-Bass, 1978).

71. Victor E. Kappeler, David Carter, and Allen Sapp, "Police Officer Higher Education, Citizen Complaints, and Departmental Rule Violation," *American Journal of Police* 11, no. 2 (1992): pp. 37–54.

72. National Academy of Sciences, *Fairness and Effectiveness in Policing: The Evidence,* pp. 141–47.

73. Skolnick, *Justice Without Trial,* pp. 199–23.

74. Myron Orfield, "The Exclusionary Rule and Deterrence: An Empirical Study of Chicago Narcotics Officers," *University of Chicago Law Review* 54 (Summer 1987): pp. 1016–55.

75. Elizabeth Reuss-Ianni, *The Two Cultures of Policing* (New Brunswick, NJ: Transaction Books, 1983).

76. Neal A. Milner, *The Court and Local Law Enforcement: The Impact of Miranda* (Beverly Hills, CA: Sage, 1971).

77. Wesley G. Skogan and Susan M. Hartnett, *Community Policing, Chicago Style,* (New York: Oxford University Press, 1997), pp. 80, 83.

78. Ibid., pp. 85–86.

79. Arthur J. Lurigio and Dennis P. Rosenbaum, "The Impact of Community Policing on Police Personnel," in Dennis P. Rosenbaum, ed., *The Challenge of Community Policing* (Thousand Oaks, CA: Sage, 1994), pp. 147–63.

80. Albert J. Reiss, Jr., *The Police and the Public* (New Haven: Yale University Press, 1971), p. 147.

81. National Academy of Sciences, *Fairness and Effectiveness in Policing: The Evidence,* p. 135.

82. William Terrill and Stephen D. Mastrofski, "Situational and Officer-Based Determinants of Police Coercion," *Justice Quarterly* 19 (June 2002): pp. 215–49.

83. Robert Friedrich, "Racial Prejudice and Police Treatment of Blacks," in Ralph Baker and Fred. A. Meyer, Jr., eds., *Evaluating Alternative Law Enforcement Policies* (Lexington: Lexington Books, 1979).

84. Steve Herbert, "Police Subculture Reconsidered," *Criminology* 36, no. 2 (1998): pp. 355–56.

85. Joan R. Petersilia Allan Abrahamse, and James Q. Wilson, *Police Performance and Case Attrition* (Santa Monica, CA: Rand, 1987).

86. David H. Bayley and James Garofalo, "The Management of Violence by Police Patrol Officers," *Criminology* 27 (February 1989): pp. 1–25.

87. Comparative salary data are available in Bureau of Justice Statistics, *Law Enforcement Management and Administrative Statistics, 1999* (Washington DC: Government Printing Office, 2001). www.ncjrs.org. NCJ 184481.

88. Bureau of Justice Statistics, *Law Enforcement Management and Administrative Statistics, 2000*, p. xiv.

89. North Carolina, Criminal Justice Education and Training Standards Commission, In-Service Training, *Frequently Asked Questions, 2008* (Updated 6/1/07). www.ncdoj.com.

90. National Academy of Sciences, *Fairness and Effectiveness in Policing: The Evidence*, pp. 141–47.

91. "Chief's Scholar Program at UC to Aid City Cops," Cincinnati.com, December 28, 2008. Cincinnati Police Department, *Strategic Plan* (May 2007), p. 15. Lincoln Police Department, *Five Year Strategic Plan, 2007–2012.* (Lincoln, NE: Lincoln Police Department, 2007).

92. Police Executive Research Forum, *Survey of Police Operational and Administrative Practices—1981* (Washington DC: PERF, 1981), pp. 378–82.

93. Police Executive Research Forum, *Survey of Police Operational and Administrative Practices—1981*, pp. 342–46.

94. Carol A. Archbold and Dorothy Moses Schulz, "Making Rank: The Lingering Effects of Tokenism on Female Police Officers' Promotion Aspirations," *Police Quarterly* 11 (March 2008): pp. 50–73.

95. Dorothy Guyot, "Bending Granite: Attempts to Change the Rank Structure of American Police Departments," *Journal of Police Science and Administration* 7, no. 3 (1979): pp. 253–84.

96. Merrick Bobb, *6th Semiannual Report* (Los Angeles: Los Angeles Sheriff's Department, 1996), pp. 50–61. www.parc.info.

97. Minneapolis Police Department Web site: www.ci.minneapolis.mn.us/police. Herman Goldstein, *Policing a Free Society* (Cambridge, MA: Ballinger, 1977), pp. 241–43.

98. See the LAPD Web site: www.lapdonline.org.

99. Albert J. Reiss, *Private Employment of Public Police* (Washington DC: Department of Justice, 1988).

100. William F. Walsh, "Patrol Officer Arrest Rates: A Study of the Social Organization of Police Work," *Justice Quarterly* 3 (September 1986): p. 276.

101. Reiss, *Private Employment of Public Police*.

102. San Jose Independent Police Auditor, *Annual Report,* www.cityofsanjose.gov/ipa/.

103. Mollen Commission, *Commission Report* (New York: City of New York: 1994), p. 81. Available at www.parc.info.

104. Standard 35.1.2, Commission on Accreditation for Law Enforcement Agencies, *Standards for Law Enforcement Agencies*, 4th ed. (Fairfax, VA: CALEA, 1999), p. 35–1.

105. Christopher Commission, *Report of the Independent Commission on the Los Angeles Police Department* (Los Angeles: Christopher Commission, 1991). www.parc.info.

106. Los Angeles Police Department, Rampart Area Corruption Incident: Public Report (Los Angles Police Department, 2000), *Executive Summary,* p. 7.

107. *United States v. City of Pittsburgh* (W.D. Pa., 1997). Available at www.usdoj.gov/crt/slt; Samuel Walker and Morgan Macdonald, "An Alternative Remedy for Police Misconduct: A Model State "Pattern or Practice" Statute," *George Mason University Civil Rights Law Journal* 19, no. 3 (2009): pp. 479–552.

108. Frank J. Landy, *Performance Appraisal in Police Departments* (Washington DC: The Police Foundation, 1977), p. 1.

109. Timothy N. Oettmeier and Mary Ann Wycoff, *Personnel Performance Evaluation in the Community Policing Context* (Washington DC: Community Policing Consortium, 1997), p. 5.

110. Landy, *Performance Appraisal in Police Departments*.

111. Martin and Jurik, *Doing Justice, Doing Gender,* pp. 86–87.

112. Joan Petersilia, *Police Performance and Case Attrition* (Santa Monica: Rand Corporation, 1987).

113. McNamara, "Uncertainties in Police Work," pp. 177–178.

114. Bayley and Garofalo, "The Management of Violence by Police Patrol Officers."

115. Ibid.

116. Jerome E. McElroy, Colleen A. Cosgrove, and Susan Sadd, *Community Policing: The CPOP in New York* (Newbury Park, CA: Sage, 1993), p. 27.

117. See the categories used in Jack R. Greene, "Police Officer Job Satisfaction and Community Perceptions: Implications for Community-Oriented Policing," *Journal of Research in Crime and Delinquency* 26 (May, 1984): pp. 168–83.

118. Eve Buzawa, Thomas Austin, and James Bannon, "The Role of Selected Sociodemographic and Job-Specific Variables in Predicting Patrol Officer Job Satisfaction," *American Journal of Police* 13 no. 2 (1994): p. 70.

119. Arthur Niederhoffer, *The Police Family* (Lexington, MA: Lexington Books, 1978).

120. Bureau of Justice Statistics, *Policing and Homicide, 1976–98: Justifiable Homicide by Police, Police Officers Murdered by Felons;* Federal Bureau of Investigation, *Law Enforcement Officers Killed and Assaulted* (Washington DC: Department of Justice, annual).

121. Ibid.; Bureau of Census, *Statistical Abstract of the United States, 2002* (Washington, DC: Government Printing Office, 2002), Table 626.

122. O'Neill and Cushing, *The Impact of Shift Work.*

123. Martin and Jurik, *Doing Justice, Doing Gender,* p. 95.

124. David C. Brody, Christianne DeMarco, and Nicholas P. Lovrich, "Community Policing and Job Satisfaction: Suggestive Evidence of Positive Workforce Effects from a Multijurisdictional Comparison in Washington State," *Police Quarterly* 5, no. 2 (2002), pp. 181–205.

125. Gail A. Goolkasian, *Coping with Police Stress* (Washington DC: Government Printing Office, 1985), pp. 11–12.

126. Peter Finn and Julie Esselman Tomz, *Developing a Law Enforcement Stress Program for Officers and Their Families* (Washington DC: Government Printing Office, 1997).

127. Ibid., pp. 79–88.

128. *Garrity v. New Jersey,* 385 U.S. 493 (1966).

129. Gilda Brancato and Eliot E. Polebaum, *The Rights of Police Officers* (New York: Avon Books, 1981).

130. Kevin Keenan and Samuel Walker, "An Impediment to Police Accountability?: An Analysis of Statutory Law Enforcement Officers Bill of Rights," *Boston University Public Interest Law Journal* 14 (Spring 2005): pp. 185–244.

131. President's Commission on Law Enforcement and Administration of Justice, *Task Force Report: The Police,* p. 9.

132. Martin, *On the Move.*

133. William G. Doerner, "Officer Retention Patterns: An Affirmative Action Concern for Police Agencies?" *American Journal of Police* XIV, no. 3/4 (1995): pp. 197–210.

134. Jerry Sparger and David Giacopassi, "Swearing In and Swearing Off: A Comparison of Cops' and Ex-Cops' Attitudes toward the Workplace," *Police and Law Enforcement,* eds. Daniel B. Kennedy and Robert J. Homer (New York: AMS, 1987), pp. 35–54.

# Police Work

# Patrol: The Backbone of Policing

Patrol is the **backbone of policing,** the central feature of police operations. This chapter examines the nature of patrol work in contemporary American policing: how patrol is organized and delivered, the nature of citizen calls for service, the effectiveness of patrol in deterring crime, and programs designed to improve patrol services.

**backbone of policing**

# The Central Role of Patrol

The cop on the beat is both the symbol of American policing and the center of police activity. First, the majority of police officers are assigned to patrol, and in that capacity deliver the bulk of police services to the public.

Second, the marked patrol car and the uniformed patrol officer are the visible symbols of the police. They are a lightning rod for public attitudes about the role of the police in society.

Third, patrol officers are the most important decision makers in policing and the gatekeepers of the entire criminal justice system. James Q. Wilson points out that police departments are unique in that discretion increases as one moves *down* the organizational hierarchy. In deciding whether or not to make an arrest, or how to handle a domestic disturbance, patrol officers are the real policy makers in policing. Making decisions that affect people's lives, they are "street-level bureaucrats."[1]

Fourth, experience on patrol is a formative part of a police officer's career. In virtually all American police departments, assignments are based on seniority. New officers start out on patrol duty, usually on the evening shift and in the highest-crime neighborhoods. This street experience becomes an important part of the police officer subculture, forging a bond of common experience among officers.

Despite its central role, patrol duty has generally been considered the least desirable assignment, and career advancement usually means promotion or assignment to something more desirable, especially detective work. The National Advisory Commission on Criminal Justice Standards and Goals comments that "the patrolman is usually the lowest-paid, least-consulted, most taken-for-granted member of the force. His duty is looked on as routine and boring." Community policing seeks to correct this long-standing problem by giving patrol officers more decision-making authority as problem solvers who respond to neighborhood problems (see Chapter 10).[2]

# The Functions of Patrol

**functions of patrol**

For a full discussion of Robert Peel and the creation of the modern police, see Chapter 2.

Robert Peel, creator of the modern police, defined the functions of police patrol.[3] The three basic **functions of patrol** are:

1. To deter crime.
2. To enhance feelings of public safety.
3. To make officers available for service.

O. W. Wilson, for decades the leading expert on police management, explained that patrol seeks to deter crime by creating "an impression of omnipresence" that will eliminate "the actual opportunity (or the belief that the opportunity exists) for successful misconduct."[4]

The second function of patrol is to maintain feelings of public safety. The visible presence of patrol officers seeks to assure law-abiding citizens they are being protected against crime. Most people believe that patrol deters crime, and when asked to suggest improvements in policing, they want more police and/or more patrol in their neighborhood.[5]

The third function of patrol is to make officers available for service by dispersing officers throughout the community. Albert Reiss observes that "no other professional operates in a comparable setting."[6] The clients of other professionals—doctors, lawyers, and dentists—must go to the professionals' offices. The police may be the last profession to make house calls.

# The Organization and Delivery of Patrol

Visit different police departments and you will find that patrol is carried out in different ways. New York City uses a lot of foot patrol: 39 percent of all patrol units, according to the 1997 LEMAS data. The San Jose, California, police department, meanwhile, uses no foot patrol units. In Florida, one-third of all patrol units in St. Petersburg involve officers on motorcycles, compared with only 5 percent in Miami.[7]

## Factors Affecting the Delivery of Patrol Services

When people say they want more police protection, they generally mean more *patrol* officers, and usually more patrol officers *in their neighborhood*. Not all police departments are efficient in organizing and delivering patrol to the public. Efficiency depends on the following factors: the number of sworn officers; the percentage of officers assigned to patrol; the distribution of patrol officers by time of day and area; the type of patrol used (automobile versus foot); one-officer versus two-officer patrols; and the work styles of patrol officers.

## Number of Sworn Officers

How many officers should a police department have? Some cities have a lot of police officers, while others have relatively few. In Washington DC, the nation's capital, there were 6.3 sworn officers for every 1,000 people in 2000. In San Jose, California, however, there were only 1.6 per 1,000. The traditional measure of the level of police protection in a community is the **police–population ratio.** The national average for larger municipal departments in 2000 was 2.6 officers per 1,000 population.[8] (See Exhibit 7–1.)

**police–population ratio**

Does a higher police–population ratio mean that a city receives better police protection? Although the ratio is widely used as a measure of the amount of police service, cities with more police per population do not necessarily have lower crime rates. The reverse is often true: cities with high crime rates often have more police officers, as high crime rates produce public demand for more police.[9]

Washington DC, with the highest police–population ratio, does not have a correspondingly low crime rate. Failure to utilize patrol officers efficiently results in fewer officers being available on the street to respond to calls for service. Exhibit 7–2 compares two hypothetical police departments in cities of the same size. The department in City A has 50 percent more officers than City B does and a higher police–population ratio: 1.8 per 1,000 versus 1.2 per 1,000. Because it utilizes its officers in a more efficient manner, City B actually enjoys more officers on patrol during the high crime period between 4 PM and midnight. How does this happen? First, City B assigns a higher percentage of its officers to patrol. Then it assigns a higher percentage of its patrol officers to the busy 4 PM to midnight shift when more officers are needed. Finally, it puts most of its patrol officers in one-officer patrol cars (with some two-officer patrols for the very high crime areas).

## EXHIBIT 7–1

### Police–Population Ratios, Selected Cities, 2000

| City | Sworn Officers per 1,000 Residents |
|------|:----------------------------------:|
| Washington DC | 6.3 |
| New York City | 5.0 |
| Detroit | 4.4 |
| Baltimore | 2.3 |
| San Diego | 1.7 |
| San Antonio | 1.6 |
| San Jose | 1.6 |

*Source:* Bureau of Justice Statistics, *Local Police Departments, 2000* (Washington DC: Government Printing Office, 2003), Appendix A.

## EXHIBIT 7–2

### Deployment of Patrol Officers in Two Hypothetical Cities

|                                                  | City A  | City B  |
|--------------------------------------------------|---------|---------|
| Population                                       | 500,000 | 500,000 |
| Sworn officers                                   | 900     | 600     |
| Percentage of officers assigned to patrol        | 50%     | 70%     |
| Officers assigned to patrol                      | 450     | 420     |
| Percentage of patrol officers assigned to 4 PM–12 AM shift | 33%     | 50%     |
| Patrol officers, 4 PM–12 AM shift                | 148     | 210     |
| One-officer patrols                              | 20      | 190     |
| Two-officer patrols                              | 64      | 10      |
| Total patrols, 4 PM–12 AM                        | 84      | 200     |

The result of efficient management? City B spends less on police services but gets more actual police protection on the street. This analysis also demonstrates why the official police–population ratio is not a good measure of the level of police services.

## Assignment to Patrol

As a first step, a certain percentage of officers must be assigned to patrol duty. Surprisingly, this varies by a wide margin from department to department. Some departments place as many as 80 percent of all their officers on patrol (including traffic units), while others are able to place only 50 or 65 percent. Many of those departments have sworn officers in assignments that other departments have civilianized.

## The Distribution of Patrol Officers

Officers assigned to patrol need to be allocated to shifts and areas, based on a workload formula, involving citizen calls for service and reported crimes.[10]

Most serious crimes occur at night, as do the majority of disturbances (family disputes, bar fights, and so on). Exhibit 7–3 indicates the distribution of 911 calls for service and the assignment of officers by shift in Omaha, Nebraska.[11] The data indicate that the assignment of officers is reasonably related to the workload. All police departments do not operate in a rational manner, however. A 1987 investigation of the Philadelphia police found that "the same number of officers are on the street at all times—during the early morning, when there is practically no activity, and on weekend evenings, when the calls for service are heaviest."[12]

Some departments utilize a fourth patrol shift, beginning in the late afternoon and ending in the early morning (e.g., 6 PM to 2 AM).[13] This approach provides additional officers on the evening shift, when the number of calls is highest, and avoids overstaffing in the early morning hours, when the number of calls is at its lowest.

# EXHIBIT 7–3

## Distribution of 911 Calls, Omaha, Nebraska

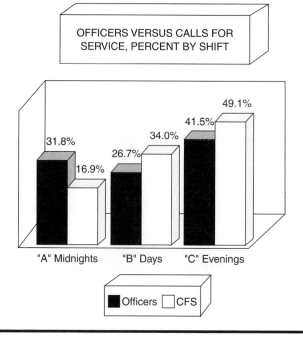

OFFICERS VERSUS CALLS FOR SERVICE, PERCENT BY SHIFT

31.8%   16.9%   26.7%   34.0%   41.5%   49.1%

"A" Midnights     "B" Days     "C" Evenings

■ Officers   □ CFS

Crime and disorder are not evenly distributed throughout the community. In his study of deadly force by New York City police officers, James J. Fyfe found that the police department gave precincts different experience ratings. The A precincts were classified as high-experience assignments because they were high crime areas. B precincts were medium-experience assignments, and C precincts were low-experience. Fyfe described C precincts as "residential 'country clubs' that place comparatively few demands on their police."[14]

Crime is more prevalent in poorer neighborhoods, and low-income people are the heaviest users of police services for order maintenance and general assistance. A National Crime Victimization Survey reports that the property crime rate for the poorest households (income of $7,500 or less) was 197.1 per 1,000, compared with 176.5 per 1,000 for households with incomes over $75,000.[15]

Low-income people are also the heaviest users of police services for noncrime events: medical emergencies and other types of situations requiring assistance. And because a disproportionate number of racial and ethnic minorities live in low-income neighborhoods, more police are generally assigned to minority neighborhoods.

Some departments fail to redraw beat boundaries regularly to adjust for social change. Neighborhoods grow or decline in population. Some deteriorate economically; as a neighborhood shifts from middle income to low income, crime and calls for service generally increase. The 1987 report on Philadelphia found that the department had not redrawn its boundaries in 16 years. Partly as a result, officers in the

Thirty-Fifth District handled an average of 494 calls, while officers in the Fifth District handled only 225. The disparity in workload was even greater in terms of serious crime: officers in the Thirty-Fifth District handled an average of 38 major offenses per year, compared with only 8 offenses for officers in the Fifth District.[16]

## Assignment of Patrol Officers

Police departments use a variety of methods for assigning patrol officers to particular shifts and patrol areas. Some assign officers on the basis of a strict seniority system and permit bidding for new assignments every six months or annually.

The issue of how often to change patrol officers' assignments involves conflicting principles. Many experts favor keeping officers in the same assignment for long periods of time. This allows patrol officers to get to know the people and the problems of their area. Some community policing programs are based on this principle. At the same time, however, it may cause officers to become bored and frustrated at the lack of new opportunities. As an anticorruption measure, some experts recommend frequent assignment changes to keep officers from developing too close relations with potentially corrupting influences.

Some departments rotate officers through different shifts every month, or on an even shorter time frame. A PERF report concludes that frequent change in shift "is deleterious to the physical and psychological health of the individual and to the well-being of the organization."[17]

Problems include loss of sleep, cardiovascular and other health problems, on-the-job accidents, disrupted family lives, and low morale. The report recommends steady shift assignments, based primarily on seniority, but with some managerial discretion in assignment based on performance and workload needs.

## "Hot Spots"

Patrol Beat 144 in Kansas City was one of the most dangerous areas in the nation. In 1991 the homicide rate was 177 per 100,000, about 20 times the national rate. Partly for this reason, the beat was chosen as the site for the Kansas City Gun Experiment, an innovative program to remove guns from the streets.[18]

**hot spot**

Beat 144 is a classic example of a **"hot spot":** an area that receives a disproportionate number of calls for police service and/or has a very high crime rate. A study of calls for service to the Minneapolis police department found that only 5 percent of the addresses in the city accounted for 64 percent of all calls. Meanwhile, 60 percent of the addresses never called the police for any reason. Routine police work is heavily skewed: a relatively small number of citizens in a community are extremely high consumers of police services.[19] Focusing police activities on "hot spots" is one of the most important innovations in policing, particularly in community policing and problem-oriented policing programs (see Chapter 10).

For a discussion of the impact of the patrol car on policing, see Chapter 2.

## Types of Patrol

Most (84 percent) police patrol in the United States today involves automobile patrol. Only 4 percent of all patrol is done on foot, 5 percent is done on motorcycle, and another 5 percent on bicycles.[20] Automobile patrol provides more efficient coverage than foot patrol. A patrol car can cover more area, pass each point more often, return to particular spots in an unpredictable manner if necessary, and respond quickly to calls for service. The efficiency of the patrol car in this regard is the reason why police departments converted from foot patrol to car patrol between the 1920s and the 1950s.

Efficiency comes at a price, however. An officer in patrol car loses direct contact with most citizens, especially law-abiding people. As a result, some people begin to see the police as an occupying army. William A. Westley was probably the first expert to notice this effect of automobile patrol. In his 1950 study of Gary, Indiana, he noted that "in contrast to the man on the beat, the man in the car is isolated from the community."[21] A decade and a half later, when riots were erupting across the country, no one could ignore the problem. The President's Crime Commission observed in 1967 that "the most significant weakness in American motor patrol operations today is the general lack of contact with citizens except when an officer has responded to a call. Forced to stay near the car's radio, awaiting an assignment, most patrol officers have few opportunities to develop closer relationships with persons living in the district."[22]

## Foot Patrol

**Foot patrol** involves a difficult trade-off between efficiency and community relations. An officer on foot cannot cover as much territory as an officer in a patrol car. This inefficiency is offset, however, by positive gains in community relations. They can have more personal contact with neighborhood residents, and this can help build trust. The Newark Foot Patrol Experiment, meanwhile, found that an increase in the number of foot patrol officers in an area resulted in people having less fear of crime and more positive attitudes toward the police.

**foot patrol**

For this reason, many community policing programs include a foot patrol element. But because of their limited mobility, it is not possible for a department to put all its patrol officers on foot patrol. Only about 4 percent of all patrol officers in the United States today patrol on foot.[23]

Striking the proper balance between efficiency and better community relations is a difficult issue. The Santa Barbara, California, police department utilizes both bicycle and foot patrol as part of its Tactical Patrol Force. These patrols are deployed on a regular basis in the central business district and the beach area; they are also used for special events such as parades or athletic events. The department regards them as an effective approach to both community relations and the police operations.[24]

## One-Officer versus Two-Officer Cars

**one-officer versus two-officer cars**

The outcry from patrol officers was predictable. One angrily accused the mayor of "jeopardizing the lives of cops." The cause of this outburst was a 1996 proposal in New York City to convert from two-officer to one-officer patrols in low-crime districts.[25] Many rank-and-file officers have opposed one-officer patrol assignments on the grounds that this approach endangers their safety.

Most patrol units—89 percent of all patrols in municipal police departments—involve single police officers. One-officer patrols are more efficient than two-officer patrols: two one-officer cars can patrol twice as much area and be available for twice as many calls as one two-officer car. Some police departments, however, still rely primarily on two-officer patrols: 90 percent of all patrol units in Buffalo, New York, for example, once involved two officers.[26]

Although some rank-and-file officers favor two-officer cars, believing that they are safer, a Police Foundation study of patrol staffing in San Diego found that officers in one-officer units were assaulted less often and were less involved in resisting arrest incidents than those in two-officer units. The one-officer patrol units, moreover, made more arrests and wrote more crime reports than two-officer units. Police officer concern about safety appears to be exaggerated. In 56.5 percent of the incidents where backup officers were dispatched in San Diego, it was later determined that they were not needed. Meanwhile, only 2.8 percent of the incidents were underdispatched, in the sense that the officers responding to the call had to request backup after they had arrived at the scene.[27]

Some police departments have been very slow to convert to one-officer patrols. At 6:00 AM on July 16, 2003, the Buffalo Police Department converted from two-officer to one-officer patrol cars. Buffalo was one of the last cities in the United States to rely exclusively on two-officer patrols. The mayor of Buffalo said, "This is an exciting time in the history of our city." The Police Commissioner estimated that the change would result in a 25 percent increase in the number of cars patrolling the city. The plan would allow the city to reduce the size of the police department and save an estimated $10 to $12 million per year for the financially strapped city.[28]

## Staffing Patrol Beats

Robert Peel's original ideal called for a patrol officer (or more than one) on every beat. The reality of policing is very different. On any given night, no officer is available for many patrol beats. When investigators for a mayor's Task Force in Philadelphia went out on a randomly selected Saturday night, they were shocked at the actual level of police patrol. Less than half (47 percent of all patrol sectors: 190 out of 450) were fully staffed with the assigned number of patrol officers.[29]

Police patrol is an extremely expensive, labor-intensive enterprise. Staffing a single patrol beat around the clock, seven days a week, requires almost five (4.8) officers. In addition to the three officers assigned to each shift, almost two others are needed because of days off, vacations, illness, and injuries. In practice, police departments are often shorthanded and have a difficult time fully staffing patrol beats.

# Styles of Patrol

## Individual Styles

How much work do patrol officers do? A New York City police officer explained that "it depends on what [you] want to make of it . . . You can make it as easy or difficult as you want. If it's done the way it's probably supposed to be done, it's probably not easy at all. But, it's the type of assignment you can also 'skate' in."[30]

In short, the actual amount of police work done by patrol officers depends on their work style. Some officers initiate more activity than others. **Officer-initiated activity** includes stopping, questioning, and frisking suspicious citizens; making informal contacts with law-abiding citizens; stopping vehicles for possible violations; writing traffic tickets; checking suspicious events; and making arrests. The amount

**officer-initiated activity**

**EXHIBIT 7–4**

## Ratio of Dispatch-Initiated to Self-Initiated Contacts with Citizens, Six Departments

| Department | Ratio |
|------------|-------|
| A | 3.8:1 |
| B | 3.6:1 |
| C | 1.5:1 |
| D | 1.2:1 |
| E | 1.1:1 |
| F | 1.0:1 |

*Source:* Stephen D. Mastrofski, Roger B. Parks, Albert J. Reiss, Jr., Robert E. Worden, Dhristina DeJong, Jeffrey Snipes, and William Terrill, Systematic Observation of Public Police (Washington DC: Department of Justice, 1998), Exhibit 6.

of officer-initiated contact with citizens varies considerably from department to department. Exhibit 7–4 indicates the ratio of dispatch-initiated to officer-initiated contacts with citizens in six police departments. The 1:1 ratio for Department F means that half of all citizen contacts are officer-initiated. In Departments A and B, only about 20 percent of all contacts are officer-initiated.

In citizen-initiated calls for service, some officers initiate more activity than others. Bayley and Garofalo found that some officers were likely to simply observe the situation and leave, while others took control over the situation, asked probing questions, and had citizens explain themselves.[31] The National Crime Victimization Survey (NCVS) found that in 20 percent of all reported property crimes, police officers only "looked around." They took a report in only about half of all property crimes.[32]

## Supervisors' Styles

The level of an officer's activity can also be shaped by his or her supervisor's style. This issue is discussed in detail in the next section.

## Organizational Styles

Patrol officer activity is also affected by different departmental styles of policing. James Q. Wilson identified three distinct organizational styles. The **watchman style** emphasizes peacekeeping, without aggressive law enforcement and with few controls over rank-and-file officers. The **legalistic style** emphasizes aggressive crime fighting and attempts to control officer behavior through a rule-bound, by-the-book administrative approach. The **service style** emphasizes responsiveness to community expectations and is generally found in suburban police departments where there is relatively little crime.[33] The Los Angeles police department has traditionally had an organizational culture that emphasizes aggressive police work, including high rates of officer-initiated contacts with citizens and high arrest rates.[34]

Some departments attempt to influence the work activity of patrol officers through quotas for traffic tickets, arrests, or field interrogations. Most experts, however, believe that numerical quotas are not related to the quality of police work.[35]

**watchman style**

**legalistic style**

**service style**

## Patrol Supervision

### The Role of the Sergeant

Some New York City police officers preferred the department's community-policing program (CPOP) because you "have more freedom . . . [you] aren't monitored by the radio and have only one sergeant who spends most of his time doing administrative work."[36] Standard police management texts call for close supervision of patrol officers by their sergeants. Community policing (see Chapter 10), on the other hand, generally involves less direct supervision and more discretion and control over time for officers on the street.

The style of supervision affects the amount of work performed by patrol officers. The basic unit of police patrol consists of a sergeant and a crew of patrol officers. The principle of the *span of control* holds that a supervisor can effectively manage only a limited number of people. In policing, the general standard is a span of control of one sergeant to eight patrol officers.[37]

An improper span of control can have a tremendous impact on the quality of police work. A sergeant cannot keep in touch regularly with his or her officers, and most importantly, cannot respond to critical incidents. The Special Counsel to the Los Angeles Sheriff's Department (LASD) found that a high rate of shootings by officers assigned to the Century Station was due in part to the fact that the span of control in that station was at times as high as 20 or 25 officers per sergeant, far in excess of the department's own recommended standard of 8 to 1.[38]

## The Communications Center

### The Nerve Center of Policing

**911 communications center**

Peter Manning's visit to a police **911 communications center** was a powerful experience: "My impressions of the communications center remain vivid and powerful. It was a smelly, smoky, poorly lit room reeling under the glare of harsh flickering fluorescent lights. Windowless, stuffy, with restricted exit and entry, few amenities. Nervous anxiety and worry was the prevalent tone . . . I have rarely endured such an unpleasant field work experience."[39]

The communications center is the real nerve center of the modern police department. Patrol work, in fact, is dominated by modern communications technology: the telephone, the two-way radio, and the patrol car. Contemporary 911-driven police work is (1) citizen-dominated, (2) reactive, and (3) incident-based. Critics call this system "dial a cop" and argue that the 911 system runs the police department, preventing any rational planning and proactive police response to problems.[40]

The communications center receives incoming calls from citizens, makes a series of discretionary decisions about how to handle those calls, and in many but not all cases dispatches police cars to the scene of the incident. The decisions by communications center personnel play a major role in shaping police work.[41] Antunes and Scott argue that the operator is "the key decision maker in the police bureaucracy."[42]

## EXHIBIT 7–5

### 911 Communications Center

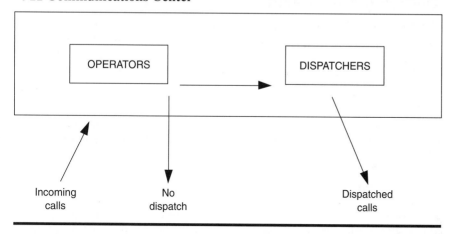

Exhibit 7–5 offers a schematic diagram of a police communications center. In most large police departments today, the communications system is staffed by civilians rather than sworn officers. In many departments they are not employed by the police department itself. Some states have only recently considered legislation to require training and licensing of communications center personnel.[43]

## 911 Systems

The 911 emergency number was introduced by the American Telephone and Telegraph (AT&T) Company in 1968. The first system went into operation in Haleyville, Alabama. Today, almost all police departments participate in a 911 system.[44]

Because of their convenience, and because police departments advertise the number, 911 systems have contributed to the great increase in calls for service. Some departments experienced increases of over 50 percent in the first 12 months after the 911 system was installed. To manage the overload, departments assigned priorities to incoming calls based on the seriousness of the problem and the need for an immediate response. Aided by CAD's call stacking capabilities, police were able to more efficiently manage delayed responses to certain nonemergency calls.[45]

## Processing Calls for Service

The 911 system is an information processing system. The **communications center operators,** dispatchers, and patrol officers are "information brokers" who receive citizen calls and translate them into official bureaucratic responses.[46] The operator obtains information from the caller and then makes a decision about the appropriate response. If he or she decides that the call requires a police response, the call is communicated to the dispatcher. The dispatcher then communicates information about the call to a patrol officer.

**communications center operators**

**SIDEBAR      7 – 1**

## Supervisors' Styles of Work

### Traditional Supervisors

Traditional supervisors expect aggressive enforcement from subordinates rather than engagement in community-oriented activities or policing of minor disorders. They are more likely than other types of supervisors to make decisions because they tend to take over encounters with citizens or tell officers how to handle those incidents.

Traditional sergeants and lieutenants are highly task oriented and expect subordinates to produce measurable outcomes—particularly arrests and citations—along with paperwork and documentation. Traditional supervisors give more instruction to subordinates and are less likely to reward and more likely to punish patrol officers. The traditional supervisor's ultimate concern is to control subordinate behavior.

### Innovative Supervisors

Innovative supervisors are characterized by a tendency to form relationships (i.e., they consider more officers to be friends), a low level of task orientation, and more positive views of subordinates. These supervisors are considered innovative because they generally encourage their officers to embrace new philosophies and methods of policing.

### Supportive Supervisors

These supervisors support subordinates by protecting them from discipline or punishment perceived as "unfair" and by providing inspirational motivation. They often serve as a buffer between officers and management to protect officers from criticism and discipline. They believe this gives their officers space to perform duties without constant worry of disciplinary action for honest mistakes.

### Active Supervisors

Active supervisors embrace a philosophy of leading by example. Their goal is to be heavily involved in the field alongside subordinates while controlling patrol officer behavior, thus performing the dual function of street officer and supervisor. They take a relatively positive view of subordinates. Active supervisors also give importance to engaging in patrol work themselves.

*Source:* Robin Shepard Engel, *How Police Supervisory Styles Influence Patrol Officer Behavior* (Washington DC: U.S. Justice Department, 2003).

Operators exercise tremendous discretion, just as police officers do. Manning illustrates the processing of calls with a description of a call reporting an alleged kidnapping. The operator has available four different kidnapping-related codes, but "there are no rules given to determine selection among these options." The operators have a 300-page procedure manual, but it "is virtually never used" because it is too large and there is no room for it on the operators' consoles.[47]

The 911 call workload has certain peak periods. To cope with this, the Communications Section in Seattle has two extra shifts of operators. In addition to the three basic shifts—First Watch (11:45 PM–7:45 AM); Second Watch (7:45 AM–3:45 PM); Third Watch (3:45 PM–11:45 PM)—there are two overlapping watches—Fourth Watch (7:45 PM–3:45 PM) Fifth Watch (11:45 AM–7:45 PM) during peak hours.[48]

Only about half of all calls received by 911 communications centers result in the dispatch of a police officer. The Police Services Study (PSS) found that 17 percent of all calls are referred to another agency. The operator takes information from the citizen in 16 percent of all calls and gives information to the citizen in 9 percent. In the remaining 14 percent of the calls, the citizen is told that the police cannot handle the call, the call is transferred, or some other response is given.[49]

Obtaining information from citizen callers is often difficult. Callers frequently provide vague, incomplete, or inaccurate information. Many are confused or frightened. Some are intoxicated or mentally disturbed. A situation that a caller describes as a "disturbance" could range from a party with only loud noise to an armed or mentally disordered person. The information is often incorrect. Bayley and Garofalo, for example, found that a weapon was actually present in only 25 percent of the reported "weapon present" calls.[50]

Gilsinan observed 911 operators in a large Midwestern city handling 265 calls over one 24-hour period. He found that operators interpret incoming information from callers and translate it into a category that fits an established bureaucratic response. Operators interact with callers in a problem-solving process, especially asking for more details, to reach the final determination.[51]

The dispatcher also exercises tremendous discretion in making important decisions. The basic decision involves which patrol unit to dispatch. The unit assigned to a particular beat is often not available: either "out of service" handling another call or not on duty at all that day. Consequently, officers are routinely assigned to calls outside their beat.[52] The most critical decision is whether the situation is an emergency and requires an expedited patrol response. Exhibit 7–6 indicates the processing of calls for service to the Los Angeles Police Department in 1999. Almost three million calls were received at the department's communications center. Only 28 percent resulted in the dispatch of a police unit. Two-thirds of the dispatches were either "emergency" or "urgent" status; only one-third were dispatched as routine incidents.

A discussion of 911 services for callers who do not speak English is covered later in this chapter.

## EXHIBIT 7–6

### Calls for Service and Police Units Dispatched, Los Angeles Police Department, 1999

| | | |
|---|---|---|
| **Total Calls for Service** | **2,976,559** | |
| Spanish language calls for service | 220,209 | |
| Percentage of total calls | 7.4% | |
| **Police Units Dispatched** | **842,317** | |
| Percentage of calls for service | 28% | |
| **Dispatch Status** | | **Percentage of Total Dispatches** |
| Emergency | 187,093 | 22% |
| Urgent | 361,546 | 43% |
| Routine | 293,678 | 35% |

*Source:* Los Angeles Police Department Web site, www.lapdonline.org.

Patrol officers process the information they receive from dispatchers, which is limited and often inaccurate. Thus, patrol officers respond to calls in the context of great uncertainty. They are dependent upon the information as given by the caller, interpreted by the operator, communicated to the dispatcher, communicated to the patrol officer, and interpreted by the patrol officer. In most departments, patrol officers are not required to provide detailed records of how they handle calls. Reports are often limited to "service rendered" or "no police action required."[53]

## Operator–Citizen Interactions

Obtaining information from a caller is one of the most important aspects of the 911 communications system. The system needs to provide a dispatched police officer with as much accurate information as possible. The process of asking questions of a caller can create problems, however. A study of 911 calls in "Citywest" analyzed operator–citizen interactions in terms of "face," defined as the desire of people to maintain a desirable public image and not experience humiliation or embarrassment (that is, to "save face").[54] The study found that many interactions are lengthy, involving many questions. Operators are trained to engage in "persistent repetition" when they cannot obtain clear or consistent information from a caller. This created problems in some calls, however.

Some questions can be perceived as threats to a caller's trustworthiness. In one call, for example, the caller finally asked, "Why are you asking [about what clothes he was wearing]." The operator explained that the responding officers needed to be able to identify who had requested help. Some questions can be perceived as threats to a caller's intelligence. In one call, for example, the operator asked, "What do you mean . . . ?" This could be interpreted as meaning that the caller did not make any sense.

Some questions can be perceived as threats to a caller's personal character. In one call the operator asked the caller, "You don't know your own sister's name?" implying a dysfunctional family relationship. Some questions can be perceived as questioning the caller's judgment. Operators are trained to determine whether or not an emergency actually exists. Some callers believe they know that an emergency exists and object to what they see as unnecessary questions.

In short, questions do more than elicit information. They can communicate—or appear to communicate—messages that affect the person being asked in a negative way. The study found that the different roles of the operator (call-taker) and dispatcher can conflict. Dispatchers want as much information as possible, but having operators ask many questions can alienate callers.

## The Systematic Study of Police Patrol

Patrol work is the most important aspect of policing. It is the point of most police–citizen interactions. Because of the decentralized nature of the job, with officers dispersed throughout the community, studying patrol systematically is extremely difficult and expensive.[55]

There have been four major observational studies of police patrol over the past fifty years. Sidebar 7–2 indicates the title, year, methodology, principal findings, and major publications from each one.

## Studies of Police Patrol

### American Bar Foundation Survey, 1956–1957

*Methodology:* direct observation, qualitative

*Sites:* Kansas, Michigan, Wisconsin

*Major findings:* pervasive exercise of discretion; complexity of police role; use of criminal law for purposes other than prosecution

*Publications:* Wayne Lafave, *Arrest* (Boston: Little Brown, 1966). Donald Newman, *Conviction* (Boston: Little, Brown, 1966).

### President's Crime Commission, 1965–1967

*Methodology:* direct observation, quantitative

*Sites:* Boston, Chicago, Washington DC

*Major findings:* quantitative analysis of patrol activities and exercise of discretion; situational factors in the exercise of discretion; officer use of force

*Publications:* Albert J. Reiss, *The Police and the Public* (New Haven: Yale University Press, 1971). Donald J. Black, *The Manners and Customs of the Police* (New York: Academic Press, 1980).

### Police Services Study, 1977

*Methodology:* direct observation, quantitative

*Sites:* metropolitan areas in St. Louis, MO; Rochester, NY; St. Petersburg, FL

*Major findings:* 911 call workload; race and gender in the exercise of discretion

*Publication:* Christy A. Visher, "Gender, Police, Arrest Decisions, and Notions of Chivalry," *Criminology* 21 (February 1983): pp. 5–28; Douglas A. Smith, Christy A. Visher, Laura A. Davidson, "Equity and Discretionary Justice: The Influence of Race on Police Arrest Decisions," *Journal of Criminal Law and Criminology* 75 (No. 1, 1984).

### Project on Policing Neighborhoods, 1996–1997

*Methodology:* direct observation, quantitative

*Sites:* Indianapolis, St. Petersburg

*Major findings:* activities of community-policing versus non-community-policing officers; citizen compliance with officer requests

*Publication:* Steven Mastrofski et al., *Systematic Observation of Public Police* (Washington DC: Department of Justice, 1998); Stephen D. Mastrofski, Michael Reisig, John D. McCluskey, "Police Disrespect Toward the Public: An Encounter-Based Analysis," *Criminology* 40 (March 2006): 519–52.

## Standards for Systematic Social Observation

Police patrol is an extremely complex activity. Relying on single incidents or impressions will not produce an accurate picture. The process of **systematic social observation** (SSO) is designed to provide an accurate, representative picture.[56]

systematic social
observation

SSO of police patrol work is accomplished by trained observers who accompany police officers at work in their cars, on foot, or even on bicycles. The expectation is that an observer accompanies the assigned officer everywhere that officer goes. Officers are told that they may direct their observer not to accompany them if they believe that safety is at issue. In our experiences, such instances occur rarely and officers quickly acclimate to the observer's presence throughout the shift.

While accompanying their assigned officer, observers may make field notes to help them reconstruct what they observe. These are written on a small notepad that is easily carried in a pocket or purse. Observers quickly develop their own shorthand for recording information that will assist their recall of the who-when-where-how of what happened. Officers are allowed, even encouraged, to read the notes made by their observer, but these notes may not be shown to or discussed with those outside the research team. Because the observed officer may ask to read the observer's notes at any time, observers are careful not to record anything the officer may find objectionable. While some might think that observer notetaking is too obtrusive, perhaps making officers nervous or self-conscious, others find that when done judiciously it can enhance rapport. Observers simply explain it as a part of their job, likening it to the reports that officers are required to complete. Most officers readily understand and accept this.

## The Call Service Workload

### The Volume of Calls

They are called the "Twin Cities," but the 911 workloads of Minneapolis and St. Paul patrol officers are very different. According to the 1997 LEMAS data, Minneapolis patrol officers handle twice as many calls per year as St. Paul officers: 550 versus 221. The Chicago police, meanwhile, handle 282 calls per year per officer, compared with 489 in the San Francisco police department.[57] In short, even though the basic technology of 911 systems is the same, the resulting workload varies tremendously.

### Types of Calls

"When you're in [patrol] you handle all kinds of jobs—maybe ones that just happened," explained a New York City patrol officer. Also, "you don't get to stay at a job for very long . . . the job is over in 15 minutes."[58]

Routine patrol work involves handling "anything and everything" that comes in over the 911 system. Each call is an isolated incident that the officer handles as quickly as possible before moving on. Studies of the 911 call workload give us a comprehensive picture of routine police patrol work. The most important finding is that only 20 to 30 percent of all calls for service involve criminal law enforcement. Most calls are **order maintenance calls** or **service calls.** Exhibit 7–7 presents the Police Services Study (PSS) data on calls for service to twenty-four police departments in three metropolitan areas. Other studies of 911 calls have found a similar distribution of calls.

Several basic points emerge from these data. First, criminal law enforcement represents a minority of all calls for service. The police are not primarily crime fighters but are peacekeepers and problem solvers.

Second, the vast majority of crime-related calls involve property crimes. Only 3 percent of all calls in Exhibit 7–7 involve a violent crime. Thus, the media image of policing that emphasizes the crime-fighting role, with a particular emphasis on violent crime and dangerous criminals, is a distortion of routine police work.

**order maintenance calls**

**service calls**

For a discussion of the crime-fighting and order maintenance roles of the police, see Chapter 1.

## EXHIBIT 7–7

## Crime and Noncrime Incidents and Their Distribution in Police Services Study

| | Percentage of All Encounters |
|---|---|
| **Crime incidents** | |
| *Violent crimes.* | |
| Murder, robbery, assault, kidnapping, rape, child abuse | 3.0 |
| *Nonviolent crimes.* | |
| Theft, selling or receiving stolen goods, breaking and entering, burglary, vandalism, arson, fraud, leaving the scene, false report, nonsupport | 15.0 |
| *Morals crimes.* | |
| Drug violations, gambling, prostitution, obscene behavior, pornography | 1.3 |
| *Suspicious circumstances.* | |
| Reports or observations of prowlers, gunshots, screams, suspicious persons or conditions | 9.8 |
| Total | 29.1 |
| **Noncrime incidents** | |
| *Traffic (regulation and enforcement).* | |
| Violation of traffic laws, traffic-flow problem, accidents, abandoned vehicles | 24.1 |
| *Disputes.* | |
| Fights, arguments, disturbances involving interpersonal conflict | 8.6 |
| *Nuisances.* | |
| Annoyance, harassment, noise disturbance, trespassing, minor juvenile problem, ordinance violation | 10.7 |
| *Dependent persons.* | |
| Drunks, missing persons, juvenile runaway, mentally disordered, other person unable to care for self | 3.4 |
| *Medical.* | |
| Injured accident victims, suicide and attempts, deaths, others needing medical attention | 1.9 |
| *Information request.* | |
| Road *directions*, referral, police or government procedures, miscellaneous requests where no additional police action mentioned | 4.0 |
| *Information offer.* | |
| Return property, missing or stolen property, false alarm report, complaint or compliment about police, general information provision | 2.8 |
| *General assistance.* | |
| Animal problem, lost or damaged property, utility problem, fire or other disaster, assist motorist, lockouts, companionship, irrational or crank call, house check, escort, transportation | 9.2 |
| *Miscellaneous.* | |
| Internal legal procedures, assistance request, officer wants to give information, officer wants information, officer assists, courier | 4.4 |
| *Gone on arrival.* | |
| Dispatched calls where parties to the problem are not at the scene | 1.8 |
| Total | 70.9 |

*Source:* Stephen Mastrofski, "The Police and Noncrime Services," in G. Whitaker and C. Phillips, eds., *Evaluating the Performance of Criminal Justice Agencies* (Beverly Hills, CA: Sage, 1983), p. 40.

Third, most police work involves order maintenance, or conflict management, and service. For this reason, policing is best characterized as peacekeeping (see Chapter 1). Cumming, Cumming, and Edell characterize the police officer as "a philosopher, guide, and friend."[59]

Fourth, many situations are ambiguous and require the exercise of discretion by the officers. It is not clear what the best response should be to situations classified as interpersonal conflict or public nuisance. Many calls that citizens characterize as crime-related do not necessarily involve an actual criminal incident. The caller may believe a crime has been committed, but there may not be sufficient evidence to support that belief. Reiss found that citizens defined 58 percent of all incidents as a criminal matter, but responding police officers recorded only 17 percent as crime-related. Reiss argues that "many citizens have only a vague understanding of the difference between civil, private, and criminal matters."[60] Officers need to use their judgment based on the particular circumstances of each situation.

Police discretion is examined in detail in Chapter 11.

Fifth, many of the order maintenance and service calls involve family problems that occur in private homes. The 911 system allows people to invite the police into their homes, which the police would normally not have a legal right to enter.[61] As a result, the police encounter, firsthand, the most intimate human problems: family disputes, mental illness, alcoholism, and so on.

Sixth, calls for service do not come from a representative sample of the community. Some people are very heavy users of police services; others rarely, if ever, call the police. Low-income people are the heaviest users of police services.[62] A study of calls for service in Minneapolis during one twelve-month period found that 5 percent of the addresses accounted for 64 percent of all the calls. These areas are now referred to as "hot spots." Some individuals or households have chronic problems and call the police repeatedly within a period of a few months. Meanwhile, 60 percent of the addresses in the Minneapolis study never called the police.[63]

# Aspects of Patrol Work

## Response Time

response time

Getting to the scene of a crime quickly has traditionally been a top police priority. Quick **response time** to calls is a part of the folk wisdom of policing. Both police and citizens believe that it will (1) increase the probability of an arrest and (2) increase public satisfaction. The standard model emphasized the fastest possible response to all calls for service.

Unfortunately, research has not supported the folk wisdom about rapid response time. Several studies have found that response time has little effect on clearance rates.[64] The total amount of time between the commission of a crime and the moment a police officer arrives on the scene includes separate parts:

1. *Discovery time*. The interval between the commission of the crime and its discovery.
2. *Reporting time*. The interval between discovery and when the citizen calls the police.

3. *Processing time*. The interval between the call and the dispatch of a patrol car.
4. *Travel time*. The length of time it takes patrol officers to reach the scene.

A Police Foundation study found that processing time took an average of 2 minutes and 50 seconds, while travel time averaged 5 minutes and 34 seconds. Cordner, Greene, and Bynum found similar times in a study of calls to the Pontiac, Michigan, police department.[65]

The police cannot control **discovery time,** reporting time, or processing time (Items 1, 2, and 3). A PERF study found that 75 percent of all reported crimes are discovery or cold crimes, and only 25 percent are involvement crimes (e.g., a confrontation between the victim and the offender). Most burglaries, for example, are not discovered until hours after they occurred. Cordner, Greene, and Bynum found that the discovery delay, the interval between the time the crime occurred or was discovered and reported, was measured in hours for property crimes and about 30 minutes for personal crimes of violence. In this context, the police travel time (item 4) is largely irrelevant in terms of catching the offender on the premises.[66]

In involvement crimes, the PERF study found that victims took an average of 4.0 to 5.5 minutes to call the police. Of these involvement crimes, 13 percent were reported while the crime was in progress and 14 percent were reported within the first minute after it was committed. Victim delay in calling the police undermines any potential gain by a faster police travel time. The study concluded that between 80 and 90 percent of serious crimes were reported to the police "too slowly for a response-related arrest to be made, even if the police response time was zero."[67]

Citizens delay calling the police for several different reasons:

- To verify that a crime has actually occurred (e.g., was anything stolen).
- To regain their composure.
- To call a friend or family member first.
- To decide whether they want to involve the police.
- A telephone is not immediately available (as in a street robbery).

Citizen satisfaction with police service is affected by response time. Furstenburg and Wellford found that citizens who had to wait more than 15 minutes for the police to arrive were significantly less satisfied than those who obtained a faster response. For both black and white citizens, satisfaction dropped steadily as response time increased from 5 to more than 15 minutes.[68]

Satisfaction is a function of citizen *expectations* about how soon the police will arrive. Citizens are most likely to be dissatisfied when they expect a quick response but do not receive it. Experiments with differential response to calls (see below) found that citizens were satisfied if they were informed that the police would not be there immediately.[69]

There have been no studies of the impact of the effect of faster response time on the crime rate. The National Academy of Sciences speculated that there might be some marginal impact on crime if the average offender noticed quicker response times and perceived an increased risk of arrest. The Academy report noted, however, that this is a "remote possibility," since offenders generally have "limited or sometimes even invalid information on police activity."[70]

**discovery time**

# Officer Use of Patrol Time

One of the traditional negative stereotypes about police officers involves the donut shop: that officers spend all their time eating donuts instead of patrolling and doing police work. This stereotype raises the crucial question of how patrol officers use their time. What does a typical patrol officer do during a typical eight-hour shift? How much "real" police work does he or she do? Another stereotype about policing is that the job is highly stressful, and that officers are continually rushing from one call to another. Is that stereotype valid?

How officers spend their time is also important from a cost standpoint. Personnel costs consume 80 to 90 percent of a police department's budget. Maximizing the productivity of a police department requires getting patrol officers to do as much work as possible.

The Project on Policing Neighborhoods (POPN) is the most thorough study of routine police work. It found that regular patrol officers spend only about 20 percent of their time in encounters with citizens. That translates into about an hour and a half per shift. They spend an average of slightly more than 20 percent of their time per shift on "general patrol," and about 15 percent traveling to locations. As expected, community policing officers spent less time in general patrol, but, surprisingly, they also spent less time than regular patrol officers in encounters with citizens.[71]

In Baltimore, patrol officers handled an average of about five calls per shift, with calls averaging twenty minutes each. This left about six and a half hours per shift of unassigned time. The authors concluded that patrol officers "have an inordinant amount of discretionary time." The study also found that only about 6 percent of unassigned time activities were directed by supervisors, dispatchers, other officers, or citizens. Also, when patrol officers were directed by supervisors to engage in an activity, the directives were very vague and generally did not involve problem solving or other proactive strategies.[72]

Arrests have a major impact on patrol officers' use of time. An arrest can take one and a half to two hours to process. Many arrests require two or more officers, depending on a department's standard operating procedures.[73] Each arrest removes the patrol officer from the street, thereby reducing the amount of time available for preventive patrol and for responding to calls.

## Evading Duty

Despite the fact that the two-way radio allows direct communication with patrol officers, officers are still able to avoid work. The easiest way is to delay reporting the completion of a call. A dispatcher assumes that an officer is still busy with the call (committed) until he or she reports that the call has been completed. Officers can create free time for themselves by simply delaying that call.[74]

## High-Speed Pursuits

High-speed pursuits are a major problem in police patrol. A pursuit is defined as a situation where a police officer attempts to stop a vehicle and the suspect knowingly flees at a high rate of speed. Pursuits are fairly common and pose serious risks to police officers, the persons being pursued, and other drivers and bystanders.[75]

Alpert and Dunham's study of pursuits by the Metro-Dade, Florida, police found that 33 percent resulted in accidents and 17 percent resulted in injuries. Slightly less than 1 percent resulted in the death of the suspect. Other studies have found even higher accident rates (44 percent in one study, but 18 percent in another). Studies have found injury rates that range from a high of 24 percent to a low of 5 percent of all pursuits.[76]

Studying and attempting to control high-speed pursuits is made difficult because all pursuits may not be reported by officers. In most departments, officers are required to complete an official report on every pursuit. Yet, many pursuits are of very short duration, and it is possible that officers do not report some of these. Officers may also not report pursuits where they know they have violated the department's pursuit policy (e.g., pursuing when road conditions are hazardous).

Until recently, patrol officers had complete discretion to initiate a pursuit. Most police departments today, however, attempt to control pursuits through written policies. These policies fall into three general categories. In 2000, 60 percent of all departments had *restrictive* policies limiting discretion by specifying the conditions under which pursuits may or may not be initiated. Another 7 percent had *discouraging* policies that advise officers against pursuits in certain situations but are not as limiting as restrictive policies. Finally, 23 percent of all departments had *discretionary* or *judgmental* policies that give officers broad discretion about whether to engage in pursuits.[77]

For a complete discussion of police discretion, see Chapter 11.

The Miami-Dade police department policy prohibits pursuits in less serious crimes: traffic offenses, misdemeanors, and nonviolent felonies where the identity of the violator is known.[78] Many experts argue that the potential risks involved are not justified in the case of minor offenses. Other departments restrict pursuits where bad weather creates unsafe driving conditions or where pedestrians are present.

# The Effectiveness of Patrol

Since the time of Robert Peel, the basic assumption of policing has been that a visible police presence deters crime. A related assumption is that increasing the number of officers on patrol will increase the deterrent effect. Until the early 1970s, however, there were no scientific experiments testing these assumptions.

## Initial Experiments

Initial experiments designed to test the effectiveness of patrol in the 1950s and 1960s did not meet contemporary standards of scientific research. In Operation 25, the New York City police department doubled the number of patrol officers in the Twenty-Fifth Precinct for four months during 1954. The department claimed that the increased patrol reduced muggings (street robberies) by 90 percent over the same period a year before, and that auto thefts declined by two-thirds.[79]

The Operation 25 experiment was methodologically flawed, however. It was not independently evaluated, raising the possibility that department officials manipulated the Uniform Crime Reports (UCR) figures on reported crime to achieve the desired results. The research design did not control for the possible displacement of crime to other areas or for other variables that might have affected criminal activity.

In another New York City experiment, the city more than doubled the number of police officers on the subways (from 1,200 to 3,100) between 8 PM and 4 AM. After a short-term decline, crime began to increase rapidly. By 1970 there were six times as many subway robberies as in 1965, before the additional police were deployed. Moreover, it was later discovered that the transit police deliberately manipulated the crime reports to lower the number of reported crimes during the experimental period.[80]

## The Kansas City Preventive Patrol Experiment

In 1972, Kansas City Police Chief Clarence M. Kelley decided to take a dangerous gamble. No chief had ever been willing to experiment with different levels of police patrol over a long period of time. And most dangerously, from a political standpoint, no chief had ever been willing to endorse an experiment where some patrol beats would receive *less* than the normal amount of patrol. There was always the possibility of a public backlash that could cost the chief his job. The experiment was also professionally risky. What if the experiment found that routine police patrol made no difference in the crime rate? Kelley was willing to take the risks, however. He was a strong chief who had brought many reforms to the Kansas City police department. In recognition of his leadership qualities, he was appointed director of the FBI in 1973, before the patrol experiment was completed.

**Kansas City Preventive Patrol Experiment**

The **Kansas City Preventive Patrol Experiment** (1972–1973) was a landmark event in American policing. It was the first experiment testing the effectiveness of patrol that met minimum standards of scientific research. The Police Foundation, a private and independent organization, funded the experiment, provided the expertise in research design, and ensured that the evaluation was independent and objective.[81]

The research design involved fifteen of the twenty-four beats in the South Patrol Division (nine were eliminated as unrepresentative of the area). They were matched on the basis of crime data, number of calls for service, ethnic composition, median income, and transiency of population and separated into five groups of three each. Beats were assigned one of three levels of patrol: (1) reactive beats received "no preventive patrol" as such; police vehicles assigned to these beats entered them only in response to calls for service; noncommitted time was spent patrolling other beats; (2) proactive beats received two or three times the normal level of patrol; (3) control beats were assigned the normal level of patrol (one car per beat).

The experiment investigated the following questions:

- Would citizens notice changes in the level of police patrol?
- Would different levels of police patrol affect the level of crime, as measured by UCR data or victimization surveys?
- Would different levels of patrol affect citizen fear of crime and if so would there be any changes in behavior or lifestyle?
- Would different levels of patrol affect citizen satisfaction with the police?

The experiment measured the impact of different levels of patrol on (1) criminal activity, (2) community perceptions and attitudes, and (3) police officer behavior and police department practices. Criminal activity was measured through official UCR data on reported crime and arrest, and through a victimization survey.

This was one of the first important applications of the relatively new victimization survey technique. The victimization survey was used to measure criminal victimization, citizen fear of crime, protective measures taken by citizens, protective measures taken by businesses, and citizen attitudes toward the police. Data were also gathered on police response time, arrest practices, police officer use of time, and officer attitudes. No previous police experiment had investigated such a wide range of issues, used such a variety of data sources, or relied on data independent of official departmental records. The experiment began in July 1972 but was suspended within a month when it was discovered that the experimental conditions were not being maintained. After being reorganized, it was resumed in October 1972 and ran for 12 months.

## Findings and Implications of the Kansas City Experiment

The experiment's findings were extremely important, and had enormous implications for police policy. The major findings were that:

- *Variations in the level of patrol had no significant impact on crime.*
- *Variations in the level of patrol had no significant impact on citizen feelings of safety.*
- *There were no significant changes in behavior or lifestyle because of perceived changes in police protection.*
- *Variations in the level of patrol did not affect attitudes toward the police.*

The findings challenged traditional assumptions about routine patrol. More patrol did not reduce crime, and lower levels of patrol did not lead to an increase in crime. Nor did citizens notice the different levels of police patrol. Since there was never any area that had absolutely no police presence, the experiment *did not prove that routine patrol has no effect on crime.* Patrol cars entered the reactive beats in response to calls, and marked police cars from other units also entered these areas.

Why did different levels of patrol have no impact on either crime or public perceptions? There are several reasons. First, as Sherman and Weisburd point out, patrol is spread so thin under normal conditions that doubling it is not likely to have any measurable impact.[82] Second, many crimes are not likely to be deterred by patrol because they occur indoors and are often impulsive acts. National Crime Victimization Survey (NCVS) data indicate that 33.7 percent of all sexual assaults occur at home, while another 21.3 percent occur at, in, or near someone else's house. More assaults occur inside a home, restaurant, or commercial building than occur on the street.[83]

About 60 percent of all murders, meanwhile, are between people who know each other. Crimes that occur indoors are not likely to be suppressed by the level of patrol on the street. Moreover, many of the offenders in these crimes do not rationally calculate the risk of arrest and punishment and, in particular, do not assess the level of police patrol in the area. In short, the traditional approach to police patrol has grossly exaggerated the extent to which many crimes are suppressible, or capable of being deterred by patrol.[84]

Third, people did not perceive the different levels of patrol coverage in Kansas City in part because of the "phantom effect," or what criminologists call **residual deterrence**.[85] Most people believe the police are present even when there is no patrol

**residual deterrence**

in the area. They have seen the police at some other time or place (e.g., the day before or in another area) and assume that the police are patrolling their area at the present moment. The initial perception has a residual effect, carrying over to other times and places.

Fourth, the Kansas City experiment tested only the *level* of police patrol. It did not study what patrol officers actually *do*—what activities they engage in. Community policing and problem-oriented policing (see Chapter 10) are important innovations primarily because they emphasize police activities that are different from traditional patrol. Critics found some flaws in the Kansas City experiment. Larson points out that police vehicles from other specialized units (which were not part of the experiment) operated in the reactive beats, thus adding to a visible police presence. Officers in the reactive beats engaged in more self-initiated activities (such as vehicle stops) and used their sirens and lights more often in responding to calls. There was also a higher incidence of two or more cars responding to a call for service in those beats. All of these actions may have created the perception of a greater police presence than actually existed.[86]

One of the most important implications of the data was that officers' uncommitted time (about 60 percent of their time on duty) might be used more effectively. Anthony Pate argues that since reduced patrol levels do not result in increased crime, "patrol can be removed, at least temporarily, without incurring negative consequences" and officers can be redeployed to other areas for specific purposes.[87]

## The Newark Foot Patrol Experiment

**Newark Foot Patrol Experiment**

The Kansas City experiment involved officers patrolling in cars. The findings quickly stimulated questions about whether or not foot patrol might have a different effect on crime and public attitudes. These questions led to the **Newark Foot Patrol Experiment** (1978–1979). The design of the experiment was similar to the Kansas City experiment. Some beats received additional foot patrol, others received less foot patrol, and others served as control beats. The experiment tested the effect of different levels of foot patrol on crime, arrest rates, and community attitudes.[88]

The Newark Foot Patrol Experiment found that additional foot patrol did not reduce serious crime: "Generally, crime levels . . . are not affected by foot patrol for residents or commercial respondents at a significant level." Different levels of foot patrol did, however, have a significant effect on citizen attitudes. Citizens were "acutely aware" of the different levels of foot patrol, and residents in beats with added foot patrol consistently saw "the severity of crime problems diminishing in their neighborhoods at levels greater than other areas studied."[89]

Increased foot patrol had other positive effects. Reduced fear of crime was also associated with more positive attitudes toward the police, including other police activities unrelated to foot patrol. At the same time, foot patrol officers reported more positive attitudes about citizens, believing them to be more supportive of the police. Foot patrol officers ranked "helping the public" as the second most important part of their job, while motor patrol officers ranked it fifth. The data suggest that the positive benefits of foot patrol on attitudes are a two-way street.

## New Questions, New Approaches

The Kansas City and Newark patrol experiments were major watersheds in thinking about the police. By questioning the traditional assumptions about patrol, the experiments encouraged creative new thinking. The finding that foot patrol reduced fear was encouraging. Also, as some observers pointed out, the experiments only tested the level of patrol and did not examine what patrol officers actually did while on duty. This new thinking led directly to the new idea of community policing.[90]

Community policing and other innovations are discussed in Chapter 10.

# Improving Traditional Patrol

In addition to community policing, many police departments have introduced innovations designed to improve the efficiency and effectiveness of traditional patrol. The most important innovations are discussed in this section.

## Differential Response to Calls

Do the police really have to respond immediately to every call for service? As patrol officers have always known, many calls involve trivial matters. In addition to the proverbial "cat in a tree" call, most property crimes are cold crimes where the responding officer just takes a crime report. Given the huge volume of 911 calls and the burden they place on the police, is there a better way of providing service to the public?

Some police departments have responded to this issue by attempting to manage the calls-for-service workload more effectively. This approach rejects the traditional assumption that the police should respond as quickly as possible to every call.

**Differential response** involves classifying calls according to their seriousness. Calls receive either (1) an immediate response by a sworn officer; (2) a delayed response by a sworn officer; or (3) no police response, with reports taken over the telephone, by mail, or by having the person come to a police station in person. Implementing differential response requires written guidelines and careful training for communications center personnel.[91]

**differential response**

An evaluation of differential response experiments found it to be successful. In Greensboro, North Carolina, only about half (53.6 percent) of all calls received an immediate dispatch of a police officer; 19.5 percent received no dispatched officer at all (most were cold larcenies where a report was taken over the telephone), and another 26.9 percent received a delayed response. Both police officers and citizens were satisfied with differential response. Greensboro citizens expressed satisfaction with 90 percent of the alternative responses, except for walk-in reports. In the case of delayed police response, citizen satisfaction was directly related to "whether the caller was informed that a delay might occur." This finding confirmed earlier research suggesting that citizen expectations are not a fixed entity but are dependent on what the police tell people to expect.[92]

The evaluation also found that differential response improved the overall quality of the call-for-service system. The new procedures "(1) increased the amount of information obtained from callers; (2) provided callers with more accurate information on what to expect in terms of response to their calls; and (3) provided patrol officers with more detailed information on calls prior to arrival at the scene."[93]

Robert Worden's study of differential response in Lansing, Michigan, found that it was both efficient and equitable. Cold crimes and other low-priority calls received a delayed response, with a median response time of 16 minutes. Over 90 percent of the citizens were satisfied with this service. Other calls were handled by taking reports over the telephone (almost all were larceny and vandalism incidents). Over 90 percent of the citizens were satisfied with this service. Differential response was equitable in the sense that whites and racial and ethnic minorities were just as likely to be satisfied (although there was some variation in intensity: satisfied versus very satisfied).[94]

## Telephone Reporting Units

Telephone reporting units (TRUs) handle calls by taking reports over the phone. Almost half of all reported crimes are larcenies and almost all of those are cold crimes in which the patrol officer would do nothing more than take a report. Many TRUs are staffed by officers on light duty due to injury. The TRUs handle anywhere from 10 to 20 percent of all calls on some shifts and up to 35 percent of all crime reports. One department found that TRUs took only half as long to take reports as patrol officers (16 versus 34 minutes).[95]

## 311 Nonemergency Numbers

Do patrol officers really need to respond to all the minor calls that come through the 911 system? When researchers first began studying routine patrol, one of the main things they noticed was how many calls involved minor incidents that really did not require a sworn officer with arrest powers. They also noticed that these calls consumed much of a patrol officer's time. As a result, experts began thinking about ways to relieve the police of this burden. One recent solution is the development of 311 call systems for less serious situations.

The Baltimore police department pioneered with an experimental 311 system in 1996. Only those calls that require the immediate presence of a police officer are routed to a 911 system dispatcher. Others are routed to the 311 system and are either referred to other agencies or receive a delayed police response. According to the city's 311 Web site, calls routed to the 311 system include calls about crimes not in progress, removing a dead animal, rodent problems, problems with traffic signs or signals, graffiti removal, sanitation problems, and other nonemergency situations.[96]

For a full discussion of the police and racial and ethnic minority groups, see Chapter 12.

What happened as a result? Did the 311 system reduce the call workload for patrol officers as expected? Did officers have more time for serious crimes? The changes in call patterns in Baltimore were dramatic. The evidence indicates that most low-priority calls (priority categories 3, 4, and 5) shifted from 911 to 311. The number of 911 calls for the most serious situations (category 1) did increase, but the total number of 911-only calls fell by 35 percent (from 2 million to 1.3 million). An evaluation found that the overall impact of the 311 system was limited because the police department did not completely change its operations. It continued to dispatch officers to all calls, 311 and 911, thereby nullifying one of the most important goals of the 311 system: freeing officers from low-priority calls. Partly as a result, response times were not lowered. And for the same reason, officers did not experience an increase in uncommitted blocks of time.[97]

# Non-English 911 Call Services

The face of America is changing. Immigration continues to bring to this country people from many different countries and cultures. A growing number of people in America do not speak English or have only weak command of English. This creates a major problem for the police, since they need to be able to receive and respond to calls from non-English speakers. Language barriers are one of the reasons why Hispanic Americans are less likely to call the police for service. Police departments can subscribe to 24-hour translation services, which are offered for a fee by private companies. The largest company currently offers on-the-spot translation of 150 different languages. A patrol officer can call the toll-free number (the department pays an annual fee) and get a translator almost immediately.

# Reverse 911

New communications and crime mapping technology has created reverse 911 systems. Instead of citizens calling the police, a reverse 911 system allows the police to call citizens. If a police department has important information about an event in a particular neighborhood, the system can identify telephone numbers in that area and call the residents. In Beech Grove, Indiana, for example, the system alerted businesses about a series of burglaries in their neighborhood. In another city a missing child was located within thirty minutes by alerting people in the area. A reverse 911 system can be activated within five minutes following a reported incident and can flood the affected area with hundreds of calls an hour.[98]

# Computers and Video Cameras in Patrol Cars

To enhance the efficiency of patrol operations, police departments are placing computers in patrol cars. Computer terminals allow officers to both obtain information and file reports efficiently. In 2000, 75 percent of all police officers had access to a computer in their patrol cars, up from 30 percent in 1990.[99]

Police departments are also placing video cameras in patrol cars, primarily as an accountability measure. In New Jersey, a consent decree settling a suit over racial profiling requires the state police to record all traffic stops. Videotapes of controversial incidents document the behavior of both citizens and officers and can help to resolve controversies over, for example, whether an officer used excessive force. By 2000, 45 percent of city police departments had video cameras in police cars.[100]

# Police Aides or Cadets

An alternative method of handling low-priority calls is to use nonsworn personnel, or **police aides.** Not all police tasks involve the need for a sworn police officer. The President's Crime Commission recommended the creation of a community service officer (CSO) to handle many of these routine assignments, thus freeing sworn officers for more critical tasks.[101] This approach is similar to the way other professions operate: delegating routine tasks to subprofessionals in training (e.g., lawyers use law clerks, college professors use graduate assistants).

**police aides**

SIDEBAR        7 – 3

## Nonemergency Police Services (NEPS) in the Charlotte-Mecklenburg, North Carolina, Police Department

In partnership with 311, a citizen should call 311 in order to contact the Crime Reporting Unit. 311 personnel are trained to answer a wide variety of Police related questions, but will transfer the caller to the CRU if a police report is needed to be filed. 311 will also connect a caller with the CRU if they need to add something to a police report which has previously been filed.

### Types of Non-Emergency Crime Reports
#### Telephone Crime Reporting

☐ Breaking and/or Entering of Storage/Utility Shed, or Detached Garage

☐ Breaking and/or Entering of Vehicle

☐ Communicating Threats

☐ Damage to Property

☐ Financial Identity Fraud

☐ Fraud

☐ Harassing Telephone Calls

☐ Indecent Exposure

☐ Larceny

☐ Simple Assault (Non-Domestic Violence Related)

☐ Supplements to Existing Police Reports

☐ Unauthorized Use of Motor Vehicle

☐ Worthless Check over $2000.00

*Source:* Charlotte–Mecklenburg Police Department Web site: www.charmeck.org/Departments/Police/Home.htm.

---

In an experiment in Worcester, Massachusetts, police service aides (PSAs) handled 24.7 percent of all calls and assisted in another 8.2 percent. These were nonemergency calls that did not require the presence of a sworn police officer. Citizens expressed satisfaction with the service they received from the PSAs and did not object to not having a sworn officer respond.[102] A Seattle CSO program was established in 1991; by 1993 it employed seventeen CSOs supervised by a sworn sergeant and a sworn lieutenant. CSOs were specially trained in social services and worked primarily with street people. CSOs patrolled the downtown area on foot and referred homeless people to agencies providing shelter, food, clothing, and alcohol or drug abuse treatment.[103]

Police cadet programs are now common across the country. The Portland, Oregon, Police Cadet Program is typical of most programs. Cadets must be between the age of 16 and 20, maintain a C average in high school with no failures, have no arrests or convictions, and be a U.S. citizen or have a valid immigration green card. Cadets participate in ride alongs; assist sworn officers at crime scenes, traffic accidents, and traffic speed watches; and help with vacation house checks, parades, and other miscellaneous duties. Cadets do not have police powers, but receive training on ethics, cultural awareness, defensive tactics, driving techniques, Oregon law, and other subjects.[104]

## Street Skills Training for Patrol Officers

In 2001 the Seattle police department introduced a special Street Skills training program. The two-day course focused on "high-risk, low-frequency" events such as high-stress driving and on shooting tactics. The first class was offered to officers on a voluntary basis. The response was so positive that the department expanded it into a mandatory four-day course for all officers. One officer commented, "It's as real as it gets." The expanded course covers additional subjects, including defensive tactics, handcuffing, and demonstration management. The course also includes ways to improve customer service, including exploration of why citizens file complaints and how to reduce them. By the end of 2001, 216 patrol officers had taken the four-day course, while 153 detectives had attended a two-day course.[105]

## Directed Patrol and "Hot Spots"

Directed patrol gives patrol officers specific duties to perform during a specified time period while they are freed from normal 911 dispatches. Traditional patrol gives officers only a general mandate to patrol their beats and to respond to calls for service. A **directed patrol** program might, for example, involve instruction to look for specific persons or types of crimes, or to patrol certain areas intensively.[106]

**directed patrol**

Cordner's evaluation of directed patrol in Pontiac, Michigan, found mixed results. There was some evidence that aggressive anticrime activities under the program may have reduced or displaced some kinds of criminal activity. The exact nature of this effect was difficult to determine conclusively, however. Cordner argues that the evidence does lend support to the view that what police officers actually do is more important than the number of officers on patrol.[107]

A more recent version of directed patrol focuses on "hot spots," or those areas that receive a very high volume of calls for service. An experiment in Minneapolis used a crack-down/back-off technique in which patrol officers would intensively patrol hot spots for short periods of time. The underlying assumption was that the impact of a short-term police presence would carry over because of residual deterrence.[108]

## Customer Feedback

The Seattle Police Department surveyed people who had called 911 to assess their satisfaction with the services they received. The customer feedback survey is a technique that many businesses—automobile dealers, hospitals—use today to assess how they are doing and how they can improve their services.

Seattle surveyed 200 people who had received a dispatched police officer. Respondents were guaranteed confidentiality. In April 2007, 77 percent were satisfied with their experience with the Seattle Police Department, and only 5 percent were dissatisfied. Equally important, the percentage who were "extremely satisfied" increased from the June 2006 survey (from 38 to 49 percent).[109]

## Beyond Traditional Patrol

The most important innovations in policing look beyond traditional patrol. Advocates of community policing and problem-oriented policing argue that 911-driven policing is reactive and limited to isolated incidents. They argue that the police should be more proactive and, working closely with community residents, focus on underlying problems. Community policing and problem-oriented policing are covered in detail in Chapter 10.

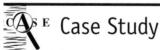 Case Study

*Kansas City (MO) Gun Experiment (Excerpt)*

### Program Type or Federal Program Source

Program to deter gun carrying in high crime hot spot areas; Offices of Weed and Seed.

### Program Goal

To reduce crime by seizures of illegal guns.

### Specific Groups Targeted by the Strategy

Violent perpetrators carrying guns.

### Geographical Area Targeted by the Strategy

Eighty-block area of Kansas City, Missouri.

The Kansas City Gun Experiment used intensive police patrols directed to an 80-block hot spot area where the homicide rate was 20 times the national average. Patrol officers seized guns by frisking individuals who were arrested and by making plain view sightings of firearms during routine traffic violation or safety stops. Traffic stops were most effective in locating illegal guns, with one gun found per 28 stops. Gun crimes, including drive-by shootings and homicides, declined significantly during the 29-week experimental period between July 1992 and January 1993. Drive-by shootings dropped from 7 to 1 in the target area, while increasing from 6 to 12 in a comparison area. Overall gun crimes dropped 49 percent (169 to 86) and criminal homicide declined 67 percent (30 to 10) from the 29 weeks before the patrols to the 29-week experiment period. However, there was no effect on other crime indicators, including calls for police service, calls about violence, property or disorder crimes, and total offense reports within the target area. Significantly, there did not appear to be a displacement effect (i.e., gun crimes did not increase in any of the seven surrounding patrol beats).

Evaluated by: Department of Criminology, University of Maryland; Department of Criminal Justice, University of Texas. Years of Operation: 1992–1993.

# Summary

Patrol is the backbone of policing. Despite many recent innovations in community policing, most police work involves patrol officers who patrol their assigned beats and respond to citizen calls for service. The patrol workload is dominated by calls for service and primarily involves noncriminal incidents. Thus, police work is best described as peacekeeping rather than crime fighting. The evidence suggests that increases in the level of patrol do not deter crime more effectively than lower levels of patrol. Innovations in patrol emphasize making more efficient use of patrol personnel and reducing the high volume of calls for service.

# Key Terms

backbone of policing, 191
functions of patrol, 192
police–population ratio, 193
hot spot, 196
foot patrol, 197
one-officer versus two-officer cars, 197
officer-initiated activity, 198
watchman style, 199
legalistic style, 199

service style, 199
911 communications center, 200
communications center operators, 201
systematic social observation, 205
order maintenance calls, 206
service calls, 206
response time, 208

discovery time, 209
use of patrol time, 210
Kansas City Preventive Patrol Experiment, 212
residual deterrence, 213
Newark Foot Patrol Experiment, 214
differential response, 215
police aides, 217
directed patrol, 219

# For Discussion

1. The Kansas City Gun Experiment represented a unique approach to crime prevention through patrol. Discuss how this approach is different from traditional patrol. What are the key elements of the experiment? What do patrol officers in this experiment do that is different from what basic patrol officers do? What is the relationship between the officers in this experiment and other patrol officers?

2. This experiment was a one-time special project. Discuss how this approach could be integrated into a police department on a permanent basis.

What problems would you anticipate? How could those problems be overcome through careful planning and administration?

3. You are the police chief in a department that is overwhelmed by 911 calls. Patrol officers have almost no time between calls and are frequently delayed in responding to calls. You have decided to adopt a 311 call system. What calls will be placed in the low priority category? Which calls will receive top priority? How would you treat a "suspicious noise" call? What about a "noise next door" call?

# Internet Exercises

What kinds of innovative patrol programs are currently operating around the country? Do a Web search of police departments using **www.officer.com** as your starting point. Divide the class into teams and assign each team a different group of departments to research. For example, you might assign teams different regions, or different size departments, or a range of departments of different sizes within particular regions.

Identify specific innovative patrol programs. Are there any programs listed on department Web sites? Describe the programs you find. Are they similar to programs described in this chapter? Or are they different in important ways? How are they different? Do the Web sites provide much detail about them?

Are there any obvious patterns related to where these programs exist? Big departments versus small departments? One region of the country rather than others?

## Notes

1. James Q. Wilson, *Varieties of Police Behavior* (New York: Atheneum, 1973), p. 7. Michael Lipsky, *Street-Level Bureaucracy* (New York: Russell Sage, 1980).

2. National Advisory Commission on Criminal Justice Standards and Goals, *Police* (Washington DC: Government Printing Office, 1973), p. 189. Wesley G. Skogan and Susan M. Hartnett, *Community Policing, Chicago Style* (New York: Oxford University Press, 1997), Ch. 4.

3. T. A. Critchley, *A History of Police in England and Wales,* 2nd ed. (Montclair, NJ: Patterson Smith, 1972), p. 52.

4. O. W. Wilson and Roy C. McLaren, *Police Administration,* 4th ed. (New York: McGraw-Hill, 1977), p. 320.

5. U.S. Department of Justice, *The Police and Public Opinion* (Washington DC: Government Printing Office, 1977), pp. 39–40.

6. Albert Reiss, *The Police and the Public* (New Haven, CT: Yale University Press, 1971), p. 3.

7. Bureau of Justice Statistics, *Law Enforcement Management and Administrative Statistics, 1997* (Washington DC: Department of Justice, 1999), Table 8a.

8. Ibid.

9. Thomas B. Marvell and Carlisle E. Moody, "Specification Problems, Police Levels, and Crime Rates," *Criminology 34* (November 1996): pp. 609–46.

10. The original workload formula was developed by O. W. Wilson in 1941. See O. W. Wilson, *Distribution of Police Patrol Force* (Chicago: Public Administration Service, 1941). Excerpts are found in Wilson and McLaren, *Police Administration,* 4th ed., pp. 633–55, Appendix J.

11. Police Executive Research Forum, *Organizational Evaluation of the Omaha Police Division* (Washington DC: PERF, 1992).

12. Philadelphia Police Study Task Force, *Philadelphia and Its Police* (Philadelphia: The City, 1987), p. 49.

13. Police Executive Research Forum and the Police Foundation, *Survey of Police Operational and Administrative Practices–1981* (Washington DC: PERF, 1981), pp. 428–32.

14. James J. Fyfe, "Who Shoots? A Look at Officer Race and Police Shooting," *Journal of Police Science and Administration* 9 (December 1981): p. 373.

15. Bureau of Justice Statistics, *Criminal Victimization in the United States,* 2004 (Washington DC Department of Justice, 2005). Available at www. ncjrs.org, NCJ 210674.

16. Philadelphia Police Study Task Force, *Philadelphia and Its Police,* pp. 48–49.

17. James L. O'Neill and Michael A. Cushing, *The Impact of Shift Work on Police Officers* (Washington DC: Police Executive Research Forum, 1991).

18. Lawrence W. Sherman, James W. Shaw, and Dennis P. Rogan, *The Kansas City Gun Experiment* (Washington DC: Department of Justice, 1995).

19. Lawrence W. Sherman, Patrick R. Gartin, and Michael E. Buerger, "Hot Spots of Predatory Crime: Routine Activities and the Criminology of Place," *Criminology* 27, no. 2 (1989): pp. 27–55.

20. Bureau of Justice Statistics, *Law Enforcement Management and Administrative Statistics, 1997,* p. xv.

21. William A. Westley, *Violence and the Police* (Cambridge, MA: MIT Press, 1970), p. 35.

22. President's Commission on Law Enforcement and Administration of Justice, *Task Force Report: The Police* (Washington DC: Government Printing Office, 1967), p. 54.

23. Bureau of Justice Statistics, *Local Police Departments 1997* (Washington DC: Government Printing Office, 2000).

24. Santa Barbara Police Department, "Tactical Patrol Force." Available at www.sbpc.com.

25. "Officers Denounce Proposal for One-Person Patrol Cars," *New York Times* (February 16, 1996).

26. Bureau of Justice Statistics, *Law Enforcement Management and Administrative Statistics, 1997,* Table 8a.

27. John E. Bodystun, Michael E. Sherry, and Nicholas Moelter, *Police Staffing in San Diego: One- or*

*Two-Officer Units* (Washington DC: The Police Foundation, 1977).

28. City of Buffalo, Press Release, July 17, 2003.

29. Philadelphia Police Task Force, *Philadelphia and Its Police,* p. 48.

30. Quoted in Jerome E. McElroy, Colleen A. Cosgrove, and Susan Sadd, *Community Policing: The CPOP in New York* (Newbury Park, CA: Sage, 1993), p. 133.

31. David H. Bayley and James Garofalo, "The Management of Violence by Police Patrol Officers," *Criminology* 27 (February 1989): pp. 1–25.

32. Bureau of Justice Statistics, *Criminal Victimization in the United States, 1994,* p. 100.

33. Wilson, *Varieties of Police Behavior.*

34. Christopher Commission, *Report of the Independent Commission on the Los Angeles Police Department* (Los Angeles: The Commission, 1991); Erwin Chermerinsky, *An Independent Analysis of the Los Angeles Police Department's Board of Inquiry Report on the Rampart Scandal* (Los Angeles: Police Protective League, 2000).

35. Bureau of Justice Statistics, *Performance Measures for the Criminal Justice System* (Washington DC: Government Printing Office, 1993), pp. 109–40. Available at www.ncjrs.org, NCJ 193505.

36. McElroy, Cosgrove, and Sadd, *Community Policing: The CPOP in New York City,* p. 138.

37. Wilson and McLaren, *Police Administration,* p. 83.

38. Special Counsel to the Los Angeles Sheriff's Department, *9th Semiannual Report* (Los Angeles: Special Counsel, June 1998), p. 23.

39. Peter K. Manning, *Symbolic Communication: Signifying Calls and the Police Response* (Cambridge, MA: MIT Press, 1988), p. xiii.

40. Malcolm K. Sparrow, Mark H. Moore, and David M. Kennedy, *Beyond 911: A New Era for Policing* (New York: Basic Books, 1990).

41. Manning, *Symbolic Communication: Signifying Calls and the Police Response.*

42. George Antunes and Eric J. Scott, "Calling the Cops: Police Telephone Operators and Citizen Calls for Service," *Journal of Criminal Justice* 9, no. 2 (1981): p. 167.

43. "Licensing May Loom for 911 Dispatchers in Pa.," *Law Enforcement News* (May 15, 1995), p. 1.

44. Kent W. Colton, Margaret L. Brandeau, and James M. Tien, *A National Assessment of Police Command, Control, and Communications Systems* (Washington DC: Government Printing Office,

1983); Bureau of Justice Statistics, *Local Police Departments, 2003* (Washington DC: Government Printing Office, 2006), p. 11. Available at www.ncjrs.org, NCJ 210118.

45. Tom McEwen, Deborah Spence, Russell Wolff, Julie Wartell, and Barbara Webster, *Call Management and Community Policing: A Guidebook for Law Enforcement* (Washington DC: U.S. Department of Justice, 2003), p. 7.

46. Peter K. Manning, "Information Technologies and the Police," in Michael Tonry and Norval Morris, eds., *Modern Policing* (Chicago: University of Chicago Press, 1992), pp. 349–98.

47. Manning, *Symbolic Communication,* p. 145.

48. Seattle Police Department, at www.cityofseattle.net/police/.

49. Eric J. Scott, *Calls for Service: Citizen Demand and Initial Police Response* (Washington DC: Government Printing Office, 1981).

50. Bayley and Garofalo, "The Management of Violence," p. 7.

51. James F. Gilsinan, "They Is Clowning Tough: 911 and the Social Construction of Reality," *Criminology* 27 (May 1989): pp. 329–44.

52. Ibid., p. 99.

53. Manning, "Information Technologies and the Police," p. 371.

54. Sarah J. Tracy, "When Questioning Turns to Face Threat: An Interactional Sensitivity in 911 Call-Taking," *Western Journal of Communication* 66 (Spring 2002): pp. 129–57.

55. Stephen D. Mastrofski, Roger B. Parks, Albert J. Reiss, Jr., Robert E. Worden, Christina DeJong, Jeffrey B. Snipes, and William Terrill, *Systematic Observation of Public Police* (Washington DC: Government Printing Office, 1998), p. 25.

56. Ibid.

57. Bureau of Justice Statistics, *Law Enforcement Management and Administrative Statistics, 1997,* Table 9a.

58. McElroy, Cosgrove, and Sadd, *Community Policing: The CPOP in New York City,* pp. 132–33.

59. Elaine Cumming, Ian Cumming, and Laura Edell, "Policeman as Philosopher, Guide, and Friend," *Social Problems* 12 (Winter 1965): pp. 276–86.

60. Reiss, *The Police and the Public,* p. 73.

61. Arthur L. Stinchcombe, "Institutions of Privacy in the Determination of Police Administrative Practice," *American Journal of Sociology* 69 (September 1963): pp. 150–60.

62. Reiss, *The Police and the Public,* p. 63.

63. Sherman, Gartin, and Buerger, "Hot Spots of Predatory Crime."

64. William Spelman and Dale K. Brown, *Calling the Police: Citizen Reporting of Serious Crime* (Washington DC: Government Printing Office, 1984).

65. Kansas City Police Department, *Response Time Analysis: Executive Summary* (Washington DC: Government Printing Office, 1978), p. 6; Gary W. Cordner, Jack R. Greene, and Tim S. Bynum, "The Sooner the Better: Some Effects of Police Response Time," in Richard R. Bennett, ed., *Police at Work* (Beverly Hills, CA: Sage, 1983), pp. 145–64.

66. Cordner, Greene, and Bynum, "The Sooner the Better."

67. Spelman and Brown, *Calling the Police*, p. 74.

68. Frank F. Furstenburg, Jr., and Charles F. Wellford, "Calling the Police: The Evaluation of Police Service," *Law and Society Review* 7 (Spring 1973): pp. 393–406.

69. J. Thomas McEwen, Edward F. Connors III, and Marica Cohen, *Evaluation of the Differential Police Response Field Test* (Washington DC: Government Printing Office, 1986).

70. National Academy of Sciences, *Fairness and Effectiveness in Policing: The Evidence*, p. 227.

71. Parks, Mastrofski, DeJong, and Gray, "How Officers Spend Their Time with the Community."

72. Christine N. Famega, James Frank, and Lorraine Mazerolle, "Managing Police Patrol Time: The Role of Supervisor Directives," *Justice Quarterly* 22 (December 2005): 540–59.

73. Herman Goldstein, The Drinking Drive in Madison: Project on the Development of a Problem-Oriented Approach to the Improvement of Policing, V.2 (Madison: University of Wisconsin Law School, 1982), pp. 67–68.

74. Jonathan Rubenstein, *City Police* (New York: Ballantine, 1974), pp. 117–19.

75. National Institute of Justice, *Restrictive Policies for High-Speed Police Pursuits* (Washington DC: Government Printing Office, 1989), p. 1.

76. Geoffrey P. Alpert and Roger D. Dunham, *Police Pursuit Driving: Controlling Responses to Emergency Situations* (New York: Greenwood Press, 1990), p. 37.; L. Edward Wells and David N. Falcone, "Organizational Variables in Vehicle Pursuits by Police: The Impact of Policy on Practice," *Criminal Justice Policy Review* 6, no. 4. (1992): p. 317.

77. Wells and Falcone, "Organizational Variables in Vehicle Pursuits by Police," pp. 324–25; Bureau

78. Alpert and Dunham, *Police Pursuit Driving*, p. 80.

79. Experiments regarding the effectiveness of patrol are reviewed in University of Maryland, *Preventing Crime: What Works, What Doesn't, What's Promising* (Washington DC: Government Printing Office, 1997), Ch. 8, "Policing for Crime Prevention"; see also John Eck and Edward Maguire, "Have Changes in Policing Reduced Violent Crime?" in A. Blumstein and J. Wallman, eds., *The Crime Drop in America* (New York: Cambridge University Press, 2000), Ch. 7.

80. Discussed in James Q. Wilson, Thinking About Crime (New York: Basic Books, 1975), Ch. 4.

81. George Kelling et al., *The Kansas City Preventive Patrol Experiment* (Washington DC: The Police Foundation, 1974).

82. Lawrence W. Sherman and David Weisburd, "General Deterrent Effects of Police Patrol in Crime 'Hot Spots': A Randomized Controlled Trial," *Justice Quarterly* 12 (December 1995): pp. 627–28.

83. Bureau of Justice Statistics, *Criminal Victimization in the United States, 1994* (Washington DC: Government Printing Office, 1997), p. 59.

84. Wesley G. Skogan and George E. Antunes, "Information, Apprehension, and Deterrence: Exploring the Limits of Police Productivity," *Journal of Criminal Justice* 7 (Fall 1979): p. 229.

85. Lawrence W. Sherman, "Police Crackdowns: Initial and Residual Deterrence," in Michael Tonry and Norval Morris, eds., *Crime and Justice: A Review of Research* (Chicago: University of Chicago, 1990), pp. 1–48.

86. Richard C. Larson, "What Happened to Patrol Operations in Kansas City?" *Journal of Criminal Justice* 3, no. 4 (1975): p. 273.

87. Anthony M. Pate, "Experimenting with Foot Patrol: The Newark Experience," in Dennis P. Rosenbaum, ed., *Community Crime Prevention: Does It Work?* (Beverly Hills, CA: Sage, 1986), p. 155.

88. The Police Foundation, *The Newark Foot Patrol Experiment* (Washington DC: The Police Foundation, 1981); Pate, "Experimenting with Foot Patrol."

89. The Police Foundation, *The Newark Foot Patrol Experiment*, pp. 4–5.

90. James Q. Wilson and George L. Kelling, "Broken Windows: The Police and Neighborhood Safety," *Atlantic Monthly* 249 (March 1982): pp. 29–38.

of Justice Statistics, *Local Police Departments 2000*, p. iv.

91. J. Thomas McEwen, Edward F. Connors III, and Marcia I. Cohen, *Evaluation of the Differential Police Response Field Test* (Washington DC: Government Printing Office, 1986).

92. Ibid., p. 102. Scott, *Calls for Service,* p. 97.

93. McEwen, Connors, and Cohen, *Evaluation of the Differential Police Response Field Test,* p. 8.

94. Robert E. Worden, "Toward Equity and Efficiency in Law Enforcement: Differential Police Response," *American Journal of Police* XII, no. 1. (1993): pp. 1–32.

95. Margaret J. Levine and J. Thomas McEwen, *Patrol Deployment* (Washington DC: Government Printing Office, 1985), pp. 40–41.

96. U.S. Department of Justice, COPS Office, *311 for Non-Emergencies: Helping Communities One Call at a Time* (Washington DC: U.S. Justice Department, August, 2003), p. 20.

97. Lorraine Mazerolle, Dennis Rogan, James Frank, Christine Famega, and John E. Eck, *Managing Calls to the Police with 911/311 Systems* (Washington DC: Department of Justice, 2005), NCJ 206256.

98. Mike Johnson, "A New Twist on 911 Capability," *American City and County 112* (December 1997): p. 10.

99. Bureau of Justice Statistics, *Local Police Departments, 2000,* p. iv.

100. Ibid.

101. President's Commission on Law Enforcement and Administration of Justice, *The Challenge of Crime in a Free Society* (Washington DC: Government Printing Office, 1967), pp. 108–9.

102. James M. Tien and Richard C. Larson, "Police Service Aides: Paraprofessionals for Police," *Journal of Criminal Justice* 6 (Summer 1978): pp. 117–31.

103. Martha R. Plotkin and Ortwin A. "Tony" Narr, *The Police Response to the Homeless: A Status Report* (Washington DC: Police Executive Research Forum, 1993), pp. 116–17, Appendix C, pp. 85–90.

104. Portland Police Bureau at www.portlandonline.com/police/.

105. Seattle Police Department, *2001 Annual Report* (Seattle: Seattle Police Department, 2002), p. 6.

106. Department of Justice, *Improving Patrol Productivity* (Washington DC: Government Printing Office, 1977), Ch. 4.

107. Gary W. Cordner, "The Effects of Directed Patrol: A Natural Quasi-Experiment in Pontiac," in James J. Fyfe, ed., *Contemporary Issues in Law Enforcement* (Beverly Hills, CA: Sage, 1981), pp. 37–58.

108. Lawrence W. Sherman and David Weisburd, "General Deterrent Effects of Police Patrol in Crime 'Hot Spots': A Randomized, Controlled Trial," *Justice Quarterly* 12 (December 1995): pp. 625–48.

109. Seattle Police Department, *How Are We Doing? Getting Feedback from the People We Serve.* Available at www.cityofseattle.net/police.

# Peacekeeping and Order Maintenance

Most police work involves peacekeeping and order maintenance, rather than crime fighting. People call the police for an infinite range of problems: arguments, fights, and domestic disputes; medical emergencies, including deaths, suicides, and injuries; assistance for dependent persons, including drunks, missing persons, and juvenile runaways; public nuisances, including noise, trespassing, and suspicious persons. Exhibit 7–6 in the previous chapter (p. 203) provides the PSS data on the frequency of these various calls for service. Many order maintenance situations involve what are referred to as "special populations": the mentally ill, juveniles, and the homeless.[1] This chapter examines the peacekeeping and order maintenance activities of the police. It gives special attention to several specific situations that frequently arise and looks at the different police responses to them.

## The Police Role

**Order maintenance** calls raise important questions about the police role. As we discussed in Chapter 1, some people view the police as crime fighters and think the noncrime calls are unimportant. Many police officers adopt this view and regard order maintenance calls as "garbage," "social work," or "bullshit."[2] This disparity between what the police actually do and what they value produces role conflict.

order maintenance

Some people, meanwhile, believe that noncrime calls are important, but primarily because they contribute to effective crime fighting. Stephen Mastrofski identifies four different ways that noncrime calls for service can help improve police effectiveness in dealing with crime: (1) The **crime prophylactic model** holds that police intervention can defuse potentially violent situations and prevent them from escalating into criminal violence; (2) the **police knowledge model** holds that noncrime calls give officers a broader exposure to the community with the result that they have more knowledge that will help them solve crimes; (3) the **social work model** holds that the latent coercive power of the police can help to steer potential lawbreakers into law-abiding behavior; (4) the **community cooperation model** holds that effective responses to noncrime calls can help the police to establish greater credibility with the public.[3]

crime prophylactic model

police knowledge model

social work model

community cooperation model

All of these models, however, assume that crime fighting is the central part of the police role and that noncrime calls are subordinate to it. Most experts on policing today, however, argue that order maintenance is at least as important as crime fighting, if not more important.[4] It is a legitimate role for the police to resolve problems that people believe exist. An orderly and peaceful society is a better society. If the police did not respond to these problems, someone else would have to. Community

For a full discussion on the role of policing order maintenance in crime control, see Chapter 9.

policing, problem-oriented policing, and zero-tolerance policing (see Chapter 10) are based on the idea that the police should focus on community problems, not all of which are crime-related.[5]

---

# Calling the Police

## Public Expectations

For a full discussion on the influence of communication technology see Chapter 2.

In a classic analysis, Egon Bittner describes police work in terms of situations involving "something-that-ought-not-to-be-happening-and-about-which-someone-had-better-do-something-now!"[6] In short, a citizen believes there is a problem and wants something done about it. The modern police communications technology encouraged this expectation by creating the possibility that someone could respond to problems. The police encouraged people to call, and over time, people were socialized into the habit of "calling the cops."[7]

Citizens have different reasons for calling the police in noncrime situations. John C. Meyer identified four specific expectations.[8]

1. **To Maintain a Social Boundary.** People often want the police to remove someone they believe does not belong there. The victim of domestic violence, for example, may call the police to remove the assailant. Homeowners may want the police to disperse a group of teenagers from the front of their homes. In many of these situations, no actual crime has occurred: it is no crime to assemble peacefully on the street. In response, police officers often ask, encourage, or order people to leave. To a great extent, people comply with such requests even when they are not legally required to.
2. **To Relieve Unpleasant Situations.** In many situations, someone calls the police because of noise, an argument, a family problem, or a dispute with neighbors. The role of the police is to restore order and keep the peace.

**counterpunching**

3. **Counterpunching.** In some disputes, someone calls the police about another person as a way of diverting attention away from his or her own behavior.
4. **To Obtain an Emergency Service.** People frequently call the police for emergency services: missing children, medical crises, suicide attempts, being locked out of their car or home, and so on.

## Police Response

Police officers exercise great discretion in handling noncrime incidents. Typically, they handle situations informally and take no official action (e.g., arrest). Informal responses include a wide variety of verbal and nonverbal tactics. In their landmark study of New York City police officers, Bayley and Garofalo identified 20 different tactics that officers use in handling situations (Exhibit 8–1).[9] The authors compared one group of experimental subject officers (ESO) to a group of comparison subject officers (CSO). The ESOs were nominated by other officers in the department to be especially skilled at handling conflict, and the CSOs were other officers who were randomly selected for the study.

## EXHIBIT 8-1

### Specific Actions Taken During Contact Stage by ESOs and CSOs—311 Nontraffic Encounters

| Action* | ESOs | | CSOs | |
|---|---|---|---|---|
| | % | # | % | # |
| Observed, stood by, took notes | 4.4 | 20 | 14.6 | 26 |
| Sought identity, relationships of parties | 15.4 | 70 | 19.1 | 34 |
| Questioned to elicit nature of problem | 30.8 | 140 | 30.9 | 55 |
| Asked citizens to "explain themselves" | 16.0 | 73 | 7.3 | 13 |
| Stated problem as police saw it | 3.5 | 16 | 3.4 | 6 |
| Verbally tried to defuse, "cool out" situation | 11.0 | 50 | 4.5 | 8 |
| Verbally restrained citizens (gave controlling orders) | 5.9 | 27 | 2.8 | 5 |
| Physically restrained citizens | 2.2 | 10 | 0.6 | 1 |
| Threatened physical force | 1.1 | 5 | 2.2 | 4 |
| Separated disputants in a nonphysical manner | 2.9 | 13 | 4.5 | 8 |
| Physically separated disputants | 1.1 | 5 | 0.0 | 0 |
| Requested dispersal of citizens | 1.1 | 5 | 0.6 | 1 |
| Ordered dispersal of citizens | 0.7 | 3 | 2.8 | 5 |
| Other | 3.9 | 18 | 6.8 | 11 |
| Total | 100.0 | 455 | 100.0 | 177 |

*Up to five actions were coded for each officer.

Some officers are more active than others. Bayley and Garofalo found that the passive officers did nothing more than observe and take notes. The more active officers took control of the situation by asking questions, giving advice or information, or warning the persons involved. Some officers accepted the complainant's definition of the situation, while others rejected it.

Citizens generally comply with specific police requests. Mastrofski, Snipes, and Supina found that citizens comply with police requests in 80 percent of all encounters. These incidents include requests to leave other people alone, to calm down and cease creating a disorder, to stop illegal behavior, and other miscellaneous requests. Compliance varied with the nature of the situation, the behavior of the officer, and the condition of the citizen. The more serious the situation, the less likely citizens are to comply. They are also less likely to comply with officers who approach the situation with a high degree of authoritativeness and/or who are disrespectful, and are less likely to comply in situations occurring in private rather than in public places.[10]

# Traffic Enforcement

Traffic enforcement activity is perhaps the most common type of order maintenance activity carried out by the police. Whereas citizen-initiated calls for service are heavily skewed toward a relatively small segment of any community, virtually all

## EXHIBIT 8-2

### Number and Percent of Drivers Stopped by Police in 2005, by Demographic Characteristics

| Characteristic of Stopped Driver | Drivers Stopped by Police During Most Recent Contact | |
|---|---|---|
| | Number (in millions) | Percent |
| Total | 17.8 | 8.8 |
| Gender | | |
| Male | 11.0 | 10.8 |
| Female | 6.9 | 6.8 |
| Ethnicity | | |
| White | 13.4 | 8.9 |
| African American | 1.6 | 8.1 |
| Hispanic | 1.8 | 8.9 |
| Other | 0.8 | 8.1 |
| Two or more races | 0.2 | 12.4 |
| Age | | |
| 16–19 | 1.5 | 13.2 |
| 20–29 | 5.0 | 13.7 |
| 30–39 | 3.8 | 10.1 |
| 40–49 | 3.7 | 8.8 |
| 50–59 | 2.4 | 6.8 |
| 60 or older | 1.4 | 3.6 |

*Note:* Detail may not add to total because of rounding.

*Source:* Bureau of Justice Statistics, *Contacts between Police and the Public, 2005* (Washington DC: Government Printing Office, 2007).

adult citizens drive cars, and minor violations of traffic laws are common. For example, about 9 percent of licensed drivers are stopped by the police each year (see Exhibit 8–2). About half of these stops are for speeding.[11]

Traffic stops are the source of low-level but significant friction between the police and the public. At the time of the stop citizens resent being stopped, asked to produce identification, and ticketed. Because of the resentment by citizens at the time of the stop, police officers, in general, find traffic enforcement a distasteful task. However, research suggests that the public, after being stopped, understand why they are pulled over. About 86 percent of those stopped by the police believed that they were stopped for a legitimate reason—with whites and those stopped for speeding being the most likely to believe that they were stopped for a legitimate reason (see Exhibit 8–3).[12]

Traffic stops are also one of the most dangerous police tasks, in terms of officers killed or injured on duty, because some stops involve armed and dangerous criminals. Lichtenburg and Smith reported that since 1988 about 13 percent of police

## EXHIBIT 8-3

### Percent of Stopped Drivers, by Ethnicity, Who Felt Police Stopped Them for a Legitimate Reason

| Reason for Traffic Stop | Total | White | African American | Hispanic |
|---|---|---|---|---|
| All reasons | 86.2 | 87.6 | 76.8 | 85.1 |
| Speeding | 90.8 | 91.5 | 86.3 | 89.0 |
| Vehicle defect | 85.7 | 90.5 | 66.5 | 85.5 |
| Record check | 88.6 | 91.8 | 72.2 | 85.4 |
| Roadside check for drunk drivers | 81.2 | 80.3 | 77.5 | 100.0 |
| Seatbelt violation | 84.2 | 84.0 | 87.0 | 82.0 |
| Illegal turn or lane change | 81.5 | 80.5 | 81.8 | 83.8 |
| Stop sign/light violation | 74.2 | 77.1 | 56.8 | 72.3 |

*Source:* Bureau of Justice Statistics, *Contacts between Police and the Public, 2005* (Washington DC: Government Printing Office, 2007).

deaths have occurred during routine traffic stops. During that same period, 9.4 percent of assaults on police were committed during traffic stops.[13]

The enforcement of traffic law violations varies widely from department to department. For example, in Glendale, Arizona, police officers write 50 percent more tickets than officers in Scottsdale, Arizona, even though both cities are approximately the same size and are located in the same metropolitan area.[14] James Q. Wilson found similar variations in traffic law enforcement in his historic study of police organizations.[15]

Traffic enforcement policy is generally the result of formal or informal department policies. In some instances, community pressure dictates vigorous enforcement. In others, it is the decision of the top police administrator. Some departments have formal or informal quotas on traffic tickets for officers.[16] Police departments occasionally engage in highly publicized traffic enforcement crackdowns. There is mixed evidence about whether such efforts effectively reduce traffic accidents or other crimes. For example, in Dayton, Ohio, the police department intensified enforcement in one high-traffic precinct over a six-month period. Officers were instructed to write many traffic tickets and to make frequent and highly visible traffic stops. This particular precinct and another comparable precinct where no crackdown occurred, were compared in terms of crime, arrests, and traffic accidents; the department found that the crackdown had no significant impact on any of these areas.[17]

There are three possible reasons why the crackdown had no effect. First, it is possible that there is no relationship between enforcement effort and crime. That is to say, increased enforcement has no deterrent effect. Second, it is possible that the increased level of enforcement was too small to make any difference. (The same issue arose with respect to the Kansas City patrol experiment.) Third, it is possible that some effect occurred but that the methods used in the evaluation lacked sufficient

For a full discussion on the Kansas City Preventive Patrol Experiment, see Chapter 7.

statistical power to detect it.[18] Similar problems arise in other studies of police law enforcement programs.

## Drunk-Driving Crackdowns

In the 1980s, public concern led to a national crusade against drunk driving. Most states increased the penalties for drunk driving, federal regulations forced states to raise the legal drinking age to 21,[19] and local police departments intensified enforcement efforts. Drunk-driving crackdowns included such tactics as random stops of drivers and roadblocks to stop all drivers. The goals were to apprehend actual drunk drivers and deter potential drunk drivers.

There is considerable debate over whether enforcement crackdowns reduce drunk driving. Evaluations of crackdowns in England and Scandinavia found short-term reductions in traffic fatalities followed by a return to previous levels.[20] Several factors appear to contribute to this phenomenon. The publicity surrounding a tough enforcement effort may cause changes in people's behavior. People drink less, or ask someone else to drive them home, or a friend stops them from driving. As the publicity surrounding the crackdown wears off, however, people return to their previous behavior patterns and drunk-driving fatalities increase.

The actual risk of arrest for drunk driving is extremely low. The probability of a police officer spotting a drunk driver is limited by several factors. First, a very small percentage of all drivers are drunk: an estimated 5 percent of all drivers on an average evening, with a higher percentage on weekends. Second, there are relatively few police officers on duty at any given moment relative to the number of cars on the road. Third, not all drivers who are in fact drunk exhibit impaired driving.[21]

Each arrest, meanwhile, sharply reduces the probability of catching other drunk drivers. An arrest is an extremely time-consuming event, involving one or more officers for anywhere from one to four hours. For the duration, each officer is out of service, unable to make further arrests or to deter drunk driving through patrol. Finally, crackdowns are difficult to sustain. Police officers, like drinkers, slip back into their normal routine and reduce their level of arrest activity.

For a full discussion on the types of calls for service that the police receive, see Chapter 7.

The rate of alcohol-related traffic fatalities (based on the number of licensed vehicles and/or drivers) has declined steadily since the 1920s (see Exhibit 8–4 for a summary of the years 1982–2007). Experts believe that several factors have contributed to this trend: safer cars, better roads and traffic safety measures, seat belts, air bags, and most recently the increase in the legal drinking age. The tough anti-drunk-driving enforcement programs have made, at best, some contribution to this trend, but they are only one part of a larger social control effort.[22]

## Policing Domestic Disputes

Domestic disputes are an important order maintenance situation. Domestic incidents represented 4.5 percent of all calls in the PSS data.[23] Police response to domestic incidents has been a matter of great controversy over the past 25 years. A revolution in public attitudes about domestic violence has led to new laws and policies, including

**EXHIBIT 8 – 4**

### Alcohol Related Traffic Deaths from 1982 to 2007

| Calendar Year | Total Drivers Killed in Traffic Crashes | Drivers Killed Who Had Alcohol in System | Percent of Drivers Killed in Alcohol-Related Crashes |
|---|---|---|---|
| 1982 | 24,690 | 13,675 | 55% |
| 1985 | 25,337 | 12,377 | 49% |
| 1988 | 27,253 | 12,835 | 47% |
| 1989 | 26,389 | 12,143 | 46% |
| 1990 | 25,750 | 11,892 | 46% |
| 1991 | 23,930 | 10,792 | 45% |
| 1992 | 22,584 | 9,678 | 43% |
| 1993 | 23,142 | 9,490 | 41% |
| 1994 | 23,691 | 9,079 | 38% |
| 1995 | 24,390 | 9,549 | 39% |
| 1996 | 24,534 | 9,400 | 38% |
| 1997 | 24,667 | 8,997 | 36% |
| 1998 | 24,743 | 9,005 | 36% |
| 1999 | 25,257 | 9,131 | 36% |
| 2000 | 25,567 | 9,451 | 37% |
| 2001 | 25,869 | 9,537 | 37% |
| 2002 | 26,659 | 9,796 | 37% |
| 2003 | 26,779 | 9,672 | 36% |
| 2004 | 26,871 | 9,421 | 35% |
| 2005 | 27,491 | 9,863 | 36% |
| 2006 | 27,348 | 10,033 | 37% |
| 2007 | 26,480 | 9,941 | 38% |

*Source*: National Highway Traffic Safety Administration, Traffic Safety Facts 2007 (National Center for Statistics and Analysis: Washington DC: 2008).

increased criminal penalties, the development of intervention and treatment programs for batterers, and changes in police department policies.[24]

## Defining Our Terms

There is much confusion about the police response to domestic incidents in part because many people fail to distinguish between disputes and violent incidents. The police handle many situations that are labeled *disturbances*. These include bar fights, arguments between neighbors, and many other kinds of problems. A **domestic disturbance** is one involving two or more people engaged in an intimate relationship. This includes married or divorced couples, live-in lovers, or people who are on a first date. It includes problems between adults and their children, or adults and their elderly parents. It also includes same-sex relationships. Only some of those—an estimated 33 percent—involve some form of *violence*.[25] The violence is usually an assault.

**domestic disturbance**

## The Prevalence of Domestic Violence

The National Crime Victimization Survey (NCVS) estimated that in 2007, 578,350 nonfatal violent crimes were committed against persons by their spouses, ex-spouses, boyfriends, or girlfriends.[26] Murray Straus and Richard Gelles, the two leading experts on the subject, have conducted a number of national surveys on domestic violence. They estimate that about 13 percent of all wives have experienced some form of **domestic violence,** and one-third of these have experienced severe violence.[27]

**domestic violence**

The Bureau of Justice Statistics reported that in 2007 intimate partner violence made up 23 percent of all violent incidents against women. Researchers have reported that intimate partner violence has decreased substantially from 1993 to 2007. In particular, they have reported that intimate partner violence against women decreased by about 50 percent during this time period, with 1.1 million women being victimized in 1993, compared with 554,260 in 2007. Victimization rates for women also declined during this period, falling from 9.8 per 1,000 women victimized to 4.2 per 1,000 women victimized.[28]

## Calling the Police

Many domestic violence victims do not call the police. NCVS data show that female victims called the police only about 62 percent of the time.[29] The reporting of domestic violence varies by the status of the victim. Low-income people call the police most frequently. In the Omaha domestic violence study, 50 percent of the victims and 31 percent of the suspects were unemployed at the time of the police call. Only 7.4 percent of all calls to the police came from the western half of the city, which includes the middle- and upper-middle-class residential neighborhoods.[30] The NCVS survey found that nonwhite female victims are substantially more likely to call the police than white female victims.[31]

Middle-class women are more likely to turn to private sources for help: a friend, a family member, a religious counselor, or a social worker. They are also more likely to be embarrassed about calling the police and worried about what neighbors or friends might think. Finally, the middle-income woman is more likely to be economically dependent upon her spouse (especially if she is a housewife and he is the sole source of income). The low-income woman is more likely to have relatively more economic equality to her husband or male friend.[32]

There are several reasons why victims of domestic violence do not call the police. According to NCVS data, only about 28 percent of victims report the incident to the police (see Exhibit 8–5). Most did not call the police because they regarded it as either a private or trivial matter. About 4 percent did not call the police because they thought it was not important to the police, 3.4 percent did not call because they feared reprisal, and 2.9 percent did not call to protect the offender.[33]

Domestic violence is concentrated in certain families and nonexistent in most families. Consequently, repeat calls to the same address are a common occurrence. In the Omaha study, 65 percent of the suspects had previously been arrested for some offense; 11 percent had been arrested for a past offense against the victim; and 3 percent had been arrested for an offense against the victim in the

### EXHIBIT 8–5

### Factors Influencing Reporting Domestic Violence to the Police

| Variable | Category | Incidents Reported | Incidents Not Reported |
|---|---|---|---|
| Calling the Police | | | |
| | Yes | 28.1% | — |
| | No | — | 71.9% |
| Most Important Reason for Calling the Police | | | |
| | It was a crime | 30.2 | — |
| | Protection from future attack | 19.9 | — |
| | To stop the incident | 16.7 | — |
| | Protection of others from future attack | 5.4 | — |
| | To punish the offender | 3.5 | — |
| | Duty to tell the police | 2.6 | — |
| | To catch the offender | 2.1 | — |
| | Other | 19.6 | |
| Most Important Reason for Not Calling the Police | | | |
| | Private matter | — | 22.8 |
| | Trivial matter | — | 18.1 |
| | Not important to police | — | 4.0 |
| | Fear of reprisal | — | 3.4 |
| | Protecting the offender | — | 2.9 |
| | Other | — | 48.8 |

*Source*: Richard Felson, Steven Messner, Anthony Hoskin, and Glenn Deane, "Reasons for Reporting and Not Reporting Domestic Violence to the Police," *Criminology* 40, 30 (2002): pp. 617–47.

previous six months.[34] Gelles and Straus found the average female victim was battered three times a year.[35]

# Police Response to Domestic Disturbances

Police officers exercise great discretion in handling domestic disturbances. The alternative responses include (1) arrest, (2) mediation, (3) separating the parties, (4) referral to a social service agency, or (5) no action at all. Arrest is not the most common response. As Mastrofski, Snipes, and Supina's study of police encounters (including all types of situations) found, rather than make an arrest, police officers often ask a person to cease illegal behavior.[36] Studies have found arrest rates ranging

> ### SIDEBAR     8 - 1
>
> ## Danger to Police in Domestic Disturbances
>
> There is considerable controversy over the extent to which domestic disturbance calls pose a danger to police officers. Joel Garner and Elizabeth Clemmer's analysis of FBI data on officers killed or assaulted in the line of duty found that domestic disturbance calls ranked very low in terms of officers killed. Robbery and burglary were consistently the most dangerous kinds of incidents. There was mixed evidence with respect to assaults on officers. Some data indicate that domestic calls are the most dangerous situations, while others indicate that they rank third or lower.[1] Hirschel, Dean, and Lumb analyzed assault and injury rates relative to the frequency of calls for service for ten categories of police activity. They found that "domestic disturbances ranked fourth in risk of officer assault and fifth in risk of officer injury."[2]
>
> Domestic disturbances are often more frustrating than dangerous. The police are frequently able to resolve the immediate dispute, but they cannot do anything about the underlying cause—unemployment, alcohol or drug abuse, or psychological trouble. Black found that some officers deliberately drove slowly to a domestic disturbance, hoping the dispute would resolve itself before they arrived.[3]
>
> [1]Joel Garner and Elizabeth Clemmer, *Danger to Police in Domestic Disturbances—A New Look* (Washington DC: Government Printing Office, 1986).
> [2]J. David Hirschel, Charles Dean, and Richard Lumb, "The Relative Contribution of Domestic Violence to Assault and Injury of Police Officers, *Justice Quarterly* 11 (1994), pp. 99–117.
> [3]Donald Black, "Dispute Settlement by the Police," in Black, *The Manners and Customs of the Police* (New York: Academic Press, 1980), p. 146.

from a high of about 40 percent of all incidents to a low of about 12 percent. (Some studies, however, have not distinguished between violent incidents and disturbances, where no law has been broken and arrest is not an option.) The Kentucky domestic violence study found arrests in 41 percent of all violent incidents, but Donald Black's earlier study found arrests in only 25 percent of all violent felonies and 20 percent of all violent misdemeanors.[37]

Mediation includes a variety of kinds of verbal responses: talking sympathetically, talking in an unsympathetic or hostile manner, asking the complainant what she or he would like done, ordering the parties to be quiet, threatening arrest. Officers often separate the parties to a dispute by asking one of them to leave the premises. If a person is the legal resident of the house or apartment, the police have no legal right to force him or her to leave. Again, to a great extent, people comply with police requests that they leave. In the Omaha domestic violence study, virtually all people left the premises when asked; moreover, couples remained apart an average of three days (70 hours), and 87 percent of the victims reported that the police intervention helped resolve the problem they were having.[38]

Police officers may also refer one or more of the parties to the dispute to social services: marriage counseling, alcohol or drug treatment, or legal aid (for those contemplating separation, divorce, and other legal matters). While many departments provide officers with a list of social agencies, a police officer has no legal power to compel someone to seek professional help. One study found that officers chose this alternative in only 5 percent of all incidents.[39]

A police officer can also take no action whatsoever. One study examining the Boulder County Police reported that in about 20 percent of the cases the police left the scene without taking any action.[40]

## Factors Influencing the Arrest Decision

Historically, several factors have discouraged officers from making arrests in domestic violence situations. First, some officers regard domestic violence as a private matter—something to be dealt with by the family. Second, many officers have learned from experience that domestic violence arrests are often dismissed because the victim refuses to pursue the case. Third, victims of domestic violence often call the police for help, but ask them to do something other than make an arrest.[41] Fourth, an arrest is work. It requires the officer to perform many tasks (taking the suspect into custody, writing reports), some of which are potentially dangerous. An arrest also raises the visibility of the officer's work, bringing it to the attention of other officials who might find it improper. If an officer does not make an arrest, on the other hand, the situation remains hidden from others. As is true in other occupations, police officers often try to reduce their workload.[42] Fifth, police departments have traditionally not valued domestic violence arrests (which are regarded as order maintenance activities), placing a higher value on arrests for murder, rape, robbery, or narcotics.

## A Revolution in Policy: Mandatory Arrest

A revolution in public attitudes toward domestic violence began in the 1970s. The women's movement identified spouse abuse as a major problem and demanded protection for victimized women. In two important lawsuits, women's groups in New York City and Oakland sued the local police departments, charging that they had denied women equal protection of the law by failing to arrest persons who had committed domestic assaults. The suits led to new department policies on police handling of domestic violence.[43] In *Bruno v. Codd* (1978) the New York City police agreed to adopt a written policy mandating arrest in cases of felonious assault (Exhibit 8–6). The *Scott v. Hart* (1979) suit against the Oakland police resulted in a similar policy.[44]

For a full discussion on administrative rulemaking see Chapter 11.

Mandatory arrest policies represent one of the first attempts to control officer arrest discretion. The strategy of using written policies is called administrative rulemaking, and it has also been used to control officer discretion in the use of deadly force, high-speed pursuits, and other areas of policing.[45]

## The Impact of Arrest on Domestic Violence

Many people believe that arrest deters future domestic violence. The **Minneapolis Domestic Violence Experiment** (1981–1982) sought to determine the relative deterrent effect of arrest, mediation, and separation in misdemeanor domestic violence incidents. Cases were randomly assigned to one of the three treatments. Each officer carried a color-coded pad of report forms and handled each case according to the approach indicated by the top form. Investigators measured repeat violence over the

**Minneapolis Domestic Violence Experiment**

## EXHIBIT 8–6

### Summary of Results of Six Immediate Arrest Experiments, for Repeat Violence Against the Same Victim

| Finding | City | | | | | |
|---|---|---|---|---|---|---|
| | **Minneapolis** | **Omaha** | **Charlotte** | **Milwaukee** | **Colorado Springs** | **Miami** |
| 6 month deterrence, official measures | yes | no | no | no | no | 1 of 2 |
| 6 month deterrence, victim interviews | yes | border | no | no | yes | yes |
| 6–12 month escalation, official measures | no | yes | yes | yes | no | no |
| 6–12 month escalation, victim interviews | * | no | no | no | no | no |
| 30–60 day deterrence, official measures (any or same victim) | yes | no | border | yes | no | 1 of 2 |
| 30–60 day deterrence, victim interviews | yes | border | no | yes | * | yes |
| Escalation effect for unemployed | * | yes | * | yes | yes | * |
| Deterrence for employed | * | yes | * | yes | yes | * |

*Key: relationship not reported.

*Source:* Lawrence W. Sherman with the assistance of Janell D. Schmidt and Dennis P. Rogan, Policing Domestic Violence: Experiments and Dilemmas, Table 6.1, page 129 (New York: Free Press, 1992).

next six months through follow-up interviews with victims and police department records of calls to the same address.[46]

The Minneapolis study found that arrest produced lower rates of repeat violence than separation or mediation. Rearrest occurred in 10 percent of the arrest cases, compared with 19 percent of the mediation incidents and 24 percent of the separation incidents. The experiment received considerable national attention and had a major impact on public policy. Between 1984 and 1986 the percentage of big-city police departments with "arrest preferred" policies increased from 10 to 46 percent.[47] Today, 99 percent of all municipal police departments have a written policy on domestic disputes (although not necessarily a mandatory arrest policy) and 46 percent have a special domestic violence unit.[48]

Critics have raised a number of serious questions about the Minneapolis experiment. Some police officers violated the integrity of the experiment by failing to handle the cases as directed, thereby undermining the random assignment of cases. A very small percentage of the participating officers produced the majority of the arrests. They were also more likely to follow the rules of the experiment. When only their cases were examined, the deterrent effect disappeared.[49] There was also

---

**S I D E B A R        8 – 2**

## Studying Your Local Police

Do the major law enforcement agencies in your area have written domestic violence policies? Obtain copies of those policies and compare them. Are they *mandatory* arrest or arrest *preferred* policies? How much discretion do they leave to the officer? Do any of the agencies have special domestic violence units or programs? What do these programs involve?

---

a great deal of attrition among the subjects. Only 62 percent of the victims (205 out of 330) could be located for an initial interview, and only 49 percent completed all 12 of the interviews.

Some critics argue that Sherman, the director of the experiment, had "prematurely and unduly publicized" the results. It is unwise, they argue, to recommend major changes in public policy on the basis of only one study that had not yet been replicated.[50] The lack of replication is a general problem in police research. Many of the most important experiments, such as the Kansas City Preventive Patrol Experiment (see Chapter 7), have not been replicated at all. It is dangerous to base public policy on one or even a small number of experiments.[51]

Replications of the Minneapolis experiment in other cities, in fact, failed to find a consistent deterrent effect of arrest. In Omaha, Charlotte, Colorado Springs, and Milwaukee there was no deterrent effect found for arrest. Some of the findings of the Omaha, Milwaukee, and Colorado Springs experiments were particularly disturbing (see Exhibit 8–6). Arrest appeared to *escalate* violence among unemployed persons compared with those who were employed. These data clearly indicate that arrest—at least from domestic violence—has different effects on different kinds of people.[52]

## Impact of Mandatory Arrest Laws and Policies

Today, there are three primary approaches that legislatures have taken with respect to incidents involving domestic violence: arrest is mandatory, arrest is preferred, and arrest is at the officer's discretion.[53] Hirschel et al. recently reported that 22 states and the District of Columbia have statutes mandating arrest, 6 have statutes that state that the preferred response is arrest, and 11 states have statutes that grant the officers discretion in incidents involving domestic violence.[54]

The full impact of mandatory arrest laws and policies is still not known. First, some commentators have warned that mandatory arrest may discourage calls by persons who only want the police to calm the immediate situation. For example, early research by Martin reported that following the implementation of a mandatory arrest statute in Connecticut, a dual arrest (meaning arresting both the offender and victim) was made in 33 percent of all police contacts for domestic violence. More recent research supported these findings.[55] Hirschel, in his national study of dual arrest, reported that while dual arrest was substantially less frequent than Martin suggested, statutes that mandate arrest result in an increased likelihood that the police arrest, both individuals involved in the dispute.[56] Accordingly, mandatory arrest laws may have the unintended impact of deterring people from calling the police for fear that they themselves may be arrested.[57] Second, mandatory arrest is likely to have a disproportionate impact on lower-class men, and poor African American men in particular.[58] This is because these individuals often have no one to turn to for help other than the police. On the other hand, the traditional no-arrest approach had a negative effect primarily on poor, African American women by denying them equal protection of the law.

## Other Laws and Policies

In addition to mandatory arrest policies, many departments have added special training for their officers in how to handle family violence situations. Surveys of victims, however, have failed to find greater satisfaction among those victims served by specially trained officers than among those served by officers who have not received special training.[59]

At the same time, many states have revised their laws on domestic violence. For example, Iowa law directs the officer to identify and arrest the primary aggressor. At least eight states now require law enforcement agencies to develop written policies on the handling of domestic violence. Several other states expanded the arrest power, allowing the police to arrest in the case of misdemeanor assaults that did not occur in their presence.[60] Eighteen states mandate that police officers make an arrest for violation of a protection order. Traditionally, police did not have the power to arrest in these situations, with the result that many women's advocates regarded protection orders as worthless pieces of paper.[61]

## The Future of Domestic Violence Policy

The future of police policy toward domestic disturbances and domestic violence is not clear. Mandatory arrest policies remain extremely popular, but the full impact of these policies is uncertain. In a comprehensive review of domestic violence policies,

---

**SIDEBAR     8 – 3**

### *Domestic Violence by Police Officers*

**Lautenberg Amendment**

A 1996 federal law (known as the **Lautenberg Amendment**) prohibits anyone with a conviction for domestic violence from owning a firearm. The law has serious implications for both the police and the military, since possession and possible use of a weapon is an essential part of the job. Police departments have been wrestling with how to respond to this law.

The law presents several questions for consideration:

1. Is the law good social policy? Is it appropriate to deny firearms to people with a record of domestic violence?

2. Is it fair, or even constitutional, for a law to be applied retroactively?

3. Should a person with any kind of criminal conviction be employed as a police officer?

Jeffrey Fagan concludes that there is "weak or inconsistent evidence" on the deterrent effect of arrest, prosecution, protection orders, and batterer treatment.[62] Lawrence W. Sherman, who directed the original Minneapolis experiment, no longer supports mandatory arrest in all situations.[63]

# Policing Vice

Policing vice requires law enforcement to regulate activities associated with public morality, such as prostitution, pornography, liquor laws, and other sexually oriented businesses. **Crimes of vice** present special enforcement problems because they are "victimless crimes," with no complaining party.[64] First, the police must initiate investigations on their own. Wiretaps, informants, undercover work, and other covert investigative techniques raise a number of difficult legal and moral questions. Second, victimless crimes involve behavior that many people regard as legitimate, or at least a private matter. The result is conflicting public attitudes about how vigorously the laws should be enforced. Last, victimless crimes are often statutorily defined as misdemeanor offenses. Enforcement, consequently, is often selective, inconsistent, and arbitrary. Many large police departments across the county have a specialized vice unit. These units typically enforce laws pertaining to prostitution. Below we discuss the nature of prostitution and the police response to it.

**crimes of vice**

## Prostitution

Prostitution is a common problem in many communities across the country. It is estimated that there are about 250,000 full-time prostitutes in the nation who serve about 1.5 million customers a week. Gross revenue from prostitution is estimated at $7.2 billion to $9 billion a year in the United States.[65] Miethe and McCorkle note that there are five different types of prostitutes, including streetwalkers, brothel prostitutes, bar girls, skeezers, and call girls.

    **Streetwalkers,** otherwise known as hustlers and hookers, work on the open streets. These prostitutes are the most visible to the public and police, and are at the lower end of the social and economic scale of prostitution. Many streetwalkers are poor, minority women who have few other options for employment.[66]

**streetwalkers**

    **Bar girls,** or b-girls, typically work out of bars or other entertainment establishments with the cooperation of management. Managers typically receive a percentage of the bar girls' revenue as a "referral" fee or sell bar girls overpriced drinks, which are paid for by the client. Bars near military bases have been a particularly popular location for bar girls to operate.[67]

**bar girls**

    **Skeezers** are the newest type of prostitute, emerging in the 1980s with the introduction of crack cocaine. These prostitutes trade sex for crack cocaine and are almost always "crack addicts."[68] Research suggests that those who engage in sex for drugs are often the victims of major trauma and have serious mental health problems.[69]

**skeezers**

    **Brothel prostitutes** typically work in large establishments owned by a single person or groups of individuals. While legal brothels only exist in a few counties in Nevada, massage parlors and escort services have emerged as a new front

**brothel prostitutes**

for prostitutes. Many illegal brothels operate through a system of referrals and informal social networks.[70]

**Call girls** represent the upper end of the economic scale of prostitution. They cater to a more affluent customer and generally make their arrangements over the telephone. Because they are not on the street, their activities are not visible to either the public or the police. Prostitution of this sort may, however, come to the public's attention if the prostitutes are working out of a motel or apartment complex in a way that causes other people to notice, take offense, and complain.[71]

In most cities, police departments concentrate their enforcement efforts on streetwalkers—in part because streetwalkers are the most visible, but also because other types of prostitutes are more difficult to apprehend. However, with this said, in many cities, low-level streetwalking is also tolerated by the police. It is usually confined to certain parts of the central business district where it is not seen by most of the public.

For instance, prostitution in Phoenix, Arizona, is primarily restricted to a two-mile strip of a major thoroughfare in the central part of the city. The police have reported that the area is fairly well organized in terms of the services offered by the prostitutes. One area of the strip consists of female prostitutes, a second area consists of male prostitutes, and a third area consists of transvestites. Historically, prostitution has been somewhat tolerated by the community as long as it is restricted to this area of the city and is not too obvious.

As such, for the patrol officer, streetwalking is essentially an order maintenance problem similar to the policing of skid row. The primary police objectives are (1) to keep streetwalking confined to a limited area (containment) and (2) to prevent related disorders from breaking out (keep the peace).[72]

Prostitution is often accompanied by an ancillary crime: a more serious offense that results from prostitution. "Johns" may be robbed, or a prostitute may be assaulted by a pimp or manager. This problem has been magnified in the media as a consequence of the Craigslist killer, who was suspected of killing at least one prostitute and harming several others. The case not only brought attention to the growing role of the Internet in prostitution, but also the risks that johns and prostitutes take when participating in such activity.

Arrests of prostitutes typically involve different motives. Conviction and punishment is not always the primary goal. Many arrests are designed to control streetwalking, either by confining it to a certain area or deterring it altogether. Convictions are usually for misdemeanors, with a sentence of, at most, several hundred dollars in fines and a few weeks or months in the county jail. The prostitutes themselves regard this as a routine business expense.[73]

Periodically, streetwalking increases to the point where it becomes more visible to the public. The resulting public outcry leads to a police crackdown: sweep arrests of all prostitutes. Like crackdowns related to other crimes, they have a short-term impact, after which things return to normal.

Prostitution arrests pose a number of legal problems for the police. The most difficult is the issue of entrapment, which occurs if the police officer initiates the idea of payment for sex. Also, equal protection problems are raised by the traditional police practice of arresting only the prostitute (usually female) and ignoring the customer (usually male), even though both are guilty of violating the law against commercialized sex. Finally, the informal practice of confining street-walking to a certain area of a city involves an illegal form of selective enforcement: enforcing the law in some areas but not others.[74]

# Policing the Homeless

Homeless people represent another order maintenance problem for the police. The homeless problem increased significantly in the 1980s. There has been much controversy over the actual number of homeless people. In the best study of the subject, Christopher Jencks estimated the total at about 400,000 people who are homeless (far less than the numbers used by some homeless advocates, but more than some government estimates).[75] The new homeless population includes more families than in the past, including more women and children. Some observers also believe there are more mentally ill persons among the homeless than in the past because of changes in mental health services.

Skid row in Los Angeles in the 1990s included a designated "sleeping zone," an area of 50 square blocks where the homeless are allowed to sleep on the streets. A newspaper account found on one night a 69-year-old grandmother and a 32-year-old woman, pregnant with twins, struggling to get into their cardboard boxes for the night. An estimated 12,000 people live in the neighborhood, most in single-room occupancy hotels, although no one knows exactly how many homeless people sleep on the streets.[76]

The **homeless problem** creates a number of challenges for the police. Homeless people establish semipermanent camps in public parks, resist transport to homeless shelters, and sleep in bus stations and subways in some cities. Advocates for the homeless have filed lawsuits challenging both police actions and local ordinances designed to restrict the homeless. Some but not all of these suits have been successful.[77] The Police Executive Research Forum (PERF) surveyed police departments to determine how they were responding to the homeless problem. Over 70 percent of the departments located in large metropolitan areas reported that homeless people posed a major or moderate problem in the community.[78]

**homeless problem**

The current police response to the homeless problem, however, is little different than it was in the past. First, it is reactive, with the police responding to calls for service about a problem with a homeless person. This has led to a police strategy that places primary emphasis on addressing complainant concerns rather than proactively working on behalf of the homeless to prevent problems from occurring in the first place. Second, the current police strategy is based on the idea of containment. Police attempt to contain the homeless problem to one area of a community to minimize disorder and to keep the homeless out of public view.[79]

However, some police agencies have begun to use proactive strategies to address problems related to the homeless. For example, the Seattle police department uses community service officers (CSOs) to handle many of the homeless-related situations. A CSO street team refers homeless persons to shelters, alcohol and drug abuse treatment programs, and financial assistance services. During extremely cold weather CSOs distribute clothes and sleeping bags that have been donated and patrol alleys looking for people who are in danger of death through exposure.[80]

## Policing the Mentally Ill

Mentally ill persons represent another important order maintenance problem for the police. The police usually become involved because someone defines the situation as a problem and there is no other solution available. The exact frequency of mental illness incidents is difficult to determine precisely because of different definitions of mental illness. Most studies estimate that 7 percent to 10 percent of police contacts are with mentally ill persons.[81] Furthermore, those with mental illnesses are responsible for a large proportion of repeat calls for service.[82]

## Police in Focus

### *Natural Disasters, Mass Exodus, and Displaced Criminals Living in Houston, Texas*

Hurricane Katrina displaced hundreds of thousands of families from Louisiana and Mississippi. Federal officials estimated that 600,000 families needed to find alternative shelter because their homes were either completely destroyed or were so badly damaged they could no longer be lived in.[1] This resulted in victims of Hurricane Katrina being evacuated to cities across the United States. The majority of them (over 300,000 people) were relocated by FEMA to Houston, Texas.[2]

In the aftermath of the hurricane, most public officials were simply concerned about finding shelter for displaced victims. However, as time passed some federal law enforcement officers began to question the effect of displaced violent criminals on the communities they were being taken to. New Orleans had historically been one of the country's most deadly cities, and in August 2005, it was on pace to be the murder capital of the United States. Many of those that were displaced were from the poorest areas of New Orleans where violent crime was concentrated.[3]

It was not long after evacuees arrived in Houston that police officials noticed changes in crime patterns. Drug markets began to emerge in areas where evacuees were housed, and homicide rates in these areas substantially increased. In the nine months following the hurricane, the Houston police department reported that 30 Katrina evacuees were the victims of homicide and 33 were suspected of committing a homicide in their city. In one month alone the Houston police department expended $6.5 million on overtime pay to respond to homicides involving Hurricane Katrina evacuees as either victims or suspects.[4]

Law enforcement officials associated with the FBI, the New Orleans police department, and other local police agencies have begun sharing intelligence on the most violent chronic offenders that were displaced and relocated across the country. A list of 112 "baddest bad guys" was disseminated among the agencies, and thus far law enforcement officials have been able to locate about 80 people on the list. One of the major lessons learned from Hurricane Katrina was that police in communities faced with mass exodus need to identify their community's chronic offenders and provide this information to those jurisdictions receiving displaced persons. Additionally, FEMA officials need to work more closely with the police and provide them with information on where they have relocated displaced persons—something that FEMA officials were unwilling to do for the first few months because of their concerns for privacy rights.[5]

[1]Barbara Sard and Douglas Rice, Changes Needed in Katrina Transitional Housing Plan to Meet Families' Needs (Washington DC: Center on Budget and Policy Priorities, October 13, 2005).
[2]http://www.cnn.com/SPECIALS/2005/katrina/people/, accessed on June 2, 2006.
[3]Amanda Ripley, "What Happened to the Gangs of New Orleans?" *Time*, May 22, 2006, pp. 54–61.
[4]Ibid.
[5]Ibid.

# Police Response to the Mentally Ill

The police come into contact with the mentally ill in a number of ways. The most common way is in response to calls from family members (32 percent). Family members often try to handle problems by themselves, and when the situation becomes uncontrollable, they call the police. Businesspersons and landlords calling the police account for about one-third of cases involving police contact with mentally ill persons. Because mentally ill persons often live in and around the central business district, businesspersons often call the police to "shoo away" a mentally ill person who may be interfering with business.[83]

Mentally ill persons are also much more likely to be the victims of crime, and, therefore, are more likely to come to the attention of the police. Teplin and her colleagues reported that over 25 percent of persons with severe mental illness were the victim of a crime in the past year. Even after controlling for demographic characteristics, those with serious mental illness were 11 times more likely to be the victim of a crime and 4 times more likely to be the victim of a serious violent crime than the general population.[84]

However, more typically the police are called to the scene because a mentally ill person is seen as threatening. In one study, almost half of all incidents involving a mentally ill person involved the person having a weapon of some kind. Property damage also occurred in about 33 percent of police contacts with mentally ill persons.[85]

Because of the complexities of handling problems associated with mentally ill persons, a great amount of time is often required. Pogrebin found that the average length of time for handling a mental health call was 74 minutes, which is significantly longer than other order maintenance calls.[86]

Police officers exercise great discretion in handling the mentally ill. The basic options include (1) hospitalization, (2) arrest, and (3) informal disposition. One study found that 75 percent of contacts between the police and the mentally ill are handled through informal disposition. This typically involves the officer using informal tactics to calm a person down. Some have referred to this practice as **"psychiatric first aid."**[87]

**psychiatric first aid**

When the situation cannot be handled informally, the officer may have to take a person with a mental illness to a hospital or jail. A number of factors are involved in making a decision of whether an individual should be hospitalized or arrested. These factors include the seriousness of the offense, officer training, alcohol or drug intoxication, and the offender's state of mind.[88] However, in communities with few mental health resources, police officers are sometimes inclined to arrest a mentally ill person for a misdemeanor. This practice is known as a **"mercy booking."** In many jurisdictions, mental health care is more readily accessible in jails than in the community. In these communities, police officers make an arrest for a minor offense to ensure that a mentally ill person receives services to get the care that is needed.[89]

**mercy booking**

Depending on the circumstances and the community resources available, a mentally ill person might also be hospitalized by the police. One study reported that individuals who are hospitalized often exhibit suicidal behavior, have a history of violence, are in need of psychotropic medication, have a mood disorder, or have a family history of mental illness.[90] (See Exhibit 8–7.)

## EXHIBIT 8-7

### Characteristics of Patients Referred to a Psychiatric Emergency Service by Police

| Reason for Referral | Percent |
| --- | --- |
| Violence or threat toward officer | 32 |
| Suicidal behavior | 51 |
| Other | 17 |
| Violence in the emergency room | 11 |
| History of violence | 49 |
| Need for psychotropic medication in the emergency room | 32 |
| Need for restraint in the emergency room | 8 |
| Intoxicated | 25 |
| Suicidal in the emergency room | 27 |
| Diagnosis | |
|     Mood disorder | 37 |
|     Psychosis | 18 |
|     Substance use disorder | 24 |
| Axis IV pathology | |
|     Mild | 1 |
|     Moderate | 66 |
|     Severe | 33 |
| Family history of mental illness | 55 |

*Source:* Robert Redondo and Glenn Currier, "Characteristics of Patients Referred by Police to a Psychiatric Emergency Service," *Psychiatric Services* 54, 6 (2003): pp. 804–6.

Several institutional and legal factors have an impact on the police response. First, the law limits the ability of the police to commit someone to a mental health facility involuntarily. A person can be committed only if he or she is a danger to self or to others. The paperwork required to meet this standard discourages officers from trying to commit people except in the most extreme cases.[91]

Second, mental health services are highly fragmented, consisting of a variety of hospitals, homeless shelters, and detoxification facilities. Most have their own admission criteria and refuse to accept people the police bring to them. In some instances, police officers go from one agency to another looking for one that will accept the mentally disordered person.

## Old Problems/New Programs

Problems arising from overreliance on arrest and the prevalence of use of force in encounters with mentally ill persons led a number of police agencies to institute special policies, personnel, and procedures to improve the police response to mentally ill persons in crisis. The first generation of efforts during the 1980s focused largely on officer training. Today, almost all police agencies provide at least some training to their recruits on mental health issues. However, the amount of time dedicated to these issues during academy training is quite limited—typically less than 6.5 hours—and most agencies provide less than one hour of postacademy in-service training per year on responding to mental health calls.[92]

The second generation of efforts during the 1990s aimed at improving the police response to problems involving the mentally ill by providing more specialized and focused responses. Today, about one-third of large police departments report that they have some type of specialized response for calls involving mentally ill persons. These specialized responses typically meet three criteria: (1) provide police officers with several options that are tailor fit to meet the needs of those with mental illnesses, (2) they link the mentally ill individual with community-based services, and (3) they take place in police agencies that have strong ties with mental health organizations, community members, and other criminal justice agencies.[93]

These agencies typically employ one of the three models.[94]

### Police-Based Specialized Response

This model involves sworn officers who have extensive training in responding to problems involving the mentally ill. These officers are responsible for responding to calls for service involving mentally ill persons and serve as a liaison to mental health agencies.

### Police-Based Specialized Mental Health Response

This model involves utilizing mental health professionals, not sworn officers, who are employed by the police department to respond to problems involving the mentally ill. The mental health professionals provide on-location and telephone advice to officers in the field.

### Mental-Health-Based Specialized Mental Health Response

This model involves formal agreements and arrangements between police departments and community mental health organizations. The model is based on the use of mental health crisis teams (MCTs) that are dispatched by police officers to provide field-level services to those in need.

# Policing People with Aids

In the 1980s acquired immunodeficiency syndrome (AIDS) presented the police with a new set of problems. Because police officers often handle people with AIDS, there is some risk of infection. Most of the risk involves police officers coming into contact with blood. While HIV has been found in saliva or "spit," there is no known case in which an officer has contracted AIDS from saliva. AIDS cannot be transmitted through casual physical contact such as touching.[95]

The Centers for Disease Control (CDC) estimates that about 1.1 million people in the U.S. are living with HIV or AIDS.[96] While the spread of the disease has been declining in general, it has been increasing in some populations, such as minorities and females. While no studies to date have systematically assessed the risk to police officers of being exposed to HIV, recent research examining HIV/

AIDS among arrestees—a group of individuals with whom the police have frequent contact—shows that police officers' potential for exposure is higher than it is in many other occupations. This is largely a consequence of the shift in policy toward more aggressive enforcement involving substance abusers. In most cities across the country, about 60 to 70 percent of those who are arrested by the police are current drug users, many of whom are injection drug users, placing them at higher risk for HIV infection.[97]

While the concern among police officers about contracting AIDS is high, few if any officers have contracted the disease. A survey by the FBI reports that between 1981 and 1991 seven police officers contracted HIV from a work-related exposure. However, recent research conducted by the Centers for Disease Control (CDC) found that not a single officer in the United States has ever contracted HIV/AIDS as a result of a work-related exposure.[98]

Flavin points out that even though the risk of contracting HIV/AIDS is low for police officers, it poses a unique threat. First, HIV/AIDS is contracted through a small microbe rather than a readily observable threat, such as a person or situation. Second, if an officer is exposed to HIV, it takes three to six months to know whether or not the officer has contracted the virus. Third, unlike most threats that the police are exposed to, HIV/AIDS is an incurable and deadly disease.[99]

As a consequence of the fear of contracting HIV/AIDS, a number of officers have become reluctant to render medical assistance. In a study of one police department, 30 percent of officers stated that they avoid helping people because of their fear of contracting HIV/AIDS.[100] In other studies researchers have found that most police officers attempt to take precautions to minimize their chances of contracting the disease, such as wearing latex gloves when assisting someone who is bleeding. However, with this said, precautions are not always possible, and as a result, officers sometimes do not render assistance and instead wait for medical personnel to take care of any medical problems.[101]

The fear of contracting HIV/AIDS has also led a number of police agencies to unofficially keep records of infected individuals. When the police agency receives a call for service, the dispatcher will notify the responding officer if the individual with whom the officer will be coming into contact is HIV positive. This practice is intended to protect officers from unknowingly placing themselves at risk. However, the collection of such information may lead to the violation of a person's right to privacy. Persons with HIV/AIDS are often the subject of prejudice and discrimination. For example, in Kokomo, Indiana, a waiter lost his job as a consequence of a police officer's informing the restaurant's management that the waiter was HIV positive—information that the officer had obtained while working on the job. The waiter later sued the City of Kokomo and was awarded $60,000, and the police department was ordered to educate its officers on issues of confidentiality.[102]

A Justice Department report recommended that all law enforcement agencies provide HIV/AIDS-related education and training for their officers, and develop formal policies for the handling of HIV-positive individuals in routine encounters, arrest situations, and police lock-ups.[103] Approximately 86 percent of state police departments offer HIV/AIDS training to recruits during basic training and 78 percent offer it through in-service training.[104] Almost half of all agencies are required to offer such training to meet state legal requirements.

# Policing Juveniles

Juveniles represent a special set of problems for the police. First, the police have a high level of contact with people under the age of 18. Young people are more likely than adults to be out on the street, where the police observe them. "Hanging out" on the corner or "cruising" in cars often produces citizen conflict over the proper use of public spaces.

Second, young people consistently express more negative attitudes toward the police than older people. For example, one survey reported that 72 percent of people between the ages of 18 and 29 expressed favorable attitudes with respect to the fairness of the police, compared with 90 percent for people in the 40- to 49-year-old age group.[105]

Third, juveniles represent a significant aspect of the crime problem in the United States: 16 percent of all violent index crime arrests and 26 percent of all property crime arrests. Juveniles are involved in three crimes at a particularly high rate: 47.4 percent of all arson arrests, 38.3 percent of all vandalism arrests, and 25 percent of all motor vehicle theft arrests.[106]

## Controversy over the Police Role

There is significant controversy over the proper police role toward juveniles. Some people favor a strict law enforcement role, emphasizing the arrest of offenders. Others prefer a crime prevention role, arguing that the police should emphasize helping young people who are at risk with advice, counseling, and alternatives to arrest.[107] However, because of increased public fear of crime and violent juvenile crime in particular, police departments have given greater emphasis to the law enforcement role in recent years. With the exception of programs such as G.R.E.A.T. traditional crime prevention programs have been deemphasized.

For a discussion on G.R.E.A.T. see Chapter 9.

Uncertain or conflicting department policies regarding juveniles often cause role conflict in police officers on the street. One report on police–juvenile operations pointed out that "crime prevention can be viewed as 'social work,' a role that police often see as taking time away from what they consider to be their primary role—the apprehension of criminals."[108]

Police response to juveniles is complicated by conflicting police responsibilities. The case of kids hanging out on the streets illustrates the problem. On the one hand, the police are expected to maintain order. To this end, a number of cities have passed curfews for juveniles and/or "gang loitering" ordinances. At the same time, however, the police have a responsibility to respect the rights of citizens. Young people have a First Amendment right to assemble in public.

For a discussion on gangs, see Chapter 9.

## Specialized Juvenile Units

Most police contacts with juveniles are divided between two units within the department: patrol and specialized juvenile units. Patrol officers have the most contact with juveniles as part of their normal patrol duty. They regularly see and have contact with groups of kids hanging out on the street corner, people they suspect to be gang members, and so on.

**S I D E B A R      8 – 4**

## Do Juvenile Curfew Laws Work?

Today 80 percent of large-sized cities (cities with a population of 100,000 or more) and 75 percent of medium-sized cities (cities with a population between 10,000 and 100,000) have juvenile curfew laws. These laws are intended to decrease the opportunity for youths to commit delinquency by prohibiting them from being in public areas in the evening and at night unless an adult accompanies them. The idea is that curfew laws will lead to the reduction of delinquency by decreasing youth access to environments associated with delinquency and by increasing the amount of parental supervision. However, research has found curfew laws to be ineffective in reducing delinquency. Most of the research has indicated that curfew laws have no impact on victimization or juvenile arrests or that crime is displaced to time periods that are not impacted by curfew laws.[1]

These findings present several questions for consideration:

1. Why are these laws popular?

2. Why are these laws ineffective?

3. Does your city have a curfew law? If so, how many youths a year are arrested for a curfew violation?

[1]K. Michael Reynolds, Ruth Seydlitz, and Pamela Jenkins, "Do Juvenile Curfew Laws Work? A Time-Series Analysis of the New Orleans Law," *Justice Quarterly* 17, no. 1 (2000): pp. 205–30.

Most large police departments have special juvenile units. They are often referred to by such names as the juvenile division, the youth division, or the crime prevention bureau. About 72 percent of all municipal police departments have a special juvenile unit. Many departments also have special child abuse and missing children units. The D.A.R.E. (Drug Abuse Resistance Education) program, where police officers provide drug education in the schools, is extremely popular. Currently, about 71 percent of all police departments have a special unit for drug education in the schools.[109]

The responsibilities of traditional juvenile units typically include (1) investigating reports of juvenile crime, (2) arresting delinquents, (3) preparing cases for court, and (4) appearing in court. However, some juvenile units have other responsibilities as well. For example, the Ross, Pennsylvania, police department's juvenile unit is responsible not only for investigating juvenile criminal behavior and the processing of cases but also for (1) investigating offenses against children, including abuse, neglect, or exploitation; (2) acting as a liaison to juvenile justice agencies (e.g., courts and probation) and schools; and (3) maintaining all juvenile records within the police department.[110]

Specialized juvenile units typically do not handle gang problems. These problems are often dealt with by a specialized gang unit.

## On-the-Street Encounters

In their historic study examining police encounters with juveniles, Black and Reiss found that 72 percent of all encounters between police and juveniles were initiated by a telephone call. Officers appear to initiate contacts with juveniles at a slightly higher rate (28 percent of all contacts) than with adults.[111] This is due to the fact that young people are more likely to be out on the street than adults, and the police are more likely to regard juveniles as criminal suspects.

As is the case with all other police activities, officers exercise great discretion in dealing with juveniles on the street. The alternative police responses include the following:[112]

For a full discussion on police discretion, see Chapter 11.

1.  Taking no official action. This is the most common outcome. As is the case with domestic disputes and allegedly mentally disturbed people, the police dispose of situations informally, mainly just by talking with people. Talking may involve advising, warning, mediating disputes, or simply listening. In many instances no arrest is made even though there are sufficient legal grounds to make an arrest.
2.  Taking a juvenile into custody but releasing him or her to a parent or guardian. About 25 to 30 percent of all juveniles taken into custody are released in this fashion.[113]
3.  Taking the juvenile into custody and releasing him or her to another law enforcement or social service agency. About 3 percent of all juveniles taken into custody are released in this fashion.[114]
4.  Arresting the juvenile and referring him or her to juvenile court. About 71 percent of all juveniles taken into custody are referred to juvenile court. Some (about 7 percent of the total) are referred to criminal court for prosecution as adults.[115]

Arrest discretion involving juveniles is influenced by the same situational factors that affect encounters with adults. These factors include the seriousness of the offense, the preference of the victim or complaining party, the relationship between complainant and suspect, and the demeanor of the suspect.[116]

For a full discussion on the allocation and distribution of officers, see Chapter 7.

## The Issue of Race Discrimination

The police arrest proportionately far more African American juveniles than white. Several factors account for this disparity. First, police departments generally assign more patrol officers to minority neighborhoods than white neighborhoods and, consequently, observe minority youths more frequently.[117]

Second, minority youths are stopped and questioned at a higher rate than whites. Many racial profiling studies have found that minority youth are stopped, frisked, and their vehicles searched at rates disproportionate to their presence in particular neighborhoods.[118]

Third, the racial disparity in arrests is associated with other factors that influence arrest decisions. Black and Reiss found that the higher arrest rate was explained in large part by greater African American involvement in serious crime. When seriousness of the suspected offense was controlled, blacks and whites were arrested at similar rates.[119] Lundman, meanwhile, found that black adults are more likely to ask the police to arrest the suspect than are white adults. Since most complainant–suspect situations are intraracial, black juveniles are arrested at a higher rate.[120]

Smith, Visher, and Davidson, in a study of arrests involving persons of all ages, found that police are slightly more likely to make an arrest when the victim is white rather than African American. Other studies have also suggested that the police are more likely to arrest a juvenile when an adult is the complaining party.[121]

The demeanor of the suspect also influences police arrest decisions. In separate studies, Black and Reiss and also Piliavin and Briar found that African American juveniles expressed hostility toward the police more often than did whites and, as a consequence, were arrested at higher rates. Piliavin and Briar described the phenomenon as the "self-fulfilling consequences of the original set of police attitudes and behavior toward black youth." The police expect black juveniles to engage in more law breaking, stop and question them at a higher rate, and as a consequence create the perception of harassment and generate more hostile reactions.[122] David Klinger, however, has raised new questions about the role of demeanor in arrests, arguing that these earlier studies did not control for hostile behavior that occurred after the arrest and therefore could not have influenced the arrest itself.[123]

## Crime Prevention Programs

Police crime prevention efforts have traditionally involved programs designed to steer juveniles away from criminal activity through education, counseling, or role modeling. The basic idea is for the police to present themselves as friends and helpers rather than as law enforcers.

Today it is not uncommon for a police department to coordinate several youth-oriented programs as part of their prevention efforts. Examples include police athletic leagues, midnight basketball, wilderness clubs, and explorer and mentoring programs. Some current crime prevention programs are part of community policing. Under this model, police agencies work to build the capacity of neighborhoods to prevent crime. This is often accomplished by the police department coordinating community and social service organizations to focus on youth and neighborhoods that are at the highest risk for delinquency. In other words, the police department acts as a social service broker to ensure that those who need the most help have an opportunity to receive it.[124]

The most popular current crime prevention programs are D.A.R.E. and G.R.E.A.T., which attempt to prevent drug use, delinquency, and involvement in gangs and gang crime. These crime prevention strategies are covered in Chapter 9.

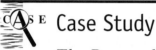 **Case Study**

### *The Demand Side of Prostitution—"Johns"*

In an NIJ-funded study, Martin A. Monto explored the types of sex-related behavior characteristics of men who solicited prostitutes. The study examined the effects of the First Offender Prostitution Program (FOPP) in San Francisco, California, and similar programs in other cities. These programs offered johns an opportunity to pay a fine and attend a daylong seminar. Participants were advised that no further legal action would be taken against them if they successfully avoided rearrest for a year. If there was a subsequent offense, however, the individual was prosecuted for the new offense and the original charge was reinstated.

Monto surveyed 1,291 men arrested for soliciting street prostitutes before they participated in FOPP and in similar johns programs in Las Vegas, Nevada; Portland, Oregon; and Santa Clara, California. He compared the data on why these men visit prostitutes, their attitudes regarding violence against women, and the consequences of conceiving of sexuality as a commodity.

Monto found that 72 percent of the men surveyed had attended some college. They ranged in age from 18 to 84 years, with a median age of 37, and were less likely to be married. Although their motives for seeking sex with a prostitute differed, there were similarities among certain groups. Married clients and college graduates were more likely to want a different kind of sex than they had with their regular partners. Unmarried clients and non-college graduates reportedly felt shy and awkward when trying to meet women but did not feel intimidated by prostitutes.

Monto also explored the clients' attitudes toward "rape myths"—that is, attitudes that have been used to support sexual violence against women. Less than one-half of 1 percent of those surveyed indicated acceptance of all eight rape myths. On the other hand, 20 percent indicated acceptance of four or more items. Researchers believe that this latter group may be responsible for perpetrating violent acts against women for hire.

Next, Monto measured the degree to which clients regarded sexuality as a commercial commodity. Monto found that the greater a client's belief that women and sex were commercial products, the more frequently he would visit prostitutes. This mindset was also a strong predictor of the acceptance of rape myths, less frequent condom use with prostitutes, and a disinclination to view prostitution as a demeaning profession for women.

Researchers also conducted a limited recidivism study of those clients who participated in the San Francisco and Portland programs. Although both programs had a recidivism rate of about 2 percent, researchers acknowledge that conclusions about the programs' efficacy in reducing recidivism were hampered by a lack of available baseline data for comparative purposes. The recidivism rate was not computed for men who were arrested but did not attend the program.

*Source:* Adapted from Marilyn Moses, Understanding and Applying Research on Prostitution, *NIJ Journal* 255, November 2006.

# Summary

Order maintenance and peacekeeping is an important part of policing for the simple reason that most calls for service fall in this category. How the police respond to these calls raises the basic issues about the police role that we discussed in Chapter 1. How do we think about the police? What do we want them to do?

Traditionally, police officers regarded order maintenance calls as garbage and social work, placing a higher value on crime fighting. Most experts today, however, argue that maintaining order and keeping the peace is a central aspect of policing. Community policing, problem-oriented policing, and zero-tolerance policing place a high value on dealing with noncrime problems. Many order maintenance situations, moreover, involve special populations: the homeless, the mentally ill, juveniles. If we think of the police in terms proposed by Herman Goldstein, as a general service agency providing a wide range of services to the public, it becomes important for police departments to develop special programs and procedures to improve the handling of these problem situations.[125]

## Key Terms

order maintenance, 227
crime prophylactic model, 227
police knowledge model, 227
social work model, 227
community cooperation
    model, 227
counterpunching, 228

domestic disturbance, 233
domestic violence, 234
Minneapolis Domestic Violence
    Experiment, 237
Lautenberg Amendment, 240
crimes of vice, 241
streetwalkers, 241

bar girls, 241
skeezers, 241
brothel prostitutes, 241
call girls, 242
homeless problem, 243
psychiatric first aid, 245
mercy booking, 245

## For Discussion

1. Describe four reasons why the public calls the police in situations not involving a crime.
2. Briefly explain why deaths involving drunken driving have declined over the past 50 years.
3. Explain how domestic violence policies evolved in local police departments across the United States.
4. Discuss the research findings on the impact of mandatory arrest for misdemeanor domestic violence.
5. Explain the difference between streetwalkers and call girls, and discuss how each might have an impact on order maintenance and peacekeeping.

## Internet Exercises

**Exercise 1** Go to the Web site **http://www.usatday. com/educate/college/firstyear/articles/20060226. htm** to learn more about the personal choices New Orleans police officers had to face during Hurricane Katrina. As a class, discuss what you think about police officers who left their jobs to take care of their family members and what the police department might have done to address the problem before it happened. **Exercise 2** Check out the Web site http://www. jrsainfo.org/dvsa-drc/index.html. This site has a number of resources regarding domestic violence.

**Exercise 3** Go to the Web site http://www.college-drinkingprevention.gov/ to view the site College Drinking: Changing the Culture, created by the National Institute on Alcohol Abuse and Alcoholism (NIAAA). The site provides information on issues related to alcohol use among college students. Review the site and discuss as a class whether you believe such a Web site impacts college student alcohol use and other risky behavior such as drunk driving.

# Notes

1. Peter E. Finn and Monique Sullivan, *Police Response to Special Populations* (Washington DC: Government Printing Office, 1988).
2. David Bayley, *Police for the Future* (New York: Oxford University Press, 1994).
3. Stephen Mastrofski, "The Police and Non-crime Services," in G. Whitaker and C. Phillips, eds., *Evaluating the Performance of Criminal Justice Agencies* (Beverly Hills, CA: Sage, 1983), pp. 44–47.
4. Charles M. Katz, Vincent Webb, and David Schaefer, "An Assessment of the Impact of Quality of Life Policing on Crime and Disorder," *Justice Quarterly* 18 (4) (2001): pp. 826–76.
5. Ibid.
6. Egon Bittner, "Florence Nightingale in Pursuit of Willie Sutton: A Theory of the Police," in Herbert Jacob, ed., *The Potential for Reform of Criminal Justice* (Beverly Hills, CA: Sage, 1974), pp. 1–25.
7. Samuel Walker, *Popular Justice: A History of American Criminal Justice,* 2nd ed. (New York: Oxford University Press, 1998), pp. 165–67.
8. John C. Meyer, "Patterns of Reporting Noncriminal Incidents to the Police," *Criminology* 12 (May 1974): pp. 70–83.
9. David H. Bayley and James Garofalo, "The Management of Violence by Police Patrol Officers," *Criminology* 27 (February 1989): pp. 1–25.
10. Stephen D. Mastrofski, Jeffrey B. Snipes, and Anne E. Supina, "Compliance on Demand: The Public's Response to Specific Requests," *Journal of Research in Crime and Delinquency* 33 (August 1996): pp. 269–305; John McCluskey, Stephen Mastrofski, and Roger Parks, "To Acquiesce or Rebel: Predicting Citizen Compliance with Police Requests," *Police Quarterly* 2, no. 4 (1999): pp. 389–416.
11. Bureau of Justice Statistics, *Contacts between Police & the Public, 2002* (Washington DC: Government Printing Office, 2005).
12. Ibid.
13. Illya Lichtenberg and Alisa Smith, "How Dangerous Are Routine Police-Citizen Traffic Stops?" *Journal of Criminal Justice* 29 (2001): pp. 419–28.
14. Arizona Criminal Justice Commission, *Crime and the Criminal Justice System in Arizona, The 2003 White Paper* (Phoenix: Arizona Criminal Justice Commission, 2003).
15. James Q. Wilson, *Varieties of Police Behavior* (New York: Atheneum, 1973), pp. 95–99.
16. Ibid.
17. Alexander Weiss and Sally Freels, "The Effects of Aggressive Policing: The Dayton Traffic Enforcement Experiment," *American Journal of Police* XV, no. 3 (1996): pp. 45–64.
18. Ibid.
19. James B. Jacobs, *Drunk Driving: An American Dilemma* (Chicago: University of Chicago Press, 1989); H. Laurence Ross, *Confronting Drunk Driving: Social Policy for Saving Lives* (New Haven, CT: Yale University Press, 1992).
20. Ross, *Confronting Drunk Driving.*
21. Ross, *Confronting Drunk Driving;* Jacobs, *Drunk Driving.*
22. Ibid.
23. Eric J. Scott, *Calls for Service: Citizen Demand and Initial Police Response* (Washington DC: Government Printing Office, 1981); Craig D. Uchida, Laure Brooks, and Christopher S. Kopers, "Danger to Police during Domestic Encounters: Assaults on Baltimore County Police, 1984–1986," *Criminal Justice Policy Review* 2 (1987): pp. 357–71.
24. Jeffrey Fagan, *The Criminalization of Domestic Violence: Promises and Limits* (Washington DC: Government Printing Office, 1996); Lawrence W. Sherman, *Policing Domestic Violence: Experiments and Dilemmas* (New York: The Free Press, 1992).
25. Lawrence Sherman, *Policing Domestic Violence.*
26. Shannon Catalano, *Criminal Victimization, 2004* (Washington DC: Bureau of Justice Statistics, 2005).
27. Murray A. Straus and Richard J. Gelles, *Physical Violence in American Families: Risk Factors and Adaptation to Violence in 8,145 Families* (New Brunswick, NJ: Transaction, 1990).
28. Callie Marie Rennison, *Intimate Partner Violence, 1993–2001* (Washington DC: Bureau of Justice Statistics, 2003); Michael Rand, *Criminal Victimization, 2007* (Washington DC: Bureau of Justice Statistics: 2008); Shannan Catalano, *Intimate Partner Violence in the U.S.,* (Washington DC: Bureau of Justice Statistics, 2008) obtained at http://www.ojp.usdoj.gov/bjs/intimate/victims.htm on May 12, 2009.
29. Catalano, *Intimate Partner Violence.*
30. Franklyn W. Dunford, David Huizinga, and Delbert S. Elliot, "The Role of Arrest in Domestic Assault: The Omaha Police Experiment," *Criminology* 28

(May 1990): pp. 183–206. Some of these data appear in the unpublished technical report.

31. Catalano, *Intimate Partner Violence.*
32. Donald Black, "Dispute Settlement by the Police," pp. 125–26 in Black, *Manners and Customs of the Police* (New York: Academic Press, 1980).
33. Richard Felson, Steven Messner, Anthony Hoskin, and Glenn Deane, "Reasons for Reporting and Not Reporting Domestic Violence to the Police," *Criminology* 40, 30 (2002): pp. 617–47.
34. Dunford, Huizinga, and Elliot, "The Role of Arrest in Domestic Assault."
35. Richard J. Gelles and Murray A. Straus, *Intimate Violence: The causes and consequences of abuse in the American family* (New York: Simon & Schuster, 1988), p. 104.
36. Mastrofski, Snipes, and Supina, "Compliance on Demand."
37. Ibid., p. 181.
38. Dunford, Huizinga, and Elliot, "The Role of Arrest in Domestic Assault."
39. Lynette Feder, "Police Handling of Domestic Violence Calls: An Overview and Further Investigation," *Women and Criminal Justice* 10, 2 (1999): pp. 49–68.
40. Dana Jones and Joanne Belknap, "Police Responses to Battering in a Progressive Pro-Arrest Jurisdiction," *Justice Quarterly* 16, 2 (1999): pp. 249–74.
41. Sherman, *Policing Domestic Violence,* 1992.
42. Albert Reiss, *The Police and the Public* (New Haven, CT: Yale University Press, 1971), p. 14.
43. Nancy Loving, *Responding to Spouse Abuse and Wife Beating: A Guide for Police;* Laurie Woods, "Litigation on Behalf of Battered Women," *Women's Rights Law Reporter* 5 (Fall 1978): pp. 7–34.
44. Loving, *Responding to Spouse Abuse and Wife Beating.*
45. Samuel Walker, *Taming the System: The Control of Discretion in Criminal Justice, 1950–1990* (New York: Oxford University Press, 1993).
46. Lawrence W. Sherman and Richard A. Berk, "The Specific Deterrent Effect of Arrest for Domestic Assault," *American Sociological Review* 49, no. 2 (1984): pp. 261–72; Sherman, *Policing Domestic Violence,* pp. 91–96.
47. Sherman, *Policing Domestic Violence,* p. 110.
48. Bureau of Justice Statistics, *Law Enforcement Management and Administrative Statistics, 2000* (Washington DC: Government Printing Office, 2004).
49. Patrick R. Gartin, "Examining Differential Officer Effects in the Minneapolis Domestic Violence

Experiment," *American Journal of Police* 14, no. 3/4 (1995): pp. 93–110.
50. Richard E. Lempert, "From the Editor," *Law and Society Review* 18, no. 4 (1984): pp. 505–13; Lawrence W. Sherman and Ellen Cohn, "The Impact of Research on Legal Policy: The Minneapolis Domestic Violence Experiment," *Law and Society Review* 23, no. 1 (1989): pp. 117–44; Richard Lempert, "Humility as a Virtue: On the Publicization of Policy-Relevant Research," *Law and Society Review* 23, no. 1 (1989): pp. 145–61; Sherman, *Policing Domestic Violence,* pp. 92–124.
51. University of Maryland, *Preventing Crime* (Washington DC: Government Printing Office, 1997), Ch. 8.
52. Lawrence Sherman, Janell Schmidt, and Dennis Rogan, *Policing Domestic Violence: Experiments and Dilemmas* (New York: Free Press, 1992).
53. David Hirschel, Eve Buzawa, April Pattavina, Don Faggiani, and Melissa Reuland, *Explaining the Prevalence, Context, and Consequences of Dual Arrest in Intimate Partner Cases* (Washington DC: National Institute of Justice, 2007).
54. Ibid.
55. M. Martin, "Double Your Trouble: Dual Arrest in Family Violence," *Journal of Family Violence* 12, no. 2 (1997): pp. 139–57.
56. Hirschel et al., *Explaining the Prevalence, Context, and Consequences of Dual Arrest.*
57. M. Martin, "Double Your Trouble."
58. Susan L. Miller, "Unintended Side Effects of Pro-Arrest Policies and Their Race and Class Implications for Battered Women: A Cautionary Note," *Criminal Justice Policy Review* 3, no. 3 (1989): pp. 299–317.
59. National Institute of Justice, *Evaluation of Family Violence Training Programs* (Washington DC: Government Printing Office, 1995).
60. Joan Zorza, "The Criminal Law of Misdemeanor Domestic Violence, 1970–1990," *Journal of Criminal Law and Criminology* 83 (1992): pp. 240–79.
61. Barbara J. Hart, *State Codes on Domestic Violence* (Reno, NV: National Council of Juvenile and Family Court Judges, 1992); Eve Buzawa and Carl Buzawa, *Domestic Violence: The Criminal Justice Response* (Newbury Park, CA: Sage, 1990), pp. 110–35.
62. Fagan, *The Criminalization of Domestic Violence,* p. 1.
63. Sherman, *Policing Domestic Violence,* p. 253.

64. Robert F. Meier and Gilbert Geis, *Victimless Crime?* (Los Angeles: Roxbury, 1997).

65. Terance Miethe and Richard McCorkle, *Crime Profiles: The Anatomy of Dangerous Persons, Places, and Situations* (Los Angeles: Roxbury, 2001).

66. Ibid.

67. Ibid.

68. Ibid.

69. Mindy Fullilove, Anne Lown, and Robert Fullilove, "Crack Hos and Skeezers: Traumatic Experiences of Women Crack Users," *Journal of Sex Research* 29, 2 (1992): pp. 275–87.

70. Miethe and McCorkle, *Crime Profiles: The Anatomy of Dangerous Persons, Places, and Situations,* pp. 223–26.

71. Ibid.

72. Egon Bittner, "The Police on Skid Row: A Study of Peacekeeping," in Bittner, *Aspects of Police Work* (Boston: Northeastern University Press, 1990), pp. 30–62.

73. LaFave, "Arrest to Control the Prostitute," in *Arrest,* pp. 450–64. Frederique Delacoste and Priscilla Alexander. *Sex Work* (San Francisco: Cleis Press, 1998); Michael Scott, *Street Prostitution* (Washington DC: Government Printing Office, 2002).

74. LaFave, "Arrest to Control the Prostitute."

75. Christopher Jencks, *The Homeless* (Cambridge, MA: Harvard University Press, 1994).

76. "Redevelopment Plans May Hem in Skid Row," *New York Times* (October 23, 1997), p. 1.

77. George L. Kelling and Catherine M. Coles, *Fixing Broken Windows* (New York: The Free Press, 1996).

78. Colleen Cosgrove and Anne Grant, *National Survey of Municipal Police Departments on Urban Quality-of-Life Initiatives,* in Tara O'Connor Shelley and Anne C. Grant, eds., *Problem-Oriented Policing: Crime-Specific Problems, Critical Issues and Making POP Work* (Washington DC: PERF, 1998).

79. David Snow and Leon Anderson, *Down on Their Luck* (Berkeley, CA: University of California Press, 1993).

80. Martha R. Plotkin and Ortwin A. Narr, *The Police Response to the Homeless: A Status Report* (Washington DC: Police Executive Research Forum, 1993), Appendix, C-85–C-116.

81. Judy Hails and Randy Borum, "Police Training and Specialized Approaches to Respond to People with Mental Illnesses," *Crime and Delinquency* 49, 1 (2003): pp. 52–61.

82. Elizabeth Biebel and Gary Cordner, "Repeat Calls for People with Mental Illness: An Application of Hot Spot Analysis," *Police Forum* 13, 3 (July 2003): pp. 1–3.

83. Robert Panzarella and Justin Alicea, "Police Tactics in Incidents with Mentally Disturbed Persons," *Policing: International Journal of Police Strategies and Management* 20, no. 2 (1997): pp. 339–56.

84. Linda Teplin, Gary McClelland, Karen Abram, and Dana Weiner, "Crime Victimization in Adults with Severe Mental Illness: Comparison with the National Crime Victimization Survey," Archives of General Psychiatry 62 (8): 911–21.

85. Robert Panzarella and Justin Alicea, "Police Tactics in Incidents with Mentally Disturbed Persons," *Policing: International Journal of Police Strategies and Management* 20, no. 2 (1997): pp. 339–56.

86. M. Pogrebin, "Police Responses for Mental Health Assistance," *Psychiatric Quarterly* 58, no. 1 (1986–87): pp. 66–73.

87. Richard Lamb, Linda Weinberger, and Walter DeCuir, "The Police and Mental Health," *Psychiatric Services* 53, 10 (2002): pp. 1266–71.

88. Ibid.

89. Ibid.

90. Robert Redondo and Glenn Currier, "Characteristics of Patients Referred by Police to a Psychiatric Emergency Service," *Psychiatric Services* 54, 6 (2003): pp. 804–6.

91. Lamb, Weinberger, and DeCuir, "The Police and Mental Health."

92. Judy Hails and Randy Borum, "Police Training and Specialized Approaches to Respond to People with Mental Illnesses," *Crime & Delinquency* 2003 49: 52–61.

93. Melissa Reuland and Matt Schwarzfeld, "Improving Responses to People with Mental Illness (New York: Council of State Governments Justice Center, 2008).

94. Ibid.

95. Minnesota Department of Health, *Facts of AIDS: A Law Enforcement Guide* (Minneapolis, MN: Department of Health, July 2003).

96. HIV/AIDS in the United States: HIV/AIDS Fact Sheet, Revised August 2008. Retrieved from http://www.cdc.gov/hiv/resources/factsheets/us.htm on May 22, 2009.

97. National Institute of Justice, *Annualized Site Reports, 2002* (Washington DC: National Institute of Justice, 2003).

98. R. Alan Thompson and James Marquart, "Law Enforcement Responses to the HIV/AIDS Epidemic," *Policing: An International Journal of Police Strategies and Management* 21, no. 4 (1998): pp. 648–65; Jeanne Flavin, "Police and HIV/AIDS: The Risk, the Reality, the Response," *American Journal of Criminal Justice* 23, no. 1 (1998): pp. 33–58.

99. Flavin, "Police and HIV/AIDS: The Risk, the Reality, the Response."

100. C. Herlitz and B. Brorsson, "Facing AIDS: Reactions among Police Officers, Nurses and the General Public in Sweden," *Social Science Medicine* 30 (1990): pp. 913–18.

101. Flavin, "Police and HIV/AIDS: The Risk, the Reality, the Response."

102. Ibid.

103. Theodore M. Hammett, *AIDS and the Law Enforcement Officer: Concerns and Policy Responses,* National Institute of Justice—Issues and Practices (1987), p. 31.

104. Terry Edwards and Richard Tewksbury, "HIV/AIDS: State Police Training Practices and Personnel Policies," *American Journal of Police* 15, no. 1 (1996): pp. 45–62.

105. W. S. Wilson Huang and Michael S. Vaughn, "Support and Confidence: Public Attitudes toward the Police," in Timothy J. Flanagan and Dennis R. Longmire, eds., *Americans View Crime and Justice: A National Public Opinion Survey* (Newbury Park, CA: Sage Publications, 1996), p. 40.

106. Bureau of Justice Statistics, *Sourcebook of Criminal Justice Statistics—2007,* obtained at http://www.albany.edu/sourcebook/index.html on May 22, 2009.

107. National Institute for Juvenile Justice and Delinquency Prevention, *Police-Juvenile Operations: A Comparative Analysis of Standards and Practices,* vol. 2 (Washington DC: Government Printing Office, nd), pp. 3–10.

108. National Institute for Juvenile Justice, *Police-Juvenile Operations,* vol. 2, p. 3.

109. Bureau of Justice Statistics, *Law Enforcement Management and Administrative Statistics, 2000* (Washington DC: Government Printing Office, 2004).

110. See http://trfn.clpgh.org/rosspd.

111. Donald Black and Albert J. Reiss, "Police Control of Juveniles," *American Sociological Review* 35 (February 1970): pp. 63–77.

112. Adapted from Office of Juvenile Justice and Delinquency Prevention, *Police-Juvenile Operations,* vol. 2, p. 57.

113. OJJDP, *Juvenile Offenders and Victims: A National Report* (Washington DC: Government Printing Office, 1995).

114. Ibid.

115. OJJDP, *Juvenile Offenders and Victims: 2006 National Report* (Washington DC: Government Printing Office, 2006).

116. Black and Reiss, "Police Control of Juveniles."

117. Samuel Walker, Cassia Spohn, and Miriam DeLone, *The Color of Justice,* 2nd ed. (Belmont, CA: Wadsworth, 2000), Ch. 4.

118. J. McMahon, J. Garner, R. Davis, and A. Kraus, *How to Correctly Collect and Analyze Racial Profiling Data* (Washington DC: Government Printing Office, 2002).

119. Black and Reiss, "Police Control of Juveniles."

120. Richard J. Lundman, "Police Control of Juveniles: A Replication," *Journal of Research in Crime and Delinquency* 15 (1978): pp. 74–91.

121. Douglas A. Smith, Christy A. Visher, and Laura A. Davidson, "Equity and Discretionary Justice: The Influence of Race on Police Arrest Decisions," *Journal of Criminal Law and Criminology* 75 (Spring 1984): pp. 234–49.

122. Carl Werthman and Irving Piliavin, "Gang Members and the Police," in David J. Bordua, ed., *The Police: Six Sociological Essays* (New York: Jorn Riley, 1968), pp. 58–59.

123. David Klinger, "Demeanor or Crime? Why 'Hostile' Citizens Are More Likely to be Arrested," *Criminology* 32 (1994): pp. 475–93.

124. Gordon Bazemore and Scott Senjo, "Police Encounters with Juveniles Revisited," *Policing: An International Journal of Police Strategies and Management* 20, 1 (1997): pp. 60–82.

125. Goldstein, *Policing a Free Society.*

# The Police and Crime

Crime control is one of the major responsibilities of the police. This involves several specific activities in responding to criminal incidents, conducting criminal investigations, and arresting offenders.

This chapter examines the crime control activities of the police. It describes what the police do and gives special attention to the popular myths that surround the subject of the police and crime.

# The Police and Crime

People usually think about the subject of the police and crime in terms of patrol and arrests. The subject is actually far more complex, involving a number of different assumptions and strategies.

## Crime Control Strategies

Lawrence W. Sherman provides the most systematic classification of the different crime control strategies used by the police or potentially available to them.[1]

### *Proactive versus Reactive*

Some police anticrime strategies are **proactive,** in the sense that the police themselves initiate them. This reflects the police department's own sense of priorities. Most drug enforcement, for example, is proactive. Other strategies are **reactive,** in the sense that they occur in response to a citizen request for service. Citizen calls to report crimes involve a reactive police response.

**proactive crime strategies**

**reactive crime strategies**

### *General versus Specific*

Some police activities are general in the sense that they are directed at the community at large and not at any particular crime. Routine preventive patrol is the most important general crime control strategy. Specific crime control activities, on the other hand, are directed at particular crimes, places, offenders, or victims.

### *Particular Crimes*

Routine patrol and the 911 system are general service activities that respond to any and all types of crimes. Other programs are directed at particular crimes. These include drunk-driving crackdowns, drug or gang crackdowns, or stakeouts designed to catch robbers.

### *Specific Places*

Routine patrol serves the community at large with no particular geographic focus. "Hot spots" programs, on the other hand, are directed at specific places that are believed to be the centers of high levels of criminal activity.

### *Specific Offenders*

Some anticrime activities are directed at particular offenders. The best examples are the repeat offender programs that target people suspected of currently committing high rates of serious crime.

### *Specific Victims*

Some anticrime programs are directed at victims rather than offenders. The most important of these are the domestic violence programs and policies adopted by many police departments. Mandatory arrest policies, for example, are designed to protect victims of domestic assault against future violence.

## Crime Control Assumptions

### *Police and Citizens*

One of the basic issues with respect to the police and crime involves the underlying assumptions about the role of the police in relation to other social control mechanisms. Many people see the police, and the entire criminal justice system, as society's primary mechanism for controlling crime. As part of the professionalization movement, the police emphasized their crime-fighting role and staked out crime as their professional domain.[2] Many experts today believe that this definition of professionalism isolated the police and cut them off from the public. To correct this problem, advocates of community policing emphasize the development of close working relationships with neighborhood residents.[3] This approach is based on the assumption that citizens are coproducers of police services, including crime-fighting activities.[4]

## *Police and Other Social Institutions*

A report on crime prevention programs by the University of Maryland places police activities in the context of other social institutions. The report argues that the traditional distinction between law enforcement and crime prevention is not valid. Law enforcement tactics such as arrest are designed to prevent crime, through either deterrence or incapacitation. Thus, it is appropriate to place all programs and institutions on a single crime prevention continuum.[5]

The report identified seven institutions that play a role in preventing crime. They include communities, families, schools, labor markets, places (in the sense of specific locales), the police, and other criminal justice programs. This innovative approach makes two important points about crime prevention. First, it indicates that the police are only one of several institutions with some impact on crime and cannot be expected to bear the primary responsibility. Second, the report emphasizes the interdependence of the different institutions. Thus, effective school-based crime prevention programs depend upon strong families, which in turn depend on healthy communities and good labor markets. Just as school programs are dependent upon this larger social network, so is the effectiveness of police crime control programs.[6]

## Measuring Effectiveness

Measuring the effectiveness of police crime control programs requires both meaningful definitions of what is to be measured as well as valid and reliable data on the expected outcomes. As is discussed below, there are serious problems with the traditional measures of police effectiveness. Moreover, the move toward community policing and problem-oriented policing involves different assumptions about what the police do and, consequently, different measures of effectiveness.[7]

## Summary

The different police activities covered in this chapter can be classified according to strategy, the underlying assumptions, and performance measures.

---

# Preventing Crime

The primary crime prevention activity of the police is routine patrol. As Chapter 7 explained, the visible presence of police officers in the community is designed to deter individuals from committing a crime.

Apart from officers who are responsible for random preventative patrol, many police agencies today have officers allocated toward crime prevention efforts—although their numbers are very small. In the United States today officers assigned to specialized crime prevention units account for only 3 percent of total officers.[8] Crime prevention officers are often responsible for meeting with citizens to explain how they can protect themselves against crime, working alongside neighborhood groups to establish and maintain neighborhood watch groups, and educating youth about drugs, crime, and gangs. These officers are typically housed in community relations units.

For a full discussion on the effectiveness of random preventative patrol, see Chapter 7.

For a full discussion on community relations, see Chapter 12.

For a full discussion on community and problem-oriented policing, see Chapter 10.

Police crime prevention strategies have undergone a revolution since the early 1980s. Instead of a peripheral activity, separated from the basic functions of patrol and criminal investigation, crime prevention is now seen as a central police activity.[9]

Crime prevention is a basic element of community policing and many problem-oriented policing programs.[10] The basic principle of community policing is that the police need to establish a better partnership with neighborhood residents. The underlying assumption is that citizens are coproducers of police services. This view of policing rejects the professional model of policing, which holds that the police and only the police have primary responsibility for crime control.[11]

Community-based crime prevention programs include efforts to build neighborhood organizations, to improve the physical appearance of the neighborhood, to eradicate centers of drug activity, to reduce truancy, and so on. In these programs, police officers act as planners, problem solvers, community organizers, and information exchange brokers. Their role is not to fight crime in the traditional manner (e.g., patrol, arrests) but to help citizens mobilize resources to prevent crime.[12]

Because community policing and problem-oriented policing crime prevention programs are so varied and are such an important part of contemporary policing, they are covered in detail in Chapter 10.

## Apprehending Criminals

The second major crime-fighting responsibility of the police is to apprehend criminals once a crime has been committed. This process involves a complex set of social and organizational factors. The police must first learn that a crime has been committed, officially record it as a crime, and then attempt to identify and arrest a suspect.

### Citizen Reporting of Crime

Police learn about crimes through (1) citizen reports, (2) police officer on-view observations, and (3) police-initiated investigations. The first two are reactive responses; the third is a proactive response.

Most of the crimes that come to the attention of the police are the result of a citizen report. Reporting a crime is one of the most important discretionary decisions in the criminal process. In this sense, citizens are the real "gatekeepers" of the criminal justice system. Patrol officers rarely discover crimes in progress.

Victims, however, do not report most crimes to the police. According to the National Crime Victimization Survey (NCVS), only 46 percent of victims of violent crimes and 37 percent of victims of property crimes report the crime to the police.[13] The nonreporting of crime has important implications for the police, since they cannot be held responsible for solving crimes they do not know about.

The reporting of crime varies according to the type of crime and situational factors related to individual crimes (see Exhibit 9–1, Exhibit 9–2, and Exhibit 9–3). Generally, citizens are more likely to report serious crimes than minor crimes, violent crimes rather than property crimes, crimes where there is personal injury rather than those without injury, crimes involving a high dollar loss more than those with little loss, and so on. African Americans and those with lower incomes are more likely to report a crime when compared with whites and those with higher incomes. Women

## EXHIBIT 9 – 1

### Reporting of Crime to the Police

|  | Percent Reported to Police |
|---|---|
| **Violent Crime** | **46.3** |
| Rape/sexual assault | 41.6 |
| Robbery | 65.6 |
| Aggravated assault | 57.2 |
| Simple assault | 40.6 |
| **Property Crime** | **37.2** |
| Burglary | 50.1 |
| Motor vehicle theft | 85.3 |
| Theft | 30.6 |

*Source:* Bureau of Justice Statistics, *Criminal Victimization, 2007* (Washington DC: Government Printing Office, 2008).

## EXHIBIT 9 – 2

### Factors Associated with Reporting Crime to the Police, 1992–2000

| | Likelihood of Reporting to the Police | |
|---|---|---|
| **Characteristics of Crime** | **Increased** | **Decreased** |
| Type | Violent | Property |
| Completion | Completed | Attempted |
| Victim injury | Injured | Not injured |
| Weapon | Present | Not present |
| **Characteristics of Victim** | | |
| Gender | Female | Male |
| Race | Black | White |
| Age | Age 25 and older | Under 25 |
| Income | Lower | Higher |
| Marital Status | Married | Never Married |
| **Offender** | | |
| Race | Black | White |
| Age | Older | Younger |
| Number | More than one | One |
| Relation to victim | Stranger | Nonstranger |
| Drug/alcohol use | Under the influence | Not under the influence |

*Sourec:* Bureau of Justice Statistics, *Reporting Crime to the Police, 1992–2000* (Washington DC: Government Printing Office, 2003).

## Reasons Why Violence Was Not Reported to the Police

| Reason for Not Reporting | Percent |
| --- | --- |
| Private or personal matter | 20.7 |
| Object recovered; offender unsuccessful | 17.3 |
| Reported to another official | 13.0 |
| Fear of reprisal | 7.3 |
| Police would not want to be bothered | 6.3 |
| Not important enough | 6.2 |
| Too inconvenient or time consuming | 4.7 |
| Police inefficient, ineffective, or biased | 4.6 |
| Lack of proof | 3.4 |
| Not aware crime occurred until later | 0.4 |
| Unable to recover property; no ID no. | 0.3 |
| Insurance would not cover it | 0.1 |
| Other reasons | 15.7 |

*Sourec:* Bureau of Justice Statistics, *Criminal Victimization in the United States, 2006: Statistical Tables* (Washington DC: Government Printing Office, 2008).

## *What If All Crimes Were Reported*

What would happen if victims reported all crimes to the police? Would it result in more arrests and fewer crimes? Probably not. First, the police workload would increase enormously. There would be many more calls for service and about 200 percent more reported crimes. Patrol officers and detectives would be swamped. Second, most of these additional crimes would be the less serious crimes. The NCVS data indicate that victims report the more serious crimes at a relatively high rate. Third, there is no reason to assume that there would be that many more arrests. As we will see later (pp. 273–274), the police are able to solve crimes when there is a good lead at the outset. There is no reason to assume that they would solve many of the additional burglaries and larcenies where there are no good leads.

In short, are we better off because citizens use their discretion not to report most crimes?

report property crimes at about the same rate as males but are about 10 percent more likely to report a violent crime to the police. Except for teenagers, who report crime at a significantly lower rate, age does not influence the reporting of crime.[14]

For the most part, victims do not report crimes primarily because they do not think the crime is that important or because they do not think anything can be done about it. Victims also regard certain crimes as private or personal matters. Perception of the police also affects the decision not to report a crime. According to the NCVS, about 6 percent of those not reporting a victimization indicated that they thought the police would not think the incident was important.[15]

# Reporting and Unfounding Crimes

After a citizen reports a crime, the police must make an official record of it in order to enter it in the Uniform Crime Reports (UCR) system. Police officers often do not complete a crime report, however. This is called **unfounding a crime.**   unfounding a crime
Donald Black found that police completed official crime reports in 64 percent of all crimes where no suspect was present, even though the complainant alleged a crime had occurred.[16] Meanwhile, crime victims told the NCVS that the police made reports in only 39.3 percent of all violent crimes and 49.3 percent of all property crimes.[17]

There is no penalty—in the law, in FBI regulations, or in police department policy—for a police officer not completing a crime report. This is an area of unregulated police discretion.

A police officer's decision to complete a crime report is affected by the same factors that influence arrest decisions. Black found that the police were more likely to record serious crimes, crimes where the complainant clearly expressed a preference for a crime report, crimes committed by strangers, and crimes where the complainant was deferential to the officer.[18]

There are several reasons why a police officer might unfound a crime. First, citizens do not always understand the criminal law and may believe that something is a crime when in fact it is not. For example, in Chicago 58 percent of all calls to the police were defined as a crime by the citizen, but only 17 percent of all calls to the police were recorded as crime-related by the police.[19]

Second, there may be insufficient evidence to convince the officer that a crime was committed. For instance, a citizen may report an attempted break-in, but the officer finds no physical evidence to support this allegation. The resident may have heard a storm door banging in the wind. These examples represent the proper exercise of discretion.

Third, officers may also abuse their discretion in unfounding crimes. A police officer may unfound a report of assault, for example, because of bias against the victim. Police officers may not make an arrest in a suspected assault incident when they perceive nonconforming behavior on the part of the victim: drinking or using drugs, being in the "wrong place," or being involved in questionable activity.

On a number of occasions, police departments have been caught systematically unfounding crimes to lower their crime rate. For example, most recently police agencies in Atlanta, Baltimore, New Orleans, New York, and Philadelphia have been identified as fudging crime reports in an effort to demonstrate that they have been successful in fighting crime.[20]

Crime reports can also be altered later. A crime can be either unfounded completely or changed to a lesser criminal offense. Thus, a rape can be changed to an assault, or a robbery to a larceny or an assault. If the change is based on new information about the crime, it is legitimate. If it is done simply to lower the crime rate, however, it is illegitimate. Recording a crime in a lower category can alter the public's perception of community safety. The news media and the public tend to focus their attention on a few "high fear" crimes: murder, robbery, rape, and burglary. Recording a robbery as a larceny makes the community appear safer than it really is.

# Criminal Investigation

Once a crime has come to the attention of the police, it has been officially recorded, and no suspect has been immediately arrested, the criminal investigation process begins.

## Myths about Detective Work

Criminal investigation, or detective work, is surrounded by myths. Movies and television police shows usually portray detective work as exciting and dangerous. Individual detectives are presented as heroic characters, possessing either great personal courage or extraordinary skill. The media often foster the idea that a good detective "can solve any crime," if he or she is only given the freedom and enough time to do it.[21]

There is no empirical basis for any of these myths. Moreover, they have several harmful effects on the public and the police. First, they create unreasonable public expectations about the ability of the police to control crime. This results in public dissatisfaction when the police fail to solve a crime. Second, the glamorous image of detective work leads many officers to regard it as *real* police work and devalue routine patrol work.[22] Some detectives, in fact, imitate the behavior they see in the movies. Herman Goldstein observes that "many of the techniques employed by detectives today are more heavily influenced by a desire to imitate stereotypes than by a rational plan for solving crimes."[23]

## The Organization of Detective Work

Criminal investigation is typically located in a separate unit of the department (except in small departments). Nationally, only about 15 percent of all sworn officers are assigned to detective units.[24] Large departments have specialized units devoted to particular types of crime (e.g., homicide, property crimes). Medium-sized departments usually have a separate but unspecialized unit in which detectives handle all types of crime. Very small departments often have no specialized detective unit.

Assignment as a detective is generally considered a high-status assignment by most police officers. In most departments it is a discretionary assignment, and one of the greatest rewards that a police chief has to hand out. In 40 percent of departments it is a separate rank, with higher pay than patrol officers, and must be obtained through a competitive process.[25]

Detective work appeals to officers for several reasons. It offers greater opportunity to control one's work and to exercise initiative. Patrol work, by contrast, is largely reactive, in response to citizen calls. (Community policing, meanwhile, is designed to give patrol officers more responsibility for initiating activity.) Detectives have considerable discretion over which cases to work on, how much time to spend on each case, and how to investigate it. Working in civilian clothes enhances the sense of individuality and frees detectives from stereotyped reactions from citizens based on the uniform.

Criminal investigation also offers a clearly defined measure of success: arrest of the suspect. The quality of work can be measured in terms of the number of arrests, the importance of a particular arrest (for example, an arrest related to a highly publicized crime), and the percentage of arrests resulting in conviction.[26] Patrol work, by contrast, involves mainly order maintenance and peacekeeping activities, for which there have never been any real performance measures.[27]

For a full discussion of order maintenance policing and peacekeeping, see Chapter 7.

Not all detective assignments are the same, however. William B. Sanders points out that "the status of an individual detective is linked to the kinds of crimes he investigates."[28] Homicide traditionally occupies the highest status, followed by robbery and sexual assault. Investigating the more serious crimes carries greater moral significance because of the harm involved. Homicide units also have the smallest workload and the highest clearance rate. Property crime units (burglary and larceny), on the other hand, rank lowest in terms of moral significance, and also have the highest workloads and the lowest clearance rates.

Vice units (narcotics, gambling, prostitution) are a special case. Because they involve victimless crimes, they require proactive police work, asking officers to exercise initiative. Undercover work also requires special skill, involves the greatest dangers, and poses the greatest moral hazards. Traditionally, the worst police corruption has been found in vice units.[29] For these reasons, some police officers do not seek assignment in vice units (see below).[30]

For a full discussion of police corruption, see Chapter 13.

# The Investigation Process

The process of investigating a crime consists of two basic stages: the preliminary investigation and the follow-up investigation.

## The Preliminary Investigation

The **preliminary investigation** consists of five basic steps: (1) identifying and arresting any suspects, (2) providing aid to any victims in need of medical attention, (3) securing the crime scene to prevent loss of evidence, (4) collecting all relevant physical evidence, and (5) preparing a preliminary report.[31]

**preliminary investigation**

In practice, patrol officers rather than detectives make about 80 percent of all arrests.[32] The explanation for this is simple. Most arrests occur because a suspect is on the scene or immediately identifiable and nearby. For those crimes where the suspect is not immediately arrested and there is no good information about him or her, arrests are relatively rare. Patrol officers, in short, handle the easy arrests, while detectives are assigned those that are inherently difficult to solve.

## Arrest Discretion

Police officers exercise great discretion in making arrests. Black found that officers make arrests in only about half of the situations where there is sufficient legal basis for an arrest.[33] In a number of situations officers simply ask the person to stop the illegal behavior. For example, in Indianapolis, Indiana, and St. Petersburg, Florida, 80 percent of the citizens were compliant with the officer's request.[34]

The decision to arrest is influenced by a number of situational factors. Generally, the probability of arrest rises when the evidence is relatively strong, the crime is more serious in nature, the victim requests an arrest, the victim and suspect are strangers rather than acquaintances, and the suspect is hostile or disrespectful toward the officer.[35] Smith, Visher, and Davidson also found that arrest is more likely in lower income neighborhoods, regardless of the race of the suspect.[36] Arrest discretion with respect to domestic violence situations and juveniles is discussed in more detail in Chapter 8.

## Follow-Up Investigations

A case is assigned to the detective bureau for follow-up investigation after an arrest has been made or if there has been no arrest. The Police Executive Research Forum (PERF) study divided follow-up investigations into three categories of activities: routine, secondary, and tertiary activities.[37]

Routine activities include interviewing victims and checking the crime scene. These steps are taken in about 90 percent of all burglaries and robberies. Secondary activities include canvassing for witnesses, interviewing other people, interviewing witnesses, discussing the case with supervisors, and collecting physical evidence. Tertiary activities include discussing the case with patrol officers, interviewing suspects, discussing the case with other detectives, checking department records, checking the National Crime Information Center (NCIC) computer files, checking other records, interviewing informants, and conducting stakeouts.

## The Reality of Detective Work

Contrary to popular belief, detective work is neither glamorous nor exciting. The Rand Corporation conducted the first detailed evaluation of detective units in the early 1970s, surveying 153 police departments by mail and interviewing officials in 29 departments. The study found detective work to be superficial, routine, and nonproductive. Many crimes receive only "superficial" attention, and some are not investigated at all. For example, detectives worked only 30 percent of all residential burglaries and 18 percent of all larcenies. Moreover, most investigative work involves "reviewing reports, documenting files, and attempting to locate and interview victims."[38] Most cases receive one day or less of investigative work, and most of that work involves paperwork: transferring information from one set of reports to another.

A PERF study of burglary and robbery investigations, meanwhile, found that about 25 percent of all burglary cases receive slightly less than two hours of investigative work, and only 11.9 percent are investigated for three days or more (at an average of about one hour per day). Only 24.8 percent of the robberies, meanwhile, are investigated for two days or more.[39] Harold Pepinsky argues that "most detectives spend the bulk of their time at their desks, going through papers and using the telephone."[40]

## Case Screening

In practice, detectives routinely screen cases, deciding how much effort to put into different cases. Screening decisions are based primarily on the seriousness of the crime and the existence of evidence that is likely to lead to an arrest. Some police agencies have adopted formal screening procedures based on "case solvability factors." These factors have in the past been shown to be highly related to the probability that a crime will be solved. Research has shown that when taken together case solvability factors can accurately predict 67 to 93 percent of investigative outcomes. These procedures are most often used by burglary, robbery, and auto theft detectives.[41]

The PERF study found that a detective's caseload actually consists of three components. The **nominal caseload** includes all cases assigned to that officer. The **workable caseload** includes those cases "that have sufficient leads and therefore are worth attempting to solve." Finally, the **actual caseload** includes those cases "actually worked by detectives."[42]

**nominal caseload**

**workable caseload**

**actual caseload**

# Measuring the Effectiveness of Criminal Investigation

## The Clearance Rate

The traditional measure of success in criminal investigation is the **clearance rate.**[43] The FBI defines a crime as cleared when the police have "identified the offender, have sufficient evidence to charge him, and actually take him into custody, or in exceptional instances, when some element beyond police control precludes taking the offender into custody."[44]

**clearance rate**

Nationally, only about 21 percent of all reported Index crimes are cleared. Exhibit 9–4 indicates national clearance rates for the eight UCR Index crimes for 2008.

The clearance rate is not a reliable performance measure for several reasons.[45] First, it is based on reported crimes, and since only about 39 percent of all crimes are reported, the *true* clearance rate is much lower than the *official* rate. Only 51 percent of all burglaries are reported, and therefore, the police actually clear only about 6 percent of all burglaries, rather than 12 percent.

Second, despite the UCR guidelines, police departments do not use the same criteria for clearing crimes. The PERF study, for example, found that in one city, only 58 percent of the burglary cases recorded as cleared were actually cleared by an arrest.[46]

---

### EXHIBIT 9–4

### Crimes Cleared by Arrest or Exceptional Means, 2008

| | |
|---|---|
| All Index Crimes | 20.8 |
| Murder and nonnegligent manslaughter | 63.6 |
| Forcible rape | 40.4 |
| Robbery | 26.8 |
| Aggravated assault | 54.9 |
| Burglary | 12.5 |
| Larceny-theft | 19.9 |
| Motor vehicle theft | 12.0 |

---

*Source:* Federal Bureau of Investigation, *Crime in the United States, 2008* (Washington DC: Government Printing Office, 2009).

Third, the data can be manipulated to produce an artificially higher official clearance rate.[47] If officials unfound a large number of crimes, for example, this will lower the denominator and produce a higher percentage of crimes cleared. Alternatively, officials can attribute additional crimes to a suspect in custody and record them as cleared. This also raises the official clearance rate. In some instances attributing additional crimes to a suspect is legitimate. There may be some evidence that the suspect did commit these other crimes, but not enough to present to the prosecutor. In this situation, there is no reason to look for another suspect. Last, police can manipulate the official clearance rate by the misuse of exceptional clearance. In other words, detectives may clear crimes even though there is no evidence to connect them with any suspect. For example, the Maricopa County Sheriff's Office was found to be clearing cases without even investigating them. One report indicated that between 75 to 82 percent of solved crimes between 2006 and 2008 were cleared by exception.[48]

Clearance rate data, along with the entire UCR system, are not audited by outsiders. A Police Foundation study, for example, found wide variation in the quality of arrest data,[49] and there is good reason for assuming that similar variations exist with respect to official clearance rate data.

## Defining an Arrest

Official data on arrests are also extremely problematic. The event referred to as an arrest has four different dimensions: legal, behavioral, subjective, and official.[50]

**legally arrested**

An individual is **legally arrested** or in custody when deprived of his or her liberty by legal authority. A police officer must have the intent to arrest, must communicate that intent to the person, and must actually take the person into custody.[51] Many people are detained on the street and then released. Others are taken to the police station and later released. During the time they were in the custody of the police and not free to leave, they were legally under arrest.[52]

**behaviorally arrested**

Someone is **behaviorally arrested** when a police officer performs any of a number of actions: A stop (in which the officer tells the individual not to leave), a verbal statement that the person is "under arrest," or physically restraining a person.

**subjectively arrested**

Someone is **subjectively arrested** whenever he or she believes they are not free to go. A police officer may regard an encounter as only a stop, but the individual may believe he or she is under arrest.

**officially arrested**

An individual is **officially arrested** only when the police make an official arrest report of it. Practices on maintaining arrest records vary greatly from department to department, however, and may even vary within individual departments. Departments do not make arrest reports at the same stage in the process as detaining and taking someone into custody. A Police Foundation study found that only 16 percent of police departments always record an arrest whenever any restraint has been imposed on the suspect; only 11 percent always record an arrest whenever a suspect is brought to the station house. All departments make a record whenever the suspect is booked.[53]

The result is that in many departments, a lot of people are legally arrested (in custody on the street or at the station house) but no official record is made of these arrests. The lack of standard procedures makes it difficult if not impossible to use arrest data to compare departments. A police department that records all arrests at an early stage, for example, will appear to be working harder and engaging in more aggressive crime fighting than one that records arrests only at the booking stage. In fact, the two departments might be taking people into custody at exactly the same rate. The official data are not a reliable indicator of their real levels of activity.

# Success and Failure in Solving Crimes

The police solve only 20 percent of all Index crimes each year. As Exhibit 9–4 indicates, they are far more successful in solving some crimes than others. Researchers have focused on three **case solvability factors** to examine their influence on investigative effectiveness: case structural factors, organizational factors, and environmental factors.

**case solvability factors**

## Case Structural Factors

Case structural factors are related to the crime that was committed and that the police are investigating. For example, the presence or absence of a good lead is a structural factor, in the sense that it is related to the nature of the crime and independent of police effort. Research has repeatedly shown that the single most important factor in solving a crime is whether the police immediately obtain the name or description of a suspect. For instance, the data in Exhibit 9–5 represent a sample of 1,905 crimes

---

**EXHIBIT 9 – 5**

### Crimes Cleared by the Los Angeles Police

Named Suspects

| Unnamed Suspects

Uncleared Cases = 48
Rate = 14%

Cleared Cases = 301
Rate = 86%

Uncleared Cases = 1,375
Rate = 88%

Cleared Cases = 181
Rate = 12%

◄──────────────────────── Total Cases = 1,905 ────────────────────────►

Total Clearance Rate = 25%

investigated by the Los Angeles police department. The LAPD cleared 86.2 percent of the 349 crimes in which a suspect was named, but only 11.6 percent of those in which a suspect was not named.[54]

Reiss and Bordua argue that most cleared crimes "solve themselves in the sense that the violator is 'known' to the complainant or to the police at the time the crime initially comes to the attention of the police."[55] Clearance rates are highest for violent crime because they involve direct contact between offender and victim. Few property crimes involve the same kind of direct contact and, consequently, have low clearance rates. Robbery is a violent crime, but is usually committed by a stranger, resulting in low rates of identification and low clearance rates.

Detective screening of cases (see above) is based primarily on whether or not there is a good lead at the outset. Sanders found that "robberies, rapes, and assaults were typified as having leads, since the victim serves as a witness."[56] Burglaries and thefts, on the other hand, were routinely considered not to have leads.

## Organizational Factors

The impact of organizational factors on the success and failure in solving crimes has also been closely examined. Many of these studies have found that changes in police effort—more detectives, more or different levels of training, different management practices—have little effect on clearance rates. The Rand study of criminal investigation concluded that clearance rates are not higher where there are more detectives or where they put more effort into cases, or where they receive more training.[57] Even though detectives complain about being overworked, and do in fact have very heavy caseloads, the lack of resources is not the primary factor that keeps clearance rates low.

However, subsequent research by Eck, and also Brandl and Frank, reached less pessimistic conclusions than the Rand study of criminal investigation. These investigators argue that investigative effort does make a difference. Their analyses involve a "triage" model that categorizes cases according to the strength of the evidence: weak, moderate, or strong. Brandl and Frank found that the probability of arrest in moderate evidence burglary and robbery cases increased as a result of more investigative effort.[58]

## Environmental Factors

Environmental factors, while rarely discussed, have a significant impact on clearance rates—even though the police have no control over them. Environmental factors are those characteristics of the community in which the police work. These might include the size of the community, the types of crimes committed in the community, the economic structure of the community, and the characteristics of the residents living in the community. Cordner examined the influence of organizational and environmental factors on clearance rates. He concluded that "environment-level variables have more influence than organization-level variables on police agency investigative effectiveness."[59]

Cordner points out that community size is perhaps the most important environmental factor. Small communities have many advantages when it comes to solving crimes. In small communities, residents are more likely to observe and recognize suspicious behavior and recognize suspects than residents in large cities are. Likewise, officers in small communities are more likely to be knowledgeable about crime patterns and are more familiar with those who are more likely to be involved in criminal activity.

A study conducted by the Phoenix police department exemplifies the influence of community environment on case solvability. Since 2000, the police department's homicide clearance rate had been hovering between 30 and 50 percent, compared with 60 percent for similar-sized cities. Police officials found that the city's poor clearance rate was largely attributable to homicides involving Hispanic residents. Hispanics accounted for 61 percent of homicides, of which only 21 percent were solved. Police officials believed that their inability to solve these crimes was a result of the lack of community cohesion in the Hispanic community and problems surrounding the immigration of Mexicans into Arizona.[60]

## Officer Productivity

There are significant differences in the productivity of detectives, as measured in terms of the number of arrests. Some make far more arrests than others. Productivity depends on a number of factors. Detectives assigned to high-solvability crimes such as robbery will have more chances to make arrests than those assigned to low-solvability crimes such as burglary. Nonetheless, it is also clear that, given the same assignment, some officers work harder and make more arrests than others. Riccio and Heaphy found that the number of arrests for Index crimes ranges from a low of 2.18 to a high of 12.06 per officer.[61]

More important than the total number of arrests is the *quality* of arrests—that is, whether the arrests lead to prosecution and conviction for a felony. For example, the Institute of Law and Society found that in one department 15 percent of the officers made over half of the arrests that resulted in a conviction.[62]

## The Problem of Case Attrition

Only about half of all felony arrests result in conviction of the suspect.[63] These data raise serious questions about whether the attrition is the result of poor police work or some other factor. In California it was determined that 11 percent of persons arrested were released by the police; 15 percent of those arrested were declined for prosecution by prosecutors; and 18 percent of the cases resulted in dismissal or acquittal.[64] The total attrition rate was 44 percent. (And this analysis did not take into account persons who were legally arrested by the police but for whom no arrest report was made.) Petersilia, Abrahamse, and Wilson attempted to identify those aspects of police work that were associated with high case attrition rates. They found that department practices explained little of the variation among the 25 departments studied. These practices included a case-screening process, a modus operandi (MO) file, a known offender file, a special victim/witness program, and other elements. Departments that used arrest statistics as a performance measure actually had lower clearance rates than departments that did not. The report did find that attrition rates were somewhat lower in cities that spent more money per arrest, a figure that seemed to indicate a connection between clearance rates and the availability of greater resources.[65]

An INSLAW study found that detectives expressed little interest in the performance measures associated with low attrition rates. None of the detectives interviewed knew what percentage of their cases were rejected by prosecutors. No supervisor reported evaluating detectives on the basis of the percentage of cases that resulted in convictions. None of the detectives expressed interest in feedback from prosecutors about the quality of their work.[66]

# The Use of Eyewitness Identification, Criminalistics, and DNA in Investigations

## Eyewitness Identification

Although victim and witness identification of suspects is extremely important in solving crimes, eyewitness identifications are also very problematic. The victim is often traumatized by the crime, frequently has only an incomplete description of the suspect, may exaggerate certain features (such as height or weight), or may resort to stereotyping in the sense of being unable to distinguish the individual features of a member of a certain racial or ethnic group. Psychologist Elizabeth Loftus, the leading expert on the subject, warns that despite the importance of eyewitness identifications, they are "not always reliable," due to all the problems associated with human perception and memory.[67] While it is unclear how often eye witnesses are wrong, one recent study indicated that of 230 people who have been exonerated through DNA testing procedures over 75 percent involved cases of mistaken identification.[68]

## Criminalistics

Technical specialists from the crime lab may be used in some investigations. Large departments maintain their own criminalistics specialists, while the smaller departments utilize the services of either a neighboring large department or a state police agency. Virtually all police departments, including the smallest, have technical services available to them through cooperative arrangements with other agencies.[69]

Despite the great publicity they receive, fingerprints are rarely an important factor in solving crimes. A major part of the problem is that it is difficult to obtain useful prints. For example, New York City police are able to obtain a usable print in only 10 percent of all burglaries. Even when prints were obtained, only 3 percent led to an arrest. This meant that of the 126,028 burglaries occurring in New York City (in the year of the study), only 300 resulted in an arrest as a result of using fingerprints.[70]

## DNA

Since the late 1980s, scientists have been able to use forensic DNA to accurately identify those from whom the DNA was obtained. DNA exists in all cellular material—such as blood, skin, bone, semen, saliva, and perspiration. Officers can collect DNA from many items, such as napkins, clothing, glasses, and many objects that humans come into contact with. The FBI notes that it only takes a few cells from a person to recover DNA.[71]

All DNA data obtained from local, state, and federal law enforcement officers is forwarded to the FBI. To manage all of the data, the FBI created a National DNA Indexing System (NDIS). The system was designed to store two types of data. The first is **forensic index** data, which contains DNA profiles from genetic evidence gathered from crime scenes. The second type of data stored by the NDIS system is **convicted offender index** data. Convicted offender index data contains genetic information on offenders who have been required to provide blood samples for genetic typing. All states today collect DNA data from offenders convicted of particular crimes. Some states, such as Louisiana, allow the police to take DNA from any arrestee.[72] As part of this program, scientists working for the FBI store genetic profiles in a computer database. Forensic laboratories exchange this data electronically so that if a match results, the FBI can notify the agency investigating the crime. The process typically takes only three to seven days.[73]

While the use of DNA evidence has garnered a great deal of attention in the media, the extent of influence that it has had on police investigations is still unclear. One study in New York City reported that DNA was rarely used in homicide investigations, and that when it was used it did not increase the probability of the case being solved. The authors reported that during the study period (1996 through 2003) DNA was collected, analyzed, and available for use in only 6.7 percent of the cases, and detectives only used the evidence as a "tool of last resort."[74] On the other hand, another study reported that DNA was helpful in clearing burglary cases. Specifically, the researchers worked with five police departments across the county and asked them to collect biological samples from a randomly selected number of burglary cases. The authors reported that when DNA evidence was used in addition to traditional investigative techniques cases were twice as likely to result in an arrest of a suspect.[75]

*forensic index*

*convicted offender index*

## Improving Criminal Investigations

Today, the most dramatic proposals for improving criminal investigations have been related to community policing. While community policing will be discussed at greater length in Chapter 10, here we present the three major changes in investigations that have been inspired by community policing to improve the effectiveness of detectives.[76]

First, the movement toward community policing has resulted in **structural changes** involving investigative units. While criminal investigators in the past were typically assigned to "headquarters," many of today's investigators have been moved out of the office and into the field by being assigned to a particular geographic area such as a beat or precinct. This change is an effort by departments to increase communication and cooperation between investigators and patrol officers and the public. It is believed that assigning investigators to a particular area will result in the investigators becoming more knowledgeable about crime patterns and developing stronger relationships with the residents and officers who live and work in the area to which the investigator is assigned.

*structural changes*

For example, in Albuquerque, New Mexico, the police department abolished all specialized investigative units such as homicide, robbery, and burglary units and created general investigative units within each command area. Detectives were then responsible for investigating all crimes within the command area to which they were assigned, rather than being responsible for investigating only one type of crime. This, the chief argued, would lead to greater cooperation between the patrol officers and the detectives and would result in commanders being geographically accountable for all crime in their command area.[77]

**procedural changes**

Second, many departments have made **procedural changes** consistent with community policing in an effort to be more successful in their criminal investigations. In particular, many agencies are adopting procedures and practices that permit greater intergovernmental cooperation. In the past, most agencies, and their investigators, rarely permitted "outsiders" to assist them in investigating and developing responses to crimes. However, as community policing began to permeate into police investigations, police organizations and investigators began to appreciate the assistance of other criminal justice organizations and community service organizations in developing broader responses to crime. Today, for example, it is not uncommon to have homicide review teams that are comprised of local, state, and federal officials from a variety of agencies, who review homicide files to develop more effective strategies to investigate and respond to homicides.

**functional changes**

Third, some of the most innovative departments are making **functional changes** to the role and responsibility of the investigator. For example, the Spokane County Sheriff's Office has given primary responsibility for problem solving to detectives. The administration believed that detectives had the most flexibility in their schedules and had the most complete and readily available information on crimes in the department. Other agencies, such as the Mesa, Arizona, police department, are requiring investigators (who have large amounts of readily available information at their fingertips because of their role in neighborhood investigations) to attend community meetings to educate residents about crimes and how to prevent them.

# Special Investigative Techniques

## Undercover Police Work

Undercover police work presents a number of special problems for the police.[78] First, it involves deliberate deception by the officer: lying about who he or she is. The danger is that officers become socialized into the habit of lying and may be tempted to lie in other contexts as well, such as when testifying under oath.

Second, an officer working undercover associates with criminals and attempts to become their friend. This socialization can erode the values and standards of policing. Ties to peer officers and family are weakened. Some officers have "gone native," embraced the criminal subculture, and become criminals themselves.

Third, undercover officers are often subject to less direct supervision than other officers. This is particularly true of deep undercover operations where the officer must spend weeks or months attempting to penetrate a criminal enterprise. The Knapp Commission found that detectives in the New York City Special Investigative Unit (SIU), for example, did not see their supervisors for weeks, and this contributed to the corruption.[79]

Traditionally, police departments have had few if any meaningful controls over undercover work. Officers learned how to work undercover through informal training by veteran officers.[80]

To prevent possible abuses, police departments have instituted formal controls over undercover work. The Commission on Accreditation requires law enforcement agencies to have "written procedures for conducting vice, drug, and organized crime surveillance, undercover, decoy, and raid operations." These procedures should cover such activities as "supplying officers with false identity, disguises, and necessary credentials," "designating a single person as supervisor and coordinator," and "providing close supervision."[81]

## Informants

Informants are an important source of information about criminal activity. They are especially useful in victimless crimes and other covert criminal activity. Informants have special knowledge because they are often criminals themselves or are associated with criminals. Developing a group of informants is part of the art of police work. Jonathan Rubinstein observes that "vice information is a commodity, and the patrolman learns that he must buy it on a restricted market."[82]

The use of informants creates a number of potential problems. First, the police are involved in an exchange relationship with someone who is usually a known criminal offender. The police must give something in order to obtain the information they want. The most valuable commodity is a promise of leniency: an agreement either not to arrest or to recommend leniency to the prosecutor or judge. With respect to not arresting an offender, there are serious moral questions about the police knowingly overlooking criminal activity. Critics argue that the relationship compromises the integrity of the police and sets the stage for corruption. New York City police officers in the 1970s provided their informants with drugs, thereby turning the officers into drug dealers.[83] The information provided by informants may be questionable. Informants may invent information simply to please their handlers or provide information only against their enemies. Jerome Skolnick found that in "Westville" narcotics detectives allowed their informants to steal, while burglary detectives allowed their informants to engage in drug dealing.[84] The danger, as Gary Marx points out, is that the informer begins "to control the sworn agent rather than the reverse."[85]

To control the potential problems involved in the use of informants, the CALEA (Commission on Accreditation for Law Enforcement Agencies) accreditation standards require that police departments maintain a set of "policies and procedures" covering the master file of informants, the "security of the informant file," "criteria for paying informants," and other "precautions to be taken with informants."[86] A joint Bureau of Justice Assistance–Police Executive Research Forum report recommended that "all understandings with a criminal informant should be put in the form of a written agreement."[87]

## Policing Drugs

By the end of the 1980s, drugs represented the most serious problem facing the police, the criminal justice system, and American society as a whole. An epidemic of crack cocaine usage led to unstable drug markets in many large urban cities across the United States. The competition for control of drug markets produced a dramatic increase in homicides. While the subculture of crack use has declined over the past ten years, and along with it general levels of violence, the nation still expends a substantial amount of resources toward combating the drug problem.[88] According to the Office of National Drug Control Policy, the United States spends about $12.9 billion on domestic enforcement, interdiction, and international drug control efforts; $3.8 billion on drug treatment; and $2.5 billion on drug prevention.[89] Nonetheless, U.S. residents still spent an estimated $62.4 billion on illicit drugs in the same year.[90]

## Drug Enforcement Strategies

**supply reduction strategy**

Local police employ two basic strategies to combat illegal drug trafficking and use. The traditional **supply reduction strategy** includes four different tactics. The first is the simple buy-and-bust strategy: undercover officers purchase drugs and then arrest the dealers. A second and related strategy is to attempt to disrupt the drug syndicate by "trading up": arresting low-level dealers and offering them leniency in return for information about higher-level dealers.[91] A third strategy involves penetrating the drug syndicate through long-term undercover work. The fourth is the

---

**SIDEBAR        9 – 2**

### *Drug Use among Arrestees*

Data collected as part of the Arizona Arrestee Information Network (AARIN) shows that police officers have regular contact with the drug-using population. Analysis of urine specimens taken from a random sample of recently booked male arrestees in Maricopa County, Arizona, found that 35.6 percent tested positive for marijuana, 20.1 percent for cocaine, 20.7 percent for methamphetamines, and 6 percent for heroin.

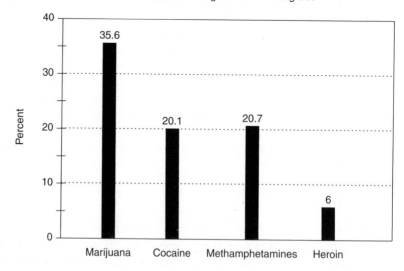

Arrestees Testing Positive for Drug Use

*Sourec:* Michael White, AARIN Annual Adult Report, Arizona State University: Phoenix (April 2008).

drug crackdown, an intensive enforcement effort concentrated in a specific area over a limited period of time.[92]

The **demand reduction strategy** involves attempting to reduce the demand for drugs on the part of potential users. This strategy includes drug education programs such as D.A.R.E.

**demand reduction strategy**

The traditional supply reduction strategies have never proved to be effective. Illegal drug use continues to remain at high levels, and in the poorest neighborhoods drug trafficking is open and rampant. Several reasons explain this failure.

First, there is no persuasive evidence that the threat of arrest, per se, deters drug use or sale (or deters any other form of criminal activity, for that matter). Second, through what is known as the "replacement effect," new drug dealers quickly replace those who are arrested. Particularly in poor neighborhoods where legitimate career opportunities are limited, the incapacitation of dealers does not affect the demand reduction strategy behavior of other new potential dealers. Third, the strategy of arresting low-level dealers and trading up to get key individuals in drug trafficking organizations has never proved to be effective in disrupting these organizations.[93]

An important question is, "Why do the police continue to engage in these activities despite their apparent ineffectiveness?" Peter Manning argues that drug arrests are made for their "dramaturgical effect": they generate publicity and create the appearance of doing something about the drug problem.[94] As Crank and Langworthy argue, police organizations exist in a larger social and political environment and need to create at least the impression that they are handling the problems that are within their professional domain.[95]

## Minorities and the War on Drugs

There is a significant disparity in the arrest of racial and ethnic minorities for drug offenses. The National Household Survey has found that African Americans are only somewhat more likely than whites to be using illegal drugs in any given month.[96] Yet, as Exhibit 9–6 indicates, African Americans are significantly more likely to be arrested for drug offenses. Jerome Miller argues that the entire criminal justice system's policy toward young African American men represents a "search and destroy" mission.[97]

Many critics argue that the racial disparity in drug arrests is the result of department policies that deliberately target minority neighborhoods. As Castellano and Uchida point out, "Drug arrests are largely police-initiated (proactive) rather than citizen-initiated (reactive)." As a result, "local drug arrest rates and patterns are largely dependent upon the arrest policies and enforcement priorities in police departments."[98] That is to say, it is not the result of discriminatory decisions by individual officers on the street, but of policy decisions made by commanders.

## Demand Reduction: The D.A.R.E. Program

The most popular demand reduction strategy is the drug education program known as **D.A.R.E.** (Drug Abuse Resistance Education). D.A.R.E. originated with the Los Angeles police department in cooperation with the Los Angeles public schools in 1983. The program consists of 17 hour-long classroom sessions conducted by a

**D.A.R.E.**

# EXHIBIT 9–6

## African Americans and Drug Possession

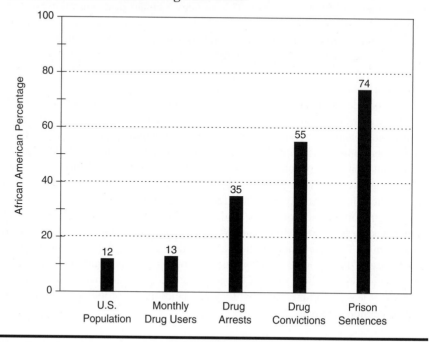

*Sourec:* The Sentencing Project, *Young Black Americans and the Criminal Justice System: Five Years Later*
(Washington DC: The Sentencing Project, 2001). Obtained from http://www.sentencingproject.org/pdfs/9070smy.pdf
on January 15, 2004.

sworn police officer. The content of the program involves both information about illegal drugs and their consequences and training in social skills to help resist illegal
drug use.[99]

The D.A.R.E. program is extremely popular. Today it is operating in about
70 percent of all public school systems at an annual cost of $750 million per year.
The program has also been adopted in 44 foreign countries.[100] Several factors explain
the program's popularity. First, it addresses parent concerns about juvenile drug
abuse. Second, there is a widespread belief that education is an effective approach.
Third, both police and public school officials want to appear to be doing something
about the drug problem.

Most evaluations of D.A.R.E. have not found any significant reduction in actual drug use as a result of the program. Critics have claimed, however, that most of
these evaluations have been limited to one-year follow-up periods.[101] Recently, however, two major studies that examined the long-term impact of the D.A.R.E. program
have been published. One of them examined the effects of the D.A.R.E. program
6 years after it had been administered, and the other, 10 years after it was administered.
Both studies randomly assigned students to either a group that received the D.A.R.E.
program or a group that did not receive the program. Both studies also measured the

effects of D.A.R.E. on students' attitudes, beliefs, social skills, and drug use behaviors. They both found that the program had no measurable impact on those who participated, compared with those who did not participate in the program.[102]

# Policing Gangs and Gang-Related Crime

In 1982 Walter Miller reported that only 27 percent of cities with populations of 100,000 or more had a gang problem, noting that the gang problem was largely isolated in America's largest cities.[103] Today, however, the street gang can be found in every state and in almost every major city throughout the United States. The National Youth Gang Survey, a survey of police departments across the country, reported that youth gangs are active in about 86 percent of large cities. Additionally, the survey reported that 26,500 gangs and 785,000 gang members are active in the United States.[104]

As a result, public officials and researchers have claimed that the increase in gangs is responsible for much of the rise in youth violence and drug use among youth. These claims have been substantiated in that studies of official records have consistently found that gang members are disproportionately involved in criminal activity. For example, in Mesa, Arizona, the police department discovered that when comparing the arrest records of documented gang members with a similar group of nondocumented delinquent youth, gang members were about twice as likely to have ever been arrested for a violent, weapon, drug, or status offense. Additionally, gang members were arrested for these offenses about four times as often as nondocumented delinquent youth.[105]

Local police rely on two strategies to combat gang problems. One strategy is suppression; the other relies on prevention.

## Gang Suppression

The growth of gangs during the last two decades has been accompanied by the development and growth of specialized law enforcement responses to gangs. Traditionally, the police response to gangs and gang-related problems was to assign responsibility for gang control to existing units, such as patrol, juvenile bureaus, community relations, investigations, and crime prevention.[106] However, in the 1980s many police departments established specialized units for gang control, including what is commonly referred to as the police gang unit. A police gang unit is a secondary or tertiary functional division within a police organization. It has at least one sworn officer whose sole function is to engage in gang control efforts.[107] Therefore, by their very nature, police gang units are specialized, have their own unique administrative policies and procedures, which are often distinct from the rest of the department, and have a front line of experts who are uniquely trained and dedicated to perform specific and focused duties.

The Law Enforcement and Management Administrative Statistics (LEMAS) survey reported that among large agencies with 100 or more sworn officers, special gang units existed in 48 percent of all municipal police departments, 41 percent of all sheriffs' departments, 55 percent of all county police agencies, and 18 percent of all state law enforcement agencies.[108] These findings led to an estimate of approximately

347 police gang units in the country. The recency of this phenomenon can be further seen by the fact that over 85 percent of specialized gang units have been established in the past 10 years.[109]

While specialized police gang units represent a new feature in American policing, they are part of an overall trend among many police departments to create specialized units to address unique law enforcement problems such as repeat offenders, domestic violence, and hate crimes. Such units are created to focus departmental resources, energy, and skill on the reduction of gangs and gang-related activity. Additionally, such an approach is intended to be a symbolic act, signifying to the community, gang members, and police officers that the police department is taking the gang problem seriously.[110]

Not only do gang units symbolize the commitment the police have toward eradicating the gang problem, but they are also symbolic of a moral crusade in which the police are battling against gangs. This is often conveyed to the public through the unit's name. For example, the San Bernardino County interagency task force uses SMASH (San Bernardino County Movement Against Street Hoodlums), and the Los Angeles sheriff's department uses GET (Gang Enforcement Team). Such acronyms express a Hollywood-like image that the police are at war with gangs, and that the gang problem can be solved as long as we intensify our efforts against them.

One of the few studies to examine the effectiveness of police gang units was conducted by Klein and his colleagues in Los Angeles. The authors compared gang-designated homicide cases to non-gang-designated homicide cases in both the Los Angeles police department and the Los Angeles sheriff's department. The authors reported that gang-designated cases were significantly more likely to have a greater number of (1) pages of investigation, (2) interviews conducted, (3) witness addresses, and (4) suspects charged than non-gang-designated cases. Klein and his colleagues also reported that in both departments, homicide cases that were investigated by the special gang unit were significantly more likely to be cleared, compared with those that were not investigated by the special gang unit. As a result, it appears, at least initially, that gang units may contribute special knowledge that aids in the investigation of gang crimes.[111]

## Gang Prevention: The G.R.E.A.T. Program

G.R.E.A.T

The most popular police-led gang prevention program is called the Gang Resistance Education and Training (G.R.E.A.T.) program. The Phoenix police department established the program in 1991, modeling it after the D.A.R.E. program. **G.R.E.A.T.** is a nine-week class, led by a uniformed police officer, offered once a week to middle school students. The program introduces students to conflict resolution skills, cultural sensitivity, and the problems that are associated with gangs and gang-related behavior. Today G.R.E.A.T. operates in all 50 states and several foreign countries.[112]

As of yet there have been few evaluations of the G.R.E.A.T. program. One of the most thorough studies used a multisite longitudinal design to evaluate the effectiveness of the program. The researchers compared about 1,750 eighth-grade students from 22 schools who had completed the G.R.E.A.T. program with a comparable group of students who had not participated in the program. Both groups were surveyed four times over four years. Over the study period, students who participated in the G.R.E.A.T. program were no less likely to have joined a gang, compared with those who had not been exposed to the gang prevention program. Furthermore, the researchers reported that the program had no impact on delinquent activity.[113]

# Policing Career Criminals

In the 1980s several police departments experimented with programs to target career criminals, defined as people believed to be currently committing a high rate of offenses. This idea was based on the Wolfgang birth cohort study, which estimated that a very small number of people (6 percent of any group of young men) commit an extremely high percentage of all serious crime.[114] Arresting, convicting, and imprisoning these career criminals, it was argued, would yield tremendous payoff in terms of crime reduction.[115]

Repeat offender programs consist of three different types: (1) targeting suspected high-rate offenders for surveillance and arrest, (2) special warrant service for suspected high-rate offenders who have outstanding warrants or are wanted for probation or parole violations, and (3) case-enhancement programs to provide prosecutors with full information about the criminal histories of high-rate offenders.[116]

The Repeat Offender Program (ROP) in Washington DC involved a team of 88 officers (later reduced to 60) assigned to locate and arrest persons believed to be committing five or more Index crimes per week. The suspects were selected on the basis of information provided by other police department units. Suspects remained on the list for 72 hours. Officers in the ROP team sought to locate the suspect through information in existing criminal records, supplemented by information available from the Department of Motor Vehicles, the phone company, and other sources. Many of the targeted individuals were already being sought on outstanding arrest warrants.[117]

An evaluation of ROP by the Police Foundation compared 212 suspects assigned to the ROP unit with a group of 212 similar suspects. The arrest activity of ROP unit officers was also compared with the activity of a control group of officers. The evaluation found that ROP "increased the likelihood of arrest of targeted repeat offenders." Half of the suspects in the experimental group (106 out of 212) were arrested by ROP officers (another 17 were arrested by other officers), compared with only 4 percent (8 out of 212) in the control group.

Other data, however, raised some questions about the efficiency of the program. ROP officers made fewer arrests than comparison officers (although most of the additional arrests by the comparison officers were for nonserious crimes). The ROP program cost $60,000 in direct expenses and took officers away from other police responsibilities, raising serious questions about the cost-effectiveness of the program.[118]

# Policing Guns and Gun Crimes

Firearms, particularly handguns, are a serious problem in the United States. Messner and Rosenfeld note that the United States stands above all other industrialized nations with regard to the number and rate in which guns are used in crime.[119] However, gun crime is down. The National Crime Victimization Survey (NCVS) indicates that between 1993 and 2007 gun crime decreased by 70.6 percent. Still,

## EXHIBIT 9–7

### Gun Crime Victimizations per 1,000 Persons Age 12 or Older by Ethnicity, Gender, and Age

| Ethnicity | Rate |
|---|---|
| White | 2.8 |
| Black | 8.4 |
| American Indian | 7.7 |
| Asian | 2.7 |
| Hispanic | 6.0 |
| Gender | |
| Male | 5.4 |
| Female | 2.4 |
| Age | |
| 12 to 14 | 2.4 |
| 15 to 17 | 8.1 |
| 18 to 20 | 11.8 |
| 21 to 24 | 8.4 |
| 25 to 34 | 5.0 |
| 35 to 49 | 3.2 |
| 50 to 64 | 1.4 |
| 65 or older | 0.6 |

about 71 percent of homicides, 25 percent of robberies, and 5 percent of assaults are committed with a gun.

Victims of gun crime are more likely to be Black, American Indian, and Hispanic, followed by Whites and Asians. Men are twice as likely to be a victim of a gun crime compared to women. Similarly, young people are at greater risk to be victimized than older people (see Exhibit 9–7).

## Gun Suppression

While police agencies have experimented with a number of strategies to reduce gun crime, such as gun buyback programs and vigorously enforcing gun-related laws, these strategies have typically met with failure.[120] Today, some of the most innovative strategies to address gun violence have focused on directed patrol and the formation of interagency task forces.

**Kansas City Gun Experiment**

The **Kansas City Gun Experiment** is perhaps the best-known directed patrol effort aimed at reducing gun violence. The experiment represented a combination of both problem-oriented policing, by focusing on a particular problem, and directed patrol, by concentrating on particular areas of high criminal activity.[121]

The experiment targeted a high-crime precinct of Kansas City where the murder rate in 1991 was 177 per 100,000, compared with a national rate of about 10 per 100,000. For a period of 29 weeks in 1992 and 1993, an extra pair of two-officer patrol cars patrolled the area for six hours at night between 7 PM and 1 AM.

The officers were directed to stop vehicles with people they believed to be carrying illegal handguns. The officers were directed to make only legally justified stops (e.g., traffic law violations) and then make legally justified searches for weapons (e.g., search incident to an arrest). The underlying assumption was that this program would reduce crime both by removing guns from the streets and by sending a deterrent message about aggressive enforcement in the area.

During the course of the experiment, the special unit officers seized 29 guns, and another 47 guns were seized in the target beat by other officers. Gun crimes fell by 49 percent in the target beat, compared with a 4 percent increase in a control beat. Changes in gun crimes in other beats across the city were mixed. There was no evidence of either displacement of gun crimes or the diffusion of benefits. The experiment suggested the potential positive effect of hot-spots-oriented anticrime programs. A replication of the gun experiment in Indianapolis found similar results.[122]

Another example of an innovative gun violence reduction project is Project Safe Neighborhood (PSN). The program was established by President Bush in 2001 to encourage criminal justice agencies to work together to reduce gun violence. The goals of this program are: (1) to increase the capacity of PSN Task Forces to design data-driven strategies that produce measurable decreases in firearm-related violent crime, and (2) to improve the long-term ability of federal, state, and local partners (including police agencies) to work together to understand, prosecute, and prevent firearm-related violent crime within their jurisdictions. Over 90 local projects based on the PSN model were funded by the Bush administration.[123]

An example of a PSN project is Project EFFECT in Las Vegas, Nevada. The program involves a task force made up of members from the Las Vegas metropolitan police department; the Bureau of Alcohol, Tobacco, and Firearms (BATF); the United States Attorney's office; and the Clark County Prosecutor's office. The purpose of the task force is to subject violent gun offenders to federal prosecution by having the local police department submit cases to the United States Attorney's office through the BATF. This strategy, if successful, results in lengthier prison sentences than if the case were prosecuted through the county court system.

# Policing Hate Crime

**Hate crimes,** or bias motivated crimes, represent a relatively new problem for the police. This is because hate crimes are not separate and distinct crimes, per se, but are offenses that are *motivated* by the offender's bias. The Hate Crimes Statistics Act of 1990 defined a hate crime as "a criminal offense against a person or property motivated in whole or in part by the offender's bias against a race, religion, disability, ethnic/national origin, or sexual orientation."[124] Because motivation is subjective, it is often difficult for police officers to determine if an offense was motivated by bias.

**hate crimes**

## The Scope and Nature of Hate Crime

In 2007, 2,025 law enforcement agencies reported 7,625 bias crime incidents to the Federal Bureau of Investigation. Most of these crimes were motivated by racial bias (50.8 percent), religious bias (18.4 percent), sexual orientation bias (16.6 percent), and ethnic/national origin bias (13.2 percent). Roughly 69 percent of the racial bias crimes were committed against blacks, 68 percent of the religious bias crimes were committed against Jews, and about 59 percent of the sexual orientation bias crimes were committed against male homosexuals.[125]

The Federal Bureau of Investigation notes that there are five characteristics of hate crimes: (1) hate crimes involve a higher level of assaults against persons than crimes generally; (2) hate crimes are generally more violent—about two-thirds of bias crime incidents are crimes against persons and the remaining one-third are crimes against property; (3) attacks are often preceded by a series of confrontations and incidents that escalate in severity; (4) hate crimes are more likely than other criminal activity to be committed by groups of perpetrators; and (5) most crimes against persons are committed by someone the victim knows, whereas hate crimes are more likely to be committed by strangers.

## The Police Response to Hate Crime

In response to a rising concern about bias crimes, a number of police departments have created specialized bias crime units. These units, like gang units, are intended to focus departmental resources and energy in an effort to increase the effectiveness of the department in combating hate crimes and to signify to the community that the police department is taking hate crimes seriously. Susan Martin argues that there are three other reasons for singling out hate crimes for special attention.

> First, because these offenses are based on who the victims are, they tend to cause victims greater difficulty in coming to terms with their victimization. Second, hate crimes appear to have particularly deleterious effects on communities, raising levels of mistrust, fear, and intergroup tensions. Third, because many of these crimes are not very serious in terms of penal law, they would otherwise receive very little or no police attention.[126]

A number of alternative organizational structures have been established by police departments to combat hate crimes. For example, the New York City Bias Crime Incident Investigation Unit (BIIU) is a centralized unit with a number of bureaucratic features. Officers who encounter what they believe to be a bias crime are required to notify their supervisors, who are in turn required to notify their commander. The commander then performs a preliminary investigation, and if the offense is verified, the Operations Unit is notified, which in turn notifies the Bias Crimes Unit.[127]

Conversely, the Baltimore County police department uses a decentralized strategy. The department did not establish a specialized bias crime unit, but rather delegates patrol officers, as part of their community policing duties, to address such problems. If the precinct commander believes that an incident requires additional attention, the commander may request assistance from the Investigations, Community Relations, or Intelligence Divisions.[128]

External evaluations have been conducted in both departments to determine the effectiveness of their strategies. In New York City, it was found that investigators in the special bias crime unit investigated more allegations of bias crimes and cleared more bias crimes than investigators assigned to a comparable group of nonbias crimes. Additionally, the victims of bias crimes expressed higher rates of satisfaction with the police response than victims in the comparison group. The higher clearance rate was particularly surprising, since bias crimes are usually committed by strangers, whereas nonbias crimes are often committed by someone the victim knows. The fact that the investigators were able to clear offenses with less evidence suggests that the intensive investigative efforts by the special unit resulted in the higher clearance rate.[129]

Similarly, in Baltimore verified bias crimes received more extensive and intensive investigation and were more likely to be cleared when compared with similar nonbias crimes. The researchers found that the administration had communicated to patrol officers that bias crimes were to be taken seriously and that the patrol officers took the problem seriously.[130]

# Policing and Terrorism

## The Scope and Nature of Terrorism

**Terrorism** is defined by the FBI as "the unlawful use of force or violence against persons or property to intimidate or coerce a government, the civilian population, or any segment thereof in furtherance of political or social objectives."[131] There are two types of terrorism: domestic and foreign.

**terrorism**

## Domestic Terrorism

**Domestic terrorism** is planned and carried out by Americans on American soil. This is by far the most common type of terrorism, accounting for about 80 percent of terrorist incidents and 90 percent of deaths prior to September 11.[132] Christopher Hewitt examined all domestic terrorist incidents between 1954 and 2000 and classified them into five categories by their ideological type (see Exhibit 9–8). The three

**domestic terrorism**

---

### EXHIBIT 9–8

#### Terrorist Incidents and Fatalities by Those Responsible, 1954–2000 (%)

| Type of Terrorism | Incidents | Fatalities |
|---|---|---|
| **Domestic Terrorism** | | |
| White racist/Rightist | 31.2 | 51.6 |
| Revolutionary left | 21.2 | 2.0 |
| Black militants | 14.7 | 25.0 |
| Antiabortion | 6.2 | 0.9 |
| Jewish | 3.6 | 0.8 |
| Other domestic/unknown | 2.8 | 8.1 |
| **Foreign** | | |
| Cuban émigré | 5.2 | 1.5 |
| Puerto Rican | 11.9 | 4.3 |
| Islamic | 1.1 | 1.7 |
| Other foreign | 2.1 | 4.1 |
| Total # of Incidents and Fatalities | 3,228 | 661 |

*Source:* Christopher Hewitt, *Understanding Terrorism in America* (New York: Routledge, 2003), p. 15.

most significant types of domestic terrorist groups today are (1) white racist/right, (2) revolutionary left, and (3) antiabortionist.

White racist/right terrorist attacks largely began in the 1950s with incidents involving the Ku Klux Klan (KKK). The KKK was primarily involved in violent attacks against civil rights activists in attempts to stop their efforts. Since the 1970s, however, the KKK has been involved in few terrorist activities. Instead, today, members of far right political groups, primarily groups who are concerned with the role of the federal government and "American Values," play a more dominant role in domestic terrorism. One of the most prolific examples was the bombing of the Oklahoma City Federal Court Building by Timothy McVeigh.

Revolutionary left terrorist attacks began in the late 1960s and peaked in 1971. These groups were primarily formed in opposition to the Vietnam War and social injustice, and engaged in activities that would result in media attention. They were responsible for over 500 bombings, 37 robberies, 10 shootings, and a kidnapping.

Most of their attacks targeted the military–industrial complex or large corporations. In the 1990s, a new form of left-oriented terrorism began in the form of eco-terrorism. These terrorist groups, such as Earth Liberation Front (ELF), oppose forest destruction, new development, SUVs, and globalization in general. They also concern themselves with issues involving animal rights. In 2003, ELF credited themselves with engaging in 75 illegal direct actions in North America. They estimate that they alone caused $55 million dollars in damage in a series of anti-SUV attacks.[133] More recently, in 2008 they were associated with the destruction of three luxury homes valued at $7 million near Seattle, Washington.[134]

Antiabortion terrorist groups began to emerge in the late 1970s and continue today. These groups, in their attempt to stop abortions from taking place, primarily target abortion clinics and abortion doctors with violence. One of the most well known groups is the Army of God. On January 29, 1998 the group bombed the New Woman All Women Health Care Clinic in Birmingham, Alabama. The explosion killed a police officer who was working part-time at the clinic and severely injured a clinic employee. The suspect, Eric Rudolph, was a member of the Army of God. In letters to the media, the Army of God claimed responsibility for the bombing and also claimed responsibility for bombing an abortion clinic and a gay night club in 1997. In October 1998, Rudolph was charged with these incidents along with the Centennial Park bombing during the 1996 Summer Olympics in Atlanta. Rudolph was captured on May 31, 2003, in North Carolina.[135] A more recent example was the killing of Dr. George Tiller, who was one of the few doctors in the country who performed late term abortions.

## Foreign Terrorism

**foreign terrorism**

**Foreign terrorism** involves terrorist activities coordinated and perpetrated by foreign persons or countries against the United States. These terrorist attacks take place both within and outside the borders of the United States. The worst foreign terrorist attack in United States history took place on September 11, 2001, involving four separate but coordinated aircraft hijackings by al-Qaida operatives. Just fewer than 3,000 persons were killed—many of whom were firefighters and police officers.

The consequences of the September 11th attacks were not limited to the victims and their families. Citizens across the country were substantially impacted. A Rand survey showed that after the attack 11 percent of adult Americans had trouble sleeping, 14 percent had difficulty concentrating, and 30 percent felt very upset when something reminded them of what happened. Additionally, 47 percent of children in the country were worried about their own and their family's safety.[136]

This attack was not the first involving foreign terrorists in general or Islamic terrorists in particular. For example, Ramzi Ahmed and Eyad Mahmoud Ismail Najim bombed the World Trade Center in 1993, and embassies in Kenya and Tanzania were bombed in 1998.[137]

## Responding to Terrorism

In response to the terrorist attacks on September 11, President Bush created the Department of Homeland Security. The Department of Homeland Security is responsible for coordinating twenty-two previously separate agencies for the purpose of protecting the country against terrorist attacks. As part of its mission the Department of Homeland Security is also responsible for facilitating President Bush's plan to strengthen homeland security.

For a full discussion on the Department of Homeland Security, see Chapter 3.

First, the president's plan provided $3.5 billion dollars to first responders, such as police, firefighters, and medical personnel to pay for training, equipment, and local anti-terrorism planning. Second, about $11 billion dollars was allocated toward enhanced border security. Particular emphasis was placed on increasing the number of U.S. Coast Guard and Customs Service personnel and creating an enhanced entry-exit visa database and tracking system. Third, $6 billion dollars was dedicated to defending the country against bioterrorism. In particular, the monies were used to boost research on new vaccines and medicines and to develop diagnostic tests to detect bioterrorist attacks. Last, $700 million dollars was used to improve the federal government's capacity to gather and share intelligence with other federal agencies as well as with state and city governments.[138]

The FBI also made a number of changes to respond to terrorism in the wake of September 11. Most significant, it created an Office of Intelligence, which is focused on increasing the FBI's intelligence and analysis capacity related to terrorism. The FBI increased the number of analysts focusing on international terrorism by 400 percent. The Office of Intelligence also hired "report officers," who are responsible for identifying key trends and distributing the intelligence to key personnel, and brought twenty-five Central Intelligence Agency officers to the FBI offices to help facilitate the identification and dissemination of intelligence related to terrorism.[139]

The FBI also created a Counterterrorism Watch (CT Watch), which is a 24-hour global command center that is responsible for the prevention of terrorism. Terrorism threats are continually reviewed and evaluated by CT Watch personnel and information that appears to be credible is disseminated to FBI investigators for immediate response. CT Watch also produced daily reports for the president and other national security policymakers.[140]

While there has been extensive discussion about the federal government's reorganization to prevent and respond to terrorism, little national attention has focused on the role of the local police to prevent and respond to terrorism. This is somewhat surprising given that citizens are more likely to report suspected terrorist activities to their local police department than to a federal law enforcement agency. One study conducted in the Phoenix metropolitan area reported that 95 percent of residents were likely to report suspected terrorist activity to local police officials, whereas only 61 percent stated that they would be likely to report suspected terrorist activity to a federal law enforcement agency.[141]

Local police are typically the first to respond to a terrorist event. However, little is known about local law enforcement's capacity to respond to terrorism. A nationwide survey of local agencies indicates that only about 19 percent have made extensive changes in preparation for a terrorist attack. Most have made only modest changes (47 percent) or no changes at all (9 percent). Most of those surveyed point to politics and turf battles as the biggest barrier to becoming more effective in their response to terrorism.[142]

Problems related to turf battles have perhaps been most pronounced between local and federal agencies. Local police officials have been very vocal about their belief that federal law enforcement agencies are unwilling to share critical information with them. Some local police departments have threatened to no longer participate in Homeland Security Department's information sharing programs unless they are given greater and more timely access to intelligence. Police chiefs from the largest cities in the nation state that they are treated like second-class citizens by the Department of Homeland Security but at the same time are responsible for ensuring the safety of their residents and are expected to be the first to respond to a security threat. Officials from the Department of Homeland Security agree that local agencies need access to high-level intelligence but fear that the intelligence will be misused or that it will be leaked to the public.[143]

---

 # Case Study

## *High Point's Overt Drug Market Strategy*

### How was the Overt Drug Market Strategy Created?

Street-level drug dealing is toxic to a neighborhood because of the direct nexus between drug dealing and violence. A prime example of this was a home invasion robbery homicide committed by three young street drug dealers in the West End community of High Point in October 2003. Like many other agencies, our response to drug-infested areas has been to conduct crackdowns and drug sweeps, making multiple arrests. In spite of this, targeted neighborhoods have had consistently high rates of drug trafficking, leaving residents without access to basic law and order within their own neighborhoods.

Determined to make a difference, the executive staff of the High Point Police Department met with Professor David Kennedy, then of Harvard University, to discuss alternative drug traffic control strategies. Kennedy proposed the concept of a law enforcement and community partnership, which would comprehensively dissuade street level drug dealers from dealing in open-air markets. The strategy acts on multiple levels as a deterrent for those impacting the community, leaving offenders with little choice but to modify their behavior. The end result is a dramatic reduction in drug-related and violent crime and a safer community.

## What is Innovative about the Overt Drug Market Strategy?

The Overt Drug Market Strategy has eleven key elements: 1) mapping, to determine where the most serious offenses are concentrated; 2) mobilizing commitment of community through public meetings to identify and inform community stakeholders; 3) surveying by police and probation officers to identify those involved in street drug dealing; 4) formal identification of offenders and their areas of activity; 5) incident review; 6) undercover investigation of each location and offender; 7) contact with the offender's family to invite them to join law enforcement in asking offenders to quit; 8) the call-in, involving a face-to-face call between offenders and law enforcement, and the community (to overcome anonymity); 9) a deadline issued for three days after the call-in for offenders to quit dealing; 10) enforcement; and 11) follow-up visits about a month after call-in to ensure that former offenders are being given the help they need to resist returning to drug dealing.

The strategy identifies or selects neighborhoods for implementation based on intense analysis of crime data, followed by interviewing/surveying patrol officers, probation officers, street narcotics officers and community members for their list of "persons of interest." This careful preparation takes a minimum of three months: building cases, identifying key players, determining which offenders need to be arrested or removed immediately and which ones to invite to the notification session. To date, forty offenders have been called in or notified for the Overt Drug Market Strategy in three neighborhoods.

By identifying known drug dealers and encouraging them to give up dealing, the High Point police department is improving access to justice on two fronts. Offenders can now access public programs and resources to assist them to find livelihoods without breaking the law, while community members have access to safer streets and a more responsive criminal justice system.

## What Obstacles were Encountered?

The most significant obstacle to High Point's Overt Drug Market Strategy is the lack of employment opportunities for notified offenders. Jobs are scarce across the board, and most street-level drug offenders have minimal qualifications. These social issues are not going to be solved quickly; however, working in collaboration with area service providers, we approach each offender's situation by offering support for whatever is requested, including mentoring, partially funded apprenticeship programs, training, or treatment needs.

While employment heads the list of needs, smaller issues come into play as well—problems such as transportation and education. For example, a notified offender might need a GED to be considered for employment but have no means to get to class unless the Resource Coordinator provides a bus pass. A local African American congregation has partnered with us, providing mentors willing to walk with offenders for as long as necessary, providing help in any way possible.

## What were the Results of the Innovation?

The single most important achievement of High Point's Street Drug Strategy has been the collapse of drug markets in the targeted neighborhoods. This is not to say drugs are not still being sold—police cannot control consumption—but the associated violence and visible danger to residents on sidewalks and street corners has vanished. Children can safely play outside; folks can walk to neighborhood stores or sit on their front porches without fear of violence or having to witness criminal activity. Rush-hour traffic jams caused by people buying drugs on their way home have disappeared. This was accomplished with very few arrests. In fact, arrests in the West End have declined 12 percent.

The 1998 institution of the violent offender notification process, on which the Overt Drug Market Strategy is based, resulted in consistent reductions in High Point's violent crime rate as it decreased 47 percent from 1,302.5 in 1997 to 681.5 in 2005. In the two years following the Drug Market call-in in the West End neighborhood, site of the first Overt Drug Market Strategy implementation, crime of all kinds remained more than 25 percent lower than before strategy implementation. Citywide, violent crime decreased 20 percent in the same two years.

*Source:* James Fealy, "Overt Drug Market Strategy, High Point, North Carolina." Presented at the Improving Access to Public Services Conference, November 6–8, 2007, The Hague The Netherlands. Accessed at http://www.innovations. harvard.edu/cache/documents/698/69851.pdf on June 8, 2009.

## Summary

Crime control is one of the major responsibilities of the police. Crime-related programs involve a number of different strategies and assumptions. There is mixed evidence about the effectiveness of these strategies in reducing crime, however. Patrol has only limited deterrent effect on crime. The police clear or solve only about 20 percent of all crimes that come to their attention. They are able to solve a high percentage of those crimes where a suspect is immediately known. Many experts today argue that the most promising programs are crime prevention efforts embodied in community policing and problem-oriented policing programs.

## Key Terms

proactive crime strategies, 261
reactive crime strategies, 261
unfounding a crime, 267
preliminary investigation, 269
nominal caseload, 271
workable caseload, 271
actual caseload, 271
clearance rate, 271
legally arrested, 272
behaviorally arrested, 272

subjectively arrested, 272
officially arrested, 272
case solvability
    factors, 273
forensic index, 277
convicted offender
    index, 277
structural changes, 277
procedural changes, 278
functional changes, 278

supply reduction strategy, 280
demand reduction strategy, 281
D.A.R.E., 281
G.R.E.A.T., 284
Kansas City Gun
    Experiment, 286
hate crimes, 287
terrorism, 289
domestic terrorism, 289
foreign terrorism, 290

# For Discussion

1. Get into groups and discuss what a hate crime is and whether you believe that police agencies should police "hate."
2. As discussed in the text, there are two primary strategies used by the police to reduce drug use: supply reduction and demand reduction. As a class, discuss which strategy you think works best, and how you, if you were a chief of police, would handle your community's drug problem.
3. As a class, discuss possible reasons that D.A.R.E. has continued to be used in classrooms across the country.
4. Check with your campus police department and find out how much (school) crime occurs on your campus. Discuss the types of crimes that occur most frequently and what you think the university should do to address these problems (if anything).
5. As a class, watch a television program or movie that focuses on an investigator or detective working in a local police department. Discuss the accuracy of the portrayal of the detective's work in light of what you have learned in class.

# Internet Exercises

**Exercise 1** Check out recent clearance rate data on the Web. Check the most recent FBI UCR data. Have national clearance rates changed for any crimes? Check out the Web sites for some local police departments. Do they provide their clearance rates? If so, how do different departments compare with the national clearance rates for particular crimes?

**Exercise 2** To learn more about trends in gang-related crime, go to the Web sites of the Chicago police department and the Los Angeles police department. Also check out the site **http://www.streetgangs.com** to learn about gangs in Los Angeles and to access other Web sites on gangs.

**Exercise 3** Go to the National Counterterrorism Center's Worldwide Incidents Tracking Center, **http://wits.nctc.gov/,** to examine current trends in terrorism around the globe.

# Notes

1. Lawrence W. Sherman, "Attacking Crime: Police and Crime Control," in Michael Tonry and Norval Morris, eds., *Modern Policing* (Chicago: University of Chicago Press, 1992), pp. 159–230.
2. Jihong Zhoa, Ni He, and Nicholas Lovrich, "Community Policing: Did It Change the Basic Functions of Policing in the 1990s? A National Follow-Up Study." *Justice Quarterly* 20, 4 (2003): pp. 697–794.
3. Vincent J. Webb and Charles M. Katz, "Citizen Ratings of the Importance of Community Policing," *Policing* 20, 1 (1997): pp. 7–24.
4. Ibid.
5. Lawrence W. Sherman et al., *Preventing Crime* (Washington DC: Government Printing Office, 1997).
6. Ibid.
7. Edward Maguire, "Measuring the Performance of Law Enforcement Agencies," CALEA Update Online, accessed at http://www.calea.org/newweb/newsletter/No83/ measurement.htm on January 7, 2004.
8. David Bayley, *Police for the Future* (New York: Oxford University Press, 1994).
9. Ibid.
10. Jeffrey Roth, Jan Roehl, and Calvin Johnson, "Trends in the Adoption of Community Policing," in Wesley Skogan, ed., *Community Policing: Can It Work* (Belmont, CA: Wadsworth, 2004).
11. Jihong Zhoa, Ni He, and Nicholas Lovrich, "Community Policing: Did It Change the Basic Functions of Policing in the 1990s?"
12. Wesley Skogan and Jeffrey Roth, "Introduction," in Wesley Skogan, ed., *Community Policing: Can*

*It Work* (Belmont, CA: Wadsworth, 2004), pp. xvii–xxxiv.

13. Bureau of Justice Statistics, *Criminal Victimization, 2007* (Washington DC: Government Printing Office, 2008).

14. Bureau of Justice Statistics, *Reporting Crime to the Police, 1992–2000* (Washington DC: Government Printing Office, 2003).

15. Bureau of Justice Statistics, *Reporting Crime to the Police, 1992–2000;* Bureau of Justice Statistics, *Criminal Victimization, 2002* (Washington DC: Government Printing Office, 2003).

16. Donald Black, "Production of Crime Rates," in Donald Black, ed., *The Manners and Customs of the Police* (New York: Academic Press, 1980), p. 69.

17. Bureau of Justice Statistics, *Criminal Victimization in the United States, 1995,* p. 115.

18. Black, "Production of Crime Rates."

19. Albert J. Reiss, Jr., *The Police and the Public* (New Haven, CT: Yale University Press, 1974), p. 95.

20. Fred Grimm, Cops' number game not unique, *The Miami Herald,* page 6b, March 9, 2004.

21. Herman Goldstein, *Policing a Free Society* (Cambridge, MA: Ballinger, 1977), pp. 55–57. For example, see Carmine Motto and Dale June, *Undercover* (Boca Raton, FL: CRC Press, 2000), pp. 1–2.

22. William A. Westley, *Violence and the Police* (Cambridge, MA: MIT Press, 1970), p. 36. For example, see Motto and June, *Undercover.*

23. Goldstein, *Policing a Free Society,* p. 55. For example, see Motto and June, *Undercover.*

24. Bayley, *Police for the Future.*

25. Mary Ann Wycoff and Colleen Cosgrove, *Investigations in the Community Policing Context: Final Report* (Washington DC: Police Executive Research Forum, 2001).

26. William B. Sanders, *Detective Work: A Study of Criminal Investigations* (New York: The Free Press, 1977), pp. 39–47.

27. Geoffrey Alpert and Mark H. Moore, "Measuring Police Performance in the New Paradigm of Policing." In Bureau of Justice Statistics, *Performance Measures for the Criminal Justice System* (Washington DC: Government Printing Office, 1993), pp. 109–40.

28. Sanders, *Detective Work.*

29. Victor Kappeler, Richard Sluder, and Geoffrey Albert, *Forces of Deviance,* 2nd ed. (Prospect Heights, IL: Waveland Press, 1998); John Dombrink, "The Touchables: Vice and Police Corruption in the 1980s," in *Police Deviance,* 3rd ed. (Cincinnati: Anderson, 1994), pp. 61–97.

30. David Giacapassi and Jerry Sparger, "Cognitive Dissonance in Vice Enforcement," *American Journal of Police* 10, 2 (1991): pp. 39–51.

31. John E. Eck, *Solving Crimes: The Investigation of Burglary and Robbery* (Washington DC: Police Executive Research Forum, 1983), pp. 69–93.

32. Reiss, *The Police and the Public,* p. 104.

33. Donald Black, *Manners and Customs of the Police* (San Diego, CA: Academic Press, 1980).

34. John McCluskey, Stephen Mastrofski, and Rodger Parks, "To Acquiesce or Rebel: Predicting Citizen Compliance with Police Requests," *Police Quarterly* 2 (1999): pp. 389–416.

35. Donald Black, "The Social Organization of Arrest," in W. Clinton Terry III, ed., *Policing Society* (New York: John Wiley, 1985), pp. 290–309.

36. Douglas A. Smith, Christy A. Visher, and Laura A. Davidson, "Equity and Discretionary Justice: The Influence of Race on Police Arrest Decisions," *Journal of Criminal Law and Criminology* 75 (Spring 1984): pp. 234–49.

37. Eck, *Solving Crimes,* pp. 124–27.

38. Peter W. Greenwood et al., *The Criminal Investigation Process,* vol. 1, *Summary and Policy Implications* (Santa Monica, CA: Rand, 1975), p. 35.

39. Eck, *Solving Crimes,* pp. 106–10.

40. Harold E. Pepinsky, "Police Decision Making," in Don Gottfredson, ed., *Decision Making in the Criminal Justice System* (Washington DC: Government Printing Office, 1975), p. 27.

41. Wycoff and Cosgrove, *Investigations in the Community Policing Context: Final Report.*

42. Eck, *Solving Crimes,* p. 250. In Edward Maguire, "Measuring the Performance of Law Enforcement Agencies," CALEA Update Online.

43. Alpert and Moore, "Measuring Police Performance in the New Paradigm of Policing."

44. Federal Bureau of Investigation, *Crime in the United States, 1999* (Washington DC: Government Printing Office, 2000).

45. Greenwood et al., *The Criminal Investigation Process,* p. 32.

46. Eck, *Solving Crimes,* p. 203.

47. Black, "The Production of Crime Rates"; In Edward Maguire, "Measuring the Performance of Law Enforcement Agencies," CALEA Update Online.

48. Clint Bolick, "Justice Denied: The Improper Clearance of Unsolved Crimes by the Maricopa

County Sheriff's Office" (Phoenix, AZ: Goldwater Institute, 2009).

49. Lawrence W. Sherman and Barry D. Glick, *The Quality of Police Arrest Statistics* (Washington DC: The Police Foundation, 1984).

50. Edna Erez, "On the 'Dark Figure' of Arrest," *Journal of Police Science and Administration* 12 (December 1984): pp. 431–40.

51. Steven H. Gifis, *Law Dictionary,* 2nd ed. (New York: Barron's, 1984), pp. 28–29.

52. Floyd Feeney, *Arrests without Conviction* (Washington DC: Government Printing Office, 1983).

53. Sherman and Glick, *The Quality of Police Arrest Statistics.*

54. President's Commission on Law Enforcement and Administration of Justice, *Task Force Report: The Police* (Washington DC: Government Printing Office, 1967), p. 8.

55. Albert Reiss and David J. Bordua, "Environment and Organization: A Perspective on the Police," in D. J. Bordua, ed., *The Police: Six Sociological Essays* (New York: John Wiley, 1967), p. 43.

56. Sanders, *Detective Work,* p. 96.

57. Greenwood et al., *The Criminal Investigation Process,* vol. 1, *Summary and Policy Implications.*

58. Steven G. Brandl and James Frank, "The Relationship between Evidence, Detective Effort, and the Disposition of Burglary and Robbery Investigations," *American Journal of Police* XIII, no. 3 (1994): pp. 149–68.

59. Gary Cordner, "Police Agency Size and Investigative Effectiveness," *Journal of Criminal Justice* 17 (1989): pp. 145–55.

60. Judi Villa and Ryan Konig, "Murders Go Unsolved as Smuggling Grows," *Arizona Republic,* November 9, 2003, p. 1.

61. Lucius J. Riccio and John F. Heaphy, "Apprehension Productivity of Police in Large U.S. Cities," *Journal of Criminal Justice* 5 (Winter 1977): pp. 271–78.

62. Brian Forst et al., *Arrest Convictability as a Measure of Police Performance* (Washington DC: Government Printing Office, 1982).

63. Bureau of Justice Statistics, *Felony Defendants in Large Urban Counties, 2000* (Washington DC: Government Printing Office, 2003).

64. Joan Petersilia, *Racial Disparities in the Criminal Justice System* (Santa Monica, CA: Rand, 1983), p. 21.

65. Joan Petersilia, Allan Abrahamse, and James Q. Wilson, *Police Performance and Case Attrition* (Santa Monica, CA: Rand, 1987).

66. Brian Forst, Judith Lucianovic, and Sarah J. Cox, *What Happens after Arrest?* (Washington DC: INSLAW, 1977).

67. Elizabeth Loftus, *Eyewitness Testimony* (Cambridge, MA: Harvard University Press, 1979), p. 7.

68. Gary Wells and Deah Quinlivan, "Suggestive Eyewitness Identification Procedures and the Supreme Court's Reliability Test in Light of Eyewitness Science: 30 Years Later." *Law and Human Behavior* 33 (2009), pp. 1–24.

69. Elinor Ostrom et al., *Patterns of Metropolitan Policing* (Cambridge, MA: Ballinger, 1977), Ch. 7.

70. *New York Times,* August 17, 1986.

71. John Smialek, Charlotte Word, and Arthur Westveer, "The Microscopic Slide: A Potential DNA Reservoir," *FBI Law Enforcement Bulletin* 69 (November 2000), pp. 18–21.

72. Barry Fisher, *Techniques of Crime Scene Investigation* (Boca Raton, FL: CRC Press, 2004).

73. Smialek, Word, and Westveer, "The Microscopic Slide."

74. David Schroeder and Michael White, "Exploring the Use of DNA Evidence in Homicide Investigations: Implications for Detective Work and Case Clearance," *Police Quarterly* 12 (September 2009), pp. 319–342.

75. Nancy Ritter, "DNA Solves Property Crimes," *National Institute of Justice Journal* 261 (October 2008).

76. Wycoff and Cosgrove, *Investigations in the Community Policing Context: Final Report.*

77. Personal communication with Chief Galvin of the Albuquerque Police Department, 1999.

78. Gary T. Marx, *Undercover: Police Surveillance in America* (Berkeley: University of California Press, 1988).

79. Knapp Commission, *Report on Police Corruption* (New York: Braziller, 1973).

80. Marx, *Undercover,* pp. 188–90.

81. Commission on Accreditation for Law Enforcement Agencies, *Standards for Law Enforcement Agencies,* 4th ed. (Fairfax, VA: CALEA, 1999), Standard 43.1.6.

82. Jonathan Rubenstein, *City Police* (New York: Ballantine, 1973), p. 381.

83. Robert Daley, *Prince of the City* (Boston: Houghton Mifflin, 1978).

84. Jerome Skolnick, *Justice without Trial* (New York: Macmillan, 1994), p. 129.

85. Gary Marx, *Undercover: Police Surveillance in America.*

86. Commission on Law Enforcement Accreditation, *Standards for Law Enforcement Agencies*, 4th ed., Standard 42.2.9.

87. Bureau of Justice Assistance, *Informants and Undercover Investigations* (Washington DC: Government Printing Office, 1990), p. 16.

88. Elliot Currie, *Reckoning: Drugs, the Cities, and the American Future* (New York: Hill and Wang, 1993); Bruce Johnson, Andrew Golub, and Eloise Dunlap, "The Rise and Decline of Hard Drugs, Drug Markets, and Violence in Inner-City New York," in Alfred Blumstein and Joel Wallman, eds., *The Crime Drop in America* (Cambridge, United Kingdom: Cambridge Press, 2000).

89. Center for Substance Abuse Research, "Two-Thirds of National Drug Control Budget Dedicated to Domestic Enforcement, Interdiction, and International Efforts," *CESAR FAX* 9 (College Park, University of Maryland: May 1, 2000).

90. Center for Substance Abuse Research, "U.S. Illicit Drug Expenditures Stable at about $65 Billion," *CESAR FAX* 10 (College Park, University of Maryland: March 5, 2001).

91. Mark H. Moore, *Buy and Bust* (Lexington, MA: Lexington Books, 1977).

92. Lawrence W. Sherman, "Police Crackdowns: Initial and Residual Deterrence," in Michael Tonry and Norval Morris, eds., *Crime and Justice: A Review of Research* 12 (Chicago: University of Chicago Press, 1990), pp. 1–48.

93. Currie, *Reckoning;* Arnold S. Trebach, *The Great Drug War* (New York: Macmillan, 1987).

94. Peter K. Manning, *The Narcs' Game* (Prospect Heights, IL: Waveland, 2004).

95. John Crank and Robert Langworthy, "An Institutional Perspective of Policy," *Journal of Criminal Law and Criminology* 83, no. 2 (1992), pp. 338–63.

96. Department of Health and Human Services, *Results from the 2002 National Survey on Drug Use and Health* (Washington DC: Government Printing Office, 2003).

97. Jerome G. Miller, *Search and Destroy: African-American Males in the Criminal Justice System* (New York: Cambridge University Press, 1996).

98. Thomas C. Castellano and Craig G. Uchida, "Local Drug Enforcement, Prosecutors and Case Attrition: Theoretical Perspectives for the Drug War," *American Journal of Police* IX, no. 1 (1990): p. 147.

99. U.S. Bureau of Justice Assistance, *An Introduction to DARE: Drug Abuse Resistance Education,* 2nd ed. (Washington DC: Government Printing Office, 1991).

100. Law Enforcement News, "When It Comes to the Young, Anti-Drug Efforts Are Going to Pot," *Law Enforcement News* 22, pp. 441–47.

101. Susan T. Emmett et al., "How Effective Is Drug Abuse Resistance Education?: A Meta-Analysis of Project DARE Outcome Evaluations," *American Journal of Public Health* 84 (September 1994): pp. 1394–1401.

102. Dennis Rosenbaum and Gordon Hanson, "Assessing the Effects of School-Based Drug Education: A Six-Year Multi-Level Analysis of Project D.A.R.E" (Unpublished manuscript: University of Illinois at Chicago, 1998); Donald Lynam et al., "Project DARE: No Effects at 10-Year Follow-Up," *Journal of Consulting and Clinical Psychology* 67 (1999): pp. 590–93.

103. Walter Miller, *Crime by Youth Gangs and Groups in the United States* (Washington DC: Government Printing Office, 1982).

104. Arlen Egley and Christina O'Donnell, *Highlights of the 2006 National Youth Gang Survey* (Washington DC: Office of Juvenile Justice Delinquency Prevention, 2008).

105. Charles M. Katz, Vincent J. Webb, and David R. Schaefer, "The Validity of Police Gang Intelligence Lists: Examining the Differences in Delinquency between Documented Gang Members and Non-documented Delinquent Youth," *Police Quarterly* 3 (2000): pp. 413–37.

106. C. Ronald Huff, *Gangs in America* (Newbury Park, CA: Sage, 1993); Jerome Needle and William Stapleton, *Police Handling of Youth Gangs. Reports of the National Juvenile Justice Assessment Centers* (Washington DC: Government Printing Office, 1983).

107. Charles M. Katz, Edward R. Maguire, and Dennis Roncek, "A Macro-Level Analysis of the Creation of Specialized Police Gang Units: An Examination of Rational, Social Threat, and Resource Dependency Perspectives" (Unpublished manuscript: Arizona State University West, 2000), p. 14.

108. Bureau of Justice Statistics, *Law Enforcement Management and Administrative Statistics, 2000: Data for Individual State and Local Agencies with 100 or More Officers* (Washington DC: Government Printing Office, 2004).

109. Katz, Maguire, and Roncek, "A Macro-Level Analysis of the Creation of Specialized Police Gang Units."

110. Charles M. Katz, "The Establishment of a Police Gang Unit: An Examination of Organizational and Environmental Factors," *Criminology* 39, no. 1 (2001): pp. 37–73.

111. Malcolm Klein, Margaret Gordon, and Cheryl Maxson, "The Impact of Police Investigations on Police Reported Rates of Gang and Nongang Homicides," *Criminology* 24 (1986): pp. 489–511.

112. Finn-Aage Esbensen, *Preventing Adolescent Gang Involvement* (Washington DC: Office of Juvenile Justice and Delinquency Prevention, 2000).

113. Finn-Aage Esbensen, D. Wayne Osgood, Terrance J. Taylor, Dana Peterson, and Adrienne Oreng, "How Great Is G.R.E.A.T.? Results from a Longitudinal Quasi-Experimental Design," *Criminology and Public Policy* 1, 1 (2001): pp. 87–118.

114. Marvin E. Wolfgang, Robert Figlio, and Thorsten Sellin, *Delinquency in a Birth Cohort* (Chicago: University of Chicago Press, 1972).

115. William Spelman, *Repeat Offender Programs for Law Enforcement* (Washington DC: PERF, 1990).

116. Ibid., pp. 25–26.

117. Susan E. Martin and Lawrence W. Sherman, *Catching Career Criminals: The Washington DC Repeat Offender Project* (Washington DC: The Police Foundation, 1986).

118. Ibid.

119. Steven Messner and Richard Rosenfeld, *Crime and the American Dream* (Belmont, CA: Wadsworth, 1997).

120. Samuel Walker, *Sense and Nonsense about Crime and Drugs* (Belmont, CA: Wadsworth, 2000).

121. Lawrence W. Sherman, James W. Shaw, and Dennis P. Rogan, *The Kansas City Gun Experiment* (Washington DC: Government Printing Office, 1995).

122. Edmund McGarrell, Steven Chermak, Alexander Weiss, and Jeremy Wilson, "Reducing Firearms Violence through Directed Police Patrol," *Criminology and Public Policy* 1, 1 (2001): pp. 119–48.

123. U.S. Department of Justice, "Project Safe Neighborhoods," *USA Bulletin* 50, 1 (January 2002).

124. http://www.fbi.gov/hq/cid/civilrights/overview.htm, accessed on 11/19/09.

125. Federal Bureau of Investigation, Hate Crime Statistics, 2007. Accessed at http://www.fbi.gov/ucr/hc2007/incidents.htm on June 8, 2009.

126. Susan Martin, "Police and the Production of Hate Crimes: Continuity and Change in One Jurisdiction," *Police Quarterly* 2 (1999): pp. 417–37.

127. James Garofalo and Susan Martin, *Bias-Motivated Crimes: Their Characteristics and the Law Enforcement Response* (Carbondale: Southern Illinois University, 1993).

128. Ibid.

129. Ibid.

130. Ibid.

131. Terrorist Research and Analytical Center, Counter-Terrorism Section Intelligence Division, *Terrorism in the United States 1982–1992* (Washington DC: U.S. Department of Justice, Federal Bureau of Investigations, 1993).

132. Christopher Hewitt, *Understanding Terrorism in America* (New York: Routledge, 2003).

133. Found at http://www.earthliberationfront.com/news/2004/011304r.shtml on January 20, 2004.

134. Miyoko Ohtake, From Green to Black, *Newsweek,* March 6, 2008.

135. Federal Bureau of Investigation, *Terrorism in the United States, 1998* (Washington DC: Federal Bureau of Investigation, 1999).

136. Found at http://www.RAND.org/publications/RB/RB4546/index.html on January 16, 2004.

137. Federal Bureau of Investigation, *Terrorism in the United States, 1999,* found at http://www.fbi.gov/publications/terror/terror99.pdf on January 20, 2004.

138. Found at http://www.dhs.gov/dhspublic/display?theme=12&content=19 on January 20, 2004.

139. Found at http://www.fbi.gov/terrorinfo/counterterrorism/analysis.htm on January 20, 2004.

140. Ibid.

141. Stephen Schnebly, Steve Ballance, and Charles Katz, *Data Sharing between the Police and the Public* (Phoenix: Arizona State University, 2006).

142. National Crime Prevention Council, *Building the Homeland Security Network: What Will It Take? The Wirthlin Report* (Washington DC: National Crime Prevention Council, 2002).

143. Robert Block, "Big-City Police Chiefs Assail Homeland Security's Secrecy," *Wall Street Journal Online* (June 30, 2006, page B1).

# Innovations in Police Strategy

For almost 20 years community policing and its many variations have become the new orthodoxy of policing.[1] Community policing, its advocates argue, represents a new philosophy of policing aimed at increasing the quality of police efforts.[2]

This chapter examines community policing, along with its variations—problem-oriented policing and zero-tolerance policing—and discusses its assumptions, characteristics, and impacts.

# Impetus for Change in Policing

Both community policing and problem-oriented policing originated in the late 1970s and early 1980s as a result of a series of crises in policing. First, the police–community relations problems of the 1960s had created a crisis of legitimacy. Local police departments were isolated and alienated from important segments of the community, particularly racial and ethnic minority populations.[3]

For a full discussion on the effectiveness of traditional police patrol, see Chapter 7.

Second, recent research had undermined the assumptions of traditional police management and police reform. The Kansas City Preventive Patrol Experiment found that there were limits to the ability of traditional police patrol to deter crime. Studies of the criminal investigation process raised doubts about the ability of the police to significantly increase the number of arrests. Furthermore, research showed that faster response time does not usually increase the likelihood of arrests. In short, the traditional reforms of more police, more patrol, more detectives, and faster response time were seen as not likely to improve policing. At the same time, the traditional police goal of providing an immediate response to all citizen calls for service, regardless of the nature of the call, burdened the police with an enormous workload.

For a full discussion on the effectiveness of criminal investigations, see Chapter 9.

Third, experts recognized that the police role is extremely complex, involving many different tasks and responsibilities. It was discovered that only a small part of police work was related to criminal law enforcement and that most police work involved order maintenance and service activities. As a consequence, experts recognized that if the police were to become more effective, they were going to have to broaden their characterization of police work from one that exclusively focused on crime control to one that also focused on such issues as community quality of life, order maintenance, and fear of crime.

For a full discussion on the police–community relations crisis of the 1960s, see Chapter 2.

For a full discussion
on response time, see
Chapter 7.

For a full discussion on
the realities of policing,
see Chapter 1.

Fourth, experts began to recognize the importance of citizens as coproducers of police services.[4] The police depend on citizens to report crime and to request help in dealing with disorder. The decision to arrest is heavily influenced by the expressed preference for arrest on the part of a citizen. Successful prosecution of offenders depends heavily on the cooperation of victims and witnesses. Even more important, informal social control at the neighborhood level was increasingly recognized as the key to limiting crime and disorder. In short, there was growing recognition that the police cannot control crime by themselves.

## The Roots of Community Policing: The Broken Windows Hypothesis

James Q. Wilson and George L. Kelling influenced the history of policing forever when they teamed together and wrote an essay entitled "Broken Windows" for *Atlantic Monthly* magazine. They argued that the police should focus their resources on disorder problems affecting the quality of neighborhood life.[5] In particular, they emphasized that the police should address those problems that create fear of crime and lead to neighborhood decay. The image of **broken windows** symbolizes the relationship among disorder, neighborhood decay, and crime. A broken window, Wilson and Kelling argue, is a sign that nobody cares about the appearance of the property. Left unrepaired, it encourages other neighborhood residents to neglect their property. This sets in motion a downward spiral of deterioration. Houses deteriorate, homeowners move out, residential buildings are converted to rental properties, houses are converted from single-family to multifamily dwellings, and some houses are abandoned. As the income level of the neighborhood declines, neighborhood stores close and property values decline. Gradually, crime in the neighborhood increases.[6] (See Exhibit 10–1.)

**broken windows**

For a full discussion on
the actual type of work
performed by the
police, see Chapter 7.

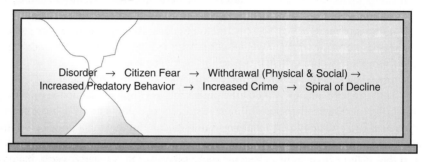

### EXHIBIT 10–1

**Broken Windows Hypothesis**

Disorder  →  Citizen Fear  →  Withdrawal (Physical & Social) →
Increased Predatory Behavior  →  Increased Crime  →  Spiral of Decline

*Source:* George Kelling and William Bratton, "Declining Crime Rates: Insiders' Views of the New York City Story,"
Reprinted by special permission of Northwestern University School of Law, *The Journal of Criminal Law and Criminology.*

These initial signs of disorder include drunks hanging out on the street or groups of teenagers on street corners. Such events create fear for personal safety in the minds of law-abiding residents in the neighborhood. Out of fear, they stay at home and withdraw from active participation in the neighborhood. In extreme cases they move out of the neighborhood altogether. The withdrawal of law-abiding citizens undermines the fabric of neighborhood life. The disorderly elements gain control of public areas, street corners, and parks; and the process of deterioration accelerates. The ultimate end of this process is serious predatory crime, such as burglary and robbery.

Wilson and Kelling maintain that traditional policing focuses on the end result of this process: serious crime. Yet the evidence indicates that the police officer's ability to fight crime is very limited. They argue that the police should intervene at the beginning of the process of neighborhood deterioration—at the first signs of neglect and disorder.

## Types of Disorder

Wilson and Kelling emphasize the importance of disorder rather than serious crime. Disorder is an extremely broad category. Wesley Skogan has distinguished between two major subcategories of disorder: (1) social and (2) physical. **Social disorder** includes such issues as public drinking, street corner gangs, street harassment, street-level drug sale and use, noisy neighbors, and commercial sex. **Physical disorder,** meanwhile, includes such problems as vandalism, dilapidation and abandonment of buildings, and rubbish.[7]

**social disorder**

**physical disorder**

## Characteristics of Community Policing

While **community policing** has been ushered into police departments across the nation, studies have illustrated that few understand the underlying concept. For example, one national survey of law enforcement agencies found that only about 50 percent of the police chiefs and sheriffs queried had a clear understanding of what community policing means.[8] Therefore, it should not be surprising that community policing has come to mean different things to different people. Popular strategies include instituting foot or bicycle patrols, establishing neighborhood police substations, identifying neighborhood problems, dealing with disorder, organizing community meetings, or conducting community surveys.[9] In fact, because the label of community policing has been attached to such a variety of activities and programs, some reformers express concern that community policing has come to mean anything that is new and innovative in American policing.[10]

**community policing**

Despite this confusion, there does appear to be a consensus about some of the basic elements of community policing, and how it differs from previous policing strategies. The most important difference is that community policing represents a *major change in the role of the police*. While the police have traditionally defined their primary mission in terms of crime control, community policing seeks to broaden the police role to include dealing with such issues as fear of crime, order maintenance, conflict resolution, neighborhood decay, and social and physical disorder as basic functions of the police.

---

**SIDEBAR     10 – 1**

## Broken Windows or Broken Theory?

While there has been a great deal of discussion surrounding the broken windows hypothesis, little research has actually examined the relationship among disorder, fear, and serious crime. One of the few studies to examine this theory is Wesley Skogan's research that examined disorder and crime in forty neighborhoods in six major cities. He found that perceptions of crime, fear of crime, and victimization are all related to physical and social disorder.[1]

However, Harcourt reexamined Skogan's data and found that his findings were largely driven by a few neighborhoods in which the relationship between disorder and crime was strong.[2] In particular, he found that if Skogan had excluded the neighborhoods of Newark, New Jersey, from his analyses, he would not have found a relationship between disorder and crime. Harcourt referred to this as the "Newark effect."

Eck and Maguire, addressing this debate, analyzed the data once again. They reported that had Skogan removed other neighborhoods from his analysis, outliers in which there was no relationship between disorder and crime, Skogan's finding of a relationship between disorder and crime would have been even stronger. They concluded that "Skogan's results are extremely sensitive to outliers and therefore do not provide a sound basis for policy."[3]

Sampson and Raudenbush examined the issue further in Chicago and reported that disorder and crime is related to the same issue—social cohesion. Specifically, they found that when neighbors were less likely to intervene and help one another both disorder and crime increased simultaneously.[4] Xu, Fiedler, and Flaming, on the other hand, controlled for social cohesion in their study of the relationship between broken windows and crime in Colorado Springs, Colorado. The authors paid particular attention to the role of social cohesion and reported that physical and moral decay in a community both indirectly and directly resulted in crime.[5]

As a consequence, the proverbial jury is still out. There is no definitive evidence on whether disorder leads to crime or whether the connection between the two is spurious.

[1]Wesley G. Skogan, *Disorder and Decline: Crime and the Spiral of Decay in American Neighborhoods* (New York: Free Press, 1990), pp. 21–50.
[2]Bernard Harcourt, "Reflecting on the Subject: A Critique of the Social Influence Conception of Deterrence, the Broken Windows Theory, and Order-Maintenance Policing New York Style," *Michigan Law Review* 97 (1998): pp. 1–51.
[3]John Eck and Edward Maguire, "Have Changes in Policing Reduced Violent Crime? An Assessment of the Evidence," in Alfred Blumstein and Joel Wallman, eds., *The Crime Drop in America* (Cambridge: Cambridge University Press, 2000), pp. 207–65.
[4]Robert Sampson and Stephen Raudenbush, "Neighborhoods and Violent Crime: A Multi-Level Study of Collective Efficacy," *Science* 277 (1997): 918–25.
[5]Yily Xu, Mora Fiedler, and Karl Flaming, "Discovering the Impact of Community Policing: The Broken Windows Thesis, Collective Efficacy, and Citizens' Judgment," *Journal of Research in Crime and Delinquency* 42 (2005): pp. 147–86.

---

Mastrofski argues that this shift in primary mission of the police from serious crime to order maintenance is justified in two ways. First, reducing minor disorder may lead to a decrease in serious crime. The broken windows hypothesis, as discussed above, asserts that an increase in community decay produces an increase in serious crime, and only by redirecting police services toward neighborhood deterioration and disorder can a community prevent crime. Second, he asserts that order maintenance is "justifiable in its own right in that it contributes to the establishment of a civil, livable environment in which citizens may, without fear, exercise their right to pursue their livelihood."[11]

In an ideal sense, then, community policing seeks to change the basic tenets most Americans, including the police, hold regarding police functions and priorities. Because the implementation of community policing involves a number of philosophical, organizational, strategic, and tactical changes,[12] it is helpful to focus on the three most commonly discussed targets of community policing reform: (1) community partnerships, (2) organizational change, and (3) problem solving.

## Community Partnerships

Community-policing advocates assert that the most effective way of reducing community decay and disorder is through a collaborative relationship between the police and the community. This broadened view recognizes that cooperation between the police and the public will give police greater access to information provided by the community, which in turn will lead the police to be more responsive to the community's needs.[13] Accordingly, the community-policing model stresses greater interaction between the police and the public, so that both entities act as **coproducers of crime control** and prevention.[14] Such a model, in an ideal sense, seeks to create a two-way working relationship between the community and the police, in which the police become more integrated into the local community and citizens assume an active role in crime control and prevention.[15]

**coproducers of crime control**

Bayley, in his seminal book *The Police for the Future,* maintains that two elements are needed to successfully implement **community partnerships** between the police and the public: consultation and mobilization.

**community partnerships**

### *Consultation*

Under community policing, agencies have sought to improve the quality of their crime control and prevention efforts by consulting with citizens in their community. This strategy is intended to help the community and police define and prioritize problems.

**Consultation** between the police and the public, usually done in the form of community meetings, serves four functions: (1) it provides a forum for citizens to express their problems and needs, (2) it allows the police to educate citizens about crime and disorder in their community, (3) it allows citizens to express complaints involving the police, and (4) it provides a forum for the police to inform the community about their successes and failures.[16] Most police agencies meet with community groups of one type or another (see Exhibit 10–2).[17]

**consultation**

For example, the Miami-Dade police department created the Marine Advisory Support Team (MAST) project as "an effort to facilitate community participation . . . and to bring together concerned parties to provide input and identify ways to improve service to the boating public and related interests." Representatives on the team included residents and businesses that lived and operated in and around Biscayne Bay as well as federal, state, and local law enforcement agencies that had jurisdiction over the bay. Once a month MAST team members meet to discuss crime and disorder.

## EXHIBIT 10–2

### Percentage of Agencies Meeting with the Following Types of Groups

| | Total | County Police | Municipal Police | Sheriff | State Law Enforcement |
|---|---|---|---|---|---|
| Advocacy groups | 54 | 55 | 55 | 52 | 33 |
| Business groups | 69 | 77 | 73 | 69 | 43 |
| Domestic violence groups | 64 | 65 | 62 | 67 | 37 |
| Local public agencies | 62 | 58 | 62 | 64 | 57 |
| Neighborhood associations | 89 | 87 | 92 | 84 | 43 |
| Religious groups | 46 | 39 | 48 | 42 | 20 |
| School groups | 79 | 24 | 79 | 81 | 65 |
| Tenants associations | 59 | 74 | 56 | 63 | 37 |
| Youth services organizations | 45 | 61 | 50 | 30 | 14 |
| Senior citizen groups | 54 | 45 | 56 | 50 | 33 |

*Source:* Bureau of Justice Statistics, *Law Enforcement Management and Administrative Statistics, 2000* (Washington DC: Government Printing Office, 2004).

Aside from making agencies aware of problems, the meetings have also led to the prioritization of community problems and to the sharing of resources to address the problems.[18]

While ideally all four of the functions are fulfilled, research has found that partnerships between the police and the public vary in terms of the level of involvement of each partner and the expectations that each has of the other. In some agencies community members are simply encouraged to act as the eyes and ears of the police. In other agencies police officers speak at community meetings or work alongside citizen volunteers. In still other agencies, formal relationships are established between the police and citizens in which the community works alongside the police to identify problems, develop possible solutions, and actively participate in responding to problems.[19]

Regardless, a distinctive characteristic of the police under community policing is that the police seek to reposition themselves so that they become an integral part of community life rather than remain distant and alienated from the community as in years past. By embedding themselves within the community "it is asserted that the police and public actually co-produce public safety."[20]

### *Mobilization*

mobilization

Because the police have recognized their own limitations in preventing crime and disorder, police agencies that have embraced community policing have mobilized the community for assistance. **Mobilization** comes in the form of such programs as Neighborhood Watch, Operation ID, and Crime Stoppers. These community organization strategies not only are a deterrent mechanism but also increase neighborhood cohesion and provide a forum for the police to inform the community of crime prevention techniques.[21] Bayley adds that while the majority of mobilization efforts have dealt with the general public, other municipal agencies can play a critical role in the prevention of crime: "Sanitation departments can haul away abandoned cars, parks and recreation agencies [can] open facilities at night or develop programs for young people, [and] fire and building inspectors [can] condemn abandoned buildings."[22]

Accordingly, under community policing the police expand the number of tools available to them, taking them beyond a reliance on arrest to solve problems. For example, they also use civil and administrative law to broaden their capacity to address quality-of-life concerns in neighborhoods. Many police agencies today work closely with zoning inspectors and other city officials to deal with problems related to local businesses that detract from a neighborhood's quality of life (e.g., commercial sex shops, bars) as well as landlords and homeowners who fail to properly maintain their property.[23] In many communities today it is not unusual for the police to partner with another agency within the city to address city code violations such as weeds, debris, inoperable vehicles, and graffiti to ensure the quality of life in neighborhoods.

For instance, in Portland, Oregon, the police department saw the number of drug houses increase from just a few to over 200 in a single year. The police department did not have the time, or the resources, to address the problem using traditional methods such as undercover work. As an alternative strategy they decided to mobilize landlords, the individuals who would be able to evict drug-dealing renters. In particular, the police department embarked on a program that educated and trained landlords about their rights and responsibilities. They taught landlords how to screen applicants, identify drug activity, evict tenants, and work with neighbors and the police. Over a two-year period more than 5,750 landlords, who oversaw 100,000 rental units, had received training.[24]

As such, community policing is largely focused on establishing and maintaining relationships between the police and the community—whether it be with citizens, community groups, or other public or private agencies—to address neighborhood crime and disorder problems. The police seek to broaden their role to one that is "seen as shifting from first government responder to social diagnostician and community mobilizer." Building linkages and relationships with others in the community allows the police to bring together a variety of services to address a specific issue or problem that may affect community safety.[25]

## The Effectiveness of Community Partnerships

### *Foot Patrol*

One of the most common ways police agencies have attempted to bring the police and citizenry together while at the same time attempting to reduce crime has been through the use of foot patrol. A number of evaluations that examined foot patrol in the 1980s reported that while additional foot patrol did not reduce crime, it did increase feelings of safety. Moreover, citizens generalized these positive feelings to the police department—and not just to the foot patrol officers but to the department as a whole.[26] This finding has led some researchers to speculate that while the police might not be able to reduce crime, perhaps they can reduce fear of crime. And if people are less fearful, they might not withdraw from the communities, and the process of neighborhood deterioration might not begin.[27]

### S I D E B A R          10 – 2

## The Police Want Your Opinion!

Many police agencies across the country are using citizen surveys to gather information from the public to help direct their agencies efforts. Local law enforcement agencies are more likely than state law enforcement agencies to collect information from citizens. The three most common reasons for surveying the public are to assess citizen satisfaction with police services, gather information relating to public perceptions of crime and disorder, and examine citizens experiences with crime.

### Percentage of Agencies Conducting Citizen Surveys, by Agency

|  | Total | County Police | Municipal Police | Sheriff | State Law Enforcement |
|---|---|---|---|---|---|
| Public perceptions of crime and disorder problems | 39 | 42 | 41 | 31 | 18 |
| Personal crime experiences | 25 | 29 | 26 | 24 | 14 |
| Satisfaction with police services | 47 | 52 | 49 | 42 | 35 |

Source: Bureau of Justice Statistics, *Law Enforcement Management and Administrative Statistics, 2000* (Washington DC: Government Printing Office, 2004).

Other studies examining police efforts at increasing police–citizen interaction, however, have found that such strategies can be effective in reducing crime. For example, in Oakland and Birmingham researchers found that both fear of crime and violent crime substantially decreased in beats where police officers made door-to-door contacts with residents.[28] In Houston researchers examining community policing found that home visits by the police led to a decrease in violent crime and disorder in the city.[29]

### Neighborhood Watch

Neighborhood Crime Watch programs are another popular community partnership strategy. Neighborhood Watch programs, however, have repeatedly been found to have little impact on crime.[30] Research conducted in Britain, where some of the most comprehensive studies have taken place, has shown that "there is no strong evidence that Neighborhood Watch has prevented a single crime in Britain since its inception in the early 1980s."[31] These studies have found that Neighborhood Watch programs are typically more active, and have a closer working relationship with the police, in affluent suburban areas with little crime. Residents who live in areas with more crime, and who live in inner-city minority neighborhoods, have been less willing to participate in Neighborhood Watch programs or any other activities that involve partnership with the police.[32]

## *Policing Where "Community" Has Collapsed*

One of the major questions surrounding community policing is whether it is a realistic strategy for the poorest and most crime-ravaged neighborhoods. Community organizing assumes that there is a viable community to help organize. The worst neighborhoods of many big cities—what some commentators call the "underclass"—are so devastated by unemployment, crime, and all the related social problems that no meaningful community remains. Most of the natural community leaders have left: those with stable employment, with families, and with a commitment to their neighborhood. In the absence of positive influences, gangs often become a focal point for young men's lives.

In their contribution to the *Perspectives on Policing* series, Hubert Williams and Patrick V. Murphy warned that "community-oriented approaches that are effective in most neighborhoods work less well, or not at all, in areas inhabited by low-income blacks and other minority groups."[33] Their point was confirmed by a University of Maryland report, *Preventing Crime.* Sherman and his colleagues found that programs directed at families, schools, and communities tend to be most effective where they are needed least. They are least effective in the families, schools, and communities that need the most help. The Maryland report made a very significant contribution to our understanding of crime prevention by emphasizing the interrelationship among families, schools, neighborhoods, and economic opportunities (what it called "labor markets").[34]

At the same time, communities in the traditional sense often do not exist in some newer and rapidly expanding cities. The Houston fear reduction experiment found that the city had an "almost nonexistent neighborhood life."[35]

It may be that community-organizing efforts may help organize only the middle class. The fear reduction experiment in Houston and the community-organizing programs in Minneapolis encountered the same phenomenon: They were more successful among middle-income people, homeowners, and whites than among the really poor, renters, and racial minorities.[36] Successful community organizing among white homeowners may be motivated by racism: their fear of blacks and Hispanics moving into the neighborhood. If this is the case, police-sponsored community-organizing activities may heighten racial conflict. A review of community-organizing efforts, in fact, reached the disturbing conclusion that the strongest community organizations it could identify "arose in response to impending or actual racial change." It would be tragic if community-policing efforts assisted resistance to equal housing opportunity.[37]

Community partnership efforts in Chicago have begun to challenge this often-cited criticism of community policing. New research conducted by Wesley Skogan suggests that after four years of intensive efforts by the police to partner with the community, residents in crime-blighted areas in Chicago are beginning to participate in neighborhood crime programs. They found that attendance at community meetings was highest among blacks who lived in high-crime areas and made less than $15,000 a year.[38]

## Organizational Change

Community policing also calls for organizational change. Eck and Maguire argue that organizational change in agencies moving toward community policing is necessary for two reasons: "first, to stimulate and encourage officers to perform community policing functions; [and] second, to make the organization more flexible and amenable to developing community partnerships and creative problem solving strategies."[39] The authors maintain that there are three organizational areas in which agencies need to make changes if they are to successfully implement community policing: (1) organizational structure, (2) organizational culture, and (3) management.

### *Organizational Structure*

While traditionally police departments have been characterized by a highly centralized organizational design, community-policing organizations are decentralized. This means that they have fewer levels of management, have less specialization, and allow for more discretion on the part of the line officer.[40] A key assumption of community policing is that police agencies must remain flexible so that they can handle a variety of problems in different communities. Therefore, to accomplish this, line officers are given a great deal of discretion in diagnosing local problems.[41]

The community-policing organization is also characterized by consistently assigning officers to a particular neighborhood or geographic area. This strategy not only is intended to foster a sense of geographic responsibility but also is a means of holding officers accountable for what takes place in their beat. Community-policing advocates also argue that this tactic "is necessary in order to take advantage of the particular knowledge that can come through greater police involvement in the community and feedback from it."[42]

### *Organizational Culture*

Traditional police organizational culture stressed the importance of crime fighting. As a consequence, the transition to community policing has largely been a battle for the hearts and minds of police officers.[43] Many advocates of community policing articulate that with the implementation of community policing will come a "new breed" of police officers who will be much more knowledgeable about, and experienced in, problem solving and community interaction, and who will be much more productive and satisfied with their work.[44]

For a full discussion on participative management, see Chapter 4.

A number of police departments have attempted to change their agency's organizational culture by implementing organizational reforms such as using participative management styles that embrace police officer input in departmental decision making; providing formal training to officers on community partnerships, problem solving, and other community-policing tactics; changing promotional standards so that officers who embrace community policing are advanced within the organization; and changing departmental evaluation standards so that evaluations reinforce the value of community-policing activities.[45]

### *Management*

The adoption of community policing also affects police management. In the past police managers focused primarily on issues of control through discipline by emphasizing departmental rules and regulations.[46] In community policing, managers are expected to assist the neighborhood officer in developing community contacts, counsel the neighborhood officer on political issues, assist the neighborhood officer in acquiring resources, and facilitate training opportunities for the neighborhood officer. Therefore, community-policing organizations are characterized by having more managers and fewer supervisors.[47]

For example, in St. Petersburg, Chief Goliath Davis made a number of management-oriented changes in an effort to enhance the department's community-policing efforts. Prior to the changes sergeants were responsible for supervising officers who were responding to calls for service, which coincidently conflicted with the sergeants' responsibility for supervising community-policing officers. As such, the supervisors had little time to assist the officers with projects or train new community-policing officers on community policing. After a police and community retreat Chief Davis made a number of organizational changes, including the addition of a shift community-police sergeant. This sergeant reported directly to the district major, instead of the lieutenant and captain as regular patrol sergeants were required to do, and was solely responsible for managing community-policing officers. This strategy, the chief argued, allowed the sergeants much more free time to work alongside officers and allowed them greater access to resources that were required to address neighborhood crime and disorder.[48]

## Evidence of Organizational Change

There has been very little evidence suggesting that police organizations have changed their organizational structure as a consequence of implementing community policing. One study of police organizations found that police organizational structures had not changed significantly since 1987. In particular, the study found that police organizations were no more likely to have fewer rules or policies or fewer supervisory levels since the inception of community policing.[49]

Likewise, another national study suggested that the police have not changed their priorities to correspond with community policing principals. Zhao examined the organizational priorities and core functions of over 200 municipal police departments. He reported that "the core functional priorities of American policing largely remain closely modeled after the professional model; these priorities were not affected significantly by changes such as the addition of officers, the provision of funds for COP training, or the adoption of COP programs."[50]

On the other hand, altering the structure of the organization so that officers are permanently assigned to a beat has been found to have some beneficial effects. For example, permanent beat assignment in Chicago neighborhoods resulted in residents' reporting increased levels of police visibility, which was attributed to increased officer activity taking place as a consequence of the officers becoming more knowledgeable about the areas they were policing.[51] Similar findings were reported in Philadelphia, where police officers were permanently assigned to public housing areas. In particular, officers who were permanently assigned to a public housing site were significantly more likely to initiate investigations, indicating an increased sense of officer ownership and responsibility, than officers who were not permanently assigned to a site.[52]

Research has shown that the occupational culture in many police agencies has changed significantly because of the implementation of community policing.

Zhao and associates surveyed officers in one northwestern police department that was well known for practicing community policing. He found that the officers' occupational values changed significantly after the implementation of community policing. The researchers reported an increase in the values reflecting personal happiness, comfort, and security.[53] Other studies have similarly found that after community policing has been implemented in an agency, police officers' attitudes toward community policing gradually improve along with knowledge about community policing.[54]

Many police agencies have incorporated community-policing-related principles in their academy training curricula to help facilitate cultural change. Haarr's research examining training in Arizona found that while being given training in community-policing principles has the desired effect, its impact quickly dissipates after the officer leaves the academy and is exposed to the work environment. The research also found that community-policing principles were not reinforced during the recruits' field training experience.[55]

Generally, these findings suggest that training alone may not have an impact on fostering a police culture that is supportive of community policing, but they do suggest that police culture can change with the implementation of community policing, although the change will take a great deal of time.

Studies examining the changing role of management in community-policing organizations have generally been positive. Mastrofski's examination of community policing in Indianapolis found that community policing may have changed the role of supervisors. Sergeants in Indianapolis were found to believe that performing supportive activities, such as helping officers work through problems in their neighborhoods, was much more important than performing constraining activities, such as enforcing departmental policies or monitoring officers.[56]

## Problem Solving

**problem solving**

The last element of community policing is **problem solving.** Here, the police and the community engage in a cooperative effort to solve neighborhood problems. The defining feature of problem solving is that it requires the participants to identify the underlying causes of problems rather than simply respond to the problems themselves. Problem solving can be enacted in a number of ways: it can involve the police mobilizing and consulting with neighborhood residents; it can involve neighborhood residents (typically through neighborhood associations) identifying the root cause of a problem and mobilizing the police or another governmental service to address the problem; or it can be done by a neighborhood police officer who regularly confers with neighborhood residents as part of his or her regular duties.

About 58 percent of local police agencies today encourage officers to engage in problem-solving projects, and 50 percent of agencies have formed problem-solving partnerships through written agreement. However, only about 34 percent of agencies actually evaluate officers based on their involvement and success with problem solving (see Exhibit 10–3).[57]

Cordner notes that problem solving, as performed in the course of community policing, is often confused with problem-oriented policing (discussed in the next section). Problem solving, he articulates, was adopted as part of community policing

---

**E X H I B I T   1 0 – 3**

### Local Police Agency Involvement in Problem Solving

| | |
|---|---|
| Actively encouraged patrol officers to engage in problem-solving project | 58% |
| Formed problem-solving partnerships through written agreements | 50 |
| Included problem-solving projects in criteria for evaluating patrol officers | 34 |

---

*Source:* Bureau of Justice Statistics, *Law Enforcement Management and Administrative Statistics, 2000* (Washington DC: Government Printing Office, 2004).

as a neighborhood-level strategy to address chronic problems. As such, he argues that problem-solving activities tend to be small in nature.[58] With this said, problem-oriented policing has become an important part of community policing in many police departments across the country. In practice, problem-oriented policing can be implemented alone or as part of community policing.

Because problem solving and problem-oriented policing are often intertwined and examined together, we discuss their differences, characteristics, and impacts in greater detail in the following section.

# Pulling It All Together: Implementing Community Policing at the Departmental Level

While community policing has been said to be implemented in police agencies across the country, there has been little consensus about the extent to which community policing has been implemented on a department-wide basis. Maguire and Katz, using data supplied by the Police Foundation, examined community policing in 1,600 police agencies. They found that agencies that claimed to have implemented community policing were more likely to embrace some elements of community policing than others. In particular, they found that police departments that had implemented community policing were more likely to perform patrol-level and organizational activities associated with community policing than they were to perform citizen and management activities associated with community policing. The authors conclude that "changes in the role of mid-management and citizens in community policing may be particularly difficult to implement because they require that police agencies make real and substantial changes in the way that they do business."[59]

## Chicago Alternative Policing Strategy (CAPS) Program

Chicago Alternative Policing Strategy (CAPS) represents one of the most ambitious community-policing efforts in the nation. With over 13,000 sworn officers, the Chicago police department is the second largest in the country. An ongoing evaluation by Wesley Skogan provides valuable insights into both the possibilities and the problems of implementing a new policing philosophy throughout a big-city department.[60]

## The CAPS Plan

CAPS began with extensive planning, involving a number of experts from outside the police department. After much discussion and revision, CAPS was designed around six basic points:

1.  Involvement of the entire police department and the entire city. Some community-policing programs, by contrast, involve specialized units separate from the basic operations of the department and/or particular neighborhoods.
2.  Permanent beat assignments for officers. To enhance officer knowledge of and involvement in neighborhood problems, officers would be given permanent beat assignments.
3.  A serious commitment to training. If community policing truly represents a different philosophy, it is necessary to train officers regarding the new expectations about their job.
4.  Significant community involvement. One of the basic principles of community policing is that it involves a high level of citizen input and partnership with the police.
5.  A close link between policing and the delivery of other city services. CAPS was intended to address neighborhood problems by helping citizens mobilize other city agencies to improve the delivery of services.
6.  Emphasis on crime analysis. A heavy emphasis was placed on geographic analysis of crime patterns, using sophisticated computer analysis, to identify problems.

CAPS leaders assumed at the outset that the program would take three to five years to implement. Although CAPS was implemented citywide, five districts were selected as prototype districts and were subject to extensive evaluation. Each of these districts had a population of approximately 500,000 people—about the size of many big cities.

## Obstacles to Change

Implementation of CAPS involved a number of major obstacles. The first was the problem of resources. Strong public opposition killed a proposed tax increase. Consultants, however, identified 1,600 officers in the department who could be reassigned to provide more efficient police services. Finally, the city obtained federal and state grants to hire more officers and support CAPS.

A second and related problem was strong public opposition to the planned closing of precinct station houses. Although designed as an efficiency measure, many residents felt that they were losing "their" police presence, and the proposal was killed.

A third and major problem involved getting the rank-and-file officers committed to CAPS. Unlike some other community-policing programs, CAPS did not rely on volunteers. The police culture is highly resistant to change. Surveys of Chicago officers, however, found significant differences in attitudes within the rank and file. Generally, older officers, racial and ethnic minority officers, and female officers were more open to change than younger, white, and male officers. A majority of all officers were extremely pessimistic at the outset, believing that community policing would blur the lines of authority between police and citizens and put unreasonable demands on the police to solve all community problems.

The attitudes of the rank and file were related to another serious problem: supervision and performance evaluations. Since CAPS represented a new philosophy and a new role for the police, it required new forms of supervision and performance evaluation. Rank-and-file officers understandably asked what they were expected to do under CAPS and how they would be evaluated. This proved to be a major controversy and was never fully resolved.

Another major problem was the 911 system. The traditional approach to calls for service would pull officers away from problem-solving activities and dispatch officers outside their beats (thereby violating the beat integrity principle of the program). CAPS attempted to address this extremely difficult problem in several ways. First, it capped the number of times officers could be dispatched out of their beats. Second, it created special rapid-response teams to handle critical incidents. Third, it attempted to limit the number of calls by developing new dispatching priorities.[61]

## *CAPS in Action*

The heart of CAPS was citizen interaction with the police. This was attempted through a regular series of beat meetings, where citizens and beat officers would be able to discuss neighborhood problems and possible solutions.

As Skogan and Hartnett point out, "Making beat meetings work was hard."[62] Officers thought meetings took time away from "real" police work. The typical meeting involved about twenty-five citizens and five officers, and took about an hour and a half. The agenda for each meeting was "just frank talk."[63] Attendance tended to be higher in African American neighborhoods, primarily because of concern about crime.

Exhibit 10–4 indicates the problems identified at beat meetings in five districts evaluated by Skogan. Drugs were clearly the problem of greatest concern. Other crime-related issues were also frequently mentioned. Many of the problems fell into the disorder category: youth problems, loud music, and the like. Significantly, police disregard for citizens was the fourth most frequently mentioned problem, indicating that CAPS faced a significant problem in public distrust.

Observations of beat meetings found that the goal of police–citizen partnerships was not met. Police officers generally dominated meetings and controlled the agenda. The goals were met at a higher rate in some neighborhoods (Rogers Park) than in others (Morgan Park).

Getting other city agencies involved in problem solving was a major problem in Chicago. This has also been found to be a common problem in other cities that have attempted to implement community policing. An evaluation of community policing in eight cities, for example, had found that this effort failed in seven of them.[64] In Chicago, a special Mayor's Office of Inquiry and Information (MOII) was responsible for seeing that other agencies cooperated with CAPS. The key instrument was a one-page service request form, which indicated a problem and the agency responsible for it. Specific requests involved replacement of missing street signs, closing or demolition of abandoned buildings, removal of graffiti,

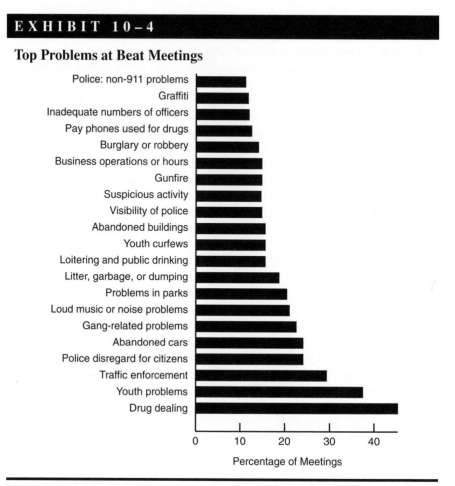

**EXHIBIT 10-4**

### Top Problems at Beat Meetings

*Source:* Wesley G. Skogan and Susan M. Hartnett, *Community Policing: Chicago Style* (New York: Oxford University Press), p. 121, Figure 5–1.

and towing of abandoned vehicles. These involved the physical decay category of disorder.

CAPS produced a number of different problem-solving activities. Under Operation Beat Feet, sixty residents in Rogers Park marched through part of the neighborhood at night in a form of "positive loitering" to deter potential criminals. Members of the Englewood community also conducted a march against drugs. Rogers Park residents initiated court action against the owner of a building that was the center of criminal activity. Morgan Park developed a Beatlink program that allowed business owners to contact patrol officers directly through beepers.

### *Evaluation of CAPS*

A wide-ranging evaluation of CAPS found mixed results. Telephone surveys found a relatively high level of awareness of the program, but it also found that awareness did not increase as time went on. Citizens in most of the evaluation districts also reported seeing police officers more often than before. In most of the evaluation districts there was also an increase in the visibility of informal contacts between police and citizens. There were significant increases as well in public perceptions that the police were responding to their concerns and dealing with crime, along with reduced fear of crime. Especially important, over 80 percent of the respondents indicated that police stopping too many people and being too tough was not a problem in their area. Consistent with previous surveys, African Americans (13 percent) were far more likely than whites (3 percent) to say that police use of excessive force was a problem.

In the end, CAPS met some but not all of its goals. Most important, officers did change the way they went about their jobs, spending more time on problem solving. There were significant perceived changes in the quality of life in the prototype districts: less crime, less fear, fewer gangs, and a greater sense of police responsiveness. The police department did not, however, succeed in fully implementing its crime-mapping program. There were also problems in achieving the desired level of citizen involvement.

The major achievement in Chicago is that some small but notable changes were accomplished in a citywide reorientation of policing. Most community-policing projects in other cities have been small pilot projects, focusing on limited areas or problems, and usually involving volunteers. The CAPS experience suggested that a reorientation of a major police department was possible.

The one major failure of CAPS was the inability to include some segments of the community. Latino renters, low-income households, and high school nongraduates in Chicago were the least aware of and least involved in CAPS. This is partially consistent with other community-oriented projects, which are generally more effective with whites and homeowners than racial and ethnic minorities and renters (see Exhibit 10–5).

# Community Policing: Problems and Prospects

Although community policing is an important development, many unanswered questions about it remain.[65] Some advocates maintain that the era of community policing has already arrived.[66] Critics argue, however, that it is premature to claim that community policing either dominates contemporary policing or has proved to be a long-term success. There are a number of key questions about community policing that need to be addressed.

## A Legitimate Police Role?

One key issue in the community-policing debate involves the question of the proper police role. Should police officers function as community organizers and work on housing problems and cleaning up vacant lots? Is this the proper role for a police officer with arrest power? Or should police officers spend their time and energy on serious crime?

There is no right or wrong answer to this question. It is a matter of policy choice. A community may define the police role in those terms, if it wishes to do so.

### EXHIBIT 10–5

## Personal Background and Awareness of CAPS

|  | 1996 | 1998 | 2003 |
|---|---|---|---|
| % Aware of CAPS | 53 | 79 | 80 |
| Whites | 52 | 78 | 81 |
| Blacks | 58 | 84 | 89 |
| Latinos | 51 | 73 | 70 |
| Spanish | 47 | 65 | 56 |
| English | 54 | 80 | 86 |
| Age 18–29 | 46 | 76 | 69 |
| Age 30–49 | 61 | 83 | 84 |
| Age 50–64 | 53 | 80 | 86 |
| Age 65+ | 46 | 65 | 77 |
| No. of Cases | 1,868 | 2,937 | 3,141 |
| Renters | 50 | 75 | 74 |
| Homeowners | 58 | 83 | 85 |
| Low income | 48 | 69 | 68 |
| Moderate income | 59 | 84 | 86 |
| Nongraduates | 41 | 62 | 65 |
| High school graduates | 56 | 82 | 83 |
| Females | 50 | 76 | 80 |
| Males | 59 | 87 | 79 |

*Note:* All subgroup percentages are based on data weighted to standardize the racial composition of the samples across the years.

*Source:* Wesley Skogan, *Community Policing in Chicago, Year Ten: An Evaluation of Chicago's Alternative Policing Strategy* (Chicago: Illinois Criminal Justice Information Authority, 2004).

For a full discussion on changes in the role of the police, see Chapter 2.

Another community may prefer the more traditional police role. The fact that the police role has been defined one way for many years does not mean that it cannot be defined in a different way. Change is not impossible. As historians of the police point out, the crime-attack role that dominates today is not as traditional as many people think. In fact, it developed only over the last 50 years.

## A Political Police?

David Bayley warns that one aspect of changing the police role is the danger of involving the police in politics. One of the basic principles of Anglo-American law is the idea of clearly defined limits on all government power, and on the police in particular. Bayley refers to this as the "minimalist" tradition of policing.[67] These limits are embodied in the Bill of Rights. Community policing, however, expands the police role and erodes the traditional limits. Bayley refers to this as "maximalist" policing. Should police officers, for example, be going door to door, calling on law-abiding citizens when those people have not called the police? If the police organize community groups, there is the danger that they will turn into political advocacy groups that will lobby for candidates or issues that the police support.[68]

Furthermore, Bayley adds, the deeper the police delve into social structural issues to uncover the root causes of neighborhood problems, the greater the probability that they will place limitations on individual liberties. For example, after police officers in Portland, Oregon, researched the nature of increased citizen complaints about disorderly conduct around neighborhood mini-marts, they found that the sale of malt liquor and cheap wine was attracting gang members and transients. To remedy the problem the officers asked the shop owners to voluntarily stop selling the malt liquor and cheap wine. However, the shop owners, who were all members of a single ethnic group, believed that the police had discriminatorily singled them out. While the issue was eventually resolved, the police officers learned that while encouraging social responsibility is part of their role within the community, it can have negative side effects.[69]

For a full discussion on controlling corruption, see Chapter 13.

## Decentralization and Accountability

One of the basic principles of community policing is decentralized decision making: giving rank-and-file officers more authority to decide what problems to work on and how to use their time. Decentralization, however, creates the problem of potential loss of control over police behavior, resulting in abuse of authority. As Herman Goldstein puts it, "How free should community officers be to select alternatives for solving problems?"[70]

Most of the gains in controlling police misconduct, including corruption and the use of force, have been achieved through centralized command and control. One major device has been administrative rulemaking: providing officers with written rules about what kinds of conduct are not permitted.

For a full discussion on administrative rulemaking, see Chapter 11.

An evaluation of the New York City CPOP program found that the traditional methods of supervising patrol officers were inappropriate for community policing. These methods are bureaucratic in nature, asking officers to account for the use of their time and their contacts with the public, and designed primarily to control misbehavior. In New York City there was special concern that giving officers too much leeway would lead to corruption—a recurring problem in the department. The CPOP program required sergeants to play more of a manager role than a strictly disciplinarian role. Sergeants had to assist officers in problem solving, represent the CPOP unit to the rest of the department (where there was some hostility), and represent it to the community.[71]

George Kelling and James Stewart warn of the dangers inherent in encouraging police officers to be responsive to community residents. A majority of the residents may demand things that are illegal or improper. Kelling and Stewart point out that "a neighborhood anti-crime group that consists exclusively of home owning whites in a racially mixed neighborhood" may only increase the level of racial conflict in the area.[72] Critics of community policing point to the "kick ass" policing style described in Wilson and Kelling's "Broken Windows." In that article, a

Chicago police officer explains how the police remove gang members from a public housing project: "We kick ass." Wilson and Kelling note that this approach is not consistent "with any conception of due process and fair treatment."[73] The issue here is the tension between community demands for order and the requirements of due process and equal protection.

## Impact on Poor and Minority Communities

Websdale notes that community policing is particularly intrusive into the lives of poor, minority citizens. He explains that community policing increases surveillance in these communities through increased police presence mandates for those who live in public housing, and cracking down on minor "quality of life" infractions. He argues that the increased attention on poor minority communities, while welcome by some, results in increased arrests and subsequently the number of individuals incarcerated, leaving the community oftentimes with fewer men, who when released are even less likely to find jobs because of their criminal record.[74]

## Conflicting Community Interests

Working with the community sounds wonderful in theory, but Michael Buerger's study of the Minneapolis RECAP program found that in some instances community interests conflicted with the objectives of an innovative police program. One program targeted shoplifting at convenience stores. It turned out, however, that corporate officials were more worried about potential lawsuits from customers than about shoplifting, which they tended to regard as a normal business expense. Some store owners, meanwhile, were afraid that a strong police presence would alienate and scare off their good customers. A proposal to exclude juveniles from stores after curfews conflicted with a larger corporate program to provide safe havens to children. The police also tried to discourage landlords from renting to suspected drug dealers. But many landlords preferred some drug dealers because they paid their rent on time, in cash, and generally tried to avoid attracting attention. In short, conflicting interests—especially financial interests—of some community residents can obstruct creative programs to solve community problems.[75]

## But Does Community Policing Work?

While a number of questions remain, the future of community policing appears bright. The Office of Community Oriented Policing Services (COPS) commissioned a number of studies examining the effectiveness of community policing, the largest of which was conducted by Zhao and Thurman. The researchers examined 6,100 cities over a six-year period to determine the impact on crime of community policing hiring initiatives (funded by the COPS Office). The authors concluded that the community policing strategy implemented under the Clinton administration was extremely effective. They noted that "an increase in one dollar of innovative grant funding per resident has contributed to a decline of 12.26 violent crimes and 43.85 property crimes per 100,000 persons."[76]

# The Roots of Problem-Oriented Policing

Herman Goldstein pioneered a new approach to the police role in 1979 with his concept of **problem-oriented policing**.[77] Goldstein had played a pivotal role in recognizing the complexity of the police role through his work with the American Bar Foundation Survey of Criminal Justice in the 1950s.[78] He then helped draft the American Bar Association (ABA) standards that emphasized the many different responsibilities of the police.[79] In his 1977 book, *Policing a Free Society,* Goldstein argues that we should think of the police as a government agency providing a wide range of miscellaneous services.[80]

**problem-oriented policing**

The central idea in Goldstein's initial article on problem-oriented policing was that the police had traditionally defined their role in terms of vague and general categories: crime, order maintenance, and service. In practice, however, each of these general categories includes many different kinds of problems. The category of crime, for example, includes murder, burglary, and drunk driving, each of which is a very different kind of social event. The category of disorder includes domestic disputes, mental health problems, public drunkenness, and many other problems. Goldstein argues that the police should take these categories and break them down into discrete problems and then develop specific responses to each one—in short, problem-oriented policing.[81]

Goldstein also points out that the traditional measures of police effectiveness are not useful. Not only are the data in the official Uniform Crime Reports (UCR) system extremely problematic, but the UCR system collapses all crimes into one global category. A problem-oriented approach would require specific measures of effectiveness for specific problems.[82]

Along with a growing number of experts, Goldstein argues that the police are the prisoners of their communications system. The 911 system forces them into a reactive role: devoting most of their resources to responding to calls for service.[83] This reactive role means that the police think in terms of isolated incidents (calls). Goldstein argues that this prevents any serious planning with respect to underlying problems.

Exhibit 10–6 illustrates the differences between traditional, 911-driven, incident-based policing and problem-oriented policing. Under the traditional approach, each incident is handled as an isolated event. Police officers are concerned only with responding to each and every incident. Problem-oriented policing, on the other hand, emphasizes the analysis of problems and developing appropriate solutions to respond to the problems. Such a model necessitates the decentralization of power within the police department so that line-level officers not only have the ability to identify problems but also are empowered to do something about them.[84]

Problem-oriented policing is often confused with community-oriented policing or is implemented as part of a department-wide community-policing strategy. However, as seen in Exhibit 10–10, on page 329, what differentiates problem-oriented policing from community policing is its emphasis on the end product of policing rather than the means by which policing is done.[85] Eck and Maguire note that "simply put, in community policing building a strong positive relationship between the public and the police is the goal. Addressing problems is secondary. Whereas in

# EXHIBIT 10–6

## Traditional versus Problem-Oriented Policing

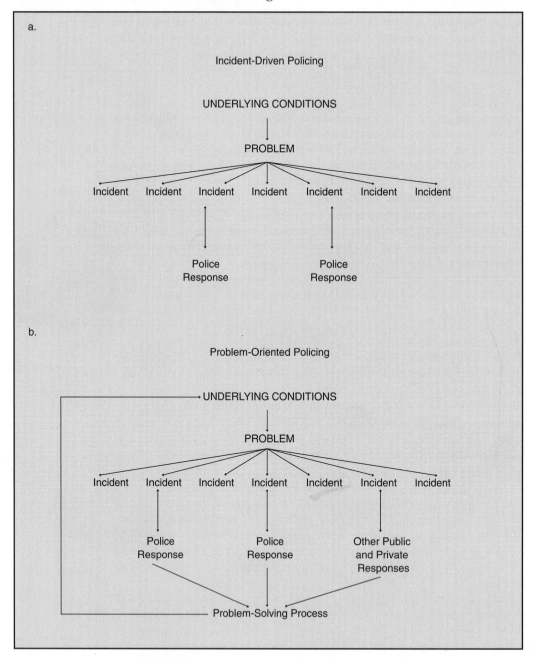

*Source:* John Eck and William Spelman, *Problem Solving: Problem-oriented Policing in Newport News* (Washington DC: PERF, 1987), Figure 1, p. 4.

problem-oriented policing the goal is to reduce problems of concern to the public. Close community partnerships are often important elements in addressing problems, but they are not the final objective."[86]

# The Problem-Solving Process

Eck and Spelman point out that problem-oriented policing is typically implemented through a four-stage process known as **SARA:** (1) scanning, (2) analysis, (3) response, and (4) assessment (see Exhibit 10–7).

**SARA**

## Scanning

The first stage of the SARA model is **scanning.** Scanning can be done in a number of ways. For example, over the course of their shift, the officers can look for and identify possible problems in their beat. Another strategy is for the officers to review calls for service and complaints to identify potential problems. Still another scanning strategy is to consult with residents who live or work in the officers' assigned area. However, the problems that are to be identified under the SARA model are not individual incidents with no association with one another, but rather problems that share some underlying cause.

**scanning**

## Analysis

The second stage of the SARA model is **analysis.** This stage requires the police to collect information about the problem in an attempt to identify its scope, nature, and cause. This often leads to the police focusing on "three categories of problem characteristics: actors (victims, offenders, third parties); incidents (physical setting, social context, sequence of events); and past responses (by the community and its institutions)."[87]

**analysis**

## Response

The third stage of the SARA model is **response.** The data collected during the analysis stage are used to develop a strategy to address the problem and implement a response. The response typically includes the use of alternative solutions that often incorporate the assistance of residents, other units within the police department, other governmental agencies, local businesses, private organizations, or any other person or group that might be able to help with the needed response. Problem-oriented policing emphasizes that the response should go beyond traditional crime-control strategies and use strategies and tactics that will have an impact on the conditions that generate crime and disorder— rather than just treat the symptom itself (i.e., crime and disorder). Such a strategy then attempts to include a greater number of tools on the tool belt of the police.

**response**

## Assessment

The last stage of the SARA model is **assessment.** The assessment involves an evaluation of the effectiveness of the response. It is intended to go beyond impressionistic or anecdotal evidence of success and incorporate rigorous feedback that allows the police to revise their response if it is not successful. The feedback also allows the

**assessment**

**E X H I B I T   1 0 – 7**

## SARA Problem-Solving Model

**Summary of Scanning Steps**

Step 1
- Laundry list of potential problems.

Step 2
- Problems identified.

Step 3
- Problems prioritized.

Step 4
- State the specific problem.
- List examples of where the problem occurs.
- Which setting is causing the most difficulty?

**Review and Preparation for Analysis**

Hypothesis
- From what you already know, what do you think is causing the problem?
- General goal statement.
- How will data be gathered and reported?
- When will data collection begin?

**Summary of Analysis Steps**

Step 1
- What conditions or events precede the problem?
- What conditions or events accompany the problem?
- What are the problem's consequences?
- What harms result from the problem?

Step 2
- How often does the problem occur?
- How long has this been a problem?
- What is the duration of each occurrence of the problem?

**Now that the data have been collected, should you continue with analysis or return to scanning and restate the problem?**

Step 3
- Define a tentative goal.
- Identify resources that may be of assistance in solving the problem.
- What procedures, policies, or rules have been established to address the problem?

**Summary of Response Steps**

Step 1
- Brainstorm possible interventions.

Step 2
- Consider feasibility and choose among alternatives.
- What needs to be done before the plan is implemented?
- Who will be responsible for preliminary actions?

Step 3
- Outline the plan and who might be responsible for each part.
- Will this plan accomplish all or part of the goal?

**EXHIBIT  10-7    (continued)**

- State the specific goals this plan will accomplish.
- What are some ways data might be collected?

Step 4

- Realistically, what are the most likely problems with implementing the plan?
- What are some possible procedures to follow when the plan is not working or when it is not being implemented correctly?

**Implement the Plan**

**Summary of Assessment Steps**

Step 1

- Was the plan implemented?
- What was the goal as specified in the response?
- Was the goal attained?
- How do you know if the goal was attained?

Step 2

- What is likely to happen if the plan is removed?
- What is likely to happen if the plan remains in place?
- Identify new strategies to increase the effectiveness of the plan.
- How can the plan be monitored in the future?

Step 3

- Post-implementation planning
- Plan modification
- Follow-up assessment

*Source:* Police Executive Research Forum, *SARA Problem Solving Model,* http://www.policeforum.org/sara.html.

police the opportunity to reexamine whether or not they identified the problem correctly. Because the police use a wide variety of responses, as a consequence of the wide variety of problems that they are required to address, no single type of assessment is possible. As such, the police are sometimes required to go beyond using existing data sources, such as calls for service, to measure, for example, changes in crime, and must collect and analyze nontraditional data, such as photographs, to measure, for example, changes in physical disorder.

# Effectiveness of Problem-Oriented Policing

Evaluations of problem-oriented policing have generally been more positive than evaluations of community policing. This section reviews those projects that have used the strongest research designs or that have received a significant amount of national attention.

## Problem-Oriented Policing in Newport News

The first significant problem-oriented policing experiment occurred in Newport News, Virginia. For several years the police there had faced a high rate of burglaries in the New Briarfield apartment complex. Increased police presence in the area reduced reported burglaries by 60 percent, but when the officers were transferred to other areas, the burglary rate increased again. By 1984 the apartment complex was generating more calls for service than any other residential area in the city. At this point, the police department decided to abandon traditional methods and to experiment with problem-oriented policing.[88]

The project utilized the SARA model. The scanning phase began with an analysis of crime patterns in the area and an opinion survey of apartment residents. The survey helped reveal the extent to which the physical deterioration in the buildings contributed to burglaries. The police department task force assigned to New Briarfield responded with tactics that addressed the physical condition of the buildings. The police also organized a meeting of the various government agencies that had some responsibility for the housing project. Exhibit 10–8 lists the public agencies contacted. The purpose of the meeting was to develop a coordinated strategy to improve conditions in the complex. A police officer assigned to the project helped organize a tenants' group, which put pressure on city officials to make improvements in the apartments. Ultimately, however, a decision was made to demolish the apartments and relocate the residents.

---

## EXHIBIT 10–8

### Public Agencies Contacted for Information on the New Briarfield Burglary Problem

**Newport News City Agencies**

Office of Business Licenses—business license records

Clerk of Courts—deed records

Department of Codes Compliance—building safety information

Fire Department—fire and arson data

Planning Department—land use and census data

Department of Public Works—street cleaning and sanitation information

Redevelopment and Housing Authority—data on housing subsidy programs

Tax Assessor's Office—property values and tax payments

**State Agencies**

Virginia Corporation Commission—corporate records

California Corporation Commission—corporate records

**Federal Agencies**

Federal Bureau of Investigation (local office)—fraud investigation issues

Internal Revenue Service—ownership patterns

Department of Housing and Urban Development (Washington DC, central office)—
    housing standards and loan default data

Office of Management and Budget—multifamily housing problems and HUD assistance
    programs

---

*Source:* John E. Eck and William Spelman, *Problem-Solving: Problem-Oriented Policing in Newport News* (Washington DC: Police Executive Research Forum, 1987), Table 9, p. 70.

Official statistics did indicate a drop in reported crime because of problem-oriented policing. More important, the activities of the officers represented a new role for the police in problem-oriented and community policing: conducting surveys of public opinion to identify neighborhood problems. By initiating the meetings about the apartment complex, police officers were acting as community organizers or brokers of government services.

## Problem-Oriented Policing in San Diego

The San Diego Police Department is widely recognized as a national leader in problem-oriented policing throughout the world. They have won national awards for problem-oriented policing projects, serve as the site for the annual international conference on problem-oriented policing, and are frequently used as a demonstration site for those wanting to learn how to engage in problem-oriented policing.

Gary Cordner conducted one of the most thorough evaluations of the implementation of problem-oriented policing in San Diego by interviewing 320 officers throughout each of the agency's eight police districts and surveying about a quarter of the agency's patrol officers and their sergeants.[89]

He found that problem-oriented policing had had a major influence on the way policing was conducted in San Diego. For example, about 70 percent of officers indicated that they had used at least some principles of problem-oriented policing recently, and almost half stated that problem-oriented policing was a very important part of policing. Police officers also expressed that their supervisors were supportive and encouraged their POP efforts. Of particular interest was the finding that police officers in San Diego, while often relying on traditional policing strategies, frequently took advantage of a wide range of response options such as collaborating with other government agencies and working with the community to address a specific problem.

However, Cordner noted that most POP projects were not carried out in a "text book fashion." For example, most officers did not engage in very sophisticated forms of scanning and analysis. Problems were mostly identified though personal observations and speaking with people. Very few of the officers engaged in any form of crime analysis. Most of the officers focused on small-scale problems associated with drugs, transient/special populations, and public order. Less than 10 percent of officers worked on problems addressing crimes (other than drug-related problems).

Cordner's research in San Diego lead him to conclude that, after almost two decades of implementing problem-oriented policing, officers had learned to implement the strategy, but did not do so as formally or completely as that idealized by academics and policymakers.[90]

## The Boston Gun Project: Operation Cease Fire

The Boston Gun Project was a problem-solving project that involved the Boston police department; the Bureau of Alcohol, Tobacco, and Firearms; federal and county prosecutors; county probation and patrol; City of Boston outreach workers; the Boston school police; and youth corrections. In the early 1990s Boston was overwhelmed with an increase in youth homicides. Crime analysis revealed that there were, on average, forty-three youth homicides per year in Boston between 1991 and 1995. After a thorough analysis facilitated by researchers at Harvard University, project participants found a strong illicit gun market providing firearms to youths. They also found that about 60 percent of the youths involved in the homicides were also associated with gangs that lived in three Boston neighborhoods.

The analyses led the project participants to believe that a successful response would have to include an attack on both the supply and demand for guns. A message was sent out to gang members that unless the shooting stopped gang members would be closely scrutinized by law enforcement officials and there would be serious repercussions. "Gang members were told that drug markets would be shut down, warrants would be served, the street would swarm with law enforcement officials (including federal presence), bed checks would be performed on probationers, rooms would be searched by parole officers, unregistered cars would be taken away, and disorder offenses such as drinking in public would be pursued." In one case a gang member who had been arrested on numerous other occasions for violent gang activity was found with a single bullet in his pocket. Because of his prior felony convictions he was prosecuted as a career criminal and received twenty years in prison.[91]

The assessment found that the project had an impact on crime, fear of crime, and resident satisfaction with the police. Two years after the operation went into effect, youth gang homicides dropped by 70 percent. Fear of crime among residents who lived in the impacted areas decreased by 21 percent, and the number of residents having faith in the police to prevent crime increased by about 33 percent.[92] The federal government has funded twenty-seven Youth Crime Gun Interdiction initiatives based on the results of the Boston Gun Project.[93]

## Characteristics of Zero-Tolerance Policing

**zero-tolerance policing**

**Zero-tolerance policing** is based on broken windows theory. It calls for the police to primarily focus on disorder, minor crime, and the appearance of crime.[94] It is characterized by interventions that aggressively enforce criminal and civil laws and that are conducted for the purpose of restoring order to communities. It is believed that through aggressive enforcement of laws aimed at combating disorder, residents will be more inclined to care for their community, which will increase order, which in turn will lead to a reduction in the fear of crime and ultimately signal to potential criminals that law breaking will not be tolerated (see Exhibit 10–9).[95]

As shown in Exhibit 10–10, zero-tolerance policing differs from other policing strategies in a number of important ways. First, community policing and

---

### EXHIBIT 10–9

**The Social Influence of Zero-Tolerance Policing**

| Police Conduct→ | Social Meaning→ | Social Norm→ | Impact on Community |
|---|---|---|---|
| Police remove visible signs of disorder | Community cares and criminals are no longer in control | Orderliness | Law-abiders feel safe and criminals stop committing crimes |

*Source:* Dorothy Roberts, "Forward: Race, Vagueness, and the Social Meaning of Order-Maintenance Policing," Reprinted by special permission of Northwestern University School of Law, *The Journal of Criminal Law and Criminology.*

EXHIBIT 10–10

## Comparisons of Social Interactions and Structural Components of Various Forms of Policing

| Social Interaction or Structural Dimension | Traditional Policing | Community Policing | Problem-Oriented Policing | Zero-Tolerance Policing |
|---|---|---|---|---|
| Focus of policing | Law enforcement | Community building through crime prevention | Law, order, and fear problems | Order problems |
| Forms of intervention | Reactive, based on criminal law | Proactive, on criminal, civil, and administrative law | Mixed, on criminal, civil, and administrative law | Proactive, uses criminal, civil, and administrative law |
| Range of police activity | Narrow, crime focused | Broad, crime, order, fear, and quality-of-life focused | Narrow to broad, problem focused | Narrow, location and behavior focused |
| Level of discretion at line level | High and unaccountable | High and accountable to the community and local commanders | High and primarily accountable to the police administration | Low, but primarily accountable to the police administration |
| Focus of police culture | Inward, rejecting community | Outward, building partnerships | Mixed depending on problem, but analysis focused | Inward, focused on attacking the target problem |
| Locus of decision making | Police directed, minimizes the involvement of others | Community-police coproduction, joint responsibility and assessment | Varied, police identify problems but with community involvement/action | Police directed, some linkage to others agencies where necessary |
| Communication flow | Downward from police to community | Horizontal between police and community | Horizontal between police and community | Downward from police to community |
| Range of community involvement | Low and passive | High and active | Mixed, depending on problem set | Low and passive |
| Linkage with other agencies | Poor and intermittent | Participative and integrative in the overarching process | Participative and integrative depending on the problem set | Moderate and intermittent |
| Type of organization and command focus | Centralized command and control | Decentralized with community linkage | Decentralized with local command accountability to central administration | Centralized or decentralized but internal focus |
| Implications for organizational change/development | Few, static organization fending off the environment | Many, dynamic organization focused on the environment and environmental interactions | Varied, focused on problem resolution but with import for organization intelligence and structure | Few, limited interventions focused on target many traditional problems, using methods |
| Measurement of success | Arrest and crime rates, particularly serious Part 1 crimes | Varied, crime, calls for service, fear reduction, use of public places, community linkages and contacts, safer neighborhoods | Varied, problems solved, minimized, displaced | Arrests, field stops, activity, location-specific reductions in targeted activity |

Source: Jack R. Green, "Community Policing in America: Changing the Nature, Structure, and Function of the Police," in Julie Horney, ed., *Policies, Processes, and Decisions of the Criminal Justice System, Criminal Justice 2000, vol. 3* (Washington DC: Government Printing Office, 2000), p. 311.

problem-oriented policing are based on the notion that the police should focus on crime prevention, whereas zero-tolerance policing focuses on a crime attack model.[96] As such, Green notes that "zero tolerance policing has its roots in the suppressive aspect of policing. In some respects it returns the police to a more traditional stance vis-à-vis law enforcement, a direction that is actively supported within many American police departments."[97]

Second, the strategy differentiates itself from community policing in that it is based on the presumption that the communities that need the police the most are also the least likely to have strong community social institutions. Therefore, while community policing is based on the idea that the community is a primary coproducer of crime control, zero-tolerance policing is based on the idea that the community may not be able to provide support for crime control strategies and that the police must take primary responsibility for crime control.[98]

Third, zero-tolerance policing differs from problem-oriented policing in that it does not attempt to carefully identify problems or thoroughly analyze the cause of problems.[99] Rather, zero-tolerance policing focuses on specific types of behavior. Minor crimes and disorder, such as urinating in public, fare-beating (not paying the fare on the subway by jumping the turnstiles), prostitution, loitering, aggressive panhandling, graffiti, and "squeegeeing" (boys and young men who wash the windows of cars stopped at traffic lights), are a major focus.[100]

Fourth, zero-tolerance policing is characterized by its focus on place-specific interventions. Prior studies examining hot spots have found that a small proportion of addresses account for a disproportionate amount of crime and disorder (Chapter 7). Accordingly, a number of police departments across the country have begun to map crime, which allows them to direct zero-tolerance policing to hot spots.[101]

Fifth, zero-tolerance policing differentiates itself from other police innovations because it culturally and organizationally represents a back-to-the-basics strategy. Its crime-fighting emphasis lends itself to a more militaristic organizational design that is both centralized and internally focused (information flowing from the administration to the line officer)—a mission and organizational structure that many police are more comfortable and familiar with. Additionally, unlike community policing and problem-oriented policing, because of the emphasis on proactive law enforcement it does not require the police to make a fundamental change in police culture.[102]

# The Effectiveness of Zero-Tolerance Policing

While quality-of-life policing has enjoyed much support among law enforcement officials, there has been little focus on its effectiveness. Below we discuss police efforts in two cities in which zero-tolerance policing has been implemented and subjected to independent evaluation.

## Zero-Tolerance Policing in New York City

Perhaps the best-known implementation of zero-tolerance policing has taken place in New York City. On the basis of the broken windows theory, Police Commissioner William Bratton and Mayor Rudolph Giuliani instituted a zero-tolerance policing strategy in 1993. Prior to this time New York City was characterized by social disorder (unlicensed peddlers, homelessness, street-level drug use), physical disorder (graffiti), and crime. There was an overall sense that the city was out of control.[103] Commissioner Bratton commented that, "I can recall coming in from the airport, flying in to LaGuardia, and coming down that highway. It looked like something out of a futuristic movie in terms of graffiti on every highway wall, dirt on rubber tires that look like they have not been cleaned in years, burned out cars, litter everywhere."[104]

To address these problems the New York City police department instituted a zero-tolerance strategy that focused enforcement efforts on order maintenance offenses such as aggressive panhandling, vandalism, public drunkenness, public urination, and prostitution.[105] The strategy was, once again, based on the notion that by focusing police resources on disorder and minor crime, the police department could restore order, which would eventually lead to a reduction in crime. An analysis of crime data suggests that the department's shift in philosophy had a significant impact on the behavior of the officers. The number of misdemeanor arrests in New York City jumped dramatically from 1993 through 1996, increasing from 133,446 to 205,277.[106]

Many observers credit the new policing strategy with the drop in serious crime in New York City in the mid- to late 1990s. Since 1993, the overall crime rate has dropped by 27 percent, homicides have dropped by 40 percent (to their lowest level in 30 years), robbery has dropped by 30 percent, and burglary has dropped by 25 percent. These drops in crime are twice the national average. These findings have led a number of experts to conclude that order maintenance policing is more effective than other police strategies.[107]

However, there is much controversy over whether zero-tolerance policing deserves credit for this accomplishment. While William Bratton, the police commissioner who instituted the policy, and criminologist George Kelling claimed that zero tolerance was directly responsible,[108] former New York City Mayor David Dinkins and former Police Commissioner Lee P. Brown claimed that the community policing program (CPOP) they initiated in the 1980s set in motion the reduction in crime.

A number of criminologists have also pointed out that serious crime was declining in other cities, and that the reduction in New York City was part of a general trend. Serious crime fell in Washington DC, for example, where the police department was marked by scandals and inefficiency. It also fell in Los Angeles, where officers were making fewer arrests in the aftermath of the 1991 Rodney King incident.[109] Richard Rosenfeld and his associates tested this hypothesis. Specifically, they examined whether New York City's aggressive order maintenance policing strategy was associated with a reduction in homicides by comparing its homicide trend to ninety-five of the largest U.S. cities and controlling for factors known to be associated with violent crime. Their analysis indicated that New York City's homicide trend did not vary significantly from the national average prior to the implementation of zero-tolerance policing, and its reduction in homicides after its implementation was not "atypical" of other large cities during that time.[110]

## Operation Restoration

A more systematic examination of the effects of zero-tolerance policing was conducted in Chandler, Arizona.[111] In 1995, it became clear to the Chandler City Council that the innermost part of the city had experienced an increase in physical and social disorder. The area was characterized by homes with broken and missing windows, doors falling off hinges, and trash and debris cluttering properties. The area was also well known for having high crime rates, street-level drug dealing, and prostitution.

The city responded by moving the zoning enforcement responsibilities from the planning and development department to the police department. This unit became responsible for the reduction of physical disorder by enforcing city code violations. The police department also established a specialized unit to aggressively enforce order maintenance laws. The two units worked in tandem, focusing their resources on four zones that were each approximately one square mile in size. This project became known as Operation Restoration and was theoretically based on the broken windows hypothesis.

Findings from the study suggested that the project had a significant impact on public morals crimes (e.g., prostitution), disorderly conduct, and physical disorder. Similar trends were also observed in the areas adjacent to the targeted area, suggesting that the project also had an impact on the surrounding area. These findings led the authors to conclude that cracking down on disorder and minor crime may not have a substantial impact on serious crime, but the benefits of such an approach may be limited to those problems that the project specifically focuses on—namely, physical and social disorder. It also led the researchers to question the theoretical foundations of zero-tolerance policing.

## Potential Problems with Zero-Tolerance Policing

While zero-tolerance policing is quickly becoming a popular policing strategy across the country, a number of important questions remain. A number of critics have argued that there is no clear evidence that the strategy is effective in reducing crime. Others have questioned the negative impact that the strategy might have on communities.

### *Conflict between the Police and the Public*

Zero-tolerance policing has been heavily criticized for encouraging officers to be overly aggressive. Some have gone as far as to refer to the policing strategy as "harassment policing."[112] Harcourt reports that since the inception of zero-tolerance policing in New York City, the police department has seen a dramatic rise in the number of citizen complaints. From 1994 to 1996 the city received 8,316 abuse complaints, representing a 39 percent increase over the previous three years. Furthermore, these complaints have led to a 46 percent increase in settlements or judgments, with the city paying out about $70 million from 1994 to 1996 for police misconduct, compared with $48 million in the previous three years.[113]

Amnesty International has reported similar findings. Citizens filing police misconduct charges against New York City police officers increased from 977 in 1987 to more than 2,000 in 1994. They further reported that the monetary awards granted to citizens in cases of police brutality increased from $13.5 million in 1992 to over

$24 million in 1994.[114] In 2001 New York City agreed to pay $50 million to 58,000 people who were arrested in 1996 and 1997 as part of the department's zero-tolerance practices. During the case, several men and women who had never been arrested before complained that instead of being issued a ticket for the minor offense (which was the policy in the past) they were booked and detained in a police detention center where they were required to disrobe, to lift their breasts or genitals, and to squat and cough.[115]

Some have alleged that the rise in complaints is largely a consequence of increases in arrests due to the zero-tolerance strategy. However, New York City's Civilian Complaint Review Board has reported that individuals who were not arrested by the officers made most of the complaints, and further reported that many of those who complained had never been arrested before.[116]

### *Increase in Crime in the Long Run*

Sherman points out that while zero-tolerance policing might have a short-term impact on the reduction of crime, it may also result in an increase in serious crime in the long term. He argues that an arrest record can have a significant impact on a person's immediate and future employment. Additionally, he points out that arrests for minor offenses can lead to further, more serious crime by making a person angrier and more defiant.[117]

### *Impact on Poor and Minority Communities*

Harcourt argues that because zero-tolerance policing is focused on minor offenses such as loitering, panhandling, and public drinking, it will primarily be directed toward poorer communities, which, in turn, means minority communities. An examination of misdemeanor arrests shows that minorities are disproportionately arrested for misdemeanor offenses when compared with the percentage of minorities in the population. This trend is particularly strong for offenses, such as arrest for suspicion, that call for a great deal of discretion on the part of police officers. Accordingly, zero-tolerance policing may lead the police back down the path of losing legitimacy in the eyes of minorities and minorities again seeing the police as a punitive occupying force.[118]

Harcourt emphasizes that the ultra-poor, minorities, and other "cultural outsiders" may be the most impacted. He states that "by handing over the informal power to define deviance to police officers and some community members, we may be enabling the repression of political, cultural, or sexual outsiders in a way that is antithetical to our conceptions of democratic theory or constitutional principles."[119]

An example of this can be found in Chandler, Arizona, where local businesses wanted day laborers—many of whom were illegal immigrants—removed from the streets for pandering because of their disruption of local business. In response, thirty Chandler police officers and six INS officers performed a crackdown for five days on illegal immigrants. The response team searched houses, stopped drivers, detained pedestrians, and interrogated children on their way to school to inquire about citizenship. In all, 432 immigrants and two United States citizens were deported. After the roundup several of the searches were found by the state's attorney general to have been conducted illegally, and a number of residents came forward and complained of being harassed and beaten by the police because of their nationality. Official arrest records detailed the extent of the discrimination. One INS agent justifying an arrest in his report stated that he "immediately noticed a lack of personal hygiene displayed by the subject, and a strong odor common to illegal immigrants." The crackdown led to a $35-million lawsuit that was later settled out of court. (For a full discussion, see the section on the effectiveness of zero-tolerance policing in Chandler, Arizona, pp. 332.)[120]

The verdict is still out on the impact of zero-tolerance policing. There have been few studies examining its effectiveness. Future research is needed to assess whether or not this policing style is promising and whether or not there may be long-term negative consequences of its use.

 # Case Study

## *Indio Police Department Tackles the Foreclosure Crisis*

Between 2002 and 2007, the city of Indio, California, experienced a housing boom, but by late 2007 found itself on the leading edge of what is now a national foreclosure crisis. Faced with increasing numbers of citizen complaints of poorly maintained properties as well as concerns that neighborhood blight was leading to more serious crime and disorder, the Indio Police Department launched a multi-pronged project to contain the impact of vacant properties on the surrounding neighborhoods.

### Indio and Its Foreclosure Problem

Indio, California, is a city of 84,000 people located 120 miles southeast of Los Angeles in Riverside County. Although not a new city—it incorporated in the 1930s—approximately 40 percent of the current housing stock was built in the most recent housing boom. Typical of the time, much of it was bought and financed through loans that were eventually packaged together into mortgage-backed securities. The rapid escalation of home prices brought an increase in investment purchasers and non-owner-occupied homes. By January 2008, 1,400 homes were in foreclosure or preforeclosure, representing 4 percent of the city's housing stock, at a time when the national rate was still less than 1 percent. The number of foreclosures continued to grow throughout the year, so that by January 2009 the rate had increased to 8 percent of Indio's homes.

As the number of foreclosed properties increased, so too did the number of vacant properties. Approximately one-third of the foreclosure properties were vacant and both the neighbors and the police were taking notice. According to Lieutenant Rich Bitonti of the Shadow Hills District, "In some of our neighborhoods you could drive down the street and see as many as 10 foreclosed properties on the same street. The overgrown yards, damaged gates, and broken windows made it very inviting for local thieves." Citizen complaints of code violations were climbing steadily and increases in property crimes associated with these properties, in particular metal theft, were tying up police time. Even within gated communities, the Indio Police Department was seeing entire homes stripped down to the drywall of anything of value. This was making these properties harder to resell and causing them to stay on the market without capable guardianship for longer periods.

## The Police Department Responds

The Indio Police Department is the largest, most visible branch of the city government, with eighty-five sworn officers, sixty civilians, and a tradition of incorporating partnerships and problem-solving activities into its work. Somewhat unusually, the police department is also responsible for enforcing all municipal and public nuisance laws, and maintains a twelve-member code enforcement team for that purpose. It was logical that the department would take the lead in developing a response to the city's foreclosure problem. It also was no surprise to others in the city that this response would result in the shifting and sharing of responsibilities with the city council, social services, and even the banking industry.

To start, the Indio Police Department wanted to better understand the nature of the problem. Department personnel analyzed code enforcement data, citizen complaints of nuisance violations, and conducted windshield surveys to determine the locations and conditions of foreclosure properties. They found no patterns to the foreclosures, which crossed the city and affected every neighborhood and every economic class. They established that properties that were vacant were a bigger source of disorder problems than those that were still occupied. They also knew from experiences in the economic downturn of the mid-1990s that getting banks to take responsibility for the conditions of vacant properties would be a serious challenge. They researched the state foreclosure laws and discovered a gap that resulted in lenders not being required to secure or maintain properties during the foreclosure, a process that typically takes more than 300 days to complete. They also found that there was no one source of accurate and timely information about property owners. "This lack of information meant that staff were spending a tremendous amount of time and resources trying to track down the responsible parties," said Jason Anderson, an Indio code enforcement officer.

From this work, Indio Police Department personnel developed a three-pronged solution: (1) they created a comprehensive foreclosure registration and maintenance ordinance; (2) they ensured that the Code Enforcement Team had the necessary tools to enforce the new ordinance; and (3) they created a Housing Resource Center focused on keeping people in their homes so that the properties would not become vacant. A media blitz, continuing education programs, and ongoing informal meetings helped inform lenders, homeowners associations, and the general public of the program.

The foreclosure registration and maintenance ordinance was passed by the city council in February 2008. It requires lenders to inspect a property prior to filing a Notice of Default or Deed of Trust and determine if it is vacant. The lender must then register all vacant properties with the police department so that code enforcement has accurate records of who is responsible for the property's maintenance. The information is stored in the department's CAD system so that officers responding to calls for service to those properties know whom to contact. The ordinance further holds the lenders responsible for securing and monitoring the property against criminal activity and blight. Lenders pay a registration fee for each property to offset the cost of enforcement. Violations of the ordinance are misdemeanors and can result in arrest and/or administrative fines up to $25,000 per violation.

The Code Enforcement Team took the lead in educating lenders, Realtors, and community members about the new ordinance. They built partnerships with local Realtors, property managers, and homeowners associations, recognizing that they were the local individuals who would have the most vested interests in the maintenance of the properties. They also increased their enforcement efforts, establishing that noncompliance would not be tolerated.

Code enforcement officers also took an active role in promoting the third prong of the approach—referring homeowners at risk of foreclosure to the new Housing Resource Center. The Center, the first city-sponsored housing resource center in the region, opened in August 2008. Trained housing counselors from the Inland Fair Housing and Mediation Board (a HUD-certified, nonprofit housing agency) provide free, confidential default- and foreclosure-prevention counseling services. The Indio Redevelopment Agency provides office space for the Center, as well as funding for facility maintenance and advertising.

## The Signs of Success

In the short time since the project was fully implemented, the Indio Police Department has already seen results. In accordance with the new ordinance, 250 properties have been registered, resulting in the collection of $41,250 in registration fees. During the last quarter of 2008, the Code Enforcement Team inspected more than 5,000 properties in the city. More than 500 notices were issued on vacant properties, and more than 200 administrative citations (totaling more than $30,000 in fines) were issued to lenders, realtors, and property managers. Even the largest national lenders have begun to actively maintain their foreclosure properties to avoid the administrative citation and fine.

The department has discovered that realtors are a key partner in their success. Realtor-listed homes registered and maintained in accordance with the ordinance are selling faster and at higher prices than bank-sold foreclosures, so there is a strong financial incentive for realtors to work with these otherwise undesirable properties.

The Housing Resource Center has conducted 140 formal counseling sessions and has helped keep 139 families in their homes. It has also received more than 450 phone calls and more than 200 walk-ins from homeowners interested in receiving counseling or foreclosure process information. As a result of this immediate success, the city intends to continue funding the operation of the Center.

## Lessons Learned

The Indio Police Department believes that without these efforts the city would have seen an increase in the number of families displaced from their community, the number of unmaintained vacant homes, and the number of crimes associated with those properties. Based on these experiences, the department suggests that the development of a national foreclosure policy and registry is warranted. Allowing for local governments to obtain accurate information in a timely manner would be a huge first step in helping local law enforcement agencies understand their foreclosure problem. In addition, as Officer Anderson noted, "having accurate information is vital when an officer responds to a call and needs to know who is responsible for the property then and there, not after hours of research."

Adapted from Deborah Spence, "Indio Police Department Tackles the Foreclosure Crisis," *Community Policing Dispatch* 2, 3 (March 2009), obtained at http://www.cops.usdoj.gov/html/dispatch/March_2009/indio.htm.

## Summary: A New Era in Policing?

For many police officials, community policing, problem-oriented policing, and zero-tolerance policing are simply buzzwords that mask traditional policing, or policing that many police officers believe they have been practicing for decades.[121]

Nonetheless, it is clear that the ideas of community policing, problem-oriented policing, and zero-tolerance policing have inspired a remarkable level of innovation in American policing. Bayley concludes that the last decade of the twentieth century may be the most creative period in policing since the modern police officer was put onto the streets of London in 1829.[122]

As a final note, Goldstein and Skolnick and Bayley all point out that we should not be too quick to argue that the innovations under these strategies have not proved to be effective. Neither have most of the activities labeled "traditional" policing. As we have already learned, patrol (Chapter 7), criminal investigation (Chapter 9), and other activities are rarely subjected to rigorous evaluations, and even fewer evaluations have proved them to be effective.[123]

## Key Terms

broken windows, 302
social disorder, 303
physical disorder, 303
community policing, 303
coproducers of crime
    control, 305

community partnerships, 305
consultation, 305
mobilization, 306
problem solving, 312
problem-oriented
    policing, 321

SARA, 323
scanning, 323
analysis, 323
response, 323
assessment, 323
zero-tolerance policing, 328

## For Discussion

*Are the law enforcement agencies in your community doing community policing, problem-oriented policing, or zero-tolerance policing? Discuss the activities of your local agency:*

1. What label is used to describe the program (COP, POP)?
2. What is the content of the program (community meetings, intensive drug enforcement, coordinated activities with non-criminal-justice programs)?
3. Is the program department-wide or operated by a special unit?
4. Has it been evaluated, and if so, what were the results of that evaluation?
5. If your agency is not engaged in community policing, problem-oriented policing, or zero-tolerance policing, find out why.

# Internet Exercises

**Exercise 1** The Herman Goldstein Award recognizes outstanding police officers and police agencies around the world that engage in cutting-edge problem-solving efforts that prove to be effective in reducing crime and related problems. Visit the Center for Problem-Oriented Policing Web site, and review the award recipients for the past two years. Its Web site is **www.popcenter.org/library-goldstein. htm.** Compare awards that were received by those outside of the United States with those that were made to officers and agencies in the United States. What are their similarities and differences?

**Exercise 2** Go to **http://www.cops.usdoj.gov/html/ dispatch/June_2009/index.htm** and click on the

most recent version of the Office of Community Oriented Policing's online magazine Community Policing Dispatch to find out about community-policing projects that have been recognized as important. Pick one project and discuss how it makes an important contribution to policing today.

**Exercise 3** Many police agencies describe their community policing, problem-oriented policing, and zero-tolerance policing programs on the Web. Check out the Web sites for several departments in your region of the country. What can you learn? Do they describe their programs in detail that is useful to you?

# Notes

1. John Eck and Dennis Rosenbaum, "The New Police Order: Effectiveness, Equity, and Efficiency in Community Policing," in Dennis Rosenbaum, ed., *The Challenge of Community Policing: Testing the Promises* (Thousand Oaks, CA: Sage Publications, 1994).

2. Jack R. Greene and Stephen D. Mastrofski, *Community Policing: Rhetoric or Reality* (New York: Praeger, 1988).

3. George L. Kelling and Mark H. Moore, "The Evolving Strategy of Policing," *Perspectives on Policing,* no. 4 (Washington DC: Government Printing Office, 1988), p. 8; John P. Crank, "Watchman and Community: Myth and Institutionalization in Policing," *Law and Society Review* 28, no. 2 (1994): pp. 325–51.

4. Wesley G. Skogan and George E. Antunes, "Information, Apprehension, and Deterrence: Exploring the Limits of Police Productivity," *Journal of Criminal Justice* 7 (Fall 1979): p. 232; James Frank, Steven G. Brandl, Robert E. Worden, and Timothy S. Bynum, "Citizen Involvement in the Coproduction of Police Outputs," *Journal of Crime and Justice* XIX, no. 2 (1996): pp. 1–30.

5. James Q. Wilson and George L. Kelling, "Broken Windows: The Police and Neighborhood Safety," *Atlantic Monthly* 249 (March 1982): pp. 29–38.

6. Wesley G. Skogan, *Disorder and Decline: Crime and the Spiral of Decay in American*

*Neighborhoods* (New York: Free Press, 1990), pp. 21–50.

7. Ibid.

8. Mary Ann Wycoff, *Community Policing Strategies* (Washington DC: National Institute of Justice, 1995).

9. Dennis Rosenbaum, ed., *The Challenge of Community Policing: Testing the Promises* (Thousand Oaks, CA: Sage, 1994).

10. David Bayley, *Policing in America: Assessment and Prospects* (Washington DC: Police Foundation, 1998); Jerome Skolnick and David Bayley, "Theme and Variation in Community Policing," in Michael Tonry and Norval Morris, eds., *Crime and Justice: A Review of the Research* (Chicago: University of Chicago Press, 1988).

11. Stephen Mastrofski, "Community Policing as Reform: A Cautionary Tale," in Stephen Mastrofski and Jack Greene, eds., *Community Policing: Rhetoric or Reality* (New York: Praeger, 1988); the above section was taken from a paper presented by Edward Maguire and Charles Katz entitled *The Validity and Reliability of Police Agencies' Community Policing Claims,* presented on November 22, 1997, at the annual meeting of the American Society of Criminology in San Diego, California.

12. Gary Cordner, "Community Policing: Elements and Effects," in Roger Dunham and Geoffrey Alpert, eds., *Critical Issues in Policing* (Prospect Heights, IL: Waveland, 1997).

13. Community Policing Consortium, *Understanding Community Policing: A Framework for Action* (Washington DC: Bureau of Justice Assistance, 1994).

14. Jerome Skolnick and David Bayley, *The New Blue Line: Police Innovation in Six American Cities* (New York: The Free Press, 1986).

15. The above paragraph was taken from a paper presented by Edward Maguire and Charles Katz entitled *The Validity and Reliability of Police Agencies' Community Policing Claims.*

16. David Bayley, *Police for the Future* (New York: Oxford Press, 1994).

17. Bureau of Justice Statistics, *Law Enforcement Management and Administrative Statistics, 2000* (Washington DC: Government Printing Office, 2004).

18. Daniel W. Flynn, *Defining the "Community" in Community Policing* (Washington DC: PERF, 1998).

19. Community Policing Consortium, *Understanding Community Policing: A Framework for Action.*

20. Jack Green, "Community Policing in America: Changing the Nature, Structure, and Function of the Police," in Julie Horney, ed., *Policies, Processes, and Decisions of the Criminal Justice System* (Washington DC: National Institute of Justice, 2000).

21. David Carter, "Community Alliance," in Larry Hoover, ed., *Police Management: Issues and Perspectives* (Washington DC: PERF, 1992).

22. David Bayley, *Police for the Future;* the above paragraph was taken from a paper presented by Edward Maguire and Charles Katz entitled *The Validity and Reliability of Police Agencies' Community Policing Claims.*

23. Green, "Community Policing in America: Changing the Nature, Structure, and Function of the Police."

24. E. J. Williams, "Enforcing Social Responsibility and the Expanding Domain of the Police: Notes from the Portland Experience," *Crime & Delinquency* 42, no. 2 (1996): pp. 309–23.

25. Green, "Community Policing in America: Changing the Nature, Structure, and Function of the Police." p. 314.

26. The Police Foundation, *The Newark Foot Patrol Experiment* (Washington DC: The Police Foundation, 1981).

27. James Q. Wilson and George L. Kelling, "Making Neighborhoods Safe," *Atlantic Monthly* 263 (1989): pp. 46–53.

28. Craig Uchida, Brian Forst, and Sampson Annon, *Modern Policing and the Control of Illegal Drugs: Testing New Strategies in Two American Cities,* Final Report (Washington DC: Police Foundation, 1992).

29. Wesley Skogan, "The Impact of Community Policing on Neighborhood Residents: A Cross-Site Analysis," in Dennis Rosenbaum, ed., *The Challenge of Community Policing* (Thousand Oaks, CA: Sage, 1994), pp. 167–81.

30. David Kessler and Sheila Duncan, "The Impact of Community Policing in Four Houston Neighborhoods," *Evaluation Review* 20 (1996): pp. 627–69.

31. Trevor Bennett, "Community Policing on the Ground: Developments in Britain," in Dennis Rosenbaum, ed., *The Challenge of Community Policing* (Thousand Oaks, CA: Sage, 1994) p. 240.

32. Ibid.

33. Hubert Williams and Patrick V. Murphy, "The Evolving Strategy of Police: A Minority View," *Perspectives on Policing* no. 13 (1990): p. 12.

34. University of Maryland, *Preventing Crime: What Works, What Doesn't, What's Promising—A Report to the Attorney General of the United States* (Washington DC: U.S. Department of Justice, Office of Justice Programs, 1997), pp. 8–1 to 8–58.

35. Skogan, *Disorder and Decline,* p. 95.

36. Ibid., p. 148.

37. Wesley G. Skogan, "Fear of Crime and Neighborhood Change," in Albert Reiss and Michael Tonry, eds., *Communities and Crime* (Chicago: University of Chicago Press, 1986), p. 222.

38. Wesley Skogan, Susan Hartnett, Jill DuBois, Jennifer Comey, Karla Twedt-Ball, and Erik Gudell, *Public Involvement: Community Policing in Chicago* (Washington DC: National Institute of Justice, 2000).

39. John Eck and Edward Maguire, "Have Changes in Policing Reduced Violent Crime? An Assessment of the Evidence," in Alfred Blumstein and Joel Wallman, eds., *The Crime Drop in America* (Cambridge: Cambridge University Press, 2000), pp. 207–65.

40. Green, "Community Policing in America: Changing the Nature, Structure, and Function of the Police."

41. Jerome Skolnick and David Bayley, *Community Policing: Issues and Practices around the World* (Washington DC: National Institute of Justice, 1988); Bayley, *Police for the Future.*

42. Ibid., p. 14.

43. Arthur Lurigio and Wesley Skogan, "Winning the Hearts and Minds of Police Officers," in Ronald Glensor, Mark Correia, and Kenneth Peak, eds., *Policing Communities* (Los Angeles: Roxbury Publishing, 2000).

44. Ibid.

45. Deb Weisel and John Eck, "Toward a Practical Approach to Organizational Change," in Ronald Glensor, Mark Correia, and Kenneth Peak, eds., *Policing Communities* (Los Angeles: Roxbury Publishing, 2000).

46. Stephen Mastrofski, Roger Parks, and Robert Worden, *Community Policing in Action: Lessons from an Observational Study* (Washington DC: National Institute of Justice, 1998).

47. R. Trojanowicz and B. Bucqueroux, *Toward Development of Meaningful and Effective Performance Evaluations* (East Lansing, MI: National Center for Community Policing, 1992); Bayley, *Police for the Future.*

48. Dennis J. Stevens, *Case Studies in Community Policing* (Upper Saddle River, NJ: Prentice Hall, 2000–2001).

49. Edward Maguire, "Structural Change in Large Municipal Police Organizations during the Community Policing Era," *Justice Quarterly* 14, no. 3 (1997): pp. 547–76.

50. Jihong Zhao, Nicholas Lovrich, and Hank Robinson, "Community Policing: Is It Changing the Basic Functions of Policing?" *Journal of Criminal Justice* 29 (2001): pp. 373–400.

51. Wesley G. Skogan and Susan M. Hartnett, *Community Policing, Chicago Style* (New York: Oxford University Press, 1997).

52. Robert Kane, "Permanent Beat Assignment in Association with Community Policing: Assessing the Impact on Police Officers' Field Activity," *Justice Quarterly* 17, no. 2 (2000): pp. 259–80.

53. Jihong Zhao, Ni He, and Nicholas Lovrich, "Value Change among Police Officers at a Time of Organizational Reform: A Follow-Up Study Using Rokeach Values," *Policing: An International Journal of Police Strategies and Management* 22, no. 2 (1999).

54. Dennis Rosenbaum, Sandy Yeh, and Deanna Wilkinson, "Impact of Community Policing on Police Personnel: A Quasi-Experimental Test," *Crime and Delinquency* 40, no. 3 (1994): pp. 331–53.

55. Robin Haarr, *The Impact of Community Policing Training and Program Implementation on Police Personnel: A Final Report,* presented to the National Institute of Justice, 2000.

56. Mastrofski, Parks, and Worden, *Community Policing in Action: Lessons from an Observational Study.*

57. Source: Bureau of Justice Statistics, *Law Enforcement Management and Administrative Statistics, 2000* (Washington DC: Government Printing Office, 2004).

58. Gary Cordner, "Problem-Oriented Policing vs. Zero Tolerance," in Tara O'Connor Shelly and Anne Grant, eds., *Problem Oriented Policing* (Washington DC: Police Executive Research Forum, 1998).

59. Edward R. Maguire and Charles M. Katz, *Community Policing, Loose Coupling and Sensemaking in American Police Agencies,* presented at the annual meeting of the American Society of Criminology in San Diego, California, 1997.

60. Skogan and Hartnett, *Community Policing: Chicago Style.*

61. Ibid., pp. 67–68.

62. Ibid., p. 113.

63. Ibid., p. 114.

64. Susan Sadd and Randolph Grinc, "Innovative Neighborhood Policing: An Evaluation of Community Policing Programs in Eight Cities," in Dennis P. Rosenbaum, ed., *The Challenge of Community Policing: Testing the Promises* (Thousand Oaks, CA: Sage, 1994), pp. 27–52.

65. David Bayley, "Community Policing: A Report from the Devil's Advocate," in Greene and Mastrofski, eds., *Community Policing: Rhetoric or Reality,* pp. 225–37.

66. George L. Kelling and Mark H. Moore, "The Evolving Strategy of Policing," *Perspective on Policing* no. 4 (Washington DC: Government Printing Office, 1988).

67. Bayley, *Police for the Future,* pp. 126–28.

68. Bayley, "Community Policing: A Report from the Devil's Advocate."

69. Williams, "Enforcing Social Responsibility and the Expanding Domain of the Police: Notes from the Portland Experience."

70. Herman Goldstein, "Toward Community-Oriented Policing," *Crime and Delinquency* 33 (January 1987): p. 12.

71. Jerome McElroy, Colleen Cosgrove, and Susan Sadd, *Community Policing: The CPOP in New York* (Newbury Park, CA: Sage, 1993).

72. George L. Kelling and James K. Stewart, "Neighborhoods and Police: The Maintenance of Civil Authority," *Perspectives on Policing* no. 10 (Washington DC: Government Printing Office, 1989), p. 4.

73. Wilson and Kelling, "Broken Windows."

74. Neil Websdale, "Policing the Poor." (Boston: Northeastern University, 2001).

75. Michael E. Buerger, "The Problems of Problem-Solving: Resistance, Interdependencies, and Conflicting Interests," *American Journal of Police* XIII, no. 3 (1994), pp. 1–36.

76. Jihong "Solomon" Zhao and Quint Thurman, *A National Evaluation of the Effects of COPS Grants on Crime from 1994 to 1999* (Omaha: University of Nebraska at Omaha, December 2001), p. 2.

77. Herman Goldstein, "Improving Policing: A Problem-Oriented Approach," *Crime and Delinquency* 25 (1979): pp. 236–58; Herman Goldstein, *Problem-Oriented Policing* (New York: McGraw-Hill, 1990).

78. Samuel Walker, "Origins of the Contemporary Criminal Justice Paradigm: The American Bar Foundation Survey, 1953–1969," *Justice Quarterly* 9 (March 1992): pp. 47–76.

79. American Bar Association, *Standards Relating to the Urban Police Function,* 2nd ed. (Boston: Little, Brown, 1980), Standard 1–2.2.

80. Herman Goldstein, *Policing a Free Society* (Cambridge, MA: Ballinger, 1977).

81. Goldstein, "Improving Policing."

82. See the discussion in Geoffrey Alpert and Mark H. Moore, "Measuring Police Performance in the New Paradigm of Policing," in Department of Justice, *Performance Measures for the Criminal Justice System* (Washington DC: Government Printing Office, 1993), pp. 109–40.

83. Malcolm K. Sparrow, Mark H. Moore, and David M. Kennedy, *Beyond 911* (New York: Basic Books, 1990).

84. Green, "Community Policing in America."

85. John Eck and William Spelman, "Who Ya Gonna Call: The Police as Problem Busters," *Crime and Delinquency* 33 (1987): pp. 31–52.

86. Eck and Maguire, "Have Changes in Policing Reduced Violent Crime? An Assessment of the Evidence," pp. 47–48.

87. John Eck and William Spelman, *Problem Solving: Problem-Oriented Policing in Newport News* (Washington DC: Police Executive Research Forum, 1987), p. 47.

88. Ibid.

89. Gary Cordner and Elizabeth Perkins Biebel, "Problem-Oriented Policing in Practice," *Criminology and Public Policy* 4, no. 2 (2005), pp. 155–80.

90. Ibid.

91. David Kennedy, *Juvenile Gun Violence and Gun Markets in Boston* (Washington DC: National Institute of Justice, 1997).

92. *Operation Cease Fire* (Boston: Boston Police Department, 1998).

93. Ibid.

94. Cordner, "Problem-Oriented Policing vs. Zero Tolerance."

95. Dorothy Roberts, "Forward: Race, Vagueness, and the Social Meaning of Order-Maintenance Policing," *Journal of Criminal Law & Criminology* 89, no. 3 (1992): p. 811.

96. Green, "Community Policing in America."

97. Ibid., p. 318.

98. Ibid.

99. Cordner, "Problem-Oriented Policing vs. Zero Tolerance."

100. George Kelling and Catherine Coles, *Fixing Broken Windows* (New York: The Free Press, 1996).

101. Green, "Community Policing in America."

102. Ibid.

103. William Bratton, "Remark: New Strategies for Combating Crime in New York City," *Fordham Urban Journal* 23 (1996): pp. 781–85.

104. Ibid.

105. Dan Kahn, "Social Influence, Social Meaning, and Deterrence," *Virginia Law Review* 83, (1997): pp. 349–95.

106. Bernard Harcourt, "Reflecting on the Subject: A Critique of the Social Influence Conception of Deterrence, the Broken Windows Theory, and Order Maintenance Policing New York Style," *Michigan Law Review* 97 (1998): pp. 291–389.

107. Dan Kahn, "Social Influence, Social Meaning, and Deterrence."

108. William Bratton, *Turnaround: How America's Top Cop Reversed the Crime Epidemic* (New York: Random House, 1998).

109. Kelling and Coles, *Fixing Broken Windows;* Samuel Walker, *Sense and Nonsense about Crime,* 4th ed. (Belmont, CA: Wadsworth, 1998), pp. 273–79.

110. Richard Rosenfeld, Robert Fornango, and Eric Baumer, "Did Cease Fire, COMPSTAT, and EXILE Reduce Homicide," *Criminology and Public Policy* 4, no. 3 (2005): pp. 414–77.

111. Charles M. Katz, Vincent J. Webb, David R. Schaefer, "An Assessment of the Impact of Quality-of-Life Policing on Crime and Disorder," *Justice Quarterly* 18, 4 (2001): pp. 825–76.

112. Robert Panzarella, "Bratton Reinvents 'Harassment Model' of Policing," *Law Enforcement News* (June 15–30, 1998): pp. 13–15.

113. Harcourt, "Reflecting on the Subject: A Critique of the Social Influence Conception of Deterrence, the Broken Windows Theory, and Order Maintenance Policing New York Style."

114. Amnesty International, *United States of America: Police Brutality and Excessive Use of Force in the New York City Police Department* (New York: Amnesty International, 1996).

115. Benjamin Weiser, "N.Y. Agrees to Pay $50 Million over Strip Searches in Minor Offenses," *International Herald Tribune* January 11, 2001, p. 3.

116. Harcourt, "Reflecting on the Subject: A Critique of the Social Influence Conception of Deterrence, the Broken Windows Theory, and Order Maintenance Policing New York Style."

117. Lawrence Sherman, "Policing for Crime Prevention," *Preventing Crime: What Works, What Doesn't, What's Promising—A Report to the Attorney General of the United States,* pp. 8–1 to 8–58.

118. Green, "Community Policing in America: Changing the Nature, Structure, and Function of the Police."

119. Harcourt, "Reflecting on the Subject: A Critique of the Social Influence Conception of Deterrence, the Broken Windows Theory, and Order Maintenance Policing New York Style," p. 48.

120. Christian Parenti, *Lockdown America: Police and Prisons in the Age of Crisis* (New York: Verso, 2000).

121. R. D. Hunter and T. Barker, "BS and Buzzwords: The New Police Operational Style," *American Journal of Police* 12, no. 3 (1993), pp. 157–68.

122. Bayley, *Police for the Future,* p. 101.

123. Goldstein, "Toward Community-Oriented Policing," p. 27; Skolnick and Bayley, *The New Blue Line.*

P A R T  **IV**

# Issues in Policing

# Police Discretion

Police officers routinely exercise discretion while doing their jobs. They make important decisions that affect citizens' lives: whether or not to stop a car, whether or not to make an arrest, and so on. This chapter examines the phenomenon of police discretion. It examines the underlying reasons for discretion, how discretion is used, the problems that result from its misuse, and different strategies for controlling it.

# Discretion in Police Work

A police officer patrolling a city park sees three young men hanging out together. He investigates and finds they are drinking beer in public in violation of a local ordinance. At least one and possibly two of them may be underage. The officer confiscates the beer, pours it out, and tells them to get out of the park. He could have issued citations but exercised his discretion not to do so.

This incident is typical of police discretion. Officers routinely decide not to arrest people who are obviously breaking the law. Far more seriously, they make critical decisions involving the life and liberty of citizens. Some examples include:

- **Domestic Dispute Arrests.** Donald Black found that police arrested only 58 percent of people suspected of committing felonious assault in domestic violence situations.[1]
- **Mental Health Commitments.** Linda Teplin reported that only 11.8 percent of persons judged mentally disordered were referred to a medical facility.[2]
- **Traffic Enforcement.** According to the Police–Public Contact Survey, about one-quarter of all drivers stopped for speeding were issued a warning rather than a ticket.[3]
- **Juvenile Court Referrals.** Nathan Goldman found that in one city 8.6 percent of arrested juveniles were referred to juvenile court, compared with 71.2 percent in another city.[4]
- **Deadly Force.** The decision to use deadly force is the ultimate life-and-death decision made by police officers.[5]

# A Definition of Discretion

**discretion**

**Discretion** is defined as (1) an official action (2) by a criminal justice official (3) based on that individual's judgment about the best course of action.[6]

Discretion pervades the entire criminal justice system. Wayne LaFave argues that "it is helpful to look at the total criminal justice system as a series of interrelated discretionary choices."[7] The administration of justice is essentially the sum total of a series of discretionary decisions, from arrest through prosecution, trial, sentencing, and parole release.

# Aspects of Police Discretion

## Street-Level Bureaucrats

The 911 center receives a call about a disturbance in an apartment, and two patrol officers are dispatched to the scene. They arrive to find clear evidence of a physical assault; the woman is bruised and the man may also have been hit. The department has a mandatory arrest policy directing officers to make an arrest where there is evidence of a felonious assault. It is about twenty minutes until shift change, the officers are tired from a busy night of calls, and so they just give the two people a verbal warning and leave. In effect, the officers have undermined the department's mandatory arrest policy.

**street-level bureaucrats**

This example illustrates one of the special features of policing: The lowest-ranking employees—patrol officers—exercise the greatest amount of discretion. James Q. Wilson comments that, in policing, "discretion increases as one moves down the organizational hierarchy."[8] For this reason, patrol officers have been described as **"street-level bureaucrats."** They make the decisions that produce actual police policy as it affects citizens.[9] Through their discretion to arrest or not arrest, police officers are the gatekeepers of the entire criminal justice system. They determine the system's workload. If they do not arrest, there is no case for the rest of the system to handle. Police discretion also determines public policy. If police officers systematically do not make arrests for possession of small amounts of marijuana, for example, they effectively decriminalize that offense.

## Potential Abuse of Discretion

Discretion can be misused in several different ways.

- **Discrimination.** The misuse of discretion can involve discrimination against racial or ethnic minorities. Racial profiling is an obvious example.[10]
- **Denial of Due Process.** Deliberately harassing suspected drug dealers, prostitutes, and pimps to chase them out of the neighborhood rather than arresting them is an abuse of discretion.[11]
- **Systematic Underenforcement of the Law.** Systematic underenforcement of the law—for example, tolerating after-hours clubs in a certain neighborhood—can damage the quality of life in that area. Historically, the police tolerated gambling, prostitution, and after-hours clubs in poor and racial minority neighborhoods.[12]

For a full discussion of police–community relations, see Chapter 12.

- **Poor Personnel Management.** Effective supervision requires clear performance standards. Officers need to be provided clear guidelines regarding how they are to handle different situations. If there are no guidelines and discretion is completely unregulated, it is impossible to fairly evaluate the officers' performance.[13]
- **Inconsistent Policy.** If officers on the street make decisions inconsistent with department policy, the policy will not be carried out.

## Proper Exercise of Discretion

A patrol officer is dispatched to an attempted burglary call at 1 AM. The residents were sleeping and heard the sound of a break-in. The officer investigates, but finds no evidence of an attempted break-in (e.g., no marks on any door or window). He tells the people it must have been some noise, does not complete a crime report, and leaves. The officer has used his or her discretion to "unfound" a crime because of a lack of evidence. This is an example of a **positive use of discretion.**

Discretion can be used in proper ways, to promote effective and efficient police work. Examples include:

**positive uses of discretion**

- **The Use of Good Judgment.** In the example given above, the police officer exercised his professional judgment in determining that no crime had been committed and that he should not fill out a crime report. In this case, there was no objective evidence of a crime and therefore no basis for a crime report.
- **Efficient Use of Scarce Police Resources.** The police cannot possibly enforce all of the criminal laws. They do not have enough officers to arrest everyone who violates the law, and the courts could not handle all of the cases.[14] By using good judgment to concentrate on the more serious crimes (robberies) and disregard less serious ones (kids drinking in the park), the police can make efficient use of their time. According to Davis, "The common sense of the officers very often prevails over the legislative excesses in criminal legislation."[15]
- **Individualized Justice.** The proper use of discretion can allow officers to individualize justice and choose the best course of action for particular events. A juvenile may have in fact violated the law, but in the case of a relatively minor offense, an arrest might not be the best response for that individual.
- **Sound Public Policy.** The proper use of discretion can allow police departments to make sound judgments about public policy. Many homeless people, for example, do things that could justify an arrest (e.g., lying down in the street, where they might be technically obstructing the sidewalk). Arresting them, however, might not be the best way to treat homeless people.

For a full discussion on innovative problem-solving police programs that do not rely on arrest, see Chapter 10.

# Decision Points and Decision Makers

Police discretion is not limited to arrest. Officers at different ranks make discretionary decisions covering a wide range of actions. The following is a list of some of the major discretionary decisions made by officers in different assignments.[16]

## Patrol Officer Decisions

Discretionary decisions by patrol officers related to *crime* situations include:

- To patrol an area more intensively than normal.
- To conduct a high-speed pursuit.
- To stop, question, or frisk a suspect.
- To write a crime report.
- To make an arrest.
- To use physical or deadly force.

Decisions by patrol officers in *order maintenance* situations include:

- To mediate a domestic dispute rather than make an arrest.
- To suggest that one party to a dispute leave the premises.
- To refer a person to a social service agency (e.g., alcohol abuse treatment).
- To commit a mentally disturbed person to a mental health facility.

For a discussion of discretionary searches and possible racial profiling, see Chapter 12.

## Detectives' Decisions

Decisions by detectives related to *criminal investigations* include:

- To stop investigating a crime because of a lack of leads.
- To seek a warrant for a search.
- To conduct a stakeout.
- To question or not question a potential suspect.

For a full discussion of criminal investigation strategies and tactics, see Chapter 9.

## Police Managers' Decisions

Police managers make discretionary decisions about *law enforcement policy* and priorities. These include:

- To adopt community policing or problem-oriented policing.
- To give high priority to traffic law violations.
- To ignore minor drug offenses such as possession of small amounts of marijuana.
- To crack down on prostitution.
- To give social gambling low priority.

# Underlying Sources of Police Discretion

Discretion is the result of several sources related to the nature of policing itself.

## The Nature of the Criminal Law

Two officers are dispatched to a bar on the basis of a reported disorder. They arrive and calm things down. It is clear that hostile words were exchanged between two people. One of them probably said something about "getting" the other guy. Did these words constitute a threat to do bodily harm? The guy who made the remark had a pool cue in his hand and may have moved it in a threatening manner. Did this constitute threat with a dangerous weapon? The responding officers have to make a decision about whether to make any arrests.

The nature of the criminal law demands that officers exercise discretion. The law defines particular crimes—assault, for example—but officers on the street have to determine whether the facts of a particular case fit the definition. Offenses such as disorderly conduct are particularly vague, and open the door for the greatest exercise of discretion—and potential abuse. LaFave argues that "no legislature has succeeded in formulating a substantive criminal code which clearly encompasses all conduct intended to be made criminal and which clearly excludes all other conduct."[17]

## Conflicting Public Expectations

The criminal law in the United States reflects conflicting public expectations about what behavior should be illegal. The law criminalizes a lot of activity that many people also regard as acceptable recreation: gambling, drinking, certain forms of private sexual behavior. Officers are often caught between these conflicting expectations and use their discretion about the best course of action.[18]

## Social and Medical Issues

The criminal law is widely used to deal with social and medical issues such as homelessness, chronic alcohol abuse, or mental health problems.[19] Police officers on the street have to use their discretion about whether to arrest a mentally disturbed person, refer him to a social service program, or simply restore order to the situation and leave.

## The Work Environment of Policing

The **work environment of policing** contributes to the exercise of discretion. Skolnick observes that "police work constitutes the most secluded part of an already secluded system of criminal justice and therefore offers the greatest opportunity for arbitrary behavior."[20] Three aspects of the work environment contribute to the exercise of discretion:

**work environment of policing**

- Patrol officers work alone or in pairs. (The Project on Policing Neighborhoods observed patrol work in two cities and found that in half of all encounters with citizens only one officer was present.)[21]
- In many critical incidents there is no direct supervision by a sergeant (often the sergeant arrives after the important decisions are made).
- The majority of police–citizen encounters occur in private places, with no other observers present—observers who might be able to testify about the officer's behavior.[22]

For all these reasons, policing has been described as **low-visibility work**.[23] Hidden from public view, police officers have tremendous opportunity to choose whatever course of action they prefer, and this work environment creates the opportunity for using and potentially abusing discretion.

**low-visibility work**

## Limited Police Resources

It is Saturday night, and the 911 communications center is flooded with calls for service. Patrol officers are running from one call to another, and for about two hours there are always several calls waiting for dispatch. On one call, the patrol officer could make an arrest for disorderly conduct in a parking lot outside of a bar. But there are other calls waiting, some of which are probably more serious, so the officer gives the person a stern warning and moves on to another call.

There are only so many officers, and they have only so much time during a regular shift. In addition, they are often short-handed because of sick leave or vacations by other members of their unit. Calls continue to come into the 911 system. They cannot possibly handle every situation that comes up, and they have to exercise their discretion about how to use their time.[24]

Adding to the problem is the simple fact that an arrest is a time-consuming event. Arresting, transporting, and booking a suspect may take between one and three hours. Some arrests, moreover, may involve more than one officer.[25]

# Factors Limiting Patrol Officer Discretion

The discretion of a patrol officer is not completely unlimited. It is shaped by a number of legal and bureaucratic factors. They include:[26]

## Legal Factors

- **Supreme Court Decisions.** An officer has to worry that a defense attorney will challenge the evidence at trial and have the judge exclude it because of an illegal search.
- **State Court Decisions.** There may be decisions by the state supreme court similar to *Mapp* or related to other police actions.
- **State Law.** Iowa has a state law governing arrest discretion in domestic violence incidents. An officer has to worry about not violating the mandatory arrest part of that law.

## Administrative Factors

- **Department Policy.** Department policy may limit high-speed pursuits. An officer has to be concerned about complying with the policy in certain situations.
- **Supervision.** Typically, a sergeant signs off on all arrests. An officer has to worry that his or her supervisor will not sign off on an arrest where there is very limited evidence, or which appears to involve racial bias.

## Organizational Culture Factors

- **Peer Officer Culture.** Example: The peer officer culture in a department does not tolerate pushing people around for no reason. An officer has to worry that a peer officer will report him or her for this. Alternatively, in another department, the peer culture does tolerate it, and offers regularly engage in low-level uses of force.

# Factors Influencing Discretionary Decisions

The exercise of discretion in particular situations is the result of several different possible influences.

## Situational Factors

Police discretion is influenced by the circumstances of each situation. Studies of the decision to arrest, for example, have found that it is affected by the following **situational factors.**

**situational factors**

- **Seriousness of the Crime.** The more serious the crime, the more likely the officer is to make an arrest. Black found that officers made arrests in 58 percent of suspected felonies but in only 44 percent of suspected misdemeanors. He concluded that "the probability of arrest is higher in legally serious crime situations than those of a relatively minor nature."[27] Seriousness of the situation also affects the handling of mental illness incidents. The more serious the disorder, or the more likely it is to offend other people, the higher the probability of arrest or commitment to a medical facility.[28]

- **Strength of the Evidence.** The police are more likely to arrest in situations where the evidence of the crime is strong. In crimes against persons, and in many property crimes, the primary evidence is the testimony of a victim or witness. When that kind of evidence or testimony does not exist, arrest is much less likely.[29]

- **Preference of the Victim.** Two officers respond to a domestic disturbance call. There is some evidence that the man hit the woman. One of the officers asks the woman, "Do you want us to take him in?" She says "no." The other officer asks, "Are you sure? We can, you know." She says "no" again. The officers warn the man and leave.

  **preference of the victim**

  A number of studies have found that an arrest is more likely when the victim or complaining party asks for an arrest. Conversely, police are unlikely to arrest when the victim clearly indicates that he or she does not want an arrest. Black found that "arrest practices sharply reflect the preferences of citizen complainants."[30]

- **Relationship between Victim and Suspect.** Arrests are more likely when the victim and offender are strangers, and are less likely when the two parties are married. Police officers traditionally regarded these incidents as private matters.[31] There has been much controversy and some litigation over the failure of the police to arrest in domestic violence situations involving married couples (Chapter 8). Recent mandatory arrest policies are designed to ensure arrest in all felonious assault cases regardless of the relationship of the two parties.

- **Demeanor of the Suspect.** Black and others found that the **demeanor of the suspect** is a very important factor in arrest decisions: "The probability of arrest and officer use of force increases when a suspect is disrespectful toward the police."[32]

  **demeanor of the suspect**

  The demeanor of the suspect is a complex phenomenon, however. Klinger argues that in many situations the disrespect occurred after the arrest and, therefore, was a consequence and not a cause of the arrest.[33] At the same time, citizen hostility or disrespect can be triggered by the officer's demeanor or action.

In an important breakthrough, Dunham and Alpert studied the sequence of events in a set of police–citizen interactions. They found that the demeanor of both officers and citizens changed as the encounter developed. In about one quarter of the encounters, the officer's demeanor changed. In half of those cases, the officer's demeanor changed for the better (i.e., became more respectful), and in the other half changed for the worse (i.e., less respectful). Meanwhile, in slightly more than half of all encounters (52 percent), the citizen's demeanor improved, while in the other 48 percent it got worse.[34]

The significant insight in Dunham and Alpert's study is that police-citizen encounters are *fluid,* with attitudes and behavior on both sides often changing. It misrepresents reality to record things at a single moment in time.

Most police–citizen interactions are routine and uneventful, with neither side exhibiting disrespect to the other or using force. Mastrofski, Snipes, and Supina investigated the extent to which citizens comply with requests from police officers by observing 346 interactions where officers asked or told a citizen (or citizens) to do something: (1) leave another person or persons alone, (2) calm down or cease being disorderly, or (3) cease illegal behavior. Citizens complied with officer requests in 78 percent of the observed cases. Failure to comply increased the chances of arrest. In 28 percent of the failure to comply cases, the officer made an arrest.[35]

- **Characteristics of the Victim.** Some decisions are based on characteristics of the victim, reflecting a moral judgment about the victim by the police officer. LaFree found substantial evidence that police officers discounted the allegations of rape victims whose lifestyle was nonconformist.[36] This involved women who did not fit traditional middle-class standards of women's behavior.
- **Race, Ethnicity, and Gender of the Citizen.** There is also some evidence that arrest decisions are based on race. Smith, Visher, and Davidson found that police officers were more responsive to white victims who complained about black suspects, particularly in property crimes.[37] Donald Black, however, did not find any direct evidence of race discrimination in arrests, but did find some indication that black officers were more responsive to complaints by black victims and, thus, more likely to arrest in those situations.[38]

The "driving while black" controversy suggests that in some traffic enforcement situations, decisions to stop drivers are heavily influenced by race and ethnicity. In Maryland and New Jersey, data indicate that state troopers were stopping a disproportionate number of African American drivers on Interstate highways.[39]

Visher found some evidence that the gender of the suspect influenced arrest decisions, although this depended on the perceived behavior of the woman. Women who conform to traditional gender role stereotypes are likely to be treated more leniently than men who are suspected of the same offense. Women who violate gender role expectations, however, do not receive preferential treatment.[40]

For a full discussion of the racial profiling controversy, see Chapter 12.

- **Characteristics of the Neighborhood.** The immediate work environment also influences police discretion. Fyfe found that officers working in high-crime neighborhoods fired their weapons more than twice as often as officers working in low-crime areas.[41] Higher-crime areas have more incidents (especially robberies) in which an officer is likely to confront an armed criminal and use deadly force in response.

    Smith, Visher, and Davidson, meanwhile, found that police officers were more likely to make arrests in low-income neighborhoods than in higher-income areas, with the result that poor whites and poor blacks were both more likely to be arrested than people in higher-income areas.[42] Arrests for vagrancy are rare on skid row but more common when a homeless person wanders into the central business district.[43]

- **Characteristics of the Individual Officer.** Many people believe that different kinds of officers will act differently on the street—meaning that they will exercise their discretion in a different manner. We have already discussed this in Chapter 6, but it is important to review it again here. Do white and African American officers use their discretion in different ways? Do their decisions result in different outcomes? Do male and female officers make different decisions in the same kind of situations? Do they use their discretion differently?

    The characteristics of individual officers do not appear to have a major influence on police behavior. The evidence strongly suggests that the behavior of white, African American, and Hispanic officers is remarkably similar with regard to arrests, use of physical force, and the use of deadly force. (see Chapter 6 for a review of the evidence). Similarly, the evidence indicates that there are no significant differences between the behavior of male and female officers. As discussed in Chapter 6, however, there is some evidence that male officers are more likely to engage in extremely inappropriate behavior (e.g., they are more likely to receive citizen complaints and be the subject of lawsuits alleging excessive force). Finally, there is no evidence suggesting that higher levels of education result in better police conduct—and presumably better use of discretion.

---

**SIDEBAR        11 – 1**

## *Discussion: Legal and Extralegal Factors in Officer Discretion*

The situational factors affecting police discretion fall into two categories: legal and extralegal. Legal factors are those related to the legality of the conduct involved, such as the seriousness of the crime and the strength of the evidence. Extralegal factors are those that have nothing to do with legality of the conduct involved, such as the preference of the victim.

Most experts argue that legal factors are appropriate for an officer to take into consideration.

Do you agree?

Is it appropriate for an officer to take into consideration the seriousness of the crime when deciding whether or not to make an arrest? Explain why. If you think it isn't, explain why.

Is it appropriate for an officer to take into consideration the strength of the evidence when deciding whether to make an arrest? Explain why. If you think it is not, explain why.

# Organizational Factors

- **Official Department Policy.** Official department policies have a powerful influence over police discretion. Fyfe found that a restrictive shooting policy adopted by the New York City police department in 1972 reduced firearms discharges 30 percent over the next three and a half years.[44] Shootings of fleeing felons in Memphis disappeared following the adoption of a restrictive shooting policy.[45] Restrictive policies on high-speed pursuits reduce the number of pursuits. Alpert found that pursuits in the Miami-Dade police department declined 82 percent after the introduction of a restrictive policy. In Omaha, meanwhile, pursuits increased 600 percent after a permissive policy was reintroduced.[46]

    The impact of written department policies on police discretion is discussed in more detail in the section on control of discretion and in Chapter 14 on police accountability.

**informal organizational culture**

- **Informal Organizational Culture.** Police departments also have their own informal organizational culture that influences officer discretion. In his classic study *Varieties of Police Behavior,* Wilson identifies three different organizational styles of policing: watchman, legalistic, and service.[47]

    Historically, the Los Angeles police department had a reputation for a legalistic style that involved aggressive crime-fighting tactics (e.g., high rates of field interrogations and arrests).[48] The organizational culture of a police department is not necessarily established by written policy. It is more the impact of values and traditions that are communicated informally among officers. In a comparison of six police departments, the Project on Policing Neighborhoods found that the percentage of officer-initiated contacts with citizens ranged from a low of about 20 percent to a high of 50 percent. These different patterns of work activity obviously reflect different informal norms about patrol activity in the six departments.[49]

# Social and Political Factors

**local political culture**

- **Local Political Culture.** In almost every state there are small towns where, according to local folklore, you want to be sure to drive right at the speed limit. These towns have reputations for making a lot of arrests for speeding.

    Police officer discretion is also influenced by the local political culture. One community might place a high priority on, for example, traffic enforcement, with the result that the police department engages in aggressive enforcement.[50] Another community might place a very high priority on order maintenance, with the result that the police aggressively enforce laws on disturbing the peace, loitering, and so on. Local political culture influences police departments informally (e.g., through communication from elected officials or other community leaders), and not necessarily through written policy. Although experts believe that local political culture is an important influence on the police, it has not been studied in detail.[51]

# The Control of Discretion

## The Need for Control

Virtually all experts agree on the need to control police discretion in order to prevent abuse of police authority. Both Davis and Goldstein argue that the first step toward controlling police discretion is admitting that it exists, that it can create problems, and that control is necessary.[52] Historically, the police denied that they exercise discretion, claiming, instead, that they fully enforce all laws.

**myth of full enforcement**

The so-called **myth of full enforcement** exists for several reasons.[53] First, the police want to maintain a public image of authority. Admitting that they sometimes do not enforce the law would undermine their authority in encounters with citizens. It would give suspects a basis for challenging an arrest, with comments like "Why me?" and "You don't arrest everyone."

Second, if the police admitted that they do not arrest everyone, it would raise serious questions about equal protection of the law. Third, to admit that the police exercise discretion in enforcing certain laws would raise questions about all police policies and how departments determine what their enforcement policies are. Fourth, most states have laws requiring the police to enforce all laws fully. Some states have criminal penalties for police and other officials who do not enforce the law. For this reason, some legal scholars have questioned whether police discretion is legal.[54]

For a discussion of Supreme Court decisions limiting the discretion of police officers, see Chapter 14.

Finally, denying that discretion exists allows supervisors to avoid closely reviewing officer behavior and developing performance expectations. Commanders can justify this neglect on the grounds that they trust the professional judgment of officers on the street. Uviller's study of New York City officers found that supervisors approve of the exercise of discretion far more than the officers under their command believe.[55]

Davis, Goldstein, and other experts argue that the myth of full enforcement creates a number of serious problems. Most important, it represents a denial of the basic reality of police work. As mentioned earlier, it creates potential due process and equal protection problems, increases the likelihood of police–community relations problems, makes it difficult to manage personnel effectively, and makes meaningful planning impossible.[56]

There are three basic strategies for controlling discretion: abolishing it, enhancing the professional judgment of police officers, and regulating it through written policies.

## Abolish Discretion?

In one of the first studies of police discretion, Joseph Goldstein concluded that it was illegal and should be abolished.[57] He and others have argued that the police do not have the legal authority to nullify the criminal law by not arresting a criminal offender. Virtually all other experts have rejected the idea of abolishing discretion. They argue that discretion is both inevitable and, as was pointed out earlier in this chapter, can often be used for positive purposes.

The debate over abolishing police discretion parallels similar debates over how to control discretion in other parts of the criminal justice system: plea bargaining, sentencing, parole release, and so forth. In those other areas, there is now a general consensus that attempting to abolish discretion is both unwise in principle and impossible in practice. The consensus is that the best response is to regulate and control discretion through written rules. Sentencing guidelines that leave judges some room for discretion are a good example of this approach.[58]

## Enhancing Professional Judgment

When you go to a doctor because of some symptoms that worry you, the doctor asks a series of questions and decides what tests to give you. He or she decides whether to refer you to a specialist for further tests and decides what medication to prescribe. The doctor does not follow any rigid set of rules in making these decisions, but uses professional judgment.

For a full discussion of police training, see Chapter 5.

Enhancing the professional judgment of police officers is another means of controlling discretion. This represents the professional model employed by the professions of medicine, law, and education. In these occupations, practitioners are granted broad discretion to make judgments about how to handle specific incidents. Control is exercised through the process of screening, training, and socializing members of the profession. Admission standards to medical schools, for example, are very high; medical school training is long and rigorous; and the training process serves to socialize prospective doctors into the culture of the profession. Once a doctor is licensed, he or she is expected to make professional judgments without direct supervision.[59]

Presumably, education and training should improve the exercise of discretion by police officers. This argument holds that better educated and trained officers would be better able to understand the complexity of the situations they encounter, better able to understand the human and social consequences of certain actions, and better able to understand and comply with court rulings and department policies governing their use of discretion. Unfortunately, the impact of education and training on police officer use of discretion is not known. The National Academy of Sciences report *Fairness and Effectiveness in Policing: The Evidence* found that there have been few well-designed studies that isolated and measured the impact of either the level of education or the training that officers have received. It found, for example, that "few studies evaluate the impact of training programs on actual performance of the job."[60]

Many critics argue that the traditional professional model does not apply to policing. First, recruitment standards are low, compared with law and medicine. Preservice training is very short (six months even in the best departments), compared with these other professions (three years for law school). Second, the peer culture of policing has often tolerated and even covered up improper behavior.[61] Third, policing has been described as a craft rather than a profession. That is to say, it involves a set of skills that are learned through practice. There is no body of specialized professional knowledge equivalent to the body of knowledge that the tax lawyer or the heart specialist possesses. Police officers are generalists rather than specialists. For all these reasons, James Q. Wilson argues that "the police are not in any of these senses professionals."[62] Consequently, the traditional professional model of controlling discretion is not applicable to policing.

## Informal Bureaucratic Controls

To a certain extent, police discretion is controlled by the bureaucratic setting of the criminal justice system. An arrest, for example, raises the "visibility" of a police officer's behavior. The arrest is reviewed by a supervisor, a prosecutor, a defense attorney, and one or more judges. A competent defense attorney will challenge improper or illegal behavior and may succeed in persuading the judge to dismiss the case. In short, a police officer is not totally free to act out his or her prejudices. Reiss, for example, found that about 75 percent of the officers in his field study made verbal expressions of racial prejudice in the presence of the observers. Yet the data on arrests did not indicate any direct pattern of race discrimination.[63] In short, police officer attitudes do not automatically translate into behavior. Bureaucratic procedures, involving routine review by other persons, constrain officers' behavior. (The relationship between police officer attitudes and behavior is discussed in more detail in Chapter 6.)

## Written Policies

The method of control that has evolved is through the use of written policies that guide the police officer's exercise of discretion. This approach is called administrative rulemaking. Because it is currently the dominant approach in American police management, it is discussed at length below.

# Administrative Rulemaking

**Administrative rulemaking** seeks to guide the exercise of police discretion through written departmental policies. These policies typically specify (1) what an officer must do in certain situations, (2) what he or she may not do in those situations, and (3) where an officer may properly exercise discretion. Virtually all experts on policing endorse this approach. The Commission on Accreditation for Law Enforcement Agencies (CALEA) accreditation *Standards for Law Enforcement Agencies* require that "a written directive governs procedures for assuring compliance with all applicable constitutional requirements."[64] The American Bar Association *Standards* for police include a similar recommendation (Exhibit 11–1).[65]

**administrative rulemaking**

## Examples of Administrative Rulemaking

- **Deadly Force.** The defense-of-life standard for the use of deadly force clearly spells out when deadly force may be used (threat to the life of the officer or another person) and when it may not be used (an unarmed fleeing felon).[66] Many department policies also include specific prohibitions on the use of warning shots, shots to wound, or shots at moving vehicles. (See Exhibit 11–2.)

### EXHIBIT 11–1

#### ABA Standard 1–4.3 Administrative Rule Making

Police discretion can best be structured and controlled through the process of administrative rule making by police agencies. Police administrators should, therefore, give the highest priority to the formulation of administrative rules governing the exercise of discretion, particularly in the areas of selective enforcement, investigative techniques, and enforcement methods.

## EXHIBIT 11–2

### International Association of Chiefs of Police: Model Policy, Use of Deadly Force (excerpts)

**I. PURPOSE**

The purpose of this policy is to provide law enforcement officers of this agency with guidelines for the use of deadly and non-deadly force.

**II. POLICY**

It is the policy of this law enforcement agency that officers use only the force that reasonably appears necessary to effectively bring an incident under control, while protecting the lives of the officer and others.

**III. DEFINITIONS**

*Deadly Force:* Any use of force that is reasonably likely to cause death.

*Non-Deadly Force:* Any use of force other than that which is considered deadly force. This includes any physical effort used to control or restrain another, or to overcome the resistance of another.

*Objectively Reasonable:* This term means that, in determining the necessity for force and the appropriate level of force, officers shall evaluate each situation in light of the known circumstances, including, but not limited to, the seriousness of the crime, the level of threat or resistance presented by the subject, and the danger to the community.

**IV. PROCEDURES**

   A.  Use of Deadly Force

      1.  Law enforcement officers are authorized to use deadly force to:

          a.  Protect the officer or others from what is reasonably believed to be a threat of death or serious bodily harm; and/or

          b.  To prevent the escape of a fleeing violent felon whom the officer has probable cause to believe will pose a significant threat of death or serious physical injury to the officer or others. Where practicable prior to discharge of the firearm, officers shall identify themselves as law enforcement officers and state their intent to shoot.

   B.  Deadly Force Restrictions

      1.  Officers may use deadly force to destroy an animal that represents a threat to public safety, or as a humanitarian measure where the animal is seriously injured when the officer reasonably believes that deadly force can be used without harm to the officer or others.

      2.  Warning shots may be fired if an officer is authorized to use deadly force and only if the officer reasonably believes a warning shot can be fired safely in light of all circumstances of the encounter.

      3.  Decisions to discharge a firearm at or from a moving vehicle shall be governed by this use-of-force policy and are prohibited if they present an unreasonable risk to the officer or others.

- **Domestic Violence.** Mandatory arrest policies on domestic violence instruct police officers that they must make an arrest when a felonious assault has occurred. Arrest-preferred policies state that arrest is the expected action, but allow the officers a range of discretion depending on various circumstances.[67]
- **High-Speed Pursuits.** Department policies on high-speed pursuits instruct officers to consider road conditions, the presence of pedestrians, and other potential risks before initiating a pursuit.[68]

## Principles of Administrative Rulemaking

Kenneth Davis, a leading authority on administrative law, describes the principles of administrative rulemaking in terms of a strategy to fill the gap between law and practice.[69] Laws are written in very broad language. The criminal law, for example, describes categories of criminal behavior in general terms ("threat to do serious bodily harm"). In practice, someone has to use his or her discretion to apply these general definitions to a specific situation. Administrative rulemaking is designed to fill in the gap by providing additional detail on how to handle specific situations. The specific objectives of administrative rulemaking, according to Davis, are to confine, structure, and check discretion.[70]

- **Confining Discretion.** Rules confine discretion by "fixing the boundaries." The defense-of-life standard on the use of deadly force, for example, fixes the boundaries by clearly indicating situations where an officer may not shoot. A mandatory arrest policy on domestic violence fixes the boundaries by instructing officers that an arrest is required if there is a felonious assault.
- **Structuring Discretion.** Discretion is structured, according to Davis, when there is a rational system for developing policies. Such a system calls for open policy statements and open rules. This approach is designed to eliminate the secrecy surrounding discretion. With respect to policing, it informs the public about what official policy is. It also offers an opportunity to object to an existing policy. Both Davis and Herman Goldstein argue that a system of open rulemaking would create an atmosphere of openness that would have a positive effect on police–community relations.[71]
- **Checking Discretion.** Discretion is checked when decisions are reviewed by another person. The use of deadly force is checked by the requirement that officers fill out reports after each firearms discharge and by having those reports automatically reviewed by supervisors.[72] This process puts officers on notice that their decisions will be examined by other people, including the chief of police.

For a discussion of the internal review use-of-force reports as a means of achieving police accountability, see Chapter 14.

## Contributions of Written Rules

A patrol officer sees a car he believes is stolen and starts to make a traffic stop by turning on his flashing lights. Suddenly, the suspect car accelerates in an obvious attempt to flee. The officer has to make a quick decision: pursue or not pursue? He knows the roads are wet and dangerously slick and sees that the fleeing vehicle is headed for an area with a lot of traffic. The officer remembers that the department's high-speed pursuit policy advises against pursuits where road conditions and traffic levels might pose a danger to innocent bystanders. He does not pursue, but calls in the identity of the fleeing vehicle to the 911 dispatcher.

Written rules offer obvious advantages. They provide direction for officers on how to handle critical incidents. In a Justice Department report, *"Broken Windows" and Police Discretion,* George L. Kelling argues that in order for the police to effectively address quality-of-life issues in neighborhoods, officers need clear guidance in the form of rules that tell them both what they should do and what they should not do.[73]

Written policies promote consistent performance throughout the department. This, in turn, helps ensure equal protection of the law. Written policies provide the basis for effective supervision. Officers can be rewarded for following policy and can be disciplined for violations.[74] Finally, officers are more likely to respect and comply with rules that are developed internally by the department than rules imposed on them by outsiders.[75]

One of the main arguments in favor of administrative rulemaking is that it is more effective than other means. Abolishing discretion is not realistic. Allowing unlimited discretion opens the door to potential abuse, for example, in the form of inappropriate use of force or discrimination.

## The Impact of Administrative Rulemaking

There is persuasive evidence that administrative rulemaking has produced some significant improvements in policing. After a comprehensive review of police research, the National Academy of Sciences concluded that "clear administrative guidelines regarding the use of force, coupled with consistently imposed sanctions for misconduct, reduces the incidence of excessive force."[76] For example:

- Fyfe found that a restrictive policy on deadly force adopted by the New York City police department in 1972 reduced the weekly average number of firearms discharges by about one-third (29.1 percent).[77]
- Alpert's study of high-speed pursuit policies found that where restrictive policies were adopted, there was a reduction in the number of pursuits, accidents, and injuries to both officers and citizens.[78]
- In the Los Angeles Sheriff's Department the number of citizens bitten by canine unit dogs declined by 90 percent after the department put in place new controls over how the dogs could be deployed.

## Ensuring Compliance with Rules

**CALEA accreditation standards**

A major issue in the control of discretion is whether officers comply with departmental policies. The principal strategy for ensuring compliance is to require officers to file a written report after each incident, and to have each report automatically reviewed by supervisors. The **CALEA accreditation standards,** for example, require a police officer to file a written report whenever he or she "discharges a firearm," causes "injury or death of another person," uses "lethal or less-than-lethal weapons," or "applies physical force as defined by the agency."[79]

Another factor influencing compliance is the immediate work setting. Firearms discharges are, by definition, high visibility events: they occur in public areas and are accompanied by a loud noise and the presence of at least one citizen, along with other potential witnesses. High-speed pursuits also are public events, obviously occurring in the streets where they are observed by many people. High visibility and the presence of potential witnesses encourage officers to complete reports as required. There is always the possibility of a witness reporting an incident the officer failed to report, or providing evidence that contradicts the officer's report.

Domestic violence incidents, however, are very low visibility events. They typically occur in private homes, usually with no witnesses other than the immediate parties. Thus, it is easier for the officer to ignore both the policy and the reporting requirement.[80]

## Codifying Rules: The Standard Operation Procedure (SOP) Manual

Written rules and policies are collected and codified in a department's **standard operation procedure manual (SOP).** The SOP manual is the central tool of modern police management. The typical SOP manual in a big-city department is several hundred pages long.

standard operation procedure manual

Many police departments now place their SOP manuals on their Web sites. The Minneapolis, Kansas City, and Los Angeles police departments are three examples. (See Sidebar 11–2.)

Placing SOP manuals on Web sites has several advantages. First, it is a step in the direction of greater openness and transparency. It allows citizens to know what their department's policies are. This increases public understanding and trust. This promotes better police-community relations (see Chapter 12). Second, it promotes reform. Citizens and local professional groups can compare their department's policy on a particular subject. They might find that the policy—use of Tasers, for example— is not consistent with most other departments and should be changed.

SOP manuals have certain limits. First, they have traditionally overemphasized relatively trivial issues (such as proper uniforms) and ignored critical issues in the use of law enforcement power (such as arrest and deadly force). In recent years, although departments have adopted written policies on deadly force and pursuits, other

---

**SIDEBAR    11 – 2**

### SOPs on the Web

An increasing number of police departments place their policy and procedure manuals on the Web. They include:

Los Angeles Police Department: www.lapdonline.org

Minneapolis Police Department: www.ci.minneapolis.mn.us/police/about (go to "Inside MPD")

Charlotte-Mecklenburg Police Department: www.charmeck.org/CMPD (go to "Inside CMPD," "CMPD Directives")

Phoenix Police Department: www.phoenixpolice.com (Go to "About Us," "Operations Manual")

important issues remain uncovered by a policy. Many departments still do not have policies on the use of informants or on arrest discretion in situations other than domestic violence.

A second problem is the "crisis management" process by which manuals develop. New policies are typically adopted in response to an immediate crisis: a lawsuit or a community protest. Peter Manning quotes a British police sergeant as saying that his department's procedures manual represented "140 years of screw-ups. Every time something goes wrong, they make a rule about it."[81] The result of crisis management is that SOP manuals are generally unsystematic. Some areas of police discretion are covered, but many are not. Manuals are often not revised for many years, and, as a result, important subjects are not reviewed or updated.

## Systematic Rulemaking

Leading experts on police discretion have urged the police to engage in systematic rulemaking. Davis and Goldstein argue that a systematic approach allows the police

---

## EXHIBIT 11–3

### Policymaking Process in the Madison, Wisconsin, Police Department

**Madison Police Department Policy 1-300 Development of Policy**

It is important that all members of the department have an adequate opportunity to comment and suggest revisions to policy. In some cases, the need for a specific policy will first be identified by personnel not assigned to policy development. Therefore, it is important to standardize the procedure to be used in order that persons having suggestions for policy development will know the most effective method for submitting their suggestions. Furthermore, a specific procedure encourages exposure of developing policy to those it will directly concern before it becomes effective.

The following procedure will be used in the development of policy:

Personnel having suggestions for policy, or concern with areas not adequately addressed, or modifications needed to present policy, should contact the Chief of Police, or designee. The suggestion may be in written form or may be a verbal explanation of the problem and possible solution. All available information that is relevant to the problem should be presented.

The suggestion will be developed into a draft policy using other resource people designated by the Chief or designee.

Efforts will be made to get comments from department members who may be affected by this policy. It may be advantageous to seek comments from persons outside the department who may have expertise in, or who may be directly affected by the suggested policy.

The draft policy will be reviewed by Professional Standards and the OAC. The draft will then be taken to the Management Team for review and finalization.

After the Management Team review, the completed policy will be approved by the Chief of Police and distributed to affected personnel.

---

*Source:* Police Department, Madison, Wisconsin, Policies and Procedures Manual. Available at www.ci.madison.wi.us/police.

to anticipate problems before they become crises and represents a professional approach to planning. Despite these recommendations, police departments have not engaged in systematic planning. Davis points out that the "research and planning" units in many police departments are usually occupied with trivial matters.[82]

Several attempts have been made to encourage systematic rulemaking. The CALEA accreditation *Standards for Law Enforcement Agencies* require accredited departments to have a system of written directives governing police policy.[83] Accreditation, however, is a voluntary system, and by 2006 only about 500 of the nearly 18,000 law enforcement agencies in the United States were accredited. In 1987 the International Association of Chiefs of Police (IACP) established the National Law Enforcement Policy Center, which began publishing model policies on specific discretionary decision points.[84] The Police Executive Research Forum (PERF) also develops model policies on various aspects of police work. Finally, a number of citizen review agencies engage in policy review, recommending new policies in areas that have generated citizen complaints.[85]

Wayne Schmidt proposes that to make administrative rulemaking systematic, each state create an administrative council on law enforcement. This agency would have the authority to develop policies for all local police departments in the state.[86] Walker recommends that states enact laws requiring police departments to develop rules on a specific set of critical decision points.[87] To a certain extent, this approach already exists for some decisions. Police use of deadly force, for example, is covered by state statute. The 1985 Supreme Court decision in *Tennessee v. Garner* ruled as unconstitutional state laws embodying the "fleeing felon" standard. Some states have enacted laws governing police pursuits. Walker's proposal would require the police to adopt rules on a broader range of police decision points.

## Citizen Oversight and Policymaking

Some citizen oversight agencies also contribute to rulemaking through a process known as *policy review*. (See Chapter 14 on policy review by police auditors.) Individual citizen complaints are analyzed to determine whether the underlying cause was a lack of policy (or a bad policy) on the part of the police department, and then recommendations for new policy are sent to the department. The San Francisco Office of Citizen Complaints and the San Diego County Citizens Law Enforcement Review Board develop several policy recommendations each year. Walker argues that policy review is one of the most important functions of citizen oversight of the police.[88]

## The Limits of Administrative Rulemaking

Administrative rulemaking also has some important limitations. First, it is impossible to write a rule that covers every possible situation. Although a policy can confine discretion, in the end there will always be ambiguous situations where an officer will have to exercise some discretion.

Second, formal rules may encourage evasion or lying. The exclusionary rule, for example, may encourage officers to lie about how they obtain evidence. With respect to narcotics, observers cited the "dropsy" phenomenon: officers lied, claiming that the suspect dropped the narcotics on the ground (thus making the seizure legal).[89] Fyfe found that in New York City the number of reported "accidental" firearms discharges increased after the restrictive shooting policy was implemented, suggesting that officers were using this category to cover improper shootings. But accidents as a percentage of all shootings increased only from 3 to 9 percent of all discharges, suggesting that if this did represent an attempt to evade policy, it was still rather limited.[90]

Third, as Michael K. Brown argues in *Working the Street,* complex written rules may only make the situation worse, creating more uncertainty for the police officer rather than less. He observes that "simply enveloping policemen in a maze of institutional controls without grappling with the grimy realities of police work does not necessarily promote accountability and may only exacerbate matters."[91]

Harold Pepinsky agrees, citing the example of the *Miranda decision.* He argues that the decision created more uncertainty. When is the suspect "in custody"? What is an "interrogation"? Advocates of written rules reply that a police officer's job is easier when clear, written guidelines are provided on how to handle critical incidents. Although some incidents still leave room for discretion, the range of situations is greatly limited. Davis sees this as the major contribution of confining discretion.[92]

Finally, elaborate rules may only create a negative atmosphere in the department where officers believe that the rules only exist to "get" them and, as a result, the officers do as little work as possible. As Kelling argues, in this kind of organizational environment officers are unlikely to engage in any creative, proactive police work.[93]

Police organizations have been characterized as punishment-centered bureaucracies, with many rules that tell officers what not to do and few rewards for positive police work. Part of the reason for this is that, historically, police managers have been concerned with control, in the sense of keeping officers from inappropriate behavior, with too little attention to guiding officers on the proper courses of action.

Walker replies to these criticisms by arguing that uncertainty is inherent in the nature of policing, that some rules are better than no rules at all, and that if officers evade rules, the task is to ensure greater compliance and not to throw out the rules altogether.[94]

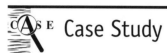 Case Study

*"Broken Windows" and Police Discretion*

### IV. Philosophy of Order Maintenance Practices

The New Haven Police Department will always use the least forceful means possible to achieve its purposes. While we will not hesitate to cite or arrest offenders, our approach, at all levels of organization, will be to attempt to get citizens to obey laws and ordinances as unintrusively as possible.

The first level of intervention, whether by managers, supervisors, or by police officers, will be to educate the public about civility, the consequences of incivility, and the laws that oblige citizens to behave in particular ways. This can be done in neighborhood meetings, in schools, or in interactions with citizens. Some citizens do not fully understand their obligations, and if those obligations—for example, regarding a noisy car or public drinking in parks—are patiently explained, they will adhere to the law.

The second level of intervention will be to remind citizens of their responsibilities if they are disorderly—that is, that they are breaking the law and subject to penalties if they persist. This too can be done in a variety of ways. It could be done by visiting a problem location and warning people that if their behavior continues they will be subject to penalties. Similarly, owners of locations that are chronic problems could be so warned by individual officers.

The final level of intervention will be law enforcement—the use of citation and arrest.

Having said that the least intrusive means of intervention will always be used should not be read to mean that in every incident police must start with education. Since police deal with incidents that have histories (for example, with problems), it may well be that in a particular incident the offenders might have a history of outrageous behavior that warrants forceful action at the outset of the encounter (for example, warning or citation).

*Source:* Excerpt from George Kelling, *"Broken Windows" and Police Discretion*, p. 50.

## Summary

Discretion is a pervasive part of policing. Officers routinely make critical decisions affecting the life and liberty of citizens. Uncontrolled discretion results in serious problems, including denial of due process and equal protection of the law.

Discretion can be controlled through formal written policies adopted by police departments. Written policies do not completely eliminate discretion; they guide it by providing directions on what the officer should or should not do in certain situations. There is evidence that written policies have reduced the number of persons shot and killed by police. Some controversy remains, however, over whether written policies can effectively control all discretionary decisions.[95]

## Key Terms

discretion, 346
street-level bureaucrats, 346
positive uses of discretion, 347
work environment of
    policing, 349
low-visibility work, 349

situational factors, 351
preference of the victim, 351
demeanor of the suspect 351
informal organizational
    culture, 354
local political culture, 354

myth of full enforcement, 355
administrative rulemaking, 357
CALEA accreditation
    standards, 360
standard operation procedure
    manual, 361

## For Discussion

*The New Haven police department policy calls for police officers to use a three-stage process in exercising discretion: (1) educate, (2) remind, and finally (3) enforce the law. As an in-class project, discuss experiences and perceptions regarding police discretion, following these steps:*

1. As an in-class discussion, identify several different order maintenance situations where the police intervened (e.g., party with loud noise).

2. Survey the experiences of students in the class by having each student complete an anonymous report of (a) their experience with one or more of these situations and (b) their experience/observation of the police response (e.g., warning, arrest, lecture).

3. With the instructor reading the anonymous reports, discuss the responses in class.

## Internet Exercises

**Exercise 1** Find three big-city police departments that have their SOP manuals on the Web.

1. Compare their use of force policies. Are there significant differences among the three departments? Are some more detailed than others?

2. Compare their high-speed vehicle pursuit policies. Are some more restrictive than others? Do the policies permit or prohibit pursuits of people suspected of traffic violations (as opposed to violent or property crimes)?

3. Compare their domestic violence policies. Do any of them mandate arrest in certain situations? What kinds of situations? Do any of the departments not have a policy on arrests in domestic violence incidents?

**Exercise 2** In response to allegations of racial profiling (an abuse of discretion), a number of law enforcement agencies have adopted new policies and procedures to control traffic enforcement activities by their officers.

What departments have taken these steps? Exactly what do these policies and procedures involve? Some policies involve only the collection of data on traffic stops. What other kinds of controls have been adopted?

Search the Web for reports on racial profiling. Try key words "racial profiling" or "driving while black." Also, go to **www.officer.com** and look for some agency reports.

In class, discuss what policies and procedures you found. Do you think they will be effective in controlling discretion? Will data collection control discretion? That is, will officers avoid questionable actions if they know they have to report them? Or will data collection deter them from taking any kind of law enforcement action?

**Exercise 3** One important area of police discretion involves the handling of domestic violence situations. A number of states have addressed this issue by enacting laws attempting to control police discretion. Some of these are "mandatory arrest" laws; some others are "arrest preferred" laws.

Research the law in your state. Is there a state statute related to domestic violence? Does it cover police discretion? Is it a mandatory arrest law? If not, how would you characterize it? Does the law provide guidelines for police officer handling of domestic violence? What do those guidelines say? In your opinion, do you think this law provides clear and effective guidance for police officers?

If your state does not have such a law, find one that does and study it with regard to the questions above.

State statutes can be found through some of the legal resource sites on the Web. One starting point would be the Reference Desk site (**www.refdesk.com**). Another way to find states that have domestic violence laws would be to do a Web search under the subject of domestic violence. See if any of those sites have reference material on state statutes.

# Notes

1. Donald Black, "The Social Organization of Arrest," in D. Black, *The Manners and Customs of the Police* (New York: Academic Press, 1980), p. 90.

2. Linda Teplin, *Keeping the Peace: Parameters of Police Discretion in Relation to the Mentally Disordered* (Washington DC: Government Printing Office, 1986).

3. Bureau of Justice Statistics, *Contact between Police and the Public: Findings from the 2002 National Survey* (Washington DC: U.S. Justice Department, 2005), Table 9.

4. Nathan Goldman, *The Differential Selection of Juvenile Offenders for Court Appearance* (New York: National Council on Crime and Delinquency, 1963).

5. William A. Geller and Michael Scott, *Deadly Force: What We Know* (Washington DC: Police Executive Research Forum, 1992).

6. Kenneth Culp Davis, *Discretionary Justice: A Preliminary Inquiry* (Urbana: University of Illinois, 1971), p. 4.

7. Wayne R. LaFave, *Arrest* (Boston, Little, Brown, 1965), p. 9.

8. James Q. Wilson, *Varieties of Police Behavior* (New York: Atheneum, 1973), p. 21.

9. Michael Lipsky, Street-Level Bureaucracy (New York: Russell Sage, 1968); Janet Coble Vinzant and Lane Crothers, *Street-Level Leadership: Discretion and Legitimacy in Front-Line Public Service* (Washington DC: Georgetown University Press, 1998).

10. ACLU, *Driving While Black: Racial Profiling on Our Nation's Highways* (New York: ACLU, 1999).

11. Kenneth C. Davis, *Police Discretion* (St. Paul, MN: West, 1975).

12. Samuel Walker, Cassia Spohn, and Miriam DeLone, *The Color of Justice*, 4th ed. (Belmont, CA: Wadsworth, 2007).

13. Frank J. Landy, *Performance Appraisal in Police Departments* (Washington DC: The Police Foundation, 1977); Timothy N. Oettmeier and Mary Ann Wycoff, *Personnel Performance Evaluation in the Community Policing Context* (Washington DC: PERF, 1997).

14. Herman Goldstein, *Policing a Free Society* (Cambridge, MA: Ballinger, 1977), p. 9.

15. Davis, *Police Discretion,* pp. 62–66.

16. Herman Goldstein, *Policing a Free Society,* pp. 94–101; Albert J. Reiss, Jr. "Consequences of Compliance and Deterrence Models of Law Enforcement for the Exercise of Discretion," *Law and Contemporary Problems* 47 (Autumn 1984): pp. 88–89.

17. LaFave, *Arrest*, pp. 70, 84–87.

18. Ibid., pp. 83–101.

19. Raymond T. Nimmer, *Two Million Unnecessary Arrests* (Chicago: American Bar Foundation, 1971).

20. Jerome Skolnick, *Justice without Trial,* 3rd ed. (New York: Macmillan, 1994), p. 13.

21. Albert Reiss, *The Police and the Public* (New Haven, CT: Yale University Press, 1971); Stephen D. Mastrofski, Roger B. Parks, Albert J. Reiss, Jr., Robert E. Worden, Christina DeJong, Jeffrey B. Snipes, and William Terrill, *Systematic Observation of Public Police: Applying Field Research Methods to Policy Issues* (Washington, Department of Justice, 1998), p. 25.

22. Herman Goldstein, "Administrative Problems in Controlling the Exercise of Police Authority," *Journal of Criminal Law, Criminology, and Police Science* 58, no. 2 (1997): p. 165.

23. Joseph Goldstein, "Police Discretion Not to Invoke the Criminal Process: Low Visibility Decisions in the Administration of Justice," *Yale Law Journal* 69, no. 4 (1960): pp. 543–88.

24. Herman Goldstein, *Policing a Free Society,* p. 9.

25. Davis, *Police Discretion,* pp. 62–66.

26. Steve Herbert, "Police Subculture Reconsidered," Criminology 36 (No. 2, 1998): pp. 343–368.

27. Black, "The Social Organization of Arrest."

28. Teplin, *Keeping the Peace.*

29. Black, "The Social Organization of Arrest."

30. Ibid., p. 101.

31. Ibid., p. 104.

32. Ibid., pp. 107–8; Albert Reiss, "Police Brutality—Answers to Key Questions," *Transaction* 5 (July–August 1968): pp. 10–19.

33. David A. Klinger, "Demeanor or Crime? Why 'Hostile' Citizens Are More Likely to Be Arrested," *Criminology* 32, no. 3 (1994): pp. 475–93.

34. Roger G. Dunham and Geoffrey P. Alpert, "Officer and Suspect Demeanor: A Qualitative Analysis of Change," *Police Quarterly* 12 (March 2009): pp. 6–21.

35. Stephen D. Mastrofski, Jeffrey B. Snipes, and Anne E. Supina, "Compliance on Demand: The Public's Response to Specific Police Requests," *Journal of Research in Crime and Delinquency* 33 (August 1996): pp. 269–305.

36. Gary LaFree, *Rape and Criminal Justice* (Belmont, CA: Wadsworth, 1989), p. 76.

37. Douglas A. Smith, Christy A. Visher, and Laura A. Davidson, "Equity and Discretionary Justice: The Influence of Race on Police Arrest Decisions," *Journal of Criminal Law and Criminology* 75 (Spring 1984): pp. 234–49.

38. Black, "The Social Organization of Arrest," pp. 107–8.

39. ACLU, *Driving while Black*.

40. Christy A. Visher, "Gender, Police Arrest Decisions, and Notions of Chivalry," *Criminology* 21 (February 1983): pp. 5–28.

41. James J. Fyfe, "Who Shoots? A Look at Officer Race and Police Shooting," *Journal of Police Science and Administration* 9 (December 1981): pp. 367–82.

42. Smith, Visher, and Davidson, "Equity and Discretionary Justice."

43. Egon Bittner, "The Police on Skid Row: A Study in Peacekeeping," in Bittner, *Aspects of Police Work* (Boston: Northeastern University Press, 1990), pp. 30–62.

44. James J. Fyfe, "Administrative Interventions on Police Shooting Discretion: An Empirical Examination," *Journal of Criminal Justice* 7 (Winter 1979): pp. 309–23.

45. Jerry R. Sparger and David J. Giacopassi, "Memphis Revisited: A Reexamination of Police Shootings after the Garner Decision," *Justice Quarterly* 9 (June 1992): pp. 211–25.

46. Geoffrey P. Alpert, *Police Pursuit: Policies and Training* (Washington DC: Department of Justice, 1997).

47. Wilson, *Varieties of Police Behavior*.

48. Lou Cannon, *Official Negligence* (New York: Times Books, 1997), Ch. 3.

49. Mastrofski et al., *Systematic Observation of Public Police,* p. 25.

50. John A. Gardiner, *Traffic and the Police: Variations in Law-Enforcement Policy* (Cambridge, MA: Harvard University Press, 1969).

51. Wilson, *Varieties of Police Behavior*.

52. Herman Goldstein, *Policing a Free Society,* pp. 93–130; Davis, *Police Discretion,* pp. 70–78.

53. Davis, *Police Discretion,* pp. 52–78.

54. Ibid.; Ronald Allen, "The Police and Substantive Rulemaking: Reconciling Principle and Expediency," *University of Pennsylvania Law Review* 125 (Spring 1976): pp. 62–118.

55. H. Richard Uviller, "The Unworthy Victim: Police Discretion in the Credibility Call," *Law and Contemporary Problems* 47 (Autumn 1984): p. 28.

56. Davis, *Police Discretion,* pp. 70–78; Joseph Goldstein, "Police Discretion Not to Invoke the Criminal Process," pp. 146–47.

57. Joseph Goldstein, "Police Discretion Not to Invoke the Criminal Process."

58. Samuel Walker, *Taming the System: The Control of Discretion in Criminal Justice, 1950–1990* (New York: Oxford University Press, 1993).

59. Wilbert E. Moore, *The Professions: Roles and Rules* (New York: Russell Sage, 1970).

60. The National Academy of Sciences, *Fairness and Effectiveness in Policing: The Evidence* (Washington DC: National Academy Press, 2004), p. 141.

61. William A. Westley, *Violence and the Police* (Cambridge, MA: MIT Press, 1970).

62. Wilson, *Varieties of Police Behavior,* p. 20.

63. Reiss, *The Police and the Public,* p. 147.

64. Commission on Accreditation for Law Enforcement Agencies, *Standards for Law Enforcement Agencies,* 4th ed. (Fairfax, VA: CALEA, 1999), Standard 1.2.2.

65. American Bar Association, *Standards Relating to the Urban Function,* 2nd. Ed. (Boston: Little, Brown, 1980), Standard 1-4.3.

66. Fyfe, "Administrative Interventions on Police Shooting Discretion."

67. Lawrence W. Sherman, *Policing Domestic Violence* (New York: Free Pres, 1992).

68. Geoffrey P. Alpert and Roger D. Dunham, *Police Pursuit Driving: Controlling Responses to Emergency Situations* (New York: Greenwood, 1990).

69. Davis, *Discretionary Justice*.

70. Ibid.

71. Davis, *Police Discretion;* Herman Goldstein, *Policing a Free Society,* pp. 119–20.

72. Fyfe, "Adminstrative Interventions on Police Shooting Discretion."

73. George L. Kelling, *"Broken Windows" and Police Discretion* (Washington DC: Department of Justice, 1999).

74. Walker, *Taming the System*.

75. Herman Goldstein, "Administrative Problems in Controlling the Exercise of Police Authority."

76. The National Academy of Sciences, *Fairness and Effectiveness in Policing: The Evidence,* p. 282.

77. Fyfe, "Administrative Interventions on Police Shooting Discretion."

78. Geoffrey P. Alpert, *Pursuit Policies and Training* (Washington DC: Government Printing Office, 1997).

79. CALEA, Standards for Law Enforcement Agencies, Standard 1.3.6.

80. Walker, *Taming the System.*

81. Peter K. Manning, *Police Work* (Cambridge, MA: MIT Press, 1977), p. 165.

82. Davis, *Police Discretion,* pp. 32–33.

83. CALEA, *Standards for Law Enforcement Agencies,* Ch. 1.

84. National Law Enforcement Policy Center, *Policy Review* (Washington DC: IACP, 1987).

85. Ibid.

86. Wayne Schmidt, "A Proposal for a Statewide Law Enforcement Administrative Law Council," *Journal of Police Science and Administration* 2, no. 2 (1974): pp. 330–38.

87. Samuel Walker, "Controlling the Cops: A Legislative Approach to Police Rulemaking," *University of Detroit Law Review* 63 (Spring 1986): pp. 361–91.

88. Samuel Walker, *Police Accountability: The Role of Citizen Oversight* (Belmont, CA: Wadsworth, 2001).

89. Dallin H. Oaks, "Studying the Exclusionary Rule in Search and Seizure," *University of Chicago Law Review* 37 (1970): pp. 665–757.

90. Fyfe, "Administrative Interventions on Police Shooting Discretion."

91. Michael K. Brown, *Working the Street: Police Discretion and the Dilemmas of Reform* (New York: Russell Sage, 1981).

92. Davis, *Discretionary Justice,* pp. 52–96; Harold E. Pepinsky, "Better Living through Police Discretion," *Law and Contemporary Problems* 47 (Autumn 1984): 249–67.

93. Kelling, *"Broken Windows" and Police Discretion,* pp. 1–2.

94. Walker, *Taming the System.*

95. New Haven Police Division, Order Maintenance Training Bulletin 96-1, in Kelling, *"Broken Windows" and Police Discretion,* pp. 49–50.

# Police–Community Relations

Conflict between the police and racial and ethnic minority communities continues to be one of the most serious problems in American policing. In recent years attention has focused on the issue of "driving while black" (DWB)—the allegation that the police single out African American or Hispanic drivers for traffic stops on the basis of their race or ethnicity rather than suspected criminal conduct.[1] A 2004 Gallup Poll found that 53 percent of all Americans and 67 percent of African Americans believe that racial profiling is "widespread."[2]

The DWB controversy is only one part of the larger problem of police–community relations in America. There are persistent allegations that racial and ethnic minorities are the victims of unwarranted stops and frisks, discriminatory arrest patterns, and excessive use of both physical and deadly force. In addition, people of color are underrepresented among sworn officers in most police departments.

This chapter examines the police–community relations (PCR) problem. It reviews the history of the problem, public attitudes toward the police, the different aspects of policing that affect racial and ethnic minorities, and programs designed to solve the problem.

# A Definition of Police–Community Relations

A 1999 *New York Times Magazine* article declared that "the way cops perceive blacks—and how those perceptions shape and misshape crime fighting—is now the most charged racial issue in America." "Neither side understands the other," it continued. "The innocent black man, jacked-up and humiliated during a stop and frisk or a pretext stop, asks: whatever happened to the Fourth Amendment?" The police officer responds by asking, "Why shouldn't I look at race when I'm looking for crime? It's no state secret that blacks commit a disproportionate amount of crime, so 'racial profiling' is simply good police work."[3] Conflicting perceptions based on race or what constitutes fair treatment of people and/or good police work are at the heart of the police–community relations problem.

**police–community relations**

**Police–community relations** (PCR) refers primarily to *relations between the police and racial and ethnic minority communities*. Relations between the white majority and the police have generally been fairly positive. The PCR problem is one aspect of the larger problem of racial and ethnic inequality in America. Walker, Spohn, and DeLone argue that "the criminal justice system is characterized by obvious disparities based on race and ethnicity."[4]

## From PCR to Legitimacy

Thinking about relations between the police and community groups has evolved dramatically in the last twenty years. The catalyst was the community policing movement (see Chapter 10), which emphasizes developing working partnerships with community groups. Gradually, police experts redefined the problem into one of *legitimacy*. Racial and ethnic minorities are only one part of the community the police serve. The concept of legitimacy holds that the police need to establish trust and cooperation with all segments of the community they serve. Legitimacy is discussed in detail at the end of this chapter.

## Policing a Multicultural Society

The changing demographic face of America creates new challenges for all social institutions, including the police. A report on *Policing a Multicultural Community* by the Police Executive Research Forum concludes that "preventing, mitigating, and negotiating intergroup conflict in the community must become an integral part of police practice. To remain effective, indeed to increase effectiveness, police must become skilled inter-cultural craftspeople."[5]

While the most serious PCR problems have historically involved the African American community, similar problems also exist with respect to other racial and ethnic groups. The experiences of various racial and ethnic groups are very different. Hispanic

Americans, for example, have different experiences with and attitudes about the police than African Americans. Native Americans have a unique history in America. The term "minority groups," therefore, is not appropriate, because it fails to distinguish between race and ethnicity, and assumes that all groups have the same experience.[6]

## Definitions of Race and Ethnicity

There is much misunderstanding about the definitions of race and ethnicity. Definitions traditionally used by many people have no scientific validity.

**Race** has traditionally been defined as referring to the major biological divisions of the people of the world. The traditional categories are Caucasian, Negroid, and Mongoloid. Anthropologists today, however, do not believe that the differences in skin color, hair texture, and body proportions we observe represent fundamental differences between people. There are, for example, substantial differences in physical features between people *within* each traditional racial category (e.g., light-skinned "blacks," and olive or dark-skinned "whites"). The American Anthropological Association issued an official statement in 1998, declaring that there is no scientific foundation for the traditional classification of human beings into distinct "races" that are identifiable by physical characteristics such as skin color, hair texture, and other features. Recent research on DNA, moreover, indicates that physical differences account for only 6 percent of the variation between traditional "racial" groups.[7]

**race**

**Ethnicity** refers to cultural differences, such as language, religion, family patterns, and foodways. Ethnicity is separate from race as a category. A person in the United States may be ethnically Hispanic, for example, but either white, black, or Native American in terms of race.[8]

**ethnicity**

**Official Data.** The U.S. Census is based on self-reporting, asking people to report both their race and their ethnicity. With regard to race, the official categories are: White; Black or African American; American Indian and Alaska Native; Asian; Native Hawaiian and other Pacific Islander, or some other race. A person of mixed racial background can indicate two or more races. With respect to ethnicity, the categories are Hispanic or Non-Hispanic. (See Exhibit 12–1). As a result, a person can self-report as Black/Non-Hispanic, or Black/Hispanic, or White/Non-Hispanic, or White/Hispanic.

## EXHIBIT 12–1

### Official U.S. Census Categories, Race and Ethnicity, 2000

| Race | Ethnicity |
|---|---|
| One Race | Hispanic or Latino (of any race) |
|   White | Not Hispanic or Latino |
|   Black or African American | |
|   American Indian and Alaska Native | |
|   Asian | |
|   Native Hawaiian and other Pacific Islander | |
|   Some other race | |
| Two or more races | |

Official criminal justice data are problematic, because state and local agencies use their own categories, determined by agency officials (rather than self-reports). The result is inconsistency and confusion. The report *Donde esta la justicia?* gives the hypothetical example of "Juanita," whose father is Puerto Rican and whose mother is African American. In Arizona she would define her own race and ethnicity; in California she would be classified as African American; and in Ohio she would be listed as "biracial."[9]

# The Major Racial and Ethnic Minority Groups

## The African American Community

The African American community has long been the major focus of the police–community relations problem. Between 1964 and 1968 major riots occurred in cities all across the country. Most were provoked by an incident involving the police. The 1965 Watts riot in Los Angeles, for example, began with a simple traffic stop on a hot August night. Tensions between the police and the African American community involve allegations of unjustified fatal shootings, use of excessive force, overly aggressive police tactics in stops and frisks, discrimination in traffic stops ("driving while black"), and employment discrimination.[10]

## The Hispanic/Latino Community

PCR problems exist with respect to the Hispanic/Latino American community. A report by the National Council of La Raza declared that "relations between the Hispanic community and local police across the country have grown tense as the Latino population has increased both in number and as a proportion of those reporting civil rights abuses."[11] The Hispanic community experiences particular problems related to the enforcement of federal immigration laws. In addition to abuses by federal agents along the U.S.–Mexican border, Hispanics have been subject to workplace raids at places of employment across the country. In some of these incidents, local police officers have worked in cooperation with the federal Immigration and Customs Enforcement (ICE) Agency.

The Hispanic/Latino community in the United States is growing rapidly, and is now the largest minority community. In 2007 it represented 15 percent of the American population, surpassing the African American community which stood at 13.5 percent. The Hispanic/Latino community is extremely diverse, and consists of several different nationality groups, including people whose country of origin is Mexico, Puerto Rico, Cuba, Haiti, or other Central American or South American country. Each group is divided among recent immigrants and people who have resided in the United States for one or more generations, and between people who are fluent in English and people with limited or no command of English. Finally, the immigrant population is divided among documented and undocumented people.

There is no consensus on the proper label for the Hispanic/Latino community. The *2002 National Survey of Latinos* found that 34 percent preferred the term Hispanic, 13 percent preferred Latino, and half (53 percent) expressed no preference. With respect to racial identity, 55 percent of all Cuban Americans preferred to be considered "white," compared with only 17 percent of Mexican Americans. Spanish was the dominant language among 47 percent of all Latinos; 28 percent were bilingual; and for 25 percent English was the dominant language.[12]

## The Native American Community

Police–community relations problems also exist between the police and Native Americans, both in urban areas and on Native American reservations. Special problems exist with respect to Native American reservations that are served by tribal police departments. A Justice Department report found that crime rates are much higher on reservations than in the general American population. Many tribal police departments are understaffed and lack sufficient equipment and resources to provide adequate police protection on reservations that encompass large geographic areas. In addition, there are often jurisdictional problems between tribal police and local police and sheriffs' departments regarding who has authority over offenses committed on reservations by Anglo Americans.[13]

## The Asian American Community

The Asian American community is also very diverse, including people whose national origin is Japan, China, Vietnam, Laos, Cambodia, or other countries. Each national origins group is divided among long-time U.S. residents and recent immigrants, and between people who speak fluent English and people with limited or no command of English. Finally, immigrants are divided among documented and undocumented.

## The Arab American Community

Arab Americans are also an extremely diverse group, which includes people with different national origins, different languages, and different ethnic traditions. Almost half of all Arab Americans (47 percent) trace their background to Lebanon, 15 percent to Syria, and 9 percent to Egypt. Most Arab Americans are native-born Americans, and an estimated 82 percent are American citizens. In terms of religion, many are Muslim, but others are Christian or members of other religious groups. The U.S. Census Bureau classifies Arab Americans as "white" or "caucasian." There is no definitive estimate of the Arab American population, however.[14]

## The Police and Recent Immigrants

Immigration and the increasing number of people whose primary language is not English pose special challenges for the police and the rest of the criminal justice system. A National Institute of Justice survey found that immigrants report crimes at lower rates than other Americans. As a result, many offenders remain unpunished and many victims are vulnerable to repeat victimization. Language and cultural barriers make it difficult for many immigrants to contact and communicate with officials, in addition to difficulties understanding the criminal justice system.[15]

How different immigrant groups relate to the police and to crime problems depends in part on how well they are assimilated into the local political power structure. A survey of six racial and ethnic groups in New York City found significant differences in how they respond to an incident of family violence, for example. Among Dominicans and Colombians, about 80 percent said they would be "very likely" to report it to the police. Only 66 percent of African Americans and 65 percent of Asian Indians said they would report it. There were similar differences in the likelihood of reporting a break-in or a drug sale. The key factor in explaining these differences was the degree to which a group had a sense of community empowerment. Members of groups were more likely to report a crime if they believed their racial or ethnic community "was likely to work together to solve local problems" and also if they believed their community had political power. Feelings of powerlessness reduced the likelihood of reporting crimes. In short, racial and ethnic groups have very different experiences in this country, and these differences explain how they relate to the police.[16]

Police departments are responding to the changing demographics of their communities in different ways. One of the most important is ensuring that officers can communicate with people who do not speak English. Some police departments, for example, offer incentive pay to bilingual officers. The National Crime Prevention Council, meanwhile, urges police departments to hire officers from recently arrived immigrant groups who can serve as liaisons between the police and newly arrived ethnic communities.[17]

Some departments offer training in "street Spanish" to equip their officers with the basic words and phrases necessary for police work. As mentioned in Chapter 7, departments have the option of subscribing to 911 translation services to handle calls from people who speak different languages. Citizen oversight agencies publish informational material and complaint forms in various languages for people who want to file a complaint against a police officer. The Seattle Office of Professional Accountability publishes brochures in eight languages other than English, including Spanish, Korean, and Arabic, on how to file a complaint against a police officer.[18]

To help overcome communications problems, the Charlotte-Mecklenburg, North Carolina, police department created a special International Unit to help the department respond more effectively to all the new immigrant groups in the community, which include Hispanic, Hmong, Vietnamese, and Asian Indians.[19]

## Not Just Race and Ethnicity: Gender and Sexual Preference

Police–community relations problems also exist with regard to other groups in society, particularly women, gay men, lesbians, and transgendered persons. With regard to women, there is a specific problem of some police officers targeting young women for traffic stops as a form of harassment. With regard to gay men, lesbians, and transgendered persons, the problem is one of disrespect and physical abuse.[20]

## Discrimination versus Disparity

**discrimination**

**disparity**

PCR issues involve allegations of discrimination against racial and ethnic minority groups. **Discrimination** is defined as *differential treatment* based on some extralegal category such as race, ethnicity, or gender. If an employer refuses to hire members of a certain ethnic group, for example, that represents discrimination. **Disparity,** on the other hand, refers to *different outcomes* that are not necessarily caused by differential

---

**E X H I B I T   1 2 – 2**

**Discrimination–Disparity Continuum**

| Systematic Discrimination | Institutionalized Discrimination | Contextual Discrimination | Individual Acts of Discrimination | Pure Justice |
|---|---|---|---|---|

**Definitions**

*Systematic discrimination*—Discrimination at all stages of the criminal justice system, at all times, and in all places.

*Institutionalized discrimination*—Racial and ethnic disparities in outcomes that are the result of the application of racially neutral factors such as prior criminal record, employment status, demeanor, etc.

*Contextual discrimination*—Discrimination found in particular contexts or circumstances (e.g., certain regions, particular crimes, special victim–offender relationships).

*Individual acts of discrimination*—Discrimination that results from the acts of particular individuals but is not characteristic of entire agencies or the criminal justice system as a whole.

*Pure justice*—No racial or ethnic discrimination at all.

*Source:* Samuel Walker, Cassia Spohn, and Miriam DeLone, *The Color of Justice: Race, Ethnicity, and Crime in America,* 4th ed. (Belmont, CA: Wadsworth, 2007), p. 19.

---

treatment. Most college students, for example, are between the age of eighteen and early twenties. This is not the result of discrimination, but because of the normal life course: younger people have not completed high school, and middle-aged people have either finished college or do not plan to attend.

There are different forms and degrees of discrimination. Exhibit 12–2 represents the discrimination–disparity continuum developed by Walker, Spohn, and DeLone.

# A Contextual Approach to Police–Citizen Interactions

Interactions between police and citizens occur in different contexts. A contextual approach helps us to understand the complexity of policing in America. Experiences with the police vary according to the department, the type of police action (e.g., traffic stop, use of deadly force), the departmental unit involved (patrol, gang unit, traffic unit), and so on.[21]

Some departments have better relations with people of color minority communities than others. In some departments, community policing officers may have good relations with the people, while special units such as gang or drug units have very bad relations because they use aggressive tactics. In short, what is true for one context may not be true in a different one.

The most serious examples of racial profiling that have been documented involve traffic stops by state police officers on interstate highways in Maryland and New Jersey. Additionally, the pattern of stops in these cases appears directly related to drug enforcement. This evidence lends support to the contextual approach to police–citizen interactions: the argument that interactions are different according to location, police unit, enforcement activity, and so on. This approach holds that police–community relations problems will also be concentrated in certain contexts.

# Public Opinion and the Police

Many national and local public opinion surveys of attitudes toward the police have been conducted since the 1960s (see Exhibit 12–3). Attitudes have been remarkably stable over time, with data not changing significantly in forty years.[22] Surveys consistently find that most Americans are satisfied with the police in their communities. In 2008, 88 percent of all Americans reported to have a "great deal" or "some" confidence in the police. This represented 91 percent of white Americans and 75 percent of African Americans. Negative attitudes toward the police are concentrated among particular groups of people or involve particular issues, such as the use of force.[23]

## Race and Ethnicity

There are significant differences in the attitudes of different racial and ethnic groups toward the police. In the 2008 survey, 25 percent of African Americans had little

## EXHIBIT 12–3

### Attitudes Toward the Police, 2008
### Reported Confidence in the Police, 2008

| Demographic Characteristic | Great Deal/ Quite a Lot | Some | Very Little | None |
|---|---|---|---|---|
| **Race** | | | | |
| White | 62% | 29% | 8% | 1% |
| Nonwhite | 47 | 34 | 14 | 3 |
| Black | 36 | 39 | 21 | 4 |
| **Sex** | | | | |
| Male | 66 | 22 | 8 | 2 |
| Female | 50 | 38 | 11 | 1 |
| **Age** | | | | |
| 18–29 years | 61 | 20 | 16 | 1 |
| 30–49 | 58 | 33 | 7 | 1 |
| 50–64 | 57 | 31 | 9 | 2 |
| 65 and older | 56 | 31 | 11 | 1 |
| **Education** | | | | |
| College post-graduate | 65 | 29 | 6 | 0 |
| College graduate | 64 | 30 | 5 | 1 |
| Some college | 65 | 24 | 9 | 1 |
| High school graduate or less | 47 | 36 | 13 | 2 |
| **Income** | | | | |
| $75,000 and over | 66 | 27 | 6 | 0 |
| $30,000–$49,999 | 59 | 30 | 9 | 1 |
| Under $20,000 | 47 | 30 | 16% | 7 |

*Source:* Adapted from 2008 Gallup Poll, conducted June 9–12, 2008. N = 822 adults, 18 years of age or older. Available in *Sourcebook of Criminal Justice Statistics,* Table 2.12 2008.

to no confidence in the police compared with only 9 percent of whites. These data have hardly changed since the 1960s. Surveys have consistently found that the attitudes of Hispanics fall somewhere between those of whites and African Americans. Unfortunately, earlier surveys did not include a separate category for Hispanics, and some surveys still do not.[24]

There are also important differences within racial and ethnic communities, however. In a study of five different neighborhoods in Miami, Dunham and Alpert found that attitudes about the police role vary according to social class as well as by race and ethnicity. Thus, middle-class and lower-class African Americans do not share identical attitudes.[25]

In 2001, the Phoenix police department conducted a special survey among new immigrants in the community. The "Hablenos Con Confianza" (Call Us With Confidence) survey found that among those who had some contact with the Phoenix police department, 64 percent regarded it as positive and 36 percent as a negative experience. One-third (34%) did not know how to report a crime to the police. One-third (33%) thought the Phoenix police department was the same as the federal Immigration and Naturalization Service (now Immigration Control and Enforcement, or ICE). Among those surveyed, 19 percent said they were afraid of the Phoenix police, 71 percent said they trusted the Phoenix police, and 62 percent said that language was a problem when they call the Phoenix police.[26]

## Attitudes about Police Use of Force

**attitudes about force**

The greatest gap between the attitudes of whites, Hispanics, and African Americans exists with regard to police use of force. As Exhibit 12–4 indicates, Hispanics and African Americans are twice as likely to believe the police will use excessive force *in their communities*.

In a survey of Cincinnati residents, 46.6 percent of African Americans indicated they had been personally "hassled" by the police, compared with only 9.6 percent of whites. Hassled was defined as being "stopped or watched closely by a police officer, even when you had done nothing wrong." Additionally, 66 percent of African Americans reported that someone they knew had been hassled, compared with only 12.5 of whites.[27] Among many African American families there is much fear of the police. A *New York Times* article in 1997 described how some African American and Hispanic parents made a special effort to teach their children to be very respectful of police

---

### EXHIBIT 12–4

**Attitudes Regarding Police Use of Force, 2008**

**How Much Confidence Do You Have that the Police in Your Community Will NOT Use Excessive Force, 2008?**

|  | A Great Deal/A Fair Amount | Just Some/Very Little |
|---|---|---|
| **Whites** | 73 | 21 |
| **Hispanics** | 46 | 47 |
| **Blacks** | 38 | 48 |

*Source:* Mark Hugo Lopez, et al., *Hispanics and the Criminal Justice System: Low Confidence, High Exposure* (Los Angeles: Pew Hispanic Center, 2008).

officers, primarily because they were afraid their children might be arrested, beaten, or even shot if they displayed any disrespect to an officer.[28]

## Social Class

To a great extent race and social class interact to affect perceptions and experience with the police. In 2008, 23 percent of people with incomes below $20,000 had little to no confidence in the police, compared with only 6 to 7 percent of people with incomes of $50,000 or greater.

Weitzer interviewed 169 residents of Washington DC, representing three neighborhoods: one middle-class white, one middle-class African American, and one lower-income African American. The residents of the lower-income African American neighborhood were seven times more likely than residents of the black middle-class neighborhood to believe that the police stop people on the street in their neighborhood without good reason, and three times more likely than residents of the white middle-class neighborhood to believe this. Also, half (49 percent) of the residents of the lower-income African American neighborhood reported having seen the police use excessive force in their neighborhood, while none of the residents of the white middle-class neighborhood reported seeing excessive force incidents.[29]

## Age: Young People and the Police

"They judge people by how old they are," argued one Chicago high school student. "They think all teenagers are bad." Another charged that "they judge people by the way they look." A white female student added, "Just because you have a different color skin, or hair, or wear bizarre clothes doesn't mean you are a criminal."[30]

Age consistently ranks second to race and ethnicity as a factor in public attitudes toward the police. The 2008 survey found that 17 percent of people between the ages of 18 and 29 had little to no confidence in the police, compared with only 8 percent of people between 30 and 49. (Lack of confidence in the police increased among the elderly, however.)

## Other Demographic Factors

*Where You Live: Neighborhood Quality of Life.*    The quality of life in a neighborhood plays a major role in shaping attitudes toward the police. People who believe the police are effective in controlling crime in their neighborhood have greater confidence in the police. This is true for all racial and ethnic groups. People who feel safer in their neighborhood have more positive attitudes toward the police compared with people who feel less safe.[31]

*Crime Victimization.*    Victims of crime consistently rate the police less favorably than do people who have not been victimized.

*Gender.*    Previous surveys have generally found little difference in the attitudes of men and women toward the police. The 2008 Gallup Poll (Exhibit 12–3), however, indicates significantly less confidence in the police among women compared with

## Police–Community Relations in the Context of Professor Henry Gates Arrest

For the first time in American history, a president of the United States commented on a case of alleged police misconduct.

On July 16, 2009, Lucia Whalen called the Cambridge, Massachusetts, police and informed them an elderly woman who lived on the street had told her that she was worried about a possible burglary taking place across the street. She stated, "I don't know if they live there or they just had a hard time with their key," and then added that the men had suitcases. Ms. Whalen did not bring up the issue of race until probed by the dispatcher and then said "one looked kind of Hispanic, but I'm not rally sure."[1] Sgt. Crowley, who was white, arrived at the scene to respond to the report of a possible break in and arrested Mr. Gates, who was an African American professor at Harvard University, for disorderly conduct. The charges were dropped a few days later.

When President Barack Obama commented at a press conference that the officer acted "stupidly," controversy over the incident escalated into a major political issue.

In the police report, Sgt. Crowley wrote that he explained to Mr. Gates that there was a call about a possible break in and he requested that he step outside so that Crowley could speak with him and determine his identity. Crowley then wrote that Mr. Gates refused to step outside and demanded to know who the officer was. Sgt. Crowley stated that Mr. Gates then became uncooperative, yelled at him, and called him a racist; and as a consequence he arrested him for disorderly conduct.[2] Mr. Gates refuted the officer's allegations and said that he had returned home from a trip to China and his taxi driver had difficulty opening a jammed front door.[3] Upon being confronted by the officer he showed him his university ID. He stated that he was treated unfairly and that he was victim of racial profiling.[4]

As a class, review newspaper articles and read the police incident report at http://i.cdn.turner.com/cnn/2009/images/07/23/0498.001.pdf to learn more about the incident. Then discuss the elements of the case that might have contributed to the arrest.

What are the facts of the case, as we know them?

Did the woman who called the police act responsibly?

Did the officer act improperly?

Was Professor Gates' conduct reprehensible?

Should the President have commended on this case?

Was this a case of racial profiling?

What does the case say about police and race relations in America today?

[1]Adapted from Simmi Aujla Police release audio in Gates case. The Wall Street Journal access at http://sbk.online.wsj.com/article/SB124870309847783787.html on July 28, 2009.
[2]Adapted from John Hechinger and Simmi Aujla, Police chief responds to Obama's remark. The Wall Street Journal. Accessed at http://online.wsj.com/article/SB124839661684677777.html on July 28, 2009.
[3]Adapted from John Hechinger and Simmi Aujla, Police chief responds to Obama's remark. The Wall Street Journal. Accessed at http://online-wsj.com/article/SB124839661684677777.html on July 28, 2009.
[4]Wayne Drash, The "unfathomable" arrest of a black scholar. CNN.COM Accessed at http://edition.cnn.com/2009/US/07/22/gates.arrest.reaction/index.html on July 28, 2009.

men. It is not clear if this is an anomaly related to this survey or an indication of a shift in public attitudes.

***Level of Education.***    People with only a high school education or less consistently rate the police less favorably that people with some college or more education. In 2008, 15 percent of people with only a high school education had little confidence in the police, compared with 6 percent of college graduates.

## Community Policing

Community policing has a positive impact on citizens' attitudes toward the police. In a national survey, Ronald Weitzer and Steven Tuch found that people who believe their police department engages in community policing in their neighborhood are less likely to believe that the police use excessive force. (The study investigated only perceptions, and we don't know whether the police actually engaged in community policing in particular neighborhoods.)[32] Skogan and Hartnett found that community policing affected citizens' attitudes toward the Chicago police in a positive direction. African Americans and whites who lived in districts where community policing existed were less likely to believe that the police stopped too many people or that the use of excessive force was a problem.[33]

## Intercity Variations

There are significant variations in how the residents of different cities rate their police. The 1998 Bureau of Justice Statistics survey found that 93 percent of San Diego residents were satisfied with their police, compared with only 80 percent of Chicago residents and 78 percent of Washington DC residents. The survey also found that the attitudes of whites and African Americans parallel each other. Both groups rated the San Diego police very high, and both groups rated the Chicago and Washington DC police relatively low.[34] In short, there are important differences in public attitudes among cities that apparently reflect differences in the activities and reputations of these departments.

***The Case of Detroit.***    The major exception to the general patterns of attitudes toward the police by race is found in a survey of Detroit residents. Contrary to all prior research, more African Americans (71.8 percent) indicated they were satisfied with the police than whites (52.8 percent). The study explained this result in terms of African American domination of the local political establishment. An African American has been mayor of Detroit since 1973, and a majority of the police force is African American. Thus, African Americans are more likely than whites to identify positively with the police and other parts of the political system.[35]

## The Impact of Controversial Incidents

George Holliday never imagined that he would make the most famous videotape in the history of the police. A little after midnight on March 3, 1991, he was awakened by the noise of a police siren and screeching tires. Looking out the window, he saw an incredible scene of a white Hyundai surrounded by six police cars, all illuminated by the light from a police helicopter. Holliday got his brand new video camera and taped police officers repeatedly beating Rodney King. The tape was soon shown on television around the world, setting off a chain of events that included two criminal trials, a major riot (1992), and an independent investigation of the Los Angeles police department. This one event had a significant impact on public attitudes about the police, in Los Angeles, the United States, and the rest of the world.[36]

Public attitudes are affected by controversial incidents such as the Rodney King beating. Tuch and Weitzer found that it had a dramatic short-term effect on attitudes toward the Los Angeles police department. Prior to the incident about 70 percent of whites consistently indicated they approved of the way the LAPD did its job. From March 1991 through May 1992, responses fell into the 40 percent range. By 1993, however, responses of whites had returned to the 70 percent range. The percentage of African Americans approving of the LAPD fell even more dramatically (to only 14 percent in late March 1991). They eventually returned to previous levels but at a slower rate than for whites.[37]

# Complex Dimensions of Trust and Confidence in the Police

Trust and confidence in the police are very complex phenomena. Surveys that frame the issue in a single question (e.g., "How much confidence do you have ....") fail to capture all the different dimensions. Sara Stoutland conducted a series of focus groups and individual interviews with both residents and professional youth workers in high-crime neighborhoods in Boston, and identified four separate **dimensions of trust** in the police.[38]

**dimensions of trust**

---

**SIDEBAR 12 – 2**

## Stoutland's Dimensions of Trust

**Trust dimension 1: *Priorities.*** Do people feel that the police share their concerns about the neighborhood? Stoutland's focus groups found that many residents feel they do not, and believe the police concentrate too narrowly on short-term crime reduction rather than broader quality-of-life issues.

**Trust dimension 2: *Competence.*** Do people feel the police have the knowledge and skills to achieve their objectives? Most of the focus group participants who had noticed increased police crime-fighting efforts felt it had reduced drug-related crime.

**Trust dimension 3: *Dependability.*** Do people feel the police can be counted on to fulfill their promises? With respect to drug-related crime, most focus group participants believe the police can be depended on to follow through on their promise to reduce crime.

**Trust dimension 4: *Respect.*** Do people feel that the police treat them respectfully? Lack of respect from the police was one of the strongest themes to emerge from the focus groups. Many participants expressed anger at the way they felt the police treat them. In addition to rudeness, some participants felt the police fail to respond when called about an incident in the neighborhood. Finally, many participants felt that the police violated their rights, and in particular harassed young people.

---

One of Stoutland's most important findings is the distinction between people's feelings about police competence and their feelings about police respect for citizens. Many recognized that the police had to act in certain ways in order to fight crime, but they did not like the way the police acted in doing so. Specifically, they saw a need for the police to stop and interrogate people on the street, but they did not like the disrespectful way the police handled these stops.

**procedural justice**
Stoutland's findings are consistent with the theory of **procedural justice.** This theory holds that people distinguish between the outcomes (the grade you received in class) and the process (Did the teacher explain why you received a low grade on your term paper?). Studies consistently find that even when the outcome is unfavorable, people are more likely to be satisfied if the official explains the basis for the action. For example, a driver is less likely to be unhappy with the police if the officer explains why he or she was stopped. And drivers are likely to be unhappy if the officer explains nothing.

Skogan's study of people who had been stopped by the police showed that peoples' attitudes toward the police were much more favorable among those people who felt that officers treated them *fairly* and if the officers *explained* the situation to them, were *polite,* and *paid attention* to what they said. Skogan also found racial and ethnic differences in citizen perceptions. African Americans and Spanish-speaking Latinos, for example, were far less likely to say that the police explained the reason why they had been stopped. Less than half of the African Americans and Latinos thought the police were polite, and both groups were more likely to say the police treated them unfairly.[39]

The different dimensions of trust and confidence in the police, and particularly the aspect of procedural justice, are key elements in the legitimacy of the police (see p. 413).

# Three Perspectives on Attitudes toward the Police

## The Police and the Larger Society

Attitudes toward the police do not necessarily reflect personal experience with or even perceptions of a local police department. Albrecht and Green argue that attitudes toward the police reflect a broader set of attitudes toward society, government, and the criminal justice system. People who express the greatest dissatisfaction with the police also have the most negative attitudes toward courts and judges. They are more alienated from society and participate less in politics than people with more favorable attitudes toward the police.[40]

Public attitudes about the police reflect the symbolic role of the police as the agents of authority who represent the coercive power of the state. The badge, baton, and gun are the visible reminders of the police officer's power to use force, which Bittner argues is the defining aspect of the police role. Blumberg argues that the police are a "social lightning rod" for public attitudes about other social and political issues, while Niederhoffer calls the police officer a "Rorschach in uniform"—someone onto whom people project their fears and fantasies.[41] Thus, people who are the victims of discrimination, or who feel powerless or alienated from society, are likely to have more negative attitudes toward the police than people who feel powerful and integrated.

**EXHIBIT 12–5**

### Ratings of Honesty and Ethical Standards of Occupations, 2005

| Occupation | Percentage of Americans Rating It "Very High" or "High" |
|---|---|
| Nurses | 82 |
| Medical doctors | 65 |
| High school teachers | 64 |
| Police | 61 |
| Clergy | 54 |
| Bankers | 41 |
| Journalists | 28 |
| Lawyers | 18 |
| Car salespersons | 8 |

*Source:* Bureau of Justice Statistics, *Sourcebook of Criminal Justice Statistics, 2005* (Washington DC: Department of Justice, 2005), Table 2.17. Available at www.albany.edu/sourcebook/.

## The Police and Other Occupations

If you do a Web search for "lawyer jokes," you will quickly find many jokes. In addition, you will find several general humor sites that have a lawyer jokes category. Lawyer jokes are very popular. Most of them characterize lawyers as unethical, amoral, and greedy. Lawyer jokes may be even more common than jokes about police officers sitting in donut shops.

Despite the fact that many police officers believe they do not get adequate respect from the public, the police compare very favorably with other occupations in terms of public attitudes. As Exhibit 12–5 indicates, the police rank fairly high with regard to perceptions of their honesty and ethical standards.

## The Police in Other Countries

American police officers may complain about a lack of public respect, but they are doing very well compared with their peers in other countries. A United Nations survey found that among American, European, and Asian countries, American police enjoyed the highest level of confidence that they were doing a good job in controlling crime (Exhibit 12–6).

## Summary of Attitudes toward the Police

The available data allow us to draw several conclusions about public attitudes toward the police: (1) the vast majority of Americans have a positive attitude toward the police; (2) racial and ethnic minorities consistently rate the police less favorably than whites; (3) a majority of African Americans and Hispanics, however, give the police a generally favorable rating; (4) young people rate the police less favorably than older people; (5) poor people, less educated people, and crime victims tend to rate the police lower than other Americans rate them; (6) people who feel their

## EXHIBIT 12-6

### Confidence That the Police Are Doing a Good Job in Controlling Crime

| | |
|---|---|
| United States | 89% |
| Canada | 87 |
| New Zealand | 79 |
| Austria | 76 |
| Australia | 76 |
| United Kingdom | 72 |
| Norway | 70 |
| Japan | 69 |
| Italy | 54 |

*Source:* United Nations, *International Crime Victims Survey, 2000.* www.uncjin.org.

neighborhood is safe view the police more favorably than people who do not feel safe; (7) community policing has a positive effect on citizen attitudes toward the police; (8) there are significant differences in opinions about the police among different cities; (9) people make important distinctions regarding police actions (Are they competent? Do they treat people with respect?); and (10) attitudes toward the police reflect attitudes toward society as a whole.

These findings support the contextual interpretation of police–community relations. That is, while the police get favorable ratings from the general population, they are rated much less favorably by certain segments of the population: racial and ethnic minorities, low-income minorities in particular, and poor young male minorities especially.

## Police Perceptions of Citizens

The Rand Corporation asked Cincinnati police officers if "citizens on the street act disrespectfully" toward them. Half of the officers responded that half or more citizens do. Yet, when asked if suspects forcibly resisted being arrested, only 7 percent said "usually." The police perception of public hostility is far greater than the actual experience of physical challenges to their authority.[42]

The former police commander in a high-crime racial minority neighborhood in St. Louis made several racial references to "those people" and "that group." The department adopted community policing, and he was transferred to another assignment and replaced by a new captain. Several rank-and-file officers assigned to that neighborhood, meanwhile, talked about the need for "kick ass" policing, where officers were free to "take down" the "shit heads" who are criminals and troublemakers.[43] These views reflect the hostile attitudes some police officers develop toward the neighborhoods where they work.

Police officers generally do not have an accurate perception of public attitudes toward them. James Q. Wilson argues that police officers "probably exaggerate the extent of citizen hostility."[44] In his pioneering work on the police subculture,

William A. Westley found that 73 percent of the officers thought that the public was "against the police, or hates the police." Only 12 percent thought that the public "likes the police."[45]

## Sources of Police Attitudes

Police officer misperception of public attitudes is the result of several factors. Most important is the pattern of **selective contact** between police and public. Officers do not have regular contact with a cross section of the community. An analysis of police emergency (911) calls in Minneapolis found that 5 percent of the addresses in the city generated 64 percent of all the calls.[46] A Bureau of Justice Services survey estimates that only 21 percent of all Americans have a face-to-face encounter with a police officer each year.[47] Low-income people and racial minorities, moreover, have a disproportionate level of contact with the police. Police departments deploy more patrol officers in their neighborhoods because of higher crime levels, and they are more likely than other Americans to call the police. Finally, the police have relatively more contact with low-income young males who use public places as their recreation spots.[48]

selective contact

In addition to selective contact, police officer attitudes are shaped by **selective perception.** Most contacts between citizens and the police are civil. Only about 2 to 5 percent involve hostility or conflict. Like most people, however, police officers are more likely to remember unpleasant or traumatic events.[49] Black found that young African American men were more likely than young white men to express hostility to the police. Consequently, officers tend to stereotype young African American males in terms of what Skolnick called the "symbolic assailant" and a potential source of conflict.[50]

selective perception

# Sources of Police–Community Relations Problems

The public opinion poll data raise a number of important questions. How do we explain the apparent contradiction between the generally favorable ratings given the police by racial and ethnic minority communities and the persistence of public conflict between the police and these groups? Is it simply because the media exaggerate a small number of bad incidents? Or are there systematic problems affecting racial and ethnic minorities? One way to answer these questions is to examine specific aspects of policing: (1) the level of police protection received by different neighborhoods; (2) police officer field practices; (3) administrative practices; and (4) employment practices.

# Level of Police Protection

## Too Much or Too Little Law Enforcement?

Do the police provide too much or too little enforcement in African American and Hispanic neighborhoods? Residents voice complaints on both sides of the issue. Many young African Americans complain of harassment by overly aggressive police tactics. At the same time, many residents of the same neighborhoods complain about inadequate police protection. Where does the truth lie?

**four systems of justice**

Historically, African Americans were the victims of underenforcement of the law. Gunnar Myrdal's classic study of race relations in America found that during the period of institutionalized segregation in the South, the police disregarded many crimes in the African American community. The result was **four systems of justice,** depending on the racial components of the offender/victim relationship: (1) crimes by whites against whites were handled as "normal" crimes; (2) crimes by whites against African Americans were rarely prosecuted, if at all; (3) crimes by African Americans against whites received the harshest response; and (4) crimes by African Americans against African Americans were often ignored.[51]

Failure to enforce the law in minority neighborhoods has often involved crimes of vice. Historically, gambling, after-hours drinking, prostitution, and drugs were allowed to exist in low-income and racial minority neighborhoods. A 1986 survey of attitudes in Philadelphia found that 65 percent of Hispanic residents believed that the police underenforced gambling laws, compared with 55 percent of African Americans and 46 percent of white Philadelphians.[52]

Tolerating vice crimes harms low-income and racial-minority communities in several ways. First, it breeds disrespect for the law and the police, partly because of the corruption that usually accompanies it. The Knapp Commission investigation of police corruption in New York City found that the monthly vice payoffs to police in the predominantly African American areas of Harlem averaged $1,500, compared with $300 in predominantly white downtown precincts.[53]

Second, underenforcement of the law exposes law-abiding citizens in minority communities to criminal activity: prostitution, drug dealing, and secondary crimes such as shootings and robberies that often accompany them. These crimes expose individuals and their families to personal risk and lower the quality of life in the neighborhood. Exposure to criminal activity increases the risk that juveniles will engage in crime themselves.

Studies investigating the assignment of patrol officers by neighborhoods have generally found no pattern of racial bias. Almost all departments today assign patrol officers on the basis of official crime rates and calls for service (see Chapter 7).[54] A police department that uses the standard workload formula for assigning patrol officers (see Chapter 7) will generally assign more officers to minority neighborhoods.

The result is that, as Bayley and Mendelsohn reported forty years ago, "the police seem to play a role in the life of minority people out of all proportion to the role they play in the lives of the dominant white majority."[55] History weighs heavily on police–community relations. In a survey of Washington DC residents, Weitzer, Tuch and Skogan argue that "For African Americans—much more so than for whites—police misconduct is not an abstraction; on the contrary, it is an issue that resonates powerfully because of African Americans' long history of conflict with the police."[56]

The crucial question is what the police *do* and whether they treat minorities differently with regard to stops and frisks, arrest, and other police actions.

Weitzer and Tuch found that whites, African Americans, and Hispanics all express strong support for more police patrol and surveillance of high-crime areas. All three groups, however, are much less supportive of stopping and searching people.[57] Their findings are consistent with Stoutland's findings (pp. 383–384) that people distinguish between what the police do (aggressive crime fighting) and how they treat people (e.g., respectfully and fairly). For the police to develop legitimacy, they have to be both effective and respectful.

## Delay in Responding to Calls

Several studies of police work found that patrol officers often deliberately delayed responding to calls for service, especially in the case of family disturbances.[58]

Furstenburg and Wellford's interviews with citizens in Baltimore who had called the police found that black citizens perceived greater delays than whites. A higher percentage of whites reported the police responding in less than five minutes, while nearly twice as many blacks as whites reported that the police took more than 15 minutes to respond. A recent study of a high-crime, predominantly African American neighborhood in St. Louis found that "most complaints about policing . . . centered around poor police response." This included delayed response time and complete failure to respond to a 911 call.[59]

---

# Police Field Practices

Police field practices are the greatest source of tensions between the police and racial minorities. This category includes actions by individual police officers such as use of deadly force, physical force, arrests, stops and frisks, and verbal abuse.

## Deadly Force

Edward Garner was a slightly built, 110-pound, 15-year-old African American on October 3, 1974, but his name is now one of the most famous in criminal justice history. Garner was shot and killed by two Memphis, Tennessee, police officers while fleeing a suspected burglary. He did have a stolen purse, containing $10, in his possession. A lawsuit brought by his family eventually reached the U.S. Supreme Court and addressed the issue of whether the police were justified in shooting him for that suspected offense. The Court ruled in *Tennessee v. Garner* (1985), that the **fleeing-felon rule,** under which the Memphis officers acted, was unconstitutional. The decision accelerated the trend toward adoption of the **defense-of-life standard,** which greatly restricts the use of deadly force by police officers.[60]

**fleeing-felon rule**

**defense-of-life standard**

The use of deadly force has been the source of major conflict between minorities and the police. James Fyfe concluded that "blacks and Hispanics are everywhere overrepresented among those on the other side of police guns."[61] One of the most controversial incidents in the 1990s was the fatal shooting of Amadou Diallo by New York City police officers (and the subsequent acquittal of officers on criminal charges). Diallo was unarmed and apparently reaching for his wallet when he was shot. This shooting, together with other incidents of police misconduct, created a strong feeling among many minorities in the city that they were the target of systematic police abuse.[62]

Police use of deadly force has changed significantly over the past forty years. In the 1960s and 1970s, the ratio of African Americans to whites shot and killed by the police was as high as 6 to 1, or even 8 to 1. The disparity between whites and

African Americans, moreover, has been greatest among unarmed people—usually defined as fleeing felons. Between 1969 and 1974 Memphis police officers shot and killed thirteen unarmed and nonassaultive African Americans, but only one white person in that category.[63] Many of the riots of the 1960s were sparked by the shooting of an African American male by a white police officer (see Chapter 2).

Since the 1960s and early 1970s, the number of police shootings has declined. The major reason is that the old fleeing-felon rule, which allowed the police to shoot unarmed suspects, has been replaced by the more restrictive defense-of-life rule as a result of the U.S. Supreme Court ruling in the 1985 *Tennessee v. Garner* case. Many departments had already adopted the defense-of-life rule on their own. Fyfe found that adoption of the defense-of-life standard by the New York City police in 1972 reduced the average number of shots fired by 30 percent. The greatest reduction occurred in fleeing-felon situations.[64]

In Memphis, the introduction of a restrictive shooting policy eliminated all shootings in the unarmed and nonassaultive category, greatly reducing the racial disparity in persons shot and killed in the process. As many police departments also adopted restrictive policies, the total number of persons shot and killed per year fell significantly between the 1960s and 1980s. Even more important, the ratio of African Americans to whites shot and killed fell from 8 to 1 to 4 to 1 in that period. The data suggest that permissive shooting policies permit racially prejudiced attitudes to affect shootings, while restrictive policies, by controlling discretion, curb the impact of personal attitudes.[65] (See Chapter 11 for a discussion of the control of discretion related to deadly force.)

The important question is whether the current disparity between African Americans and whites shot and killed represents *systematic* discrimination (Exhibit 12–2), or whether it is *contextual* discrimination (e.g., certain departments), or *individual* discrimination (e.g., particular officers). Some analysts argue that the proper standard involves the number of persons in each racial and ethnic group who are at risk of a shooting incident. "At risk" may be defined in terms of involvement in serious crime. Geller and Karales examined shootings by Chicago police between 1974 and 1978. They found that African Americans were shot and killed six times as often as whites in terms of their presence in the total population. When they controlled for participation in violent crimes, however, the disparity disappeared. Whites were shot and killed at a rate of 5.6 per 1,000 arrests for forcible felonies, compared with 4.5 blacks shot per 1,000 arrests for the same category of crime.[66]

## Use of Physical Force

police brutality

Allegations of **police brutality,** defined as the use of excessive physical force by the police, represent the most common complaint voiced by minorities about the police. The videotaped beating of Rodney King in 1991 by Los Angeles police officers provided dramatic visual evidence of this problem.[67]

The issue of excessive physical force is particularly complex. Police officers are authorized by law to use force in certain situations: to protect themselves, to effect an arrest, to overcome resistance, and to bring a dangerous situation under control. The relevant question is, When is the use of force excessive? The CALEA accreditation standards state that officers "will use only the force necessary to accomplish lawful

**EXHIBIT 12-7**

## Citizen Contacts with Police, and Police Use of Force, 2002

| | | |
|---|---|---|
| Total U.S. Population (age 16 and over) | 215,536,800 | |
| Contact with police | 45,278,900 | (21% of population) |
|    Motor vehicle stop | 16,783,500 | |
|    Other contact | 8,495,400 | |
| Use of force by police | 664,502 | (1.5% of all contacts) |

Source: Bureau of Justice Statistics, *Contacts between Police and the Public: Findings from the 2002 National Survey* (Washington DC: Government Printing Office, 2004).

objectives." Excessive force is any level of force more than is necessary to fulfill a lawful objective.[68] A police officer is not justified in using physical force in response to mere disrespect, for example.

The determination of whether a certain level of force is necessary in a particular situation frequently reflects conflicting perceptions of whether a person was resisting arrest, or whether he or she posed a threat to the safety of the officer.[69] Police departments have adopted a *use of force continuum,* indicating the different levels of force appropriate for particular situations (Exhibit 12–5).

Police use of force is a statistically infrequent event. The Bureau of Justice Statistics surveyed more than 60,000 people in 2005 and found that police officers used or threatened some kind of force in 1.6 percent of all encounters with citizens.[70] Other studies have reached estimates of about 1 percent. Among all uses of force, about two-thirds are justified, given the circumstances, and about one-third are unjustified or excessive. Thus, police use excessive force in an estimated one-third of 1 percent (0.3 percent) of all encounters with citizens.[71]

Many people reject the 1 percent estimate and believe that the real incidence is much higher. The 1 percent estimate acquires a different meaning when examined more closely. The Bureau of Justice Statistics estimate of 707,520 force incidents per year translates into 1,938 per day. If we accept the conservative estimate that one-third involve excessive or unjustified use of force, the result is about 646 excessive force incidents every day of the year across the country. If we further assume that most of these incidents occur in the cities, the result is a large number of annual incidents in every city.

Moreover, as Reiss points out, use of force incidents accumulate over time with the result that "a sizeable minority of citizens experience police misconduct at one time or another."[72] And since most force incidents involve young, low-income men, with a disproportionate representation of racial and ethnic minorities, this group of people will have a very strong perception of police harassment.

## Situational Factors in the Use of Force

Police use of force is associated with certain situational factors. Officers are more likely to use force against criminal suspects (about 4 to 6 percent of all encounters with suspects). Worden's analysis of the Police Services Study (PSS) data from the 1970s found that officers were more likely to use force against male suspects, African

American males, and citizens who were drunk and antagonistic to the police. Physical resistance to a police officer significantly increased the likelihood of use of force.[73] Citizen resistance or discourtesy is highly associated with police use of force. Since officers are legally authorized to use force in certain circumstances, it is important to determine whether the officer used more force than was necessary.

To provide a meaningful analysis of police use of force, Geoffrey Alpert developed the *force factor* framework, which examines police officer behavior in relationship to the citizen's actions. If an officer used force where there was no resistance or threat on the part of the citizen, then the force would be considered excessive. Analyzing data from one police department, Alpert found that officers used more force than was indicated by citizen behavior in 19 percent of all cases and less force than was indicated in 32 percent of all cases.[74]

Many officers concede that other officers sometimes use excessive force. A national survey of police officers by the Police Foundation found that 21.7 percent agree that officers in their departments sometimes, often, or always use more force than is necessary to make an arrest. There were significant differences in the attitudes of white and African American officers in how they treat minority group citizens. Over half of the African American officers (57.1 percent) agree that officers are more likely to use physical force against blacks and other minorities than against whites in similar situations. Only 5.1 percent of the white officers agreed with that statement. African American officers also agreed more than white officers (54.4 percent versus 8.8 percent) that the police are more likely to use force against poor people than middle-class citizens.[75]

Critics of the police assume that excessive force incidents primarily involve white officer interactions with minority citizens. Reiss, however, found that white and African American officers were about equally likely to use force and were most likely to use force against members of their own race.[76] This finding is supported by citizen complaint data from San Jose and New York City, which indicate that white, African American, and Hispanic officers receive citizen complaints at rates equal to their presence on the police force.[77] In short, the use of force is primarily a function of the police role and situational factors rather than the race or ethnicity of officers.

## Use of Police Canine Units

Being bitten by a police dog is a form of police use of force. Police Canine Units have also been a police–community relations problem in some cities. Minorities believe that police dogs are used more often against them, and that they are bitten far more often than whites. The special counsel to the Los Angeles sheriff's department (LASD) found that in 1991 African Americans and Latinos were 81 percent of those bitten by the department's dogs. By 1999 the total number of bites had been reduced by 90 percent (from 58 to 5) (although all of those bitten were minorities).[78]

## Arrests

African Americans are arrested more often than whites relative to their numbers in the population. In 2007 they represented 28 percent of all arrests, 39 percent of all arrests for violent crimes, and 35 percent of all drug arrests, despite the fact that they constitute only 12 percent of the U.S. population. Arrest is an extremely common experience for young African American men in the inner city. Tillman estimates that 65.5 percent of all African American males are arrested before the age of 30, compared with 33.9 percent of white males. Meanwhile, 29.6 percent of all African American females are arrested before the age of 30, compared with only 10.1 percent of white females.[79]

Donald Black's study of arrest found that police decisions to arrest are influenced by several **situational factors** (see Chapter 11). These include (1) the strength of the evidence, (2) the seriousness of the crime, (3) the preference of the victim, (4) the **victim–suspect relationship,** and (5) the demeanor of the suspect.[80]

**situational factors**

**victim–suspect relationship**

Race was not a direct factor in arrest decisions. African Americans, however, were more likely to be disrespectful of the police and arrested for that reason.

Although the evidence is not strong, it appears that the characteristics of crime victims have some impact on the racial pattern of arrests. African American complainants request arrests more often than whites, and since most crimes are *intra*racial (the victim or complainant is the same race as the suspect), this results in more arrests of African Americans. The Police Services Study data indicate that the police are more likely to comply with the wishes of white victims when they seek the arrest of African American suspects than in other situations, particularly in property crimes.[81]

The effect of the **demeanor of the suspect** on arrests is extremely complex. Black found that African Americans were more likely to be antagonistic to the police, and more likely to be arrested for that reason. David Klinger, however, argues that these earlier studies did not control for when the antagonistic demeanor occurred. He concludes that much of it occurs after the arrest and in those instances, therefore, is a consequence and not a cause of arrest.[82]

**demeanor of the suspect**

There have been no studies, however, to determine the extent to which the demeanor of suspects is provoked by police officers. Bayley and also Mastrofski and Parks argue that police officers approach encounters with citizens with a "script" representing their preliminary perception of the situation.[83] Thus, an officer may approach an encounter with an expectation of conflict and, as a consequence, provoke a hostile response through informal cues or unconscious behavior. To the extent that officers stereotype young African American males as potential suspects,[84] they may provoke high rates of antagonistic behavior that in turn results in higher rates of arrest. New evidence suggests that both officer and citizen demeanor often changes during an encounter, and that these changes are influenced by the actions and demeanor of the other party (see Sidebar 12–3).

Several studies have found that African Americans are arrested on the basis of less stringent legal criteria than whites. Hepburn found that arrests of blacks were more likely to be declined for prosecution than arrests of whites, suggesting that the arrests were made for reasons other than law enforcement.[85] A Rand study of the criminal process in California found that African Americans were more likely to have arrest charges dropped by the police or prosecutor. Although these data might suggest greater leniency at the prosecution stage, they could also mean that African Americans were arrested on weaker evidence.[86]

The greatest racial disparities in arrest involve drug offenses. About 36 percent of all drug arrests in 2007 involved African Americans. The 2007 National Survey of

## *The Complex Dimensions of Police-Citizen Demeanor*

The patterns of demeanor of citizens and police officers are extremely complex. Dunham and Alpert point out that almost all studies measure the subjects' behavior at one point. Common sense, however, tells us that our behavior often changes in response to someone else's conduct. Dunham and Alpert confirmed this in a study of police–citizen interactions in Savannah, Georgia, where they observed the sequence of events in police–citizen encounters.

The demeanor of citizens and police officers changed in about one fourth of all encounters. With both citizens and officers, their demeanor improved (i.e., became more civil) in half the cases and changed for the worse (i.e., became less civil) in the other half. Most important, both citizen and officer demeanor changed in reaction to the demeanor or behavior of the other person.

Dunham and Alpert argue that the last point has enormous implications for police training. Officers need to be trained over how their conduct affects citizens, and taught techniques for deescalating potential confrontations and gaining cooperation. (One such technique is known as "verbal judo.") This would probably reduce the number of use-of-force incidents and citizen complaints.

*Source:* Roger G. Dunham and Geoffrey P. Alpert, "Officer and Suspect Demeanor: A Qualitative Analysis of Change," *Police Quarterly* 12 (March 2009): pp. 6–21.

Drug Use, however, estimates that the rates of illegal drug use are not that different among racial and ethnic groups, with African Americans only slightly more likely to use illegal drugs than whites, and use among Latinos lower than both of the other two groups.[87] These data suggest that the police target African Americans for drug enforcement. The National Criminal Justice Commission concludes that *"police enforcement of new drug laws . . . focus almost exclusively on low-level dealers in minority neighborhoods."*[88] (This is an example of contextual discrimination. See Exhibit 12–2.)

## Field Interrogations and Searches

An African American resident of Washington DC explained how he and his friends perceive police practices: "If they [the police] stop a white guy at three in the morning, they'll figure he was working late and he's on his way home to see his wife. [They] stop a black person at three in the morning and figure he was up to no good . . . always assuming the worst when it's someone of color."[89] The perception of harassment by the police is very strong, especially with regard to police-initiated stops on the street. These actions are referred to as pedestrian stops or field interrogations. Stops are sometimes accompanied by searches.

**field interrogations**

**Field interrogations** involve a crime control strategy of both identifying and apprehending offenders, and at the same time sending a message of deterrence to people on the street. Young racial and ethnic minority males in particular regard this practice as harassment. The President's Crime Commission found that field interrogations and "aggressive preventive patrol were a major cause of tensions between the police and minority communities."[90] In Cincinnati, 46.6 percent of African Americans reported being "hassled" by the police, compared with only 9.6 percent of whites.[91]

The most sophisticated investigation of stop and frisk practices is a study of the New York City police department by the attorney general of the state of New York. The study found, first, that African Americans were more likely to be stopped than their presence in the population would indicate. Second, to control for participation in crime, the study compared the percentage of African Americans stopped with the percentage of African Americans arrested in eight selected precincts. This analysis was based on the assumption that arrest data are a valid substitute for participation in crime (an assumption not all criminologists agree with). The study found that African Americans were stopped at a higher rate than the arrest data would predict. Third, analyzing a sample of stop and frisk reports, the study found that the police frequently lacked adequate cause for a stop. And, in fact, few stops of African Americans resulted in an arrest.[92]

## Being "Out of Place" and Getting Stopped

A white resident of Washington DC explained that "if a black person were in this neighborhood and they were walking around, the police might stop them just because of their skin color and because they look like they don't belong in the neighborhood."[93]

A number of experts believe that a certain amount of racial bias in traffic enforcement ("racial profiling") is the result of a police officer deciding that an African American or Hispanic driver is "out of place" in a white neighborhood. The officer assumes that the person does not live there and consequently must be there for some criminal purpose. (See the full discussion of racial profiling, below.)

## Discussion: Crime Fighting and Stereotyping

Traffic stops and field interrogations illustrate one of the major conflicts over goals in policing. The police regard these practices as a legitimate and effective crime-fighting tactic. These practices, however, tend to involve **stereotyping** of citizens. The problem is deeply rooted in policing. As Skolnick points out, police officers are trained to be suspicious and from experience develop a visual "shorthand" for suspects, based on visual cues. Inevitably, this involves a certain amount of stereotyping, by gender, age, and race. Skolnick concludes that "a disposition to stereotype is an integral part of the policeman's world."[94]

**stereotyping**

Stereotyping minorities as criminal suspects can be reinforced by department policy. The Christopher Commission concluded that the aggressive war-on-crime style of the Los Angeles police department "in some cases seems to become an attack on [minority] communities at large. The communities, and all within them, become painted with the brush of latent criminality."[95] Serious questions exist about the crime control effectiveness of aggressive law enforcement. Following the Rodney King incident in 1991, arrests by LAPD officers dropped from 312,870 in 1990 to 189,191 in 1995 (or 39 percent). Yet, the crime rate in Los Angeles also dropped during those years.[96]

The question of whether race or ethnicity can *ever* be used by police or other criminal justice officials is discussed later regarding racial profiling.

A social psychology experiment using video games found that racial stereotypes common to all Americans can affect a police officer's likelihood of using deadly force. Participants in the experiment were instructed to shoot when the human images in the game were armed. The human images were presented in a potentially threatening manner: crouching or appearing suddenly on the screen; some in fact had guns. They were somewhat more likely to shoot at African American images who were carrying wallets, cell phones, or cameras. Although the racial differences were small, they could help to explain how racial stereotypes influence police officers' decisions to use deadly force.[97]

## Verbal Abuse and Racial and Ethnic Slurs

The Christopher Commission, created to investigate the Los Angeles police department after the 1991 Rodney King beating, reviewed 180 days of computer-based communications among LAPD police officers. These communications were sent over the LAPD's sophisticated MDT (mobile digital transmission) system. A large number of these messages contained offensive racial stereotypes for African Americans and Hispanics, while others openly referred to use of physical force. While these messages were internal communications between officers, and not addressed directly to citizens, they indicate that the culture of the LAPD tolerated the use of offensive language.[98]

**verbal abuse**

**Verbal abuse,** particularly racial and ethnic slurs, are also a source of tension between the police and minority communities. Allegations of inappropriate language represent about 17 percent of all complaints against officers received by the Minneapolis Civilian Review Authority.[99] Reiss found that 75 percent of all police officers in his study were heard using offensive racial terms (although in conversation with other officers and not to citizens). In that study, officers "openly ridiculed and belittled" citizens in only 5 percent of all encounters.[100] Five percent is a small figure, but they tend to be concentrated among a certain segment of the population, accumulate over time, and become a part of a community's perception of the police.

## Discussion: Making Sense of Conflicting Evidence on Discrimination

There is conflicting evidence regarding the extent to which the police systematically target racial and ethnic minorities for traffic stops and field interrogations. The BJS survey of police–citizen contacts found that in 2002 whites had a higher rate of contact than either African Americans or Hispanics. This included both police-initiated and citizen-initiated contacts. About 42 percent of all contacts are citizen-initiated, with people calling to report a crime or a neighborhood problem or to ask for assistance. In terms of police-initiated traffic stops, African Americans are more likely to be stopped than either whites or Hispanics. Additionally, once they are stopped, African Americans are more likely to be given a ticket (as opposed to a warning), arrested, searched, and have force used against them.[101]

The data from the Bureau of Justice Statistics survey do not support the allegations of *systematic* racial profiling by the police, although they do indicate racial disparities. African Americans are stopped by the police at a higher rate than other racial or ethnic groups. There are several possible explanations for the apparent contradiction between the BJS data and the widespread belief that racial profiling exists. First, as Walker argues, police interactions with minorities are highly contextual. It is possible that the worst forms of profiling exist in special contexts, such as interstate highways and anti-drug crackdowns, and in a national survey these incidents are simply drowned out by the larger patterns of police–citizen interactions. Second, the psychological impact of a few racial profiling incidents may well be far greater than their statistics would predict. These incidents become surrogates for the larger patterns of racism and discrimination in American society.[102]

## Language and Cultural Barriers in Policing

An important aspect of conflict between the police and some racial and ethnic groups is a lack of **cultural competence** on the part of police officers. Cultural competence is defined as the ability to understand and respond appropriately to differences in the languages, traditions, lifestyles, and patterns of communication of different racial or ethnic groups. This is a special problem in communities that have recently experienced significant immigration of people from Latin America, Asia, or Africa. The city of Minneapolis, for example, has over 20,000 immigrants from Somalia. The Minneapolis police need to be able to communicate and understand the cultural traditions of Somali people.

**cultural competence**

The report *Donde esta la Justicia?* points out the negative impact of one difference in styles of communication: "Avoiding direct eye contact is considered respectful in many Latin nations," but in the United States doing so can be perceived as "a sign of disrespect or deceptiveness" by criminal justice officials. The report cited the case of a judge who interpreted the downcast eyes of a Latino juvenile as an admission of guilt and, consequently, gave him a long sentence.[103]

## Language Barriers

A police officer in a Midwestern city, assigned to patrol the part of town that is the center of the growing Hispanic community, explained, "The way I figure, we're here to provide a service and if you can't provide a service to a certain group of people, then you're not doing your job." The officer was referring specifically to being able to communicate with community residents who do not speak English.[104]

Because police work involves communication between people, **language barriers** create potentially serious obstructions to the delivery of high quality police services. Barriers are likely to arise when the citizen speaks a language other than English that the responding officer does not speak. If the officer is bilingual—for example, able to speak both English and Spanish—these barriers can be overcome.[105]

**language barriers**

Language skills make a big difference in how people relate to the police. Skogan conducted the first survey of English-speaking and non-English-speaking Hispanics and found significant differences in reporting crime and neighborhood problems. Hispanics who did not speak English were much less likely to report crimes: only 9 percent of respondents, compared with 35 percent of English-speaking Hispanics and 27 percent of African Americans. Non-English-speakers were also less likely to report a neighborhood problem to the police (8 percent, compared with 19 percent of English-speaking Hispanics and 14 percent of African Americans).[106]

Partly as a result, Latinos in Chicago who speak Spanish were substantially less likely to be aware of the Chicago Alternative Policing Strategy (CAPS) than were other racial and ethnic groups, including Latinos who speak English. Consequently, attendance at neighborhood beat meetings, one of the key components of CAPS, was far lower among all Latinos (both English- and Spanish-speaking) than among African Americans. Latinos were three times more likely than whites to feel that the police in their neighborhood were impolite. English-speaking Latinos perceived the crime problem to be improving, while Spanish-speaking Latinos saw crime getting worse.[107]

A study of potential Spanish-language barriers in one Midwestern city found some minor problems and delays but no serious problems because of language. Potential language barriers represented only 15 percent of all police–citizen contacts in the precinct that is the center of that city's Latino community. Delays occurred in 87 percent of those contacts, and frustration on the part of either the citizen or the officer occurred in 73 percent. Some conflict occurred in 27 percent of the calls because of language barriers, but none of those situations involved serious conflict (e.g., use of force by either party).

Generally, officers who lacked a command of Spanish "muddled through" their interactions with Spanish-speaking citizens. They either utilized "street Spanish" (a few basic phrases they had learned on the job), used command Spanish (which they had learned through formal training), or found a bystander who could translate.[108]

## Discrimination Involving Women, Gays, Lesbians, and Transgendered People

### *"Driving While Female"*

In early 2001 a Long Island, New York, police officer was placed on suspension after three women alleged that he had stopped them while driving and threatened them with arrest if they did not take off their clothes and stand naked. Immediately after these cases became public, another Long Island officer was charged with forcing a woman to perform oral sex or be arrested.[109]

These cases are examples of the problem of "driving while female" (DWF), a gender-based variation on "driving while black." The full extent of this problem is not known, but there is evidence that some male officers target young female drivers and stop them as a form of sexual harassment.

### *Young African American Women and the Police*

Most of the research on policing and people of color focuses on the experience of young African American men. Brunson and Miller included a sample of young women in their survey of African American adolescents in St. Louis. Their reported experience with the police is different from that of young men.

The most common complaint among young African American women surveyed was being stopped for curfew violations. Whereas the young men in the survey reported being stopped at all hours of the day, the young women reported being stopped mainly at night. Some reported being treated as suspects when they were in the company of young men. Complaints about a lack of police responsiveness mainly involved incidents of violence against women, suggesting bias against African American victims.[110]

### *Abuse of Sexual Minorities*

Surveys of gay and lesbian people have found a pattern of police abuse directed toward them. Reports of police abuse range from a high of 30 percent of respondents to a low of 8 percent. In addition to abuse, gay and lesbian people also experience ordinary disrespect from some police officers. Where it occurs, mistreatment of gay and lesbian people reflects, in part, prejudice against people who do not have conventional lifestyles. Abuse also reflects a sense that in many instances gay and lesbian people are vulnerable and powerless because filing a complaint or a suit would identify them as gay or lesbian. Some police departments have responded to this problem in several different ways. Some departments actively recruit gay and lesbian officers. Some have established active outreach or liaison programs with the gay and lesbian community. Many departments incorporate material on equal treatment of gay and lesbian people in their regular human relations training.[111]

# Special Topic: Racial Profiling

The major controversy in police–community relations in recent years has been the issue of racial profiling.[112] **Racial profiling** is defined as the practice of police officers stopping drivers because of their race or ethnicity and not because of a legitimate law violation. A Minnesota law defines racial profiling as

**racial profiling**

> [A]ny action initiated by law enforcement that relies upon the race, ethnicity, or national origin of an individual rather than: (1) the behavior of that individual; or (2) information that leads law enforcement to a particular individual who has been identified as being engaged in or having been engaged in criminal activity.

When profiling involves African American drivers, it is often referred to as "driving while black." Where it involves Hispanic or Latino drivers, it is referred to as "driving while brown." The racial profiling controversy came to national attention in the late 1990s as a result of lawsuits in New Jersey and Maryland alleging racial discrimination in enforcement on Interstate highways by the state police in both states. Observational data in Maryland found that African American drivers represented only 17.5 percent of all drivers observed to be speeding, but were 72.9 percent of all drivers who were stopped and searched.[113]

The racial profiling controversy involves very complex issues related to determining actual traffic enforcement practices by law enforcement agencies, the proper analysis of official traffic stop data, and the most effective remedies for racial or ethnic bias in traffic enforcement. Most important, while almost all traffic stop data reports have found evidence of racial or ethnic *disparities* in stops and searches, not all of these reports have found persuasive evidence of illegal *discrimination*.

A majority of Americans believe that racial profiling exists. According to a 2004 Gallup poll, 53 percent of all Americans believe it is "widespread." Even white Americans think it exists. The Gallup poll found that 50 percent of white Americans, 67 percent of African Americans, and 63 percent of Hispanics believe racial profiling exists. Moreover, the issue of discrimination is not limited to traffic enforcement. All racial and ethnic groups surveyed believe that racial profiling is widespread in shopping malls and stores.[114]

## Traffic Enforcement Practices

Traffic enforcement is an extremely important part of policing. The BJS Police Public Contact Survey reports that half (52 percent) of all contacts between police and citizens involve traffic stops.[115] Unfortunately, researchers ignored this critical aspect of policing for decades. The previous study was Gardiner's 1969 book, *Traffic and the Police*.[116] Large police departments typically have a special traffic enforcement unit dedicated to this activity; regular patrol officers also make traffic stops.

## Data on Traffic Enforcement Patterns

Traffic enforcement involves several different actions by the police. These include: (1) stopping a vehicle; (2) resolving the stop through an arrest, traffic citation, warning, or no action; and (3) searching the vehicle, driver, and/or passengers.

### National Data

The BJS Police–Citizen Contact Survey is the most thorough report on traffic enforcement patterns. Males were more likely to be stopped than females, and young people (age 16 to 24) were more likely to be stopped than older people. The report found some evidence of racial or ethnic bias, but no clear pattern of systematic discrimination. In the 16- to 24-year-old category, whites were actually more likely to be stopped than African Americans, and Hispanic drivers were the least likely to be stopped. Young African American males were more likely to be stopped more than once, however, with an average of 2.7 stops, compared with 1.8 for Hispanic drivers and 1.7 stops for whites.[117]

The strongest evidence of racial or ethnic disparities involved what happened *after* the initial stop. African Americans and Hispanics were far more likely to be searched than were white drivers who had been stopped. The police were almost equally likely to use force against white, African American, and Hispanic drivers (about one-third of all stops).

### State and Local Data

Many law enforcement agencies collect traffic-stop data, and several states have passed laws requiring racial profiling policies. Studies of individual departments have generally found racial and ethnic disparities with regard to drivers stopped and searched. A report by the COPS Office reviewed twenty-four reports; four found discrimination in stops and four found discrimination in searches; nine found no discrimination in stops, and four found no discrimination in searches. Two found mixed evidence on stops, and six found mixed evidence on searches.[118]

The San Jose Police Department undertook one of the first traffic stop studies by a local police department. It found that Hispanics represented 31 percent of the local population, but 43 percent of all drivers stopped by the police. Non-Hispanic whites, meanwhile, were 43 percent of the population, but only 29 percent of the drivers stopped.[119]

In their study of traffic stops in a white suburban community that bordered on a predominantly African American city, Meehan and Ponder found that *place* makes a difference (see the contextual approach, above, p. 377). First, African American drivers were somewhat more likely to be stopped. Second, they were more than twice as likely to be the subject of a query. Third and most important, African American drivers were more likely to be stopped and queried in predominantly white neighborhoods. Significantly, white drivers were queried at the same rate regardless of the location. This study supports the argument that the police are more likely to stop drivers who in their judgment are "out of place."[120]

## Interpreting Traffic-Stop Data

Interpreting traffic-stop data to determine whether or not a pattern of racial or ethnic discrimination exists is extremely difficult. The Northeastern University Institute on Race and Justice points out that at present "no 'industry standard' exists for measuring racial or gender profiling."[121] Virtually every report has found a pattern of racial or ethnic *disparity* in traffic stops, based on the residential population of the area. A disparity, however, does not necessarily mean that a pattern of *discrimination* exists.

Although most traffic stop studies use the resident population as the **benchmark** or denominator for interpreting the data, most criminologists have concluded that it is not a proper benchmark. **Population data** do not indicate who is actually driving on the roads, or who is violating a traffic law. The percentage of African American drivers may be higher or lower than the percentage of African Americans in the local population. African Americans may be violating traffic laws at a higher or lower rate than white drivers. (And in fact, whites report driving drunk at a significantly higher rate than African Americans, according to the National Survey of Drug Use and Health.)[122] The Northeastern University Institute advises that "racial or gender differences in both driving behavior and automobile type may affect rates of citations or warnings. Similarly, individuals from particular groups may be more likely to own and operate vehicles that are disproportionately subject to citations or warnings due to mechanical or registration problems."[123] Resident population data also do not reflect nonresidents who are driving into or through the area, in particular commuters who live outside the area.

Several alternative estimates of the driving population and driving behavior are available. These include official data on drivers licences by race and ethnicity, and estimates of driving habits, such as drunk driving by race and ethnicity. One useful alternative measure involves "not-at-fault" traffic accident data. Drivers who are involved in a traffic accident, but are not themselves at fault, represent a random selection of all drivers. (Drivers who are at fault are not a representative sample of all drivers, for obvious reasons.) "Not-at-fault" traffic accident data has the advantage of being readily available and inexpensive to analyze.[124]

**benchmark**

**population data**

**rolling survey**

The best data on who is at risk to be stopped while driving are derived from *direct observation*. The **rolling survey** technique was developed by John Lamberth for use in the lawsuits against the New Jersey and Maryland State Police. In a rolling survey, trained observers drive on the roadway in question and observe the racial composition of all drivers and the racial composition of those drivers observed to be breaking a traffic law. This technique provides a valid and reliable estimate of who is actually at risk for a traffic stop on that particular roadway. The rolling survey technique generates good data, but is extremely expensive to conduct and requires careful training and supervision of observers.

**internal benchmarking**

Another useful alternative involves **internal benchmarking** (IB). Internal benchmarking compares the performance of individual officers with peer officers: officers with similar assignments (shift, location, etc.). The basic assumption is that officers with the same assignment should have roughly similar work patterns. There is no reason why one officer should stop significantly more African American drivers than peer officers. Internal benchmarking tries to identify any officers who stop significantly more African American or Hispanic drivers than their peers. The data do not prove discriminatory behavior, but they raise questions about an officer's performance that become the basis for administrative review of an officer's performance. Because it involves a comparison of officers within the same department, internal benchmarking is not useful if all officers are engaging in racial profiling.[125]

## Explaining Disparities in Traffic Enforcement

Several different explanations have been offered for the racial and ethnic disparities found in traffic stops. Engel, Calnon, and Bernard point out that "the most widely used explanation" "is that officers act on the basis of prejudicial attitudes." They add, however, that no studies have investigated, much less found that prejudicial attitudes are the major factor. Some other experts blame racial profiling on the war on drugs—that is, department-level crime fighting strategies.[126] The ACLU, for example, argues that when departments emphasize drug enforcement, officers are pressured into making high rates of stops of suspected drug traffickers and that stereotypes about the involvement of African Americans in drugs leads them to stop a high rate of black drivers.[127]

*A Contextual Analysis.*    Racial profiling occurs in three different contexts. The first is the war on drugs. Drug enforcement activities often target African Americans or Hispanics because officers believe they are likely to be engaged in drug trafficking.

## EXHIBIT 12–8

### Alternative Benchmarks for Studying Traffic-Stop Data

1. **Resident population data.** Convenient, but does not measure the driving population or driving behavior.
2. **Direct observation.** Expensive, but provides good evidence on the driving population and driving behavior.
3. **Internal benchmarking.** Relatively convenient, and provides valuable comparisons of peer officer behavior.
4. **Nonfault traffic accident data.** Convenient and a useful proxy measure of driving population by demographic characteristics.
5. **Licensed driver data.** Convenient, but does not reflect actual driving population or driving behavior.

*Source:* Adapted from Lorie A. Fridell, *By the Numbers: A Guide for Analyzing Race Data from Vehicle Stops* (Washington DC: Police Executive Research Forum, 2004).

A second context involves police stopping citizens who appear to be *out of place* (see the discussion, p. 395). This might include, for example, an African American who is in a predominantly white neighborhood or a white person in a predominantly African American neighborhood. In either case, the police act because they believe it is suspicious for this person to be in this neighborhood.[128] A third context involves a general crackdown on crime. Crackdowns typically occur in poor, high-crime neighborhoods that are predominantly African American or Hispanic.

## Police Justifications for Racial and Ethnic Disparities

Police and some social scientists offer explanations for racial and ethnic disparities in traffic stops. The major argument is that African Americans and Hispanics are more likely to be engaged in criminal activity, and drug trafficking in particular. Heather MacDonald argues that racial profiling is a "myth," and that differential enforcement patterns can be explained by the greater involvement of racial and ethnic minorities in crime, especially drug trafficking.[129]

Critics argue that this explanation involves circular reasoning: racial and ethnic minorities are stopped and arrested more often than whites, producing higher arrest rates that, in turn, justify higher rates of stops and arrests. Moreover, the National Survey of Drug Use and Health consistently finds that reported use of illegal drugs among African Americans is only slightly higher than among whites, while use among Latinos is lower than both of the other groups.[130] The observational studies of traffic patterns on both Maryland and New Jersey Interstate highways found that white and African American drivers were equally likely to be speeding and that there was no justification for stopping African American drivers at a higher rate.

In its official report on traffic enforcement, the San Jose police department explained the disparities on the grounds that Hispanic and African American neighborhoods are assigned higher levels of patrol because of the higher crime rates and calls for service in those neighborhoods. Consequently, residents of those neighborhoods are more exposed to observation by police officers and therefore more likely to be stopped than drivers in areas with lower levels of police presence.[131]

## The Legitimate Use of Race and Ethnicity in Police Work

The report *Racially Biased Policing* argues that race or ethnicity can be used legitimately in police work, but only under certain circumstances. The report outlines standards for three different situations.[132]

- A police officer cannot stop or arrest a person *solely* on the basis of race or ethnicity. That is, the officer cannot make a traffic stop just because the driver is African American. Such a stop would clearly violate the Fourteenth Amendment guarantee of equal protection of the law.
- The police also cannot use race or ethnicity when it is one element in a *general profile* of criminal suspects. That is, the police cannot use a general profile including, for example, age, sex, race, and clothing. They cannot stop all African American males who are young, or who wear baggy jeans.
- The police may use race or ethnicity when it is *one element in the description of a specific criminal suspect,* and where that information is based on credible information from a reliable source. In the case of a convenience store robbery, for example, the police can rely on information from the victim that describes the suspect as a young, stocky male, with a beard, wearing a blue baseball cap, and who is African American (or white, or Hispanic).

On the use of written policies to control police officer discretion, see Chapter 11.

## Policies to Prevent Bias in Traffic Enforcement

Policies designed to prevent racial or ethnic bias in policing fall into several categories. The first approach is for law enforcement agencies to have a specific *written policy* prohibiting racial or ethnic discrimination in all aspects of police work. The Denver Police Department policy adopts the recommendation of the PERF report. It states that:[133]

> *"It is the policy of the Denver Police Department that all police-initiated actions . . . will be based on a standard of reasonable suspicion or probable cause. . . .*
>
> *Officers must be able to articulate specific facts, circumstances, and conclusions which support probable cause or reasonable suspicion. . . .*
>
> *Officers shall not consider race, ethnicity, national origin, religion, age, gender, gender identity, or sexual orientation in establishing either reasonable suspicion [or] probable cause. . . .*
>
> *Officers may take into account the reported race, ethnicity, or national origin of a specific suspect. . . ."*

A second approach is to improve *police officer training.* Such training needs to include specific coverage of traffic enforcement strategies and tactics, as well as clear indications of when race and ethnicity can be used. In 2003 the state of Virginia, following the recommendation of a state advisory Panel on Bias-based Policing, launched an antidiscrimination training program for all new law enforcement officers. Current officers would receive the same training on a phased basis as part of their regular in-service training.[134]

**SIDEBAR    12 – 5**

### Resources on Racial Profiling

#### Overview
**David Harris,** *Profiles in Injustice: Why Racial Profiling Cannot Work* (New York: The New Press, 2002).

#### National Traffic-Stop Data
**Bureau of Justice Statistics,** *Characteristics of Drivers Stopped by Police, 1999* (Washington DC: U.S. Justice Department, 2002). Available at www.ncjrs.gov, NCJ #191548.

#### Traffic-Stop Data Collection and Analysis
**Lorie Fridell,** *By the Numbers: A Guide for Analyzing Race Data from Vehicle Stops* (Washington DC: Police Executive Research Forum, 2004).

#### Law Enforcement Agency Policies
**Police Executive Research Forum,** *Racially Biased Policing: A Principled Response* (Washington DC: Police Executive Research Forum, 2001). Available at www. policeforum.org.

A third approach is traffic-stop *data collection and analysis*. This has been the approach favored by civil rights groups. As a result, several states have passed laws either prohibiting racial profiling or mandating data collection. (For a current list of state laws, go to www.racialprofilinganalysis.neu.edu.) At the same time, many law enforcement agencies have collected traffic-stop data voluntarily. The problems with analyzing traffic-stop data are discussed in the previous section. Some police chiefs oppose data collection on the grounds that it is unnecessary, expensive, time consuming, and unlikely to produce meaningful results. A report by the COPS Office, however, argues that "data collection and evaluation is an appropriate way to address the concerns of racial profiling. Anecdotal evidence is an unreliable tool upon which to make policy decisions."[135]

## Can Policies Reduce Racial and Ethnic Disparities?

Can official policies designed to reduce racial and ethnic disparities in traffic enforcement actually work? There is some evidence they do. Each year about 70 million people enter the United States from other countries; in the late 1990s, the U.S. Customs Service (since changed to the U.S. Customs and Border Protection and moved to the Department of Homeland Security) searched about 50,000 people for possible violations, such as the possession of drugs or other contraband. A report by the General Accounting Office in 2000 found serious racial, ethnic, and gender disparities in people searched. African American women were nine times more likely than white women to be X-rayed after being frisked; yet, they were the least likely to be found in possession of contraband.[136]

As a result of the report, the Customs Service developed new guidelines for deciding whom to search. First, officers must have suspicions based on a short list of behaviors by someone they might search: physiological signs of nervousness, unexplained bulges in clothing, inconsistencies in answers to questions, and so forth. In other words they could no longer search on the basis of a "hunch." Second, they have to obtain a supervisor's approval before taking certain actions. For example, an officer has to obtain the approval of an immediate supervisor before conducting a partial body search. The impact of the new rules were dramatic. The number of persons searched declined by almost half (47 percent), but the percentage of people found with contraband (the "hit rate") rose by 65 percent. Contraband was found in 5.8 percent of all searches, compared with 3.5 percent under the old rules. The racial and ethnic disparities in persons searched also declined. As some experts put it, they were working "smarter." David Harris, one of the leading experts on racial profiling, points to the GAO experience and argues that while it is difficult to change a law enforcement agency, "we know it can be done."[137]

## Problem Solving on Racial Profiling

An alternative approach to addressing racial profiling involves problem-solving (see Chapter 10 on problem-oriented policing). The Northeastern University Institute of Race and Justice describes this approach in terms of a "community–police task force" which can "open up discussion about police and community accounts of racial profiling." A COPS Office report argues that "it does not matter how accurate data collection and analysis is if the community does not feel engaged in the process."[138]

The Seattle police department undertook a series of steps to examine the issue. As a report by the department's Office of Professional Accountability (OPA) explains, the SPD has held community forums, analyzed citizen complaints alleging racial bias, and revised both department policies and training related to traffic enforcement. In short, problem solving in Seattle involves an ongoing effort of self-evaluation and policy change.[139]

**partnerships**

The Northeastern University *Practitioners Guide for Addressing Racial Profiling* explains the importance of developing community and police **partnerships** on racial profiling. First, partnerships foster trust. The guide mentions cases where police departments did their own studies of racial profiling but did not include community representatives in the planning stage. As a result, the community groups did not trust the results of the studies. Second, partnerships are a valuable avenue for two-way communication. A police department can gain useful insight into its reputation and use this information to make improvements. Community groups can also learn more about what the police department is doing. Third, partnerships can help police departments reduce the risk of engaging in unacceptable practices that might result in being sued.[140]

## Summary: The Racial Profiling Controversy

Racial profiling is an extremely important and complex issue. Discrimination on the basis of race or ethnicity is illegal. The issue is much larger than traffic enforcement, however. As the Police Executive Research Forum points out, it can occur in any aspect of police work: "Racially biased policing occurs when law enforcement inappropriately considers race or ethnicity in deciding with whom and how to intervene in an enforcement capacity."[141] That can include routine arrests, use of deadly or physical force, the handling of homeless people, undercover operations, or any other kind of police work.

# Improving Police–Community Relations

Police departments have attempted several different approaches to improving police–community relations: maintaining a diverse work force; improving the handling of citizen complaints; creating special police–community relations units, and improving training. An emerging consensus among experts is that better community relations requires changing and improving basic police operations. This includes adopting community policing and problem-oriented policing (see Chapter 10) and improving police accountability mechanisms to reduce the use of force and other field practices that create community tensions (Chapter 14).

## A Representative Police Force

**Employment discrimination** by police departments is another important cause of police–community relations tensions. Racial and ethnic minority officers are underrepresented in most police departments. Underrepresentation exists when the percentage of a minority group as sworn officers does not equal the percentage of that group in the local community served by that department. Virtually every national commission that has studied the police over the past 40 years has recommended that police departments hire more minority officers.[142]

**employment discrimination**

The CALEA accreditation standards recommend that each law enforcement agency have "minority group and female employees in the sworn law enforcement ranks in approximate proportion to the makeup of the available work force in the agency's law enforcement service community." Diversity and affirmative action are covered in detail in Chapter 5.[143]

## Handling Citizen Complaints

An African American resident of Milwaukee told the U.S. Civil Rights Commission that "people who have police complaints are literally afraid to go down to the fire and police commission and fill out these complaints."[144] A 1978 U.S. Civil Rights Commission report on Memphis found that "the single most aggravating factor . . . is the failure of the existing internal and external mechanisms which purportedly exist to prevent and combat" police misconduct. The commission cited the case of two officers who shot and killed a 16-year-old boy fleeing from the scene of a burglary. The officers were temporarily suspended for two days and then reinstated. Later, two other officers were fired for killing a dog.[145]

For a full discussion of problem solving in policing, see Chapter 10.

The perception that police departments are hostile to people who want to file complaints, do not investigate complaints thoroughly, and do not discipline officers who are guilty of misconduct is a major police-community relations problem.

Pate and Fridell found that among municipal police departments, African Americans represented an average of 21.4 percent of the population, but 42.3 percent of all people filing complaints against police officers. City police departments were also less likely to sustain complaints filed by African Americans than by whites.[146] These data lend some support to the long-standing allegations by civil rights leaders that internal police complaint procedures "whitewash" officer misconduct.

Hispanic Americans are less likely to file complaints against the police than African Americans. One possible reason is the language barrier. Persons who do not speak English are not able to access the complaint process. To overcome this barrier, a number of citizen oversight agencies publish brochures in Spanish explaining the complaint process. The Washington DC Office of Police Complaints has information about the complaint process in thirteen languages besides English on its Web site. Cultural factors are another obstacle for many ethnic groups, particularly recent immigrants. A study of citizen perceptions of the complaint process in Omaha found that Spanish-speaking Hispanic residents were extremely fearful of the police and the possible consequences of filing a complaint. Much of this fear was the result of concern about being arrested for not having proper immigration documents.[147]

**civilian review boards**

Because of distrust of police complaint procedures, civil rights leaders have demanded the creation of external or citizen oversight agencies—some of which are called **civilian review boards**—to handle citizen complaints. Many of these agencies engage in active outreach programs to reach different racial and ethnic groups. Citizen oversight is discussed in detail in Chapter 14, along with other mechanisms of police accountability.

## Community Relations and Newly Arrived Ethnic Groups

The National Crime Prevention Council makes a strong argument in favor of police departments hiring members of newly arrived ethnic groups. The council itself uses several different terms to describe members of these groups, many of whom are recent immigrants: "newcomer," "foreign-born," and "non-native."[148]

First, there are enforcement benefits to police departments. Sworn officers from newly arrived groups can alleviate the reluctance of crime victims to cooperate with the police and testify in court, can expedite case processing by facilitating communication, and on patrol duty can educate newcomers in the community about police practices.

Second, newcomer officers can help to increase public safety. In particular they can overcome misunderstandings that create dangerous situations. The council pointed out that some recent immigrants, following their own cultural traditions, leave their cars when stopped for a traffic violation and bow to show their respect. Since many police departments ask drivers to remain in their cars, some officers might interpret the driver leaving the car as a potentially threatening gesture and unnecessarily use force.

Third, there are intangible benefits. Native-born officers benefit from an enriched multicultural understanding by virtue of working with and getting to know colleagues from newcomer groups. Greater cultural understanding enhances the professionalism of the department and improves public perception of it.

## Discussion: Assign Officers on the Basis of Race?

Some people believe that it would help solve community relations problems if African American officers were assigned to the African American community and if Hispanic officers were assigned to the Hispanic community. This idea rests on the assumption that officers who police members of their own racial or ethnic group will relate better to community people and also better understand community problems. This idea is extremely unpopular with American citizens. In their national survey of public attitudes, Weitzer and Tuch found that over 90 percent of whites, African Americans, and Hispanics reject the idea.[149]

Surveys in both Washington DC and New York City, in fact, found that most people prefer mixed-race patrol teams. Moreover, they have very clear ideas about the value of mixed-race patrol teams. First, in mixed-race teams officers are likely to educate each other about differences in race, ethnicity, culture, and communities. Second, mixed-race teams are more likely to result in equal treatment of citizens. Third, mixed-race teams have an important symbolic value regarding equality and integration.[150]

## Do Citizens Care About the Color of the Officer?

The assumption that assigning racial- and ethnic-minority-group officers to minority neighborhoods will improve police–community relations is not supported by the evidence. Ron Weitzer interviewed 169 residents of three neighborhoods in Washington DC (one middle-class African American, one middle-class white, and one lower-income African American). Two-thirds of the middle-class residents, white and African American, reported that they could see no difference between white and African American officers. Residents in the lower-income African American neighborhood were more likely to see differences, but the differences they perceived were very mixed. Some residents saw white officers being more courteous and African American officers being less courteous than their counterparts. Only 13 percent of the residents of the lower-income African American neighborhood expressed a preference for having mostly African American officers in their neighborhood. Generally, the overwhelming number of respondents in all neighborhoods either expressed a preference for racially mixed teams of officers or said that the race of officers doesn't matter.[151]

The findings from Weitzer's study provide additional indirect support for Stoutland's analysis of the dimensions of trust in the police (see pp. 383–84.) She found that people notice and care about *how* police officers treat them.

## Special Police–Community Relations Units

In response to the urban riots of the 1960s, most big-city police departments created special **police–community relations (PCR) units,** which operated programs designed to improve relations with minority communities. PCR units spent most of their time speaking in schools and to community groups.[152] About half also operated **ride-along programs** that allowed citizens to spend a few hours riding in a patrol car.[153] Ride-along police cars were generally driven by a PCR unit officer, following patrol cars to calls for service. In the interests of safety and privacy, the officer did not allow citizens to observe actual encounters too closely.

Some departments also created neighborhood storefront offices, staffed by PCR unit officers, in an effort to overcome the isolation of the police and provide a

**police–community relations (PCR) units**

**ride-along programs**

more convenient access for community residents.[154] Police headquarters buildings are often forbidding places for many citizens and can be difficult to reach. The Detroit police department established fifty-two "ministations" throughout the city beginning in 1975. Each precinct had at least three, and some had four. Crime prevention officers (CPOs) assigned to the ministations did not engage in regular patrol and did not answer calls for service. Instead, they organized teenage summer employment programs, encouraged trash pickup in neglected areas, and maintained a volunteer escort service for the elderly.[155] The Houston Fear Reduction Experiment (see Chapter 10) also included neighborhood offices.[156]

Creating a special unit to address a particular problem has been characterized as a "presentational strategy" by an organization: an effort to provide external evidence of addressing an issue.[157] In many instances, however, the effort involves nothing more than creating an image with little in the way of substantive activity.

Special PCR units were not effective. The President's Crime Commission found that minorities regarded most PCR programs as "public relations puff" and a "deliberate con game."[158] Most police officers did not regard PCR units as an essential part of police operations. A Justice Department report found that PCR units "tended to be marginal to the operations of the police department," with little or no relationship to patrol or criminal investigation activities.[159]

Using 1968 public opinion data, Decker, Smith, and Uhlman found that in cities with special PCR units public attitudes toward the police were only slightly more positive than in those cities where no PCR unit existed. The existence of a program had no effect on the attitudes of whites, but did have a positive effect among those respondents who expressed the least trust in government.[160]

Ride-along programs tend to attract only those people who already have a favorable attitude toward the police and, consequently, do not reach those people who have serious complaints about the police. Many departments have abandoned their ride-along programs because of budget constraints. Some have been replaced by Citizen–Police Academies, which attempt to provide interested citizens with a more comprehensive understanding of policing.[161]

Special PCR programs tend to be more successful with those groups of people who already have favorable attitudes toward the police: whites, homeowners, and older people. In the Houston fear reduction program, as well as in many other experiments, innovations designed to improve relations with the public were less successful with racial minorities than with whites.[162] Overcoming deeply rooted racial and ethnic barriers in policing represents an extremely difficult challenge.

## Outreach to Immigrant Communities

Immigration trends are changing the face of the United States. The percentage of the population that is foreign born nearly doubled from 6.2 percent in 1980 to almost 12 percent in March 2002. The new variety of languages and cultures in American cities presents new issues for police departments.[163]

A number of departments have responded to the increased diversity of their communities by developing special outreach programs designed to establish closer relations and better understanding on the part of both the police and new immigrant communities. The Charlotte-Mecklenburg, North Carolina, police department created an International Relations Unit (IRU) in 2000, designed to reach out to all immigrant groups. The unit consists of six officers and a sergeant, all of whom are either fluent in a second language or who have an understanding of a second culture.[164]

The largest number of outreach programs involve the police and the Hispanic/ Latino community. Because of a large increase in the Hispanic population that followed the opening of a large food processing plant, the Storm Lake, Iowa, police department established a Community Service Officer (CSO) program staffed by civilians who can speak English and either Spanish or Lao, and who are responsible for parking tickets and other nonemergency calls for service. The Las Vegas metropolitan police department created a Hispanic American Resource Team (H.A.R.T.), which consists of officers who are fluent in Spanish and who are on call if needed by other units in the department. Some programs have been developed by the National Latino Peace Officers Association (NLPOA). The Minnesota chapter of the NLPOA created a reading program for first and second graders where NLPOA members read stories in both English and Spanish.[165]

## Should Local Police Enforce Federal Immigration Laws?

enforcing immigration laws

The laws relating to immigration are federal laws. Traditionally, state and local law enforcement officers have had no authority to enforce these laws—for example, to arrest an undocumented person for violating immigration law. In recent years, however, the federal government has sought to enlist local police departments in enforcing immigration laws. The 1996 Immigration Reform Act authorized the U.S. Justice Department to deputize local law enforcement officers for this purpose, but the practice was never put into effect. In 2002, however, the Justice Department issued a regulation implementing this law.

Many local police officials do not want to be involved in enforcing federal immigration laws. They argue that their many responsibilities (crime, order maintenance, service) require them to develop close relations with the communities they serve. The role of immigration enforcement, they believe, will alienate them from communities with large numbers of immigrants, especially Spanish-speaking communities. People will be reluctant to call the police to report crime or other problems and will generally be unwilling to talk with them. This will undermine all of the trust-building efforts of community policing programs. The California Police Chiefs Association sent a formal letter to the U.S. Attorney General in April 2002 opposing the federal government's new policy.[166]

## Race Relations and Human Relations Training

human relations training

Police training programs have improved dramatically over the past thirty years. Not only has the average length of preservice training more than doubled, but most police academies have either added or greatly expanded the coverage of race relations and human relations. In 1952, police academy training programs devoted an average of 4 hours to human relations; by 1982, the average was 25.3 hours.[167]

No research has established a direct connection between race relations training and either improved police officer behavior or improved public attitudes, however. A study of a police–community relations program in San Francisco found a significant change in police officer attitudes as a result of structured meetings with community residents. Officers reported more positive attitudes toward African American residents and perceived less community hostility toward them as a result of the training sessions. There was no evaluation of police officer behavior, however.[168] The Los Angeles police department instituted a program of cultural awareness training after the 1991 Rodney King incident. Five years later, however, only 2,700 of the more than 9,000 officers had undergone the training program.[169]

Speaking at a 1999 national conference on police–community relations, Billy Johnston, retired commander with the Boston police department, described his personal transformation. He joined the department in 1966 and was assigned to the riot squad. "I was trained to go to war," he recalled, "and to do so you must have an enemy." The "enemy," in this case, became the people in the community. Johnston's views underwent a dramatic change after he worked undercover as a decoy. "It was the first time I understood being different, a victim of crime, and scared." Leaving a bar known to serve gay people, he was attacked and threatened. "I realized what it meant to be hated." Johnston's views changed not because of a classroom lecture, but through a real-life experience that gave him a new perspective on police-community relations.[170]

A number of experts question the value of classroom training. A review of cultural diversity training programs for police found that the content of these programs had not changed much since the 1960s, that they tended to perpetuate negative stereotypes of racial minorities, and that they focused on individual officers and ignored problems related to the organization as a whole.[171] Alpert, Smith, and Watters argue that "mere classroom training" on issues of race relations "is insufficient." They stress the importance of on-the-street police behavior and recommend that both new recruits and veteran officers "experiment with methods of communicating with members of racial and cultural groups other than their own."[172] A Detroit crime-victims training program found that recruits' attitudes toward citizens changed dramatically after only four months on the job, suggesting that street experience is a far more powerful influence over officer attitudes than classroom training.[173]

## Training in Cultural Competence

In response to an influx of new immigrants in the community, the Charlotte-Mecklenburg, North Carolina, police department created a special International Unit. New immigrant groups in the country included Hispanics, Hmong, Vietnamese, and South Asian Indians. The International Unit produced a manual for all officers in the department. One section addressed cultural traditions that might cause misunderstandings. It explained, for example, the traditional medical practices of coining and cupping that are used in some Asian communities to treat illnesses. These practices leave marks on the body and are sometimes misinterpreted as physical abuse, including child abuse. The manual alerts officers to these practices so that they will be able to interpret physical marks correctly and not mistakenly arrest people for abuse.[174]

The New York City police department, meanwhile, prepared a *Fact Sheet* on Arab communities. It includes the section "What Codes of Conduct Should I Know When Entering an Arab's Home?" It explains that in "many Arab Muslim households [people] remove their shoes at the door because carpeting is used for prayers.[175]

# From PCR to Legitimacy: The New Paradigm

Thinking about the police role has evolved dramatically in the last two decades. Leaders of the community policing movement argued that the basic problem in American policing was the loss of legitimacy among all segments of the population. (See Chapter 10.) Traditional police–community relations efforts have always been directed toward one segment of the population: racial and ethnic minorities. The concept of legitimacy represents a new paradigm for improving policing.

Legitimacy is defined as the belief that the police as a social institution are acting properly and effectively, and deserve public support. When the community policing movement first arose, its leaders recognized that the police had lost legitimacy for two reasons: first, their apparent inability to control crime effectively; and second, practices such as excessive force that deeply alienated people. The first order of business for community policing, then, is to win back legitimacy. The Charlotte, North Carolina, Police Department explains, "one of our greatest assets is trust between police and the public. Without sufficient trust, we will not get enough information from the public about crime problems and possible offenders. Without trust, we cannot build effective problem-solving partnerships with our community."[176]

Winning legitimacy consists of two dimensions. The first involves substantive outcomes: controlling crime and disorder and providing services to the public. The second involves *how* police do their job: treating all people with respect and courtesy, and not engaging in misconduct such as discourtesy or the use of excessive force. This second dimension is referred to as *procedural justice*. If people feel the police are legitimate, they will be more likely both to obey the law and to comply with requests for help from the police.[177]

The key difference between the PCR and legitimacy paradigms is that PCR programs are directed only toward one part of the community. The legitimacy paradigm holds that the police need to direct their efforts toward the entire community.

In practice, winning legitimacy consists of two approaches. With regard to the control of crime and disorder, community policing and problem-oriented policing programs involve working closely with community groups, developing partnerships, and implementing programs that address specific neighborhood problems. These are described in Chapter 10.

The second approach involves developing accountability mechanisms that will reduce or eliminate officer misconduct. In recent years a set of "Best Practices" related to accountability has developed.

# "Best Practices": Responsive Policing and Accountability

In his introduction to the department's first traffic-stop data report, San Jose (California) Police Chief William Lansdowne explained that the department "prides itself upon being responsive to the needs and concerns of everyone" and, therefore, "has an obligation to members of the community concerned about racial profiling to look into the matter to see if there is any indication that it occurs in San Jose."[178] Along with San Diego, San Jose was one of the first police departments to undertake traffic-stop data collection and release the data. The first San Jose report included some indications of racial and ethnic disparities in traffic stops, but it was not clear if they represented discrimination, as explained earlier in this chapter.

With traffic-stop data collection, the San Jose police department adopted one of the major "best practices" in policing. A Justice Department report issued in January 2001 listed the best practices as (1) a comprehensive policy requiring officers to report all uses of force; (2) an open and accessible citizen complaint procedure; (3) an early warning system to identify potential "problem" officers (see Chapter 14); (4) improved police training; (5) traffic-stop data collection; and (6) improved recruitment, hiring, and retention of officers.[179]

## Community Policing and Improving PCR

Community policing represents a different approach to improving police–community relations in several respects. First, as Alpert, Smith, and Watters point out, it represents a comprehensive philosophy of policing. It may better address on-the-street police behavior than most of the traditional PCR programs that emerged after the riots of the 1960s and were essentially add-ons to basic police operations.[180]

Second, community policing is directed toward the community as a whole, and not just racial and ethnic minority communities. A survey of large police departments found that over 87 percent claimed that community policing had led to improved relations with minority communities.[181] Community policing programs are discussed in detail in Chapter 10.

---

 # Case Study

## *Police–Community Relations Initiatives of the East Palo Alto Police Department*

### Introduction

*East Palo Alto, California, was a community with a very high crime rate and a history of police–community relations problems. Chief Ronald L. Davis came from the Oakland, California, police department and introduced a comprehensive set of new initiatives. Some of them are excerpted here.*

*Go to the Department Web site (see source note) and read the entire Letter to the Community.*

### Questions

1. *Based on what you have learned, how would you evaluate the specific police–community relations programs described by Chief Davis?*
2. *Do you think they are likely to be effective?*
3. *What about some of the other programs described in the letter? Are they likely to help improve police–community relations? If yes, explain how and why. If no, explain why not.*

# East Palo Alto, California, Chief Ronald L. Davis, Letter to the Community, December 26, 2008

Dear Community Member:

The purpose of this report is to summarize the activities of the Police Department over the past 3 years and provide you information to gauge our progress. During this period, the Police Department has worked closely with the community and allied agencies to achieve five (5) primary goals:

1. Reduce crime and violence
2. Improve police-community relations
3. Enhance the professionalism of the Department
4. Build the internal capacity of the Department
5. Implement community policing

. . . .

## *Community Collaboration & Problem-Solving*

The community and police department have partnered to implement a comprehensive strategy designed to reduce crime and violence. Our strategy thus far has proven to be effective and serves as a national model on how to use community policing to aggressively respond to violence.

. . .

## *Improve Police-Community Relations*

Much progress has been made in this area; however, there is much more to accomplish.

Over the past 3 years the Department has engaged the community at historic levels. With the implementation of Area Command, the Department conducts 4 Beat meetings every month, which provides community members the forum to share their concerns with the police and work in partnership to solve problems.

. . .

## *Enhance Professionalism of the Department*

On the first day of my appointment as Chief of Police, I announced to the Department the newly established "Five Deadly Sins."

In other words, these violations would not be tolerated under any circumstance and violations would result in my immediate recommendation to terminate employment.

1. Brutality
2. Untruthfulness
3. Retaliation Against Witness
4. Discrimination
5. Acceptance of Gratuities

. . .

*Source:* Chief Ronald L. Davis, Chief of Police, East Palo Alto, California, Letter to the Community, December 26, 2008. www.ci,east-palo-alto.ca.us/police/pdf/Police_Department_Report.pdf

# Summary

Conflict between the police and racial and ethnic communities remains a serious problem in American policing. This problem persists despite general improvements in policing. There is evidence of racial discrimination in police field practices, such as the use of force, the handling of citizen complaints about police behavior, and police employment practices. Many of these problems are the responsibility of the police themselves. At the same time, conflict between police and minorities is a product of the larger structure of racism and racial discrimination in American society.

# Key Terms

police–community relations, 372
race, 373
ethnicity, 373
discrimination, 376
disparity, 376
attitudes about force, 379
dimensions of trust, 383
procedural justice, 384
selective contact, 387
selective perception, 387
four systems of justice, 388
fleeing-felon rule, 389

defense-of-life standard, 389
police brutality, 390
situational factors, 393
victim–suspect relationship, 393
demeanor of the suspect, 393
field interrogations, 394
stereotyping, 395
verbal abuse, 396
cultural competence, 397
language barriers, 397
racial profiling, 399
benchmark, 401

population data, 401
rolling survey, 402
internal benchmarking, 402
partnerships, 406
employment discrimination, 407
civilian review boards, 408
police–community relations (PCR) units, 409
ride-along programs, 409
enforcing immigration laws, 411
human relations training, 411

# Internet Exercises

As we learned, special1 police–community relations (PCR) programs were popular in the 1960s, but have faded away (pp. 409–10).

Pick four police departments, based on a rational selection process (four different geographical regions, four different sizes, four departments in one state, etc.).

Go on their Web sites. Search their sites to determine: (1) do they have a special PCR program or unit? (2) if not, do they have a community policing or problem-solving program that addresses the old PCR problems? (3) do they have any special programs regarding new immigrants to the community? (4) do they have any special reports or information regarding efforts to build trust and legitimacy?

Compare the information you are able to find. How would you rank these departments? Do some appear to be doing a better job than others? Does one department stand out compared with the others?

**Exercise 1** A number of police departments have active programs designed to improve police–community relations. Select ten departments and search their Web sites (**www.officer.com**) to see how many describe PCR programs.

Select your ten departments on the basis of some rational formula: geographic distribution, size (measured by number of sworn officers). For example, you might choose the ten largest in the entire country, or the two largest in each of five different regions, or ten departments from your immediate three- or four-state region.

Report your findings in class. How many departments report having any program? What do those programs consist of (citizen attitude surveys, ride-along programs, citizen police academies)?

**Exercise 2** In spring 2001 the City of Cincinnati experienced riots as a result of a fatal shooting of an African American man by a white police officer. This was the fifteenth such fatal shooting in six years.

This riot was very similar to the riots of the 1960s. Has nothing changed in Cincinnati? Have there been no improvements in police–community relations in that city? Using the Web, locate news stories and reports on the situation in Cincinnati. Some can be found through the "Archives" section of local or national newspapers.

What do these stories and reports conclude about the situation in Cincinnati? Were police–community relations significantly worse than in other cities? What factors explain the riot in the spring of 2001?

**Exercise 3** Many observers believe that, unlike in Cincinnati, police–community relations have significantly improved in Boston in recent years. Go to the Boston police department Web site. What programs do they claim to have that are concerned with police–community relations? Check other Boston-related Web sites for pertinent material. Does the mayor's office Web site describe any community relations programs? In the end, can you identify any significant differences between Cincinnati and Boston?

## Notes

1. ACLU, *Driving While Black* (New York: ACLU, 1999).
2. Gallup Poll, 2004, available in Bureau of Justice Statistics, *Sourcebook of Criminal Justice Statistics,* Table 2.26. www.albany.edu/sourcebook/.
3. Jeffrey Goldberg, "The Color of Suspicion," *New York Times Magazine* (June 20, 1999), p. 52.
4. Samuel Walker, Cassia Spohn, and Miriam DeLone, *The Color of Justice: Race, Ethnicity, and Crime in America,* 4th ed. (Belmont, CA: Wadsworth, 2007).
5. Henry I. DeGeneste and John P. Sullivan, *Policing a Multicultural Community* (Washington DC: Police Executive Research Forum, 1997).
6. Discussed in Walker, Spohn, and DeLone, *The Color of Justice.*
7. American Anthropological Association, Statement on Race, May 17, 1998. Available on the organization's Web site: www.aaanet.org.
8. Definitions of race and ethnicity are discussed in Walker, Spohn, and DeLone, *The Color of Justice,* pp. 6–12.
9. Francisco A. Villarruel and Nancy E. Walker, *Donde esta la justicia?* (Washington DC: Building Blocks for Youth, 2002), p. 46.
10. National Advisory Commission on Civil Disorders, *Report* (New York: Bantam Books, 1968).
11. Alfredo Mirande, *Gringo Justice* (Notre Dame, IN: University of Notre Dame Press, 1987); National Council of La Raza, *The Mainstreaming of Hate: A Report on Latinos and Harassment, Hate Violence, and Law Enforcement Abuse in the '90s* (Washington DC: National Council of La Raza, 1999), p. 15.
12. Pew Hispanic Center, *2002 National Survey of Latinos* (Los Angeles: Pew Hispanic Center, 2002).
13. Marianne O. Nielsen and Robert A. Silverman, eds., *Native Americans, Crime, and Justice* (Boulder, CO: Westview, 1996); Executive Committee for Indian Country Law Enforcement Improvements, *Final Report to the Attorney General and the Secretary of the Interior* (Washington DC: October 1997); Eileen Luna, "The Growth and Development of Tribal Police," *Journal of Contemporary Criminal Justice* 14 (February 1998): pp. 75–86.
14. Information is available on the Web site of the Arab-American Institute: www.aaiusa.org.
15. Robert C. Davis and Edna Erez, *Immigrant Populations as Victims: Toward a Multicultural Criminal Justice System* (Washington DC: Government Printing Office, 1998).
16. Robert C. Davis and Nicole J. Henderson, "Willingness to Report Crimes: The Role of Ethnic Group Membership and Community Efficacy," *Crime and Delinquency* 49 (October 2003): pp. 564–80.
17. National Crime Prevention Council, *Building and Crossing Bridges: Refugees and Law Enforcement Working Together* (Washington DC: National Crime Prevention Council, 1994).
18. Seattle Office of Professional Accountability, www.cityofseattle.net.

19. Charlotte-Mecklenburg Police Department, International Unit, *Law Enforcement Services to a Growing International Community* (Charlotte: Charlotte-Mecklenburg Police Department, 2004).

20. Amnesty International USA, *Stonewalled: Police Abuse and Misconduct Against Lesbian, Gay, and Transgendered People in the U.S.* (New York: Amnesty International USA, 2005).

21. Samuel Walker, *Police and Minority Group Interactions* (Washington DC: Police Executive Research Forum, 2000).

22. Steven A. Tuch and Ronald Weitzer, "Racial Differences in Attitudes toward the Police," *Public Opinion Quarterly 61* (1997): pp. 642–63.

23. Ronald Weitzer and Steven A. Tuch, *Race and Policing in America: Conflict and Reform* (New York: Cambridge University Press, 2006), p. 41.

24. Mark Hugo Lopez and Gretchen Livingston, *Hispanics and the Criminal Justice System: Low Confidence, High Exposure* (Los Angeles: Pew Hispanic Center, 2009).

25. Roger G. Dunham and Geoffrey P. Alpert, "Neighborhood Differences in Attitudes toward Policing: Evidence for a Mixed-Strategy Model of Policing in a Multi-Ethnic Setting," *Journal of Criminal Law and Criminology* 79, no. 2 (1988): pp. 504–23.

26. Available at www.phoenix.gov/police.

27. Sandra Lee Browning, Francis T. Cullen, Liqun Cao, Renee Kopache, and Thomas J. Stevenson, "Race and Getting Hassled by the Police: A Research Note," *Police Studies* 17, no. 1 (1994): pp. 1–11.

28. "From Some Parents, Warnings about Police," *New York Times* (October 23, 1997), p. A18.

29. Ronald Weitzer, "Citizens' Perceptions of Police Misconduct: Race and Neighborhood Context," *Justice Quarterly* 16 (December 1999): pp. 1101–28.

30. Warren Friedman and Marsha Hott, *Young People and the Police: Respect, Fear and the Future of Community Policing in Chicago* (Chicago: Chicago Alliance for Neighborhood Safety, 1996).

31. Weitzer and Tuch, *Race and Policing in America: Conflict and Reform,* p. 45.

32. Weitzer and Tuch, *Race and Policing in America: Conflict and Reform,* pp. 45.

33. Wesley Skogan and Susan M. Hartnett, *Community Policing, Chicago Style* (New York: Oxford University Press, 1997).

34. Bureau of Justice Statistics, *Criminal Victimization and Perceptions of Community Safety in 12 Cities,* 1998.

35. James Frank, Steven G. Brandl, Francis T. Cullen, and Amy Stichman, "Reassessing the Impact of Race on Citizens' Attitudes toward the Police: A Research Note," *Justice Quarterly* 13 (June 1996): pp. 321–34.

36. The events of March 3, 1991, are described in detail in Jerome H. Skolnick and James J. Fyfe, *Above the Law* (New York: Free Press, 1993), pp. 1–3.

37. Tuch and Weitzer, "Racial Differences in Attitudes toward the Police," pp. 647–49.

38. Sara E. Stoutland, "The Multiple Dimensions of Trust in Resident/Police Relations in Boston," *Journal of Research in Crime and Delinquency* 38 (August 2001): pp. 226–56.

39. Wesley G. Skogan, "Citizen Satisfaction with Police Encounters," *Police Quarterly* 8 (September 2005): pp. 298–321.

40. Stan L. Albrecht and Miles Green, "Attitudes toward the Police and the Larger Attitude Complex," *Criminology* 15 (May 1977): pp. 67–86.

41. Egon Bittner, "The Functions of the Police in Urban Society," in Bittner, *Aspects of Police Work* (Boston: Northeastern University Press, 1990), pp. 89–232; Abraham Blumberg, *Criminal Justice,* 2d. ed. (New York: New Viewpoints, 1979), p. 58; Arthur Niederhoffer, *Behind the Shield: The Police in Urban Society* (Garden City, NY: Anchor Books, 1967), p. 1.

42. Greg Ridgeway et al., *Police-Community Relations in Cincinnati: Year Two Evaluation Report* (Santa Monica: Rand Corporation, 2006), p. 72.

43. Carolyn M. Ward, "Policing in the Hyde Park Neighborhood, St. Louis: Racial Bias, Political Pressure, and Community Policing," *Crime, Law and Social Change* 26 (1997): pp. 172–73, 181.

44. James Q. Wilson, *Varieties of Police Behavior* (New York: Atheneum, 1973), p. 28.

45. William A. Westley, *Violence and the Police* (Cambridge, MA: MIT Press, 1970), p. 93.

46. Lawrence W. Sherman, Patrick R. Gartin, and Michael E. Buerger, "Hot Spots of Predatory Crime: Routine Activities and the Criminology of Place," *Criminology* 27, no. 1 (1989): pp. 27–55.

47. Bureau of Justice Statistics, *Contacts between Police and the Public: Findings from the 1999 National Survey* (Washington DC: Government Printing Office, 2001).

48. Albert Reiss, *The Police and the Public* (New Haven, CT: Yale University Press, 1971).

49. Robert E. Worden, "The 'Causes' of Police Brutality: Theory and Evidence," in W. A. Geller

and H. Toch, eds., *And Justice for All* (Washington DC: Police Executive Research Forum, 1995), p. 44; John A. Groeger, *Memory and Remembering: Everyday Memory in Context* (New York: Addison Wesley, 1997), pp. 189–96.

50. Irving Piliavin and Scott Briar, "Police Encounters with Juveniles," *American Journal of Sociology* 70 (September 1964): pp. 206–14; Donald Black, "The Social Organization of Arrest," in Black, *The Manners and Customs of the Police* (New York: Academic Press, 1980), pp. 85–108; Jerome Skolnick, *Justice without Trial,* 3rd ed. (New York: Macmillan, 1994).

51. Gunnar Myrdal, *An American Dilemma: The Negro Problem and Modern Democracy* (New York: Harper and Brothers, 1944); Samuel Walker, "'A Strange Atmosphere of Consistent Illegality': Myrdal on 'The Police and Other Public Contacts,'" in O. Clayton, ed., *An American Dilemma Revisited* (New York: Russell Sage, 1996), pp. 226–46; Guy B. Johnson, "The Negro and Crime," *Annals of the American Academy of Political and Social Science* 217 (September 1941): pp. 93–104.

52. Philadelphia Police Study Task Force, *Philadelphia and Its Police* (Philadelphia: The City, 1987), p. 169.

53. The Knapp Commission, *Report on Police Corruption* (New York: Braziller, 1973), p. 75.

54. These studies are summarized in National Academy of Sciences, *Fairness and Effectiveness in Policing: The Evidence* (Washington DC: National Academy Press, 2004), pp. 314–15.

55. David H. Bayley and Harold Mendelsohn, *Minorities and the Police* (New York: The Free Press, 1969), p. 109.

56. Ronald Weitzer, Steven A. Tuch, and Wesley G. Skogan, "Police-Community Relations in a Majority-Black City," *Journal of Research in Crime and Delinquency* 45 (4, 2008): p. 418.

57. Weitzer and Tuch, *Race and Policing in America,* pp. 150–52.

58. Black, *The Manners and Customs of the Police,* p. 117; Richard J. Lundman, "Domestic Police-Citizen Encounters," *Journal of Police Science and Administration* 2 (March 1974): p. 25.

59. Frank Furstenburg and Charles Wellford, "Calling the Police: The Evaluation of Police Service," *Law and Society Review* 7 (Spring 1973): p. 402; Carolyn M. Ward, "Policing in the Hyde Park Neighborhood, St. Louis: Racial Bias, Political Pressure, and Community Policing," p. 169.

60. The facts of the case are in *Tennessee v. Garner,* 471 U.S. 1 (1985).

61. James J. Fyfe, "Reducing the Use of Deadly Force: The New York Experience," in Department of Justice, *Police Use of Deadly Force* (Washington DC: Government Printing Office, 1978), p. 29.

62. U.S. Commission on Civil Rights, *Revisiting Who is Guarding the Guardians: A Report on Police Practices and Civil Rights in America* (Washington DC: U.S. Commission on Civil Rights, 2000).

63. James J. Fyfe, "Blind Justice: Police Shootings in Memphis," *Journal of Criminal Law and Criminology 73,* no. 2 (1982): pp. 707–22.

64. William A. Geller and Michael S. Scott, *Deadly Force: What We Know* (Washington DC: Police Executive Research Forum, 1992); James J. Fyfe, "Administrative Interventions on Police Shooting Discretion: An Empirical Assessment," *Journal of Criminal Justice* 7 (Winter 1979): pp. 309–23.

65. Jerry R. Sparger and David J. Giacopassi, "Memphis Revisited: A Reexamination of Police Shootings after the Garner Decision," *Justice Quarterly* 9 (June 1992): pp. 211–23; Lawrence W. Sherman and Ellen G. Cohn, *Citizens Killed by Big City Police* (Washington DC: Crime Control Institute, 1986); Geller and Scott, *Deadly Force: What We Know;* Bureau of Justice Statistics, *Policing and Homicide, 1976–1998: Justifiable Homicide by Police, Police Officers Murdered by Felons* (Washington DC: Department of Justice, 2001). Available at www.ncjrs.org, NCJ 180987; Samuel Walker, *Taming the System: The Control of Discretion in Criminal Justice*, 1950–1990 (New York: Oxford University Press, 1993) pp. 21–53.

66. William A. Geller and Kevin J. Karales, *Split-Second Decisions: Shootings of and by Chicago Police* (Chicago: Chicago Law Enforcement Study Group, 1981).

67. Lou Cannon, Official *Negligence: How Rodney King and the Riots Changes Los Angeles and the LAPD* (New York: Times Books, 1997).

68. Commission on Accreditation for Law Enforcement Agencies, *Standards for Law Enforcement Agencies,* 4th ed. (Fairfax, VA: CALEA, 1999), Standard 1.3.1.

69. Carl B. Klockars, "A Theory of Excessive Force and Its Control," in W. A. Geller and H. Toch, eds., *And Justice for All,* pp. 11–29.

70. Bureau of Justice Statistics, *Contacts between Police and the Public, 2005* (Washington DC:

Department of Justice, 2007). Available at www. ncjrs.org NCJ 215243.

71. Kenneth Adams, "Measuring the Prevalence of Police Abuse of Force," in Geller and Toch, eds., *And Justice for All,* pp. 61–97; Albert Reiss, *The Police and the Public* (New Haven, CT: Yale University Press, 1971), p. 142.

72. Reiss, *The Police and the Public,* p. 151.

73. Robert Worden, "The 'Causes' of Police Brutality: Theory and Evidence on Police Use of Force," in Geller and Toch, eds., *And Justice for All,* p. 52.

74. Geoffrey P. Alpert, "The Force Factor: Measuring and Assessing Police use of Force and Suspect Resistance," in Bureau of Justice Statistics, *Use of Force by Police: Overview of National and Local Data* (Washington DC: Government Printing Office, 1999), pp. 45–60.

75. David Weisburd and Rosann Greenspan, *Police Attitudes toward Abuse of Authority: Findings from a National Study* (Washington DC: Government Printing Office, 2000).

76. Albert Reiss, "Police Brutality—Answers to Key Questions," *Transaction 5* (July–August 1968): pp. 10–19.

77. San Jose Independent Police Auditor, Annual Report 2006 (San Jose, CA: Cityof San Jose, 2007), p. 51. New York Civilian Complaint Review Board, StatusReport, January–December 2007 (New York: CCRB, 2008), Table 11.

78. Special Counsel to the Los Angeles Sheriff's Department, *11th Semiannual Report* (Los Angeles, October 1999), p. 78. www.parc.info.

79. Robert Tillman, "The Size of the 'Criminal Population,' The Prevalence and Incidence of Adult Arrest," *Criminology* 25 (August 1987): pp. 561–79.

80. Donald Black, "The Social Organization of Arrest," in Black, *The Manners and Customs of the Police.*

81. Douglas A. Smith, Christy A. Visher, and Laura A. Davidson, "Equity and Discretionary Justice: The Influence of Race on Police Discretion," *Journal of Criminal Law and Criminology* 75 (Spring 1984): pp. 234–49.

82. Black, "The Social Organization of Arrest"; David A. Klinger, "Demeanor or Crime? Why 'Hostile' Citizens Are More Likely to Be Arrested," *Criminology 32,* no. 3 (1994): pp. 475–93.

83. David H. Bayley, "The Tactical Choices of Police Patrol Officers," *Journal of Criminal Justice* 14, no. 1 (1986): pp. 329–48; Stephen Mastrofski and Roger B. Parks, "Improving Observational

84. Skolnick, *Justice without Trial,* pp. 44–47.

85. John R. Hepburn, "Race and the Decision to Arrest: An Analysis of Warrants Issued," *Journal of Research in Crime and Delinquency* 15, no. 3 (1978): pp. 54–73.

86. Joan Petersilia, *Racial Disparities in the Criminal Justice System* (Santa Monica, CA: Rand, 1983), pp. 20–33.

87. Department of Health and Human Services, *Results from the 2007 National Survey on Drug Use and Health National Findings,* (Washington DC: Department of Health and Human Services, 2007). Available at www.samhsa.gov/oas/nhsda. htm#NHSDAinfo.

88. Steven R. Donziger, ed., *The Real War on Crime: The Report of The National Criminal Justice Commission* (New York: Harper, 1996), p. 115.

89. Quoted in Ronald Weitzer, "Racialized Policing: Residents' Perceptions in Three Neighborhoods," *Law and Society Review 34,* no. 1 (2000): p. 138.

90. President's Commission on Law Enforcement and Administration of Justice, *Task Force Report: The Police* (Washington DC: Government Printing Office, 1967), pp. 183–86.

91. Browning et al., "Race and Getting Hassled by the Police: A Research Note."

92. Eliot Spitzer, *The New York City Police Department's "Stop and Frisk" Practices* (New York: Attorney General of New York, 1999).

93. Quoted in Weitzer, "Racialized Policing," p. 137.

94. Skolnick, *The Police and the Urban Ghetto* (Chicago: American Bar Foundation, 1968).

95. Christopher Commission, *Report of the Independent Commission on the Los Angeles Police Department* (Los Angeles: The Commission, 1991), p. 74. Available at www.parc.info.

96. Merrick Bobb, Special Counsel, *Five Years Later: A Report to the Los Angeles Police Commission* (Los Angeles: The Police Commission, 1996), p. 5. www.parc.info.

97. Joshua Correll, Bernardette Park, Charles M. Judd, and Bernd Wittenbrink, "The Police Officers' Dilemma: Using Ethnicity to Disambiguate Potentially Threatening Individuals," *Journal of Personality and Social Psychology* 83 (December 2002): pp. 1314–30.

98. Christopher Commission, *Report of the Independent Commission on the Los Angeles Police Department,* pp. 48–55.

99. Minneapolis Civilian Review Authority, *1999 Annual Report* (Minneapolis, MN: Civilian Review Authority, 2000).

100. Reiss, *The Police and the Public,* p. 142.

101. Bureau of Justice Statistics, *Contacts Between Police and the Public: Findings from the 2002 National Survey* (Washington DC: Department of Justice, 2005). Available at www.ncjrs.org, NCJ 207845.

102. Walker, *Police Interactions with Racial and Ethnic Minorities.*

103. Francisco A. Villarruel and Nancy E. Walker, *Donde esta la justicia?* (Washington DC: Building Blocks for Youth, 2002), pp. 1–2.

104. Leigh Herbst and Samuel Walker, "Language Barriers in the Delivery of Police Services," *Journal of Criminal Justice* 29, no. 4 (2001): pp. 329–40.

105. Robert C. Davis and Edna Erez, *Immigrant Populations as Victims: Toward a Multicultural Criminal Justice System* (Washington DC: Government Printing Office, 1998).

106. Skogan, "Citizen Satisfaction with Police Encounters," pp. 298–321.

107. Wesley Skogan et al., *Community Policing and 'The New Immigrants': Latinos in Chicago* (Washington DC: U.S. Justice Department, 2002).

108. Herbst and Walker, "Language Barriers in the Delivery of Police Services."

109. Samuel Walker and Dawn Irlbeck, *Driving While Female: A National Problem in Police Misconduct* (Omaha: University of Nebraska at Omaha, 2002). Available at www.policeaccountability.org.

110. Rod K. Brunson and Jody Miller, "Gender, Race, and Urban Policing: The Experience of African American Youths," *Gender and Society,* 20 (August 2006): 531–52.

111. Amnesty International USA, *Stonewalled: Police Abuse and Misconduct Against Lesbian, Gay, and Transgendered People in the United States* (New York: Amnesty International USA, 2005).

112. The best single book is David Harris, *Profiles in Injustice: Why Racial Profiling Cannot Work* (New York: The New Press, 2002).

113. American Civil Liberties Union, *Driving While Black* (New York: ACLU, 1999).

114. Bureau of Justice Statistics, *Sourcebook of Criminal Justice Statistics, 2003*, Table 2.26.

115. Bureau of Justice Statistics, *Characteristics of Drivers Stopped by Police, 1999* (Washington DC: U.S. Justice Department, 2002). Available at www.ncjrs.org, NCJ 191548.

116. John A. Gardiner, *Traffic and the Police* (Cambridge: Harvard University Press, 1969).

117. Bureau of Justice Statistics, *Characteristics of Drivers Stopped by Police,* 1999.

118. Joyce McMahon, Joel Garner, Captain Ronald Davis, and Amanda Kraus, *How to Correctly Collect and Analyze Racial Profiling Data: Your Reputation Depends on It!* (Washington DC: U.S. Justice Department, 2003). Available at www.ncjrs.org, NCJ 199264.

119. San Jose Police Department, *Vehicle Stop Demographic Study: First Report* (San Jose: San Jose Police Department, 1999).

120. Albert J. Meehan and Micahel C. Ponder, "Race and Place: The Ecology of Racial Profiling African American Motorists," *Justice Quarterly* 19 (September 2002), pp. 399–430.

121. The Northeastern University Web site is www.racialprofilinganalysis.neu.edu.

122. U.S. Department of Health and Human Services, *Results from the 2003 National Survey on Drug Use and Health: National Findings* (Rockville, MD: Department of Health and Human Services, 2004), p. 254.

123. The Northeastern University Web site is www.racialprofilinganalysis.neu.edu.

124. The alternative measures are discussed in Lorie Fridell, *By the Numbers: A Guide for Analyzing Race Data from Vehicle Stops* (Washington DC: Police Executive Research Forum, 2004). Data on drunk driving behavior is reported in the *2003 National Survey on Drug Use and Health: National Findings* (Rockville, MD: Department of Health and Human Services, 2004).

125. Samuel Walker, *Internal Benchmarking for Traffic Stop Data: An Early Intervention Approach* (Omaha: University of Nebraska at Omaha, 2003). Available at www.policeaccountability.org; Fridell, *By the Numbers,* pp. 143–59.

126. Robin Shepard Engel, Jennifer Calnon, and Thomas J. Bernard, "Theory and Racial Profiling: Shortcomings and Future Directions in Research," *Justice Quarterly* 19 (June 2002): pp. 261–62.

127. ACLU, *Driving While Black.*

128. Meehan and Ponder, "Race and Place: The Ecology of Racial Profiling African American Motorists."

129. Heather MacDonald, *Are Cops Racist?* (Chicago: Ivan Dee, 2003).

130. Department of Health and Human Services, *Results from the 2007 National Survey on Drug Use and Health: National Findings* (Washington DC: Department of Health and Human Services, 2007).

Available at www.samhsa.gov/oas/nhsda. htm#NHSDAinfo.

131. San Jose Police Department, *Vehicle Stop Demographic Study: First Report* (San Jose: San Jose Police Department, 2002).

132. Police Executive Research Forum, *Racially Biased Policing: A Principled Response* (Washington DC: Police Executive Research Forum, 2001), Ch. 4.

133. *Denver Police Department Operations Manual,* Policy 118.00, "Biased Policing," Available on the Web at www.denvergov.org.

134. "Virginia to Train Police against Profiling," *Washington Post,* August 21, 2003; Virginia, Governor's Advisory Panel on Bias-based Policing, *Report to the Governor* (July 2003).

135. McMahon, et al., *How to Correctly Collect and Analyze Racial Profiling Data,* p. 9.

136. U.S. Customs Service, *Better Targeting of Airline Passenger for Personal Searches Could Produce Better Results,* GAO/GGD-00-38 (Washington DC: General Accounting Office, 2000).

137. U.S. Customs Service, Personal Search Review Commission, *Report on Personal Searches by United States Customs Service, 2003.* Harris, *Profiles in Injustice,* p. 222.

138. McMahon, et al., *How to Correctly Collect and Analyze Racial Profiling Data,* p. 2.

139. Seattle Police Department, Office of Professional Accountability, *Report on Seattle's Response to Concerns about Racially Biased Policing* (Seattle: Seattle Police Department, 2003). Available at www.cityofseattle.net/police.

140. Lamberth Consulting, *Practitioners Guide for Addressing Racial Profiling* (Boston: Northeastern University, 2005).

141. PERF, *Racially Biased Policing,* p. 5.

142. Walker, Spohn, and DeLone, *The Color of Justice,* pp. 110–16.

143. Commission on Accreditation for Law Enforcement Agencies, *Standards for Law Enforcement Agencies,* 4th ed. (Fairfax, VA: CALEA, 1994), Standard 31.2.1.

144. U.S. Civil Rights Commission, *Police Protection of the African American Community in Milwaukee,* p. 45.

145. U.S. Civil Rights Commission, Tennessee Advisory Committee, *Civic Crisis—Civic Challenge: Police Community Relations in Memphis* (Washington DC: Government Printing Office, 1978), pp. 1, 88.

146. Anthony M. Pate and Lorie A. Fridell, *Police Use of Force,* Vol. 1 (Washington DC: The Police Foundation, 1993), p. 9.

147. Ibid., p. 195; Samuel Walker, "Complaints against the Police: A Focus Group Study of Citizen Perceptions, Goals, and Expectations," *Criminal Justice Review* 22 (Autumn 1997): pp. 207–26.

148. National Crime Prevention Council, *Lengthening the Stride: Employing Peace Officers from Newly Arrived Ethnic Groups* (Washington DC: National Crime Prevention Council, 1995).

149. Weitzer and Tuch, *Race and Policing in America,* pp. 112–16.

150. Ibid, p. 116.

151. Ronald Weitzer, "White, Black, or Blue Cops? Race and Citizen Assessment of Police Officers," *Journal of Criminal Justice* 28 (2000): pp. 313–24.

152. Fred A. Klyman and Joanna Kruckenberg, "A National Survey of Police–Community Relations Units," *Journal of Police Science and Administration* 7 (March 1979): p. 74.

153. Charles E. Reasons and Bernard A. Wirth, "Police–Community Relations Units: A National Survey," *Journal of Social Issues* 31 (Winter 1975): pp. 27–34.

154. Ibid.

155. Jerome Skolnick and David Bayley, *The New Blue Line: Police Innovation in Six American Cities* (New York: Free Press, 1986), pp. 54–70.

156. Lee P. Brown and Mary Ann Wycoff, "Policing Houston: Reducing Fear and Improving Service," *Crime and Delinquency* 33 (January 1986): pp. 71–89.

157. Peter Manning, *Police Work* (Cambridge: MIT Press, 1977).

158. President's Commission on Law Enforcement and Administration of Justice, *Field Studies, IV,* Vol. 1, (Washington DC: Government Printing Office, 1967), p. 58.

159. U.S. Department of Justice, *Improving Police/ Community Relations* (Washington DC: Government Printing Office, 1973), pp. 3–4.

160. Scott H. Decker, Russell L. Smith, and Thomas M. Uhlman, "Does Anything Work? An Evaluation of Police Innovations," in Baker and Meyer, eds., *Evaluating Alternative Law Enforcement Policies,* pp. 43–54.

161. Ellen G. Cohn, "The Citizen Police Academy: A Recipe for Improving Police–Community Relations," *Journal of Criminal Justice* 24, no. 3 (1996): pp. 265–71.

162. Brown and Wycoff, "Policing Houston"; University of Maryland, *Preventing Crime* (Washington DC: Government Printing Office, 1997).

163. Bureau of the Census, *Hispanic Population in the United States: March, 2002* (Washington DC: Bureau of the Census, 2003).

164. University of Nebraska at Omaha and the National Latino Peace Officers Association, *Police Outreach to the Hispanic/Latino Community: A Survey of Programs and Activities* (Omaha: University of Nebraska at Omaha, 2002).

165. Ibid.

166. "Police Departments Balk at Idea of Becoming 'Quasi-INS Agents,'" *USA Today*, May 7, 2002. Bob McDonnell, President, California Police Chiefs Association, *Letter to Attorney General John Ashcroft,* April 10, 2002.

167. Thomas M. Frost and Magnus E. Sherry, *San Diego Community Profile: Final Report* (Washington DC: The Police Foundation, 1975).

168. John E. Boydstun and Michael E. Sherry, *San Diego Community Profile: Final Report* (Washington DC: The Police Foundation, 1975).

169. Bobb, *Five Years Later,* p. 27.

170. Quoted in the U.S. Department of Justice, *Attorney General's Conference: Strengthening Police-Community Relationships: Summary Report* (Washington DC: U.S. Department of Justice, 1999), pp. 9–10.

171. Jerome L. Blakemore, David Barlow, and Deborah L. Padgett, "From the Classroom to the Community: Introducing Process in Police Diversity Training," *Police Studies* XVIII, no. 1 (1995): pp. 71–83.

172. Geoffrey P. Alpert, William C. Smith, and Daniel Watters, "Implications of the Rodney King Beating," *Criminal Law Bulletin* 28 (September–October 1992): p. 477.

173. Arthur J. Lurigio and Dennis P. Rosenbaum, "The Travails of the Detroit Police-Victims Experiment: Assumptions and Important Lessons," *American Journal of Police* XI, no. 3 (1992): pp. 22–23.

174. Charlotte-Mecklenburg Police Department, International Unit, *Law Enforcement Services to a Growing International Community* (Charlotte: Charlotte-Mecklenburg Police Department, 2004).

175. New York City Police Department, Fact Sheet, New York City's Arab Communities. Available on the Vera Institute Web site at www.vera.org.

176. Tom R. Tyler, "Enhancing Police Legitimacy," *The Annals* 593 (May 2004): pp. 84–99; Charlotte-Mecklenburg Police Department, *Employee Conduct: Investigations and Discipline* (2005), p. 4, Available at www.charmek.org/departments/CMPD/.

177. See also, Tom R. Tyler, *Why People Obey the Law* (New Haven: Yale University Press, 1990).

178. San Jose Police Department, *Vehicle Stop Demographic Study: First Report* (San Jose, CA: San Jose Police Department, December 1999).

179. U.S. Department of Justice, *Principles for Promoting Police Integrity: Examples of Promising Police Practices and Policies* (Washington DC: U.S. Justice Department, 2001).

180. Alpert, Smith, and Watters, "Implications of the Rodney King Beating," p. 477.

181. Ibid.

# Police Corruption

"For as long as there have been police," Lawrence Sherman observes, "there has been police corruption."[1] Corruption is one of the oldest and most persistent problems in American policing. Historians have found evidence of bribery in the earliest years of colonial America. Although a number of police departments have successfully reduced it in recent years, corruption persists as a major problem in some departments today. Most recently, an investigation into the Los Angeles police department found serious corruption in the organization. Officers in the Rampart Division of the Los Angeles police depart-ment were found to be involved in the theft of drugs, bank robbery, false imprisonment, planting evidence, and the beating of arrestees.[2] In the 1990s, the Mollen Commission found serious corruption in the New York City police department. Officers were found on the payroll of drug dealers, earning up to $4,000 a week.[3] Similarly, in 1998, forty-nine police officers and jail guards in Cleveland were convicted of accepting money to protect drug shipments.[4]

This chapter examines the nature of police corruption, the factors that cause it, and strategies for controlling it.

# A Definition of Police Corruption

Herman Goldstein defines **police corruption** as "acts involving the misuse of authority by a police officer in a manner designed to produce personal gain for himself or for others."[5] The two key elements are (1) misuse of authority and (2) personal gain.

Corruption is only one form of misconduct or deviant behavior by police officers. Barker and Carter's typology of police deviance distinguishes between occupational deviance and abuse of authority. **Occupational deviance** includes criminal and noncriminal behavior "committed during the course of normal work activities or committed under the guise of the police officer's authority." This includes improper behavior that is not illegal, such as sleeping on the job. **Abuse of authority** includes an action by a police officer "that tends to injure, insult, trespass upon human dignity . . . and/or violate an inherent legal right" of a citizen.[6] An illegal arrest or use of excessive force is wrong but does not involve any personal gain. Some illegal activity by a police officer, meanwhile, is not occupational deviance. A criminal assault on a friend or family member by an off-duty police officer is a private act. Finally, some actions are unwise but not necessarily illegal. Some police departments, for example, do not allow their officers to receive free meals at restaurants. Taking a free meal is a

For a full discussion of police corruption during the early years of policing, see Chapter 2.

**police corruption**

**occupational deviance**

**abuse of authority**

425

## EXHIBIT 13–1

### Personnel Standards, Omaha Police Division

**Chapter 1: Section 18**

**Receiving or accepting any fee, reward or gift, of any kind for services rendered, or pretending to be rendered:**

No officer or employee of the Police Department shall expect or accept extra compensation in any form from any person, outside the Police Department, for services rendered as part of his official duties, unless same is approved by the Chief of Police.

No officer or employee shall solicit or accept any form of compensation or gift for the performance of, or failure to perform, an act or service which is part of his official duties. This includes, but is not limited to, accepting or soliciting free or reduced rate meals at restaurants/food establishments, or free or reduced admission into theaters/sporting events.

Any person offering anything of value to an officer or employee as an incentive to influence the action of said employee, shall be brought immediately before a Command Officer for investigation of attempted bribery.

The assurance that any law enforcement officer or employee can carry out his lawfully assigned duties in a fair and impartial manner is based completely on the premise that he is not under obligation to anyone.

*Source:* Omaha Police Department, *Standard Operating Procedure Manual,* p. 77.

violation of department policy but not a crime. Exhibit 13–1 represents an excerpt from the personnel standards of the Omaha police department, indicating behavior that is prohibited.

# The Costs of Police Corruption

Corruption imposes high costs on the police, the criminal justice system, and society. First, a corrupt act by a police officer is a criminal act. Criminal activity by a police officer undermines the basic integrity of law enforcement.

Second, corruption usually protects other criminal activity. Historically, corruption protected gambling syndicates, which were the major source of income for organized crime. However, today corruption is often related to drug trafficking. A Government Accounting Office (GAO) report revealed that about half of all police officers convicted as a consequence of FBI-led corruption cases are convicted for drug-related offenses.[7]

Third, police corruption undermines the effectiveness of the criminal justice system. The New York City Commission to Combat Police Corruption argues that "The honesty and integrity of police officers is . . . critical to the workings of the criminal justice system."[8] Officers routinely testify in court, and if they have a reputation for dishonesty, their credibility in criminal cases is damaged. In 2000, as a consequence of the Rampart scandal, hundreds of drug convictions were threatened because of revelations that police officers in Los Angeles framed individuals by planting drugs on them and then lying about it.[9]

Fourth, corruption undermines the professionalism of a police department. Effective discipline becomes impossible if supervisors are corrupt and threatened with exposure by officers under their command. Corruption encourages police lying, as officers protect one another. Lying to protect oneself or other officers can then spread to other areas of policing, such as covering up excessive use of force.[10]

Fifth, as former *New York Times* reporter David Burnham argues, corruption is "a secret tax totaling millions of dollars a year" on individual citizens of New York City.[11] In some instances, it is a direct tax, as when corrupt police extract bribes from businesses.

Sixth, corruption undermines public confidence in the police. The belief that a department is corrupt undermines respect for officers and public support for the department as a whole. This has a special impact on police–community relations. Illegal vice activities have generally been relegated to low-income and racial-minority neighborhoods. Weitzer and Tuch, in their national study of citizen perceptions of police misconduct, found that minorities were significantly more likely than whites to believe that it is very common or fairly common for police officers in their city's police department to engage in corruption.[12]

The Mollen Commission's report on police corruption in New York City addressed this issue only indirectly. It noted that the worst examples of corruption and brutality existed "particularly in crime-ridden, drug-infested precincts, often with large minority populations."[13] It did not, however, specifically discuss the point that the officers in these areas probably felt free to engage in rampant corruption and brutality because they perceived the residents to be politically powerless.

On the positive side, public opinion polls consistently indicate that the police rank relatively high compared with other occupations in terms of perceived honesty and integrity. In a 2006 Gallup poll, for example, the police ranked fifth out of 21 occupations, just ahead of clergy and much higher than senators, congresspersons, bankers, and accountants.[14]

The percentage of white Americans rating the honesty and ethical standards of the police as "high" or "very high" rose somewhat between the late 1970s and the early 1990s, but then declined slightly. The ratings by nonwhites remained consistently lower than those of whites, rising and falling over the same period.[15]

For a full discussion of police–community relations, see Chapter 12.

For a full discussion of the perceived honesty of the police, see Chapter 12, Exhibit 12–5.

## EXHIBIT 13–2

### How Common Do You Think Corruption (Such as Taking Bribes, Involvement in Drug Trade) Is in Your City's Police Department?

|  | **Whites** | **Blacks** | **Hispanics** |
|---|---|---|---|
| Very common | 6% | 22% | 9% |
| Fairly common | 11 | 26 | 20 |
| Not very common | 50 | 41 | 47 |
| Not at all common | 33 | 11 | 24 |
| Number of respondents | 613 | 555 | 592 |

*Source:* Ronald Weitzer and Steven Tuch, *Rethinking Minority Attitudes toward the Police: Final Technical Report* (Washington DC: National Institute of Justice, June 26, 2004).

## Types of Corruption

Corruption takes many different forms. Some are far more serious than others. For some activities, such as receiving free meals, there is debate over whether they should be defined as corruption. Different corrupt acts have different causes and call for different control strategies.[16]

### Gratuities

**gratuities**

The most common form of police corruption involves **gratuities:** free meals, free dry cleaning, or discounts on other purchases. Some departments prohibit gratuities, while others do not. One survey found that only half of all police departments had written policies mentioning free meals—and not all of those policies clearly prohibited the practice.[17]

Gratuities involve mixed motives on the part of businesspeople. In some cases they represent a sincere effort to thank police officers for doing a dangerous job to protect the community. In other cases, they reflect self-interest: the belief that the presence of police cars near their stores will deter robbers and burglars or the expectation that the police will return the favor by providing extra patrol coverage in the

---

## Police in Focus

### *At What Price a "Freebie"? The Real Cost of Police Corruption*

Jim Ruiz, a retired police sergeant from New Orleans turned professor, recounts his experiences with receiving gratuities as a police officer in a candid and well-framed analysis of the ethical issue. He points out that most academic discussions of police accepting gratuities focus on single events of free coffee, sodas, or a free or discounted meal, and do not frame their analysis as a percentage of an officer's income or the cumulative amount they receive from gratuities each year. Ruiz's experiences and observations led him to a conservative estimate that police officers receive approximately $8,713 a year in gratuities, and that if these "gifts" were taxed, the sum would be significantly higher. He points out that policymakers and academics should not overlook the substantial amount of gratuities that police officers cumulatively receive over a year and that gratuities comprise a substantial proportion of an officer's compensation (up to 30 to 40 percent of an officer's income).

As a class, discuss whether you believe that a police department should have a policy on gratuities and

what that policy should be. If departmental policies are believed to be needed to control the practice, discuss which strategies could be used to address the issue.

#### "Conservative List" and Cost of Common Gratuities

| Gratuities | Annual Cost |
|---|---|
| Coffee/soda | $494.00 |
| Doughnuts | 444.60 |
| Lunch | 1,482.00 |
| Cigarettes | 2002.00 |
| Alcohol | 2,496.00 |
| Laundry | 962.50 |
| Movie theater | 832.00 |
| Total annual gratuities | $8,713.10 |

*Source:* Jim Ruiz and Christine Bono, "At What Price a 'Freebie'? The Real Cost of Police Gratuities," *Criminal Justice Ethics* 23, 1 (2004): pp. 44–54.

area. For example, one survey conducted in Reno, Nevada, found that about 33 percent of those who offer police officers free gifts such as coffee and meals explicitly stated that they expected special favors in return.[18]

People who believe that the police should never be allowed to receive gratuities argue that they open the door to more serious forms of corruption.[19] Gratuities encourage officers to believe they are entitled to special privileges and may lead them to demand such privileges. The Knapp Commission, which investigated New York City corruption in the early 1970s, made a distinction between **"grass eaters"** (who passively accept what is offered to them) and **"meat eaters"** (who aggressively demand favors).[20]

**"grass eaters"**

**"meat eaters"**

A survey of North Carolina residents found very mixed opinions about police accepting gratuities (see Exhibit 13–3). Only 36 percent did not believe it was appropriate for a police officer to accept an occasional free coffee, nonalcoholic drink, or discounted meal when on duty. At the same time, however, only 23 percent thought accepting a meal when off duty was appropriate.[21]

---

## EXHIBIT 13–3

### Survey Statements, Questions, and Responses

| Statements | Strongly Agree | Agree | Disagree | Strongly Disagree |
|---|---|---|---|---|
| It is appropriate for a police officer to accept an occasional free coffee, nonalcoholic drink, or discounted meal when on duty. | 51 (5%) | 549 (59%) | 265 (28%) | 69 (8%) |
| It is appropriate for a police officer to accept free meals at restaurants when off duty. | 10 (1%) | 201 (22%) | 589 (64%) | 122 (13%) |
| It is appropriate for a police officer to accept repairs at no cost to privately owned vehicles. | 1 (0%) | 70 (8%) | 668 (71%) | 191 (21%) |
| It is appropriate for a police officer to show special consideration toward someone who has given him/her one of these favors in the past. | 4 (0%) | 79 (8%) | 608 (66%) | 246 (26%) |

| Questions | Yes | No |
|---|---|---|
| If you ran a small business such as a coffee shop, restaurant, movie theater, or automotive repair shop, would you offer police officers free gifts or discounts on items like coffee, meals, movie tickets, or vehicle repair? | 334 (37%) | 558 (63%) |
| If you offered police these gifts or discounts, and they were accepted, would you expect special consideration by the police in return, such as extra patrol or a warning on a traffic stop instead of a citation? | 242 (26%) | 689 (74%) |

| | Prohibited by the Department | Left to the Officer's Discretion |
|---|---|---|
| Do you think gratuities and favors to police officers should be prohibited by the department or left to the discretion of the officer? | 569 (64%) | 319 (36%) |

*Source:* Mark Jones, "Police Officer Gratuities and Public Opinion," *Police Forum* 4 (October 1997): p. 9.

## Bribes

**bribes**

Accepting **bribes** not to enforce the law is a far more serious form of corruption. Some bribes are isolated acts, such as when an officer takes money not to write a traffic ticket. Other bribes are more systematic, particularly regular payoffs to protect a drug operation. Historically, the most serious police corruption has involved regular payoffs to protect an ongoing illegal activity—gambling, prostitution, after-hours drinking, or narcotics. In New York City, regular payoffs were referred to as "the pad." New York City police officers "on the pad" were found to receive up to $850 a month to protect a single dealer.[22] In New Orleans 11 officers were convicted of accepting $100,000 for protecting a warehouse that was being used to store 286 pounds of cocaine.[23]

Corrupt officers can also be bribed to sell information about criminal investigations, either before or after arrests are made. A tip about an investigation may help drug dealers avoid arrest. Robert Daley reported in 1978 that New York City detectives regularly sold information to defense attorneys about pending cases. Officers took money in exchange for altering their testimony, "forgetting" important points on the witness stand, destroying evidence, or revealing important points about the prosecution's case.[24] A person engaged in a civil lawsuit against someone else may bribe a police officer for damaging information about that person contained in police files. In the past, before bail reform, police officers frequently took kickbacks for referring arrested persons to certain bail bondsmen or defense attorneys.

Some bribes protect illegal activities, while others support legitimate businesses. David Burnham found that New York City building contractors regularly paid the police $50 a week to avoid being ticketed for such violations as double-parking or blocking streets and sidewalks.[25]

It is important to point out that while bribery is still a problem in many police agencies across the country, police officers in the United States ask for bribes far less often than police officers in many other countries do. One international study that surveyed citizens on whether they had been asked to pay a bribe to a police officer found that the United States ranked seventeenth out of forty-one counties; just below many of the developed counties, but above undeveloped and third-world countries (see Exhibit 13–4).[26]

## Theft and Burglary

Theft or burglary by officers on duty is a particularly serious form of corruption. One example involves officers taking money from people arrested for drunkenness. The victim often has a hard time remembering how much money he or she actually had, much less convincing anyone that the officer stole any money. Another example involves officers who steal property, money, or drugs from the police department's property room. Between 1992 and 1996, 40 police officers in New Orleans were arrested for bank robbery, auto theft, and other illegal acts. An additional 200 officers were later reprimanded, fired, or retired as a consequence of criminal activity.[27]

Narcotics arrests offer special temptations for theft. Officers making a drug raid usually find large amounts of both money and drugs. For example, the "River Cops" case in Miami, Florida, revealed that a large number of police officers were involved in the stealing and selling of cocaine. Upon further scrutiny of police activities, 19 officers were arrested, convicted, and sentenced to prison and 70 officers were fired.[28]

## EXHIBIT 13–4

### International Survey on Bribe Payments

| Nation | Percentage of Respondents Asked to Pay a Police Officer Last Year | Nation | Percentage of Respondents Asked to Pay a Police Officer Last Year |
|---|---|---|---|
| England and Wales | 0.00% | Poland | 2.36 |
| France | 0.00 | Chechnya | 2.38 |
| Netherlands | 0.00 | Belarus | 2.61 |
| Scotland | 0.00 | Costa Rica | 2.63 |
| Sweden | 0.00 | Ukraine | 3.30 |
| Switzerland | 0.00 | South Africa | 3.50 |
| Canada | 0.16 | Paraguay | 3.92 |
| Slovenia | 0.28 | India | 4.26 |
| Botswana | 0.63 | Lithuania | 4.37 |
| Macedonia | 0.72 | Slovak Rep. | 4.61 |
| Austria | 0.75 | Kyrgyz Rep. | 5.23 |
| Mongolia | 0.77 | Croatia | 6.84 |
| Malta | 0.93 | Yugoslavia | 7.09 |
| Albania | 1.13 | Brazil | 8.90 |
| Hungary | 1.35 | Georgia | 9.18 |
| Estonia | 1.46 | Russia | 9.90 |
| **United States** | 1.50 | Bolivia | 11.34 |
| Philippines | 1.56 | Bulgaria | 13.54 |
| Romania | 1.63 | Indonesia | 17.64 |
| Latvia | 1.73 | Argentina | 20.92 |
| Zimbabwe | 2.20 | | |
| | | Average | 4.59 |

Source: Sanja Kutnjak Ivkovic, "To Serve and Collect: Measuring Police Corruption," *Journal of Criminal Law and Criminology* 93 (2003), pp. 593–649.

Similarly, the Mollen Commission found that corrupt officers in New York City stole drugs, money, and guns from drug dealers. One officer took $32,000 in money and goods in one theft. In some instances, officers arranged for phony 911 calls that allowed them to enter business premises and steal goods.[29]

## Internal Corruption

In very corrupt departments, promotions or favored assignments must be purchased with bribes. During the nineteenth century, payment for promotion was so systematic in the New York City police department that there was a printed schedule of the "price list" for each rank.[30] The Knapp Commission found a "widespread" pattern of police officers bribing other officers "to gain favorable assignments." It was rumored that a bribe of between $500 and $2,000 could gain assignment as a detective.[31]

## Corruption and Brutality

The Mollen Commission argues that a new form of corruption emerged in the 1980s and 1990s, characterized by a convergence of corruption and brutality. Officers brutally beat drug dealers, stole their drugs and money, and then sold the drugs to other dealers or other officers. Not all corruption involved brutality, and not all brutality in the department was associated with corruption. Nonetheless, the two were closely related. Particularly disturbing was the extent to which officers testified that brutality was their "rite of initiation" into other forms of misconduct: "Once the line was crossed without consequences, it was easier to abuse their authority in other ways, including corruption."[32]

The most notorious case to date may involve officers from the Los Angeles police department's Rampart Division, in which officers in 1998 and 1999 were found to be engaging in "hard core" criminal activity. Officers in the Rampart CRASH unit, which was considered an elite anti-gang squad, were found to be actively attacking known gang members and falsely accusing individuals of crimes that they did not commit. Investigation into the scandal disclosed that officers routinely choked and punched individuals for the sole purpose of intimidating them. In one case, officers used a suspect as a "human battering ram" and thrust his face continuously into a wall. In several other instances officers planted drugs on suspects to make arrests. Corrupt sergeants in the division promoted these activities by giving out awards for misdeeds. One officer was given an award for shooting an unarmed innocent person.[33]

## Levels of Corruption

The level of corruption varies from department to department. In some, corrupt acts involve only an occasional deviant officer. In others, the corruption is systemic through the department. Sherman argues that the relevant question is, Why are there different kinds and extents of police corruption in different communities, and in the same communities at different points in their history?[34]

Measuring the level of corruption is extremely difficult. By definition, it is a covert crime. Normally, there is no victim to complain, since both the officer and the person paying the officer are guilty of a crime. Surveys have found that only 5 percent of those approached by a police officer for a bribe report the activity to the police.[35]

As a consequence, there is little reliable data on the extent of police corruption. Most of the available data consists of the revelations of corruption scandals and reports of investigations that usually follow major scandals. A few researchers, however, have attempted to survey the public and police officials to examine this issue, but most of these studies have not been systematic and typically ask questions about perceptions of corruption rather than participation in it.[36]

The seminal piece of research on the topic was conducted by James J. Fyfe and Robert Kane in their analysis of the life and career histories of all officers who were involuntarily separated from the New York City Police Department from 1975 through 1996. They found that very few officers were found to have been involved in corruption or other forms of police misconduct. The data indicated that 1,543 officers (out of about 78,000 who were employed over the period) had engaged in

### EXHIBIT 13-5

#### Charge Specifications against NYPD Officers from 1975–1996

| Charge Specifications | Percent (N) |
| --- | --- |
| Administrative/Failure to Perform | 30.1 (742) |
| Drugs | 19.0 (468) |
| Profit-Motivated Crimes | 15.7 (387) |
| Off-Duty Crimes against Persons | 11.6 (286) |
| Obstruction of Justice | 10.8 (266) |
| Off-Duty Public Order Crimes | 5.8 (144) |
| On-Duty Abuses | 4.8 (119) |
| Conduct on Probation | 2.2 (53) |
| **Total** | **100.0 (2,465)** |

career-ending misconduct, which represented about two percent of all officers employed over the period.[37]

As seen in the table above (See exhibit 13–5), the 1,543 officers generated 2,465 charges. The majority of offenses against officers were administrative in nature, followed by drug offenses (e.g., sale, possession), profit-motivated crime, off-duty crimes against persons, obstruction of justice, off-duty public order crimes, on-duty abuse (i.e., excessive force), and conduct on probation. Accordingly, the authors found that very few of the officers were disciplined for activities associated with corruption.

Fyfe and Kane also examined those risk and protective factors associated with career-ending police misconduct in the New York City Police Department. They concluded that those officers who were black, had a criminal history, and had documented problems in prior jobs were the most likely to be separated from the police department for serious misconduct. Conversely, those who had an associates or baccalaureate degree and those who performed well in the Academy were significantly less likely to engage in career-ending misconduct.

## Pervasiveness of Corruption within a Police Organization

Sherman identified different levels of corruption, using a three-part typology based on "the pervasiveness of corruption, its organization, and the sources of bribes."[38]

### Type I: Rotten Apples and Rotten Pockets

The least serious form of corruption exists when it involves only a few police officers acting on their own. The **"rotten apple"** theory describes a situation where only a few officers are independently engaged in corrupt acts. A **"rotten pocket"** exists when several corrupt officers cooperate with one another. An example of a rotten pocket is a group of narcotics officers stealing money or drugs during a narcotics raid. The Mollen Commission found corruption centered in crews. In the Thirtieth Precinct of the New York City police department, for example, groups of three to five officers worked semi-independently, protecting and assisting each other.[39]

"rotten apple"

"rotten pocket"

**pervasive unorganized corruption**

## Type II: Pervasive Unorganized Corruption

Corruption reaches a higher degree of intensity when it has "a majority of personnel who are corrupt, but who have little relationship to each other."[40] Many officers may be taking bribes for not issuing traffic tickets, but the officers are not actively cooperating with one another. Here the corruption is pervasive, but unorganized.

**pervasive organized corruption**

## Type III: Pervasive Organized Corruption

The most serious form of corruption exists at an organized level that penetrates the higher levels of the department. An example is a systematic payoff to protect illegal activities, with the payoff shared among all members of a unit and their supervisors. In his study of one West Coast city, William Chambliss describes how one restaurant owner had to pay $200 a month to the beat officers (the sum was divided equally among them) and $250 a month to the higher-ranking officers (also divided among several officers). Failure to pay meant that the owner faced frequent citations for building code violations.[41] The Knapp Commission found that in New York City a newly assigned plainclothes detective was not entitled to a share of the payoffs for about two months until he was checked out for reliability. The earnings lost by this delay were made up in the form of two months' "severance pay" when the officer left the division.[42]

---

# Theories of Police Corruption

Theories of police corruption fall into six different categories, depending upon whether they focus on the individual officer, the social structure, the neighborhood, the nature of police work, the police organization, or the police subculture.

## Individual Officer Explanations

The most popular explanation of police corruption is the so-called rotten-apple theory. It is appealing because it emphasizes the moral failings of one or more individuals, provides convenient scapegoats, and avoids dealing with more difficult issues. It also points in the direction of a simple remedy.

Police officials prefer the rotten-apple theory because it allows them to blame a few individuals without having to investigate larger problems in the department. The department can appear to solve the problem by firing the guilty officers. The rotten-apple theory also appeals to private citizens, because they can understand personal guilt more easily than complex legal or organizational issues. Further, the theory allows citizens to avoid considering the extent to which police corruption may be rooted in their own preferences for gambling or other illegal activities.

Most experts, however, believe that the rotten-apple theory fails to adequately explain most police corruption. It does not account for the long history of corruption or its pervasiveness in certain departments. How could so many "bad" people be concentrated in one organization? Nor does it explain why some honest people become corrupt. Studies of police recruitment indicate that most people attracted to policing are not morally inferior; they are rather average people, attracted to policing for the same reasons that people choose other careers.[43] Finally, the rotten-apple theory does not explain why some police departments have long histories of corruption while others are relatively free of corruption. The Knapp Commission concluded that "the rotten-apple doctrine has in many ways been a basic obstacle to meaningful reform."[44]

# Social Structural Explanations

Most experts explain police corruption in terms of the American social structure. In their view, closely related aspects of the criminal law, cultural conflict, and politics encourage and sustain corruption.[45]

## *The Criminal Law*

The criminal law is a major cause of much police corruption. State and federal laws prohibit or seek to regulate many activities that people regard as legitimate recreation or matters of private choice. These include gambling, alcohol and drug consumption, and various sexual practices. The basic problem is a conflict of cultures and lifestyles. Some people believe these activities are immoral and harmful, while others believe they are acceptable and not harmful to others.[46]

Prohibition in the 1920s is an excellent example of the extent to which an industry will arise to provide products or services that have been outlawed. The providers of illegal goods and services have a self-interest in maintaining their enterprise. The profits from these nontaxed enterprises provide sufficient revenue to corrupt the administration of justice—to bribe police, prosecutors, and judges as needed. Police corruption, then, is a routine business expense—an "insurance policy" designed to guarantee continuation of the enterprise. Recently, Eric Schlosser reported that organized crime and illicit activities were a major part of the American economy. Roughly 4.6 percent of America's gross domestic product (GDP), or about $650 billion, was related to the nation's "shadow economy."[47] The greatest proportion of the revenue is believed to be generated through drug trafficking and sales. Drug sales alone are believed to total about $60 billion a year.[48]

Criminal syndicates have sufficient financial resources to support candidates for political office who, in turn, may use their power to influence the administration of justice, including, for example, blocking the investigation of certain criminal activities. In 1935 V. O. Key noted a change in the nature of police corruption as the delivery of vice services became more centralized and criminal syndicates took on the characteristics of legitimate big business enterprises.[49]

The law also includes many regulatory ordinances that contribute to police corruption. Laws prohibiting double-parking, for example, are designed to facilitate the smooth flow of traffic, but some business owners are afraid that tough enforcement will deny them some customers. Particularly in cities with congested central business districts, there have been payoffs to the police to ignore certain traffic law violations.

The example of regulatory ordinances illustrates an important distinction between different types of corruption. Some forms of corruption involve the use of deviant means to further deviant goals. An example is bribery to protect illegal drug sales. Other forms of corruption involve deviant means to achieve legitimate goals. An example is a bribe to sustain a profitable business.

William Chambliss emphasizes the intimate connection between the law, the political structure, the police, and criminal activity. "Organized crime," he argues, "becomes not something that exists outside law and government but is instead a creation of them." Chambliss adds that "the people who run the organizations which supply the vices in American cities are members of the business, political, and law enforcement communities—not simply members of a criminal society."[50]

### Cultural Conflict

The criminal law is a reflection of the cultural diversity of American society. Different groups have used the law to prohibit behavior that offends their values. Other groups, however, regard the same behavior as legitimate. McMullen argues that conflict over the goals of the legal system is a basic precondition for corruption: "A high level of corruption is the result of a wide divergence among the attitudes, aims, and methods of the government of a country and those of the society in which they operate."[51]

### Local Political Culture

The level of corruption in a police department is heavily influenced by the local political culture. Sherman argues that there will be less corruption in "communities with a more public-regarding ethos." Some communities develop traditions of efficient and honest public service, while others develop self-serving, or "private-regarding," traditions that encourage corruption.[52] Police corruption persists in New York City and New Orleans because corruption pervades other parts of government. But police corruption has been largely eliminated in cities such as Charlotte, North Carolina, and Portland, Oregon, where the local political culture emphasizes good government.

Although an important factor, the concept of political culture has not been clearly defined or investigated. It is not clear why some cities and counties have a different political culture or exactly how it affects law enforcement.

## Neighborhood Explanations

Just as some individuals are responsible for corruption, and some organizations foster corruption, Robert Kane argues that some neighborhoods influence the deviant patterns of police officers assigned to an area. He points out that since the 1930s researchers have known that crime and delinquency are strongly related to neighborhoods that are characterized by social disorganization (i.e., neighborhoods with high levels of poverty, high population turnover, high racial diversity, and low levels of informal social control). Kane maintained that because police officers work in socially disorganized neighborhoods where they are subject to many of the same neighborhood problems that lead to increases in crime among residents, such factors might also explain police misconduct.

To examine this issue he collected data on the number of police officers terminated and dismissed by the New York City police department between 1975 and 1996. He then linked this information to where the officers were assigned at the time of the incident(s) that led to their separation and whether the officer was dismissed because of police misconduct/corruption. Kane found that corruption was significantly more likely to take place in neighborhoods where there was a great amount of population turnover, poverty, and unemployment; and where there was a high proportion of foreign-born residents and persons who had low levels of education.[53]

## The Nature of Police Work

Barker argues that the "occupational setting" of police work "provides the police officer with more than ample opportunity for a wide range of deviant activities."[54]

Three aspects of police work contribute to police corruption. First, police work exposes officers to many opportunities to be corrupt. The police enforce the law, and inevitably, some people seek to avoid arrest by offering a bribe. Thus, officers face constant temptations from people seeking to corrupt them. Organized crime syndicates, in particular, have enormous financial resources at their disposal. This helps to explain why corruption has generally been worst among vice officers. The increase in drug activity in the 1980s, particularly with the advent of crack cocaine, exposed officers to greater temptations than in the past.

Second, policing is **low-visibility work.**[55] Officers generally work alone or in pairs, with no direct supervision. The risk of being caught is often very low. Detectives work with even less direct supervision than patrol officers. Thus, they face the greatest temptations and have the lowest risk of being caught.

Third, the impact of police work on officer attitudes also contributes indirectly to corruption. Herman Goldstein argues that "the average officer—especially in large cities—sees the worst side of humanity. He is exposed to a steady diet of wrongdoing. He becomes intimately familiar with the ways people prey on one another." As a result, officers easily develop a cynical attitude toward people. Constant exposure to wrongdoing can lead to the belief that "everyone does it."[56]

**low-visibility work**

## The Police Organization

Some departments have more corruption than others, while others have succeeded in reducing it. The most important organizational variable is leadership: the quality of management and supervision. Corruption flourishes in departments that tolerate it. Assuming that temptations or "invitations" to corruption are prevalent in all communities, individual officers are more likely to succumb if they believe they won't be caught or, if they are caught, the punishment will not be severe.

Carl Klockars examined the impact of organizational culture on corruption in thirty police departments across the country. He found that officers, regardless of the police organization that they worked for, ranked the seriousness of various types of corruption similarly. However, he found that officers in departments that scored high on organizational integrity were more likely to expect to be severely disciplined if caught committing a corrupt act than officers in departments that scored low on organizational integrity. He also found that officers in departments that scored high on organizational integrity were more likely to believe that officers should be severely disciplined for engaging in corrupt acts.[57] Such findings suggest that while police officers view the seriousness of various forms of corruption similarly, officers in organizations that do not tolerate corruption may be less tempted to engage in corruption.

Robin Haarr emphasizes the importance of organizational commitment and its relationship with police deviance. In her examination of patrol officers in one

Midwestern police department, she found that officers with a low level of organizational commitment were more likely to engage in work avoidance and police misconduct such as sex with prostitutes and unnecessary use of force. On the other hand, she found that officers with a high level of organizational commitment were more likely to engage in deviance *for* the organization such as falsifying arrest reports and lying in court to increase work productivity.[58]

## The Police Subculture

The occupational subculture of policing is a major factor in both creating police corruption, by initiating officers into corrupt activities, and sustaining it, by covering up corrupt activities by other officers.

In his classic study of the police subculture, Westley reported in 1970 that officers were willing to lie to cover up an illegal act by another officer.[59] Recent studies suggest that little has changed in the last 30 years. In a survey of 925 officers from 121 police departments, Weisburd and colleagues reported that 52.4 percent of officers thought that it is not unusual for a police officer to turn a blind eye to improper conduct by other officers, and only 39 percent of officers agreed that police officers would report serious criminal violations involving abuse of authority by fellow officers.[60]

This is in large part a consequence of peer pressure, which is particularly strong among police officers. The police subculture puts a high value on loyalty and group solidarity (Chapter 6). Officers defend one another in the face of criticism because they expect their colleagues to come to their aid as well. This kind of group solidarity, however, tends to foster lying and cover-ups.[61] Officers who are not loyal to other officers are often ostracized in the police department. One national survey of

---

**S I D E B A R          1 3 – 1**

### *Do the Police Have an Obligation to Participate in Internal Investigations and Research about Corruption?*

Learning the nature and extent of corruption in a police agency is a necessary first step before any response to it can take place. However, in many police departments, corruption is an unspeakable topic. Police administrators do not talk about it out of fear that a scandal might break out. Police officers, on the other hand, abide by a strict subculture that dictates that they should remain silent about issues involving police misconduct out of loyalty to fellow officers. Last, unions in many police departments have not permitted their officers to participate in research about corruption, arguing that they are just trying to protect their members.

As a class, discuss what you think about a police department's "moral obligation" to participate in internal investigations on corruption as well as research examining corruption. Should police officers be more open to insiders and/or outsiders about issues involving corruption in their department? If they were, what would be the consequences for police officers and police administrators?

*Source:* Sanja Kutnjak Ivkovich, "To Serve and Collect: Measuring Police Corruption," *Journal of Criminal Law and Criminology* 93 (2003): pp. 593–649.

police officers reported that 67 percent of police officers believed that an officer who reports another officer's misconduct is likely to be given the cold shoulder by his or her fellow officers.

# Becoming Corrupt

## The Moral Careers of Individual Officers

With very few exceptions, police officers are honest at the outset of their careers. (The exceptions are those individuals who have prior histories of criminal activity and who are not rejected during recruitment.) The Mollen Commission found that "most corrupt officers start off as honest and idealistic." In fact, "some of the most notoriously corrupt cops in the [New York City] Department were ideal recruits on paper."[62] Officers who do become corrupt typically go through a process involving a series of stages that move from lesser to greater tolerance of and/or involvement in corrupt activities. Sherman describes this process as the **"moral career" of a police officer.** [63]

"moral career" of a police officer

The moral career of a corrupt officer begins with relatively minor gratuities. The officer begins to regard free meals as a normal part of the job. Peer pressure is extremely important in this first stage. The new officer is introduced to corrupt acts by veteran officers. Sherman writes that the "moral experience about accepting these perks usually occurs in the recruit's first days on duty, and the peer pressure to accept them is great."[64] The Mollen Commission found that in New York the unpunished use of excessive force initiated many officers into patterns of misconduct, including corruption.[65]

At the same time, the officer is under pressure from citizens offering bribes. There are many stories of free meals being forced on police officers even though they are willing to pay.

The second and third stages of becoming corrupt, according to Sherman, involve regulatory offenses. An officer accepts a free drink from a bar owner and allows the bar to remain open after the legal closing hour, or the officer takes a bribe from a driver who has exceeded the speed limit. Peer pressure is important if the officer knows that other officers routinely do the same thing. At this point, the individual officer is still passively accepting such offers.

At some point, the officer becoming corrupt changes from one who only passively accepts gratuities (the "grass eater") into one who aggressively solicits bribes (the "meat eater").[66] Corrupt acts begin to involve more serious violations of the law, become more systematic, and involve larger amounts of money; the officer begins to initiate corrupt acts. The fourth, fifth, and sixth stages in Sherman's hypothetical model involve regular payoffs for the protection of such activities as prostitution and narcotics trafficking. Sherman points out that "accepting narcotics graft . . . is the most difficult moral experience of all." Officers must adjust their self-image to accept the fact that they are actively assisting the sale and distribution of what they know to be an illegal and destructive drug. At this point the moral career of the officer is complete. The officer has reached the final point of not just accepting but actively furthering illegal and harmful activities.

## Corrupting Organizations

Entire organizations become corrupt as they move through similar stages from less serious to more serious corruption. The "moral career" of a department can be viewed as moving through the various stages identified by Sherman. Initially, corruption involves isolated individuals or a few isolated groups. When virtually all officers are engaged in corrupt acts, the second and third stages have been reached. The final stages involve "pervasive organized corruption," in which virtually all officers are engaged in systematic arrangements with criminal elements. A police department becomes progressively corrupt because the department's leadership does not actively combat corruption.

# Controlling Corruption

Controlling police corruption is extremely difficult. The history of the police indicates that many apparently successful reform efforts have been only temporary. Herman Goldstein observes that "the history of reform provides many illustrations of elaborate attempts to eliminate dishonesty followed by rapid reversion to prior practices."[67] In New York City, for example, there have been corruption scandals followed by special investigations every 20 years since the 1890s (see Sidebar 13–2). Each investigation made recommendations for reform, and yet corruption continued to flourish.

At the same time, however, there are examples of police departments that have successfully reduced or eliminated corruption: Los Angeles and Oakland in the 1950s. Sherman calls the reform of the Oakland police department during the same period "one of the most lasting of any American police agency."[68]

The control of corruption involves two different tasks. The first is to prevent it from occurring in the first place. The second is to reduce and eliminate it once it exists. There are two basic approaches to the control of corruption. One involves *internal* approaches, including activities undertaken by a police department itself. The other involves *external* approaches, including agencies outside of the department.

**SIDEBAR 13 – 2**

### *Investigations of Police Corruption, New York City*

1885—Lexow Commission

1913—Curran Commission

1932—Seabury Commission

1954—Gross Commission

1973—Knapp Commission

1994—Mollen Commission

*Source:* Frank Anechiarico and James B. Jacobs, *The Pursuit of Absolute Integrity* (Chicago: University of Chicago Press, 1996), p. 157.

# Internal Corruption Control Strategies

There are several components of an effective internal corruption control program.

## The Attitude of the Chief

Experts agree that successful control of corruption begins with the attitude of the chief administrator. The head of the department must make it clear that corruption will not be tolerated. The Mollen Commission argued that "commitment to integrity cannot be just an abstract value. It must be reflected not only in the words, but in the deeds, of the Police Commissioner, the Department's top commanders, and the field supervisors who shape the attitudes of the rank and file."[69] The known examples of successful corruption control all involved strong action by chiefs: William Parker in Los Angeles, Wyman Vernon in Oakland, Clarence Kelley in Kansas City, and Patrick V. Murphy in New York City.

A police chief faces certain risks in taking a strong public stand against corruption. Open discussion of the subject is an admission of existing or possible wrongdoing. The Mollen Commission found that anticorruption mechanisms in New York City failed in part because department officials did not want any bad publicity. As a result, allegations of corruption were not investigated.[70]

## Rules and Regulations

The second step in a corruption control process involves clearly defining what actions will not be tolerated. One way to draw the line clearly is to develop written policies that specify forbidden acts. The use of written policies, or what is known as administrative rulemaking, is also used to control police discretion and to achieve police accountability. Carter and Barker argue that administrative rules on corruption serve six basic purposes. They "(1) inform officers of expected standards of behavior; (2) inform the community about those standards; (3) establish the basis for consistency in police operations; (4) provide grounds for discipline and counseling of errant officers; (5) provide standards for officer supervision; and (6) give direction for officer training."[71]

For a full discussion of administrative rulemaking, see Chapter 11.

There is much disagreement over where to draw the line on some issues.[72] Not all law enforcement officials believe that it is necessary or possible to prohibit free meals or other discounts, for example. A Police Foundation survey of Oregon state police officers found that 62 percent did not think it was proper for officers to accept discounts even if they were offered to other customers, while 20 percent thought it was acceptable.[73]

For a full discussion of police accountability, see Chapter 14.

Other leaders, however, argue that the line must be drawn prohibiting all gratuities. Patrick V. Murphy told his officers, "Except for your paycheck there is no such thing as a clean buck."[74] William Parker in Los Angeles and O. W. Wilson in Chicago believed that even a free cup of coffee compromised the integrity of the police. The argument against all gratuities is premised on the belief that this one small step creates a climate in which successively larger steps become possible. Other experts, however, argue that anticorruption efforts should focus on serious acts of corruption.

# Managing Anticorruption Investigations

The effective control of corruption requires meaningful investigation of suspected corruption by the department itself. Typically, this is the responsibility of the internal affairs unit (IAU) or office of professional standards (OPS). (See Exhibit 13–6.)

A successful anticorruption effort requires several elements. As already noted, it first needs the strong backing of the chief executive. The International Association of Chiefs of Police (IACP) recommends that the unit commander "should report directly to or have regular access to the chief," since the chief is ultimately responsible for discipline.[75] The Mollen Commission, however, found that in New York City command officers sent clear messages to corruption investigators that they should not aggressively pursue reports of corruption. The most notorious officer in that scandal, Michael Dowd, was in fact arrested on drug charges by suburban Suffolk County police, and not by New York City police.[76]

Second, an IAU needs a sufficient number of personnel to handle the investigative workload. Patrick V. Murphy increased the size of the Internal Affairs Division (IAD) in the New York City police department, bringing the ratio of investigators to officers from 1 to 533 line officers, to 1 to 64. Sherman found investigator-to-officer ratios of 1 to 110 and 1 to 216 in two other departments he studied.[77] Murphy also decentralized anticorruption by creating a network of field internal affairs

## EXHIBIT 13–6

### Internal Affairs Unit, St. Petersburg Police Department

**VI.** Internal Affairs Division

  **A.** Purpose of the Internal Affairs Division

    **1.** To conduct thorough investigations and make fair and impartial evaluations of allegations made against employees, upon receipt of an allegation or complaint of misconduct against the Department or its employees, or as may be directed by the Chief of Police.

    **2.** To make random inspections to ensure proper conduct and integrity in the following areas:

      a. Audit and destruction of controlled substances seized by the Department

      b. Use of cellular phones

      c. Bail bond procedures

      d. Wrecker service

      e. Random substance testing

  **B.** Organization and Staffing

    **1.** The Internal Affairs Division shall report directly to the Chief of Police. The Division will be staffed by such personnel as directed by the Chief and assigned to such duty hours as directed by the Division Commander.

    **2.** The Commander of the Internal Affairs Division shall advise the Chief of Police of the receipt of each Formal Complaint or potential formal complaint, as necessary. In no case shall this exceed seven (7) calendar days from the time the information was received.

*Source:* St. Petersburg Police Department Internal Affairs Report, 2005.

units (FIAUs). Twenty years later, however, the Mollen Commission found that the IAD investigated few corruption allegations, while most cases were delegated to the FIAUs, which were then too overloaded to conduct effective investigations.[78] The problem was not necessarily the structure of the anticorruption effort but the lack of administrative commitment to make it work effectively.

There is disagreement over whether anticorruption efforts should be centralized or decentralized within the department. Most police departments have centralized the management of investigations, with the commander of the IAU reporting directly to the chief. However, some agencies, such as New York City, take a different approach by decentralizing their anticorruption efforts.[79]

Staffing IAUs is a problem in many departments. Police officers generally do not like IAUs, regarding them as "snitches," and do not want the assignment themselves. Interviews with current and former internal affairs officers in one southwestern metropolitan area found many examples of the stigma attached to internal affairs assignments. One officer was told by a friend, "You're crazy, what the hell do you want to work there for?" Another was told "I thought you were better than that."[80]

From the perspective of many officers, internal affairs violates the norms of group solidarity. Also, many officers regard internal affairs investigations as more intrusive than criminal investigations. Under the *Garrity* **ruling,** an officer can be disciplined and even dismissed for refusing to answer questions by internal affairs (although anything the officer discloses cannot then be used against him or her in a criminal prosecution). Finally, many officers believe that internal affairs is biased and out to "get" certain officers.[81]

*Garrity* ruling

In some departments, because of union contracts, the chief has no choice over who is assigned to the IAU. Common sense suggests that someone who does not want the assignment, or who may have a problematic performance record, is not likely to be an aggressive anticorruption investigator. In other departments the chief has full control over assignment to the IAU, and it is a preferred assignment that is considered a key to promotion.

## Investigative Tactics

The major obstacle facing anticorruption investigations is the same one that all detectives face: obtaining credible evidence. Corruption is often a victimless crime with no complaining party. Investigators usually have to initiate investigations on their own. In corrupt departments, the major problem has always been the "blue curtain," the refusal of officers to testify against corrupt officers. Even honest officers are reluctant to inform on their colleagues.

Successful investigations have often relied on a few corrupt officers who decided to cooperate with investigators. In the New York City scandal of the 1970s, officers David Durk, Frank Serpico, and Robert Leuci provided the most important evidence for investigators. These officers did so, however, only at a tremendous personal cost: ostracism within the department and even potential threats against their lives. Similarly, in the Los Angeles Rampart scandal it was not until after officer Rafael Perez was arrested for auto theft, forgery, and the sale of cocaine, and was offered a reduced prison sentence, that he provided departmental investigators with information that broke the case open.[82]

# Cracking the "Blue Curtain"

blue curtain of silence

The so-called **blue curtain of silence**—the refusal of officers to testify against other officers—is one of the major factors protecting police corruption. In Los Angeles and New York City new initiatives have been developed to catch and punish officers who give false testimony. In Los Angeles, the inspector general for the Police Commission launched a new effort in 1997 to identify officers who give "false and misleading testimony" in investigations.[83] The Commission to Combat Police Corruption, established in the wake of the Mollen Commission investigation, reviewed the police department's handling of perjury cases and concluded that "the penalties imposed for lying are insufficient." It recommended that officers be automatically terminated for lying unless there were special circumstances.[84]

On the other hand, some police agencies have found that such policies actually serve to reinforce the code of silence. For example, in Los Angeles, the Rampart Independent Review Panel reported that there are a variety of reasons that officers do not immediately come forward to report an incident, including friendship, loyalty, and fear of retaliation. However, the panel found that officers often reconsider their decision, especially if they witness repeated misconduct by the same officer. It argued that policies that punish officers for failing to report misconduct *immediately* discourage officers from reporting misconduct later, and further serve to reinforce the need for secrecy.[85]

# Proactive Integrity Tests

The use of integrity tests is another strategy used by police departments to identify corrupt officers. This strategy involves targeting officers who are under suspicion, called directed integrity tests, or the random selection of officers, called randomized integrity tests, and attempting to stimulate officers into engaging in corruption. For example, an officer might be called to the scene of a proposed burglary. As part of the integrity test no one would be at the supposed crime scene and there might be jewelry or cash left in the open. Because of the burglary the officer might steal the jewelry or cash and attempt to "blame" the theft on the supposed offender.

For example, New York City used this strategy in the wake of both the Knapp Commission in the 1970s and the Mollen Commission in the 1990s. In the 1970s, they found that between 12 percent and 34 percent of the officers tested failed the integrity test, depending on the district. In 1995 and 1996 about 2,500 police officers were tested, of whom fewer than 1 percent failed the test. The police department believed that this was evidence of their success in combating corruption.[86]

Similarly, in response to a series of corruption scandals, the New Orleans police department created a new Public Integrity Division in the mid-1990s. The division began conducting integrity tests of police officers to identify corruption. Exhibit 13–7 represents excerpts of a report by the division on the conduct of integrity tests.

# Effective Supervision

Standards of integrity also require effective supervision of routine officer behavior. Herman Goldstein comments that "corruption thrives best in poorly run organizations where lines of authority are vague and supervision is minimal."[87] If officers

## EXHIBIT 13–7

### New Orleans Police Department Public Integrity Division, Integrity Tests

The Public Integrity Division (PID) implemented a process to ensure that employees of the New Orleans police department abide by the rules and procedures established to provide the highest level of protection to the citizens and visitors of New Orleans. The Integrity Test program is a process by which investigators observe employees performing routine law enforcement duties. Two types of tests are utilized: *directed,* where the test is focused on a specific individual or unit; and *random,* which is not directed toward a specific individual or unit.

Scenarios are set up mimicking situations common to everyday law enforcement duties and officers are summoned to the scene to conduct an investigation. The officer(s) under observation are unaware that they are being tested. Scenarios such as staged auto accidents, found personal property, and information on search warrants have been used.

**Integrity test results, 2003**

- Number of tests conducted: 48
- Number of individual employees tested: 48
- Number of employees passed: 48
- Number of employees failed: 0

*Source:* New Orleans Police Department, *2003 Annual Report* (New Orleans: City of New Orleans, 2004).

learn from experience that their day-to-day behavior is not being monitored, or that they are not being disciplined for minor neglect of duty, they will conclude that corrupt acts will not be caught. Historically, departments with reputations for pervasive corruption have also had reputations for general inefficiency. A review of the Rampart scandal in Los Angeles found that CRASH unit sergeants and watch commanders were not involved in the day-to-day operations of the unit and failed to consult on, participate in, or oversee routine officer activity.[88]

Officers themselves argue that good first-line supervision is perhaps the best way to control police deviance. For example, in one national survey "almost 90 percent of officers believed that good first-line supervisors are effective in preventing police officers from abusing their authority." In focus group sessions, supervisors agreed, articulating that supervisors, through good role modeling and mentoring, can prevent police deviance.[89]

As a means of enhancing supervision, the IACP and the Justice Department's Police Integrity conference both recommend early warning (EW) systems to identify officers with chronic problems. EW systems are designed not just to punish officers but also to "address, and hopefully resolve, problems early in their development."[90]

For a full discussion of EW Systems, see Chapter 14.

## Rewarding the Good Officers

Experts on police corruption argue that corruption flourishes because police departments fail to reward the honest officers. As Herman Goldstein points out: "Many competent officers have found that to have reported corruption even once had the effect of permanently impairing their careers."[91] The Mollen Commission argued that "reforms must focus on making honest officers feel responsible for keeping their fellow officers honest, and ridding themselves of corrupt ones." Unfortunately, it found that honest officers "were often discouraged from doing so." Officers were told not to report corruption, and when they did report corrupt officers, the information was ignored.[92]

## Personnel Recruitment

Effective screening of recruits is an important element in controlling corruption. Unfortunately, however, it is not always possible to spot potentially corrupt officers at this stage. The Mollen Commission found that some of the most corrupt officers were ideal recruits in terms of their backgrounds.[93]

The Miami, Florida, Washington DC, and Los Angeles, California, police departments have had major corruption scandals as a result of hiring officers with crime and drug-related histories. The problem, however, was that these departments were under political pressure to hire more officers and did not conduct the normal background checks.[94] For example, officers involved in the Rampart scandal in Los Angeles were found to have criminal records, financial problems, histories of violent behavior, and drug problems. Upon further investigation the department found that these officers were all hired in the late 1980s and early 1990s, a time when the department compromised its hiring protocol in an effort to quickly fill empty positions within the police department.[95]

Today, among all large local law enforcement agencies, 98 percent report using criminal record checks, 97 percent report using background investigations, and 78 percent report using credit history checks as a screening method for selecting new officers.[96] Background investigations of job applicants are regarded as an essential part of an effective anticorruption effort. Experience indicates that persons with prior arrest records (even without convictions) and particularly people with prior involvement with drugs are extremely high risk in terms of becoming corrupt if employed as police officers.

There is considerable disagreement among police departments over whether applicants should be automatically eliminated on the basis of any prior criminal activity and/or drug involvement. Virtually all agencies refuse to hire anyone with a felony conviction. With respect to drugs, the IACP argues that the ideal standard should be "no prior drug abuse of any kind."[97] However, given the extent of drug usage in contemporary society, maintaining an absolute standard would screen out a very large percentage of applicants. Generally, most departments are willing to hire individuals with some prior drug history, making distinctions between experimentation, use, and abuse. Most departments are willing to accept individuals with some minor usage or experimentation, but not recent and/or heavy use.

Many departments have initiated drug-testing programs to identify both applicants and currently employed officers who are involved with drugs. One survey of police agencies found that 89 percent of all departments gave drug-screening tests to applicants.[98] Another study reported that of those departments that had some kind of drug-testing program, several tested officers currently in or seeking transfer to "sensitive" assignments (internal affairs, vice, or narcotics units). Officers found to be using drugs were not necessarily dismissed automatically. Many departments indicated that they preferred offering counseling to the officers.[99]

# External Corruption Control Approaches

Once corruption exists in a department, it is extremely difficult to eliminate. Often, the internal mechanisms of control have broken down or, in the case of pervasive corruption, are inadequate to the task. In those situations, external corruption control strategies may be necessary.

## Special Investigations

Because of the difficulties' in investigating corruption, special investigating commissions have sometimes been used. The Knapp Commission investigated the New York City police in the early 1970s, and the Mollen Commission conducted another investigation in the 1990s. Similarly, the Christopher Commission in the 1990s investigated allegations of police abuse in Los Angeles, California.

Special commissions have the advantage of being independent of the police department. On the other hand, commissioners may lack intimate knowledge of the inner, day-to-day workings of the department. Also, external investigations arouse the hostility of the rank and file, aggravating the existing tendency of the police to close ranks and refuse to cooperate.

## Criminal Prosecution

Because police corruption involves violations of the criminal law, prosecution under state law is one potential remedy. Criminal offenses include specific corruption-related offenses, theft, possession and sale of narcotics, and perjury.

While there is no nationwide data available on the number of state prosecutions of police officers for corruption, an analysis of officers arrested, convicted, and imprisoned can shed some light on the criminal justice system's ability to convict and punish corrupt officers. Ivkovich's historical analysis of the effectiveness of this strategy suggests that very few officers are seriously punished for engaging in corruption. For example, over the course of the Knapp Commission, 137 cases involving corruption were forwarded to the prosecutor's office, in which two-thirds of defendants were convicted or pled guilty. About 61 percent of those convicted were released or given a suspended sentence, and only five officers were sentenced to prison for one year or longer.[100]

Another remedy is to prosecute cases of local police corruption using federal laws. Federal prosecutors have fewer ties to local criminal justice officials, allowing them to be more independent in their investigations. One of the most extensive studies to examine the prosecution of corruption cases was conducted by Kathryn Malee and John Gardiner. These researchers compiled data from all corruption cases prosecuted in Chicago and Cook County between 1970 and 1987. During this 16-year period there were 114 cases involving corruption. Malee and Gardiner reported that federal prosecutors were 10 times more likely to prosecute the case than county prosecutors were.[101]

## SIDEBAR    13 – 3

### *FBI Inquiries Focus on Corruption, Misconduct*

When the FBI investigates a police agency, generally the allegations involve public corruption or misconduct. Below are examples of the types of cases the FBI has brought against law enforcement agencies.

**March 2009:** FBI investigates a former Fort Mohave (AZ) police officer accused of forcing a person in custody to have sex with him and then lying about it. A federal judge sentences the former officer to two years in prison after he pleads guilty to making false statements and violating a person's civil rights.

**January 2009:** The FBI investigates the former Sheriff of Montague County, (TX), on allegations he sexually assaulted a woman after promising her he wouldn't arrest her when deputies found drug paraphernalia in her house. The former sheriff admits he assaulted the woman and pleads guilty to deprivation of civil rights.

**December 2008:** The FBI raided the offices of the Harvey (IL) Police Department just days after four officers were arrested on suspicion of providing protection for drug dealers.

**December 2008:** Two former Broward Country, (FL) sheriff's deputies busted in an FBI sting investigation plead guilty in West Palm Beach federal court to attempted possession of cocaine.

**October 2008:** The FBI arrested the Starr County (IX) sheriff, who is indicted on drug charges involving hundreds of pounds of marijuana and cocaine moved through the remote border county.

**August 2008:** Two members of the Ramsey County (MN) sheriff's Special Investigations Unit are convicted of taking money planted during an FBI integrity test.

**August 2007:** The FBI investigates whether concealed-gun permits issued by the Sacramento County (CA) Sheriff's Department were granted for political favors.

**November 2006:** FBI agents raid the Henry County (VA) Sheriff's Office and seize evidence logs, old case files and the sheriff's own computer as part of a corruption investigation.

**November 2005:** The FBI begins surveillance in 2001 on the chief deputy sheriff of Alleghany County (PA) who was suspected of taking bribes. The investigation leads to the deputy's indictment in late 2005.

*Source:* "FBI inquiries focus on corruption, misconduct," *Arizona Republic,* June 21, 2009, page A20.

Criminal prosecution of alleged corruption is in many respects easier than prosecution of excessive force complaints. It is usually easier to prove, for example, that an officer received a bribe, and had criminal intent to receive it, than that an officer had criminal intent in beating someone. Nonetheless, there are reasons to question the effectiveness of criminal prosecution, by itself, as a long-term remedy for police corruption. In almost all of the investigations of corruption in the New York City police department, officers have been prosecuted and convicted. And yet, corruption persists. The lesson appears to be that criminal prosecution can remove individual officers but cannot eliminate the factors that cause corruption.

## Mobilizing Public Opinion

Many experts argue that police corruption flourishes in certain departments because of a local political culture that tolerates it. Controlling corruption, therefore, requires mobilizing public opinion. The media play a major role in shaping public opinion about corruption. The media often expose the existence of corruption and set in motion the reform process. *New York Times* reporter David Burnham, for example, was instrumental in exposing corruption in the New York City police department in the 1970s. His front-page article on corruption on April 25, 1970, led to the Knapp Commission investigation.[102]

It is worth noting that the *Times* took up the issue only after both the mayor and high-ranking officials in the police department had refused to follow up on the allegations brought to them by officers Frank Serpico and David Durk.

Relying on the media has certain limitations, however. Media-generated scandals tend to be short-lived. Both the media and the public have very short attention spans, and they quickly turn to other crises. The media also tend to cover the most dramatic aspects of a scandal, usually focusing on individuals who become scapegoats. The underlying causes of corruption are complex and do not offer a dramatic newsworthy event. Finally, scandals tend to produce dramatic responses, such as the removal or transfer of certain officers, which does not necessarily address the underlying problem. Departments often reassign personnel in response to a scandal. Kornblum found that mass transfers in New York City affected honest officers as well as corrupt ones and failed to address the underlying causes of corruption.[103]

## Altering the External Environment

Sherman argues that police departments are not completely at the mercy of the external political environment. He cites Oakland in the 1950s, where a reform-minded police chief influenced that environment by threatening to arrest politicians who were involved in gambling and other illegal activities. The threat helped to reduce corruption both in the police department and in the city as a whole. The result was a new political environment that was less supportive of corruption.[104]

## The Limits of Anticorruption Efforts

In a recent book, Frank Anechiarico and James B. Jacobs argue that anticorruption efforts not only have been ineffective but have made government itself ineffective. In their view, rules and regulations designed to prevent corruption limit the capacity of government agencies to be creative and flexible in carrying out their basic missions.[105]

The Anechiarico-Jacobs argument is a provocative one. As they point out, corruption persists in the New York City police department despite special investigations every twenty years since the 1890s. Nonetheless, their argument suffers from two flaws. Most important, it is almost entirely specific to New York. Other cities do not have the same level of corruption as New York, and police departments in other cities have successfully reduced corruption.[106]

 E **Case Study**

### Hurricane Katrina and the New Orleans Police Department

On August 29, 2005, New Orleans experienced substantial destruction in the wake of Hurricane Katrina, which resulted in the breach of a levy and subsequent massive flooding throughout 80 percent of the city. While a mandatory evacuation resulted in most residents leaving the city, between 50,000 and 100,000 residents were left behind to largely fend for themselves. Massive numbers of police officers were needed for humanitarian and rescue efforts and to combat lawlessness in the streets following the hurricane. However, NOPD executives quickly realized that they did not have the number of officers available for service that they had anticipated. Initially it was unclear whether missing officers were attending to family problems, were simply unable to report for duty due to being stranded, or were simply absent without leave.

Following the initiation of rescue efforts Chief Compass estimated that 500 officers, or 36 percent of the department, had deserted. News reports also began to show videos of police officers looting department stores for nonessential items, such as electronics and jewelry. (For a video clip of NOPD police officers looting during Hurricane Katrina, see http://www.youtube.com/watch?v=cHcajIRcBvA.)

The latest police department statistics show that problems associated with desertion were not as problematic as initially believed. However, they do suggest that police misconduct immediately following Hurricane Katrina will have a devastating impact on the New Orleans police department for some time to come. In the end,

- 66 officers were fired for desertion.
- 11 officers were fired for neglecting their duties.
- 41 officers resigned because of police misconduct.
- an undisclosed number were suspended without pay for police misconduct.

Altogether, it is estimated that NOPD lost about 7 percent of its officers after investigations of police misconduct were completed.

*Source:* Kevin Johnson, "Katrina Made Police Choose between Duty and Loved Ones," *USA Today,* February 21, 2006. Accessed at www.usatoday.com/educate/college/firstyear/articles/20060226.htm on August 10, 2006; Willoughby Anderson, "This Isn't Representative of Our Department," unpublished manuscript.

# Summary

Police corruption remains one of the most serious problems in policing. Not only does it have a long history, but the current drug problem threatens to make it even worse. Controlling corruption is extremely difficult. Corruption is not simply the result of a few bad apples but is deeply rooted in the nature of American society and the criminal law, and is influenced by such factors as the neighborhood where the police officer works and the unit to which he or she is assigned. Despite these problems, there are some hopeful signs. A few departments have succeeded in reducing or eliminating corruption through effective control techniques.

# Key Terms

police corruption,  425
occupational deviance, 425
abuse of authority, 425
gratuities, 428
grass eaters, 429
meat eaters, 429
bribes, 430

rotten apple, 433
rotten pocket, 433
pervasive unorganized
   corruption, 434
pervasive organized
   corruption, 434

low-visibility work, 437
"moral career" of a police
   officer, 439
*Garrity* ruling, 443
blue curtain of silence, 444

# For Discussion

1. What are the costs of corruption? How could corruption cost your community?
2. What are the five types of corruption? Give an example of each.
3. What are grass eaters and meat eaters? Which type of officer causes the greatest amount of harm to a community?
4. Explain the three levels of corruption and give an example of each.
5. Identify the six different theories of police corruption. Explain which theory you believe best explains why police corruption occurs.
6. Following Hurricane Katrina, many police officers were placed in a situation where they were required to choose between their responsibilities as police officers and their responsibilities to their families. As a class, discuss the personal and professional obligations that a police officer has during a public emergency, such as Hurricane Katrina, and what departmental strategies might be implemented to address them.

# Internet Exercises

**Exercise 1** Go to the Web site **http://www. policeabuse.org.** Select one of the many telephone and video recordings in which investigators attempt to assess the quality of police departmental complaint procedures. After viewing the recording, discuss how the officer conducted him/herself. What did the officer do well? How could the officer have better handled the situation?

**Exercise 2** Do some research on corruption in your local police department by going to the city newspaper's Web site. How often has there been a corruption scandal? Have there been any patterns (e.g., involvement in drugs, prostitution, gambling)? How has the department typically handled the problems? Has the department typically blamed the problems on a few "bad apples," or have they tried to address the root causes of the problems?

**Exercise 3** Go to the New York City Police Department's Commission to Combat Police Corruption Web site (http://www.nyc.gov/html/ccpc/html/ home/home.shtml) and review the NYPD's latest report on police corruption in New York City. As a class, discuss what the agency does well with regard to addressing corruption and what they could do better.

## Notes

1. Lawrence W. Sherman, ed., *Police Corruption: A Sociological Perspective* (Garden City, NY: Anchor Books, 1974), p. 1.

2. Bernard Parks, *Rampart Area Corruption Incident: Public Report* (Los Angeles: Los Angeles Police Department, 2000).

3. Mollen Commission to Investigate Allegations of Police Corruption, *Commission Report* (New York: The Mollen Commission, 1994).

4. Richard Willing and Kevin Johnson, "More Law Enforcers Becoming Lawbreakers," *USA Today* (July 29, 1999): 4a.

5. Herman Goldstein, *Police Corruption: A Perspective on Its Nature and Control* (Washington DC: The Police Foundation, 1975), p. 3.

6. Thomas Barker and David L. Carter, "A Typology of Police Deviance," in T. Barker and D. L. Carter, eds., *Police Deviance,* 2nd ed. (Cincinnati, OH: Anderson, 1991), pp. 3–12.

7. Government Accounting Office, *Report to the Honorable Charles B. Rangel, House of Representatives, Law Enforcement: Information on Drug-Related Police Corruption* (Washington DC: Government Printing Office, 1998), p. 35.

8. New York City Commission to Combat Police Corruption, *The New York City Police Department's Disciplinary System* (New York: The Commission, 1996), p. 10.

9. Parks, *Rampart Area Corruption Incident: Public Report.*

10. William A. Westley, *Violence and the Police* (Cambridge, MA: MIT Press, 1970), pp. 109–52.

11. David Burnham, "How Police Corruption Is Built into the System—And a Few Ideas for What to Do about It," in Sherman, ed., *Police Corruption,* p. 305.

12. Ronald Weitzer and Steven Tuch, *Rethinking Minority Attitudes toward the Police: Final Technical Report* (Washington DC: National Institute of Justice, June 26, 2004).

13. Mollen Commission, *Commission Report,* p. 45.

14. The Gallup Organization, Inc., The Gallup Poll. Available at http://poll.gallup. Accessed on January 18, 2006.

15. Sanja Kutnjak Ivkovich, "To Serve and Collect: Measuring Police Corruption," *Journal of Criminal Law and Criminology* 93 (2003): pp. 593–649.

16. Goldstein, *Police Corruption,* pp. 16–22.

17. Tom Barker and Robert O. Wells, "Police Administrators' Attitudes toward the Definition and Control of Police Deviance," *Law Enforcement Bulletin* (March 1982): p. 11.

18. Robert Sigler and Timothy Dees, "Public Perception of Petty Corruption in Law Enforcement," *Journal of Police Science and Administration* 14 (1988): p. 18.

19. Richard Kania, "Should We Tell the Police to Say 'Yes' to Gratuities?" *Criminal Justice Ethics* 7, no. 2 (1982): pp. 37–49.

20. Knapp Commission, *Report on Police Corruption* (New York: George Braziller, 1973), p. 4.

21. Mark Jones, "Police Gratuities and Public Opinion," *Police Forum* (October 1997), pp. 6–11.

22. Victor Kappeler, Richard Sluder, and Geoffrey Alpert, *Forces of Deviance: Understanding the Dark Side of Policing* (Prospect Heights, IL: Waveland, 1994).

23. Government Accounting Office, *Report to the Honorable Charles B. Rangel.*

24. Robert Daley, *Prince of the City* (Boston: Houghton Mifflin, 1978).

25. David Burnham, "How Police Corruption Is Built into the System—And a Few Ideas for What to Do about It," in Sherman, ed., *Police Corruption,* p. 305.

26. Sanja Kutnjak Ivkovich, "To Serve and Collect: Measuring Police Corruption," *Journal of Criminal Law and Criminology* 93 (2003): pp. 593–649.

27. Kappeler, Sluder, and Alpert, *Forces of Deviance: Understanding the Dark Side of Policing.*

28. Ibid.

29. Mollen Commission, *Commission Report,* pp. 22–31.

30. Jay Stuart Berman, *Police Administration and Progressive Reform: Theodore Roosevelt as Police*

*Commissioner of New York* (New York: Greenwood Press, 1987).

31. Knapp Commission, *Report on Police Corruption,* pp. 3, 167–68.

32. Mollen Commission, *Commission Report,* p. 47.

33. CNN.COM, "Testimony: Alleged Corrupt LAPD Cops Gave Each Other Awards," http://www.cnn.com/2000/us/02/10/lapd.scandal/ (February 10, 2000); CNN.COM, "Outside Probe of LAPD Corruption Scandal Demanded," http://www.cnn.com/2000/us/02/16/lapd.scandal/ (February 16, 2000).

34. Sherman, ed., *Police Corruption,* p. 3.

35. Ivkovich, "To Serve and Collect: Measuring Police Corruption," pp. 593–649.

36. See the attempt to resolve this problem in Sherman, *Scandal and Reform* (Berkeley: University of California Press, 1978).

37. James J. Fyfe and Robert J. Kane (forthcoming), "Bad Cops: A Study of Career-Ending Misconduct Among New York City Police Officers." Criminology & Public Policy.

38. Sherman, ed., *Police Corruption,* p. 7.

39. Mollen Commission, *Commission Report,* p. 17.

40. Sherman, ed., *Police Corruption,* p. 9.

41. William Chambliss, "The Police and Organized Vice in a Western City," in Sherman, ed., *Police Corruption,* pp. 153–70.

42. Knapp Commission, *Report on Police Corruption,* p. 74.

43. David H. Bayley and Harold Mendelsohn, *Minorities and the Police* (New York: The Free Press, 1969), pp. 1–33.

44. Knapp Commission, *Report on Police Corruption,* p. 7.

45. Goldstein, *Police Corruption,* pp. 32–38.

46. Robert F. Meier and Gilbert Geis, *Victimless Crime?* (Los Angeles: Roxbury, 1997).

47. Eric Schlosser, *Reefer Madness* (New York: Houghton Mifflin Company, 2003).

48. Commission on Behavioral and Social Sciences and Education, National Research Council, Committee on Law and Justice, *Transnational Organized Crime: Summary of a Workshop* (Washington DC: National Academy Press, 1999).

49. V. O. Key, "Police Graft," *American Journal of Sociology* 40 (March 1935): pp. 624–36.

50. Chambliss, "The Police and Organized Vice," p. 154.

51. M. McMullen, "A Theory of Corruption," *Sociological Review* 9 (June 1961): pp. 184–85.

52. Sherman, ed., *Police Corruption,* pp. 16–17.

53. Robert Kane, "The Social Ecology of Police Misconduct," *Criminology* 40, no. 4 (2002): pp. 867–96.

54. Thomas Barker, "Peer Group Support for Police Occupational Deviance," *Criminology* 15 (November 1977): pp. 353–66.

55. Joseph Goldstein, "Police Discretion Not to Invoke the Criminal Process: Low-Visibility Decisions in the Administration of Justice," *Yale Law Journal* 69, no. 4 (1960): pp. 543–88.

56. Goldstein, *Police Corruption,* p. 25.

57. Carl Klockars, Sanja Ivkovich, William Harver, and Maria Haberfeld, *The Measurement of Police Integrity* (National Institute of Justice: Washington DC, 2000).

58. Robin Haarr, "They're Making a Bad Name for the Department: Exploring the Link between Organizational Commitment and Police Occupational Deviance in a Police Patrol Bureau," *Policing: An International Journal of Police Strategy and Management* 20, no. 4 (1997): pp. 786–817.

59. Westley, *Violence and the Police.*

60. David Weisburd and Rosann Greenspan, *Police Attitudes toward Abuse of Authority: Findings from a National Study* (Washington DC: National Institute of Justice, 2000).

61. Westley, *Violence and the Police.*

62. Mollen Commission, *Commission Report,* pp. 5, 20.

63. Lawrence W. Sherman, "Becoming Bent: Moral Careers of Corrupt Policemen," in Sherman, ed., *Police Corruption,* pp. 191–208.

64. Ibid., p. 199.

65. Mollen Commission, *Commission Report,* p. 47.

66. Knapp Commission, *Report on Police Corruption,* p. 4.

67. Goldstein, *Police Corruption,* p. 37.

68. Lawrence W. Sherman, *Scandal and Reform: Controlling Police Corruption* (Berkeley: University of California Press, 1978), p. xxxiv.

69. Mollen Commission, *Commission Report,* p. 112.

70. Ibid., pp. 70–109.

71. David L. Carter and Thomas Barker, "Administrative Guidance and Control of Police Officer Behavior: Policies, Procedures, and Rules," in Barker and Carter, eds., *Police Deviance,* 2nd ed., pp. 22–23.

72. Kania, "Should We Tell the Police to Say 'Yes' to Gratuities?"

73. Karen Amendola, *Assessing Law Enforcement Ethics: A Summary Report Based on the Study Conducted with the Oregon Department of State*

*Police* (Washington DC: The Police Foundation, 1996), p. 12.

74. Goldstein, *Police Corruption,* p. 29.

75. IACP, *Building Integrity and Reducing Drug Corruption in Police Departments,* (Washington DC: Office of Justice Programs, U.S. Department of Justice, September 1989), p. 68.

76. Mollen Commission, *Commission Report.*

77. Sherman, *Police Corruption,* p. 10.

78. Mollen Commission, *Commission Report,* pp. 85–90.

79. Sherman, *Police Corruption,* p. 8.

80. Aogán Mulcahy, "'Headhunter' or 'Real Cop': Identity in the World of Internal Affairs Officers," *Journal of Contemporary Ethnography* 24 (April 1995): pp. 99–130.

81. Ibid; *Garrity v. New Jersey,* 385 U.S. 493 (1967).

82. Parks, *Rampart Area Corruption Incident.*

83. Inspector General, *First Annual Report* (Los Angeles: Los Angeles Police Commission, 1997).

84. New York Commission to Combat Police Corruption, *The New York City Police Department's Disciplinary System: How the Department Disciplines Members Who Make False Statements* (August 1998), pp. 32, 39.

85. Richard Drooyan, *Report of the Rampart Independent Review Panel* (Los Angeles: November 16, 2000).

86. Sanja Kutnjak Ivkovich, "To Serve and Collect: Measuring Police Corruption," pp. 593–649.

87. Goldstein, *Police Corruption,* p. 42.

88. Parks, *Rampart Area Corruption Incident.*

89. David Weisburd et al., *Police Attitudes toward Abuse of Authority: Findings from a National Study,* p. 6.

90. Department of Justice, *Police Integrity* (Washington DC: Government Printing Office, 1997).

91. Goldstein, *Police Corruption,* pp. 50–51.

92. Mollen Commission, *Commission Report,* p. 5.

93. Ibid., p. 20.

94. "D.C. Police Force Still Paying for Two-Year Hiring Spree," *Washington Post* (August 28, 1994), p. 1; Parks, *Rampart Area Corruption Incident.*

95. Parks, *Rampart Area Corruption Incident.*

96. Bureau of Justice Statistics, *Law Enforcement Management and Administrative Statistics, 2000* (Washington DC: Bureau of Justice Statistics, 2004).

97. IACP, *Building Integrity and Reducing Drug Corruption in Police Departments,* p. 26.

98. Bureau of Justice Statistics, *Law Enforcement Management and Administrative Statistics, 2000.*

99. J. Thomas McEwen, Barbara Manili, and Edward Connors, *Employee Drug-Testing Policies in Police Departments* (Washington DC: Government Printing Office, 1986).

100. Sanja Kutnjak Ivkovich, "To Serve and Collect: Measuring Police Corruption," pp. 593–649.

101. Kathryn Malee and John Gardiner, "Measurement Issues in the Study of Official Corruption: A Chicago Example," *Corruption and Reform* 2 (1987): pp. 267–78.

102. David Burnham, *The Role of the Media in Controlling Corruption* (New York: John Jay College, 1977).

103. Allan Kornblum, *The Moral Hazards* (Lexington, MA: D. C. Heath, 1976), pp. 58–59.

104. Sherman, *Scandal and Reform,* pp. 140–45.

105. Frank Anechiarico and James B. Jacobs, *The Pursuit of Absolute Integrity* (Chicago: University of Chicago Press, 1996).

106. Comments, Samuel Walker, "Author Meets Critics," American Society of Criminology, Annual Meeting, 1997.

# Accountability of the Police

## Chapter Outline

In a democratic society it is essential that the police be held accountable for their actions. Accountability is an extremely complex subject, however. This chapter examines the issues of what accountability is, what the police should be accountable for, to whom they should be accountable, and specific mechanisms or procedures for ensuring accountability.

# A Definition of Accountability

**Accountability** means having to answer for your conduct. In a democratic society    **accountability**
the police and other government agencies answer to the public. Elected officials such
as mayors, governors, and presidents of the United States answer directly to the voters. In turn, they are responsible for holding law enforcement agencies under their
jurisdiction accountable for their performance.

# The Dimensions of Accountability

What are the police accountable for? The question involves two dimensions of policing. The National Academy of Sciences argues that the police in America have a dual
mandate: fairness and effectiveness.[1] They are expected to do two things simultaneously: to control crime and disorder effectively *and* also to be fair and ensure justice.

---

**SIDEBAR     14 – 1**

*The Dimensions of Accountability*

**Accountability for What Police Do**

Crime control

Order maintenance

Miscellaneous services

**Accountability for How Police Do Their Job**

*Individual Officer Level*

  Respect

  Equal treatment

  Fairness

*Departmental Level*

  High standards of professional conduct

  Equality of services for each neighborhood

---

Looking at it another way, the police should be held accountable for *what* they do: how well they control crime, maintain order, and provide services to the public. They should also be held accountable for *how* they do their job: performing their tasks in an efficient manner, complying with the law, and treating all citizens lawfully and respectfully.

## The Dilemmas of Policing in a Democracy

The principle of accountability distinguishes democratic from totalitarian societies. In totalitarian regimes, the police do not have to answer to either the public or the law. They are, literally, "lawless." When Communism collapsed in the Soviet Union and the country began the transition to democracy, criminologist Louise Shelley commented that "for the first time in seventy years . . . the regular police (*militsiia*) were expected to abide by the rule of law."[2]

One of the most serious challenges of policing in a democratic society is that the public often demands crime control techniques that are not lawful, such as rounding up "suspicious" looking people. In his classic work *Justice Without Trial,* Jerome Skolnick argues that the demand for effective crime control often conflicts with the requirements of the law.[3] If police officers beat confessions out of people, they might solve more crimes. But that would buy effectiveness at the price of legality.

## A Historical Perspective on Accountability

Until the mid-1960s, a Los Angeles police officer faced a serious internal investigation if he damaged a patrol car but no similar investigation if he shot and wounded a citizen.[4] This example illustrates the point that meaningful accountability of the police is a relatively recent development. Through most of their history, the American police were not accountable at all (see Chapter 2). Police departments were corrupt and inefficient, and individual officers evaded duty and assaulted citizens without fear of being disciplined. Elected officials used the police for graft, protection of illegal enterprises, and getting jobs for their friends. They took almost no interest in controlling officer misconduct.

Procedures for accountability began to develop slowly in the late 1950s. The Supreme Court issued a series of decisions imposing constitutional standards on routine police work such as searches and interrogations. Police departments began to develop written rules on deadly force, pursuits, and other actions, to control police officer behavior. In the 1990s, systems such as COMPSTAT and early interventions systems emerged to review both crime control effectiveness and individual officer conduct.[5]

Important aspects of the history of police accountability are covered in Chapter 2.

A January 2001 Justice Department report, *Principles for Promoting Police Integrity,* recommended a set of "best practices" to increase integrity and accountability in law enforcement agencies. The report explained that accountability is necessary for the success of community policing:[6]

# Accountability for *What* the Police Do

## The Traditional Approach

The police role involves law enforcement, order maintenance, and service (see Chapter 1). Traditionally, however, the police were held accountable primarily for their law enforcement or crime control role. The measures of effectiveness included the crime rate, the clearance rate, and response times.[7] As discussed in Chapter 9, these data are not reliable measures of police performance. The official UCR crime rate is limited to eight Index crimes and provides no data on several major categories of crime, including white-collar crime, organized crime, and narcotics offenses. For the eight Index crimes, the UCR includes only reported crime, omitting the two-thirds of all crimes that are not reported. Police officers unfound, or do not record, an unknown number of crimes reported by citizens. Also, an unknown number of crime reports are lost through inefficiency. Because of extreme variations in department practices about recording crimes and maintaining records, the UCR is not a reliable performance measure for comparing different departments.[8]

Official arrest data are also not a reliable measure for accountability because there are wide variations in how police departments record arrests. Some departments complete an official arrest report only when a suspect is booked. Others complete an arrest report whenever a suspect is detained and questioned. Because report practices are not comparable, arrest data are not reliable for comparing different departments.[9]

The clearance rate (the percentage of reported crimes solved or cleared by the police) is also not a reliable performance measure. The data are not independently audited, and there are many opportunities for manipulating the data to produce high clearance rates. Officers can unfound reported crimes or improperly count additional crimes as cleared.

For a discussion of official police data on crime, see Chapter 9.

Finally, the traditional crime rate and clearance rate data ignore the order maintenance and service-related activities of the police, which represent 70 to 80 percent of all police work. They also do not address the *quality* of police services—for example, citizen perceptions of how they are treated.

## New Measures of Police Service

The Portland, Oregon, Auditor's Office surveyed city residents in 2005 and asked if they were willing to help the police department solve neighborhood problems. The responses varied by neighborhood. In one part of town 65 percent said they were "willing" or "very willing" to help the police. But in another area only 58 percent gave these responses. Interestingly, citywide almost 40 percent were not willing or had no answer.[10]

The Portland survey is an annual effort by the City Auditor that asks residents about all government services, including the police. This practice is consistent with the community-policing idea of developing new measures of police performance. In earlier years, the Portland auditor has asked questions about feelings of neighborhood safety and whether or not people know the police officer who works in their area.

## COMPSTAT: A New Approach

Every other Thursday, about thirty officers with the Lowell, Massachusetts, police department, including the chief, top commanders, and some sergeants and patrol officers, meet in a conference room for the biweekly COMPSTAT meeting. The purpose of each meeting is to review crime data from each of the department's three districts over the past three weeks. The review is designed to identify patterns in criminal activity and develop immediate and crime-specific responses.[11]

**COMPSTAT**

COMPSTAT is one of the most important innovations in police accountability. Originally developed by the New York City police department in the 1990s, it has been adopted by many departments across the country. **COMPSTAT** has several key elements:

- A clearly *focused mission* on crime control.
- The use of *timely data* on crime and disorder (in some programs, crime data are available within 24 hours).
- A *geographic focus,* emphasizing crime patterns in particular precincts and neighborhoods.
- Increased *internal accountability,* with precinct commanders being held responsible for responding quickly to crime problems in their areas.
- Innovative *problem solving,* with precinct commanders expected to develop timely and relevant responses to crime problems.

For a full discussion of COMPSTAT and police crime-control efforts, see Chapters 4 and 9.

COMPSTAT combines several innovations in policing that have developed in the past 20 years. The geographic focus is an application of the concept of "hot spots," with its focus on particular streets or blocks where crime is concentrated (see Chapter 10). The use of time crime data is similar to the use of officer performance data in early intervention systems (see pp. 469–473). Problem solving is an application of problem-oriented policing (see Chapter 10). And increased accountability for managers is related to other accountability measures discussed in this chapter.

Does COMPSTAT work? Is it effective in reducing crime? The New York City program coincided with a significant decline in crime in the 1990s. Many people credited COMPSTAT for this accomplishment. But it also coincided with both the NYPD's zero-tolerance policing program and a large increase in the number of police officers. Additionally, serious crime fell in other cities without any of these three innovations. Consequently, it is difficult to determine the exact impact of COMPSTAT in New York City.[12]

Because it is such a major innovation, COMPSTAT raises a number of serious organizational issues. A study of the Lowell police department found a number of problems in implementing the program. COMPSTAT was successful in focusing the mission of the department on crime control. It was less successful in promoting either a geographic focus or flexible problem solving. The traditional police bureaucracy emphasizes centralization of command and standard procedures. This is the main achievement of all bureaucracies, according to the theories of the famous sociologist Max Weber. The evaluation of the Lowell COMPSTAT program concluded that there is an inherent tension between the goals of COMPSTAT and the bureaucratic structure of modern police organizations. The impact of COMPSTAT on both police organizations and crime, in short, is unclear.

# Accountability for *How* the Police Do Their Job

There are a number of different ways in which the police are held accountable for *how* they do their job. It is useful to discuss these different ways in terms of whom the police are accountable to. From this perspective, there are two basic approaches to accountability: **internal mechanisms of accountability,** meaning accountability procedures within the police department, and external mechanisms, meaning procedures that are outside the department.

**internal mechanisms of accountability**

# Internal Mechanisms of Accountability

Primary responsibility for holding police officers accountable for their actions lies with the police department itself. Herman Goldstein argues that "the nature of the police function is such that primary dependence for the control of police conduct must continue to be placed upon internal systems of control."[13] These systems include routine supervision, officers' reports on critical incidents, periodic performance evaluations, and investigation of alleged misconduct by the internal affairs unit (IAU) or the office of professional standards (OPS).

# Supervision

## Routine Supervision

A newspaper report described the midnight shift in the Suffolk County police department as the "lost battalion." It found that officers "can go for hours without speaking to a supervisor, or weeks without having contact with their precinct's top managers."[14]

The department was failing to provide routine supervision—the kind recommended in police management textbooks since the 1940s—to officers working between midnight and 8 AM. The report was prompted by a series of allegations that male officers in the department had stopped, harassed, and even abused young, single, female drivers.

**routine supervision**

**Routine supervision** is one of the central tasks of police management, and this responsibility primarily falls on sergeants. A Police Foundation survey of police officers found that almost 90 percent agree that "good first-line supervisors can help prevent police officers from abusing their authority."[15]

## The Span of Control

For a discussion of different styles of supervision among patrol sergeants, see Chapter 7.

**span of control**

In the mid-1990s the Los Angeles County sheriff's department experienced a number of officer-involved shooting incidents by officers assigned to the Century Station. An investigation by Special Counsel Merrick Bobb—the department's citizen oversight—found that the source of the problem was not a few "bad apples" but bad management practices. Most serious, Bobb found that at times each sergeant was supervising 20 to 25 officers, a ratio that far exceeded the department's own standard of 8 to 1.[16]

The ratio of sergeants to officers is referred to as the **span of control.** The theory of span of control assumes that any supervisor can effectively supervise a limited number of people.[17] In policing, the recommended span of control is between 8 and 10 patrol officers for each sergeant. When the recommended span of control is exceeded, supervision may deteriorate, and as a result officer performance may also decline.

## What Sergeants Do

Supervision by sergeants involves a number of different activities. First, they are expected to monitor officers under their command on a regular basis, either through face-to-face meetings or over the police radio. In the case of potentially serious incidents, sergeants are expected to appear at the scene, provide advice if needed, and if necessary take command of the situation. Second, sergeants review and approve officers' reports. Typically, sergeants review and sign off on arrest reports. Third, sergeants are expected to advise officers under their command whenever their performance is less than satisfactory and to instruct them on proper procedure. Fourth, if a sergeant becomes aware that an officer has violated a department policy or committed some act of misconduct, he or she is expected to file a report with the internal affairs unit or the office of professional standards, which would then investigate the allegation.[18]

Engel's analysis of supervisors' styles found different approaches to supervision and discipline. "Supportive" supervisors define their role in term of protecting officers under their command "from criticism and discipline" by upper management. "Traditional" supervisors, on the other hand, "are more likely to punish patrol officers" than are other categories of supervisors.[19] In short, in addition to different organizational cultures between departments, there are different styles of supervision within particular departments.

Sergeants often develop close personal ties with the officers under their command. This can affect their ability to supervise properly. They may become unwilling to criticize those officers and exercise the proper level of control and discipline. These relationships represent an important part of the police subculture (see Chapter 6). Departments that allow personal ties to affect supervision and discipline do not have high standards of accountability.

# Close Supervision

The commanders in the Forty-Second and Forty-Fourth precincts in the New York City police department took a hands-on approach to supervision. They personally spoke to officers who received a high number of citizen complaints, communicating a message that improper behavior toward citizens would not be tolerated. And when some of those officers received more complaints, they were reassigned from patrol to desk duty. A Vera Institute study found that this approach to close supervision helped reduce complaints and improve relations with the community.[20]

Close supervision goes beyond routine performance appraisal. It involves focusing on specific problems and taking extra steps to correct them. Both of the precinct commanders in the Vera study communicated to their officers that reducing citizen complaints was a high priority, both personally spoke at roll call sessions, and both paired younger officers with more experienced veterans. Most important, they spoke personally to officers who received citizen complaints in an effort to both help them correct their behavior and warn them about the consequences if there were more complaints or other problems. Both reassigned or passed over for promotion officers who continued to receive citizen complaints. These actions communicated to all officers in each precinct that they would be held accountable for unacceptable performance. The Vera Institute study found that citizen complaints fell in both precincts, while complaints rose for the department as a whole.

# Coaching, Mentoring, Leading

The role of supervisors in holding officers accountable includes more than imposing formal discipline. The Standard Operating Procedure of the Madison, Wisconsin, Police Department explains that: "Some of the primary tasks of supervisors are encouraging, counseling and, if necessary, disciplining or correcting the behavior of employees. The purpose of this is to direct individual effort into effective and productive action." The department further explains that some on-the-job performance problems "may be related to alcoholism, other drug dependency, emotional disorders, or other personal problems."[21] Like many departments, it maintains an **employee assistance program** (EAP) through which officers can receive professional counseling related to the specific problem. Participation in EAP programs is confidential. Informal corrective action to improve performance problems is also the key element of early intervention systems (see pp. 469–473).

**employee assistance program**

# The Impact of Organizational Culture

The Los Angeles police department delivered a devastating criticism of its own personnel evaluation system: "Our personnel evaluations have little or no credibility at any level in the organization." This criticism was delivered by the LAPD's internal Board of Inquiry report on the Rampart scandal in 2000. The report's chapter on the department's integrity systems, meanwhile, identified over thirty policies and procedures designed to ensure integrity and accountability. Yet, it concluded that all these systems had not prevented the Rampart scandal from occurring.[22]

The findings of the Board of Inquiry report raised serious questions about the effectiveness of personnel evaluations and other internal accountability mechanisms.

There is an important distinction between meaningful accountability, where actions have consequences, and superficial accountability, where an organization has elaborate policies and forms but does not use them in any meaningful way.

**organizational culture**     Whether or not meaningful discipline occurs depends on the **organizational culture** of a police department. The Chemerinsky report on the LAPD's Board of Inquiry report argued that "every police department has a culture—the unwritten rules, mores, customs, codes, values, and outlooks—that creates the policing environment and style." The culture of the LAPD, it concluded, involves the enforcement of "voluminous rules and regulations, some of them very petty." While petty rules are enforced, serious misconduct is covered up. First, the code of silence results in officers being reluctant to report misconduct by other officers. Second, when they do report misconduct, officers are not only not rewarded for doing so but often punished by the department.[23] And in fact, ninety current and former LAPD officers filed suit against the department for having been demoted or otherwise punished for reporting misconduct by other officers.

The informal organizational culture of a police department has a major impact on accountability. A report on the Baltimore police department defined organizational culture as "the collection of embraced values, activities, rules, and standards that enable it to achieve its core identity." Focus groups with 250 officers found that the positive "cultural assets" of the department included professionalism, bravery, and commitment. However, the culture also included bitterness and cynicism on the part of officers, distrust of others in the organization, and low morale. As a result, the "operating culture" of the department included "individual survival, group loyalty, frustration and resentment."[24]

## Corrective Action: Informal and Formal

One important task for supervisors is to take corrective action to improve the performance of officers under their command. Some of these actions can be very *informal*. After a police–citizen encounter, for example, a sergeant might talk to an officer, pointing out that he or she was rude to a citizen or that the officer created a potential danger for himself by the way he placed himself at the scene. A sergeant might notice that an officer appears to have a lot of things on his mind or be in a hostile mood. Like employees in other occupations, police officers are often affected by family problems. The sergeant in this case might just talk with the officer about the situation or suggest referral to a counseling program.[25]

A number of departments have *formal* programs for improving officer performance. A sergeant might refer an officer for retraining on traffic stop or use of force tactics, for example. The Los Angeles Sheriff's Department has a formal peer officer support program. This consists of officers who have received 40 hours of training and are available to talk with other officers on a strictly confidential basis. Most departments participate in a formal employee assistance program (EAP), where an officer can receive professional counseling related to depression, family problems, or substance abuse.[26]

## Written Policies and Reporting Requirements

One of the most important tools for holding officers accountable is providing written policies governing the exercise of discretion in handling critical incidents—use of deadly force, high speed pursuits, and so forth—and then to require officers to complete written reports after each incident. These reports are then reviewed by command officers to determine whether officers complied with departmental policy. If an officer violated policy, some form of discipline should result. The nature of written policies and the reporting requirement are explained in detail in Chapter 11 on Police Discretion.

For a discussion of written policies to control police discretion, see Chapter 11.

## Performance Evaluations

Regular **performance evaluations** are a standard technique for holding employees accountable. Annual (or more frequent) evaluations by an immediate supervisor are designed to provide feedback to employees by identifying areas of outstanding, acceptable, or inadequate performance. Identifying areas of inadequate performance is intended to provide feedback to the officer so that he or she has an opportunity to improve. Performance evaluations can also be used when considering employees for promotion.[27]

**performance evaluations**

The collection of traffic-stop data is an important accountability mechanism related to allegations of racial profiling. A full discussion of data collection is in Chapter 12.

Officer Michael Dowd of the New York City police department's Seventy-Fifth Precinct received excellent performance evaluations. His supervisor wrote that he "has excellent street knowledge; relates well with his peers and is empathetic to the community, [and could] easily become a role model for others to emulate." Unfortunately, Dowd was one of the most corrupt and brutal officers in the entire NYPD, and he was eventually convicted on criminal charges.[28]

Dowd's case dramatizes the fact that standard performance evaluations sometimes completely fail to accurately assess an officer's real performance. Standard performance evaluations in police departments have a number of serious problems. A 1997 report found that "most performance evaluations currently used by police do not reflect the work officers do."[29] They also suffer from a number of technical problems. Evaluation categories and criteria often lack clarity. Many reports, for example, ask supervisors to rate officers' "quality of work," without specifying either the nature of the work or how quality should be measured. Reports also suffer from the "halo" effect, meaning that a high rating in one particular area of performance tends to affect the ratings in other areas. Evaluations are also affected by the central tendency phenomenon. That is, the ratings of all officers tend to cluster around one evaluation level (e.g., everyone receives a rating of 4 on a scale of 1 to 5). Finally, there is a problem of leniency or grade inflation: virtually everyone is rated "above average," and even a rating of "average" is considered to be highly negative.[30]

Another failure is that performance evaluations are often not used effectively for purposes of promotion or selection for important assignments. In short, once the evaluations are completed, they sit in a file without being used to make decisions about the quality of different officers and whether they merit an important promotion or assignment.

The **Christopher Commission,** for example, identified forty-four Los Angeles police officers with extremely high rates of citizen complaints. Yet, many of them received excellent performance evaluations. One officer who had been accused of striking a handcuffed suspect with the butt of a shotgun for no apparent reason was evaluated as having an "easy going manner which he used to his best advantage in the field."[31]

**Christopher Commission**

# Internal Affairs/Professional Standards Units

**internal affairs unit**

An **internal affairs unit** (IAU), or office of professional standards (OPS), is responsible for investigating alleged misconduct by police officers. Investigations are either *reactive,* in response to a citizen complaint or official report, or *proactive,* in the sense that the department has some evidence of possible misconduct by an officer that needs investigation. Some police departments conduct "stings" designed to detect potential officer corruption.[32]

**CALEA accreditation standards**

An internal affairs unit, or office of professional standards, is considered an essential element of modern police management. Standard 52.1.2 of the **CALEA accreditation standards** states that "a written directive specifies that the position responsible for the internal affairs functions has the authority to report directly to the agency's chief executive officer."[33]

Internal affairs units occupy a difficult position within police departments. Because they investigate other officers, they face hostility from the rank and file. Officers assigned to IAUs are often regarded as "snitches" for the chief. A study of IAUs in a metropolitan area in the Southwest quoted an IAU lieutenant as saying, "They are a bunch of headhunters, and they're headhunters for the police chief."[34] Officers traditionally do not like to serve in internal affairs units. One officer who requested the assignment said that his friends "thought I was nuts."[35]

The effectiveness of IAUs depends on several factors. Most important are the attitude and the actions of the chief. Virtually all experts on policing agree that the chief must communicate to officers that misconduct will not be tolerated and then follow up with appropriate discipline against officers who are in fact found guilty.[36]

Internal affairs units also need sufficient resources. This is measured in terms of the number of IAU investigators per sworn officer. Following the Knapp Commission investigation of corruption in the New York City police department in the 1970s, Police Commissioner Patrick V. Murphy increased the ratio of IAU investigators to officers from 1 to 533, to 1 to 64.[37]

Training for internal affairs investigators is very important. Many departments provide no special training related to investigating citizen complaints or corruption allegations. The PERF evaluation of the Omaha police department found that "no formal training is provided, [and] all training is on the job."[38] Most IAU officers had prior experience in criminal investigation. Investigating fellow officers is very different from investigating criminals, however.

## Internal Discipline Issues

The internal discipline process involves a number of important issues.

*Staffing.*    Internal affairs units need to be adequately staffed in order to effectively investigate alleged misconduct. Following the Rampart scandal in Los Angeles, a report found the LAPD's Internal Affairs Group "underfunded and understaffed."[39]

*Training for Investigators.*    Investigating allegations of misconduct against fellow officers is difficult for internal affairs unit investigators. No one likes to investigate friends or colleagues. A report by Jayson Wechter, a staff member with the San Francisco Office of Citizen Complaints, argues that investigating citizen complaints is especially difficult. All organizations have a tendency to be self-protective in the face of outside criticisms. Investigators are naturally inclined to believe the officer rather than the citizen.[40]

Most departments do not provide special training for IAU investigators. They assume that officers' experience in criminal investigations will be sufficient. But as Wechter argues, investigating complaints against officers, especially complaints from citizens, is different. He recommends special training for IAU investigators.

*Appropriate Discipline.*    In any organization, proven misconduct requires appropriate discipline. The same principle applies in the criminal courts: serious crime needs to be punished with an appropriately severe punishment. A report by the Philadelphia Integrity and Accountability Office (IAO) found that almost half of the officers who were found guilty by the Internal Affairs Bureau between 2000 and 2003 were "never formally disciplined."[41] The Office of Independent Review (OIR) in the Los Angeles Sheriff's Department found that in about half of all minor discipline cases the officer never undertook the required action (e.g., substance abuse counseling or anger management class).[42]

The belief that police departments do not discipline officers appropriately for proven misconduct is one major source of police–community relations problems (see Chapter 12).

*Consistent and Fair Discipline.*    Discipline needs to be consistent and fair. A 2000 report to the Los Angeles Police Commission found a lack of guidelines for the Internal Affairs Group, and as a result disciplinary actions were arbitrary and inconsistent. Favoritism for certain officers and inconsistent discipline create serious morale problems among rank-and-file officers.[43] To correct this problem, a federal judge ordered the Oakland, California, police department to develop a discipline matrix. A report by the Police Professionalism Initiative argues that a discipline matrix, which is similar to sentencing guidelines, is a potentially effective tool for police accountability.[44]

## Standards of IA Citizen Complaint Procedures

The State of New Jersey has a unique law under which the state attorney general is empowered to develop standards for the citizen complaint procedures of local police departments. The 2000 Internal Affairs Policy and Procedures (IAPP) requires each department to accept complaints "from any person, including anonymous sources"; that IA should travel to the complainants home or other location for the interview if the complainant is unable to travel; that IA should investigate collateral issues of potential misconduct not alleged by the complainant (for example, IA may exonerate the officer of use of force allegations, but investigate the legality of the original arrest); officers assigned to IA should receive specific training related to the investigation of citizen complaints; and many other requirements.[45]

The New Jersey IAPP standards are important because there has been a lack of national standards for IA units and the investigation of citizen complaints. A 2009 investigation by the New Jersey ACLU, however, found that police departments were routinely violating the attorney general's guidelines. Over 60 percent of all departments, for example, require citizens to file complaints in person, in violation of the guidelines.[46]

EXHIBIT 14-1

### Innovation: Education-Based Discipline: Los Angeles Sheriff's Department

In 2008 Sheriff Lee Baca initiated an innovative program of "Education-Based Discipline" (EBD).

Sheriff Baca believed that traditional discipline in many cases involves giving the officer a certain number of days off. It is a mechanical process that "does not require the Department to engage with the employee in a way that will remediate the employee and reduce the likelihood that the policy violations will reoccur."

Under Education-Based Discipline, the officer has the choice of taking classes, conducting briefings, or writing letters of apology to people who were offended by his or her actions.

In one case, an officer was to be disciplined for submitting to a court an affidavit with inaccurate information. An investigation determined that the inaccurate information was the result of sloppy, rushed work, and was not intentional. Nonetheless, the case against the suspects was dismissed.

Instead of the usual days off punishment, the officer was given the opportunity to write a Training Bulletin on the issue and deliver conduct briefings at two precinct stations regarding the importance of accuracy in writing affidavits. The Training Bulletin and the conduct briefings were intended to be educational for the officer and the other officers who were briefed.

*Source:* Los Angeles Sheriff's Department, Office of Independent Review, *Seventh Annual Report, April 2009* (Los Angeles: Sheriff's Department, 2009), pp. 32–34.

## *Using Discipline Records in Personnel Decisions*

The 1991 Christopher Commission report on the Los Angeles police department found that the LAPD did not use officer discipline records in promotion or reassignment decisions. As a result, officers with reprimands or suspensions were being promoted.[47]

To correct this problem, the consent decree with the Oakland (California), directed the department to take into account "Prior Disciplinary History as an Aggravating Factor" in discipline cases. Specifically, it directed that "Factors which may be considered in the weighing process include, but are not limited to: . . . The nature and seriousness of any prior violation; . . . The number of prior violations; . . . The length of time between prior violations and the current case; . . . The relationship between any prior violation and the present misconduct; . . . Whether the prior history demonstrates a continuation or pattern of the same or similar misconduct; and . . . Whether the prior history demonstrates continuous misconduct, even if minor, evidencing a failure to conform to rules or to correct said behavior."[48]

## The "Code of Silence"

"code of silence"

A corrupt New York City police officer explained the **"code of silence"** in blunt terms. Asked by the Mollen Commission investigating corruption if he was ever afraid that one of his fellow officers might turn him in, he answered, "Never." "Why not?" commission investigators asked. "Because it was the Blue Wall of Silence. Cops don't tell on cops." Anyone who might report his corrupt activities would "be labeled as a rat."[49]

The code of silence is a major part of the organizational culture of policing. Many experts regard the code as the major obstacle to police accountability. The code of silence (also known as the "blue curtain") is defined as the unwillingness of police officers to report misconduct by other officers. Westley identified the code of silence in his pioneering study of the police subculture.[50] The Christopher Commission found that the code of silence was a major factor in protecting abuse of force by Los Angeles police officers.[51] A national survey of police officers by the Police Foundation in the 1990s found that slightly more than half (52.4 percent) agreed that "it is not unusual for a police officer to turn a blind eye to improper police conduct by other officers."[52]

There have been few efforts to break the code of silence and to punish officers for giving false testimony in investigations of officer misconduct. The New York City Civilian Complaint Review Board reported instances of officers lying to the New York City police department, but the department declined to act on these reports.[53]

---

# Early Intervention Systems

## Officers with Performance Problems

Two officers in the Boston police department accumulated twenty-four citizen complaints each between 1981 and 1990. For one of the officers, three of the complaints were sustained; none of the twenty-four complaints were sustained against the other officer. An investigation by the *Boston Globe* found that a very small number of officers accounted for a large percentage of all citizen complaints: 11 percent of the officers received 62 percent of all the complaints.[54] The pattern of complaints found in the Boston police department appears to exist in almost every department.

In response to this phenomenon, departments have developed **early intervention systems** as a new mechanism of police accountability. The empirical basis of early intervention (EI) systems is the evidence that in nearly every police department a small group of officers receive a disproportionate share of all citizen complaints. They are referred to as "problem prone" officers. The Christopher Commission identified 44 problem officers in the Los Angeles police department. They averaged 7.6 complaints for excessive force or improper tactics, compared with only 0.6 for all other officers; while in Kansas City, 2 percent of the officers were responsible for 50 percent of all citizen complaints.[55]

**early intervention systems**

## The Nature of EI Systems

EI systems have emerged as a "best practice" for enhancing police accountability. A report by the COPS Office defines EI systems as follows:

> *An Early Intervention (EI) system is a data-based management tool designed to identify officers whose performance exhibits problems, and then to provide interventions, usually counseling or training, to correct those performance problems. EI systems have emerged as an important mechanism for ensuring police accountability.*[56]

---

**E X H I B I T   1 4 – 2**

## Comparing COMPSTAT and Early Intervention

EI systems are very similar to COMPSTAT (see pp. 460–461). Both involve the collection and analysis of systematic data for the purpose of focusing efforts on correcting the problems that are identified.

|  | **COMPSTAT** | **Early Intervention** |
|---|---|---|
| **Subject** | Crime and disorder | Individual officer conduct |
| **Systematic Data** | Timely official data | Timely data on officer performance on crime, citizen calls for service |
| **Problem Identification** | Pattern of residential burglaries; graffiti | High level of citizen complaints |
| **Response** | Intensive patrol problem-solving effort; resident education | Informal counseling; retraining |

---

In an EI system, officer performance data are entered into a computerized data base, where they are analyzed to identify officers who have a high rate of use of force reports, many citizen complaints, or other indicators of performance problems. These officers are then subject to an intervention by the department, usually in the form of counseling by their immediate supervisor or special training designed to improve their performance. The components of an EI system are listed in Sidebar 14–2.

EI systems are included in all of the consent decrees and memoranda of understanding negotiated by the U.S. Justice Department to settle suits against law enforcement agencies for a "pattern or practice" of abuse of citizens (see pp. 482–485). In the New Jersey state police, the court-ordered EI system is known as the Management Awareness and Personnel Performance System (MAPPS); in the Cincinnati police department, it is called the Risk Management System (RMS).[57]

## Performance Indicators

Some EI systems are very large, with many performance indicators, while others are small, with only about five indicators. The Phoenix Personnel Assessment Review System (PARS) uses eighteen indicators. The most commonly used indicators include:[58]

- Officer use of force reports.
  - *a* Use of deadly force.
  - *b* Officer-involved fatal shootings.
  - *c* Use of nonlethal force.
- Citizen complaints.
  - *a* Total complaints against the officer.
  - *b* Sustained complaints.

```
S I D E B A R          1 4  —  2
```

## *The Components of an Early Intervention System*

### Identification
Performance indicators

Analysis of data

Identification of officers with performance problems

### Selection
Assessment of identified officers

Selection of officers for intervention

### Intervention
Effort to improve officer performance

Supervisor's counseling

Training

Referral to professional counseling

### Follow-up
Monitor officer's performance, postintervention

*Source:* Samuel Walker, *Early Intervention Systems for Law Enforcement Agencies: A Planning and Management Guide* (Washington DC: Department of Justice, 2003).

---

- Officer involvement in civil suits.
- Vehicle pursuits.
- Resisting arrest charges filed by the officer.
- Use of sick leave.
- Disciplinary actions against the officer.

Some of the larger systems also include all arrests, field interrogations, and traffic stops by each officer. Systems that use a large number of indicators are better able to analyze an officer's performance. But large systems are also more difficult to manage.

## Interventions

Once an EI system has identified an officer with performance problems, that officer is subject to an official intervention. Interventions are informal and not recorded as formal discipline. There is no record of the intervention in an officer's personnel file. Typically, the intervention involves individual counseling by an officer's immediate supervisor. In many cases, the officer is simply advised to improve his or her performance. The supervisor might determine that the officer needs retraining in a particular area and refer the officer to the training unit for that purpose. In some cases, the officer's performance problems may be the result of personal issues, such as family problems, alcohol abuse, or financial pressures. The sergeant may then refer the officer for professional counseling in the appropriate area.[59]

Several EI systems emphasize interventions even before an officer is identified by the EI system. A report on intervention strategies by the Police Executive Research Forum (PERF) and the COPS Office found several departments where sergeants make an effort to closely monitor officer attitudes and behavior. Many sergeants said they were able to spot potential problems early on the basis of changes such as a normally outgoing officer becoming very quiet and withdrawn, an officer whose joking with fellow officers becomes hostile, or an officer whose paperwork becomes sloppy. These are often signs of personal problems. Sergeants in these departments address them by talking informally with the officer, referring him or her to peer officers for help, or recommending professional counseling. Many officer performance problems are the result of personal problems, and it is possible for an active supervisor to notice these problems and take some action.[60]

## Goals of EI Systems

EI systems have several goals, related to different target audiences.[61]

- *Individual officers.* EI systems are designed to improve the performance of officers whose performance indicates they are having problems dealing effectively with citizens.
- *Supervisors.* EI systems are designed to improve the supervision efforts of sergeants by giving them systematic data on the performance of officers under their command; this data helps them focus their efforts on particular officers and on particular performance issues (e.g., use of force or rudeness).
- *The department.* EI systems have the capacity to improve a department as a whole by systematically identifying unacceptable officer performance and focusing efforts to reduce or eliminate those problems.
- *Police–community relations.* EI systems can improve police–community relations by reducing specific problems such as use of excessive force while at the same time communicating to the public the message that the department is seriously addressing community concerns.

## An Evolving Tool

EI systems can evolve over time and become more comprehensive accountability tools. The MAPPS system in the New Jersey state police, according to a Monitors' report, "moved beyond [a] narrow focus in its use of MAPPS to focus on systemic organizational issues and to craft solutions to those issues before they negatively impact the organization in any significant way." The NJSP had moved beyond what was required by the consent decree to engage in proactive problem-solving regarding traffic stops and other issues. For example, it was developing a data base on officer off-duty misconduct.[62]

## Effectiveness of EI Systems

An officer with a large police department in the southeastern United States had a high number of use of force incidents. After she was identified by the department's EI system, the performance review found that she had a special fear of being struck in the face. Because she was not asserting control of conflict encounters, she was frequently attacked and had to use force to gain control. The EI system intervention involved special training in defensive tactics that allowed her to assert control while feeling protected. As a result, her performance improved significantly.

The case described above is anecdotal evidence about the success of early intervention systems. Other more systematic research also indicates that they are successful in reducing officer use of force and citizen complaints.

An NIJ evaluation of three EI systems found that they were effective in identifying officers with performance problems and in correcting their performance. In both Minneapolis and Miami–Dade, the officers initially identified by the EI systems had substantially worse performance records (e.g., more complaints, more use of force reports) than their peer officers (i.e., officers in the same recruit class). Officers subject to intervention had significantly fewer citizen complaints and use of force incidents in the months following intervention.[63]

A survey of police managers who have had direct experience with EI systems found very positive assessments of their systems. The managers overwhelmingly reported that their EI systems improved management and supervision: 65 percent said it had a positive effect; 21 percent reported a "mixed" effect; and most important, only 2 percent said that it had a negative effect on management and supervision (12 percent had no opinion). Additionally, 6 percent of managers observed that their EI system had a negative impact on officer morale. Comments about the positive contributions included:

- Sergeants have been able to evaluate the strengths and weaknesses of their squads even before meeting with them.
- Managers have been able to intervene with help before misconduct occurred that required discipline.[64]

Managers also reported that their EI system helped to improve supervision. One manager remarked that the process assisted his department in identifying officers and nonsworn personnel with field responsibilities who began to demonstrate behavior not consistent with the department's policies and standards. Another explained that, by evaluating the strengths and weaknesses of their squad before meeting with them, sergeants were able to develop a proactive strategy to address personnel and leadership issues.

## Risk Management and Police Legal Advisors

**Risk management** (RM) is a process widely used in private industry and in health care agencies to reduce the cost associated with lawsuits against the organization. The basic principle of RM is that the organization collect systematic data on litigation costs, analyze the causes of the underlying lawsuits, and take steps to reduce or eliminate the causes. For example, if a department has many suits related to property damage in serving warrants (especially in no-knock warrants), the department could provide officers with training on this issue and/or develop written policies to reduce property damage.

**risk management**

Risk management has not been adopted widely in American law enforcement, however. Archbold's survey of police legal advisors and risk management units found that none of the 354 law enforcement agencies examined had a risk manager or risk management unit internal to the department. In those departments where there was a risk management unit, it was located in some other office of local government. Even worse, very few of those departments with a risk management program or a police legal advisor collect and publish data on the impact of their efforts on litigation costs.[65]

The most aggressive risk management program is operated by the special counsel to the Los Angeles sheriff's department. The special counsel regularly reports data on the number of suits filed against the department and the annual litigation costs.

**police legal advisor**

A related approach to accountability is the **police legal advisor,** a lawyer or team of lawyers employed by the police department itself. The Kansas City police department has an Office of General Counsel with a staff of two attorneys. The Charlotte-Mecklenburg, North Carolina, Police department Office of the Police Attorney has a staff of five attorneys. It publishes a police legal newsletter that summarizes recent court decisions affecting the police, along with other relevant information.[66]

The purpose of a police legal advisor is preventive: to review police policies and activities to prevent actions that might violate the law, harm citizens, or produce a law suit.

## Surveying the Community

One approach for a police department to hold itself accountable to the public is to survey residents about their experiences and perceptions of the department. Surveying citizens is one of the components of many community policing programs (see Chapter 10).

The Seattle police department surveyed citizens in 2006 and 2007 about their experiences with 911 calls. Over 70 percent were satisfied with their experience, and only 5 percent were not satisfied. On a 5-point scale, responses to the question of whether people believed the police "in your neighborhood are professional and courteous" averaged 4.2. The city auditor for Portland, Oregon, regularly evaluates the performance of all city agencies, including the police. In 2007–2008, 66 percent of those surveyed rated the quality of the police department "good" or "very good." Because the survey is done every year, the 2007–2008 report had ten-year trend data on this question.[67]

# Accreditation

## The Nature of Accreditation

**accreditation**

**Accreditation** is a process of professional self-regulation, and it is used in virtually all professions: law, medicine, education, and others. An accreditation process for law enforcement was created in 1979. A coalition of the leading professional associations created the Commission on Accreditation for Law Enforcement Agencies (CALEA). The group originally included representatives from the International Association of Chiefs of Police (IACP), the National Sheriffs' Association (NSA), the

National Organization of Black Law Enforcement Executives (NOBLE), and the
Police Executive Research Forum (PERF). CALEA published its first set of *Standards for Law Enforcement Agencies* in 1983 and accredited the first police departments in 1984. By 2009, over 500 agencies had been accredited.[68]

CALEA establishes minimum standards for all law enforcement agencies.
Some standards are mandatory; others are recommended but optional. Some standards are mandatory for large agencies, but not for small ones. The fourth edition
of the *Standards,* published in 1999, includes over 445 specific standards. Accredited departments are required, for example, to have a written policy on the use of
force and the use of deadly force, a system of written directives for all rules and
regulations, an affirmative action plan, a system for handling citizen complaints,
and so on.[69]

## Benefits of Accreditation

Advocates of accreditation argue that it is an essential aspect of any occupation that
aspires to professional status. Self-governance is preferable to regulation and control
by external groups because members of the profession know the field best.[70]

The CALEA Web site (www.calea.org) has a page titled "Accreditation Works."
It includes statements by police chiefs on how accreditation has benefited their departments. Some examples include:

- *Reduced insurance costs.* The chief of the Kingsport, Tennessee, police
  department (99 sworn officers) reported in 1997 that the accreditation
  brought a $100 per officer reduction in annual insurance costs, for a savings
  of about $10,000 per year.
- *Improved use of force reporting.* The Concord, California, police department
  reported that the accreditation process pointed out that the department
  was not following its own policy in reviewing officer use of force reports.
  Accreditation corrected this problem.
- *Improved procedures for juveniles.* At the start of the accreditation process,
  the New Orleans police department did not meet any of the CALEA standards
  related to the handling of juveniles. In response, the department secured
  $310,000 in grants to improve the Juvenile Division offices and also revised
  the policies and procedures related to handling juveniles.

## Criticisms of Accreditation

Accreditation has serious limits, however. First, it is a voluntary process. Police departments suffer no penalty for not being accredited. In education, lack of accreditation means that students' credentials may not be accepted by other institutions and
that the institution may not be eligible for federal education funds.

Second, some critics argue that accreditation standards set minimum conditions but do not define the optimum standards of excellence. That is, they define the
"floor" but not the "ceiling." Most of the CALEA standards, for example, require
that a department have a written policy on a particular issue. But with the exception
of the use of force and a few others, the CALEA standards fail to specify what that
policy should be.

**S I D E B A R          14 – 3**

## Accountability and Police Use of Force: The Need for Better Data

One of the major obstacles to greater accountability regarding police use of force is the lack of reliable, systematic data. The major research needs include:

- **Establishing Clear Definitions of Both Force and Excessive Force.** What actions by a police officer constitute the use of force? Some departments include a "control of person" action, including the use of handcuffs in a routine arrest. What constitutes excessive force?

- **Improving the Measurement of the Use of Force.** The basic source of data on police use of force is official departmental records. How reliable are those records? Are we confident that officers complete reports in every instance where they are required to? And are we confident that the reports accurately reflect what really happened?

- **Identifying Variations and Correlates in the Use of Force.** In what kinds of situations are police officers most likely to use force? Are there any officer characteristics that correlate with frequent uses of force?

- **Evaluating Use of Force Control Strategies.** Are there any management strategies that have proved to be effective in controlling officer use of force? Are some strategies more effective than others?

*Source:* Kenneth Adams, "A Research Agenda on Police Use of Force," in Bureau of Justice Statistics, *Use of Force by Police: Overview of National and Local Data* (Washington DC: Government Printing Office, 1999), pp. 61–73.

Third, some critics argue that the accreditation standards address purely formal aspects of administration, without addressing specific content, or what is called the "standard of care" in the medical field.[71]

Fourth, a number of law enforcement officials believe that the accreditation process is too expensive and time-consuming.

## External Mechanisms of Accountability

**external mechanisms of accountability**

### The Political Process

Mayors have the right to choose their police chiefs, and in most states voters elect sheriffs. On the one hand, this represents a direct way of making the police accountable to the public. On the other hand, when mayors fire police chiefs, it often represents political interference. Or the voters may elect an unqualified person as sheriff. To limit political interference, some jurisdictions limit the ability of the mayor to fire the police chief. The chief in Minneapolis serves under a three-year contract. The chief of the Los Angeles police department has a five-year contract.

Citizens control the police and other government agencies through the political process.[72] The executive branch of government—elected mayors, appointed city managers, governors, presidents—exercises control primarily by appointing police chiefs, directors of state police, and the U.S. attorney general. The legislative branch—city councils, county boards of commissioners, state legislators, the Congress—exercises control through budgets. The judicial branch serves as a check and balance on both the executive and legislative branches, by ensuring compliance with the law.

A few cities have special commissions to govern their police departments. In the 19th century this approach was very common (see Chapter 2).[73] Only a few police commissions survive today, however. The Los Angeles Police Commission, for example, consists of five members, appointed by the mayor, and has full responsibility for running the Los Angeles police department.[74] Detroit and San Francisco also have police commissions.[75]

The formal structure of governance of the police (commission, no commission; citizen oversight agency, no oversight agency) is only part of the process. Government officials have to make a commitment to high standards of professionalism for the police and communicate that commitment to police department leaders. Luna and Walker refer to this commitment as "political will." They base their argument on the citizen oversight process in Albuquerque, New Mexico, which had considerable powers but did not work effectively because the mayor and other political leaders failed to make it work.[76]

# The Courts

## The Supreme Court and the Police

In one of the most famous cases ever decided by the **U.S. Supreme Court,** Cleveland police officers barged into Dolree Mapp's house in 1957 waving what they said was a search warrant. They had previously been to the house looking for a suspect they thought was hiding there. When they could not find the suspect, they arrested Ms. Mapp for possessing some obscene literature she had in the house. Mapp was convicted, but appealed and eventually took her case to the Supreme Court. No copy of the alleged search warrant was ever found, either in police files or in any court, and there was strong suspicion that the police did not actually have a warrant. The U.S. Supreme Court overturned Mapp's conviction.

**U.S. Supreme Court**

The *Mapp v. Ohio* (1961) decision is still one of the most controversial in the history of the Supreme Court.[77] The Court ruled that the evidence against Dolree Mapp had been obtained illegally, violating her Fourth Amendment right to protection against "unreasonable searches and seizures." The Court imposed the exclusionary rule, which holds that "all evidence obtained by searches and seizures in violation of the Constitution is, by that same authority, inadmissible in a state court." The Court had previously applied the exclusionary rule to federal criminal proceedings in 1914 (*Weeks v. United States*), while a number of state supreme courts had applied it to state proceedings, including California in 1955 (*People v. Cahan*). The significant aspect of *Mapp* was that the Supreme Court applied the exclusionary rule to state and local police through the Fourteenth Amendment, which holds that no state may deprive one of its citizens due process of law. Thus, the Court set national standards for all police agencies and assumed the role of policing local police.[78]

The judicial branch of government is an important but indirect part of the political process. Although federal judges are appointed by the president and confirmed by the Senate, thereby ensuring some political control, judicial independence protects them against direct political influence once they are appointed. Courts at all levels of government play some role in holding the police accountable. At bail settings, preliminary hearings, and trials, local court judges rule on the admissibility of evidence and other issues that impact on police work.[79] The most important court with respect to police accountability is the U.S. Supreme Court. In the 1960s the Supreme Court issued a series of rulings that imposed new standards for police conduct.

## The Impact of Supreme Court Decisions

What impact do Supreme Court decisions have on the police? Do they protect the constitutional rights of citizens as intended? Has the *Mapp* decision eliminated illegal searches? Have this and other decisions, such as *Miranda v. Arizona,* requiring the police to advise citizens of their rights, helped improve policing? Or have these decisions hindered the police? Have they made it difficult for the police to fight crime and allowed criminals to go free? These questions are part of a forty-five-year debate over the Supreme Court and the police.

Law professor Paul Cassell was almost single-handedly responsible for bringing a case before the Supreme Court in 2000, asking it to overturn the original *Miranda* decision. Cassell's research estimated that *Miranda* has produced serious costs to society's ability to fight crime. Cassell did not succeed, however. In the *U.S. v. Dickerson* (2000) decision the Supreme Court rejected his argument and reaffirmed the *Miranda* warning in a 7 to 2 decision.[80]

Cassell's efforts were the latest in a long debate over the impact of the Supreme Court on the police. In this instance, Cassell's own evidence did not support his conclusion. He estimated that *Miranda* results in a net loss of convictions in only 3.8 percent of all criminal cases. Many observers did not find this to be a significant impact. And, in fact, 84 percent of the suspects in his study voluntarily waived their *Miranda* rights.[81]

Richard Leo observed interrogations in one West Coast police department (and observed videotapes of interrogations in others) and found that 78 percent of the suspects waived their *Miranda* rights and talked to the police. He also found that in 30 percent of the cases the police lied to the suspect by falsely claiming they had a confession from a partner or some other incriminating evidence. In short, the specific intent of *Miranda* is frequently undermined by both police and suspects.[82]

Milner studied four Wisconsin police departments and found considerable variation in the impact of the *Miranda* decision. Officers in the most professional of the four departments he studied were less hostile to the decision than in the other three less professional departments. The officers in all four departments indicated a high degree of knowledge of the *Miranda* requirements, and all indicated that changes had been made as a result of the decision. These changes included using new methods to gather evidence and improved education and training. The majority of officers in all departments indicated that their jobs had been changed by the *Miranda* requirements.[83]

*Miranda* and other Supreme Court decisions on police practices touched off a major political and legal controversy. The police argued that they were being "handcuffed" in their effort to control crime.[84] This argument stimulated much research on the impact of Supreme Court decisions on the police.

```
S I D E B A R        1 4 – 4
```

## The Long-Term Impact of Supreme Court Decisions: Leo's Argument

Based on his observational studies of the impact of *Miranda* on interrogations, Richard Leo argues that the decision has had four "profound" long-term effects.

First, "*Miranda* has had a civilizing influence on police behavior inside the interrogation room." The decision has helped to eliminate the brutal tactics—documented in the 1931 report *Lawlessness in Law Enforcement*—that the police used to get confessions.

Second, Leo argues, *Miranda* has helped to change and transform the culture of policing, defining a moral and legal standard that is always in the mind of officers when conducting interrogations.

Third, *Miranda* and other supreme court decisions have heightened public awareness of constitutional rights. Citizens' knowledge of their rights, meanwhile, serves as a check on police behavior, as they feel empowered to challenge unjust officer behavior.

Fourth, *Miranda* has stimulated the police to develop more sophisticated interrogation techniques. In some respects, this has been a very good development, as the police have abandoned coercive or brutal techniques. But at the same time, as Leo's research makes clear, some of the new techniques involve subtle tricks that undermine the spirit and intent of *Miranda*.

*Source:* Richard A. Leo and George C. Thomas, III, *The Miranda Debate: Law, Justice, and Policing* (Boston: Northeastern University Press, 1998), pp. 217–19.

Studies have found that the exclusionary rule does not limit the crime-fighting capacity of the police. The rule is largely confined to drug, gambling, and weapons cases that raise issues of how the police obtained the evidence. The rule has little impact on murder, robbery, rape, or burglary cases. Reviewing criminal cases in Boston, Sheldon Krantz found that "very few motions to suppress evidence are raised, and very few of these are granted." Motions to suppress evidence were raised in only 48 of 512 district court cases (or 9.4 percent), and only 10 of those 48 motions were granted. Thus, the defendant was successful in only 20.8 percent of the motions and 1.9 percent of all cases. A General Accounting Office (GAO) study found that defense attorneys filed motions to suppress evidence in only 11 percent of 2,804 cases. Less than 20 percent of those motions were successful, producing an overall success rate of 2.2 percent.[85]

Supporters of the Supreme Court decisions on the police argue that they had three positive effects. First, the Court defined basic principles of due process. Second, decisions such as *Mapp* and *Miranda* created penalties for police misconduct (excluding the evidence or the confession). This served as a basic mechanism of accountability. Third, the decisions stimulated police reform, including improvements in recruitment, training, and supervision.[86]

Orfield's interviews with Chicago narcotics officers found several positive effects of the exclusionary rule. The *Mapp* decision led to better training of officers, including closer supervision of warrants by prosecutors. Detectives were also more likely to use warrants than to conduct impulsive warrantless searches. Many officers indicated that the exclusionary rule was a good thing that helped to maintain high standards of professionalism.[87]

The Supreme Court decisions also increased public awareness about the details of police procedures. This knowledge, and the consequent tendency to demand one's rights, serves as a constraint on the police, preventing many abuses. Increased awareness of individual rights has also led to higher public expectations about police performance. The Court decisions defined an ideal against which actual performance is measured. By raising public expectations, the decisions generated pressure for continued police reform.

At the same time, there are significant limitations on the role of the Court as a mechanism of accountability. First, the Court cannot supervise day-to-day police operations. It cannot ensure that individual police officers are in fact complying with its decisions.[88] Second, most police work does not involve an arrest and, therefore, never comes before a court.[89] An individual has a remedy only if he or she is arrested and convicted. Third, the police may or may not be informed about current court decisions. Wasby found that small-town police in Massachusetts and Illinois did not receive information of Court decisions in a systematic fashion in the 1970s.[90] Fourth, some critics argue that Court-imposed rules only encourage evasion or lying by police officers. Finally, the exercise of rights may become an empty formality, with little real meaning. Both Cassell and Leo, for example, found that most suspects waive their right to silence and agree to be interrogated by the police.

## Civil Suits against the Police

**civil suits**

The City of Detroit paid out more than $124 million in **civil suits** involving police misconduct in the 1990s, an average of over $10 million a year. Despite these huge costs, almost nothing was done to reduce misconduct and the huge cost to taxpayers. Finally, in late 2000, the U.S. Justice Department stepped in, sued the department, and reached a consent decree requiring a wide range of reforms related to accountability.[91]

People who are the victims of police abuse can sue for civil damages. A person may sue in federal court under state or federal law. An 1871 federal law (now 42 U.S.C. 1983) provides that a person can sue for damages if he or she has been deprived of any rights by an official acting "under color of law" (that is, in an official capacity). Lawsuits under this law are often referred to as "1983 actions."[92]

The number of successful damage suits against the police has risen dramatically in recent years. The total damages paid by the City of Los Angeles for police-related cases increased from $7,000 in 1965 to $1.5 million in 1975 and to $8 million in 1990.[93]

The primary purpose of a damage suit is to compensate the victim or victims of police misconduct for the harm done. Lawsuits, however, are expensive, time-consuming, difficult to win, and offer a potential remedy only in cases of extreme harm. The potential damage awards in cases of minor misconduct do not make litigation worthwhile. A report on civil litigation on police misconduct found that even among those cases where the plaintiff won, the average award was only 10 percent of the initial claim. The median award, in fact, was only $8,000.[94]

Some research suggests that the strategy of suing police departments to achieve general reforms is not successful. Edward Littlejohn's study of police misconduct litigation in Detroit through the 1970s found that suits produced few reforms.[95]

A study of 149 police misconduct suits filed in Connecticut between 1970 and 1977 found that they had little apparent effect on the police. The plaintiffs rarely won, because juries tended to be sympathetic to the police, and neither the individual officers nor the department directly bore the financial cost of losing.[96]

McCoy argues that rising damage awards involving police abuse provoked an insurance crisis in many cities by the late 1970s and forced them to take steps to curb misconduct. McCoy suggests that city attorneys need to provide feedback to the police department not just in the few cases where large damages are awarded but in all cases that are filed. The director of the Institute for Liability Management argues that an effective risk management program must include training for all officers, ensuring that officers have copies of department policies, regular training for supervisors, an atmosphere of accountability in the department, constant monitoring of changes in relevant laws, and good legal advice.[97]

The rising cost of civil suits over officer misconduct has prompted some cities and counties to take proactive steps to reduce misconduct. The special counsel to the Los Angeles sheriff's department was created in 1993 for the specific purpose of investigating problems in the department, recommending reforms, and reducing the costs of misconduct litigation.[98] The special counsel represents one form of citizen oversight (see pp. 486–488). Special Counsel Merrick Bobb has investigated virtually every aspect of the department: recruitment, training, and assignment of officers; the use of deadly force and canines; sexual harassment in the workplace; and other issues. The result has been improvements in several areas. The current docket of excessive force lawsuits against the LASD fell from an average of 300 in fiscal years 1992–1993 and 1993–1994 to about 63 between 2002 and 2004. The number of "bites" by LASD canines fell from 58 in 1991 to 22 in 2001.[99]

---

**SIDEBAR        14 – 5**

## *Problems with Civil Suits as an Accountability Measure*

Many people regard civil suits for police misconduct as an accountability measure for police departments. Common sense suggests that a police department that is (1) sued more often than other departments and/or (2) pays out more in court decisions and settlements for police misconduct is worse than a department that is sued less and pays out less.

There are a number of problems with civil suits as an accountability measure, however:

1. The number of suits filed may only reflect the availability of attorneys willing to file police misconduct suits.

2. The number of suits filed may reflect a city's practice of settling suits—more suits are likely to be filed in jurisdictions where there is a practice of settling cases rather than fighting them.

3. The annual dollar amount of settlements and judgments may reflect a local legal culture that encourages high payments for police misconduct.

4. Trend data on settlements and judgments are misleading because cases are usually settled many years after the initial incident occurred; consequently, the dollar payments for the year 2002 do not reflect current police practices.

# Federal "Pattern or Practice" Suits

## Department of Justice Suits

consent decree

A 1997 **consent decree** against the Pittsburgh police department ordered sweeping changes in its management and accountability procedures. The decree ordered the department to develop a data system on all officer uses of force, to create an early intervention system, and to require officers to record the race and ethnicity of all persons they stopped for questioning, including pedestrians and motor vehicle drivers.[100]

The consent decree was one of over twenty settlements resulting from lawsuits brought by the Civil Rights Division of the U.S. Department of Justice. The 1994 Violent Crime Control Act authorized the Justice Department to bring civil suits against law enforcement agencies where there is a "pattern or practice" of abuse of citizens' rights. In addition to Pittsburgh, the Justice Department sued the New Jersey state police, the Los Angeles police department, the Cincinnati police department, and other agencies.[101]

Pattern or practice cases are settled through a consent decree, a memorandum of agreement (MOA), or an investigative findings letter. A consent decree or an MOA is supervised by a federal judge who can punish the police department if it does not implement the required reforms. The judge can convert an MOA into a consent decree in the case of noncompliance. An investigative findings letter indicates reforms that need to be made, but has no enforcement mechanism.

What, exactly, is a "pattern or practice" of police misconduct? The U.S. Justice Department explains that it is more than "sporadic bad incidents or the actions of the occasional bad officer," and requires "information indicating a pattern of misconduct or systemic practices underlying the misconduct . . . ."[102]

## State and Private Suits

pattern or practice suits

Most **pattern or practice suits** have been brought by the U.S. Justice Department. A few others, however, have been brought by state attorneys general or as private lawsuits. The Attorney General of California brought a civil suit against the Riverside, California, police department because of a series of excessive force incidents. The suit resulted in a consent decree very similar to those in the cases brought by the Justice Department.[103] The Attorney General of New York, meanwhile, sued the small town of Walkill, New York, because of a number of abuses of citizens by the police department. This suit also resulted in a consent decree and the appointment of a monitor to audit the implementation of the required reforms.[104]

## Court-Ordered Reforms

Each consent decree or MOA orders a set of management changes related to accountability, summarized in the 2001 Justice Department report *Principles for Promoting Police Integrity*[105]. They include:

- *Use of Force Reporting*. Revising the use of force reporting system to clarify the definition of force and the reporting requirement.
- *Early Intervention System*. Requiring the department to create an EI system or to revise and strengthen its existing system.

---

**SIDEBAR        14 – 6**

## Major Requirements of the New Jersey State Police Consent Decree

1. *Policy Requirements*. . . . State troopers may not rely to any degree on the race or national or ethnic origin of motorists in selecting vehicles for traffic stops. . . .

2. *Traffic Stop Documentation*. . . . State troopers engaged in patrol activities will document the race, ethnic origin, and gender of all motor vehicle drivers who are the subject of a traffic stop. . . .

3. *Supervisory Review of Individual Traffic Stops*. . . . Supervisors regularly will review trooper reports concerning post-stop enforcement actions and procedures, and patrol car videotapes of traffic stops, to ensure that troopers are employing appropriate practices and procedures.

4. *Supervisory Review of Patterns of Conduct*. . . . The State will develop and implement an early warning system, called the Management Awareness Program, that uses computerized information on traffic stops, misconduct investigations, and other matters to assist State Police supervisors to identify and modify potentially problematic behavior.

5. *Misconduct Allegations*. . . . The State Police will make complaint forms and informational materials available at a variety of locations, will institute a 24-hour toll-free telephone hotline. . . .

6. *Training*. . . . The State Police will continue to implement measures to improve training for recruits and incumbent troopers. . . .

7. *Independent Monitor*. . . . An Independent Monitor, who will be an agent of the court, will be selected by the United States and the State of New Jersey to monitor and report on the State's implementation of the Decree.

*Source: United States v. New Jersey (1999). Available at www.usdoj/gov/crt/split.*

---

- *Improved Citizen Complaint Procedures.* Virtually all of the consent decrees require the police department to revise its procedures for receiving and investigating citizen complaints.
- *Officer Training.* Consent decrees generally require improvements in training to cover new use of force policies and other departmental changes.

The situation in Cincinnati was unique because it involved separate settlements. In 2000 the City of Cincinnati experienced a riot and the imposition of martial law following the fatal shooting of the fifteenth African American male in five years. An MOA with the Justice Department ordered accountability reforms similar to the settlement in other cities. A Collaborative Agreement (in effect a consent decree) with private plaintiffs, including the ACLU and the Black United Front, ordered the police department to adopt community policing and problem-solving, and to work closely with community representatives in doing that. The Cincinnati Collaborative Agreement is the only settlement that orders a department to change its policing strategy.[106]

## Court-Appointed Independent Monitors

**independent monitor**    Federal consent decrees and MOA include the appointment by the court of an **independent monitor.** Monitors have several functions: to oversee implementation of the court-ordered reforms; to assist the department in implementing the reforms; and, to issue public reports on the progress of implementation. The monitor in Washington DC, however, found significant failures. In June 2002, for example, the monitor reported that "Despite substantial efforts in the past several months to compensate for an extraordinarily slow start, MPD has failed to accomplish virtually all of the milestones identified in the MOA within the time periods specified.[107] The Monitor played a major role in prodding and advising the department, and as a result by 2008 it had made substantial progress in implementing the required reforms.

## The Impact of Consent Decrees

Do consent decrees and MOAs achieve their intended results? Are the court-ordered reforms actually implemented, and are departments more accountable as a result? The evidence indicates that while Pittsburgh implemented its reforms quickly, delays and resistance affected some other departments. The Cincinnati police were found in "breach" of the MOA at one point, and the consent decrees over both the New Jersey State Police and the Los Angeles Police Department were extended beyond their five-year limits because of implementation delays.

Despite some implementation problems, independent evaluations found that consent decrees were successful in achieving their intended goals. A Vera Institute evaluation of Pittsburgh found that the consent decree had been successfully implemented and that many rumored negative effects had not occurred. The consent decree greatly improved the department's use of force policy. Despite rumors of morale problems among Pittsburgh police officers, the evaluation found no evidence of "depolicing," or a work slowdown as a result of the consent decree.[108]

The court appointed monitor over the New Jersey State police concluded in December 2007 that

> *The New Jersey State Police appear to have reached a watershed moment during the last two reporting periods. Ample evidence exists to suggest that the agency has become self-monitoring and self-correcting to a degree not often observed in American law enforcement.*[109]

Similarly, the monitor in Cincinnati in August 2008 found that

> *The City of Cincinnati is now in a very different situation than it was in 2002. In the five years of the MOA and the six years of the CA, the City made significant changes in the way it polices Cincinnati. The CPD has improved its training, its policies and procedures, its investigations of uses of force and citizen complaints, its risk management and its accountability.*[110]

The monitor in Washington DC concluded in January 2008 that

> *. . . with respect to the core areas of concern (weapons discharges, canine bites, use of force training, and the documentation and investigation of use of force incidents), the department has substantially transformed itself for the better since the late 1990s.*[111]

In short, the experiences of these departments suggest that court-ordered reform, supported by an independent monitor, can bring about significant change in a large police department.

## Thinking About Court-Ordered Reform

The three court-appointed monitors make bold claims for the positive impacts of the consent decrees regarding these three law enforcement agencies. The claims raise a number of important questions for consideration. Is litigation an effective tool for bringing about organizational change in law enforcement agencies? If so, is litigation an appropriate tool in all situations? What about police departments that have problems in particular areas, but do not have systemic problems?

Another important question is whether reforms will be sustained following the end of a consent decree or MOA. Will the reforms be institutionalized and permanent? Or will the department slide back into unacceptable practices? This is a basic question relevant to all forms of change in policing. Will community policing or problem-oriented policing be institutionalized in a department? What are the conditions of institutionalization? What makes reform stick?[112]

## Injunctions

In the case of police practices that systematically violate citizen rights, civil rights groups have sought injunctions against the police to stop the alleged practice. If, for example, police officers are systematically stopping, questioning, and frisking all black males in a community—without regard for individualized suspicion—members of that group can seek an injunction ordering the practice stopped. For the most part, however, injunctions have not been an effective remedy for police misconduct. In an important case involving the Philadelphia police department (*Rizzo v. Goode,* 1976), the U.S. Supreme Court held that the plaintiffs had failed to prove that the police chief and other city officials were directly responsible for the alleged police misconduct and that the plaintiffs themselves were likely to be the targets of this misconduct in the future.[113]

## Criminal Prosecution

Four New York City police officers were prosecuted for the fatal shooting of Amadou Diallo in early 1999. The shooting and the trial that followed were among the most controversial events in the city, sharply dividing people along racial and ethnic lines. Diallo, a Haitian immigrant, was unarmed and shot while standing in the doorway of his apartment. Many civil rights activists saw the shooting as an example of the police targeting racial minorities, and they demanded that the officers be convicted. At the end of the trial, however, the four officers were acquitted. The Diallo case dramatizes the role of **criminal prosecution** as a mechanism of police accountability.[114]

**criminal prosecution**

Police officers who violate the law can be prosecuted as criminals. Successful criminal prosecution of a police officer is extremely difficult, however. First, local prosecutors routinely work closely with the police and are reluctant to bring criminal charges against them. The Criminal Division of the U.S. Justice Department is extremely small and has responsibility for many other types of criminal activity.[115]

Second, in the case of allegations of police use of excessive force, it is often difficult to prove that the force was in fact excessive and that the officer had criminal intent. The officer can always claim that his or her actions were a legitimate exercise of police powers under the circumstances. In such cases it is important to distinguish between *improper* police action, which can be subject to internal departmental discipline, and *illegal* action, where the prosecution must prove criminal intent. The successful conviction on federal charges of three Los Angeles police officers involved in the Rodney King beating was a relatively rare exception. Convictions are much easier to obtain in corruption cases, where there is less ambiguity about the facts than there is in use of force cases. Third, convictions are difficult to obtain because, as a Vera Institute study found, juries are often sympathetic to police officers and "suspicious of victims" of police abuse.[116]

Criminal prosecution by itself appears to have limited deterrent effect in departments where other effective controls do not exist. A number of New York City police officers were prosecuted and convicted in the scandals of the 1970s and 1980s, and yet the Mollen Commission found serious criminal law violations in the 1990s. Evidently, the officers were not deterred by the prosecutions and convictions in the previous years.

## Citizen Oversight of the Police

Since the 1960s, civil rights groups have argued that police departments fail to investigate citizen complaints thoroughly or fairly. As an alternative, they have demanded the creation of **citizen oversight** (also called external review or civilian review) of the police. Citizen oversight is defined as a process by which people who are not sworn officers are involved in some way in the review of citizen complaints against police officers. Citizen oversight rests on the assumption that because of the police subculture police officers cannot objectively investigate complaints against fellow officers.

**citizen oversight**

Citizen oversight has grown tremendously in the last thirty years. In almost all big cities there is now some form of oversight agency. The U.S. Justice Department recommends an open citizen complaint process as one of its integrity-related "best practices." It recommends that law enforcement "agencies should provide a readily accessible process in which community and agency members can have confidence that complaints against agency actions and procedures will be given prompt and fair attention."[117]

### Two Models of Citizen Oversight

#### *Civilian Review Boards*

Citizen oversight agencies exist in two basic forms. The first is the *civilian review board*. This consists of a board of citizens that reviews individual complaints and makes a recommendation to the police chief. There are many variations on review boards. The San Francisco Office of Citizen Complaints (OCC) has its own staff of investigators and conducts the original complaint investigation. The New York Civilian Complaint Review Board (CCRB) also conducts the original investigation.[118]

## *Police Auditors*

The second form of citizen oversight is the *police auditor.* Police auditors do not in-vestigate individual citizen complaints. Their role is to audit or monitor the opera-tions of the police department. This includes the complaint process, policies, and procedures related to use of force or traffic stops and other aspects of the agency. The special counsel to the Los Angeles sheriff's department, for example, has investi-gated employment practices, civil litigation data, the canine unit, foot pursuits, and many other issues since 1993. The San Jose Independent Police Auditor also investi-gates a wide range of issues. Reviewing policies and procedures and making rec-ommendations for change are known as *policy review.* The San Jose Independent Police Auditor has made over 100 policy recommendations in its first fifteen years of operation.[119]

## *Goals and Objectives*

Both review boards and police auditors operate on the assumption that providing some *citizen input* will improve policing. Both review boards and police auditors seek to increase the openness, or *transparency,* of police departments. To increase openness, both review boards and police auditors issue *public reports* with detailed information about the police department. These reports are typically available on the oversight agency's Web site. The reports of the New York City CCRB, for example, have very detailed data about complaints, complainants, and officers who are the subject of complaints. The reports of the LASD special counsel have detailed discus-sions of policy issues, such as use of force or foot pursuits.[120]

Civilian review boards and police auditors have different goals and objectives. Review boards focus on individual complaints for the purpose of determining whether or not the police officer is guilty of abusing the citizen and/or violating department rules. The basic goal is to *ensure justice in individual cases.* Police auditors, on the other hand, focus on the organization, with the goal of bringing about *organizational change.* The long-term goal is to effect change that will prevent misconduct in the future.

Community outreach is one activity through which review boards and police auditors seek to increase public understanding. Outreach activities include neighbor-hood meetings, public forums on particular issues or controversies, publishing bro-chures explaining police operations and the complaint process, and publishing reports on issues of concern to the public. The Boise, Idaho, community ombudsman, for example, has published reports on controversial incidents that provide an independent review of the facts and an assessment of problems that need to be fixed.[121]

# Citizen Oversight: Pro and Con

Opponents of citizen oversight argue that (1) it intrudes on the professional indepen-dence of the police, (2) people who are not police officers are not qualified to review police operations, (3) it is expensive and unnecessarily duplicates the work of internal affairs, and (4) internal affairs units sustain more complaints against police officers.[122]

Advocates of citizen review, on the other hand, argue that it serves to open up police departments, ending the historic isolation from the public. They cite evidence that the number of citizen complaints is higher in cities with some form of external review,

SIDEBAR       14 – 7

## Auditing Activities of the Special Counsel to the Los Angeles Sheriff's Department (selected examples)

1993   **Officer-involved shootings and other serious uses of force**

*1st Semiannual Report* **(October 1993)**

1995   **The department canine unit**

*4th Semiannual Report* **(June 1995)**

1999   **Sexual harassment**

*11th Semiannual Report* **(October 1999)**

2002   **Risk management and litigation costs**

*15th Semiannual Report* **(July 2002)**

2003   **Review of department's foot-pursuit policy, with recommendation for new policy**

*16th Semiannual Report* **(February 2003)**

2005   **Strip Searches**

*19th Semiannual Report* **(February 2005)**

2007   **Process for Reviewing Use of Force Incidents**

*24th Semiannual Report* **(December 2007)**

*Source:* All of the special counsel reports are available at the Web site of the Police Assessment Resource Center: www.parc.info.

suggesting that it enhances public confidence in the complaint process.[123] Hudson's research on Philadelphia found that internal affairs sustained a higher percentage of complaints primarily because it generally handled violations of departmental rules, which are inherently easier to sustain than citizen complaints about use of force.[124]

There have been few evaluations of citizen review procedures. Kerstetter found that public confidence in the complaint process did improve with the existence of a citizen review procedure.[125] A Vera Institute study of the New York City Civilian Review Board (CCRB) found that both complainants and police officers thought it was biased against them.[126] The New York CCRB is regularly criticized by the New York Civil Liberties Union, the leading advocate of citizen review.[127]

In short, some forms of citizen review appear to be relatively more effective than others. Effectiveness depends upon several factors, including the agency's definition of its role, its resources, the quality of its staff, and the degree of political support it receives from the community.

## The New Paradigm: Complaints as a "Learning" Tool

Historically, police departments were hostile to citizen complaints, and often failed to investigate them thoroughly. The new paradigm today is that complaints are a "learning" tool, from which the department can gain useful information about possible problems that need to be addressed. The Charlotte-Mecklenburg, North Carolina, police department's *Employee Conduct: Investigations and Discipline* manual explains that the department might learn that an employee has "fallen into patterns of behavior or tactics that are not consistent with our expectations." It then explains the different ways of dealing with such problems, ranging from retraining through termination.[128]

## Blue-Ribbon Commissions

In a forceful statement, the 1931 Wickersham Commission concluded that "the third degree—the inflicting of pain, physical or mental, to extract confessions or statements—is widespread throughout the country." The Wickersham report on illegal use of force by police was unprecedented, and it sparked the first serious national effort to control police misconduct. Exactly sixty years later, the Christopher Commission report on use of force in the Los Angeles police department following the Rodney King incident received almost as much national attention.[129]

The Wickersham Commission and the Christopher Commission are two of the most famous examples of special **blue-ribbon commissions** in police history (see Chapter 2). Blue-ribbon commissions are a form of external accountability and serve several important functions. First, national commissions bring together the leading experts in the field and define minimum standards that can then be used to seek improvements in local departments. Second, as the President's Crime Commission (1965–1967) did, commissions can sponsor original research and generate new knowledge about policing. Third, blue-ribbon commissions are usually comprehensive in scope, addressing the full range of police issues, and not just a single problem.[130]

The greatest weakness of blue-ribbon commissions is that they are temporary agencies and are disbanded after issuing their final reports. As a result, they have no ability to do follow-up and monitor the implementation of their recommendations. Walker argues that this limitation has been overcome by the new institution of the police auditor (see p. 487).[131] A new form of citizen oversight, police auditors are permanent agencies that can monitor the implementation of their recommendations and issue follow-up reports to the public. The special counsel to the Los Angeles sheriff's department is the most successful police auditor (see the special counsel's reports at www.parc.info).

**blue-ribbon commissions**

## The News Media

*New York Times* reporter David Burnham is almost single-handedly responsible for exposing one of the biggest corruption scandals in the New York City police department. The scandal that is closely identified with officer Frank Serpico, who testified against corrupt officers, was first exposed by Burnham in a front-page *Times* story on April 25, 1970. Many people in the department and city government had known about the pattern of corruption, but no one did anything. Following Burnham's revelations, they were forced to act. The mayor appointed the Knapp Commission to investigate, a number of officers were convicted of corrupt acts, and Patrick V. Murphy was brought in as police commissioner to clean up the department.[132]

The news media play an important role in police accountability.[133] On a day-to-day basis, the media report on what the police are doing. This informs the public and, hopefully, helps them to make intelligent political choices related to policing. The media have also been important in exposing serious police problems, as they did with the New York City police scandal in 1970.

At the same time, the news media often contribute to police problems. First, they tend to emphasize sensational stories, especially violent crimes or major police misconduct. They do not provide good coverage of routine police activities because these events are not dramatic. Second, the media present a distorted picture of police work by focusing on crime and ignoring the aspects of police work not related to crime. Third, the media tend to emphasize the negative aspects of policing. They will give considerable coverage to a questionable shooting by a police officer, for example, but not cover the fact that there are long periods with no shootings. One of the unwritten rules of the news media is that good news is not news.

## Public Interest Organizations

The local chapter of the American Civil Liberties Union (ACLU) in Oakland, California, had volunteers systematically call different units of the Oakland police department in 1996 and ask about how to file a citizen complaint. The callers found that few Oakland officers handling their calls gave out correct information. Many, apparently, were simply uninformed about the department's complaint process. Some others may have deliberately not given out the right information. The ACLU report blasting the Oakland police department for this failure was only one in a long series of investigations and reports on police misconduct by that organization.[134]

**public interest organization**

The ACLU is a private, nonprofit **public interest organization.** Private groups play an important role in police accountability. For the most part, they have been involved in attacking police misconduct. The National Association for the Advancement of Colored People (NAACP) has a long record of fighting police use of excessive force against African Americans.[135] The ACLU was responsible for some of the most important Supreme Court cases involving the police. ACLU briefs were the basis for the Court's decisions in the landmark *Mapp* and *Miranda* cases, for example. The ACLU has been the leading advocate of citizen review of the police in New York City, Los Angeles, and many other cities. At the same time, the ACLU has defended the rights of police officers in cases involving, for example, grooming standards and department investigations of alleged police misconduct. The ACLU published a handbook on *The Rights of Police Officers.*[136]

## Accountability and Crime Control: A Trade-Off?

For many years, some people argued that strict accountability measures limit the crime control effectiveness of the police. In the 1960s, for example, the police argued that the *Miranda* decision requiring police to advise suspects of their rights hindered their ability to obtain confessions. Critics of citizen oversight of the police have argued that having citizen complaints reviewed by people who are not police officers involves "second-guessing" the police and will cause officers to be less aggressive in fighting crime.

The tension between accountability and crime control was best framed by Herbert Packer in his classic essay "Two Models of the Criminal Process." The crime-control model places few formal restraints on criminal justice officials (not just the police) for the purpose of effective crime control. The due-process model places many formal restraints on officials for the purpose of protecting the rights of citizens.[137]

In a recent article, David Bayley forcefully argues that the alleged conflict between accountability (including formal due-process requirements) and crime control is a false dichotomy.[138] Breaking the law or departmental rules, in fact, does little to improve crime control and actually harms the police. The major problems, Bayley argues, include the following:

- Citing several studies, he concludes that "violating the rule of law contributes marginally to deterrence." Studies of stops and frisks by New York City police and by the U.S. Customs Service, for example, show that they were very unproductive in terms of finding contraband.
- Violating the law actually reduces crime-control effectiveness. Citing a wide body of police research, Bayley argues that the police are heavily dependent on citizen cooperation (to report crime, to cooperate as witnesses, etc.). If police alienate citizens through inappropriate or illegal actions, they will undermine efforts to gain cooperation. This idea is one of the basic principles of community policing (see Chapter 10).
- Violating the law "weakens the authority of law." Citing the research by social psychologist Tom Tyler, Bayley argues that people are more likely to obey the law when they respect legal institutions, including the police.

Bayley's argument applies to all of the accountability measures covered in this chapter, including early identification systems and citizen oversight agencies.

# A Mixed Approach to Police Accountability

No single mechanism is the key to achieving police accountability. Each of the different mechanisms has its strengths and weaknesses. Internal mechanisms are both strong, because they are internal and the officials involved are close to the situation, and weak, because these same officials are too close to the officers they have to monitor. By the same token, external mechanisms are strong, because they are independent of the police, but also weak, because they are remote from the activities they attempt to monitor.

The current **mixed approach to police accountability** represents a blend of internal and external mechanisms (see Exhibit 14–3). In important respects, this reflects the concept of checks and balances, which is one of the fundamental principles of American democracy. Elected officials have significant control over police departments, but not total control. Police administrators have a great deal of autonomy, but not complete autonomy. The courts have some influence over policing, but only in limited areas. Citizens have some input, but not direct control over police operations. Viewed from a historical perspective, there has been a shift in the mix of internal and external forms of accountability. Direct political interference in policing declined as a result of the professionalization movement (see Chapter 2). Some other forms of external accountability—particularly the courts and citizen review—have grown in recent decades. At the same time, some forms of internal accountability have also grown, with the development of better mechanisms for the control of misconduct and the supervision of routine police work.

**mixed approach to police accountability**

## EXHIBIT 14–3

### Examples of a Mixed Approach to Police Accountability

**Portland, Oregon, Police Bureau**

*Internal Accountability*
  Office of Professional Standards
    Internal Affairs Division
    Risk Liability
*External Accountability*
  City Auditor
    Independent Police Review Divison
    Citizen Review Committee
  Advisory Committees

**Charlotte-Mecklenburg, North Carolina, Police Department**

*Internal Accountability*
  Internal Affairs Division
  Police Attorney's Office
*External Accountability*
  Community Relations Committee

 E  Case Study

### *Miami-Dade Police Department, Early Identification System (Excerpt)*

## III. EMPLOYEE PROFILE SYSTEM:

Instituted and operated by PCB, the system establishes a data collection source profiling departmental employees to identify patterns of stress-induced or performance problems.

A.  Profile Criteria: Profiles will document specified criteria for assessment:
  1.  Complaints.
  2.  Use of force incidents.
  3.  Commendations.
  4.  Correctional action.
  5.  Promotional status change.

B.  Report Assessment: Profile reports will be reviewed by immediate supervisors as deemed necessary. The concerned commander or designee will review profile reports annually, in conjunction with other criteria, to identify problems.

C.  Action Alternatives: Based on profile reports and relevant data, the following will result:
  1.  Referral to the Psychological Services Program for counseling or referral assistance.

2. Participation in the Stress Abatement Program for training assistance.
3. Correctional action.
4. Assessment that no problem exists, terminating further action.

*Source:* Miami-Dade Police Department, *Early Identification System* (1992).

## Summary

Holding the police accountable to the public for what they do and how they do it is an essential feature of a democratic society. In the past, few meaningful accountability mechanisms existed. The result was widespread inefficiency, abuse of citizens, and corruption. A variety of accountability mechanisms have been developed in recent years. They represent a mix of internal and external approaches.

## Key Terms

accountability, 457
COMPSTAT, 460
internal mechanisms of
    accountability, 461
routine supervision, 462
span of control, 462
employee assistance
    program, 463
organizational culture, 464
performance evaluations, 465
Christopher Commission, 465

internal affairs unit, 466
CALEA accreditation
    standards, 466
code of silence, 468
early intervention systems, 469
risk management, 473
police legal advisor, 474
accreditation, 474
external mechanisms of
    accountability, 476
U.S. Supreme Court, 477

civil suits, 480
consent decree, 482
pattern or practice suits, 482
independent monitor, 484
criminal prosecution, 485
citizen oversight, 486
blue-ribbon commissions, 489
public interest
    organization, 490
mixed approach to police
    accountability, 491

## For Discussion

The Denver police department has posted its Discipline Handbook on its Web site. Read the Handbook. What are its objectives? What principles does it articulate? What are the underlying values? What specific programs to achieve its objectives does it describe?

Discuss the Denver Discipline Handbook with reference to issues that have been covered in this book. Do any parts of the Handbook address the police subculture (Chapter 6)? Are any features likely to have an impact on police–community relations (Chapter 12)? Specifically, how do features of the discipline system seek to advance accountability (Chapter 14)?

## Internet Exercises

**Exercise 1** Several law enforcement agencies have been sued for a "pattern or practice" of abusing the rights of citizens. Some of these suits have resulted in consent decrees where the department agrees to make a series of reforms related to accountability.

Locate one of these consent decrees. *Hint:* Some of the first agencies involved are the Pittsburgh police, the New Jersey state police, and the Los Angeles police department. You can also check the Web site of the Civil Rights Division of the U.S. Department of Justice for other departments.

Study the consent decree you have found. What changes must the department make? Do you think these changes will improve accountability? What does this consent decree say about the department before the suit? What was the department not doing that, if done, would help to ensure accountability?

**Exercise 2** The San Jose Independent Police Auditor (IPA) is one important citizen oversight agency. Find the IPA's Web site and review its annual reports from 1993 to the present. What has the San Jose IPA done over the years? What does it claim as its most important achievements? Do you believe these are valuable contributions to police accountability? Do you believe any of the activities of the IPA interfere with the management of the San Jose police department? If so, which activities? Discuss in class why you think they interfere with professional management.

**Exercise 3** Do any police departments describe their COMPSTAT programs on their Web sites? Check New York City, New Orleans, and Minneapolis for a start. Some departments use different names to describe them (in Minneapolis, for example, it is CODEFOR). Can you find any other departments that say they have similar systems?

Do these departments describe their systems in detail? Do they make any claims about their effectiveness? How much do you really learn about these systems from the Web sites?

## Notes

1. National Academy of Sciences, *Fairness and Effectiveness in Policing: The Evidence* (Washington DC: National Academy Press, 2004).

2. Louise Shelley, "The Soviet Police and the Rule of Law," in David Weisburd and Craig Uchida, eds., *Police Innovation and Control of the Police* (New York: Springer-Verlag, 1993), p. 127.

3. Jerome H. Skolnick, *Justice Without Trial: Law Enforcement in Democratic Society,* 3rd. ed. (New York, Macmillan, 1994).

4. Paul Jacobs, *Prelude to Riot* (New York: Vintage Books, 1968), p. 38.

5. Samuel Walker, "Historical Roots of the Legal Control of Police Behavior," in David Weisburd and Craig Uchida, eds., *Police Innovation and Control of the Police* (New York: Springer-Verlag, 1993), pp. 32–55.

6. U.S. Department of Justice, *Principles for Promoting Police Integrity* (Washington DC: Department of Justice, 2001).

7. Geoffrey P. Alpert and Mark H. Moore, "Measuring Police Performance in the New Paradigm of Policing," in Bureau of Justice Statistics, *Performance Measures for the Criminal Justice System* (Washington DC: Government Printing Office, 1993), pp. 109–42.

8. Bureau of Justice Statistics, *Criminal Victimization, 2002* (Washington DC: Government Printing Office, 2003); Donald Black, "Production of Crime Rates," in Donald Black, *The Manners and Customs of the Police* (New York: Academic Press, 1980), pp. 65–84.

9. Lawrence W. Sherman and Barry G. Glick, *The Quality of Police Arrest Statistics* (Washington DC: The Police Foundation, 1984).

10. Portland, Office of The City Auditor, *Service Efforts and Accomplishments: 2003–05* (Portland: Office of the Auditor, 2005). Available online at www.portlandonline.com.

11. James J. Willis, Stephen D. Mastrofski, and David Weisburd, "Compstat and Bureaucracy: A Case Study of Challenges and Opportunities for Change," *Justice Quarterly* 21 (September 2004): pp. 463–96.

12. Eli Silverman, *NYPD Battles Crime: Innovative Strategies in Policing* (Boston: Northeastern University Press, 1999); William Bratton and Peter Knobler, *Turnaround: How America's Top Cop Reversed the Crime Epidemic* (New York: Random House, 1999). For a skeptical view, see Samuel Walker, *Sense and Nonsense about Crime and Drugs,* 6th ed. (Belmont, CA: Wadsworth, 2006).

13. Herman Goldstein, "Administrative Problems in Controlling the Exercise of Police Authority," *Journal of Criminal Law, Criminology, and Police Science* 58, no. 2 (1967): p. 171.

14. "The Lost Battalion," *Newsday* (February 2, 2001), p. 1.

15. David Weisburd and Rosann Greenspan, with Edwin E. Hamilton, Hubert Williams, and Kellie

A. Bryant, *Police Attitudes Toward Abuse of Authority: Findings from a National Study* (Washington DC: Department of Justice, 2000), p. 7. www.ncjrs.org. NCJ 181312.

16. Special Counsel Merrick Bobb, *9th Semiannual Report* (Los Angeles: The Special Counsel, 1998), pp. 22–23. Available at www.parc.info.

17. James J. Fyfe, Jack R. Greene, William F. Walsh, O.W. Wilson, and Roy Clinton McLaren, *Police Administration,* 5th ed. (New York: McGraw-Hill, 1997), p. 139.

18. John Van Maanen, "The Boss: First-Line Supervision in an American Police Agency," in Maurice Punch, ed., *Control in the Police Organization* (Cambridge, MA: MIT Press, 1983), pp. 275–317.

19. Robin Shepard Engel, *How Police Supervisory Styles Influence Patrol Officer Behavior* (Washington DC: Department of Justice, 2003). www.ncjrs.org. NCJ 194078.

20. Robert C. Davis and Pedro Mateu-Gelabert, *Respectful and Effective Policing: Two Examples in the South Bronx* (New York: Vera Institute of Justice, 1999).

21. Madison, Wisconsin, Police Department, *Standard Operating Procedure Manual,* Section 4-1400 Administration of Sanctions/Discipline.

22. Los Angeles Police Department, *Board of Inquiry into the Rampart Area Incident* (Los Angeles: LAPD, March 2000), Executive Summary, p. 7, Chapter 10, "Police Integrity Systems."

23. Erwin Chemerinsky, *An Independent Analysis of the Los Angeles Police Department's Board of Inquiry Report on the Rampart Scandal* (Los Angeles: September 11, 2000).

24. Baltimore, Maryland, *The Mayor's Plan to Dramatically Reduce Crime in Baltimore,* "The Cultural Diagnostic" (Baltimore, MD: The City of Baltimore, 2000).

25. Samuel Walker, Stacy Osnick Milligan, and Anna Berke, *Strategies for Intervening with Officers through Early Intervention Systems: A Guide for Front-Line Supervisors* (Washington DC: Police Executive Research Forum, 2006). Available at www.cops.usdoj.gov.

26. Ibid.

27. Fyfe et al., *Police Administration,* 5th ed., Ch. 10, "Personnel Management II: Human Resources Management," pp. 318–63.

28. Commission to Investigate Allegations of Police Corruption (Mollen Commision), *Commission Report* (New York: City of New York, 1994), p. 81. Available at www.parc.info.

29. Timothy N. Oettmeier and Mary Ann Wycoff, *Personnel Performance Evaluations in the Community Policing Context* (Washington DC: Police Executive Research Forum, 1997), p. 5.

30. Frank J. Landy, *Performance Appraisal in Police Departments* (Washington DC: The Police Foundation, 1977), pp. 11–13.

31. Christopher Commission, *Report of the Independent Commission on the Los Angeles Police Department* (Los Angeles: Christopher Commission, 1991), p. 43. Available at www.parc.info.

32. Fyfe et al., *Police Administration,* "The Internal Affairs Unit," pp. 467–75.

33. Commission on Accreditation for Law Enforcement Agencies, *Standards for Law Enforcement Agencies,* 4th ed. (Fairfax, VA: CALEA, 1999), Standard 52.1.2.

34. Aogan Mulcahy, "'Headhunter' or 'Real Cop'? Identity in the World of Internal Affairs Officers," *Journal of Contemporary Ethnography* 24 (April 1995): p. 106.

35. Ibid., p. 108.

36. Herman Goldstein, *Police Corruption* (Washington DC: The Police Foundation, 1975), pp. 40–41.

37. Lawrence W. Sherman, *Controlling Police Corruption* (Washington DC: Government Printing Office, 1978), p. 10.

38. Police Executive Research Forum, *Organization Evaluation of the Omaha Police Division* (Washington DC: PERF, 1992), p. 75.

39. Los Angeles Police Commission, *Report of the Rampart Independent Review Panel* (Los Angeles: Los Angeles Police Commission, 2000), pp. 93–96.

40. Jayson Wechter, *Investigating Citizen Complaints Is Different* (Omaha: Police Professionalism Initiative, 2004).

41. Integrity and Accountability Office, *Disciplinary System* (Philadelphia: Philadelphia Police Department, 2003).

42. Office of Independent Review, *Second Annual Report* (Los Angeles: Los Angeles Sheriff's Department, 2003), p. 63.

43. Los Angeles Police Commission, *Report of the Rampart Independent Review Panel,* pp. 97–99.

44. Samuel Walker, *The Discipline Matrix: An Effective Police Accountability Tool?* (Omaha: Police Professionalism Initiative, 2004).

45. New Jersey Attorney General, *Internal Affairs Policy and Procedures* (Rev. November 2000).

46. New Jersey ACLU, *The Crisis Inside Police Internal Affairs* (Newark: ACLU of New Jersey, 2009). www.aclu-nj.org.

47. Christopher Commission, *Report of the Independent Commission on the Los Angeles Police Department.*

48. *Denver Police Discipline Handbook: Conduct Principles and Disciplinary Guidelines* (2008). www.denvergov.org/police/.

49. Mollen Commission, *Commission Report,* p. 53.

50. William Westley, *Violence and the Police* (Cambridge, MA: MIT Press, 1970).

51. Christopher Commission, *Report of the Independent Commission,* pp. 168–71.

52. Weisburd and Greenspan, with Hamilton, Williams, and Bryant, *Police Attitudes toward Abuse of Authority: Findings from a National Study.*

53. Public Advocate for the City of New York, *Disciplining Police: Solving the Problems of Police Misconduct* (New York: The Public Advocate, 2000), pp. 31–36.

54. "Wave of Abuse Claims Laid to a Few Officers," *Boston Sunday Globe* (October 4, 1992), p. 1.

55. Christopher Commission, *Report of the Independent Commission on the Los Angeles Police Department,* pp. 39–48; "Kansas City Police Go After Their 'Bad Boys,'" *New York Times* (September 10, 1991).

56. Samuel Walker, *Early Intervention Systems for Law Enforcement Agencies: A Management and Planning Guide* (Washington DC: Department of Justice, 2003). www.ncjrs.org. NCJ 201245.

57. All the consent decrees and memoranda of understanding are available at www.usdoj.gov/crt/split.

58. Walker, *Early Intervention Systems for Law Enforcement Agencies: A Management and Planning Guide.*

59. Samuel Walker, Geoffrey P. Alpert, and Dennis J. Kenney, *Early Warning Systems: Responding to the Problem Police Officer* (Washington DC: U.S. Justice Department, 2001). Available at www.ncjrs.org, NCJ 188656.

60. Samuel Walker, Stacy Osnick Milligan, and Anna Berke, *Strategies for Intervening with Officers through Early Intervention Systems: A Guide for Law Enforcement Chief Executives* (Washington DC: Department of Justice, 2006). www.ncjrs.org. NCJ 212299.

61. Walker, *Early Intervention Systems for Law Enforcement Agencies: A Management and Planning Guide,* Ch. 4.

62. Samuel Walker, *Popular Justice: A History of American Criminal Justice,* 2nd ed. (New York: Oxford University Press, 1998); New Jersey State Police, Monitors' Seventeenth Report (April 2009), p. vii. www.nj.gov/oag/monitors.htm.

63. Walker, Alpert, and Kenney, *Early Warning Systems: Responding to the Problem Police Officer.*

64. Walker, *Early Intervention Systems for Law Enforcement Agencies.*

65. Carol A. Archbold, *Police Accountability, Risk Management, and Legal Advising* (New York: LFB Scholarly Publishing, 2004).

66. Kansas City Police Department Office of the General Counsel: www.kcpd.org/kcpd2004/legalteam.htm; Charlotte-Mecklenburg: www.charmek.org, go to Inside CMPD, Police Attorney's Office.

67. Seattle Police Department, *How Are We Doing? Getting Feedback from the People We Serve,* www.cityofseattle.net/police/; Portland, *City of Portland Service Efforts and Accomplishments, 2007–08* (Portland: City Auditor, December 2008). Available at www.portlandonline.com/auditor.

68. Current information is available on the CALEA Web site: www.calea.org.

69. CALEA, *Standards for Law Enforcement,* 4th ed.

70. Jack Pearson, "National Accreditation: A Valuable Management Tool," in James J. Fyfe, ed., *Police Management Today* (Washington DC: ICMA, 1985).

71. James J. Fyfe, comments to author.

72. Herman Goldstein, "Directing Police Agencies through the Political Process," in *Policing a Free Society* (Cambridge, MA: Ballinger, 1977), pp. 131–56.

73. Samuel Walker, *A Critical History of Police Reform* (Lexington, MA: Lexington Books, 1977).

74. C. A. Novak, *The Years of Controversy: The Los Angeles Police Commission, 1991–1993.* (Washington DC: The Police Foundation, 1995).

75. Edward Littlejohn, "The Civilian Police Commission: A Deterrent of Police Misconduct," *University of Detroit Journal of Urban Law* 59 (Fall 1981): pp. 5–62.

76. Eileen Luna and Samuel Walker. "Institutional Structure vs. Political Will: Albuquerque as a Case Study in the Effectiveness of Citizen Oversight of the Police," in Andrew Goldsmith and Colleen Lewis, eds., *Civilian Oversight of Policing: Governance, Democracy and Human Rights* (Portland, OR: Hart, 2000), pp. 83–104.

77. *Mapp v. Ohio,* 367 U.S. 643 (1961).

78. Walker, "Historical Roots of the Legal Control of Police Behavior."

79. Herman Goldstein, "Trial Judges and the Police," *Crime and Delinquency* 14 (January 1968): pp. 14–25.

80. *Dickerson v. U.S.,* No. 99-5525 (June 26, 2000).

81. Paul G. Cassell and Bret S. Hayman, "Police Interrogation in the 1990s: An Empirical Study of the Effects of Miranda," *UCLA Law Review* 43 (February 1996): p. 860.

82. Richard A. Leo, *Police Interrogations and American Justice* (Cambridge: Harvard University Press, 2008).

83. Neal Milner, *The Court and Local Law Enforcement* (Beverly Hills, CA: Sage Publications, 1971).

84. Fred Graham, *The Self-Inflicted Wound* (New York: Macmillan, 1970).

85. Samuel Walker, *Sense and Nonsense about Crime,* 6th ed. (Belmont, CA: Wadsworth, 2006), pp. 99–103; Sheldon Krantz et al., *Police Policymaking* (Lexington, MA: Lexington Books, 1979); Controller General of the United States, *Impact of the Exclusionary Rule on Federal Crime Prosecutions,* Report #GGD-79-45 (April 19, 1979).

86. Walker, "Historical Roots of Legal Control of Police Behavior."

87. Myron W. Orfield, Jr., "The Exclusionary Rule and Deterrence: An Empirical Study of Chicago Narcotics Officers," *University of Chicago Law Review* 54 (Summer 1987): pp. 1016–55.

88. Carl McGowan, "Rulemaking and the Police," *Michigan Law Review* 70 (March 1972): pp. 659–94.

89. Goldstein, "Administrative Problems in Controlling the Exercise of Police Authority," p. 168.

90. Stephen Wasby, *Small-Town Police and the Supreme Court* (Lexington, MA: Lexington Books, 1976).

91. "City Had Bad-Cop Warning," *Detroit Free Press* (December 29, 2000), p. 1; *United States v. City of Detroit and the Detroit Police Department* (June 12, 2003). Available at www.usdoj.gov/crt/split/.

92. Michael Avery, David Rudovsky, and Karen Blum, *Police Misconduct: Law and Litigation,* 3rd ed. (St. Paul, MN: West, 1997).

93. *New York Times* (March 15, 1991).

94. Charldean Newell, Janay Pollock, and Jerry Tweedy, "Financial Aspects of Police Liability," *ICMA Baseline Data Report* 24 (March–April 1992): pp. 1–8.

95. Edward J. Littlejohn, "Civil Liability and the Police Officer: The Need for New Deterrents to Police Misconduct," *University of Detroit Journal of Urban Law* 58 (1981): pp. 365–431.

96. "Project: Suing the Police in Federal Court," *Yale Law Journal* 88 (1979): pp. 781–824.

97. Candace McCoy, "Lawsuits Against Police: What Impact Do They Really Have?" *Criminal Law Bulletin 20* (January–Feburary 1984): p. 53. Cited in Newell, Pollock, and Tweedy, "Financial Aspects of Police Liability," p. 8.

98. Special Counsel, Los Angeles County Sheriff's Department, *6th Semiannual Report* (Los Angeles: Los Angeles County, 1996), pp. 33–39. Available at www.parc.info.

99. Merrick Bobb, *11th Semiannual Report* (Los Angeles: October 1999); Merrick Bobb, *15th Semiannual Report* (Los Angeles: July 2002), p. 103. Available at www.parc.info.

100. *United States v. City of Pittsburgh* (W. D. Pa., 1997).

101. Samuel Walker and Morgan Macdonald, "An Alternative Remedy for Police Misconduct: A Model State 'Pattern or Practice' Statute," *George Mason University Civil Rights Law Journal* 19, no. 3 (2009): pp. 479–552.

102. Pattern or practice suits are discussed in detail in Samuel Walker, *The New World of Police Accountability* (Thousand Oaks, CA: Sage Publications, 2005).

103. *California v. City of Riverside* (2001). Available at www.ci.riverside.ca.us/rpd.

104. *People of the State of New York v. Town of Walkill* (2001). Dean Esserman, *First Report of the Monitor* (January 2002). Available at www.parc.info.

105. U.S. Department of Justice, *Principles for Promoting Police Integrity* (Washington DC: Department of Justice, 2001). Available at www.ncjr.org, NCJ 186189.

106. *United States v. Cincinnati* (2002); Walker and Macdonald, "An Alternative Remedy for Police Misconduct."

107. Michael R. Bromwich, *Special Report of the Independent Monitor for the Metropolitan Police Department* (Washington DC: Special Monitor, June 2002). Available at www.policemonitor.org.

108. Robert C. Davis, Christopher W. Ortiz, Nicole J. Henderson, Joel Miller, and Michelle K. Massie, *Turning Necessity into Virtue: Pittsburgh's Experience with a Federal Consent Decree* (2002). Available at www.policemonitor.org.

109. New Jersey State Police, *Monitors' Sixteenth Report* (August 2007), Executive Summary. www.nj.gov/oag/monitors.htm.

110. City of Cincinnati, *Independent Monitor's Final Report* (December 2008), p. 37.

111. Independent Monitor for the Metropolitan Police Department, *Twenty-Third Quarterly Report* (January, 2008), p. 4. Available at www.policemonitor.org.

112. Trent Ikerd, Examining the Institutionallization of Problem-Oriented Policing, Ph.D. Dissertation, University of Nebraska at Omaha, 2007.

113. Avery, Rudovsky, and Blum, *Police Misconduct: Law and Litigation,* Ch. 15; Monrad G. Paulson, "Securing Police Compliance with Constitutional Limitations," *National Commission on the Causes and Prevention of Violence, Law and Order Reconsidered* (New York: Bantam Books, 1970), pp. 402–5; *Rizzo v. Goode,* 423 U.S. 362 (1976).

114. U.S. Commission on Civil Rights, *Revisiting Who Is Guarding the Guardians?* (Washington DC: Government Printing Office, 2000).

115. Vera Institute of Justice, *Prosecuting Police Misconduct* (New York: Vera Institute, 1998).

116. Ibid.; Goldstein, "Administrative Problems in Controlling the Exercise of Police Authority," p. 162; Jerome Skolnick and James J. Fyfe, *Above the Law* (New York: The Free Press, 1993).

117. U.S. Department of Justice, Special Litigation Section; Web site: www.usdoj.gov/crt/split.

118. Samuel Walker, *Police Accountability: The Role of Citizen Oversight* (Belmont: Wadsworth, 2001).

119. San Jose Independent Police Auditor, *Year End Report,* 2008 (San Jose: City of San Jose, 2009).

120. The Reports of the special counsel are available at www.parc.info.

121. Outreach activities are discussed in detail in Chapters 11, 12, and 13 in Justina Cintron Perino, ed., *Citizen Oversight of Law Enforcement* (Chicago: American Bar Association, 2006).

122. Americans for Effective Law Enforcement, *Police Civilian Review Boards AELE Defense Manual, Brief 82-3* (San Francisco: AELE, 1982); Douglas Perez, *Common Sense about Police Review* (Philadelphia: Temple University Press, 1994).

123. The arguments on both sides are reviewed in Walker, *Police Accountability: The Role of Citizen Oversight,* pp. 54–60.

124. James R. Hudson, "Organizational Aspects of Internal and External Review of the Police," *Journal of Criminal Law, Criminology, and Police Science* 63 (September 1972): pp. 427–32.

125. Wayne A. Kerstetter and Kenneth A. Rasinski, "Opening a Window into Police Internal Affairs: Impact of Procedural Justice Reform on Third-Party Attitudes," *Social Justice Research* 7, no. 2 (1994): pp. 107–27.

126. Michele Sviridoff and James E. McElroy, *Processing Complaints against Police in New York City* (New York: Vera Institute of Justice, 1989).

127. New York Civil Liberties Union, *A Third Anniversary Overview of the Civilian Complaint Review Board,* July 5, 1993–July 5, 1996 (New York: NYCLU, 1996).

128. Charlotte-Mecklenburg Police Department, *Employee Conduct: Investigations and Discipline* (2005). Available at www.charmek.org.

129. National Commission on Law Observance and Enforcement, *The Third Degree* (Washington DC: Government Printing Office, 1931), p. 153; Christopher Commission, *Report of the Independent Commission on the Los Angeles Police Department.* www.parc.info.

130. Samuel Walker, "Setting the Standards: The Efforts and Impacts of Blue-Ribbon Commissions on the Police," in W.A. Geller, ed., *Police Leadership in America: Crisis and Opportunity* (New York: Praeger, 1985), pp. 354–70.

131. Walker, *Police Accountability: The Role of Citizen Oversight.*

132. David Burnham, *The Role of the Media in Controlling Corruption* (New York: John Jay College, 1977).

133. See the contributions in "The Chief and the Media," in W.A. Geller, ed., *Police Leadership in America: Crisis and Opportunity,* pp. 99–146.

134. Walker, *Police Accountability: The Role of Citizen Oversight,* p. 128.

135. NAACP, *Beyond the Rodney King Story: An Investigation of Police Misconduct in Minority Communities* (Boston: Northeastern University Press, 1995).

136. Samuel Walker, *In Defense of American Liberties: A History of the ACLU* (New York: Oxford University Press; 1990); Gilda Brancato and Eliot E. Polebaum, *The Rights of Police Officers* (New York: Avon Books, 1981).

137. Herbert Packer, "Two Models of the Criminal Process," in Packer, *The Limits of the Criminal Sanction,* pp. 149–73.

138. David Bayley, "Law Enforcement and the Rule of Law: Is There a Tradeoff?" *Criminology and Public Policy* 2 (November 2002): pp. 133–54.

# Challenges for a New Century

**Chapter 15**

The Future of Policing in America

# The Future of Policing in America

## Chapter Outline

Previous chapters have discussed various innovations and reforms that have taken place in many agencies across the United States. In this chapter we discuss what Maguire and King refer to as large-scale macro-level trends. These are changes that have the potential to transform the landscape of policing in the future.[1] As you have probably discovered by now, there is a lot left to learn about policing today, and much more if we're to make predictions about its future. With this caveat, we discuss five areas of policing in which we believe current trends will have a profound and longstanding impact on police agencies in the future: (1) police technology, (2) employment practices in law enforcement, (3) police research, (4) demographic change, and (5) the war on terrorism.

# Police Technology

Perhaps one of the most influential changes taking place in policing today is related to information technology. Many police agencies use the Internet to convey information to the public, use cell phones to communicate with others while in the field, and use mobile computers to instantly retrieve information. However, it is clear that this is just the beginning and that advances in information technology will have a broad and powerful impact on policing in the future. For example, Tom Steele, founder of the International Association of Chiefs of Police, Law Enforcement Information Managers Section, stated:

> We are just beginning to realize the significance of what is happening. There is not one—I repeat not one—area of the enforcement culture that will go untouched. The very essence of how we do business has been impacted through greater communications and information sharing. Over the next 15 to 20 years you will see the greatest redirection, reorganization, and modification of policing since Sir Robert Peel and the Metropolitan Police.[2]

## Major Technology Applications

Jim Chu, a police manager with the Vancouver, Canada, police department and a leading expert in police-related information technology, notes that there are four major applications that are of consequence to police agencies of the future: (1) database and information technology, (2) computer-aided dispatch, (3) records management systems, and (4) mobile computing.[3]

### *Database and Information Technology*
In the past, police agencies relied on card file indexes, with cards containing such basic information on suspects as their name, date of birth, case number, and criminal history record. This system was particularly helpful to specialized units such as burglary, forgery, and vice to assist them with identifying potential suspects in an area where a crime had occurred.

Most police departments today have either developed relational databases or are on their way to doing so. Computerized relational databases operate much like a card file index, but are much more powerful. They allow the police to store and retrieve large amounts of information obtained from a variety of sources. For example, if a police officer is investigating a suspect in a crime, the officer can use a relational database to gather information from the department's criminal history records system, the gang unit's intelligence system, and the state's department of motor vehicles—all at one time.

Relational databases are not only useful for gathering and storing information on suspects and criminals, but they are also used for management purposes. They have the capacity to identify areas that need greater levels of police service and can provide trend information on criminal activity in specific neighborhoods. Relational databases can also be used to evaluate officers by tracking the number of arrests that they make, the types of arrests that they make, and the number of complaints against an officer.[4]

### Computer-Aided Dispatch

**computer-aided dispatch**

**Comuter-aided dispatch** (CAD) was first used in the 1970s as a method of more effectively and efficiently managing calls for service from the public. It was quickly realized that this system of service delivery had many advantages. First, it offered police departments a faster and more effective method of communicating with police officers in the field. Much like instant text messages, CAD systems allowed dispatchers to input relevant information into the system and send it instantaneously to officers' mobile computers. Unlike radio dispatch, the uniformity and clarity of the graphic display reduced officer confusion. Second, CAD systems enhance safety by monitoring officer status. If officers do not update their "field status" after they have responded to a call, the CAD system will automatically alert a dispatcher to contact someone to check on their safety. Third, CAD systems help dispatchers and officers prioritize calls for service. Various types of calls are precoded according to their seriousness and guide dispatchers and officers on appropriate action.

### Records Management Systems

In the past, one of the most time-consuming activities engaged in by police agencies was the management of paperwork. In large police organizations it was a hopeless effort that often resulted in frustration and loss of information. This was largely the consequence of complex processes in place for collecting, organizing, storing, and disseminating paper reports. All of the paper shuffling taking place in organizations led to too many opportunities for "lost paperwork" and resulted in administrators and officers rarely having all of the relevant information at their disposal.

**records management systems**

The advent of **records management systems** (RMS) has solved many of the problems associated with the "paper tiger." Records management systems are used to input and organize information from different types of reports in one easy-to-access format. For example, officers who work in agencies that have adopted this technology often are not required to file written reports. Instead, all information is input into a mobile terminal and is transmitted to appropriate personnel. As such, records management systems (RMS) have not only reduced the amount of time that officers spend on paper work, but they have also improved the accuracy of the information collected by the police. This is because the computer programs in place in mobile terminals have quality-control features that prompt officers for certain types of information and ensure that the data entered is consistent and accurate.

RMS programs also allow for easy access to information. Some RMS programs allow numerous types of reports, such as crime reports, field interview contacts, traffic citations, booking reports, criminal history reports, and investigation reports, to be displayed at any time, on any computer terminal—permitting officers to access information faster and more easily.[5]

## *Mobile Computing*

Two to three decades ago the only way for a supervisor or dispatcher to communicate with a police officer was through a call box or by mobile radio. It was even more difficult for a citizen to get a hold of a particular officer while he or she was in the field. Today, (and more so in the future) there are a number of different methods (see Exhibit 15–1) for communicating with an officer, with each having its own strengths and weaknesses.

On the impact of earlier technological innovations—the telephone, the two-way radio, and the police car—see Chapter 2.

Call boxes, first installed in 1877, were inefficient and ineffective compared with today's communication devices. Officers could only access call boxes at specific locations, and when they did have access to a call box, officers could only obtain or convey certain types of information—such as the location of a particular problem or the need for assistance. Mobile radios, which became popular in the 1930s, allowed officers to access communication at almost any geographic location, and permitted communication among officers, supervisors, and dispatchers at almost any time. Cellular phones further enhanced the ability of officers to communicate with those outside of the police department who do not have access to a two-way radio. For example, officers responsible for particular areas or who work closely with businesses or neighborhood groups are now able to easily communicate with members of the community. While the progression from the call box to the two-way radio and the cellular phone has substantially enhanced the capacity of police officials to communicate with each other and the community, the content of the information exchanged over these forms of media have changed

## EXHIBIT 15–1

### Communication Devices

|  | Timely | Access to All Information |
|---|---|---|
| Call box | No | Not good |
| Mobile radio | Yes | Not good |
| Cellular phone | Yes | Not good |
| Mobile data terminal | Maybe | Better |
| Mobile workstation | Maybe | Very good |
| Personal digital assistant | Yes | Very good |

*Source:* Jim Chu, *Law Enforcement Information Technology* (New York: CRC Press, 2001), p. 11.

**S I D E B A R        15 - 1**

## Current and Cutting-Edge Applications in Law Enforcement

| Function | Current | Cutting Edge |
|---|---|---|
| **Capture** Obtain information | An officer relays information verbally to a dispatcher who types the information into a terminal. | A bar code on a driver's license is scanned and the details are automatically recorded into predefined fields on a mobile computer deployed in the police vehicle. |
| **Transmit** Move information from one location to another | Information is sent from the dispatcher terminal, over a local network, to the state or city switch that is connected to local databases. | The information is automatically sent from the vehicle through a wireless connection. Results (registered owner of vehicle) are returned and the results are used to spawn new queries. The location of the stop is determined from an automatic vehicle location system. |
| **Store** Save information on a disk drive for later retrieval | The traffic stop details are recorded in the computer-aided dispatch (CAD). | The offender details are sent to a regional data warehouse that serves as a multijurisdictional investigative information repository. |
| **Retrieve** Find information needed from the disk drive | Users from the same agency access the data stored in the CAD system. | The "islands of information" that exist in many areas are eliminated as investigators quickly access city, state, and federal databases to narrow the search for suspects to a crime. |
| **Manipulate** Computer processor performs calculations | A query is made to find all traffic stops that fit a user-specified criterion. | Data mining techniques correlate CAD data with other sources (traffic flow, accident locations) to help identify patterns and areas requiring targeted enforcement. |
| **Display** Show the information on a screen or printout | Lists of CAD incidents are printed and passed around. | Electronic presentations, including maps and other graphics, are assembled for high-level executive briefings, and the material is also posted to an agency intranet for comments by others. |

*Source:* Jim Chu, *Law Enforcement Information Technology* (New York: CRC Press, 2001), p. 11.

only slightly. Typically, it is restricted to specific incidents or particular pieces of information.

Mobile computers and workstations have revolutionized the type and amount of information that patrol officers have at their disposal. In some of the most technologically advanced police departments, mobile computers and workstations are the primary mechanism that officers use to deposit and access information. For example, officers can input information that was formerly in written form directly into the computer. This not only eliminates all of the paper generated by reports but makes the information available to all other police officials almost instantaneously. Mobile computing also permits anytime, anyplace access to the department's CAD and RMS systems, which can assist officers with stops and crime scene investigations. For example, if an officer pulls a suspect over for a traffic violation, he or she can instantly access the department's CAD and RMS system by mobile computer and query information about the person who was pulled over. Officers, for example, can check the driver's criminal record, verify if the driver is the owner of the car, and determine if the person has any outstanding arrest warrants. Additionally, mobile computers facilitate investigations and information gathering by allowing officers to perform online text searches for needed information when they are in the field.[6]

## The Use of Technology in the Field

### COMPSTAT

One of the most important innovations in police crime fighting is COMPSTAT (see Chapter 4). Using computerized data management, COMPSTAT provides timely data on crime and disorder by neighborhood. In most programs, police commanders meet weekly or monthly to analyze and discuss the data. At these meetings, precinct commanders are expected to have analyzed the data, identified problems, and have already developed responses that will address new or changing patterns of crime and disorder in the areas under their command (e.g., a series of residential burglaries on one block; a sharp increase in drug arrests in one area).[7]

Through COMPSTAT, computer technology offers the opportunity for greater police effectiveness than previously. First, the data are very current. Some programs provide data on a twenty-four-hour basis. Second, computer technology facilitates analysis of trends and changes in crime and disorder. Third, the system facilitates crime mapping, allowing a focus on particular neighborhoods or even streets. Fourth, the system heightens the ability of the chief of police to hold precinct commanders accountable for crime and disorder in their areas.

### Early Intervention Systems

Early intervention (EI) systems are an application of personnel records management for the purpose of increasing the accountability of police officers (see Chapter 14). An EI system is a computerized database with performance data on each officer. Systems vary, but most include data on officer use of force, citizen complaints, commendations, and officer involvement in civil suits against the department. Some EI systems contain as many as 18 or 20 performance indicators.[8] The data permit commanders to analyze officer performance and to identify those officers who appear to have performance problems. The department can then refer these officers to some kind of intervention—informal counseling, retraining, professional counseling—designed to correct their performance problems.[9]

## *License Plate Readers*

Local police agencies across the country are beginning to use automated license plate readers, otherwise known as LPRs or tag readers. License plate readers are installed on police vehicles and fixed sites such as traffic intersections and highway entrances and exits. License plate readers became popular in the 1990s as a strategy used by the British military to deter Irish Republican Army attacks. The United States later adopted them to identify stolen cars and illegally parked cars.[10] For example, in Mesa, Arizona, LPRs are placed in patrol vehicles and on street corners to immediately alert patrol officers when a vehicle has been identified as stolen. Currently, there are five potential uses for license plate readers: (1) crime analysis, (2) alerts and hot lists, (3) tracking individuals, (4) identifying previously undetected crimes, and (5) revenue generation.

Some police departments may choose to use LPRs for tactical crime analysis. For example, an agency might have an LPR near a local bank that could help them identify vehicles that have been in an area when a robbery occurred. Police agencies can also use license plate readers to identify vehicles owned by persons of interest, or those who pose a threat to law enforcement. These lists are referred to as "hot lists." Hot lists can be generated by a variety of sources including patrol officers, the National Insurance Crime Bureau, the Department of Homeland Security, the National Crime Information Center, and Amber Alerts.

License plate readers notify police officers when a license plate on the hot list is observed so that the officer can take appropriate action. Additionally, LPRs are used to track individuals. Some jurisdictions may choose to track the movement of drug smugglers, gang members, fugitives, and those on parole or probation. The Department of Homeland Security might use the information to track the movement of those on terrorist watch lists, and local police departments could use LPRs to determine whether the license plates of registered sex offenders have entered a school or day care parking lot. License plate readers can also be used by the police to detect previously undetected crime. For instance, in many states a person can have their license suspended if he or she is found to be driving without insurance. However, this violation is rarely discovered by the police unless the person is pulled over for another reason. With the appropriate data sharing agreements in place, LPRs have the potential to be used to detect those vehicles on the road that have not been insured and could be used to identify vehicles that are associated with persons who have had their license suspended. Last, and related, some states revoke license plates and drivers' licenses because drivers failed to pay a fine or owe taxes. LPRs could be used to bring those who owe the government money to the attention of the police.[11]

There has been no research examining the effectiveness of LPRs, but preliminary evidence suggests that police officials are excited about its prospects. Some, however, question whether privacy rights are violated as a consequence of the implementation of the technology. To date there have been no legal precedents to address privacy rights issues raised by LPRs, however, police advocacy groups claim that analogous cases have been seen before the courts in the past and suggest that LPRs do not violate constitutional privacy protections.[12]

## The Future of Police Information Technology

Since 9/11, there has been increased priority placed upon building the necessary infrastructure for law enforcement agencies to share information with one another. In most agencies today the police have limited capacity to share information. One of the few exceptions is the National Crime Information Center (NCIC) run by the FBI. NCIC is a computerized database project that permits local agencies to report a limited amount of information pertaining to criminal record history, fugitives, stolen property, and missing persons to the FBI, and in turn provides the information to other agencies upon demand.[13] The program, while valued by police, permits only a very small amount of information to be shared. As a consequence, a small number of police agencies across the country are beginning to develop technology that permits sharing more detailed information.

One major innovation has been the development of the Global Justice XML Data Model (GJXDM). GJXDM allows criminal justice agencies to maintain their information in a standardized language providing for increased opportunities for data sharing in a consistent format with partners across the criminal justice field. Unfortunately, information-sharing initiatives are generally complex, which greatly increases the risk of failure. One problem is that many police agencies do not have personnel with the required skills to facilitate data integration and information-sharing projects. This requires police agencies to hire outside consultants to develop and implement information-sharing capacities, expending a substantial amount of financial resources that the police do not often have. Another problem is that these projects require a great amount of trust and a willingness to share. Police agencies are highly fragmented organizations that often do not work well with one another and are very protective about releasing information that has been gathered by their people, on their "turf." Last, researchers from COPLINK, a fairly well known company that specializes in information sharing, pointed out that agencies must see an immediate gain or benefit in order to be motivated to share information. Because information-sharing projects typically take years to plan and implement, there are almost no immediate rewards for police agencies.[14]

While information sharing is difficult to implement, there is evidence regarding its benefits to the police. For example, Zaworski examined the impact of the Automated Regional Justice Information System (ARJIS) on the performance of officers and investigators in the San Diego sheriff's department. The findings indicated that information-sharing technology in general increases effectiveness and job performance. More specifically, Zaworski reported that information-sharing technology increased arrest rates for patrol officers and improved case clearance rates for detectives. Additionally, the report indicated that officers were more satisfied with the data that they had available to them to perform their job and believed that it enhanced officer safety due to increased officer knowledge in the field.[15]

## Technologically Advanced Weapons

New technologically advanced forms of nonlethal weaponry are being developed to assist the police to subdue dangerous suspects. One rapidly emerging technology is the Thomas A. Swift electrical rifle (Taser). A **Taser** is a battery-powered electro-muscular device (EMD) that fires two metal prongs, which are attached to a wire that delivers approximately 26 watts of electricity at more than 50,000 volts. The electricity causes substantial muscular pain and typically results in the immobilization of the suspect. A short time after the electrical charges are stopped there are reportedly few lasting effects other than irritation where the probes were located.[16] (Note: The word "Taser" is trademarked by TASER International.)

Today, approximately 8,000 police agencies have purchased Tasers for departmental use.[17] The Phoenix police department has the largest number of Tasers. A departmental study of their use suggested that the implementation and use of Tasers successfully reduced injuries to suspects and officers. In one year the Phoenix police department reported that among 475 incidents where a Taser could have been employed, it was actually used 128 times. Only 9 percent of suspects Tasered were injured, compared to 33 percent of those who were not. Likewise, 2 percent of officers who used the Taser were injured, compared to 9 percent of officers who did not use the weapon.[18]

Several organizations, however, have condemned the use of Tasers. They argue that the weapon is more dangerous than the police admit or may be aware of. One report found that the weapon is 39 times more powerful than company officials claim, explaining that the Taser generated 704 watts of power compared to the 18 watts specified by the manufacturer. From 2001 through December 2008, 334 people have died after Taser use in the United States.[19] Unfortunately, to date, there has been little independent research that has examined the medical ramifications of its use. The independent research that has examined Taser use, however, has determined that only 0.3 percent of incidents involving Tasers result in moderate or serious injuries such as broken bones, loss of eye, or serious head injury.[20]

# Crime Analysis

Related to the shift in the use of technology is the employment of crime analysis by police departments. Crime analysis allows police agencies to make organizational and strategic decisions based on evidence rather than on guesswork. It allows agencies to make data-driven decisions with regard to the allocation of resources and predicting future criminal activity, and supports patrol officers and investigators in their technical decisions.

O'Shea and Nicholls state that crime analysis consists of three functions:

1. To assess the nature, extent, and distribution of crime in order to efficiently and effectively allocate resources and deploy personnel.
2. To identify crime–suspect correlations to assist investigations.
3. To identify the conditions that facilitate crime and incivility so that policymakers may make informed decisions about prevention approaches.[21]

**Taser**

To accomplish these functions, crime analysts are responsible for a number of activities related to the collection, analysis, and dissemination of crime-related data. First, crime analysts are responsible for gathering, and sometimes entering, information that comes to the police. This information is typically collected through crime reports, calls for service, arrest reports, and field interview cards. Second, crime analysts are responsible for analyzing the data to determine patterns and trends in crime. This is often accomplished through the use of databases, complex statistical packages, and mapping software that require substantial training to use. Third, after a crime analyst has identified a pattern, the information is presented to the appropriate personnel, who use it to develop a response.[22]

Today, about 75 percent of police departments having more than 100 sworn officers have assigned at least one person to conduct crime analysis. These positions are usually staffed by a civilian because of the specialized training needed for the assignment and because civilians are less costly to employ when compared to sworn officers. About 72 percent of those agencies that do have a crime analyst have placed them in a separate unit. This unit falls typically under an administrative division (44 percent), but may also fall under a detective division (27 percent) or patrol division (8 percent).[23]

## Types of Crime Analysis

Deborah Osborne and Susan Wernicke describe three of the most common types of crime analysis used by police agencies, or potentially available to them.[24]

### *Tactical Crime Analysis*

**Tactical crime analysis** typically involves the identification of specific crime problems in particular geographic areas. The goal of this type of analysis is to provide patrol officers and detectives with timely information that allows them to respond to crimes that are currently taking place. For example, a crime analyst might identify a trend of auto burglaries, determining the typical location, time, and dates of the criminal activity. This information would provide patrol officers with information about where to direct their patrol activities and the time that this strategy might be most effective in capturing or deterring the offender(s).

**tactical crime analysis**

### *Strategic Crime Analysis*

**Strategic crime analysis** focuses on long-term crime trends. This information is used to develop strategic plans to address particular problems. Strategic crime analysis is different from tactical crime analysis in that the focus is on long-term planning and larger, more complex projects. A project conducted in Scottsdale, Arizona, provides an illustration. The Scottsdale police department Crime Analysis Unit discovered that over a course of years, open-garage-door burglaries were increasing. The crime analyst coordinated with patrol, community watch groups, and neighborhood associations to develop a strategic plan to prevent open-garage-door burglaries. The plan was implemented, and the strategy employed was repeated over the course of several years.

**strategic crime analysis**

### *Administrative Crime Analysis*

administrative crime
analysis

**Administrative crime analysis** focuses on providing summary statistics and data to police managers. This information is often used by managers to better understand crime and disorder problems. For example, a chief of police might use the Uniform Crime Report data collected by the agency to compare the amount of crime in his community with that of similar jurisdictions. Similarly, a district commander might request a daily crime report to examine the amount and type of crime occurring in their district to stay better informed about crime in their area of responsibility.

For additional discussion
of hot spots, see Chapter 7.

**crime mapping**

## Crime Mapping

Over the past twenty years police experts have come to recognize that some geographic areas have more crime than others. These areas have become known as "hot spots". This has led some police departments' crime analysts to specialize in what has become known as **crime mapping.** Crime mapping permits analysts to identify spatial patterns and hot spots for different types of crimes. Today, about 13 percent of police departments engage in computerized crime mapping. About one-third of large police departments (with 100 or more sworn officers) currently use computer crime mapping, compared to 3 percent of smaller departments. One Arizona study found that even among those departments that use crime mapping, only half have crime analysts that are proficient it its use.[25] As such, the use of computerized crime mapping is still in its infancy and will take some time to be fully institutionalized within police agencies across the country.

Currently the Department of Justice (DOJ) is allocating substantial resources to assist police agencies to adopt crime mapping.[26] This is because crime mapping allows the police to allocate resources in areas that have the most crime. In the past this might have been done at the precinct and beat level by simply calculating the number of crimes that take place in each area. However, with crime maps the police are able to allocate resources to specific addresses, street corners, and blocks. Crime mapping can be used for a variety of other purposes as well. For example, it can be combined with other sources of data, such as census data, school boundary data, and property assessment data, to help the police understand the relationship between geographic areas, crime, and community-level characteristics.[27] Some agencies also provide their officers with crime maps to keep them up-to-date on where crime is occurring in their patrol area so that they can engage in proactive enforcement efforts during the time in which they are not responding to calls for service. Likewise, crime maps can be shared with the community to educate people about crime in their neighborhood.[28]

Research funded by the National Institute of Justice reported that of agencies that use computerized crime mapping, 94 percent use it to inform officers and investigators of the location of crime, 56 percent use it to make resource allocation decisions, 49 percent use it to evaluate interventions, 47 percent use it to inform residents about crime activity and changes in their community, and 44 percent use it to identify addresses where there are repeat calls for service.[29]

For an example of what crime mapping looks like, see Exhibit 15–2.

**EXHIBIT 15-2**

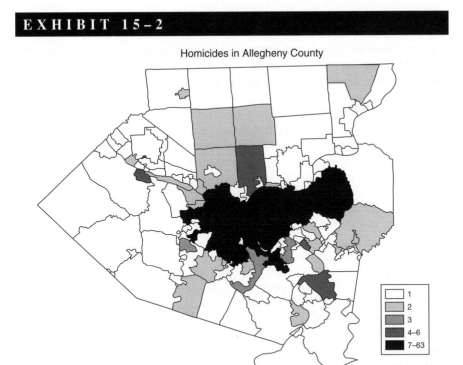

Homicides in Allegheny County

| | |
|---|---|
| | 1 |
| | 2 |
| | 3 |
| | 4–6 |
| | 7–63 |

*Source:* Erin Dalton, *"Violence in Pittsburgh: An Analysis,"* unpublished manuscript, 2005.

# The Outlook for Police Employment

The employment outlook for those interested in a career in law enforcement appears bright. Greater concern about crime and delinquency, increasing threats to homeland security, and the need to replace police officers from the baby boom generation has resulted in an increasing demand for law enforcement officers that should last for years to come. For example, the Bureau of Labor Statistics reports that the demand for police officers is projected to increase 11 percent through 2016.[30]

## Opportunities in Local, County, and State Law Enforcement

Most of the job opportunities available in law enforcement exist within city, county, and state agencies. However, it is important to point out that such jobs as a city police officer, county sheriff, or highway patrol officer are not the only job options available to you. There are a host of jobs that are available that might be of greater interest to you or might provide you with an experience you might not have considered. These jobs can not only provide you with the experience and connections that can help you get the law enforcement career that you have always wanted, but they can also offer you a career for a lifetime.

Some of the most overlooked careers in policing are jobs held by civilians. Today, about one-third of all personnel employed by local, county, and state law enforcement agencies are civilians. Many police agencies hire civilians to enforce community physical disorder ordinances, facilitate community crime prevention, and collect evidence. Civilians are also used as crime analysts, strategic planners, and technicians of various kinds.

There are also a number of state agencies that grant individuals police powers to perform various regulatory functions. These jobs range from enforcing laws related to gambling, to inspecting factories for excess pollution, to regulating livestock and other farm animals. For example, an individual who is interested in policing but also has a strong interest in outdoor activities might consider working for a state agency that protects wildlife, such as the state department of agriculture, state department of parks and recreation, or the state department of fish and game. There is an agency to fit almost anyone's interest. For example, Exhibit 15–3 lists a variety of California state agencies that employ persons who possess police power.

## Local, County, and State Salaries

The average annual salary for police and sheriff's patrol officers was about $47,460 in 2006, the last year for which these figures were available. Detectives make more

### EXHIBIT 15–3

**California State Agencies That Possess Police Power**

| | | | | |
|---|---|---|---|---|
| Department of Agriculture | Department of Employment | Department of Justice | Department of Fish and Game | California Horse Racing Board |
| Department of Alcoholic Beverage Control | Department of Finance | Department of Mental Hygiene | San Francisco Port Authority | Bureau of Investigations |
| Department of Corrections | California State Police | Department of Motor Vehicles | Harbor Police | License Bureau |
| Department of Youth Authority | Department of Industrial Welfare | Department of Professional and Vocational Standards | Department of Social Work | |
| California Disaster Office | Fair Employment Practice Commission | Department of Public Health | State Fire Marshal | |
| Department of California Highway Patrol | Department of Insurance | Department of Parks and Recreation | Office of Consumer Council | |
| Department of Education | Department of Investments | Department of Conservation | Department of Business Taxes | |

*Source:* James Stinchcomb, *Opportunities in Law Enforcement and Criminal Justice Careers* (Chicago: VGM Career Books, 2003).

## EXHIBIT 15–4

### Minimum and Maximum Salary for Police Officers by Rank

| | Minimum Annual Base Salary | Maximum Annual Base Salary |
|---|---|---|
| Police chief | $78,547 | $99,698 |
| Deputy chief | $68,797 | $87,564 |
| Police captain | $65,408 | $81,466 |
| Police lieutenant | $59,940 | $72,454 |
| Police sergeant | $53,734 | $63,564 |
| Police corporal | $44,160 | $55,183 |

Source: U.S. Department of Labor, Bureau of Labor Statistics, http://www.bls.gov/oco/ocos160.htm (earnings). Accessed March 10, 2009.

than patrol officers. In 2006, the median annual income for detectives and criminal investigators was approximately $58,260. In 2006, the International City–County Management Association's annual Police and Fire Personnel, Salaries, and Expenditures Survey examined the salaries of full-time police personnel in cities across the county. Exhibit 15–4 shows their findings.[31]

Police officers also receive paid vacation, sick leave, and medical and life insurance—benefits that many other employers do not provide to their employees. Because police officers are usually covered by pension plans, many retire at half-pay after twenty or twenty-five years of service.[32]

## Opportunities in Federal Law Enforcement

There are also ample opportunities for individuals aspiring to a career in federal law enforcement, particularly since the creation of the Department of Homeland Security. Similar to the variation within state law enforcement agencies, there are a number of federal agencies that fulfill numerous roles—those that are responsible for criminal investigations, intelligence gathering, and law enforcement, as well as those that perform compliance and security functions.[33]

Most of these agencies require that an applicant have an undergraduate degree. Those agencies that perform investigative functions often require specialized skills, such as legal training or knowledge about taxes and finance. Today, for example, the Drug Enforcement Agency is seeking persons with a background in pharmacy and the Border Patrol is looking for persons who speak Spanish.[34]

Persons interested in a career in federal law enforcement should expect to move to a different geographic area of the country. First, if a person is hired by a federal law enforcement agency, they will most likely be sent to the Federal Law Enforcement Training Center in Glynco, Georgia. Second, while most agencies try to relocate you to a geographic area of your interest, the city or state in which you will live and work is not guaranteed. About 50 percent of all federal law enforcement officers were assigned to the five locations listed in Exhibit 15–5.[35]

**EXHIBIT 15-5**

## Top Five Jurisdictions Employing Federal Officers

| Jurisdiction | Number of Federal Officers |
| --- | --- |
| California | 10,469 |
| Texas | 8,836 |
| New York | 6,556 |
| District of Columbia | 6,508 |
| Florida | 4,980 |

*Source:* Law Enforcement Career Starter, www.netlibrary.com/nlreader.dll?bookid=28378&filename=page_3.html.

## Federal Salaries

The salaries of about 75 percent of federal law enforcement officers are determined by the General Schedule (GS) pay system. The GS system is comprised of 15 grades—GS-1 through GS-15. There is also a salary range of 10 steps within each grade. The entry-level pay that a federal law enforcement officer receives varies by agency. However, some federal agents and inspectors receive law enforcement availability pay (LEAP), which increases the pay of these agents by 25 percent because of the substantial amount of overtime they are expected to work.

Individuals working for the FBI begin with a salary of about $60,199 a year. Agents who are not promoted to a supervisory position can earn as much as $94,268 a year after several years. FBI supervisors, managers, and executives earn between $111,394 and $131,033 per year, depending on their position. As with other law enforcement jobs, federal agents receive excellent benefits, including paid vacation and sick time, medical coverage, and life insurance.[36]

## The Future of Police Research

A generation ago we knew very little about policing. We did not know what patrol officers did during a typical eight-hour shift. We did not know who they arrested, or why they did not arrest some people. Everyone assumed that patrol deterred crime, but there was no scientific evidence to support that belief. We did not know if some tactics were more effective than others in preventing crime.

Today we have a lot of information related to those questions. Since the late 1960s there has been a "research revolution" in policing that has enormously expanded our knowledge base. The National Academy of Sciences concluded that "no other country has made a more concerted effort to harness the rigor of social science to the study of policing."[37] As previous chapters of this book have described in detail, we can make some informed statements about what works and what does not work in policing. The current body of research on policing is summarized and evaluated in the National Academy of Sciences report *Fairness and Effectiveness in Policing: The Evidence.*[38]

Knowledge does not come easily or cheaply. The research revolution in policing is the product of a large investment of funds in scientific research. The primary source of that funding is the federal government, though some additional research funds come from private foundations such as the Ford Foundation. Significant federal funding of research in criminal justice began in 1968 with the creation of the Law Enforcement Assistance Administration (LEAA). Today the federal government supports criminal justice research primarily through the National Institute of Justice (NIJ). Some additional research is supported by the National Science Foundation (NSF) and the COPS Office of the U.S. Justice Department.

## Does Research Do Any Good?

Many people ask whether research does any good. Does anyone actually read all of those studies—other than the professors who wrote them and the students who are assigned to read them in class? Does research have any impact on policy? Is social science research on policing worth the investment of our money?

The answer to these questions is yes. People do read research reports, and there are a number of examples of how research has influenced police policy.[39]

One of the best examples of the impact of research on policy is the development of community policing. Often characterized as a "new paradigm" for policing, community policing emerged after research discredited the assumptions of the traditional professional model of policing. Specifically:

- The Kansas City Preventive Patrol Experiment found that increasing the level of patrol did not deter crime more effectively than the normal level of patrol.
- Several studies found that faster response time to calls for service did not result in more arrests.
- The Rand Corporation study of the criminal investigation process found that traditional detective work did not increase the number of crimes solved.

Along with other research, these studies forced policy makers to rethink the role of the police and the goals of basic police operations. In this effort, they built upon some other important research findings.

For a discussion of the Kansas City Preventive Patrol Experiment, see Chapter 7.

- The Newark Foot Patrol Study found that increasing the number of foot patrol officers reduced citizen fear of crime (even though crime did not actually go down) and that citizens also had more positive feelings about the police.
- Several studies found that the police are heavily dependent on citizens for reporting crime and providing information about crime and other problems.

Synthesizing these findings, a combination of researchers and policymakers developed the idea of community policing based on research that suggested that (1) traditional police operations have not proven effective and (2) the police cannot effectively respond to crime and disorder by themselves but need good relations and close cooperation with citizens.

## The Future of Federal Support for Research

Given the enormous contributions of social science research to our understanding of policing and the reliance of research on federal funds, it is important to consider the future of federal support for police research. The future of federal support for research is very uncertain, however. The National Academy of Sciences found that even in the past the level of research support has varied considerably from year to year. This has made it difficult to develop a stable and focused research agenda. Even more serious, because of the budget problems of the federal government, support for research through the National Institute of Justice has been reduced and may be reduced even further. Given the important contributions of research in the past, this is a potentially serious problem for the future of the American police.

## Demographic Change

**demographic change**

American society is experiencing significant **demographic change,** mainly as a result of immigration. The change in the composition of American society poses new and difficult challenges for law enforcement.

The biggest change is the growth of the Hispanic/Latino population. Shortly after the 2000 census was completed, Hispanics became the largest racial or ethnic minority group in the country, edging past the African American community, at about 13 percent of the total U.S. population.[40] Many Hispanic immigrants do not speak English or have only a limited facility with English. This creates potential problems in terms of communicating with the police—through 911 systems and in on-the-street encounters. Many immigrants also bring to this country experiences with very brutal police officials, and they assume that American police officers are just as bad. Many of these immigrants are not familiar with American principles of individual rights and the right to protest government actions. They do not know, for example, that citizens can file a complaint against a police officer without having to go to court or obtaining a lawyer.

The recent growth of the Hispanic community poses a challenge for police–community relations. The history of American policing is filled with conflict between the police and racial and ethnic minorities. There is a long history of violence arising from conflict with the African American community. Conflict with the Hispanic community resulted in the Zoot Suit riot in Los Angeles in 1943.

In addition to the Hispanic community, recent immigration trends have resulted in significant African, Asian, and Latin American communities in this country. Differences in language and culture create potential problems and conflicts with the police.

Whether the history of tension and violent conflict between the police and racial and ethnic minority communities is repeated in the years ahead or good relations are established depends on what both the police and community leaders do.

## Impact of the War on Terrorism

The terrorist attacks on the World Trade Center and the Pentagon on September 11, 2001, have had a radical impact on American society. We are all subject to new security measures in airports, government buildings, and other places. The federal government has declared a **war on terrorism** that has changed our foreign policy. The war on terrorism is also having a profound effect on domestic policy in ways that directly affect state and local police agencies.

**war on terrorism**

# Role Expansion

Along with the federal government, state and local law enforcement agencies are increasingly concerned about possible terrorist activities. This includes such efforts as (1) investigating suspected terrorists; (2) preparing for and responding to specific terrorist acts such as the bombing of a building; (3) preparing for possible terrorist acts involving weapons of mass destruction (WMD), including chemical and biological weapons (CBW).

These activities involve a major expansion of the role of state and local police agencies. There is the danger that adding these new roles and responsibilities will divert personnel and effort from current responsibilities. These new responsibilities are also very costly. Training for possible terrorist acts is expensive—just as all forms of training are expensive. Maintaining a special unit or command officer responsible for coordinating antiterrorist efforts means that additional officers will have to be hired or diverted from current assignments.[41]

# Immigration Enforcement

In order to enhance national security against potential threats from immigrants to this country, the Justice Department wants state and local police to assist them in enforcing federal immigration laws. Traditionally, state and local agencies had no authority to enforce federal laws. However, after 9/11 the federal government began to advocate for the position that terrorism and related criminal activity was best responded to through a multi-agency approach that made use of expertise at the federal, state and local levels. Specifically, they articulated that local law enforcement personnel are typically the first to come into contact with criminal aliens who may pose a threat to national security or public safety and are usually the first responders when there is a terrorist attack. Today, agencies that are interested in assisting the federal government in this way can request assistance from Immigration and Customs Enforcement (ICE) through the **287(g) program.** The 287(g) agreements permit local police to enforce immigration law after they have received required training from ICE personnel. To date, sixty-three agencies have signed a 287(g) agreement with ICE.[42]

**287(g) program**

Many local police departments, however, do not want to become involved in the enforcement of federal immigration laws. In fact, recently many police chiefs, mayors, and city councils are ordering local officers not to assist federal agents in arresting people for entering the country illegally and are developing policies and procedures that limit the potential for illegal immigrants to see local police as a threat to their legal status. For example, in Chicago police officers are not permitted to ask immigrants about their legal status. In Minneapolis the mayor asked federal agents to stop identifying themselves as "police," so that immigrants would not confuse federal agencies responsible for deportation with the local police department.[43]

Local police officials and politicians are concerned that assisting federal agencies with identifying and deporting illegal immigrants would alienate them from local immigrant communities with whom they are trying to develop positive relations. They emphasized that illegal immigrants are often the most vulnerable to victimization because they are often afraid to tell the police about the crime for fear of deportation. The Major Cities Chiefs Association, which represents chiefs from fifty-seven large police departments, warned that local enforcement of immigration laws would undermine trust and cooperation.[44]

Immigration law is in the midst of potentially sweeping change. In 2006 the U.S. House of Representatives passed a bill that would make being an undocumented immigrant (e.g., entering the country illegally, being in the country with an expired visa) a crime. Under current law, violations of immigration law are civil offenses. The House bill also made it a crime to assist undocumented immigrants. The law potentially made it a crime for someone to operate a homeless shelter or a soup kitchen that serves undocumented immigrants. The U.S. Senate, meanwhile, passed an immigration bill that did not contain these provisions.

It is not clear what the future of U.S. immigration law will be. If it became law, the House bill would represent a radical shift in U.S. policy and would create large new categories of crimes that state and local police would be responsible for enforcing.

## Racial and Ethnic Profiling

For further discussion on racial profiling see Chapter 12.

The war on terrorism has resulted in an increase in stereotypes about Arab Americans in the minds of some people. The Arab American Anti-Discrimination Association has reported an increase in acts of discrimination against Arab people. Some of these acts are similar to the racial profiling experienced by African Americans. The Leadership Conference on Civil Rights (www.civilrights.org) issued a report, *Wrong Then, Wrong Now,* on the illegal profiling of Arab Americans.[45] To address some of these issues, the Department of Justice created a four-hour cultural competency course to educate local and federal law enforcement officers about Arab and Muslim cultures and customs. So far the program has resulted in about 2,000 law enforcement officers being trained.[46]

## Personnel Challenges

Following September 11, 2001, local police agencies have faced several personnel challenges. First, invasions of both Afghanistan and Iraq have resulted in the mobilization of both the National Guard and the military reserves. As a result, almost every police department has lost some personnel to military duty. This creates personnel shortages for large departments, but in small agencies it can create a critical situation. A small rural department with only three or four officers cannot afford to lose one of its officers. In some cases, the chief of police has been mobilized for military duty.

Second, local police agencies are faced with increasing demands to fulfill needs related to homeland security. For example, personnel in many jurisdictions have been diverted away from traditional patrol and investigative activities and are being used to guard critical infrastructures, such as public buildings, nuclear facilities, dams, and bridges. Additionally, they are fulfilling roles in intelligence task forces and supporting federal agencies in providing security to seaports and airports. Rand Corporation conducted a study of how the Long Beach police department has adapted to the changing service demands placed upon it after 9/11 and reported that the changes have been significant. Examples of the study's findings are presented in Exhibit 15–6.

## EXHIBIT 15–6

### Examples of How the Long Beach Police Department Has Adapted to Post-9/11 Service Demands

- Created counterterrorism unit
- Created terrorist liaison officers
- Reassigned officers to assess and protect critical infrastructures, such as the port, airport, and water treatment facilities
- Sent officers to train in new skills, such as WMD response, and signs of terrorism
- Established port police equipped with small boats
- Redistributed officers to respond to areas with high population growth
- Increased visibility and response times by switching most officers from two- to one-person patrol cars
- Reduced staffing on lower-priority programs such as Drug Abuse Resistance Education (DARE) and Community Reactions Division
- Reduced staffing on narcotics division
- Reduced foot patrols
- Requested additional resources to cover additional demand, both from the city for local needs, and from the government for national needs

*Source:* Barbara Raymond, Laura J. Hickman, Laura Miller, and Jennifer S. Wong, *Police Personnel Challenges After September 11: Anticipating Expanded Duties and a Changing Labor Pool,* Rand Corporation Occasional Paper (Santa Monica: Rand Corporation 2005).

# Case Study

## *FBI Futures Working Group*

The Futures Working Group (FWG) is a collaboration between the FBI (http://www.fbi.gov) and the Society of Police Futurists International (PFI). FWG's purpose is to develop—and encourage others to develop—forecasts and strategies to ethically maximize the effectiveness of local, state, federal, and international law enforcement bodies as they strive to maintain peace and security in the twenty-first century.

In 1991, the FBI Academy hosted the International Symposium on the Future of Law Enforcement. The symposium was attended by 250 criminal justice practitioners and educators from 20 nations. Those present voted to begin a professional association, PFI, dedicated to the future of policing.

PFI and the FBI have enjoyed a close working relationship. Following the tragic events of September 11, 2001, it became clear that law enforcement professionals would need help with the complex and difficult issues that they would be facing. In response to this need, the FBI and PFI agreed to capitalize on their collective organizational strengths by jointly forming the Futures Working Group.

In February, 2002, the Futures Working Group had its initial meeting at the FBI Academy in Quantico, Virginia. During that meeting, an organizational framework was crafted and a research agenda was sketched out. The group became a reality on April 2, 2002, when FBI Director Robert Mueller and PFI President Gerald Konkler signed the Futures Working Group Memorandum of Understanding.

*Source:* http://www.policefuturists.org/futures/fwg.htm. Accessed February 17, 2003.

## Summary

The American police face many challenges in the immediate future. Technology, demographic change, the state of the economy, and the war on terrorism will force many changes on the police. How the police will respond to these challenges and external changes is not clear. The only thing that is certain is that ten years from now—if not sooner—American policing will be different from what it is today.

## Key Terms

computer-aided dispatch, 502
records management
    systems, 502
Taser, 508

tactical crime analysis, 509
strategic crime analysis, 509
administrative crime
    analysis, 510

crime mapping, 510
demographic change, 516
war on terrorism, 516
287(g) program, 517

## For Discussion

1. Get into groups and discuss the pros and cons of technology in policing today. Think about technology's impact on police officers, police agencies, and citizens.
2. As a class, discuss whether you think police officers are paid too little or too much. Are police officers paid more or less than similar occupations? Should police officers be paid more, and if so, why?
3. As a class, discuss what role, if any, local police should have in enforcing immigration laws.

## Internet Exercises

**Exercise 1** Go to **http://www.policefuturists.org/futures/fwg.htm** to learn more about the future of policing.

**Exercise 2** Visit your local police department's Web site and look for the page describing the qualifications for becoming a police officer. Look at each of the qualifications to determine whether you fit the criteria to become a police officer in that department.

**Exercise 3** Go to **http://www.officer.com/** to learn about various jobs available in police agencies across the country. Think about whether you would be interested in working for a police agency located in another part of the country. What factors would influence your decision?

**Exercise 4** Go to **http://www.iaca.net/**, for the International Association of Crime Analysts. The site will provide you with information on how to become a crime analyst.

# Notes

1. Edward Maguire and William King, *Trends in Policing,* unpublished manuscript, Manassas, VA, 2004.
2. As quoted in Jim Chu, *Law Enforcement Information Technology* (New York: CRC Press, 2001), p. 3.
3. Chu, *Law Enforcement Information Technology,* p. 3.
4. Ibid.
5. Ibid.
6. Ibid.
7. James J. Willis, Stephen D. Mastrofski, and David Weisburd, "Compstat and Bureaucracy: A Case Study of Challenges and Opportunities for Change," *Justice Quarterly* 21 (September 2004): pp. 463–96.
8. Samuel Walker, *Early Intervention Systems for Law Enforcement Agencies: A Planning and Management Guide* (Washington DC: Department of Justice, 2003). Available at www.ncjrs.org.
9. Samuel Walker, Stacy Osnick Milligan, and Anna Berke, *Strategies for Intervening with Officers through Early Intervention Systems: A Guide for Front-Line Supervisors* (Washington DC: Police Executive Research Forum, 2006). Available at www.cops.usdoj.gov.
10. Mary Beth Sheridan, "License Plate Readers To Be Used In D.C. Area," *The Washington Post,* August 17, 2008, p. C1.
11. International Association of Chiefs of Police, Law Enforcement Information Management Section, Issue Identification: Privacy Issues Concerning the Utilization of Automated License Plate Readers, Draft, March 2009: Washington DC: International Association of Chiefs of Police.
12. Ibid.
13. Accessed at http://www.fas.org/irp/agency/doj/fbi/is/ncic.htm on June 20, 2006.
14. M. Chau, H. Atabakhsh, D. Zeng, and H. Chen, *Building an Infrastructure for Law Enforcement Information Sharing and Collaboration: Design Issues and Challenges,* National Conference on Digital Government, Los Angeles, May 21–23, 2001.
15. Martin J. Zaworski, "Assessing an Automated, Information Sharing Technology in the Post "9–11" Era—Do Local Law Enforcement Officers Think It Meets Their Needs," February 2005. Accessed at http://www.ncjrs.gov/pdffiles1/nij/grants/208757.pdf.
16. C. Uchida, "Outcomes of Police Use of Force: Evaluating the Use of Tasers in the US," unpublished manuscript, *Justice & Security Strategies: Silver Springs,* 2005, p. 2; Jim Weiss and Mickey Davis,

"The Latest TASER Technology," *Law and Order Magazine,* September 2003, pp. 1–5.
17. Michael White and Justine Ready, "The TASER as a Less Than Lethal Force Alternative," *Police Quarterly* 10 (2): pp. 170–91.
18. C. Moss, "Less than Lethal Weapons." Accessed at http://www.iejs.com/TechnologyandCrime/Law_Enforcement_Technology/less_than_lethal_ weapons.htm on June 22, 2006.
19. BBC, "New concern over TASER death tool." Accessed at http://news.bbc.co.uk/2/hi/uk_news/northern_ireland/7784665.stm on March 9, 2009.
20. William Bozeman, William E. Hauda, Joseph J. Heck, Derrel D. Graham, Brian P. Martin, and James E. Winslow, "Safety and Injury Profile of Conducted Electrical Weapons Used by Law Enforcement Officers Against Criminal Suspects." *Annals of Emergency Medicine,* In press, 2009.
21. Timothy O'Shea and Keith Nicholls, *Crime Analysis in America* (Center for Public Policy at the University of South Alabama, March 2002).
22. See http://www.iaca.net/resources/faq.html. Accessed on February 18, 2004.
23. O'Shea and Nicholls, *Crime Analysis in America.*
24. Deborah Osborne and Susan Wernicke, *Introduction to Crime Analysis* (New York: Hayworth Press, 2003).
25. Arizona Criminal Justice Commission, *Crime Mapping in Arizona Report* (Phoenix, AZ: Statistical Analysis Center, 2002).
26. See the National Institute of Justice's MAPS program at http://www.ojp.usdoj.gov/nij/maps/.
27. Arizona Criminal Justice Commission, *Crime Mapping in Arizona Report.*
28. Accessed at http://www.ojp.usdoj.gov/nij/maps/briefingbook.html on June 20, 2006.
29. Cynthia Mamalian and Nancy La Vigne, *The Use of Computerized Crime Mapping by Law Enforcement: Survey Results* (Washington DC: National Institute of Justice, 1999).
30. U.S. Department of Labor, Bureau of Labor Statistics: http://www.bls.gov/oco/ocos160.htm#outlook, accessed on March 10, 2009.
31. U.S. Department of Labor, Bureau of Labor Statistics, http://www.bls.gov/oco/ocos160.htm. Accessed March 10, 2009.
32. Ibid.
33. Thomas Ackerman, *Guide to Careers in Federal Law Enforcement* (Traverse City, MI: Sage Creek Press, 1999).

34. James Stinchcomb, *Opportunities in Law Enforcement and Criminal Justice Careers* (Chicago: VGM Career Books, 2003).

35. Law Enforcement Career Starter, www.netlibrary. com/nlreader.dll?bookid=28378&filename=page_3. html.

36. U.S. Department of Labor, Bureau of Labor Statistics. Accessed on March 10, 2009.

37. National Academy of Sciences, *Fairness and Effectiveness in Policing: The Evidence* (Washington DC: National Academy Press, 2004), p. 34.

38. Ibid.

39. This issue is discussed in Samuel Walker, "Science and Politics in Police Research: Reflections on Their Tangled Relationship," *Annals of the American Academy of Political and Social Science* V, 593 (May 2004): pp. 1–20.

40. For the most recent data, go to the Census Bureau Web site: www.census.gov.

41. U.S. Department of Justice, Office of Community Oriented Policing Services, *Local Law Enforcement Responds to Terrorism: Lessons in Prevention and Preparedness* (Washington DC: U.S. Justice Department, 2003). Available at: www.cops.usdoj.gov.

42. http://www.ice.gov/partners/287g/Section287_g.htm. Accessed March 10, 2009.

43. Judy Keen, "Big Cities Reluctant to Target Illegals," *USA Today.* Accessed at Usatoday.com on June 20, 2006.

44. Ibid.

45. Leadership Conference on Civil Rights, *Wrong Then, Wrong Now: Racial Profiling before and after September 11* (Washington DC: Leadership Conference of Civil Rights, 2003).

46. A. Khashu, R. Busch, and Z. Latif, "Building Strong Police Immigrant Community Relationships: Lessons from a New York City Project," Vera Institute of Justice, New York (August 2005).

# Glossary

## A

**abuse of authority**   Actions by a police officer, under the guise of his or her authority, that tend to injure or insult a citizen, trespass on human dignity, and/or violate a citizen's inherent civil rights.

**accountability**   Having to answer for one's conduct. Both police organizations and individual officers are distinctly accountable to the public, elected officials, and the courts for how well they control crime, maintain order, and perform these tasks while remaining in compliance with the law.

**accreditation**   The process of voluntary professional self-regulation that serves as an approach to establishing minimum national standards in policing.

**affirmative action**   Originating in 1965, a program to establish specific goals and timetables for the employment of minorities and women for any private employer or government agency receiving federal funds.

**Alice Stebbins Wells**   A leader of the policewomen's movement. Wells organized the International Association of Policewomen in 1915.

**analysis**   The second stage of the SARA model of problem-oriented policing, in which the police collect information about a problem to help identify its scope, nature, and cause.

**assessment**   The fourth stage of the SARA model of problem-oriented policing, in which the effectiveness of the response is evaluated through rigorous feedback that allows for revision if the response is not successful.

**assessment center**   A technique used in police departments to evaluate the ability of an applicant to handle the job being sought through promotion.

**August Vollmer**   Chief of police in Berkeley, California, from 1905 to 1932, known as the father of police professionalism for advocating higher education for police officers and promoting organizational reform within departments.

**authorized strength**   The maximum number of sworn officers any given law enforcement agency is authorized to employ.

## B

**bar girl**   A prostitute who works out of bars or other entertainment establishments.

**behaviorally arrested**   Occurs when taking a suspect into custody and involves a number of different actions, such as a stop (in which the officer tells the individual not to leave), a verbal statement that the person is "under arrest," or physical restraint of a person.

**blue curtain of silence**   A code of silence among police officers whereby officers refuse to testify against corrupt officers, creating a veil of secrecy around police actions.

**blue-ribbon commissions**   Commissions serving as a form of external accountability for police conduct that address a full range of police issues and bring together leading experts to help improve local departments.

**bona fide occupational qualifications**   Established qualifications that are reasonably necessary to the normal operation of that particular job.

**Boston police strike**   Occurred in 1919 when 1,117 officers went on strike and formed a police union after having received no pay raise in nearly twenty years. After violence and disorder erupted throughout Boston, the strike quickly collapsed and the striking officers were fired.

**bribe**   Something offered or given to a person in the hope of influencing that individual's views or conduct. Police bribes can include monetary payoffs to protect illegal activity, provide information on criminal investigations, remove criminal files, or alter testimony in court.

**broken windows**   Developed by James Q. Wilson and George L. Kelling, argues that police should focus their resources on disorder problems that create fear of crime and lead to neighborhood decay.

**brothel prostitutes**   Prostitutes who work for legal brothels, illegal message parlors, and escort services.

**bureaucracy**   A pyramidal model of government administration in which tasks are grouped into separate bureaus or departments and information flows up and down according to the hierarchical structure. Marked by diffuse authority, visible divisions of labor, and inflexible rules of operation, each employee answers to one supervisor, creating a uniform and clear chain of command.

# C

**case solvability factors**   Factors that have been shown in the past to be related to the probability that a crime will be solved.

**citizen oversight**   An approach designed to provide independent citizen input for complaints filed against the police through agencies that independently review citizens' complaints, monitor the complaint process, scrutinize general police practices, review department policy and recommend policy changes, and audit the quality of complaint investigations.

**civil service**   A nearly universal set of formal and legally binding procedures governing personnel decisions in police organizations, ensuring that such decisions are based on objective criteria and not on favoritism, bias, or political influence.

**civilians**   Those who follow the pursuits of civil life and are not employed as sworn officers or officials.

**clearance rate**   The traditional measure of success in criminal investigations for a police agency based on the percentage of crimes solved by arrest.

**code of silence**   Also known as the "blue curtain," a code of honor among police officers whereby officers refuse to testify against corrupt colleagues, creating a veil of secrecy around police actions.

**collective bargaining**   A method of determining conditions of employment through bilateral negotiations according to the following principles: employees have a legal right to form unions; employers must recognize employee unions; employees have a right to participate in negotiations over working conditions; and employers are required to negotiate with the union's designated representatives.

**community partnership**   A collaborative partnership that stresses increased interaction between the police and the public to make the police more responsive to the community's needs and reduce community decay and disorder.

**community policing**   A model of policing that stresses a two-way working relationship between the community and the police, in which the police become more integrated into the local community and citizens assume an active role in crime control and prevention.

**COMPSTAT**   (Computerized Statistics) An organizational model, first used by the New York City police in 1994, that allows police departments to blend timely intelligence, effective tactics, rapid deployment of personnel, and vigorous follow-up and assessment.

**constable**   A peace officer who is empowered to serve writs and warrants but has a smaller jurisdiction than a sheriff.

**containment**   A strategy used by police to confine the homeless problem to one area of a community to both minimize disorder and keep homeless people out of public view.

**contingency theory**   A theoretical framework for understanding the structures and practices of police organizations based on the underlying premise that these organizations are created and structured to achieve specific goals, such as crime control, and will ultimately fail if unable to adjust to environmental contingencies.

**convicted offender index**   One of two types of data collected by the FBI as part of their National DNA Indexing System (NDIS). The convicted offender index contains genetic information on offenders who have been required to provide blood samples for genetic typing.

**coroner**   A medical examiner responsible for aiding criminal investigations by probing deaths not thought to be of natural causes.

**corruption**   A form of misconduct or deviant behavior by police officers that involves the misuse of authority in a manner designed to produce personal gain for themselves or for others.

**counterpunching**   Occurs when someone calls the police about another person to divert attention from his or her own behavior.

**county police**   Police agencies that operate on a countywide basis and lack the non-law-enforcement roles of the county sheriff. About 1 percent of local departments are county police.

# D

**deadly force**   The legal right of police officers to use force with the intent to kill if placed in a defense-of-life situation.

**decentralize**   To place greater decision-making responsibility on rank-and-file officers at the neighborhood level and to become more responsive to neighborhood residents.

**decertification**   The process of revoking a police officer's license to work in a given state; addresses the problem of an officer who is fired from one department for misconduct and is then hired by another, but does not prevent the fired officer from being hired in another state.

**defense-of-life standard**   States that police officers are allowed to use deadly force only in situations where their own lives or the life of another person is in danger.

**deformalize**   To eliminate many of the rules and policies that stifle creativity and discourage problem solving within police organizations.

**delayerize**   To decrease the amount of social and administrative distance between the beat officer and the chief of police.

**despecialize**   To replace specialized police units with neighborhood officers who are more knowledgeable about the problems their neighborhoods face.

**differential response**   The screening of 911 calls by the police to provide responses appropriate to the nature and severity of the calls.

**discovery time**   The interval between the commission of a crime and its discovery.

**discretion**   The freedom to act on one's own judgment.

**discrimination**   Differential treatment based on some extralegal category such as race, ethnicity, or gender.

**disparity**   Differences or inequalities that are not necessarily caused by differential treatment.

**domestic disturbance**   A dispute, requiring police response, that involves two or more people engaged in an intimate relationship (married or divorced couples, live-in lovers, people on a first date, problems between adults and children, or adults and elderly parents).

**domestic terrorism**   Terrorism planned and carried out by Americans on American soil.

**domestic violence**   A disturbance between two or more people engaged in an intimate relationship that has escalated to a degree involving actual or threatened violence.

## E

**early intervention system**   A management information system that systematically compiles and analyzes data on problematic police officer behavior, citizen complaints, police officer use of force reports, and other indicators to identify officers with recurring performance problems.

**ethnicity**   The cultural differences existing that characterize a group of people.

## F

**field training**   A supplement to classroom training that allows for practical experience under the supervision of a training officer in on-the-job type situations.

**field training officer (FTO)**   An experienced police officer assigned to supervise recruits during field training.

**fleeing-felon rule**   Declared unconstitutional by the Supreme Court in 1985 (*Tennessee v. Garner*), allowed police the legal right to use deadly force in apprehending a felon attempting to escape.

**foot patrol**   Officers within a department who make neighborhood rounds on foot. While extremely expensive and able to cover only limited ground, foot patrol allows for enhanced police–community relations.

**force factor**   A framework for examining a police officer's use of force in relation to the actions of a citizen to help determine if the officer's actions were reasonable.

**foreign terrorism**   Terrorism coordinated and perpetuated by foreign persons or countries against the United States.

**forensic index**   One of two types of data collected by the FBI as part of their National DNA Indexing System (NDIS). Forensic index data contain DNA profiles from genetic evidence gathered from crime scenes.

**Fourteenth Amendment**   Guarantees equal protection under the law by stating that all persons born or naturalized in the United States are citizens therein, and no state shall make or enforce laws that deprive citizens of life, liberty, or property, without due process of law; nor deny to any person within its jurisdiction the equal protection of the laws.

**fragmented**   Broken down into separate, decentralized parts.

**functional specialization**   A form of organizational structure in which employees are assigned specific duties based on their areas of expertise, thereby allowing less critical tasks to be delegated to paraprofessionals.

## G

***Garrity* ruling**   States that a police officer can be disciplined and even dismissed for refusing to answer questions by internal affairs, but the information disclosed cannot then be used against him or her in a criminal prosecution.

**grass eater**   A police officer who passively accepts gratuities offered to him or her.

**gratuities**   The most common form of police corruption, gifts or favors given to police officers, sometimes out of a sincere effort to thank the officers but often out of self-interest with an expectation of better police service.

## H

**hate crime**   A criminal offense against a person or property motivated in whole or in part by the offender's bias against a race, religion, disability, ethnic/national origin, or sexual orientation.

**high-speed pursuit**   A situation where a police officer attempts to stop a vehicle and the suspect knowingly flees and is pursued at a high rate of speed.

**highway patrol**   Agencies having statewide authority to enforce traffic regulations and arrest non-traffic violators under their jurisdiction.

**honest law enforcement**   An approach representative of low expectations for law enforcement that states police would continue to patrol neighborhoods, answer calls for service, intervene in problem situations, and try to apprehend offenders, but would not make unjustified claims that they are preventing crime.

**horizontal cliques**   Informal networks formed between similarly ranked officers.

**hot spot**   An area that receives a disproportionate number of calls for police service and/or has a very high crime rate.

## I

**injunctions**   Court orders that prohibit a specified group from a specific course of action.

**institutional theory**   A theoretical framework for understanding the structures and practices of police organizations based on the premise that police organizations are social institutions that operate in relation to their external social and political environment.

## J

**J. Edgar Hoover**   Former director of the Federal Bureau of Investigation from 1924 to 1972; increased the size and scope of the bureau's capabilities, but is best known for systematically misusing his power and exaggerating the bureau's effectiveness.

**job stress**   Conditions associated with one's work environment that are mentally or physically disruptive; the major cause of job dissatisfaction.

**job stress coping mechanisms**   Confidential assistance programs that utilize health professionals and/or peer support groups to help employees cope with personal or work-related problems.

## K

**Kansas City Gun Experiment**   Designed to reduce gun-related crimes by removing guns from the streets of a high-crime precinct in Kansas City; represented a combination of problem-oriented policing (by focusing on a particular problem) and "hot spots" (by concentrating on particular areas of high criminal activity).

**Kansas City Preventive Patrol Experiment**   Conducted from 1972 to 1973, measured the impact of different levels of patrol on criminal activity, community perceptions, police officer behavior, and police department practices, while being the first independent and objective experiment

(that met the minimum standards of scientific research) to test the effectiveness of patrol.

**Kerner Commission**   Created in 1967 to study issues of race relations; found that hostility between the police and ghetto communities was a major cause for disorder. Officially known as the National Advisory Commission on Civil Disorders.

## L

**lateral entry**   Moving from one police department to another at either the same rank or a higher rank.

**Lautenburg Amendment**   A federal law passed in 1996 prohibiting anyone with a conviction for domestic violence from owning a firearm.

**Law of Equal Employment Opportunity**   Designed to eliminate employment discrimination by making it illegal to refuse employment to, discharge, or deny benefits and compensation to anyone on the basis of race, ethnicity, color, religion, or sex.

**legalistic style**   An organizational style used in police departments that emphasizes aggressive crime fighting and attempts to control officer behavior through a rule-bound, "by-the-book" administrative approach.

**legally arrested**   Occurs when an individual is deprived of his or her liberty by legal authority and is under arrest or simply taken into custody. A police officer must have the intent to arrest, must communicate that intent to the person, and must actually take the person into custody.

**local political control**   A tradition, inherited from England during the colonial period, that places primary responsibility for public protection with local governments, both city and county.

**local political culture**   Values and traditions, communicated informally in a particular department, town, or community, that influence the organizational structure of policing and officer discretion in that area.

**London Metropolitan Police**   Created in 1829, represents the first example of an efficient, proactive police force. Introduced three important elements of policing: the mission of crime prevention, the strategy of preventive patrol, and an organizational structure similar to the military.

## M

***Mapp v. Ohio***   A controversial Supreme Court decision that established Fourth Amendment protection against unreasonable searches and seizures by the police.

**meat eater**   A police officer who actively and aggressively demands gratuities.

**mercy booking**   Arresting a mentally ill person for a minor offense so that he or she will be booked into the county jail and receive needed mental health care.

**Minneapolis Domestic Violence Experiment** A study conducted from 1981 to 1982 to determine the relative deterrent effect of arrest, mediation, and separation in misdemeanor domestic violence incidents; found that arrest produced lower rates of repeat violence than separation or mediation.

**municipal police** Also known as *city police,* make up the most important component of American law enforcement. Representing the majority of all law enforcement agencies and sworn officers, municipal police are responsible for dealing with serious crime, difficult order maintenance problems, and a wide range of emergency services.

## N

**Newark Foot Patrol Experiment** Conducted from 1978 to 1979 to test the effect of foot patrol on crime and public perception; concluded that added foot patrol did not affect serious crime, but did have a positive impact on public perception of the police.

## O

**O. W. Wilson** Leader of the police professionalization movement from the late 1930s through the end of the 1960s. Developed a formula for efficient management of personnel by assigning patrol officers on the basis of a workload formula that reflected reported crime and calls for service.

**occupational deviance** Criminal and improper noncriminal behavior committed during the course of normal work activities or under the guise of a police officer's authority.

**officially arrested** Occurs only once the police make an official arrest report.

**order maintenance** Police intervention in incidents that do not involve actual criminal activity but often entail "interpersonal conflict" or "public nuisance."

**organizational culture** Values and traditions, communicated informally, that influence the organizational style of policing within a police department.

## P

**peace officer** A status granted to individuals who have certain powers not available to ordinary citizens and who provide certain legal protections. A peace officer can be a police, probation, parole, or corrections officer.

**physical disorder** A form of societal neglect resulting from physical decay within a neighborhood; examples include vandalism, dilapidation and abandonment of buildings, and trash buildup.

**police aides** Nonsworn personnel used by police departments to handle low-priority calls and routine assignments, freeing sworn officers for more critical tasks.

**police brutality** The use of excessive physical force by the police.

**police officer** A nonmilitary person who is employed by a government agency and has the legal status of a peace officer.

**police–community relations** Relations between the police and racial and ethnic minority communities.

**police–population ratio** The standard measure for the level of police protection in a community; usually expressed as the number of sworn officers per thousand residents.

**political patronage** The practice of politicians appointing governmental or political positions based on friendship instead of merit.

**preliminary investigation** The first stage of investigating a crime, consisting of five steps: identifying and arresting any suspects, providing aid to any victims in need of medical attention, securing the crime scene to prevent loss of evidence, collecting all relevant physical evidence, and preparing a preliminary report.

**proactive crime strategies** Anticrime strategies initiated by the police themselves, as opposed to occurring in response to a citizen request for service.

**problem-oriented policing** A model of policing that stresses planned responses to crime and disorder problems.

**promotion** Advancement in rank or responsibility usually based on merit, but sometimes the result of personal favoritism.

**psychiatric first aid** Application of immediate informal, field-based counseling by a police officer.

## R

**race** A group of people classified together on the basis of physical and biological similarities.

**racial profiling** The practice of making police stops solely on the basis of one's race or ethnicity and not because of criminal activity.

**rank hierarchy** Hierarchy based on the officer's rank.

**reactive crime strategies** Anticrime strategies used by police when responding to a civilian's request for service.

**reality shock** The astonishment a new police officer experiences when encountering the unpleasant aspects of dealing with the public, the criminal justice system, and the department during the first weeks and months on the job.

**residual deterrence**   Also called the *phantom effect,* involves assuming that the police are patrolling an area from their having been seen in the area or nearby at another time, leading to the presumption that the police are present when there is no patrol in the area.

**resource dependency theory**   A theoretical framework for understanding the structures and practices of police organizations based on the premise that such organizations must obtain resources to survive, and that to obtain these resources they must engage in exchanges with other organizations in their environment.

**response**   The third stage of the SARA model of problem-oriented policing, in which data collected during the analysis stage are used to develop a strategy to address the problem and, ultimately, implement a response.

**response time**   The total amount of time between the commission of a crime and the moment a police officer arrives on the scene.

**reverse discrimination**   Discrimination focused on whites and/or males; in violation of the 1964 Civil Rights Act and the equal protection clause of the Fourteenth Amendment.

**rewards hierarchy**   Typically corresponds with an officer's rank and seniority within the department.

**Robert Peel**   Credited as the father of modern policing, fought to improve the basic structure of law enforcement and persuaded the English Parliament to establish the London Metropolitan Police in 1829.

## S

**scanning**   The first stage of the SARA model of problem-oriented policing, in which officers take steps to identify possible problems and expose their underlying causes.

**selective contact**   A lack of cross-sectional contact and communication between police officers and a community that leads to misperceptions about public attitudes toward the police.

**selective perception**   The likelihood that police officers will remember traumatic or unpleasant incidents with citizens, even though only 2 to 5 percent of contacts involve hostility or conflict.

**seniority hierarchy**   Hierarchy based on the amount of time that the officer has been employed by the policy agency.

**sheriff**   Elected on a countywide basis in all but two states, an official serving all three components of the criminal justice system: law enforcement, courts, and corrections. Usually is directly involved in partisan politics in ways that municipal police chiefs are not.

**skeezers**   A woman who trades sex for crack cocaine.

**social control**   An organized and planned response to deviance and socially problematic behavior.

**social disorder**   A form of societal neglect resulting from the disorderly actions of individuals in a neighborhood; examples include public drinking, street corner gangs, street harassment, street-level drug sale and use, noisy neighbors, and commercial sex.

**special district police**   Police agencies designed to serve only specific government agencies. Examples include the Los Angeles School District police force and the Metropolitan Transit Police Force in the Washington, D.C., subway system.

**state police**   Agencies that have statewide police powers for both traffic regulation and criminal investigations.

**status hierarchy**   Hierarchy based on officers' assignments or jobs within the police agency.

**streetwalker**   One who represents the lower end of the social and economic scale of prostitution by soliciting on the streets, thus being highly visible to both the police and the general public.

**subjectively arrested**   Occurs when someone having an encounter with the police believes he or she is not free to go, leading to the perception of having been arrested.

## T

**terrorism**   The unlawful use of force or violence against persons or property to intimidate or coerce a government, the civilian population, or any segments thereof in furtherance of political or social objectives.

**Title VII, 1964 Civil Rights Act**   Makes it illegal to refuse to hire or to discharge any individual, or to otherwise discriminate against any individual with respect to employment on the basis of race, color, religion, sex, or national origin.

**tribal police**   Agencies whose primary responsibility is to provide general law enforcement services for Indian Nations.

**turnover**   The number of employees hired by a company or department to replace workers who have left their jobs in a given period of time.

## U

**unfounding a crime**   Failure of a police officer to complete an official crime report when a citizen reports a crime.

## V

**verbal abuse**   The use of inappropriate language, particularly racial and ethnic slurs, by police officers.

**vertical cliques**   Informal networks formed between lower and higher ranking officers.

**vice**   Victimless crimes with no complaining party and involving prostitution, gambling, or narcotics.

**victimless crime**   A crime that has no complaining party and often involves behavior that many people regard as legitimate, resulting in conflicting public attitudes about how vigorously the laws should be enforced.

## W

**the watch**   A policelike group, established in colonial times, requiring all adult males to patrol the city for crimes, fires, and disorder.

**watchman style**   An organizational style used in police departments that emphasizes peacekeeping without aggressive law enforcement and few controls over rank-and-file officers.

**Wickersham Commission**   Created in 1929 by President Herbert Hoover as the first national study of the American criminal justice system. Officially the National Commission on Law Observance and Enforcement.

## Z

**zero-tolerance policing**   Based on the belief that aggressive enforcement of laws directed at combating disorder will motivate residents to better care for their community, a policy that calls for the police to focus primarily on disorder, minor crime, and the appearance of crime through interventions that vigorously enforce criminal and civil laws and are conducted for the purpose of restoring order to communities.

# Credits

## Text/Line Art Credits

### Chapter 1

Page 8, Exhibit 1-1, Eric J. Scott, *Calls For Service: Citizen Demand and Initial Police Response* (Washington DC: Government Printing Office, 1981), pp. 28–30.

Page 10, Exhibit 1-2, Police Roles and Responsibilities: "Major Current Responsibilities" excerpted from *Standards Relating to the Urban Police Function,* 2nd Edition, 1980, published by the American Bar Association Section of Criminal Justice. Copyright 1980 © by the American Bar Association. Reprinted with permission. This information or any or portion thereof may not be copied or disseminated in any form or by any means or stored in an electronic database or retrieval system without the express written consent of the American Bar Association.

Page 12, Sidebar 1-1, The Principles of Democratic Policing: Reproduced with permission of Taylor & Francis Informa UK Ltd- Journals from The Principles of Democratic Policing: Adapted from "Policing in Transition," Jeremy Travis from *Police Practice & Research: An International Journal, 1* (1), Copyright © 2000; permission conveyed through Copyright Clearance Center, Inc.

Page 18, Case Study, Adapted from *Reality-Based Police Programs, 2000. Issue Briefs.* Studio City, CA: Mediascope Press; or it can be viewed at http://www.mediascope.org/pubs/ibriefs/rbpp.htm

### Chapter 2

Page 31, Sidebar 2-3, Alexander von Hoffman, "An Officer of the Neighborhood: A Boston Patrolman on the Beat in 1895," *Journal of Social History 26* (Winter 1992): pp. 309–30.

Page 45, Sidebar 2-5, National Academy of Science, *Fairness and Effectiveness in Policing: The Evidence* (Washington DC: National Academy Press, 2004).

Page 52, Case Study, Excerpt from the Kerner Commission Report, 1968, pp. 304–5. Emphasis added.

### Chapter 3

Page 61, Exhibit 3-2, Bureau of Justice Statistics, *Census of State and Local Law Enforcement Agencies, 2004* (Washington DC: Government Printing Office, 2007).

Page 62, Exhibit 3-3, Bureau of Justice Statistics, *Census of State and Local Law Enforcement Agencies, 2004* (Washington DC: Government Printing Office, 2007).

Page 67, Sidebar 3-3, Adapted from Edward Maguire and Rebecca Schulte-Murray, Issues and Patterns in the Comparative International Study of Police Strength, *International Journal of Comparative Sociology, 42*, 1–2 (2001): pp: 75–99. Reprinted with permission of Brill Academic Publishers.

Page 69, Sidebar 3-5, Adapted from Bureau of Justice Statistics, *Sheriff's Departments, 2003* (Washington DC: Government Printing Office, 2006).

Page 80, Exhibit 3-8, Hours of Security Guard Training Required by State. Reprinted by Permission of Service Employees International Union.

Page 83, Case Study, Adapted from Kevin J. Stro and Joe Eyeman's Interagency Coordination: A Case Study of the 2005 London Train Bombings. National Institute of Justice Journal, 260. http://www.ojp.usdoj.gov/nij/journals/260/interagency-coordination.htm , accessed on February 16, 2009.

### Chapter 4

Page 94, Sidebar 4-1, Reproduced with permission of Sage Publications Inc. Journals from The Myth of the Military Model of Leadership, Thomas Cowper, 3 (3). Copyright © 2000; permission conveyed through Copyright Clearance Center, Inc.

Page 101, Sidebar 4-2, Adapted from William R. King, "Toward a Life-Course Perspective of Police Organizations." *Journal of Research in Crime and Delinquency* 2009, 46: 213–44.

Page 104, Exhibit 4-2, Has Your Department Implemented a Compstat-Like Program? From "The Growth of Comstat in American Policing," David Weisburd, Stephen Mastrofski, Rosann Greenspa, and James Willis in *Police Foundation Reports,* April 2004. Reprinted by permission of the Police Foundation.

Page 108, Exhibit 4-3, Omaha Police Department, "Union Contract," *Standard Operating Procedure Manual,* pp. 12–13.

Exhibit 4, Page 109, Exhibit 4-4, Florida Statutes, Sec. 112.532.

Page 114, Case Study, Adapted from "Philadelphia Police Department: CompStat Meetings." The URL of the page is: http://www.ppdonline.org/hq_compstat2.php. Downloaded on April 30, 2009.

## Chapter 5

Page 121, Exhibit 5-1, Bureau of Justice Statistics, *Police Departments in Large Cities, 1990–2000* (Washington DC: U.S. Justice Department, 2002). Available at www. ncjrs.org. NCJ 175703.

Page 124, Exhibit 5-2, San Diego Police Department web site: www.sandiego.gov/police/recruiting/about/dimensions.shtml.

Page 125, Exhibit 5-3, Bureau of Justice Statistics, *Local Police Departments, 2003* (Washington DC: U.S. Justice Department, 2006). Table 16. Available at www. ncjrs.org. NCJ 210118.

Page 129, Exhibit 5-4, Bureau of Justice Statistics, *Local Police Departments, 2003* (Washington DC: Government Printing Office, 2006), p. 8.

Page 135, Police in Focus, Charlotte-Mecklenburg Police Department, at www.charmeck.org.

Page 140, Exhibit 5-5, Bureau of Justice Statistics, Local Police Departments, 2003 (Washington DC: U.S. Justice Department, 2006), Table 17.

Page 141, Police in Focus, Bureau of Justice Statistics, *State and Local Law Enforcement Training Academies, 2002* (Washington DC: Department of Justice, 2005). Available at www.ncjrs.org, NCJ 204030.

Page 142, Exhibit 5-6. Reprinted by permission of the Tampa Florida Police Department.

Page 145, Case Study, President's Commission on Law Enforcement and Administration of Justice, *The Challenge of Crime in a Free Society* (Washington DC: Government Printing Office, 1967), p. 110.

## Chapter 6

Page 155, Sidebar 6-2, Mollen Commission, *Report of the Commission to Investigate Allegations of Police Corruption and the Anti-Corruption Procedures of the Police Department* (New York: Mollen Commission, 1994). Available at www.parc.info.

Page 160, Police in Focus, Dorothy Moses Schulz, *Breaking the Brass Ceiling: Women Police Chiefs and Their Paths to the Top* (New York: Praeger, 2004).

Page 160, Exhibit 6-2, National Center for Women and Policing, Equality Denied: The Status of Women in Policing: 2001 (Los Angeles: National Center for Women and Policing, 2002). Available at www.feminist. org. Reprinted by permission of *Ms.* Magazine, © 2001.

Page 175, Sidebar 6-6, Samuel Walker, *Early Intervention Systems for Law Enforcement Agencies: A Planning and Management Guide* (Washington DC: Department of Justice, 2003).

Page 179, Sidebar 6-7, Samuel Walker, Stacy Osnick Milligan, and Anna Berke, *Supervision and Intervention within Early Intervention Systems: A Guide for Law Enforcement Chief Executives* (Washington DC: Police Executive Research Forum,2005), pp. 24–25.

Page 182, Case Study, National Center for Women and Policing, *Equality Denied* (1998), p. 5.

## Chapter 7

Page 193, Exhibit 7-1, Bureau of Justice Statistics, *Local Police Departments, 2000* (Washington DC: Government Printing Office, 2003), Appendix A.

Page 199, Exhibit 7-4.

Page 202, Sidebar 7-1, Robin Shepard Engel, *How Police Supervisory Styles Influence Patrol Officer Behavior* (Washington DC: U.S. Justice Department, 2003).

Page 203, Exhibit 7-6, Los Angeles Police Department Web site, www.lapdonline.org.

Page 207, Exhibit 7-7, Reproduced with permission of Sage Publications Inc Books from Evaluating Performance of Criminal Justice Agencies, Stephen Mastrofski, Copyright © 1983; permission conveyed through Copyright Clearance Center, Inc.

Page 218, Sidebar 7-3, Charlotte-Mecklenburg Police Department Web site: www.charmeck.org/Departments/Police/Home.htm.

Page 220, Case Study, Department of Criminology, University of Maryland; Department of Criminal Justice, University of Texas. Years of Operation: 1992–1993.

## Chapter 8

Page 230, Exhibit 8-2, Bureau of Justice Statistics, *Contacts between Police and the Public, 2005* (Washington DC: Government Printing Office, 2007).

Page 231, Exhibit 8-3, Bureau of Justice Statistics, *Contacts between Police and the Public, 2005* (Washington DC: Government Printing Office, 2007).

Page 233, Exhibit 8-4, National Highway Traffic Safety Administration, Traffic Safety Facts 2007 (National Center for Statistics and Analysis: Washington DC: 2008).

Page 235, Exhibit 8-5, Richard Felson, Steven Messner, Anthony Hoskin, and Glenn Deane, "Reasons for Reporting and Not Reporting Domestic Violence to the Police," *Criminology* 40, 30 (2002): pp. 617–47.

Page 238, Exhibit 8-6, Lawrence W. Sherman with the assistance of Janell D. Schmidt and Dennis P. Rogan, *Policing Domestic Violence: Experiments and Dilemmas,* Table 6.1, page 129 (New York: Free Press, 1992).

Page 246, Exhibit 8-7, Robert Redondo and Glenn Currier, "Characteristics of Patients Referred by Police to a Psychiatric Emergency Service," *Psychiatric Services* 54, 6 (2003): pp. 804–6.

Page 252, Case Study, Adapted from Marilyn Moses, Understanding and Applying Research on Prostitution, *NIJ Journal* 255, November 2006.

## Chapter 9

Page 265, Exhibit 9-1, Bureau of Justice Statistics, *Criminal Victimization, 2007* (Washington DC: Government Printing Office, 2008).

Page 265, Exhibit 9-2, Bureau of Justice Statistics, *Reporting Crime to the Police, 1992–2000* (Washington DC: Government Printing Office, 2003).

Page 266, Exhibit 9-3, Bureau of Justice Statistics, *Criminal Victimization in the United States, 2006: Statistical Tables* (Washington DC: Government Printing Office, 2008).

Page 271, Exhibit 9-4, Federal Bureau of Investigation, *Crime in the United States, 2007* (Washington DC: Government Printing Office, 2008).

Page 280, Sidebar 9-2, Michael White, AARIN Annual Adult Report, Arizona State University: Phoenix (April 2008).

Page 282, Exhibit 9-6, The Sentencing Project, *Young Black Americans and the Criminal Justice System: Five Years Later* (Washington DC: The Sentencing Project, 2001). Obtained from http://www.sentencingproject.org/pdfs/9070smy.pdf on January 15, 2004.

Page 289, Exhibit 9-8, Christopher Hewitt, *Understanding Terrorism in America* (New York: Routledge, 2003), p. 15.

Page 292, Case Study, James Fealy, "Overt Drug Market Strategy, High Point, North Carolina." Presented at the Improving Access to Public Services Conference, November 6–8, 2007, The Hague The Netherlands. Accessed at http://www.innovations.harvard.edu/cache/documents/698/69851.pdf on June 8, 2009.

## Chapter 10

Page 302, Exhibit 10-1, George Kelling and William Bratton, "Declining Crime Rates: Insiders' Views of the New York City Story," Reprinted by special permission of Northwestern University School of Law, The Journal of Criminal Law and Criminology.

Page 306, Exhibit 10-2, Bureau of Justice Statistics, *Law Enforcement Management and Administrative Statistics, 2000* (Washington DC: Government Printing Office, 2004).

Page 308, Sidebar 10-2, Bureau of Justice Statistics, *Law Enforcement Management and Administrative Statistics, 2000* (Washington DC: Government Printing Office, 2004).

Page 313, Exhibit 10-3, Bureau of Justice Statistics, *Law Enforcement Management and Administrative Statistics, 2000* (Washington DC: Government Printing Office, 2004).

Page 316, Exhibit 10-4, Wesley G. Skogan and Susan M. Hartnett, *Community Policing: Chicago Style* (New York: Oxford University Press), p. 121, Figure 5–1.

Page 318, Exhibit 10-5, Wesley Skogan, *Community Policing in Chicago, Year Ten: An Evaluation of Chicago's Alternative Policing Strategy* (Chicago: Illinois Criminal Justice Information Authority, 2004).

Page 322, Exhibit 10-6, John Eck and William Spelman, *Problem Solving: Problem-oriented Policing in Newport News* (Washington DC: PERF, 1987), Figure 1, p. 4.

Page 324, Exhibit 10-7, Police Executive Research Forum, *SARA Problem Solving Model,* http://www.policeforum.org/sara.html.

Page 326, Exhibit 10-8, John E. Eck and William Spelman, *Problem- Solving: Problem-oriented Policing in Newport News* (Washington DC: Police Executive Research Forum, 1987), Table 9, p. 70.

Page 328, Exhibit 10-9, Dorothy Roberts, "Forward: Race, Vagueness, and the Social Meaning of Order-Maintenance Policing." Reprinted by special permission of Northwestern University School of Law, *The Journal of Criminal Law and Criminology.*

Page 329, Exhibit 10-10, Jack R. Green, "Community Policing in America: Changing the Nature, Structure, and Function of the Police," in Julie Horney, ed., *Policies Processes, and Decisions of the Criminal Justice System, Criminal Justice 2000, vol. 3* (Washington DC: Government Printing Office, 2000), p. 311.

Page 334, Case Study, Deborah Spence, "Indio Police Department Tackles the Foreclosure Crisis," *Community Policing Dispatch* 2, 3 (March 2009), obtained at http://www.cops.usdoj.gov/html/dispatch/March_2009/indio.htm.

### Chapter 11

Page 358, Exhibit 11-2, International Association of Chiefs of Police: Model Policy, Use of Deadly Force. Reprinted from the IACP National Law Enforcement Policy Center Model Policy on Use of Force. Copyright held by the International Association of Chiefs of Police. 515 North Washington Street, Alexandria, VA 22314 USA. Further reproduction without express written permission from IACP is strictly prohibited.

Page 362, Exhibit 11-3, Police Department, Madison, Wisconsin, Policies and Procedures Manual. Available at www.ci.madison.wi.us/police.

Page 364, Case Study, Excerpt from George Kelling, *"Broken Windows" and Police Discretion,* p. 50.

### Chapter 12

Page 377, Exhibit 12-2, From WALKER/SPOHN/DELONE. *The Color of Justice,* 3e. © 2003 Wadsworth, a part of Cengage Learning, Inc. Reproduced by permission. www.cengage.com/permissions.

Page 378, Exhibit 12-3, Adapted from 2008 Gallup Poll, conducted June 9–12, 2008. N - 822 adults, 18 years of age or older. Available in *Sourcebook of Criminal Justice Statistics,* Table 2.12 2008.

Page 379, Exhibit 12-4, Mark Hugo Lopez, et al., *Hispanics and the Criminal Justice System: Low Confidence, High Exposure* (Los Angeles: Pew Hispanic Center, 2008).

Page 385, Exhibit 12-5, Bureau of Justice Statistics, *Sourcebook of Criminal Justice Statistics, 2005* (Washington DC: Department of Justice, 2005), Table 2.17. Available at www.albany.edu/sourcebook/.

Page 386, Exhibit 12-6, United Nations, *International Crime Victims Survey, 2000.* www.uncjin.org.

Page 391, Exhibit 12-7, Bureau of Justice Statistics, *Contacts between Police and the Public: Findings from the 2002 National Survey* (Washington DC: Government Printing Office, 2004).

Page 394, Sidebar 12-3, Roger G. Dunham and Geoffrey P. Alpert, "Officer and Suspect Demeanor: A Qualitative Analysis of Change," *Police Quarterly* 12 (March 2009): pp. 6–21.

Page 403, Exhibit 12-8, Adapted from Lorie A. Fridell, *By the Numbers: A Guide for Analyzing Race Data from Vehicle Stops* (Washington DC: Police Executive Research Forum, 2004).

Page 414, Case Study Chief Ronald L. Davis, Chief of Police, East Palo Alto, California, Letter to the Community, December 26, 2008. www.ci.east-palo-alto.ca.us/police/pdf/Police_Department_Report.pdf.

### Chapter 13

Page 426, Exhibit 13-1, Omaha Police Department, *Standard Operating Procedure Manual,* p. 77.

Page 427, Exhibit 13-2, Ronald Weitzer and Steven Tuch, *Rethinking Minority Attitudes toward the Police: Final Technical Report* (Washington DC: National Institute of Justice, June 26, 2004).

Page 428, Police in Focus, Jim Ruiz and Christine Bono, "At What Price a 'Freebie'? The Real Cost of Police Gratuities," *Criminal Justice Ethics* 23, 1 (2004): pp. 44–54.

Page 429, Exhibit 13-3, From "Police Officer Gratuities and Public Opinion," Mark Jones in *Police Forum,* 4, Academy of Criminal Justice Sciences, October 1997, p. 9.

Page 431, Exhibit 13-4, Sanja Kutnjak Ivkovic, "To Serve and Collect: Measuring Police Corruption," *Journal of Criminal Law and Criminology* 93 (2003), pp. 593–649. Reprinted by special permission of Northwestern University School of Law, *The Journal of Criminal Law and Criminology.*

Page 438, Sidebar 13-1, Sanja Kutnjak Ivkovich, "To Serve and Collect: Measuring Police Corruption," *Journal of Criminal Law and Criminology* 93 (2003): pp. 593–649. Reprinted by special permission of Northwestern University School of Law, *The Journal of Criminal Law and Criminology.*

Page 440, Sidebar 13-2, Frank Anechiarico and James B. Jacobs, *The Pursuit of Absolute Integrity* (Chicago: University of Chicago Press, 1996), p. 157.

Page 442, Exhibit 13-6, St. Petersburg Police Department Internal Affairs Report, 2005.

Page 445, Exhibit 13-7, New Orleans Police Department, *2003 Annual Report* (New Orleans: City of New Orleans, 2004).

Page 448, Sidebar 13-3, "FBI inquiries focus on corruption, misconduct," *Arizona Republic,* June 21, 2009, page A20.

Page 450, Case Study, Kevin Johnson, "Katrina Made Police Choose between Duty and Loved Ones," *USAToday,* February 21, 2006. Accessed at www.usatoday.com/educate/college/firstyear/articles/20060226.htm on August 10, 2006; Willoughby Anderson, "This Isn't Representative of Our Department," unpublished manuscript.

## Chapter 14

Page 468, Exhibit 14-1, Los Angeles Sheriff's Department, Office of Independent Review, *Seventh Annual Report, April 2009* (Los Angeles: Sheriff's Department, 2009), pp. 32–34.

Page 471, Sidebar 14-2, Samuel Walker, *Early Intervention Systems for Law Enforcement Agencies: A Planning and Management Guide* (Washington DC: Department of Justice, 2003).

Page 476, Sidebar 14-3, Kenneth Adams, "A Research Agenda on Police Use of Force," in Bureau of Justice Statistics, *Use of Force by Police: Overview of National and Local Data* (Washington DC: Government Printing Office, 1999), pp. 61–73.

Page 479, Sidebar 14-4, Kenneth Adams, "A Research Agenda on Police Use of Force," in Bureau of Justice Statistics, *Use of Force by Police: Overview of National and Local Data* (Washington DC: Government Printing Office, 1999), pp. 61–73.

Page 483, Sidebar 14-6, *United States v. New Jersey* (1999). Available at www.usdoj/gov/crt/split.

Page 488, Sidebar 14-7, All of the special counsel reports are available at the Web site of the Police Assessment Resource Center: www.parc.info.

Page 492, Case Study, Miami-Dade Police Department, *Early Identification System* (1992).

## Chapter 15

Page 503, Exhibit 15-1, Reproduced with permission of Taylor & Francis Group LLC—Books from *Law Enforcement Information Technology,* Jim Chu, Copyright © 2001; permission conveyed through Copyright Clearance Center, Inc.

Page 504, Sidebar 15-1, Reproduced with permission of Taylor & Francis Group LLC—Books from *Law Enforcement Information Technology,* Jim Chu, Copyright © 2001; permission conveyed through Copyright Clearance Center, Inc.

Page 511, Exhibit 15-2, from "Violence in Pittsburgh: An Analysis," by Erin Dalton, Brian Bell, LaToya Warren, published by One Vision One Life, an initiative of the Allegheny County Department of Human Services Office of Community Services.

Page 512, Exhibit 15-3, James Stinchcomb, *Opportunities in Law Enforcement and Criminal Justice Careers* (Chicago: VGM Career Books, 2003).

Page 513, Exhibit 15-4, U.S. Department of Labor, Bureau of Labor Statistics, http://www.bls.gov/oco/ocos160.htm (Earnings). Accessed March 10, 2009.

Page 514, Exhibit 15-5, Law Enforcement Career Starter, www.netlibrary.com/nlreader.dll?bookid=28378&filename=page_3.html.

Page 519, Exhibit 15-6, Reproduced with permission of Rand Corporation from *Police Personnel Challenges After September 11,* Barbara Raymond, Laura J. Hickman, Laura Miller, and Jennifer S. Wong, Copyright © 2005; permission conveyed through Copyright Clearance Center, Inc.

Chapter 15, Page 519, Case Study, http://www.policefuturists.org/futures/fwg.htm. Accessed February 17, 2003.

## Photo Credits

Page 2: Mark Karrass/Corbis; p. 22: Bettmann/Corbis; p. 58: Thinkstock/PunchStock; p. 92: Richard Mei/AP Images; p. 120: Arresting Images; p. 150: Brand X Pictures; p. 190: Lon C. Diehl/PhotoEdit; p. 226: The McGraw-Hill Companies, Inc./Christopher Kerrigan, photographer; p. 260: Brand X Pictures; p. 300: Arresting Images; p. 344: Arresting Images; p. 370: Brooks Kraft/Sygma/Corbis; p. 424: AP Images; p. 456: The McGraw-Hill Companies, Inc./John Flournoy, photographer; p. 500: Royalty-Free/Corbis.

# Name Index

# Subject Index